Southern Living
2014 Annual Recipes

Oxmoor
House®

Old-School Cranberry Salad and New-School Cranberry Salad (page 264)

Ms. Shawn's Old-School Cranberry Salad

New-School Cranberry Salad

clockwise from top left:
• The City and The Country Mac and Cheese (page 24)
• Whole Wheat Pancakes with Peanut Butter Sauce (page 30)
• Meatball Pasta Bake (page 28)
• Quick Beef Chili (page 36)

Gulf Coast Seafood Stew (page 44)

Chicken and Gnocchi
(page 50)

5

Spinach Salad with Honey
Dressing and Honeyed
Pecans (page 73)

clockwise from top left:

• Honey-and-Soy-Lacquered Ribs (page 74)
• Chipotle Scalloped Potatoes (page 77)
• Strawberry-Lemonade Layer Cake (page 95)
• Mile-High Mini Strawberry Pies (page 93)

clockwise from top left:

- Mix 'n' Match Spring Pasta Toss (page 97)
- Coconut-Almond Roulade (page 105)
- Grilled Sausage Salad Pizza (page 116)
- Cheese Grits and Roasted Tomatoes (page 119)

Grain Salad with Grilled Shrimp and Sweet Peppers (page 115)

Macerated Peaches with
Ancho-Cinnamon Sugar
(page 135)

**Honey-Balsamic-Blueberry
Pie (page 133)**

Baked Zucchini Chips and Zucchini-Carrot Salad with Catalina Dressing (page 143)

clockwise from top left:
- Grilled Pork Chops with Blueberry-Peach Salsa (page 157)
- Blueberry-and-Kale Grain Salad (page 157)
- Blackberry-Brie Pizzettas (page 156)
- Petite Blueberry Cheesecakes (page 158)

clockwise from top left:
- Smoky Black-eyed Peas with Fried Green Tomatoes (page 205)
- Pork, Mango, and Tomato Salad (page 211)
- Mexican Chocolate Pudding Cake (page 225)
- Hush Puppies (page 214)

Grilled Pork Chops with
Apple-Bourbon Glaze
(page 218)

Cast-Iron Cowboy
Steak (page 236)

Our Year at
Southern Living®

Dear Friends,

Welcome to *Southern Living 2014 Annual Recipes,* the 36th volume of our handy reference collection. It's a particularly busy time of year here at *SL* HQ where we are putting the final touches on the special December double issue, and we are delighted to share with you this year's installment of the big white cake, the cover icon that heralds the Christmas season.

As the cook in the family with two little girls at home, I have never been more excited about helping readers get dinner on the table for their families, whether supper means a quick pasta on a Wednesday night, a slow cooker tangy pork shoulder recipe, or a three course menu for a Saturday supper club. Food is not just sustenance; it's the way we cooks nourish our relationships with friends and family.

> *Food is not just sustenance; it's the way we cooks nourish our relationships with friends and family.*

We kicked off 2014 with the goal of elevating and celebrating iconic Southern dishes and ingredients, starting with a January feature on casseroles—the workhorse dishes that elicit comfort and joy. In March, we turned to congealed salads. Long-neglected, gelatin salads got a bad rap at some point in the 1980s. Well, we brought the jiggle back this year in all of its Technicolor glory by remaking classic congealed salads with modern looks and fresh ingredients.

This summer, we launched our first-ever A to Z guide to Southern food, celebrating the people, places, and recipes that are central to our heritage. The package detailed our region's return to its agricultural roots, including trends like the rise of artful vegetable plates at white tablecloth restaurants, backyard container gardening, the proliferation of farmers' markets, and more. Finally, Southern vegetables such as okra, corn, and field peas get the star treatment they deserve.

In October, we honored the most important tool in the kitchen—the cast iron skillet. More than pearls or china, it's the first heirloom we ask our grandmothers for, and it's the pan that has the power to launch 1,000 recipes. If you don't have one or if you've neglected yours and let it rust in the garage, turn to page 239 to become a convert.

This letter marks my second full year at the magazine. In this feasting season of Thanksgiving, I'm especially thankful for our food team here at *Southern Living* who work hard every day to surprise and delight you, our readers, with tried and true recipes. The way we cook and eat in the South continues to evolve as we lead ever busier lives, but I believe that the best Southern food, like the best Southern music, continues to honor the past while looking forward. Next year, I'll be taking the helm at our sister magazine *Cooking Light.* Rest assured, your *Southern Living* recipes will be in great hands. And you bet I'll be stopping by the *SL* Test Kitchen for a slice of the 2015 Christmas white cake.

Cheers,

Hunter Lewis

Contents

19

Top-Rated Recipes

Members of our food staff gather almost every day to taste-test recipes. Here we share this year's highest-rated recipes.

JANUARY

- The City and The Country Mac and Cheese (page 24) Smoky city ham and salty country ham along with a creamy cheese sauce ensure this dish delivers.
- Sweet Potato, Cauliflower, and Greens Casserole (page 25) This vegetarian dish features big flavor from sweet potatoes, cremini mushrooms, fresh greens, cheese sauce, and cumin.
- Loaded Chicken-Bacon Pot Pie (page 25) Shorten cooking time of this savory dish by using prepared ingredients.
- Skillet Pork Chops with Apples and Onions (page 34) Add complex flavor to the mustardy pan sauce by first browning the pork chops in this elegant but easy dish.
- Lemon-Rosemary-Garlic Chicken and Potatoes (page 34) Enjoy the simple yet dynamic flavors of this chicken and potatoes as a weeknight dinner.
- Peanut Butter-Banana Cream Pie (page 39) Peanut butter and bananas in this pie will send your taste buds to heaven.

FEBRUARY

- Winter Mushroom Risotto (page 48) A velvety sauce encompasses the complex earthy tones in this risotto.
- Italian Potato Salad (page 50) Add salami and a tangy-but-sweet dressing for an Italian twist on a classic side.
- Chicken and Gnocchi (page 50) Check out our favorite go-to recipe for chicken and dumplings.
- Fried Catfish with Pickled Peppers (page 52) Homemade pickled peppers and brine add flavor, color, crunch, and kick to golden fried fish.
- Lemon-Lime Pound Cake (page 54) Inspired by a classic Southern favorite, this treat uses a soft drink for baking.

- Citrus Pull-Apart Bread (page 55) Layers of sweet dough cradle a citrus filling in this recipe that makes two gorgeous loaves.
- Snap Pea Salad (page 65) Enjoy a simple salad of snap peas, cauliflower, and green onions dressed in a dilly-garlic white wine vinegar dressing.

MARCH

- Mini Tomato Aspics (page 69) Set this acidic gelatin-based condiment in mini muffin pans.
- Honey Flans (page 73) Faint floral notes from the honey add great flavor to this decadent make-ahead dessert.
- Honey-Roasted Carrots (page 73) Bourbon, honey, and thyme give these vegetables a savory yet sweet note.
- Honey-and-Soy Lacquered Ribs (page 74) Simple and sweet pork ribs absorb great flavors from a soy sauce, Asian chili-garlic sauce, dry mustard, ginger, and honey mixture.
- Honey-Pineapple Upside-Down Cake (page 75) Tangy pineapple, a sweet honey glaze made with brown sugar, and a spongy cake showcase sweet flavors in this simple dessert.
- Grapefruit-Pecan Sheet Cake (page 77) This Lone Star State-inspired dessert makes a great Texas treat for your next gathering.
- Chipotle Scalloped Potatoes (page 77) Heat up this starchy side and add bacon, nutmeg, and white Cheddar for savory flavors.
- Weekend Brisket (page 77) Though good by itself, leftovers complete an egg biscuit sandwich or taco.
- Herb-Roasted Boneless Leg of Lamb (page 84) Prepare this hearty meal on Sunday night and use leftovers throughout the week.

APRIL

- Easy Parmesan-Herb Rolls (page 88) Enhance store-bought refrigerated dough with dried herbs and cheese for homemade-style dinner rolls.
- Glazed Spiral-Cut Holiday Ham (page 89) Become inspired by one of three easy but creative glaze recipes.
- Hot Potato Salad (page 89) This dish features the perfect marriage of potato salad and bubbly, and cheesy gratin.
- Spring Pea Orzo (page 90) Mix up this pasta salad while still warm so it absorbs the maximum flavor from the dressing.
- Mega Strawberry Pie (page 93) A spin on a mini strawberry pie recipe, this pastry celebrates the arrival of spring.
- Strawberries-and-Cream Sheet Cake (page 94) Showcase the seasonal berry in this moist cake perfect for any occasion.
- Strawberry-Rhubarb Tartlets (page 94) These adorable pastries can be served as breakfast, dessert, or a snack.
- Strawberry-Lemonade Layer Cake (page 95) Alternating layers of jam, frosting, and fluffy cake make this an unbelievable dessert.
- Mosaic Tea Sandwiches (page 102) Make entertaining easy by layering cream cheese spread, seasonally fresh ingredients, and herbs for this dainty appetizer.
- Prosciutto-Asparagus Tea Sandwiches (page 102) Salty notes from the prosciutto and thinly sliced ribbons of fresh asparagus provide great taste.
- Salmon-Cucumber Tea Sandwiches (page 102) Fresh dill and crisp cucumbers give this bite-sized snack a bright flavor.
- Vegetable Medley Tea Sandwiches (page 102) Press layers of ruffles made from yellow squash, cucumbers, and radishes into cream cheese spread

smoky flavor from the ham hocks, to your go-to snacks repertoire.

- Bacon, Peach, and Basil Burgers (page 208) A tangy-sweet chutney balances the heat in these tasty burgers.
- Sloppy Joe Carolina-Style Burgers (page 208) Mounds of crunchy slaw on these over-the-top burgers add crisp texture to this weeknight dinner.
- Sweet Tea-and-Lemonade Cake (page 213) Embrace the flavors of an Arnold Palmer in this after-dinner treat.

SEPTEMBER

- Apple Stack Cake (page 217) Layer six 8-inch cakes among baked apples and drizzled with a sweet apple cider glaze.
- Carrot-Apple Soup (page 219) Preserve the bright color and flavor in this refreshing soup by skipping sautéing before creating the soup.
- Caramel Apple Cheesecake Tart (page 221) Crumbled gingersnap cookies and pecans make a flavorful crust for this creamy cheesecake.
- Cornbread Pudding with Whiskey Caramel (page 224) Gooey caramel seeps into the crevices of the savory cornbread pudding.
- Grape Focaccia (page 225) This simple baking-sheet focaccia is effortlessly gorgeous and perfect for entertaining.
- Eggs Simmered in Tomato Sauce (page 228) Serve with crusty bread to mop up the Middle Eastern-spiced tomato sauce.
- Easy Apple Butter (page 230) This fall condiment lends flavor to three bonus recipes.

OCTOBER

- Chicken-and-Wild Rice Skillet Casserole (page 234) A riff on old-school chicken and rice, new flavors update this rustic meal.
- Top-Shelf Chicken Under a Brick (page 235) Crispy skin and juicy meat are results of this new cooking technique that cuts cooking time in half.
- Cast-Iron Cowboy Steak (page 236) Heat the cast-iron skillet on the grill

to properly cook a bone-in steak.
- Braised White Turnips (page 236) Butter, honey, apple cider vinegar, and salt enhance the flavor of this simple side dish.
- Sugar-and-Spice Caramel Popcorn (page 241) Balance the sweet caramel drizzled over the popcorn with our secret ingredient.
- Tangy Slow-Cooker Pork Shoulder (page 243) Ladle on plenty of our sweet and tangy sauce over this slow-cooked, tender pulled pork.
- Zesty Pot Roast (page 247) Let this slow-cook in a Dutch oven for a tasty Sunday supper.
- Party-Perfect Meatballs (page 249) Briny olives, fresh herbs, and lemon zest revive a recipe with modern flavors.

NOVEMBER

- Cane Syrup-Glazed Acorn Squash (page 254) Add good ole fashion Southern sweetness to this seasonal side.
- Angel Biscuits (page 262) Serve these high-rising biscuits baked in a skillet alongside your holiday meal.
- Creamed Onion Tart (page 263) Give a classic recipe an inventive and stylish twist with flaky pie crust.
- Roasted Root Vegetables with Cider Glaze (page 266) Savor the simplicity of these rustic vegetables that will be a staple of any holiday meal.
- Cranberry Cheesecake with Cranberry-Orange Sauce (page 271) Spruce up a classic recipe by drizzling a sweet but tangy sauce a top.
- Tennessee Whiskey-Pecan Pie (page 274) Add some Southern flair with crunchy pecans and smoky-sweet bourbon in this pie filling.
- Pecan Spice Cake with Caramel-Rum Glaze (page 275) Finish a delicious holiday meal with a classic recipe that boasts a boozy caramel glaze.

DECEMBER

- Sweet Potato Cheesecake Tartlets (page 285) Combine seasonal favor-

ites such as pecan pie, sweet potatoes, and cheesecake for a tiny treat at a holiday open house.
- Gumbo Arancine (page 288) Prepare these party snacks ahead for an easy yet savory crowd-pleaser.
- Cream Cheese-Citrus Mints (page 293) A throwback recipe from 2003, try this modern version with bright citrus flavors.
- White Cake with Bourbon Buttercream and Seven-Minute Frosting (page 300) Dress up a simple yet loved-by-all white cake with bourbon buttercream.
- Milk Punch Tres Leches Cake (page 301) Top the cake with creamy whipped cream and freshly grated nutmeg.
- Sunday Sauce (page 305) Pork shoulder, pancetta and sweet Italian sausage add hearty ingredients for a classic meal.
- Chicken-and-Biscuit Cobbler (page 306) Using fresh herbs will assure this holiday staple feels homemade.
- Harvest Beef Soup (page 306) Add a pop of color with some unexpected vegetables in this hearty winter soup.
- Bacon-and-Cheddar Grits Quiche (page 309) Give your quiche a new spin with a bacon and cheesy grits crust.
- Parmesan-Crusted Braised Lamb Shanks (page 312) Grate aged cheese into a fine powder for a flavorful crust on this stunning lamb dish.
- Beer-Braised Turkey Legs (page 313) Welcome a change of pace from traditional holiday roasts with this Latin-inspired poultry main dish.
- Creamy Parmesan Grits (page 315) Add a salty, earthy flavor to your side dish staple with freshly grated Parmesan cheese.
- Acadian Gateau au Sirop with Roasted Pears and Caramel Sauce (page 319) Roasted pears and decadent caramel sauce add sweet and savory components to this traditional Louisiana spice cake.

January

The Cult of the Casserole

INTRODUCING NINE NEW CLASSICS FOR EVERY OCCASION, FROM THE ELEGANT TO THE EVERYDAY. SEASON WITH LOVE, POP THEM IN THE OVEN, AND BAKE UNTIL BROWNED AND BUBBLY

THE FRENCH INVENTED the casserole in the early 18th century, but it was the busy mid-20th-century housewife who turned it into *the* icon of Southern hospitality. No other dish rises to any occasion, high or low, with such graceful ease, and no other dish resonates such cozy comfort on such an elemental level. A whole lot of delicious happens when good ingredients become acquainted with one another in a bubbling hot sauce. We could go on for days about the utility and versatility of this one-pot wonder, but we'll leave you with this: A casserole baking in the oven promises something good, honest, and wholesome to come. It warms our hearts.

TENETS OF CASSEROLE COOKERY

No. 1

Make it homemade. Nothing says from the heart like a casserole.

THE CITY AND THE COUNTRY MAC AND CHEESE

Smoky cubes of brined city ham and salty bits of country ham give this main-course mac its name and savory appeal. Pasta enrobed with a creamy sauce and melting pockets of gooey cheese take it over the top. (Pictured on page 3)

- 12 oz. elbow macaroni or cavatappi pasta
- 4 cups diced smoked, fully cooked ham
- 1 cup diced country ham
- 2 Tbsp. vegetable oil
- 6 Tbsp. butter
- 1/3 cup grated onion
- 2 tsp. dry mustard
- 1/2 tsp. kosher salt
- 1/4 tsp. freshly ground black pepper
- 1/4 tsp. freshly grated nutmeg
- 1/8 tsp. ground red pepper
- 5 Tbsp. all-purpose flour
- 3 1/2 cups milk
- 1 3/4 cups heavy cream
- 2 tsp. prepared horseradish
- 2 tsp. Worcestershire sauce
- 2 cups (8 oz.) shredded extra-sharp Cheddar cheese
- 2 cups diced Gruyère or Swiss cheese
- 1 1/2 cups soft, fresh breadcrumbs (about 4 white bread slices)
- 2 Tbsp. butter, melted
- 1 Tbsp. minced fresh chives

1. Preheat oven to 350°. Prepare pasta according to package directions for al dente.

2. Stir together smoked ham and country ham. Sauté half of ham mixture in 1 Tbsp. hot oil in a large skillet 7 to 8 minutes or until lightly browned. Repeat with remaining ham mixture and oil.

3. Melt 6 Tbsp. butter in a large saucepan over medium heat. Add onion and next 5 ingredients, and sauté 30 seconds or until fragrant. Add flour, and cook, stirring constantly, 2 minutes or until golden brown and smooth. Gradually whisk in milk and cream, and bring to a boil, whisking occasionally. Reduce heat to medium-low, and simmer, whisking constantly, 5 minutes or until slightly thickened and mixture coats a spoon. Stir in horseradish and Worcestershire sauce. Remove from heat, and stir in Cheddar cheese until melted. Stir in pasta, ham, and Gruyère; pour into a lightly greased 13- x 9-inch baking dish.

4. Process breadcrumbs and 2 Tbsp. melted butter in a food processor 6 to 7 seconds to combine. Sprinkle over pasta mixture.

5. Bake on an aluminum foil-lined jelly-roll pan at 350° for 30 minutes or until bubbly and golden. Remove from oven to a wire rack, and cool 15 minutes. Top with chives.

Note: We tested with Cracker Barrel Extra Sharp Cheddar.

Makes 8 to 10 servings. Hands-on 40 min.; Total 1 hour, 25 min.

TENETS OF CASSEROLE COOKERY

No. 2

Carrying it to a friend? Write your initials with nail polish on the underside of the dish.

comfort and joy

BY SHERI CASTLE

A new baby is born. A loved one passes on. A family is forever reshaped. It is possible to take comfort. You can carry it in your hands, in a casserole dish.

When welcoming a new baby, a casserole gives the joyous, exhausted parents a glimpse of family meals yet to come. During bereavement, a casserole offers a moment of respite. In times of upheaval, a casserole is reassuringly familiar. This meal asks no more of the beleaguered than to peel back the foil.

The day of my adored grandmother Madge Marie Reece Castle's funeral was filled with equal parts immeasurable love and unspeakable loss. The family returned home to find the kitchen brimming with homemade food brought by friends and neighbors. I found my favorite chicken-and-dressing casserole, spooned some up, and picked a quiet spot where I could sit with my toddler in my lap. One bowl and one spoon for the two of us. It was the only moment all day that made any sense. When words don't come easy, a casserole says plenty: "I understand your normal life has come to a complete stop for a few days, so I'm going to pause mine long enough to make you something good to eat."

Homemade conveys heartfelt. A reliable casserole can deliver comfort and joy, but it's not the food so much as the gesture of genuine compassion. Casserole unto others as you would have them casserole unto you.

to cover any exposed filling, if necessary.) Whisk together egg and 1 Tbsp. water. Brush over pastry.
4. Bake at 400° on lower oven rack 35 to 40 minutes or until browned and bubbly. Let stand 15 minutes before serving.

Note: You can also make this in 6 (12-oz.) ramekins. Cut pastry into circles; place over ramekins after filling. Bake as directed.

Makes 6 servings. Hands-on 40 min.; Total 1 hour, 35 min.

LOADED CHICKEN-BACON POT PIE

Deli-roasted chicken and puff pastry short-cut time; bacon, white wine, and mustard give the gravy and vegetables savory punch.

- 5 thick bacon slices, diced (about 1 cup)
- 1 medium-size sweet onion, chopped
- 2 garlic cloves, chopped
- 1 cup chopped carrots
- 1 (8-oz.) package fresh mushrooms, halved
- 1/2 cup dry white wine
- 1/3 cup all-purpose flour
- 3 cups reduced-sodium or organic chicken broth
- 3/4 cup whipping cream
- 1 1/2 Tbsp. dry mustard
- 2 tsp. fresh thyme leaves
- 1 tsp. kosher salt
- 1/8 tsp. ground red pepper
- 4 cups shredded deli-roasted chicken
- 1 cup small frozen sweet peas
- 1/2 (17.3-oz.) package frozen puff pastry sheets, thawed
- 1 large egg, lightly beaten
  Garnish: fresh thyme

1. Preheat oven to 400°. Cook bacon in a Dutch oven over medium heat 8 to 10 minutes or until crisp. Drain on paper towels, reserving 3 Tbsp. drippings.
2. Add onion to hot drippings, and sauté 3 minutes. Add garlic and next 2 ingredients; sauté 4 to 5 minutes or until carrots are crisp-tender. Remove from heat, and add wine. Return to heat; cook 2 minutes. Sprinkle with flour; cook, stirring constantly, 3 minutes. Whisk in broth; bring to a boil. Boil, whisking constantly, 2 to 3 minutes or until thickened. Stir in cream and next 4 ingredients.
3. Remove from heat, and stir in chicken, peas, and bacon. Spoon mixture into a lightly greased 11- x 7-inch baking dish. Place pastry over hot filling, pressing edges to seal and trimming off excess. (Use scraps

SWEET POTATO, CAULIFLOWER, AND GREENS CASSEROLE

As a hefty vegetarian main course or as a side, this one delivers big flavor and meaty texture. (Pictured on page 164)

- 1 head cauliflower (1 1/2 to 2 lb.), cut into small florets
- 1 (8-oz.) package fresh cremini mushrooms, stemmed and halved
- 6 Tbsp. olive oil, divided
- 1 tsp. ground cumin, divided
- 1 tsp. kosher salt, divided
- 1/4 tsp. freshly ground black pepper, divided
- 3 large sweet potatoes (2 1/2 to 3 lb.), peeled and cut into 1/4-inch-thick slices
- 2 garlic cloves, minced
- 4 cups chopped fresh kale, collards, or mustard greens
- 2 tsp. red wine vinegar
- 1 (14-oz.) can butter beans, drained and rinsed (optional)
  Easy Cheese Sauce
- 1/2 cup panko (Japanese breadcrumbs)
- 1 Tbsp. chopped cilantro
- 1 tsp. extra virgin olive oil

1. Preheat oven to 475°. Toss together cauliflower, mushrooms, 2 1/2 Tbsp. oil, 1/2 tsp. cumin, 1/2 tsp. salt, and 1/8 tsp. pepper in a medium bowl. Spread cauliflower mixture in a single layer in jelly-roll pan.

SL TEST KITCHEN PICKS

USE THE RIGHT SIZE FOR THE JOB. HERE ARE FIVE FAVORITES.

ANCHOR HOCKING
13- x 9-inch workhorse, $10.39; *target.com*

12-INCH STAUB FRY PAN
Fancy-pants one-pan favorite, $149.99; *zwillingonline.com*

SOUFFLÉ DISHES
Mini 10-oz. wonders, $2.36 each; *surlatable.com*

LE CREUSET FRENCH OVEN
Functional 5 1/2-qt. beauty; $275; *lecreuset.com*

VINTAGE 2-QT. OVAL
Timeless, durable Pyrex; prices vary; *etsy.com*

---

2. Toss together sweet potatoes, 2 1/2 Tbsp. oil, and remaining cumin, salt, and pepper. Spread in a single layer in another jelly-roll pan.

3. Bake potatoes and cauliflower at 475° for 10 to 12 minutes or until browned and just tender, turning once. Cool on wire racks 10 minutes.

4. Reduce oven temperature to 375°. Heat remaining 1 Tbsp. oil in a large skillet over medium-high heat. Add garlic; cook, stirring often, 1 minute. Add kale; cook, stirring occasionally, 10 minutes or until tender. Add salt and pepper to taste; stir in vinegar.

5. Layer half each of sweet potatoes, cauliflower mixture, beans (if desired), kale, and 1 1/2 cups Easy Cheese Sauce in a lightly greased 13- x 9-inch baking dish. Repeat layers. Top with remaining 1/2 cup cheese sauce. Stir together panko, chopped cilantro, and olive oil, and sprinkle crumb mixture over casserole.

6. Bake at 375° for 20 to 25 minutes or until thoroughly heated, bubbly, and golden brown. Let stand 5 minutes before serving.

Makes 6 to 8 servings. Hands-on 55 min.; Total 1 hour, 45 min.

Easy Cheese Sauce

- 1/3 cup dry vermouth*
- 1 garlic clove, minced
- 3 cups half-and-half
- 3 Tbsp. cornstarch
- 1 tsp. kosher salt
- 1/2 tsp. freshly ground black pepper
- 2 cups (8 oz.) shredded pepper Jack cheese

1. Bring vermouth and garlic to a boil in a large skillet over medium-high heat; reduce heat to medium-low, and simmer 7 to 10 minutes or until vermouth is reduced to 1 Tbsp.

2. Whisk together half-and-half and cornstarch. Whisk half-and-half mixture, salt, and pepper into vermouth mixture; bring to a boil over medium-high heat, whisking constantly. Boil, whisking constantly, 1 minute or until mixture is thickened. Add pepper Jack cheese. Reduce heat to low, and simmer, whisking constantly, 1 minute or until cheese is melted and sauce is smooth. Remove from heat, and use immediately.

*Dry sherry may be substituted.

Makes 3 1/2 cups. Hands-on 25 min., Total 25 min.

SAUSAGE, PEPPER, AND GRITS CASSEROLE

We took a cue from shepherd's pie and used grits (in lieu of mashed potatoes) to seal in the flavor of juicy sausage in an ever-so-sweet sauce.

CHEESE GRITS CRUST

- 1 cup milk
- 1/2 cup uncooked quick-cooking grits
- 2 cups (8 oz.) shredded sharp Cheddar cheese
- 1 Tbsp. fresh thyme leaves
- 3/4 tsp. kosher salt
- 1/2 tsp. freshly ground black pepper
- 2 large eggs, lightly beaten

SAUSAGE FILLING

- 1 (19-oz.) package mild Italian sausage
- 1 Tbsp. canola oil
- 2 large red bell peppers, sliced
- 1 medium-size red onion, sliced
- 3 garlic cloves, minced
- 1 (14.5-oz.) can diced tomatoes with garlic and onion, drained
- 1/4 cup butter
- 1/4 cup all-purpose flour
- 1 1/2 cups reduced-sodium or organic chicken broth

1 1/2 Tbsp. grape jelly
1 tsp. red wine vinegar
1/2 tsp. freshly ground black pepper
1/4 tsp. kosher salt

1. Prepare Cheese Grits Crust: Bring milk and 1 cup water to a boil in a large saucepan over medium heat; add grits, and cook, stirring often, 5 minutes or until thickened. Stir in cheese and next 3 ingredients; remove from heat.
2. Gradually stir about one-fourth of hot grits mixture into eggs; add egg mixture to remaining hot grits mixture, stirring until blended.
3. Prepare Sausage Filling: Preheat oven to 375°. Cook sausage in hot oil in a Dutch oven over medium heat 7 to 8 minutes on each side or until browned. Remove sausage from Dutch oven, reserving 1 Tbsp. drippings in Dutch oven.
4. Sauté bell peppers and onion in hot drippings 5 minutes or until tender. Add garlic, and sauté 2 minutes. Cut sausage into 1/2-inch-thick slices. Stir together tomatoes, bell pepper mixture, and sausage in a large bowl.
5. Melt butter in Dutch oven over medium heat; whisk in flour, and cook, whisking constantly, 4 to 5 minutes or until smooth and medium brown. Gradually whisk in broth, and bring to a boil, whisking constantly.
6. Reduce heat to medium-low; simmer, stirring occasionally, 5 minutes or until thickened. Stir in jelly and next 3 ingredients. Stir into sausage mixture, and spoon into a lightly greased 11- x 7-inch baking dish. Gently spread Cheese Grits Crust over top.
7. Bake at 375° for 20 to 25 minutes or until lightly browned. Let casserole stand 10 minutes before serving.

Makes 6 to 8 servings. Hands-on 50 min.; Total 1 hour, 25 min.

CHICKEN ENCHILADA CASSEROLE

Layers of corn tortillas give this ultra-creamy casserole some structure. We also love it with smoky shredded BBQ brisket or pulled pork in place of the chicken, or try small cooked, peeled shrimp.

1 1/2 cups diced sweet onion
2 large poblano peppers, seeded and diced
2 Tbsp. canola oil
3 garlic cloves, minced
2 (10 3/4-oz.) cans cream of chicken soup
1 (8-oz.) container sour cream
2 (4.5-oz.) cans chopped or diced green chiles
1 cup chicken broth
1 (1-oz.) envelope taco seasoning mix
18 (6-inch) corn tortillas, quartered
6 cups shredded cooked chicken
2 cups (8 oz.) shredded extra-sharp Cheddar cheese
2 cups (8 oz.) shredded pepper Jack cheese

1. Preheat oven to 350°. Sauté first 2 ingredients in hot oil in a large skillet over medium-high heat 5 minutes or until tender. Add garlic, and sauté 1 minute. Stir in soup and next 4 ingredients; remove from heat.
2. Spread 1 cup soup mixture in a lightly greased 13- x 9-inch baking dish. Arrange 24 tortilla quarters, slightly overlapping, over soup mixture; top with 3 cups chicken, 3/4 cup each Cheddar and pepper Jack cheeses, and 1 1/2 cups soup mixture. Repeat layers. Top with remaining 24 tortilla quarters, soup mixture, and cheeses.
3. Bake at 350° for 45 to 50 minutes or until bubbly and golden. Remove from oven to a wire rack, and let stand 15 minutes before serving.

Makes 8 to 10 servings. Hands-on 30 min.; Total 1 hour, 30 min.

a casserole throw down

BY ANGELA ENGLISH

T his is a story about how we define ourselves as Southern cooks at home.

Five years ago my husband, chef Kelly English, and I had a sizable wedding in Memphis, Tennessee. The music was brass, the liquor was free-flowing, and the food embodied Memphis and NOLA traditions. The wedding party was a mix of Ole Miss Rebels and LSU Tigers, and they were rowdy to say the least.

The most memorable wedding story that's told of our special day involves a celebrity chef groomsman who was my husband's mentor, and my matron of honor. The foodies in our wedding party were in awe that this particular chef was celebrating with us. En route to the reception in the limo bus, my matron of honor introduced herself to the chef and tried to make conversation, and I guess she wasn't getting much of a response from him. (I'm sure he was trying to enjoy the festivities and keep a low profile.) She began heckling him regarding his unwillingness to talk recipes and football.

Her last words to him and everyone on the limo bus were, "I may not be a celebrity chef, but I can cook a mean casserole, and my mama can cook a mean casserole."

Meatball Pasta Bake

MEATBALL PASTA BAKE

Orange juice and fennel give this quick supper bright, fresh flavor. Chop fennel as you would an onion, or omit it, if desired. (Also pictured on page 3)

1	(16-oz.) package penne pasta
1	small sweet onion, chopped
1	medium-size fennel bulb, thinly sliced (optional)
2	Tbsp. olive oil
3	garlic cloves, minced
1	tsp. fennel seeds
2	(24-oz.) jars marinara sauce
2	(14-oz.) packages frozen beef meatballs, thawed
1	cup fresh orange juice
3/4	cup organic chicken broth
1	tsp. firmly packed orange zest
1	medium-size red bell pepper, chopped
1/2	tsp. kosher salt
1	cup torn fresh basil
1 1/2	(8-oz.) packages fresh mozzarella cheese slices
	Garnish: fresh basil leaves

1. Preheat oven to 350°. Prepare pasta according to package directions.
2. Sauté onion and fennel bulb in hot oil in a Dutch oven over medium heat 8 to 10 minutes or until tender. Add garlic and fennel seeds, and sauté 1 minute. Stir in marinara sauce and next 6 ingredients; increase heat to medium-high, and bring to a boil. Reduce heat to medium-low; cover and simmer 10 minutes. Remove from heat, and stir in basil, cooked pasta, and salt to taste. Transfer to a lightly greased 13- x 9-inch baking dish. Place dish on an aluminum foil-lined baking sheet. Top with cheese.
3. Bake at 350° for 25 minutes or until bubbly.

Note: We tested with Classico Marinara with Plum Tomatoes.

Makes 8 to 10 servings. Hands-on 30 min.; Total 1 hour, 10 min.

TENETS OF CASSEROLE COOKERY

No. 3

Texture is tantamount. Layer in ooey gooey, toothsome, and crunchy.

CHICKEN-AND-POPPY SEED CASSEROLE

Preheat oven to 350°. Stir together 2 1/2 cups **Homemade Cream of Mushroom Soup,** 5 cups chopped **deli-roasted chicken,** 1 (16-oz.) container **sour cream,** and 1 Tbsp. **poppy seeds.** Spoon into a lightly greased 11- x 7-inch baking dish. Stir together 1/4 cup **butter,** melted, and 18 **buttery round crackers,** crushed; sprinkle over casserole. Bake 35 to 40 minutes or until bubbly. Let stand 5 minutes before serving.

Makes 6 servings. Hands-on 15 min.; Total 1 hour, 20 min., including homemade soup

CREAMY POTATO-CHICKEN CASSEROLE

Preheat oven to 350°. Microwave 1 (28-oz.) package **frozen cubed potatoes with onions and peppers** at HIGH 6 to 7 minutes or until tender. Let stand 5 minutes. Meanwhile, stir together 1 1/4 cups **Homemade Cream of Mushroom Soup,** 3 cups chopped **deli-roasted chicken,** 1 (16-oz.) container **sour cream,** 2 cups (8 oz.) shredded **sharp Cheddar cheese,** and a dash of **hot sauce.** Stir in cooked potatoes. Spoon into a lightly greased 13- x 9-inch baking dish. Sprinkle with 2 cups crushed **white Cheddar cheese crackers.** Bake 45 to 50 minutes or until bubbly. Let stand 5 minutes before serving.

Makes 8 servings. Hands-on 15 min.; Total 1 hour, 30 min., including homemade soup

TENETS OF CASSEROLE COOKERY

No. 4

Always let a baked casserole stand before serving to allow it to set up.

ode to cream of mushroom

BY HANNAH HAYES

Let us now praise the famous casserole cure-all, the red-and-white-labeled silver bullet: Cream of Mushroom Soup.

Lord knows it isn't pretty, unlike the hostesses who appeared alongside the cans in early advertisements, coiffed within an inch of their lives. But when Mama poured it over chicken breasts, pork chops, or green beans, she might as well have been Julia Child herself. Campbell Soup Company created this American idol in 1934, introducing Continental cooking to resourceful Depression-era wives and mothers. In just four minutes, anyone could enjoy the concentrated essence of French cuisine for only 12 cents. While many of those early adopters didn't know Escoffier from a hill of beans, the soup base became a wartime hero, at one point accounting for 30% of the company's business. Along came Andy Warhol, diet fads, and changing family dynamics. Now, its appeal isn't convenience alone but how it comforts us, like a tin-can telephone to family dinners past. We bet if you try our homemade version (below), you'll feel like you're talking to a very familiar friend.

HOMEMADE CREAM OF MUSHROOM SOUP

This makes 5 cups, about the same as four 10.75-oz. cans. Use 1 1/4 cups of this in place of each can called for in your recipe.

1/2   **cup butter, divided**

3   **(8-oz.) packages fresh mushrooms, chopped**

1/3   **cup all-purpose flour**

2   **cups whipping cream**

1   **(8-oz.) package cream cheese, softened**

2   **(1-oz.) containers home-style concentrated chicken stock (from a 4.66-oz. package)**

1. Melt 3 Tbsp. butter in a Dutch oven over medium-high heat; add mushrooms, and sauté 10 to 12 minutes or until liquid evaporates. Transfer to a bowl.

2. Reduce heat to medium. Melt remaining 5 Tbsp. butter in Dutch oven. Whisk in flour until smooth; whisk 1 minute. Gradually whisk in cream and next 2 ingredients. Cook, whisking constantly, 2 minutes or until melted and smooth. Remove from heat; stir in mushrooms. Use immediately, or cool completely. Freeze in 1 1/4-cup portions in plastic freezer bags. Thaw before using.

Makes 5 cups. Hands-on 25 min.; Total 25 min.

Energize Your Mornings

KICK-START THE NEW YEAR AND EVERY DAY WITH OUR 13 FRESH, FAST, AND HEALTHY BREAKFAST RECIPES INSPIRED BY AUTHOR CAROLYN O'NEIL AND OUR NEW COLLABORATION WITH HER, *THE SLIM DOWN SOUTH COOKBOOK*

WHETHER YOU WAKE TO a rooster's crow or your smartphone's chime, mornings are a launchpad for the rest of the day. What's on the menu for breakfast can make or break how you feel all day and impact your lifelong health and nutrition. Think of it as a way to rev up your metabolism and provide nutrients your body and brain need.

But can breakfast be Southern and healthy? You bet your biscuits! The recipes here reflect this food philosophy in my new book, *The Slim Down South Cookbook*. They're big on whole grains and produce with a pleasing portion of protein. Most are quick and meant for dashing out the door, while others work for relaxed weekends. And because planning is key to any healthy eating plan, some are make-ahead recipes too. So wake up happy and healthy with these family-friendly breakfasts.

—CAROLYN O'NEIL

WHOLE WHEAT PANCAKES WITH PEANUT BUTTER SAUCE

Carolyn says: "Cook this batter immediately after mixing to keep the pancakes springy and light. The whole wheat adds flavor." (Pictured on page 3)

Stir together 1 cup **fat-free milk,** 2 large **egg whites,** 2 Tbsp. **dark brown sugar,** 2 Tbsp. **olive oil,** and 2 Tbsp. **apple cider vinegar** in a medium bowl. Stir in 1 cup **whole wheat flour,** 1 Tbsp. **baking powder,** and 1/4 tsp. **table salt** until just combined. Pour about 2 Tbsp. batter for each pancake onto a hot, lightly greased griddle or large skillet. Cook pancakes over medium-high heat 3 minutes or until tops are covered with bubbles and edges look dry and cooked; turn and cook other side. Microwave 1/2 cup **creamy peanut butter** in a microwave-safe bowl 45 seconds; drizzle over pancakes, and serve immediately with **sliced grapes** and **syrup.**

Makes 6 servings. Hands-on 40 min., Total 40 min.

Calories *278;* **Protein** *10.6g;* **Carbs** *25.4g;* **Fiber** *3.3g;* **Fat** *16.6g*

PEACHES-AND-CREAM REFRIGERATOR OATMEAL

Carolyn says: "Make these jars of oatmeal a day ahead. The fruit is ripe for riffs—use anything you've got in your fridge."

Stir together 2 cups uncooked **regular oats,** 1 cup **low-fat yogurt,** 1 cup **fat-free milk,** and 1/2 cup chopped **fresh peaches.** Spoon into 6 (1-pt.) **canning jars.** Cover with metal lids, and screw on bands. Shake until combined (about 30 seconds). Chill 8 to 12 hours. Top each serving with 1/4 cup chopped fresh peaches, **nectarines, or oranges** and 1 tsp. **honey.**

Makes 6 servings. Hands-on 20 min.; Total 8 hours, 20 min.

Calories *180;* **Protein** *7.1g;* **Carbs** *33.3g;* **Fiber** *3.4;* **Fat** *2.7g*

Lemon-Blueberry Quinoa Porridge

BREAKFAST TACOS

Carolyn says: "Using tongs, hold each tortilla over a gas flame 10 to 20 seconds on each side or until charred. It makes a tremendous difference in flavor."

Whisk together 2 large **eggs;** 6 large **egg whites;** 1 (4-oz.) can mild chopped **green chiles,** drained; 1/2 (8-oz.) package **reduced-fat cream cheese,** softened; 1/2 tsp. **freshly ground black pepper;** and 1/4 tsp. **table salt.** Heat 1 Tbsp. **olive oil** in a large nonstick skillet; add egg mixture, and scramble. Divide egg mixture among 6 (6-inch) slightly charred **whole wheat tortillas.** Top each with 1 Tbsp. chopped **green onions** and **hot sauce** to taste. Roll up each tortilla, and serve immediately.

Makes 6 servings. Hands-on 10 min., Total 10 min.

Calories 225; **Protein** 11.4g; **Carbs** 23.2g; **Fiber** 3.5g; **Fat** 9.4g

LEMON-BLUEBERRY QUINOA PORRIDGE

Carolyn says: "Quinoa, a nutty seed packed with protein, is great for breakfast. Its firm texture is perfect in this creamy porridge." (Also pictured on page 162)

Stir together 1 1/2 cups **almond milk*,** 1 cup uncooked **quinoa,** 1 cup **water,** 2 tsp. **granulated sugar,** 1/2 tsp. **ground cinnamon,** 1/2 tsp. **almond extract,** and 1/4 tsp. **table salt** in a medium saucepan, and bring to a boil over medium heat. Cover, reduce heat to medium-low, and simmer 15 minutes or until liquid is absorbed. Spoon into 4 bowls; top each with 1/4 cup **fresh blueberries,** 1 Tbsp. chopped toasted **almonds,** 2 Tbsp. almond milk, 1/2 tsp. **light brown sugar,** and 1/2 tsp. loosely packed **lemon zest.**

*Low-fat milk may be substituted.

Makes 4 servings. Hands-on 15 min., Total 30 min.

Calories 252; **Protein** 8g; **Carbs** 39.7g; **Fiber** 5.3g; **Fat** 7.1g

PINEAPPLE PARFAITS

Carolyn says: "Greek yogurt is a fantastic source of protein. Pair it with any tangy fruit and salted nuts for something extraordinary."

Sauté 1 1/2 cups diced **fresh pineapple** and 2 Tbsp. **light brown sugar** in 1 Tbsp. hot **olive oil** in a skillet over medium-high heat 2 to 3 minutes or until lightly browned. Remove from heat; stir in 1/4 tsp. **vanilla extract.** Spoon 1 cup **low-fat Greek yogurt** into each of 4 bowls, and top with one-fourth of pineapple mixture and 1 Tbsp. chopped salted **pistachios.**

Makes 4 servings. Hands-on 15 min., Total 15 min.

Calories 136; **Protein** 5.5g; **Carbs** 17.7g; **Fiber** 1.1g; **Fat** 5.6g

MUFFIN-CUP SOUFFLÉS

Carolyn says: "Freshly grated ginger gives the traditional bacon-and-egg breakfast duo a new, exotic flavor. You can substitute 1 tsp. ground ginger if you don't have fresh ginger available."

Preheat oven to 325°. Stir together 6 cooked **bacon slices,** chopped; 1/2 cup chopped **green onions;** 1 Tbsp. grated **fresh ginger;** and 1/4 tsp. **freshly ground black pepper.** Whisk together 6 large **eggs,** 4 large **egg whites,** 1 cup **low-fat milk,** and 1/4 tsp. **table salt** in a medium bowl. Place **paper baking cups** in a 12-cup muffin pan, and coat with **cooking spray.** Divide egg mixture among paper baking cups; top with bacon mixture. Bake 25 minutes or until tops begin to brown. Cool on a wire rack 3 minutes. Serve each soufflé with **soy sauce.**

Makes 1 dozen. Hands-on 20 min., Total 50 min.

Calories 77; **Protein** 6.6g; **Carbs** 1.7g; **Fiber** 0.1g; **Fat** 4.7g

STRAWBERRY-BASIL SMOOTHIES

Carolyn says: "Basil gives these smoothies a jolt of garden-fresh flavor. Use whatever kind of milk is in your fridge. We call for almond milk, which is lower in fat and calories than cow's milk, but both contain essential nutrients."

Process 2 cups frozen whole, hulled **strawberries,** slightly thawed; 1 ¼ cups **almond milk;** 1 cup firmly packed **fresh basil leaves;** 2 Tbsp. **honey;** and a pinch of **table salt** in a blender 30 seconds to 1 minute or until smooth.

Makes 4 servings. Hands-on 5 min.; Total 5 min.

Calories *73;* **Protein** *1g;* **Carbs** *16.2g;* **Fiber** *2.1g;* **Fat** *1.1g*

HUMMINGBIRD POWER BARS

Carolyn says: "What could be better than a breakfast that tastes like the classic Hummingbird cake without the colossal calories?"

Preheat oven to 300°. Stir together 1 ½ cups uncooked **regular oats,** 1 cup **high-fiber cereal,** 1 cup chopped toasted **walnuts,** 1 cup chopped **dried banana chips,** ½ cup chopped **dried pineapple,** ½ cup **unsweetened shredded or flaked coconut,** ½ cup **oat bran,** and ½ tsp. **table salt** in a small bowl. Microwave ¼ cup firmly packed **light brown sugar,** ¼ cup **honey,** 2 Tbsp. **light corn syrup,** 2 Tbsp. **olive oil,** and 1 tsp. **vanilla extract** in a large microwave-safe bowl at HIGH 1 minute. Pour warm honey mixture over oat mixture, stirring to coat. Whisk 2 large **egg whites,** and stir into oats mixture. Press into a lightly greased **parchment paper**-lined 9-inch square pan. Bake 50 minutes or until browned. Cool completely in pan on a wire rack (about 45 minutes). Cut into 16 squares.

Note: We tested with Fiber One for high-fiber cereal.

Makes 16 bars. Hands-on 15 min.; Total 1 hour, 50 min.

Calories *355;* **Protein** *6.4g;* **Carbs** *49g;* **Fiber** *7.7g;* **Fat** *19g*

CARROT-POPPY SEED MUFFINS

Carolyn says: "Low-fat buttermilk gives a dose of vitamin B12 and potassium in these tender, delicious muffins."

Preheat oven to 375°. Whisk together 1 ½ cups **all-purpose flour,** ¾ cup firmly packed **dark brown sugar,** 1 Tbsp. **poppy seeds,** 1 ¼ tsp. **baking powder,** ½ tsp. **baking soda,** and ½ tsp. **table salt** in a large bowl. Stir in 2 large **eggs,** 5 Tbsp. **olive oil,** and 1 Tbsp. firmly packed **orange zest.** Fold in 2 cups shredded **carrots** (about 3 large) and ¾ cup **low-fat buttermilk.** Place **paper baking cups** in a 12-cup muffin pan, and coat with **cooking spray.** Spoon batter into cups, filling two-thirds full. Bake 20 to 22 minutes or until golden brown.

Makes 1 dozen. Hands-on 15 min.; Total 35 min.

Calories *160;* **Protein** *2.9g;* **Carbs** *24.4g;* **Fiber** *0.8g;* **Fat** *6g*

Beet-Poppy Seed Muffins

Switch up the color and flavor by using shredded beets in place of carrots.

Prepare recipe as directed, substituting 1 large **fresh beet,** peeled and shredded (about 1 ½ cups), for carrots. Omit buttermilk. (Do not squeeze juice from shredded beet.)

Calories *160;* **Protein** *2.7g;* **Carbs** *24.7g;* **Fiber** *1g;* **Fat** *5.9g*

BREAKFAST COOKIES

Carolyn says: "Did someone say 'cookie'? These grab-and-go breakfast bites taste indulgent, but they're made with whole wheat flour, nuts, and dried fruit. Drizzle them with a cranberry juice-flavored glaze."

Preheat oven to 325°. Beat ½ cup softened **butter,** ¼ cup **honey,** and ½ tsp. **table salt** at medium-low speed with an electric mixer until creamy. Add 2 cups **whole wheat flour,** 1 tsp. **vanilla extract,** and ½ tsp. **baking soda,** and beat 1 minute or until blended. Stir in 2 cups coarsely chopped assorted **mixed nuts** and **dried fruit.** Shape dough into a large log (about 3 inches in diameter); wrap in plastic wrap, and chill 8 hours to 1 week. Cut dough into ½-inch-thick slices, and place on a **parchment paper**-lined baking sheet. Bake 20 minutes. Stir together ½ cup plus 2 Tbsp. **powdered sugar** and 1 Tbsp. **cranberry juice.** Drizzle glaze over cookies.

Makes 10 cookies. Hands-on 20 min.; Total 8 hours, 40 min.

Calories *357;* **Protein** *7.5g;* **Carbs** *44.8g;* **Fiber** *2.4g;* **Fat** *18.4g*

BAKED EGGS WITH SPINACH AND TOMATOES

Carolyn says: "Elegant enough for company, these take two minutes to throw together. They're fun to build, so let the kids help."

Preheat oven to 350°. Coat 6 (6- to 8-oz.) ramekins with **cooking spray.** Layer 1 Tbsp. **low-fat garlic-and-herb spreadable cheese** (such as Rondelé); 8 fresh **spinach leaves,** torn; 1 large **egg;** 2 Tbsp. **jarred pasta sauce;** 1 Tbsp. **half-and-half,** and ⅛ tsp. **freshly ground black pepper** in each ramekin. Place on a baking sheet. Bake 20 to 25 minutes or until cooked to desired firmness. Let stand 5 minutes. Serve with toast.

Makes 6 servings. Hands-on 20 min., Total 45 min.

Calories *352;* **Protein** *18.8g;* **Carbs** *43.8g;* **Fiber** *4.2g;* **Fat** *11.8g*

COUNTRY HAM-AND-EGG TOASTS

Carolyn says: "I think the tartine, an open-faced sandwich from France, is the most versatile vehicle for a healthy breakfast. Try topping with everything from poached eggs to leftover chicken." (Also pictured on page 162)

Preheat oven to 425°. Toss together 6 large **green onions,** 2 tsp. **olive oil,** and ⅛ tsp. **kosher salt** in a jelly-roll pan. Bake 10 to 12 minutes or until tender. Cool in pan 5 minutes. Cut onions into 2-inch-long pieces. Spread 2 tsp. **low-fat mayonnaise** onto each of 4 toasted **sourdough bread slices.** Layer each with one-fourth of green onions; 1 **hard-cooked egg,** sliced; and, if desired, 1 Tbsp. thinly sliced cooked **country ham.** Top with desired amount of freshly grated **Parmesan cheese.**

Makes 4 servings. Hands-on 15 min., Total 30 min.

Calories *414;* **Protein** *19.9g;* **Carbs** *58.6g;* **Fiber** *3.3g;* **Fat** *12.1g*

Baked Eggs with Spinach and Tomatoes

Country Ham-and-Egg Toasts

Feed Your Family in a Flash

THESE EIGHT FAST ONE-POT MEALS DELIVER BIG, COMFORTING FLAVOR MINUS THE MESS

SKILLET PORK CHOPS WITH APPLES AND ONIONS

Elegant and easy, this hearty dish comes with a side and a sauce all-in-one. Be sure to brown the chops well so they'll give the mustardy pan sauce deep flavor.

- 4 (6- to 8-oz.) bone-in pork rib chops (1 to 1 1/4 inches thick)
- 1 tsp. kosher salt
- 1/2 tsp. freshly ground black pepper
- 2 Tbsp. olive oil
- 2 Granny Smith apples, cut into 1/2-inch-thick wedges
- 1 medium-size yellow onion, thinly sliced (root end intact)
- 1/3 cup chicken broth
- 1 cup whipping cream
- 1/4 cup Dijon mustard
- 2 Tbsp. bourbon
- 8 small fresh thyme sprigs

1. Preheat oven to 450°. Sprinkle pork with salt and pepper. Cook in hot oil in a 12-inch cast-iron skillet over medium heat 5 to 6 minutes on each side or until golden brown. Remove from skillet.
2. Add apples and onion to skillet; cook, stirring occasionally, 4 to 5 minutes or until browned. Remove from skillet.
3. Add broth to skillet, and cook 1 to 2 minutes, stirring to loosen browned bits from bottom of skillet. Whisk together cream and mustard; add to skillet, and cook, stirring constantly, 1 to 2 minutes or until bubbly.
4. Remove skillet from heat, and stir in bourbon. Add pork, turning to coat, and top with apples, onions, and thyme.
5. Bake at 450° for 10 minutes or until liquid is just beginning to bubble. Let stand in skillet 5 minutes before serving.

Makes 4 servings. Hands-on 30 min., Total 45 min.

LEMON-ROSEMARY-GARLIC CHICKEN AND POTATOES

Nicknamed "Anytime Chicken" by Test Kitchen Specialist Vanessa McNeil Rocchio, this winner of a chicken dinner is our new favorite roasting-pan supper for weeknights or easy entertaining with friends. (Pictured on page 161)

- 1/3 cup olive oil
- 1/4 cup fresh lemon juice
- 1 (3.5-oz.) jar capers, drained
- 2 lemons, sliced
- 10 garlic cloves, smashed
- 3 Tbsp. fresh rosemary leaves
- 2 tsp. kosher salt
- 1 tsp. freshly ground black pepper
- 3 Tbsp. olive oil
- 6 chicken legs (about 1 1/2 lb.)
- 4 skin-on, bone-in chicken thighs (about 2 1/2 lb.)
- 2 lb. small red potatoes
  Crusty French bread

1. Preheat oven to 450°. Stir together first 8 ingredients in a medium bowl.
2. Place a roasting pan on stove-top over 2 burners. Add 3 Tbsp. olive oil, and heat over medium-high heat. Sprinkle chicken with desired amount of salt and pepper; place, skin sides down, in pan. Add potatoes. Cook 9 to 10 minutes or until chicken is browned. Turn chicken, and pour lemon mixture over chicken.
3. Bake at 450° for 45 to 50 minutes or until chicken is done. Serve chicken with sauce and French bread.

Makes 6 servings. Hands-on 20 min.; Total 1 hour, 5 min.

FOUR KEYS TO ONE-POT SUPPER SUCCESS

GRAB YOUR SKILLET, DUTCH OVEN, OR BAKING SHEET AND...

1. GET ORGANIZED Prep all of your ingredients before you start cooking so you can add them quickly and at the right time.
2. EMBRACE HEAT Heat your pot or pan over high heat when the recipe states to do so, and have a spoon or tongs at the ready.

3. BUILD FLAVOR Season and brown meat well to develop the foundation of flavor in the bottom of the skillet or Dutch oven.
4. SERVE SMART Most one-pot meals are meant to be served from oven or stove to table. No need to dirty extra serving dishes.

ONE-POT PASTA WITH TOMATO-BASIL SAUCE

Throw all of your ingredients into one pot over medium-high heat, and about 25 minutes later you'll have noodles perfectly coated in a luscious tomato-basil sauce. (Pictured on page 162)

- 12 oz. casarecce or fusilli pasta
- 1 (28-oz.) can diced tomatoes
- 2 cups chicken broth
- 1/2 medium-size yellow onion, sliced
- 4 garlic cloves, sliced
- 1 tsp. dried oregano
- 1/3 cup firmly packed fresh basil leaves
- 2 tsp. kosher salt
- 1 Tbsp. olive oil
- 1/4 tsp. dried crushed red pepper (optional)
- 1 (6-oz.) package fresh baby spinach
  Freshly grated Parmesan cheese

1. Place first 9 ingredients and, if desired, dried crushed red pepper in a Dutch oven in order of ingredient list. Cover and bring to a boil over medium-high heat (about 12 to 15 minutes). Reduce heat to medium-low, and cook, covered, 10 to 12 minutes or until pasta is slightly al dente, stirring at 5-minute intervals.
2. Remove from heat, and stir in spinach. Cover and let stand 10 minutes. Stir just before serving. Serve with Parmesan cheese.

Note: We tested with Garofalo Casarecce pasta.

Makes 6 servings. Hands-on 20 min., Total 50 min.

Shrimp Pasta Pot: Prepare recipe as directed, stirring in 1 lb. peeled large, raw shrimp, deveined, with spinach in Step 2.

CURRIED SHRIMP WITH PEANUTS

*"This is an updated version of my favorite dinner as a kid," says Vanessa. "Cooking the curry powder with the flour brings out the essential oils, making the dish even more flavorful." **Easy Side:** Cook 2 (8.5-oz.) pouches **ready-to-serve basmati rice** according to package directions. Stir in 1/4 cup chopped **fresh cilantro,** 1 tsp. loosely packed **lime zest,** and 1 Tbsp. **fresh lime juice.** (Pictured on page 162)*

- 2 Tbsp. butter
- 1 Tbsp. all-purpose flour
- 2 tsp. curry powder
- 3/4 cup milk
- 3/4 cup chicken broth
- 1/3 cup ketchup
- 1 Tbsp. grated fresh ginger
- 1/2 jalapeño pepper, seeded and chopped
- 1/4 tsp. dried crushed red pepper (optional)
- 2 1/2 lb. peeled large, raw shrimp, deveined
- 2 tsp. fresh lime juice
- 1/4 tsp. kosher salt
  Toppings: salted cocktail peanuts, bean sprouts, toasted unsweetened flaked coconut, cilantro

Melt butter in a heavy saucepan over low heat; whisk in flour and curry powder until smooth. Cook, whisking constantly, 1 minute. Gradually whisk in milk, next 4 ingredients, and, if desired, dried crushed red pepper. Increase heat to medium, and cook, whisking constantly, 5 to 6 minutes or until mixture is thickened and bubbly. Stir in shrimp, lime juice, and salt. Reduce heat to medium-low, and cook, stirring often, 5 minutes or just until shrimp turn pink. Serve with desired toppings.

Makes 4 to 6 servings. Hands-on 25 min., Total 25 min.

Curried Shrimp with Peanuts

ROASTED CHICKEN CAESAR SALAD

Reinvent the Caesar by roasting the lettuce to caramelize it, and jazz up store-bought dressing to make it taste like homemade.

- ¼ small red onion, thinly sliced
- 1 cup bottled refrigerated Caesar dressing
- ⅓ cup freshly grated Parmesan cheese
- 3 Tbsp. chopped fresh chives
- 2 garlic cloves, pressed
- ½ tsp. loosely packed lemon zest
- 1 Tbsp. fresh lemon juice
- 8 chicken breast tenders
- 2 romaine lettuce hearts, halved lengthwise
- 1 Tbsp. olive oil
  Toppings: Parmesan cheese, black pepper, flat-leaf parsley leaves, croutons

1. Preheat broiler with oven rack 6 inches from heat. Place onion in water to cover; chill until ready to use.
2. Whisk together Caesar dressing and next 5 ingredients.
3. Brush both sides of chicken with ⅓ cup dressing mixture. Place chicken on a lightly greased rack in an aluminum foil-lined jelly-roll pan. Broil 6 to 8 minutes or until browned. Transfer chicken to a serving platter.
4. Place lettuce, cut sides up, on rack in jelly-roll pan; brush with olive oil. Broil 3 to 5 minutes or until browned and wilted.
5. Drizzle desired amount of remaining dressing mixture over chicken and lettuce. Drain onions; pat dry. Serve salad with onions, any remaining dressing, and desired toppings.

Note: We tested with Naturally Fresh Classic Caesar Dressing.

Makes 4 servings. Hands-on 25 min., Total 35 min.

SKILLET ORZO WITH FISH AND HERBS

Cook the orzo like rice, paella-style, on the stove, then top with fish, and bake. Feel free to substitute salmon for any flaky white fish.

- 2 Tbsp. butter
- ¾ cup sliced green onions (about 5 onions), divided
- 4 tsp. pressed garlic cloves (about 3 cloves), divided
- 4 cups vegetable broth
- 2 cups orzo pasta
- ½ cup drained sun-dried tomatoes in oil, chopped
- 1 tsp. kosher salt
- 1 tsp. freshly ground black pepper
- 1½ cups loosely packed fresh flat-leaf parsley, chopped and divided
- 4 (4-oz.) skinless flaky white fish fillets (such as cod)
- 1 tsp. lemon zest
- 1 Tbsp. extra virgin olive oil
  Lemon halves

1. Preheat oven to 350°. Melt butter in a 12-inch ovenproof skillet over medium heat. Add ½ cup sliced green onions and 1 tsp. garlic; sauté 4 minutes or until tender. Stir in broth, next 4 ingredients, and ½ cup parsley. Bring to a simmer, and cook, uncovered and stirring occasionally, 15 minutes or until orzo is just tender and some liquid remains in skillet. Remove from heat.
2. Sprinkle fish with desired amount of salt and pepper. Place fish in a single layer on hot orzo mixture, and cover skillet.
3. Bake at 350° for 10 to 25 minutes or until fish flakes with a fork. (The bake time will vary depending on the thickness of the fish.)
4. Stir together lemon zest and remaining green onions, garlic, and parsley. Spoon over cooked fish; drizzle with olive oil. Serve immediately with lemon halves.

Makes 4 servings. Hands-on 30 min., Total 40 min.

QUICK BEEF CHILI

Rich, beefy petite tender, the quick-cooking foundation of this stew and a supermarket steak cut from the shoulder, looks and tastes like tenderloin but costs a third of the price. Can't find it? Try chuck-eye steak, which has good flavor but needs a little more trimming. (Pictured on page 3)

- 2 lb. beef petite tender steak (aka shoulder tender), trimmed and cut into 1-inch cubes
- 2 Tbsp. olive oil
- 1 yellow onion, chopped
- 4 garlic cloves, chopped
- 2 to 3 tsp. chipotle chile powder
- 2 tsp. dried oregano
- 2 tsp. ground cumin
- 1 (6-oz.) can tomato paste
- 5 (4.5-oz.) cans chopped green chiles
- 4 cups chicken broth
- 1 (14.5-oz.) can stewed tomatoes
- 2 Tbsp. plain yellow cornmeal
  Toppings: green onions, fried onion rings, sour cream, Cheddar cheese

1. Sprinkle beef with desired amount of salt and pepper. Cook beef in hot oil in a large enamel cast-iron Dutch oven over medium-high heat, stirring often, 5 to 6 minutes or until browned. Transfer beef to a platter.
2. Add onion to Dutch oven, and cook, stirring often, 3 minutes or until tender. Add garlic and next 3 ingredients; cook, stirring constantly, 2 minutes. Stir in tomato paste, and cook, stirring constantly, 2 minutes.
3. Add chiles, next 2 ingredients, beef, and 1 cup water; bring to a boil. Boil, stirring occasionally, 20 minutes. Add salt to taste. Sprinkle with cornmeal. Cook, stirring constantly, 5 minutes or until thickened. Serve with desired toppings.

Makes 2 qt. Hands-on 25 min., Total 55 min.

ORANGE RICE SALAD

(FROM FEBRUARY 1976)

THE ORIGINAL: a congealed salad meets rice pudding that fits modern times like a leisure suit. Can you believe we made the far-out suggestion to serve it as both salad and dessert? **THE REMAKE:** a breezy, tropical take on rice pudding with a sunshiny attitude. We cut the gelatin and replaced the canned fruit with fresh. Can you dig it?

RECIPE REVIVAL

TROPICAL RICE PUDDING

(Pictured on page 163)

- 2 cups cooked long-grain rice
- 4 cups milk
- 3/4 cup sugar
- 1/2 tsp. table salt
- 1 cup heavy cream
- 2 large eggs
- 1 cup coarsely chopped fresh pineapple*
- 1 Tbsp. firmly packed orange zest
- 1 Tbsp. firmly packed lemon zest
- 1 tsp. orange extract**
  Toppings: fresh pineapple, navel orange segments, toasted unsweetened coconut, sweetened whipped cream, ground cinnamon and cinnamon sticks, fresh mint sprigs

1. Bring first 4 ingredients to a simmer in a large saucepan over medium-high heat, stirring occasionally. Reduce heat to medium-low; simmer, stirring often, 20 to 25 minutes or until milk is reduced by half and rice is very tender.
2. Meanwhile, whisk together cream and eggs. Whisk 2 Tbsp. hot rice mixture into mixture. Reduce heat to low; stir cream mixture into remaining rice mixture. Cook, stirring constantly, 2 minutes or until begins to thicken. Remove from heat; stir in pineapple and next 3 ingredients. Serve with toppings.

*1 (8-oz.) can pineapple tidbits, drained, may be substituted.
**Vanilla extract may be substituted.

Makes 8 servings. Hands-on 40 min., Total 55 min.

OUR OWN KING OF THE KITCHEN, NORMAN KING, EXPLAINS HOW TO

COOK UNDER PRESSURE

The pressure cooker is my go-to gadget for 2014. Unlike the cookers of old, today's sleek models are all about safety. They also shortcut stews, braises, and beans that ordinarily take hours to prepare. Here are the four keys to pressure cooker success.

Test Kitchen recommended! Fissler Vitaquick, 6.4-qt., $249.95; *crateandbarrel.com*

① KNOW THY COOKER
Read the instruction manual and familiarize yourself with the unit before it touches the stove. Key parts: the latch for locking the lid and the pressure indicator.

② JUST LIKE A SAUCEPAN
One of my favorite features? The pot works on the stove, so you can sauté, boil, or simmer as your would in a saucepan or Dutch oven. Then it's time to lock down the lid and let the pressure build.

③ PRESSURIZE AND COOK
Pressure cookers cook 30 to 40 degrees hotter than water's boiling point with 8 to 15 pounds per square inch (psi) of pressure, turning hours of cook time into minutes. (See "Try It!" at right.)

④ LET OFF SOME STEAM
Release the pressure after the food is cooked. The natural release method, letting the cooker stand off the heat until the pressure is released (about 20 minutes), is the simplest and safest way.

TRY IT!
15-MINUTE RED BEANS

In just 15 minutes of hands-on time, you can pressure-cook a pot of red beans flavored with andouille that tastes like it's been simmering all afternoon. The pressure pushes the heat into the beans quickly, but they still cook up perfectly tender and intact. Test Kitchen pro Pam Lolley, our resident Cajun-phile, was dubious until she tested my recipe. Now she's a believer, and you will be too.

Go Bananas!

SPLIT WITH TRADITION WITH TWO OF OUR FAVORTE NEW DESSERTS—ONE EASY CAKE
AND A DREAMY, PEANUTTY BANANA CREAM PIE

PEANUT BUTTER-BANANA CREAM PIE

- 22 peanut butter sandwich cookies
- 1/2 cup lightly salted dry-roasted peanuts
- 1/4 cup butter, melted
- 1/2 cup granulated sugar
- 1/4 cup cornstarch
- 2 cups half-and-half
- 4 large egg yolks
- 3 Tbsp. butter
- 2 Tbsp. creamy peanut butter
- 2 tsp. vanilla extract, divided
- 2 medium bananas
- 2 cups heavy cream
- 1/2 cup powdered sugar
  Garnishes: halved peanut butter sandwich cookies, chopped lightly salted dry-roasted peanuts

1. Preheat oven to 350°. Process cookies and peanuts in a food processor about 1 minute or until finely chopped. Stir together cookie mixture and melted butter. Press mixture on bottom, up sides, and onto lip of a lightly greased 9-inch pie plate.
2. Bake at 350° for 10 to 12 minutes or until lightly browned. Transfer to a wire rack, and cool completely (about 30 minutes).
3. Whisk together granulated sugar and cornstarch in a large heavy saucepan. Whisk together half-and-half and egg yolks in a medium bowl. Gradually whisk half-and-half mixture into sugar mixture, and bring to a boil over medium heat, whisking constantly. Boil, whisking constantly, 1 minute; remove from heat.
4. Stir butter, peanut butter, and 1 tsp. vanilla into sugar mixture. Place heavy-duty plastic wrap directly on warm custard (to prevent a film from forming), and cool 30 minutes.

5. Cut bananas into 1/2-inch-thick slices; place in a single layer on bottom of crust, covering bottom completely. Spoon custard mixture over bananas; cover and chill 4 to 48 hours.
6. Beat cream at high speed with an electric mixer until foamy; gradually add powdered sugar and remaining 1 tsp. vanilla, beating until soft peaks form. Top pie with whipped cream mixture. Serve immediately, or chill up to 4 hours.

Note: We tested with Nabisco Nutter Butter peanut butter sandwich cookies.

Makes 8 servings. Hands-on 35 min.; Total 5 hours, 45 min.

BANANA SNACK CAKE

- 1/2 cup butter, softened
- 1 cup granulated sugar
- 1 cup firmly packed light brown sugar
- 3 large eggs
- 1 1/3 cups mashed very ripe bananas (about 3 medium)
- 1 tsp. vanilla extract
- 2 cups all-purpose flour
- 1 tsp. baking soda
- 1 tsp. ground cinnamon
- 1/4 tsp. ground nutmeg
- 1/4 tsp. table salt
- 1 cup chopped toasted pecans, divided
  Cream Cheese Frosting
  Glazed Banana Slices (optional)

1. Preheat oven to 350°. Beat butter at medium speed with a heavy-duty electric stand mixer 1 to 2 minutes or until creamy. Gradually add both sugars, beating well. Add eggs, 1 at a time, beating just until blended after each addition. Add mashed bananas

and vanilla, and beat at low speed just until combined.
2. Stir together flour and next 4 ingredients. Gradually add flour mixture to butter mixture, beating at low speed just until blended. Stir in 1/2 cup pecans. Spread batter in a greased and floured 15- x 10-inch jelly-roll pan.
3. Bake at 350° for 20 to 25 minutes or until a wooden pick inserted in center comes out clean. Cool completely on a wire rack (about 1 hour). Spread cake with Cream Cheese Frosting. Top with Glazed Banana Slices, if desired. Sprinkle with remaining 1/2 cup pecans.

Makes 32 servings. Hands-on 15 min.; Total 2 hours, including frosting and glazed bananas

Cream Cheese Frosting

Beat 1/2 cup **butter,** softened, and 1 (8-oz.) package **cream cheese,** softened, at medium speed with an electric mixer until creamy. Gradually add 4 cups **powdered sugar** and 2 tsp. **vanilla extract,** beating at low speed until blended. Increase speed to medium-high; beat 1 to 2 minutes or until fluffy.

Makes about 3 1/2 cups. Hands-on 10 min., Total 10 min.

Glazed Banana Slices

Preheat broiler with oven rack 5 to 6 inches from heat. Cut 4 **ripe bananas** in half crosswise; cut lengthwise into 1/4-inch-thick slices, and place in a single layer on a lightly greased aluminum foil-lined baking sheet. Brush with 1 Tbsp. **melted butter;** sprinkle with 2 Tbsp. **light brown sugar.** Broil 4 to 5 minutes or until bubbly and just beginning to brown. (Keep an eye on the bananas while broiling to make sure they don't overbrown.)

Hands-on 15 min., Total 15 min.

Community Cookbook

COMFORT YOUR FAMILY WITH OUR FAVORITE BLOGGERS' **HEARTY WINTER SOUPS**

From the Kitchen of
RUSSELL VAN KRAAYENBURG
HOUSTON, TX
CHASINGDELICIOUS.COM

"Wherever this soup came from, I'm sure glad it's become a Tex-Mex staple. I like to give it a winterized twist by adding a big ol' helping of butternut squash."

BUTTERNUT SQUASH TORTILLA SOUP
(Pictured on page 164)

Sauté 1 large **red onion,** chopped, and 1 **jalapeño pepper,** seeded and chopped, in 2 Tbsp. hot **olive oil** in a large Dutch oven over medium heat 5 minutes or until tender. Add 4 **garlic cloves,** minced; 1 Tbsp. **ground cumin;** and 1 Tbsp. **tomato paste;** sauté 2 minutes. Add 1 (2-lb.) **butternut squash,** peeled and cut into 1/2-inch cubes, and 1 (14.5-oz.) can petite **diced tomatoes,** drained. Cook, stirring often, 10 minutes. Add 6 cups **chicken broth,** and bring to a boil. Reduce heat to low, and simmer, stirring occasionally, 20 minutes or until squash is tender. Stir in 2 cups **fresh cilantro leaves.** Remove from heat, and spoon into bowls. Top with **tortilla chips** or **strips,** shredded cooked **chicken,** crumbled **feta cheese or queso fresco** (fresh Mexican cheese), diced **avocado,** and **sour cream.** Serve with **lime wedges.** MAKES about 10 cups

---

From the Kitchen of
JULIE DEILY
ORLANDO, FL
THELITTLEKITCHEN.NET

"Baked potatoes are a big favorite in our house, so I decided to turn them into a soup. This was a huge hit and added to our regular rotation. Tempering ensures the cream mixture doesn't curdle."

LOADED BAKED POTATO SOUP

Melt 4 Tbsp. **butter** in a Dutch oven over medium heat; add 1 small **yellow onion,** chopped, and cook, stirring often, 3 to 5 minutes or until tender. Sprinkle onion mixture with 3 Tbsp. **all-purpose flour,** and cook, stirring constantly, 1 minute. Gradually whisk in 6 cups **chicken broth,** 1/2 tsp. **kosher salt,** and 1/2 tsp. **freshly ground black pepper.** Add 2 medium-size **russet potatoes,** peeled and diced, and bring to a boil, stirring often. Reduce heat to medium-low; simmer, stirring occasionally, 15 minutes or until potatoes are tender. Whisk together 1/2 cup **heavy cream** and 1/2 cup **sour cream** in a bowl. Gradually stir about 1 cup hot potato mixture into cream mixture; add cream mixture to remaining hot potato mixture, stirring constantly. Stir in 1 cup (4 oz.) shredded **Cheddar cheese** and 3 cups frozen **broccoli florets,** thawed. Cook 5 minutes or until thoroughly heated. Top with chopped cooked **bacon,** sliced **green onions,** and shredded **Cheddar cheese.** MAKES 6 cups

---

From the Kitchen of
STEPHANIE GANZ
RICHMOND, VA
ONIONCLOUTE.COM

"The ingredients in this recipe are humble, but they come together to create a soup that is better than the sum of its parts."

CABBAGE, WHITE BEAN, AND POTATO SOUP

Sauté 1 large **yellow onion,** chopped, and 3 **garlic cloves,** minced, in 2 Tbsp. hot **olive oil** in a large Dutch oven over medium-high heat 5 to 7 minutes or until tender. Add 1 lb. **fingerling potatoes,** cut into 1/2-inch-thick slices; 1 tsp. **kosher salt;** and 1/2 tsp. **freshly ground black pepper.** Stir in 1/2 medium-size head **cabbage,** thinly sliced; 6 cups organic **chicken broth;** and 1 (15.5-oz.) can **cannellini beans,** drained and rinsed, and bring to a boil. Cover and reduce heat to medium-low. Simmer 15 minutes. Top each serving with shaved fresh **Parmesan cheese** and a drizzle of **extra virgin olive oil.** Serve with **garlic toast.** MAKES about 10 cups

February

The New Southern Supper Club

IF YOU RESOLVED TO ENTERTAIN MORE IN 2014, THEN A COZY WINTER NIGHT
IS THE PERFECT REASON TO GATHER FRIENDS AND START YOUR OWN SUPPER CLUB.
HERE'S OUR PROVEN STRATEGY TO MAKE THE PARTY LAST.

Rule No. 1
THE BUILD-YOUR-OWN APPETIZER BAR

The first signs of spring bring out the itch in all good Southerners. It's time to entertain again. We've survived winter's chill, all cozy at home, and our need to socialize and share runs deep. The *SL* strategy for supper-club success involves a make-ahead movable feast that starts in the kitchen—the perfect spot to welcome guests (and put them to work!). There's no better icebreaker than encouraging folks to break bread with a signature cocktail in hand as they top their crostini.

SOUTHERN 75

Stir together 1 cup **bourbon,** 1/2 cup **lemon juice,** and 1/3 cup **powdered sugar** in a pitcher until sugar dissolves (about 30 seconds). Cover and chill 3 hours. Divide among 8 Champagne flutes; top each with 1/4 cup chilled **hard cider** (such as Angry Orchard). Garnish with **apple slices, lemon curls,** or **rosemary sprigs,** if desired.

Makes 3 1/2 cups. Hands-on 5 min.; Total 3 hours, 5 min.

Make-Ahead Tip: Mix together the first 3 ingredients of this twist on a classic French 75 up to 24 hours ahead.

CROSTINI

- 1 (8- to 10-oz.) **French bread baguette, cut into 1/2-inch-thick slices (35 to 40 pieces)**
- 2 1/2 **Tbsp. extra virgin olive oil**

Preheat oven to 400°. Place bread in a single layer on a baking sheet, and brush with olive oil. Bake 7 to 8 minutes or until lightly browned. Cool completely on a wire rack (about 2 minutes).

Makes 6 to 8 servings. Hands-on 5 min., Total 15 min.

Ham-and-Greens Crostini

- 4 oz. country ham, finely chopped
- 2 Tbsp. olive oil
- 1 large bunch fresh collard greens (about 1 1/2 lb.), washed, trimmed, and finely chopped
- 1 Tbsp. butter
- 1/8 tsp. ground red pepper
  Kosher salt and freshly ground black pepper
- 1 Tbsp. half-and-half
- 1 (8-oz.) goat cheese log, softened
  Crostini (recipe at left)

1. Cook ham in 1 Tbsp. hot oil in a large skillet over medium-high heat 3 to 4 minutes or until crisp. Remove from skillet using a slotted spoon, and drain on paper towels. Reserve drippings in skillet. Add greens and remaining oil to hot drippings in skillet; cook, stirring often, 4 to 5 minutes or until slightly wilted. Add butter and red pepper, and cook, stirring occasionally, 45 seconds. Stir in ham. Add salt and pepper to taste; transfer to a bowl.
2. Stir together half-and-half and goat cheese until smooth. Stir in half of greens mixture. Reserve remaining half of greens mixture.
3. Spread about 1 Tbsp. goat cheese mixture onto each Crostini. Top each with 1 tsp. reserved greens mixture.

Makes 8 to 10 appetizer servings. Hands-on 25 min.; Total 25 min., not including crostini

Make-Ahead Tip: Refrigerate cooked greens up to 2 days.

Butternut Squash-and-Pecan Crostini

- 1 large butternut squash (about 1 1/2 lb.), halved lengthwise and seeded
- 1 Tbsp. olive oil
- 1/2 tsp. smoked paprika
  Kosher salt and freshly ground black pepper
- 1 tsp. apple cider vinegar
- 2 Tbsp. butter, melted
  Crostini (recipe at left)
  Shaved Parmesan cheese
- 1/4 cup toasted pecans, chopped
  Garnish: fresh sage leaves

1. Preheat oven to 425°. Place squash, flesh side up, in a 13- x 9-inch baking dish; drizzle with oil, and sprinkle with paprika and desired amount of salt and pepper. Turn squash, and place, flesh side down, in baking dish. Cover with heavy-duty aluminum foil. Bake 30 to 40 minutes or until tender. Cool in pan on a wire rack 5 minutes. Peel squash, and cut into large pieces.

2. Pulse squash, vinegar, and butter in a food processor 7 or 8 times or until smooth. Add salt and pepper to taste.

3. Spread 1 tsp. squash mixture onto each Crostini. Top each with a few pieces of shaved Parmesan and about 1/4 tsp. pecans.

Makes 8 to 10 appetizer servings.
Hands-on 10 min.; Total 45 min., not including crostini

Make-Ahead Tip: Chill squash mixture up to 2 days. Microwave, stirring every 30 seconds, until hot.

Pear-and-Blue Cheese Crostini

- 1 ripe pear, thinly sliced
  Crostini (recipe at left)
- 1 cup firmly packed baby arugula
- 4 oz. blue cheese, sliced
- 4 cooked bacon slices, coarsely chopped
  Honey

Place 1 pear slice on each Crostini. Top with arugula, cheese, and bacon. Drizzle with honey.

Make-Ahead Tip: Refrigerate cooked bacon up to 3 days.

MAKE AHEAD
Toasts may be made one day ahead and stored in an airtight container at room temperature.

PARTY TIMELINE

2 DAYS BEFORE
Make mousse and crostini toppings; store in fridge. Buy two dozen roses. Store in water until time to arrange.

1 DAY BEFORE
Make crostini. Make stew base, mayo, and cocktail base; store in fridge.

2-3 HOURS BEFORE
Set the table, and fill vases with roses.

1 HOUR BEFORE
Cook corn cakes; hold in a 200° oven.

15 MINUTES BEFORE
Pour yourself a cocktail—a relaxed host puts everyone at ease.

DURING APPETIZERS
Reheat stew base; add remaining uncooked seafood to cook.

DURING DINNER
Pull mousse from fridge. Pop shortbreads into a 350° oven for 5 minutes.

Rule No. 2
THE NO-FAIL MAIN DISH

Forget what you know about dinner parties past: elaborate menus with tricky themes and too many side items. There's a new breed of entertaining that's based on simplicity and marries fresh ingredients with a one-pot stove-to-table philosophy. The secret weapon? A Dutch oven. This heavy-bottomed workhorse churns out any company-worthy dish, from jambalaya to beef bourguignon. Long-simmering and full of flavor, one-pot meals serve a crowd and are a cinch to clean up. The best part? Confidence in knowing that less really is more.

MAKE AHEAD
Make the stew base one day ahead. Reheat and cook the seafood minutes before serving.

GULF COAST SEAFOOD STEW

This rustic stew was inspired by the rich, meaty flavors of a crawfish or shrimp boil. Feel free to substitute more shrimp for the crawfish, if desired. (Also pictured on page 4)

1 1/2 lb. unpeeled, medium-size raw shrimp
2 celery ribs
1 large sweet onion
2 qt. reduced-sodium fat-free chicken broth
12 oz. andouille sausage, cut into 1/2-inch pieces
1 poblano pepper, seeded and chopped
1 green bell pepper, chopped
1 Tbsp. canola oil
3 garlic cloves, chopped
1 lb. small red potatoes, halved
1 (12-oz.) bottle beer
1 Tbsp. fresh thyme leaves
2 fresh bay leaves
2 tsp. Creole seasoning
1 1/2 lb. fresh white fish fillets, (such as snapper, grouper, or catfish), cubed
1 lb. cooked crawfish tails (optional)
Kosher salt and freshly ground black pepper
Griddle Corn Cakes (recipe at right)
Spiced Mayonnaise (recipe at right)

1. Peel shrimp; place shells in a saucepan. (Refrigerate shrimp until ready to use.) Add celery ends and onion peel to pan; chop remaining celery and onion. (Using the leftover bits of onion and celery will layer the flavor and result in a flavorful broth.) Add broth; bring to a boil over medium-high heat. Reduce heat to low; simmer 30 minutes.

2. Meanwhile, cook sausage in a large Dutch oven over medium-high heat, stirring often, 7 to 8 minutes or until browned. Remove sausage; pat dry. Wipe Dutch oven clean. Sauté celery, onion, and peppers in hot oil in Dutch oven over medium-high heat 5 to 7 minutes or until onion is tender. Add garlic, and sauté 45 seconds to 1 minute or until fragrant. Stir in potatoes, next 4 ingredients, and sausage.

3. Pour broth mixture through a fine wire-mesh strainer into Dutch oven, discarding solids. Increase heat to high; bring to a boil. Reduce heat to low, and cook, stirring occasionally, 20 minutes or until potatoes are tender.

4. Add fish; cook 2 to 3 minutes or until just opaque. Add shrimp, and cook 2 to 3 minutes or just until shrimp turn pink. If desired, stir in crawfish, and cook 2 to 3 minutes or until hot. Add salt and pepper to taste.

5. Spoon seafood into warmed soup bowls. Top with desired amount of broth. Serve immediately with Griddle Corn Cakes and Spiced Mayonnaise.

Makes 6 to 8 servings. Hands-on 55 min.; Total 1 hour, 35 min., not including corn cakes and mayonnaise

GRIDDLE CORN CAKES

Smear the mayo over these cakes and encourage your guests to dunk them in the stew. Make them up to one hour ahead, and keep warm on low in the oven.

- 2 **cups plain white or yellow cornmeal**
- 1 **tsp. kosher salt**
- 1 **tsp. baking soda**
- 1 **cup buttermilk**
- 1 **large egg, lightly beaten**
- 1/4 **cup canola oil, divided**
- 1 **green onion, thinly sliced**

1. Stir together first 3 ingredients in a small bowl.

2. Stir together buttermilk, egg, and 2 Tbsp. oil. Stir into cornmeal mixture just until blended. Stir in green onion.

3. Brush 1 Tbsp. oil on a hot griddle. Drop cornmeal mixture by 1/8 cupfuls onto hot griddle. Flatten to 1/2 inch thick, and cook 1 1/2 to 2 minutes on each side or until golden. Repeat process with remaining batter and oil.

Makes 20 cakes. Hands-on 10 min.; Total 10 min.

MAKE AHEAD
Cook corn cakes up to one hour ahead, then hold in a 200° oven. Serve them on a platter with a bowl of the spiced mayo.

SIX MORE SECRETS TO SUPPER CLUB SUCCESS

WHAT'S THE RIGHT NUMBER OF PEOPLE? Eight is enough. It keeps the group intimate, means less food to buy, and is easier to fit everyone around a table.

ASSIGNED SEATING: YES OR NO? We say yes. Otherwise two scenarios are possible: couples sit together or you revert to the 7th grade with genders separated. Mix up your guests: Separate couples and close friends. Put big talkers next to quieter types, and sit Republicans next to Democrats. (No, never!)

HOW DO I ADDRESS THE "WHAT CAN I BRING?" QUESTION? Don't be shy! A bottle of wine is always easy, but be specific. Tell guests the kind of grape that will go best with the meal. Have 4 bottles (two chilled whites and two reds) ready, and then open guests' bottles if necessary. For the menu on these pages, we recommend a New Zealand Sauvignon Blanc or Muscadet for white and Pinot Noir or Côtes du Rhône for red.

WHAT TO DO ABOUT DIETARY RESTRICTIONS? Learn your friends' life choices but not their preferences. For example, adapt your menu if you're feeding a vegetarian, but don't worry if John likes mushrooms or not.

HOW DO YOU AVOID STALL-OUT? It's all about frequency. The most successful supper club meets seven times a year: January, February, April, May, August, September, and October. Take Spring Break and summer months off, and don't even think about squeezing it in during the holidays. Thursdays are a good night—not too busy and it gives you all week to prep.

WHAT DO YOU THINK OF POT-LUCKS? Whether one host cooks all of the food or people are assigned courses is up to each group. We know one thing for sure: Set a menu (like ours) and stick to it. Otherwise you risk having seven-layer dip paired with lasagna.

SHOULD YOU BRING THE HOST A GIFT? That depends if your mama raised you right. (Kidding!) You'll never go wrong with a small, thoughtful gesture. Our pick: a set of festive letterpress coasters ($8 for 12; *dinglewooddesign.etsy.com*) with a handwritten tag that says thank you.

SPICED MAYONNAISE

Portion control may be a problem, as this flavored mayo is so tasty that folks will want more. Feel free to double the recipe and use it just like plain mayonnaise.

- 1/4 **cup Gulf Coast Seafood Stew broth (recipe at left)***
  Pinch of ground saffron (optional)
- 1 **cup mayonnaise with olive oil (such as Hellmann's with Olive Oil)**
- 2 **garlic cloves, minced**

Stir together broth and saffron; let stand 5 minutes. Stir together mayonnaise and garlic in a small bowl. Whisk in broth mixture, 2 Tbsp. at a time, until smooth and mixture is desired consistency.

Makes 1 cup. Hands-on 5 min.; Total 10 min., not including broth

*Bottled clam juice or chicken broth may be substituted.

Rule No. 3
THE EVERYDAY TABLE SETTING

Have no fear—there's no fine china here. Just a can't-believe-it's-so-easy formula for a stylish place setting that starts with a basic white plate. Yep, you heard us. So whether you have a brand-new set or mix-and-match collection, we suggest you put the dinner plates to use. Layer a charger (in lieu of a place mat) underneath. To offset the crispness of the white, we love using antique chargers or textured ones made of rattan or bamboo. Because the main dish is a stew, top the setting off with a vibrant bowl. A simple soup spoon and two clear glass goblets (for water and wine) round out the essentials. Don't stress over a complicated centerpiece. Buy 2 dozen roses in bright hues from the grocery store. (Tip: Pick them up a few days before to allow them to fully open.) Place a single stem or three in tiny glass bottles down the center of the table. Tie a handwritten tag around a bottle for a quick and easy place card. Turn down the lights and add votives for a sparkly glow.

Rule No. 4
THE MAKE-AHEAD DESSERT

Some of life's best moments are spent gathered around a dinner table. Yet there's always that split second at the end of a meal that can cause a party to break up early. Change the scenery and energy by moving the after-party to a cozy living room or den, preferably centered on a roaring fire, where an after-dinner drink (say, bourbon or dark rum) and rich dessert will give folks a reason to linger. The beauty of this chocolate mousse is that it can be made days ahead and brought out just in time for coffee and tea.

MOCHA CHOCOLATE MOUSSE

This seriously easy and decadent mousse hides a smart secret: reduced-sodium soy sauce. Just 1/2 tsp. elevates the deep, rich flavor of the dark chocolate. Add crunch with cookies to contrast the mousse's silky texture. Heating store-bought shortbread in the oven opens up the flavors of the buttery cookies.

- 3 (4-oz.) bittersweet chocolate baking bars (60% cacao), chopped
- 2/3 cup strong-brewed coffee
- 1/4 cup bourbon
- 1/2 tsp. vanilla extract
- 1/2 tsp. reduced-sodium soy sauce
- 1 2/3 cups heavy cream, divided
- 1/4 cup sugar
- Store-bought shortbread cookies (optional)
- Toppings: sweetened whipped cream, fresh raspberries, chocolate shavings

1. Microwave chocolate in a large microwave-safe bowl at HIGH 1 minute or until slightly melted.
2. Bring coffee, next 3 ingredients, and $^{2}/_{3}$ cup cream to a simmer in a small saucepan over medium heat. Pour cream mixture over chocolate in bowl. Let stand 15 seconds, and stir until smooth. Cool completely (about 30 minutes).
3. Beat remaining 1 cup cream at high speed with a heavy-duty electric stand mixer, using a whisk attachment, until foamy; gradually add sugar, beating until soft peaks form. Stir in $^{1}/_{2}$ cup coffee mixture until blended; gradually fold in remaining coffee mixture. (Mixture will be loose.)
4. Spoon chocolate mixture into a shallow 2-qt. bowl or 6 (8- to 10-oz.) glasses. Cover with plastic wrap (without touching mousse), and chill 2 to 3 hours. Serve with cookies, if desired, and toppings.

Note: We tested with Walkers Pure Butter Assorted Shortbread cookies. Warm shortbread in the oven at 350° for 5 minutes so they taste freshly baked.

Makes 6 servings. Hands-on 25 min.; Total 2 hours, 55 min.

Make-Ahead Tip: Refrigerate mousse, without desired toppings, up to 2 days.

WORTH THE SPLURGE! We love the vivid colors and timeless quality of Le Creuset cookware. Pretty enough to display, it's the new family heirloom.

Rule No. 5
THE PARTY ESSENTIALS

Here at *Southern Living*, one of our mottoes is "blue-and-white is always right." It's a no-fail combo we love to use when setting a table because it's classic and modern at the same time and never goes out of style. Add rustic wood and shiny brass accents to give it an instant update.

1. DOMINOES SET $19; *westelm.com*

2. RAW WOOD BOARDS Blue Dip, Medium, $39; *westelm.com*

3. LE CREUSET SIGNATURE INDIGO ROUND FRENCH OVEN $239.95; *surlatable.com*

4. DOMUS FRENCH PRESS COFFEE POT Large with Wicker Handle by Nick Munro; $155; *shophorne.com*

5. LINEN TOWEL in White/Navy, $15; *jayson-home.com*

6. GOLD COCKTAIL SPOONS $29/set of 4; *westelm.com*

7. BLUE DON KARAKUSA DESIGN BOWL $42.50/set of 5; *pearlriver.com*

Ciao Down!

THEY SAY POLENTA. WE SAY GRITS. THEY SAY PANCETTA. WE SAY BACON.
THE LANGUAGE IS DIFFERENT, BUT ITALY AND THE SOUTH SHARE SOME SERIOUSLY TASTY TRADITIONS.
MEMPHIS CHEFS ANDREW TICER AND MICHAEL HUDMAN MAKE THEIR NONNAS PROUD
BY SHARING THEIR SOUTHERN SPINS ON ITALIAN TRADITION.

Braised greens, tender beans, and a deep, abiding love of pork are just a few of the ties that bind two of the world's most soul-satisfying cuisines. The American South and Italy may be an ocean and a world apart, but the pleasures they share at the table are surprisingly similar. From their mutual humble origins and culinary traditions to their robust pantries and reverence for seasonal ingredients, the intersection of two great cultures is the perfect place to find a comforting recipe to feed family and friends.

Nowhere is this confluence of culinary styles more pronounced, or delicious, than in East Memphis (yes, you read that right). Here, chefs Andrew Ticer and Michael Hudman, lifelong friends who grew up in big, boisterous Italian families, serve a unique and very personal hybrid of Southern American-Italian cooking at their two acclaimed restaurants: the upscale Andrew Michael Italian Kitchen, which opened in 2008, and the casually hip Hog & Hominy, one of our favorites since it opened in 2012. Their recipes—often inspired by their Italian *nonnas*—are showcased in a new cookbook, *Collards & Carbonara* (Olive Press, 2013), and the new recipes that follow in these pages were created exclusively for *Southern Living* readers.

On a recent rainy evening in Memphis, we cooked dinner at Andy's house. As we sipped Negronis and feasted on several courses of Parmesan-dusted deliciousness, we talked about how Italian and Southern American cuisines meld so easily on the plate. By the time the bubbling Baked Ziti with Sausage emerged from the oven, our clatter of forks—and the happy quiet that ensued—revealed yet another shared sentiment: Nothing beats gathering friends and family around a table to feast on honest food prepared with love and gratitude for what's been handed down. *Salute* to the ties that bind.

WINTER MUSHROOM RISOTTO

We love the complex depth of flavor chicken livers lend (think dirty rice), but feel free to leave them out. Remember, the key to a creamy risotto is to stir, stir, stir. All that action releases the rice's natural starches, which make the sauce thick and velvety.

- 9 cups reduced-sodium fat-free chicken broth
- 2 (8-oz.) packages fresh cremini mushrooms
- 6 fresh thyme sprigs
- 1 bunch fresh flat-leaf parsley
- 2 1/2 oz. chicken livers or gizzards
- 2 Tbsp. olive oil
- 6 Tbsp. unsalted butter, divided
- 1 large yellow onion, minced
- 2 celery ribs, minced
- 1 1/2 cups uncooked Arborio (short grain) rice
- 1 cup dry white wine
- 1/3 cup freshly grated Parmesan cheese
- 2 tsp. chopped fresh thyme

1. Bring broth to a simmer in a large saucepan over medium-high heat. Meanwhile, remove stems from mushrooms. Add thyme sprigs, mushroom stems, and half of parsley to broth. Reduce heat to low; gently simmer until ready to use. Remove leaves from remaining parsley, and coarsely chop. Discard stems.

2. Sauté livers in hot oil in a Dutch oven over medium heat 5 minutes or until cooked. Remove livers, and finely chop. Add 4 Tbsp. butter and mushroom caps to Dutch oven, and sauté 10 minutes or until deep golden brown. Remove from Dutch oven using a slotted spoon. Add onion, and sauté 10 minutes or until tender. Add celery, and sauté 5 minutes or until softened.

3. Add rice, and cook, stirring constantly, 1 minute or until fragrant. Stir in wine, and cook, stirring often, 3 minutes. Add 1 cup hot broth mixture (discarding mushroom stems and herb sprigs), and cook, stirring constantly, until liquid is absorbed. Repeat procedure with remaining broth mixture, 1 cup at a time, until liquid is absorbed. (Total cooking time is 30 to 35 minutes.) Remove from heat.

4. Stir in livers, cheese, chopped thyme, chopped parsley, remaining 2 Tbsp. butter, and salt and pepper to taste. Serve immediately.

Makes 6 to 8 servings. Hands-on 1 hour, 25 min.; Total 1 hour, 30 min.

THE TIE THAT BINDS
Rice

Rice abounds in the coastal South. It soaks up our rich gravies and pan juices and adds ballast to stews and étouffée. Arborio rice, a shorter grain grown in Italy with a higher starch content, absorbs stocks in a different manner: The cooking liquid is added warm, in small increments, and stirred until the grain takes on a creamy consistency and becomes risotto.

Braised Beans with Collard Greens and Ham

BRAISED BEANS WITH COLLARD GREENS AND HAM

Smoked ham hocks are inexpensive and give the dish rich flavor; substitute with ham steak if you prefer. This dish defines easy, relaxed cooking, so don't stress over measurements.

- 1 lb. dried cannellini beans
- 1 medium-size yellow onion, diced
- 9 cups reduced-sodium fat-free chicken broth, divided
- 6 fresh thyme sprigs
- 5 fresh flat-leaf parsley sprigs
- 2 bay leaves
- 3 fresh sage sprigs (optional)
- 3 fresh basil sprigs (optional)
  Kitchen string
- 2 (1-lb.) smoked ham hocks
- 1 Parmigiano-Reggiano cheese rind (optional)
- 4 cups chopped fresh collard greens
- 2 garlic cloves, chopped
- 1 Tbsp. olive oil
- 1 (14.5-oz.) can fire-roasted diced tomatoes

1. Rinse and sort beans according to package directions. Place beans in a large bowl; add water to 2 inches above beans. Cover and chill 8 to 12 hours.

2. Drain beans, and place in a large saucepan. Add onion and 8 cups broth. Tie together thyme, parsley, bay leaves, and, if desired, sage and basil with string; add to bean mixture. Add ham hocks and, if desired, rind. Bring to a boil over medium-high heat. Reduce heat to low, and simmer, uncovered and stirring occasionally, 1 hour or until beans are tender but hold their shape. Skim off foam with a spoon.

3. Remove hocks, and cool 5 minutes. Remove meat from bones; discard bones. Return meat to bean mixture. Add collards, and cook, stirring occasionally, 15 to 20 minutes or until collards are tender.

4. Sauté garlic in hot oil in a large skillet over medium-low heat 2 minutes or until light golden. Add tomatoes, and sauté 5 minutes. Stir tomato mixture and remaining 1 cup broth into beans, and cook, stirring often, 5 minutes or until liquid is reduced by half. Discard herb bundle and cheese rind; season beans with salt and pepper to taste. Serve immediately.

Makes 6 to 8 servings. Hands-on 40 min., Total 10 hours

THE TIE THAT BINDS
Beans 'n' Greens

In the South, cold-weather comfort means collards and turnip greens slow-simmered in a potlikker, often served with beans or field peas. In Italy, bitter greens like escarole and chicory are braised with cannellini beans. You'll love this easy one-pot main course that takes its smoky flavor from canned fire-roasted tomatoes and ham hocks.

FRIED CATFISH WITH PICKLED PEPPERS

Rethink store-bought sauce: Spoon spicy, quick-pickled peppers and their kicky brine over fish to add flavor, color, and crunch. (Pictured on page 165)

- 1½ cups all-purpose flour
- 2¼ tsp. table salt
- 2 tsp. freshly ground black pepper
- 4 large eggs
- 1½ cups plain yellow cornmeal
- 4 (6-oz.) catfish fillets
  Vegetable oil
  Pickled Peppers

Combine flour and 1 tsp. each salt and pepper in a shallow dish. Whisk together eggs and 2 Tbsp. water in another dish. Combine cornmeal, 1 tsp. salt, and remaining 1 tsp. pepper in a third dish. Sprinkle catfish with remaining ¼ tsp. salt. Dredge fillets, 1 at a time, in flour mixture, shaking off excess; dip in egg mixture, and dredge in cornmeal mixture, shaking off excess. Place on a wire rack in a jelly-roll pan. Pour oil to depth of 2 inches in a cast-iron Dutch oven. Heat over medium-high heat to 350°. Fry fillets, 2 at a time, in hot oil 6 minutes or until done. Drain on a wire rack over paper towels. Serve with Pickled Peppers.

Makes 4 servings. Hands-on 20 min.; Total 20 min., not including peppers

---

THE TIE THAT BINDS
Peppers

Colorful, piquant peppers win the best supporting ingredient role in both Italian and Southern cooking. Dependable dishes like tomato sauce and fried fish wouldn't taste as good without the subtly sweet kick a pepper lends, particularly when it's pickled. Serve them on any antipasti platter or proper Southern sideboard.

Pickled Peppers

We used sweet mini bell peppers and jalapeños, but any variety like serrano, Fresno, Thai, or poblano peppers will also work well.

- 12 oz. assorted hot and sweet peppers, sliced (such as jalapeño peppers and sweet mini bell peppers)
- 2 cups white wine vinegar
- ¾ cup white vinegar
- ½ large Spanish onion, thinly sliced
- 3 garlic cloves, smashed
- 1½ Tbsp. kosher salt
- 1½ Tbsp. sugar
- 1 Tbsp. black peppercorns
- 1 Tbsp. coriander seeds
- 1 tsp. dill seeds
- 3 bay leaves

Divide peppers among 3 (1-pt.) canning jars. Bring white wine vinegar and next 9 ingredients to a boil in a medium saucepan over medium-high heat. Reduce heat to medium, and simmer, stirring occasionally, 5 minutes. Divide hot mixture among jars. Cover with lids; screw on bands. Let stand 30 minutes. Chill 12 hours before serving. Store up to 3 weeks.

Makes 3 pt. Hands-on 15 min.; Total 12 hr., 50 min.

MEATBALLS WITH TOMATO RAGU AND CREAMY POLENTA

Baking the meatballs sets their shape so they'll stay whole when simmered in the tomato sauce.

MEATBALLS

- 1 cup soft, fresh breadcrumbs
- ¼ cup milk
- 1 large egg, lightly beaten
- ⅓ cup fresh flat-leaf parsley leaves, finely chopped
- 2 oz. thick bacon slices, minced
- ¼ cup freshly grated Parmesan cheese
- 1 Tbsp. minced fresh thyme
- 1 Tbsp. minced fresh rosemary
- 2 garlic cloves, minced
- ½ tsp. loosely packed lemon zest
- 2 tsp. fresh lemon juice
- 1½ tsp. kosher salt
- 1 tsp. freshly ground black pepper
- ¼ to ½ tsp. dried crushed red pepper
- 1 lb. ground pork

RAGU

- 1 large yellow onion, coarsely chopped
- 2 celery ribs, coarsely chopped
- 1 large carrot, coarsely chopped
- 2 garlic cloves
- 2 (28-oz.) cans whole plum tomatoes
- ¼ cup olive oil
- 1 cup dry red wine
- 1 tsp. kosher salt
- 2 cups vegetable broth
- 1 (1-oz.) package fresh basil
- 2 tsp. lemon zest

POLENTA

- 1¼ tsp. kosher salt
- 2 cups uncooked polenta or grits
- 1 cup whipping cream
- ½ cup freshly grated Parmesan cheese
- 2 Tbsp. butter

1. Prepare Meatballs: Preheat oven to 400°. Combine first 2 ingredients in a bowl; let stand 10 minutes. Stir in egg and next 11 ingredients until blended. Add pork; combine using your hands. (Do not overmix.) Shape into 36 (1-inch) balls. Lightly grease a jelly-roll pan with cooking spray. Place meatballs in pan. Bake 10 minutes.

2. Prepare Ragu: Process onion and next 3 ingredients in a food processor 20 seconds or until finely chopped; transfer to a bowl. Process tomatoes, in batches, until smooth.

3. Sauté onion mixture in hot oil in a Dutch oven over medium heat 17 to 20 minutes or until tender. Add wine and $\frac{1}{4}$ tsp. salt, and cook, stirring occasionally, 3 minutes. Stir in broth, basil, tomatoes, and remaining $\frac{3}{4}$ tsp. salt. Bring to a boil; reduce heat to low, and simmer, stirring occasionally, 35 minutes; add meatballs, and cook 10 minutes. Discard basil. Stir in lemon zest and salt and pepper to taste.

4. Prepare Polenta: Bring 8 cups water and 1 $\frac{1}{4}$ tsp. kosher salt to a boil in a 4-qt. saucepan over medium-high heat; gradually whisk in polenta. Reduce heat to medium-low; cook, stirring occasionally, 20 to 25 minutes or until creamy. Remove from heat; stir in cream, cheese, and butter. Add salt and pepper to taste. Serve immediately with ragu.

Makes 6 to 8 servings. Hands-on 1 hour, 20 min.; Total 2 hours, 35 min.

THE TIE THAT BINDS
Cornmeal

Grits are both the quiet star and the workhorse of the Southern table. Across the pond, they've got polenta (the chefs' uncles call them "Italian grits"), grits' finely ground sister that's also the rich, creamy anchor of a meal. In addition, both cultures use cornmeal as a dredge for frying and as a flavorful, textured base for cookies, cakes, pastries, and breads.

Meatballs with Tomato Ragu and Creamy Polenta

Pucker Up for Sunny Sweets

BRIGHTEN WINTER'S LAST BLUSTERY DAYS WITH THE FRESH KISS OF CITRUS
AND SEVEN NEW SPINS ON FAVORITE SOUTHERN DESSERTS

LEMON-LIME POUND CAKE

This recipe is based on a classic Southern favorite called 7UP Pound Cake, which was created around the 1950s when it became popular to use soft drinks instead of other liquid in many recipes, but especially for baking. (Pictured on page 168)

1 1/2   **cups butter, softened**
   3   **cups sugar**
   5   **large eggs**
   2   **Tbsp. lemon zest**
   1   **tsp. vanilla extract**
   1   **tsp. lemon extract**
   3   **cups all-purpose flour**
   1   **cup lemon-lime soft drink (such as 7UP)**
       Shortening
       Lemon-Lime Glaze
       Candied Lemons (optional)
       Garnish: lime twists

Lemon-Lime Pound Cake
with Lemon-Lime Glaze
and Candied Lemons

1. Preheat oven to 350°. Beat butter at medium speed with a heavy-duty electric stand mixer until creamy. Gradually add sugar; beat at medium speed 3 to 5 minutes or until light and fluffy. Add eggs, 1 at a time, beating just until blended after each addition. Stir in lemon zest and extracts.
2. Add flour to butter mixture alternately with lemon-lime soft drink, beginning and ending with flour. Beat at low speed just until blended after each addition. Pour batter into a greased (with shortening) and floured 10-inch Bundt pan.
3. Bake at 350° for 1 hour and 5 minutes to 1 hour and 15 minutes or until a long wooden pick inserted in center comes out clean, shielding with aluminum foil after 45 to 50 minutes to prevent excessive browning. Cool in

pan on a wire rack 10 minutes; remove cake from pan to wire rack.
4. Spoon Lemon-Lime Glaze over warm or room temperature cake. Top cake with Candied Lemons, if desired.

Makes 12 servings. Hands-on 20 min.;
Total 1 hour, 35 min., not including glaze or
candied lemons

Lemon-Lime Glaze

Whisk together 2 cups **powdered sugar,** 2 tsp. **lemon zest,** 1 1/2 Tbsp. **fresh lemon juice,** and 1 Tbsp. **fresh lime juice** in a bowl until blended and smooth. (For a thinner glaze, stir in an additional 1 Tbsp. fresh lemon juice, 1 tsp. at a time, if desired.)

Makes about 1 cup. Hands-on 5 min.,
Total 5 min.

Candied Lemons

Save the syrup to sweeten tea.

Cut 2 medium **lemons** into 1/8-inch-thick slices; discard seeds. Stir together 4 cups **water** and 2 cups **granulated sugar** in a large, heavy saucepan. Bring to a light boil, stirring just until sugar dissolves. Add lemons; reduce heat to medium-low. Gently simmer 45 minutes or until rinds are very soft and lemons are translucent, turning lemons every 15 minutes. Remove with a slotted spoon, and place in a single layer on a wire rack. Cool completely.

Hands-on 15 min., Total 1 hour

SHAKER ORANGE PIE

This is the pie for you marmalade fans out there. Although the homemade pastry is well worth the effort, use a refrigerated piecrust if you want a shortcut.

- 2 **medium-size oranges**
- 2 **cups sugar**
- 1 1/2 **cups all-purpose flour**
- 1/2 **cup cold unsalted butter, cut into small pieces**
- 1 1/4 **tsp. kosher salt, divided**
- 1/4 **cup ice-cold water**
- 1/2 **(8-oz.) package cream cheese, softened**
- 1 **tsp. vanilla extract**
- 3 **large eggs, lightly beaten**
- 2 **Tbsp. cornstarch**
- 2 **Tbsp. fresh lemon juice**

1. Grate zest from oranges to equal 2 Tbsp. Cut oranges in half lengthwise, and thinly slice. Bring sugar, orange slices, zest, and 1 cup water to a boil in a medium saucepan over medium heat. Reduce heat to medium-low, and simmer 1 hour or until oranges are translucent. Remove from heat; cool completely.

2. Meanwhile, pulse flour, butter, and 1 tsp. salt in a food processor just until mixture resembles coarse meal. With processor running, pour 1/4 cup ice-cold water through food chute; pulse until dough forms a ball and pulls away from sides of bowl. Wrap dough in plastic wrap. Chill 1 hour.

3. Preheat oven to 425°. Remove dough from plastic wrap; roll into a 13-inch circle on a lightly floured surface. Lightly grease a 9-inch pie plate with cooking spray. Fit dough into prepared pie plate. Fold edges under, and crimp. Prick bottom and sides of piecrust with a fork. Freeze 20 minutes. Line piecrust with aluminum foil, and fill with pie weights or dried beans.

4. Bake at 425° for 15 minutes. Remove weights and foil, and bake 10 minutes.

5. Reduce oven temperature to 375°. Beat cream cheese, vanilla, and remaining 1/4 tsp. salt at medium speed with an electric mixer just until smooth. Spread mixture into prepared crust.

6. Whisk together eggs and next 2 ingredients until smooth; stir into orange mixture. Pour cream cheese mixture in piecrust, and arrange oranges evenly. Cover loosely with foil.

7. Bake at 375° for 30 minutes. Remove foil, and bake 30 more minutes or until set. Cool completely on a wire rack before slicing (about 1 hour).

Makes 8 servings. Hands-on 45 min.; Total 5 hours, 30 min.

CITRUS PULL-APART BREAD

This makes two gorgeous loaves for breakfast, tea, or coffee. Keep one, and share the other.

- 1/4 **cup warm water (100° to 110°)**
- 1 **(1/4-oz.) envelope active dry yeast**
- 1 **tsp. granulated sugar**
- 1 **cup butter, softened and divided**
- 1/2 **cup granulated sugar**
- 1 **tsp. table salt**
- 2 **large eggs, lightly beaten**
- 1 **cup milk**
- 1 **Tbsp. fresh lemon juice**
- 4 1/2 **cups bread flour**
- 1/4 **tsp. ground nutmeg**
  Citrus Filling (recipe, page 56)
- 2/3 **cup powdered sugar**
- 1/4 **cup butter, melted**
- 2 **Tbsp. honey**
- 1 **large egg white**
  Fresh Citrus Glaze (recipe, page 56)

1. Combine first 3 ingredients in a 1-cup glass measuring cup, and let stand 5 minutes.

2. Beat 1/2 cup butter at medium speed with a heavy-duty electric stand mixer until creamy. Gradually add 1/2 cup granulated sugar and 1 tsp. salt; beat 3 minutes or until light and fluffy. Beat in eggs and next 2 ingredients. Stir in yeast mixture.

3. Combine bread flour and nutmeg. Gradually add to butter mixture, and beat at low speed 2 minutes or until well blended.

4. Sprinkle a flat surface generously with bread flour. Turn dough out; knead until smooth and elastic (about 5 minutes), sprinkling surface with bread flour as needed. Coat a large bowl with cooking spray. Place dough in bowl, turning to grease top. Cover with plastic wrap; let rise in a warm place (80° to 85°) 1 1/2 to 2 hours or until doubled in bulk.

5. Punch dough down; turn out onto lightly floured surface. Divide dough in half. Roll 1 dough portion into a 20- x 12-inch rectangle. Spread with 1/4 cup softened butter, and cut into 5 (12- x 4-inch) strips. Sprinkle 2 Tbsp. Citrus Filling over 1 strip, and top with a second strip. Repeat with remaining strips and filling, stacking strips as you go. Cut stack into 6 (4- x 2-inch) rectangles.

6. Lightly grease 2 (9- x 5-inch) loaf pans with cooking spray. Place stacked rectangles, cut sides up, into 1 prepared pan. Repeat procedure with remaining dough, 1/4 cup softened butter, Citrus Filling, and second pan. Sprinkle any remaining filling over loaves.

7. Whisk together powdered sugar, melted butter, honey, and egg white until blended. Spoon over loaves. Cover loosely with plastic wrap; let rise in a warm place (80° to 85°) 1 hour or until doubled in bulk.

8. Preheat oven to 350°. Bake 30 to 35 minutes or until golden brown, shielding with aluminum foil after 25 minutes to prevent excessive browning, if necessary. Cool in pans on a wire rack 10 minutes. Remove from pans to a wire rack; brush with Fresh Citrus Glaze. Cool 5 minutes.

Makes 2 loaves. Hands-on 55 min.; Total 4 hours, 35 min., including filling and glaze

Citrus Filling

Stir together 1 cup **sugar**, 4 Tbsp. **orange zest**, and 2 Tbsp. **lemon zest** until combined.

Makes about 1 1/4 cups. Hands-on 10 min.; Total 10 min.

Fresh Citrus Glaze

Beat 2 cups **powdered sugar** and 2 Tbsp. softened **butter** at medium speed with an electric mixer until blended. Add 2 tsp. **orange zest,** 2 Tbsp. **fresh orange juice,** and 1 Tbsp. **fresh lemon juice;** beat until smooth. (Stir in an additional 1 Tbsp. orange juice, 1 tsp. at a time, if desired.)

Makes 3/4 cup. Hands-on 10 min., Total 10 min.

LEMON MELTAWAYS

(Pictured on page 168)

- 3/4 cup plus 2 Tbsp. **butter,** softened
- 1 1/2 cups **powdered sugar,** divided
- 1 Tbsp. **lemon zest**
- 2 Tbsp. **fresh lemon juice**
- 1 1/2 cups **all-purpose flour**
- 1/4 cup **cornstarch**
- 1/4 tsp. **table salt**
- **Parchment paper**

1. Preheat oven to 350°. Beat butter at medium speed with a heavy-duty electric stand mixer until creamy. Add 1/2 cup powdered sugar; beat at medium speed until light and fluffy. Stir in zest and juice. Whisk together flour and next 2 ingredients. Gradually add flour mixture to butter mixture, beating at low speed just until blended. Cover and chill 1 hour.
2. Drop dough by level spoonfuls 2 inches apart onto parchment paper-lined baking sheets, using a 1-inch cookie scoop.
3. Bake at 350° for 13 minutes or until lightly browned around edges. Cool on baking sheets 5 minutes.
4. Toss together warm cookies and remaining 1 cup powdered sugar in a small bowl.

Makes about 3 1/2 dozen. Hands-on 30 min., Total 2 hours

TANGERINE PUDDING

You'll need about six to eight tangerines for the 2 cups juice in this recipe. Feel free to substitute any variety of oranges or mandarins if you'd like.

- 1/2 cup sugar
- 3 Tbsp. cornstarch
- 1/4 tsp. table salt
- 2 cups fresh tangerine juice
- 1 medium tangerine
- 3 large eggs
- 3 Tbsp. butter
- 2 tsp. fresh lemon juice
- 1/4 tsp. vanilla extract
- **Sweetened whipped cream**
- **Garnishes: citrus slices, pineapple mint**

1. Whisk together first 3 ingredients in a 3-qt. heavy saucepan. Whisk in tangerine juice until smooth. Remove 1 (2-inch) strip of peel from tangerine, using a vegetable peeler, and add to pan. Bring to a boil over medium-low heat, stirring occasionally; boil, stirring constantly, 1 minute or until mixture is thick and bubbly. Remove pan from heat.
2. Whisk eggs until frothy. Gradually whisk 1/4 cup hot juice mixture into eggs; add egg mixture to remaining hot juice mixture, whisking constantly. Return to heat, and cook, stirring constantly, 2 minutes or until thickened. Transfer mixture to a medium bowl; stir in butter and next 2 ingredients until butter is melted. Place heavy-duty plastic wrap directly onto warm custard (to prevent a film from forming); chill 2 hours. (Mixture will thicken as it chills.) Discard peel, if desired. Serve with whipped cream.

Makes 4 to 6 servings. Hands-on 30 min.; Total 2 hours, 30 min.

Tangerine Pudding

LEMON-ALMOND BARS

For quick cleanup and easy serving, line the bottom and sides of the pan with foil before adding the dough.

- 2 3/4 cups granulated sugar, divided
- 3/4 cup butter, softened
- 2 Tbsp. plus 1 tsp. lemon zest, divided
- 3 1/4 cups all-purpose flour, divided
- 1/2 tsp. table salt, divided
- 6 large eggs
- 1/4 cup chopped crystallized ginger
- 1 tsp. baking powder
- 2/3 cup fresh lemon juice
- 1/4 cup butter, melted
- 1/2 cup sliced almonds

1. Preheat oven to 350°. Beat 1/4 cup granulated sugar, butter, and 1 tsp. zest at medium speed with a heavy-duty electric stand mixer 2 minutes or until creamy. Stir together 2 cups flour and 1/4 tsp. salt. Gradually add to butter mixture, beating until just blended. Coat a 13- x 9-inch pan with cooking spray. Press dough into bottom of prepared pan. Chill 15 minutes.

2. Bake at 350° for 15 to 20 minutes or until lightly browned. Remove from oven; reduce oven temperature to 325°.

3. Whisk together eggs and 2 cups sugar. Process ginger and 1/2 cup flour in a food processor 1 minute or until ginger is finely chopped. Stir in baking powder. Whisk ginger mixture into egg mixture. Whisk in lemon juice and remaining 2 Tbsp. lemon zest; pour over crust.

4. Bake at 325° for 15 to 20 minutes or until filling is just set. Remove from oven.

5. Stir together remaining 3/4 cup flour, 1/2 cup sugar, and 1/4 tsp. salt in a small bowl. Stir in melted butter until well blended. Stir in almonds. Sprinkle over hot lemon mixture, and bake 20 to 25 more minutes or just until lightly golden. Cool completely in pan on a wire rack (about 1 hour). Cut into squares.

Makes 32 bars. Hands-on 30 min.; Total 2 hours, 35 min.

Citrus Shortcakes

CITÀS SHORTCAKES

Use any combination of your favorite citrus segments in this shortcake spin. Be sure to start with a total of 6 cups of fruit. (Pictured on page 167)

SHORTCAKES

- 2 cups all-purpose flour
- 1/4 cup granulated sugar
- 2 Tbsp. lemon zest
- 1 Tbsp. baking powder
- 1/4 tsp. table salt
- 1/2 cup cold butter, cubed
- 1 cup plus 3 Tbsp. heavy cream, divided
- 1/2 tsp. lemon extract
  Parchment paper
- 1 large egg yolk
- 2 Tbsp. sparkling sugar

TOPPING

- 1 1/2 cups heavy cream
- 1/4 tsp. lemon extract
- 3/4 cup powdered sugar
- 3 cups orange segments
- 3 cups red grapefruit segments
- 1/4 cup torn fresh mint
- 1/4 cup granulated sugar

1. Prepare Shortcakes: Preheat oven to 425°. Stir together first 5 ingredients in a large bowl. Cut butter into flour mixture with a pastry blender or fork until mixture resembles coarse meal.

Make a well in center of mixture.

2. Stir together 1 cup cream and 1/2 tsp. lemon extract. Add to dry ingredients, stirring just until dough comes together.

3. Turn dough out onto a lightly floured surface; knead lightly 2 or 3 times. Pat or roll dough to 1-inch thickness; cut into 8 rounds with a 2 1/4-inch round cutter. Place 2 inches apart on a parchment paper-lined baking sheet.

4. Stir together egg yolk and remaining 3 Tbsp. cream; brush over tops of shortcakes. Sprinkle with sparkling sugar.

5. Bake at 425° for 15 minutes or until golden. Cool completely (about 30 minutes).

6. Prepare Topping: Beat 1 1/2 cups heavy cream and 1/4 tsp. lemon extract at medium speed with an electric mixer until foamy. Gradually add powdered sugar, beating until soft peaks form.

7. Toss together oranges, grapefruit, mint, and 1/4 cup granulated sugar. Split shortcakes in half horizontally. Top bottom halves of shortcakes with half of fruit mixture and whipped cream. Cover with top halves of shortcakes, and top with remaining fruit mixture and whipped cream.

Makes 8 servings. Hands-on 20 min.; Total 1 hour, 5 min.

THE *SL* TEST KITCHEN ACADEMY

OUR OWN KING OF THE KITCHEN, NORMAN KING, EXPLAINS HOW TO

MAXIMIZE YOUR CITRUS

This season, brighten your winter cooking and squeeze the most flavor out of your citrus by using every inch of the fruit, from the flesh and juice to the peel and pith. I even roast leftover peels to grind for homemade seasoning salts. (See recipe below.)

BOOST YOUR JUICE AND EMPOWER THE PEEL

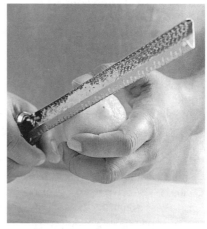

① SQUEEZE MORE JUICE
A handheld juicer is a must in the *SL* Test Kitchen. Not only does it extract more juice (about 4 Tbsp. per large lemon and 2 1/2 Tbsp. per large lime), but also it releases essential oils into the juice from the peel, adding even more citrus flavor. Lemon Juicer, $13.95; *surlatable.com*

② ADD A TWIST
Get bartender-perfect citrus twists by using a tool known as a channel knife. For extra-long twists, start at the stem and peel all the way through the peel and pith around the fruit from top to bottom. This ensures the twist will hold its curly shape. Easy Grip Zester, $7.99; *zyliss.com*

③ ZEST A BETTER WAY
Hold a rasp grater upside down to zest citrus. This way, you can see how much zest has been grated. Hold the grater in your dominant hand and the fruit in the other hand, with the grating surface facing the fruit. Rotate the fruit as you grate. Microplane rasp grater, $12.95; *microplane.com*

TRY IT!
MAKE YOUR OWN CITRUS SALT

LEMON-PEPPER SEASONING SALT
Preheat oven to 225°. Remove peels in strips from 8 **lemons** (or 4 oranges or 12 clementines) using a vegetable peeler. Place peels, pith sides up, in a single layer on a **parchment paper**-lined jelly-roll pan. Bake 1 hour and 30 minutes to 1 hour and 45 minutes or until dried and fragrant; cool completely. Grind to a coarse powder in a spice grinder or mortar and pestle. Stir together 2 Tbsp. ground roasted citrus peels, 1 Tbsp. **kosher salt,** and 2 tsp. **freshly ground black pepper** in a small bowl. Store in an airtight container up to 2 months. Use to season fish, meat, or vegetables before, during, or after cooking.

Makes 3 Tbsp. Hands-on 15 min.; Total 2 hours, 5 min.

Transform Taco Night

BREAK OUT OF THE BOX WITH FOUR ULTRA-FRESH WEEKNIGHT COMBOS THAT WILL LIVEN UP YOUR FAMILY DINNER

STEAK TACOS WITH CHARRED SALSA

Here's a fresh serving idea: Assemble and serve tortillas in parchment paper-lined cups.

- 4 ears fresh corn, husked
- 1 medium-size onion, cut into eighths
- 7 sweet mini bell peppers or 1 red bell pepper
- 1 large poblano pepper
- 1 lb. grape tomatoes
- 1/4 cup olive oil, divided
- 2 lb. skirt or flank steak
- 2 Tbsp. Montreal steak seasoning or your favorite steak rub
- 2 garlic cloves, pressed
- 2 Tbsp. fresh lime juice
- 3/4 tsp. kosher salt
- 12 (6-inch) corn tortillas, warmed
  Toppings: fresh cilantro leaves, crumbled queso fresco or feta cheese

1. Heat a grill pan over medium-high heat. Brush first 5 ingredients with 2 Tbsp. olive oil. Cook corn and onion in hot pan, turning occasionally, 5 to 6 minutes or until charred. Remove from pan. Cook peppers in pan 5 to 6 minutes or until charred. Remove from pan. Cook tomatoes in pan 2 to 3 minutes or until charred.
2. Rub steak with steak seasoning, and cook in pan over medium-high heat 5 to 6 minutes on each side or to desired degree of doneness. Remove from pan, and let stand 5 minutes. Chop steak.
3. Cut corn kernels from cobs, and place in a large bowl. Discard cobs. Chop onion, mini peppers, poblano, and tomatoes. Stir together garlic, next 2 ingredients, remaining 2 Tbsp. olive oil, and chopped vegetables. Serve steak and salsa in tortillas with desired toppings.

Makes 6 servings. Hands-on 40 min., Total 45 min.

FRIED CHICKEN TACOS WITH BUTTERMILK-JALAPEÑO SAUCE

Use this creamy sauce to dress up store-bought fried chicken or as a salad dressing or dip for wings.

Process 1/2 cup refrigerated **light Ranch dressing**; 1 large **jalapeño pepper**, stemmed; 1 bunch **fresh cilantro** (about 1 1/2 cups loosely packed); 2 **garlic cloves**, chopped; and 1 Tbsp. **fresh lime juice** in a blender or food processor 2 to 3 seconds or until smooth, stopping to scrape down sides as needed. Place 1 **fried chicken breast tender** in each of 12 (6-inch) **corn tortillas**, warmed. Serve with dressing and sliced **radishes**.

Makes 6 servings. Hands-on 15 min., Total 15 min.

GREEK CHICKEN TACOS

Crisp lettuce cups offer a light, refreshing spin to this Greek salad-inspired taco, but feel free to use warm flour tortillas or pitas instead.

Stir together 1/2 pt. **grape tomatoes**, quartered; 4 oz. **feta cheese**, crumbled; 1/2 **English cucumber**, chopped; 1/2 cup **green olives**, chopped; 1/3 cup thinly sliced **red onion**; 3 **pepperoncini salad peppers**, chopped; 2 Tbsp. chopped **fresh flat-leaf parsley**; 2 Tbsp. **fresh lemon juice**; 2 Tbsp. **olive oil**; 1 **garlic clove**, pressed; and 1/2 tsp. **kosher salt**. Place 1/4 cup shredded **deli-roasted chicken** in each of 12 **lettuce leaves** such as butter or romaine; add tomato mixture.

Makes 6 servings. Hands-on 15 min., Total 15 min.

CARIBBEAN PORK TACOS

The combination of salty char-grilled meat with fiery-sweet salsa makes this a favorite of Test Kitchen Specialist Vanessa McNeil Rocchio's family.

Heat a nonstick grill pan over medium-high heat. Rub 2 (1-lb.) **pork tenderloins** with 2 Tbsp. **Caribbean jerk seasoning.** Cook pork in pan 8 to 10 minutes on each side or until done. Let stand 5 minutes. Meanwhile, stir together 1 1/3 cups chopped **fresh pineapple**; 1 small **jicama**, peeled and cut into thin sticks; 1 **jalapeño pepper**, seeded and chopped; 2 **green onions**, sliced; 2 **garlic cloves**, pressed; 1/4 cup **fresh lime juice**; 2 Tbsp. **olive oil**; and 3/4 tsp. **kosher salt.** Thinly slice pork; serve with salsa in 6 (6-inch) **flour tortillas,** warmed.

Makes 6 servings. Hands-on 35 min., Total 35 min.

EASY SIDE!

SPICY GREEN RICE

Melt 3 Tbsp. **butter** in a 3-qt. saucepan over medium-high heat; add 1 medium **jalapeño pepper,** seeded and minced. Sauté 2 to 3 minutes or until tender. Add 2 cups uncooked **quick-cooking rice;** cook, stirring constantly, 5 minutes or until golden brown. Stir in 1 (10 1/2-oz.) can **condensed chicken broth,** undiluted, and 1 (7-oz.) can **salsa verde;** bring to a boil. Cover and remove from heat; let stand 5 minutes. Stir in 1/4 cup chopped **fresh cilantro.**

Makes 4 servings. Hands-on 15 min.; Total 20 min.

Spin Sunday Supper into Leftover Gold

CYNTHIA GRAUBART SETS THE TABLE FOR THREE FAMILY MEALS: ONE SIMPLE SUNDAY ROASTED CHICKEN DINNER AND TWO FAST AND HEARTY WEEKNIGHT MEALS

MANY COOKS TODAY LIVE DOUBLE LIVES. We slow down on the weekend, spending more time in the kitchen cooking and challenging ourselves with new recipes and techniques. Most important, we spend more time at the table with family and friends. But when the Monday morning rooster crows, we are back to our overbooked schedules and in need of quick and easy meals.

As the author of four cookbooks, I know the power a recipe has in creating less stress in the kitchen. I've made a career out of teaching others to cook and use a little advance planning to make mealtime more productive and the week run more smoothly. Why not enjoy the more leisurely cooking on the weekend and ease the weeknight burden at the same time?

The New Sunday Supper does just that. We'll use the Sunday meal to create the base for two fast and delicious weeknight dinners. This month, we roast two chickens flavored with rosemary and lemon that give them a seductive aroma. The classic recipe saves time, yielding enough meat for three dinners for a family of four. A side of green beans, first served with roast chicken on day one, makes enough for Easy Biscuit-Topped Chicken Pot Pie on day two, topped with a quick, two-ingredient biscuit.

Take the dish over the top with homemade chicken stock. To make it—and add value to the chickens you've already bought—toss the bones from both roasted chickens in a slow cooker; add two carrots, a celery rib, and a quartered onion; cover with water; and cook on low for 8 hours or so. Strain and freeze in 1/2-cup portions for future use.

For the third dinner, toss the remaining chicken in homemade or bottled barbecue sauce, and serve on Texas toast with an easy slaw.

One Sunday supper and a head start on two weeknight dinners. Enjoy!

SUNDAY NIGHT
CLASSIC DOUBLE ROAST CHICKENS

- 4 tsp. kosher salt
- 2 tsp. freshly ground black pepper
- 2 (4- to 5-lb.) whole chickens
- 2 lemons, halved
- 2 fresh rosemary sprigs
- 1 Tbsp. olive oil

1. Preheat oven to 375°. Stir together salt and pepper. If applicable, remove necks and giblets from chickens, and reserve for another use. Pat chickens dry.

2. Sprinkle 1/2 tsp. salt mixture inside cavity of each chicken. Place 2 lemon halves and 1 rosemary sprig inside cavity of each chicken. Rub 1 1/2 tsp. olive oil into skin of each chicken. Sprinkle with remaining salt mixture; rub into skin. Tuck chicken wings under, if desired. Lightly grease a wire rack in a 17- x 12-inch jelly-roll pan with cooking spray. Place chickens, breast sides up and facing in opposite directions (for even browning), on wire rack.

3. Bake at 375° for 1 1/2 hours or until a meat thermometer inserted in thigh registers 180°. Cover and let stand 10 minutes before slicing.

Makes 2 chickens. Hands-on 20 min., Total 2 hours

Green Beans with Tomato Sauce

Steam 2 (16-oz.) packages frozen cut **pole beans** according to package directions. (Reserve 1 cup cooked beans for Easy Biscuit-Topped Chicken Pot Pie, if desired.) Melt 1 Tbsp. **butter** in a large skillet over medium-high heat; add 1 Tbsp. minced **shallot;** cook 30 seconds. Stir in beans. Stir in 1 (24-oz.) jar **pasta sauce** (such as Bertolli Olive Oil and Garlic) and 2 tsp. fresh **thyme leaves.** Cook, stirring often, 2 to 3 minutes or until hot. Add **table salt** and **freshly ground black pepper** to taste.

Makes 4 to 6 servings. Hands-on 15 min., Total 15 min.

MONDAY NIGHT

USE SUNDAY'S CHICKEN AND GREEN BEANS

EASY BISCUIT-TOPPED CHICKEN POT PIE

- 1 cup sliced carrots
- 2 Tbsp. butter
- 1 cup chopped sweet onion
- 1/2 (8-oz.) package fresh mushrooms, quartered
- 1 cup frozen cut pole beans, thawed
- 3 Tbsp. all-purpose flour
- 1 tsp. kosher salt
- 1/4 tsp. freshly ground black pepper
- 1 1/2 cups chicken broth
- 2 cups shredded or diced cooked chicken
- 1 cup self-rising soft wheat flour
- 1/2 cup whipping cream

Preheat oven to 375°. Microwave carrots and 2 Tbsp. water in a microwave-safe glass bowl at HIGH 1 to 2 minutes or until crisp-tender. Drain. Melt butter in a medium skillet over medium-high heat; add onion, and sauté 2 minutes. Add mushrooms; cook, stirring constantly, 2 minutes. Add beans and carrots, and cook 2 minutes. Sprinkle all-purpose flour, salt, and pepper over vegetables. Cook, stirring constantly, 1 minute or until smooth. Gradually stir in broth; cook over medium-high heat, stirring constantly, 8 to 10 minutes or until mixture is thickened and bubbly. Stir in chicken. Stir together self-rising flour and cream just until dry ingredients are moistened. Turn dough out onto a lightly floured surface, and knead lightly 3 or 4 times. Pat or roll dough to 1/2-inch thickness; cut with a 3-inch round cutter to make 4 biscuits, reshaping once, if necessary. (Do not twist cutter as you cut.) Place 4 (10-oz.) ovenproof bowls in a jelly-roll pan. Divide hot chicken mixture among bowls, and top each with a biscuit. Bake at 375° for 20 minutes or until biscuits are golden brown.

Note: We tested with White Lily Enriched Unbleached Self-Rising Flour.

Makes 4 servings. Hands-on 45 min.; Total 1 hour, 5 min.

TUESDAY NIGHT

READY IN 25 MINUTES!

BARBECUE CHICKEN SANDWICHES WITH CREAMY SLAW

- 1/2 cup mayonnaise
- 1 Tbsp. lemon juice
- 1/2 tsp. granulated sugar
- 1 (12-oz.) package angel hair coleslaw mix or broccoli slaw mix
- 1/3 cup chopped fresh flat-leaf parsley
- 1 1/2 cups ketchup
- 1/4 cup spicy brown mustard
- 1 Tbsp. apple cider vinegar
- 1 Tbsp. Worcestershire sauce
- 1 tsp. light brown sugar
- 1/2 tsp. garlic powder
- 1/2 tsp. onion powder
- 1/4 tsp. kosher salt
- 2 cups shredded cooked chicken
- 4 Texas toast slices

Prepare slaw: Stir together mayonnaise, lemon juice, and granulated sugar until smooth. Stir in coleslaw mix and parsley. Add table salt and freshly ground black pepper to taste. Prepare sauce: Stir together ketchup and next 7 ingredients in a medium saucepan. Cook over medium-low heat, stirring occasionally, 15 minutes or until bubbly. Stir together 1/2 cup barbecue sauce and chicken in a bowl. Spoon mixture over Texas toast slices. Serve with slaw and remaining barbecue sauce.

Makes 4 servings. Hands-on 25 min., Total 25 min.

Biscuits to the Rescue

TURN SUPERMARKET CANNED BISCUITS INTO SPEEDY MEALS AND SNACKS ANYTIME DURING THE DAY

Breakfast
SAUSAGE, BISCUIT, AND GRAVY BAKE

Preheat oven to 350°. Cook 1 lb. **ground pork sausage** in 2 tsp. **canola oil** in a large skillet over medium-high heat 8 minutes or until meat crumbles and is no longer pink; remove from skillet, and drain. Melt 5 Tbsp. **butter** in skillet; whisk in 1/4 cup **all-purpose flour.** Whisk constantly 1 minute. Gradually whisk in 3 cups **milk,** 3/4 tsp. **table salt,** and 1/2 tsp. **freshly ground black pepper.** Bring to a boil, whisking constantly; cook 2 minutes. Stir in sausage. Grease an 11- x 7-inch baking dish with **cooking spray;** place dish on a baking sheet. Split 8 **refrigerated jumbo biscuits** in half horizontally; place 8 halves in baking dish. Top with half of sausage mixture and 1/4 cup chopped **green onions.** Repeat layers. Sprinkle with 3/4 cup shredded **sharp Cheddar cheese.** Bake 40 minutes or until golden.

Makes 6 to 8 servings. Total 1 hour

Lunch
BBQ IN A BLANKET WITH BUTTERMILK-RANCH SAUCE

Preheat oven to 425°. Toss together 1 cup **pulled barbecued pork** (without sauce) and 1/2 cup of your favorite bottled **barbecue sauce.** Press 8 **refrigerated jumbo biscuits** into triangles (about 5 inches on each side); spoon 2 Tbsp. pork mixture along 1 edge of each triangle. Roll up triangles. Place rolls, seam sides down, 2 inches apart on a **parchment paper**-lined baking sheet. Bake 10 to 12 minutes or until golden. Meanwhile, prepare Buttermilk Ranch Sauce: Stir together 1/4 cup **buttermilk,** 1/4 cup **mayonnaise,** 1 Tbsp. **bottled barbecue sauce,** 1 tsp. **Ranch**

Chicken Salad Empanadas

dressing mix, and 1/4 tsp. **table salt** until smooth. Serve creamy Buttermilk Ranch sauce with BBQ in a Blanket.

Makes 4 servings. Total 30 min.

Dinner
CHICKEN SALAD EMPANADAS

Preheat oven to 350°. Stir together 2 cups shredded cooked **chicken,** 1/2 cup **mayonnaise,** 1/3 cup chopped toasted **pecans,** 1/4 cup chopped **celery,** 2 Tbsp. **fresh lemon juice,** 3/4 tsp. **table salt,** and 1/4 tsp. **freshly ground black pepper.** Roll 8 **refrigerated jumbo biscuits** into 6-inch circles. Place 1/4 cup chicken mixture in center of each circle; fold dough over mixture. Press edges with a fork or crimp to seal. Cut slits in tops of pies to allow steam to escape, if desired. Place pies on a **parchment paper**-lined baking sheet. Bake 20 to 25 minutes or until golden.

Makes 8 servings. Total 40 min.

Anytime Snack
PESTO BISCUIT PIZZA

Preheat oven to 450°. Roll 8 **refrigerated jumbo biscuits** into 6-inch rounds; place 2 inches apart on 2 **parchment paper**-lined baking sheets. Spread 1 1/2 Tbsp. **refrigerated basil pesto** on each round. Cut 10 **cherry tomatoes** in half; top pizzas with tomatoes. Top each pizza with 2 Tbsp. crumbled **feta cheese.** Bake 5 minutes. Rotate pans, and switch from top to bottom racks; bake 4 to 5 more minutes or until golden.

Makes 4 servings. Total 25 min.

BABA AU RHUM

(FROM JANUARY 1975)

❝ THE ORIGINAL: A sophisticated French confection that became *très chic* in America when Julia Child was the crème de la crème of cooks. We love the classic yeast recipe—except for its whopping 6 hours of prep time! **THE REMAKE:** A shortcut version that'll earn "ooh la las" from your luncheon or teatime crowd. Whipped egg whites give it *baba au ruhm*'s signature airy crumb, the perfect texture to soak up a divine rum syrup.

RECIPE REVIVAL ➡

COFFEE *BABA AU RHUM*

6	large eggs, separated
1 1/4	cups granulated sugar
1	tsp. coffee extract
2	cups all-purpose flour
1	Tbsp. baking powder
1	Tbsp. finely ground coffee
1	tsp. kosher salt
3/4	cup butter, melted
1/2	cup milk
3	cups firmly packed light brown sugar
3	cups brewed coffee
1/2	cup rum*

Garnishes: whipped cream, fresh raspberries, powdered sugar

1. Preheat oven to 350°. Whisk together yolks and granulated sugar until mixture is thick and pale (about 2 minutes). Stir in coffee extract. Sift together flour and next 3 ingredients; gently stir into yolk mixture until just blended. Stir in butter and milk until just blended.

2. Whisk egg whites until stiff peaks form. Fold one-third egg whites into yolk mixture. Fold in remaining egg whites. Pour into a well-buttered 10-cup Bundt pan.

3. Bake at 350° for 50 minutes or until a wooden pick inserted in center comes out clean. Cool in pan on a wire rack 10 minutes. (Do not remove from pan.)

4. Meanwhile, bring brown sugar and brewed coffee to a boil in a medium saucepan. Reduce heat to low, and simmer, stirring occasionally, 20 minutes. Remove from heat; stir in rum. Reserve 2 cups syrup. Return pan to stove-top; cook over medium-low heat, stirring occasionally, 15 minutes or until slightly thickened.

5. Pierce cake 10 to 15 times using a skewer. Pour reserved 2 cups thin syrup over cake. Let stand 15 minutes. Invert cake onto a serving platter. Spoon desired amount of thickened syrup over cake. Reserve remaining syrup for another use (such as topping pancakes).

Makes 12 servings. Hands-on 35 min.; Total 2 hours, 10 min.

*The rum is optional. Replace it with an additional 1/2 cup brewed coffee, if desired.

Swoon over Chocolate

IMPRESS YOUR SWEETHEART WITH EASY AND ELEGANT MINI CHOCOLATE COOKIE CAKES

CHOCOLATE SHORTBREAD CAKE

This dessert, prepped in just 30 minutes, is all about the crisp cookies and luscious chocolate.

- 15 oz. milk chocolate morsels (about 2 1/2 cups)
- 3/4 cup butter
- 3 Tbsp. honey
- 1/3 cup heavy cream
- 1 Tbsp. bourbon
- 2 cups coarsely chopped butter cookies
  Parchment paper
  Easy Ganache

1. Line each compartment of a 6-mold mini cheesecake pan (or jumbo-size muffin pan) with plastic wrap.

2. Pour water to depth of 1 inch into bottom of a double boiler over medium heat; bring to a boil. Reduce heat, and simmer; place chocolate and next 2 ingredients in top of double boiler over simmering water. Cook, stirring occasionally, 5 to 6 minutes or until chocolate is melted. Whisk in cream and bourbon.

3. Remove from heat. Gently stir cookies into chocolate mixture, and pour into prepared pan (about 3/4 cup in each mold). Chill 2 to 24 hours or until set.

4. Remove cakes from pan to a wire rack in a parchment paper-lined jelly-roll pan; discard plastic wrap. Slowly pour warm Easy Ganache over cakes, spreading to edges and on sides. Chill 1 hour before serving.

Note: We tested with LU Le Petit Beurre cookies. Store any leftover ganache in the refrigerator. Reheat in the microwave; drizzle over ice cream or your favorite pound cake.

Makes 12 servings (2 per cake). Hands-on 30 min.; Total 4 hours, including ganache

Easy Ganache

Heat 1 cup **heavy cream** in a saucepan over medium heat just until cream begins to boil. Pour over 8 oz. **semisweet chocolate morsels** (about 1 1/4 cups) in a heatproof bowl; stir until smooth. Stir in 1 Tbsp. **bourbon,** 1 Tbsp. **honey,** and 1/2 tsp. **kosher salt.** Let stand 10 minutes or until spreading consistency.

Makes about 1 3/4 cups. Hands-on 10 min.; Total 20 min.

TEST KITCHEN TIP
Letting the ganache stand 10 minutes is the key to a glossy, lacquered look.

Plant Your Peas, Please

THE MOST FLAVORFUL ONES ARE PICKED FRESH FROM THE VINE

Garden peas, often called English peas or just plain "peas," love cool weather. There are three types to plant. Grow **shelling peas** for the large peas that form inside tough, inedible pods (try 'Green Arrow,' 'Mr. Big,' or 'Wando'). Plant **snow peas** for their edible pods (try 'Mammoth Melting Sugar,' 'Oregon Giant,' or 'Avalanche'). You can enjoy the sweet immature pods of **snap peas** whole, or you can wait for your peas to mature and eat the peas in the pods or serve the peas alone (try 'Sugar Ann,' 'Sugar Daddy,' or 'Sugar Sprint').

Grow

Besides great flavor, peas have pretty flowers—usually white but sometimes purple. Some also have colorful pods, such as purple 'Shiraz' or yellow 'Golden Sweet.' To speed up germination, soak seeds overnight before planting in slightly moist soil. Sow directly into your garden or raised beds. Don't thin seedlings. In the Upper South, sow seeds as soon as the ground can be worked in spring. In the Middle and Lower South, plant in late winter for spring harvest or late summer for fall harvest. In the Coastal and Tropical South, start in early winter. For a good selection online, try *southernexposure.com* or *johnnyseeds.com.*

Train

You can buy vining or dwarf selections of garden peas. Peas climb by tendrils, so purchase a trellis (*gardeners.com*) to provide support for taller, climbing selections and make harvesting easier. Or build your own trellis using deciduous branches cut from the yard. Vines are brittle and can be damaged easily, so use scissors or small snips to harvest gently. Pick peas regularly to encourage production.

SNAP PEA SALAD

Cut 8 oz. **sugar snap peas** into 1-inch pieces. Cook in boiling water to cover 15 seconds; plunge in ice water. Drain. Toss together peas, 2 cups **mâche,** 2 cups chopped fresh **cauliflower,** ½ cup chopped **green onions,** 3 Tbsp. chopped fresh **dill weed,** 1 minced **garlic clove,** 1 Tbsp. each **olive oil** and **white wine vinegar,** and 1 tsp. **table salt.**

get growing!
PEAS

SOIL
Well-drained soil, amended with organic matter to retain moisture

MULCH
After seedlings emerge, add a layer of straw or finely shredded bark to keep roots cool and soil moisture consistent.

| LIGHT FULL | WATER MEDIUM | CARE MEDIUM |

These 'Super Sugar Snap' peas are sweet, crunchy, and loaded with vitamins.

Community Cookbook

KICK OFF YOUR GAME-DAY PARTY WITH OUR FAVORITE BLOGGERS' **SUPER BOWL SNACKS**

From the Kitchen of
COURTNEY CHAMPION
RICHMOND, VA
COOKLIKEACHAMPIONBLOG.COM

....

"This is so addictive, I've never seen it stick around at parties for more than a few minutes!"

....

BAKED TEX-MEX RED PEPPER CHEESE DIP

Preheat oven to 325°. Stir together 2 cups (8 oz.) shredded extra-sharp **Cheddar cheese;** 2 cups (8 oz.) shredded **pepper Jack cheese;** 3/4 (8-oz.) package **cream cheese,** softened; 3/4 cup **roasted red bell peppers,** chopped; 1/2 cup **mayonnaise;** 1/3 cup chopped **fresh cilantro;** 3 **green onions,** finely chopped; 2 **jalapeño peppers,** seeded and finely chopped; 1 tsp. **Worcestershire sauce;** 1/4 tsp. **dried crushed red pepper;** and **table salt** and **freshly ground black pepper** to taste.

Lightly grease a 2-qt. baking dish with **cooking spray;** spread cheese mixture in prepared dish. Bake 20 to 25 minutes or until thoroughly heated and bubbly. **MAKES** 6 to 8 servings

From the Kitchen of
ROBYN STONE
CARROLLTON, GA
ADDAPINCH.COM

....

"These pot stickers are hearty while still being the perfect size for snacking."

....

BUFFALO CHICKEN POT STICKERS

Stir together 4 cups shredded cooked **chicken;** 3/4 cup **Buffalo-style hot sauce;** 3 **green onions,** chopped (about 1/2 cup); and 1/2 tsp. **freshly ground black pepper** in a medium bowl. Spoon 2 tsp. chicken mixture in center of each of 48 **wonton wrappers.** Moisten edges of each wonton with water; fold corners over mixture to form a triangle. Press edges to seal. Heat 1 Tbsp. **olive oil** in a large nonstick skillet over medium heat. Cook wontons, 12 at a time, in hot oil 2 minutes or until golden. (Do not turn.) Add 1/3 cup **water;** cover and cook 2 more minutes. Transfer to a **parchment paper**-lined baking sheet, and keep warm in a 200° oven until ready to serve. **MAKES** 4 dozen

From the Kitchen of
GENÊT HOGAN
WOODSTOCK, GA
RAISEDONAROUX.COM

....

"These combine all-American flair with the deeply traditional flavors of South Louisiana."

....

CAJUN CORN PUPS

Whisk together 1 (7.5-oz.) package **corn muffin mix;** 1/3 cup cold **beer;** 1 large **egg,** lightly beaten; 1 1/4 tsp. **Creole seasoning;** and 1/4 tsp. **garlic powder** in a medium bowl. Cut 1 (1-lb.) package **andouille sausage** into 1-inch slices. Dip sausages in batter, coating well. Pour **vegetable oil** to depth of 1 inch into a Dutch oven; heat over medium-high heat to 340°. Fry sausages, in batches, 2 minutes on each side or until golden brown. Drain on paper towels. Keep warm on a wire rack in an aluminum foil-lined jelly-roll pan in a 200° oven. Serve with Creole mustard. **MAKES** 6 to 8 servings

From the Kitchen of
EMILY NABORS HALL
BIRMINGHAM, AL
FOODBLOGSOUTH.COM

ROASTED RED PEPPER DIP

Process 1 (12-oz.) jar **roasted red bell peppers,** drained and patted dry; 1 (4-oz.) **goat cheese log,** softened; 1/2 cup **mayonnaise;** 1 Tbsp. **fresh lemon juice;** 1 **garlic clove;** and 1/2 tsp. each **kosher salt** and **freshly ground black pepper** in a food processor 15 seconds or until smooth. Add 1/4 cup chopped toasted **pecans;** 1 Tbsp. finely chopped, seeded **jalapeño pepper;** and 2 tsp. each chopped **fresh chives** and **fresh flatleaf parsley;** pulse until combined. Transfer to a bowl; chill 4 hours. Drizzle with 1 Tbsp. **olive oil.** Serve with **pita chips** or **crudités.** **MAKES** 1 1/2 cups

March

Southern Congealiality

GELATIN SALADS MAY BRING BACK TECHNICOLOR MEMORIES OF SUPPER AT GRANDMA'S, BUT GUESS WHAT? THE JIGGLY WONDERS ARE BACK AND TASTIER THAN EVER.

DEAR CONGEALED SALAD,

A confession: For years—well, decades—we ignored you. Maybe it's because we couldn't tell Grandma, your BFF, that your goopy mayonnaise topping and bizarre sweet-savory flavor combo turned us off. Our silence didn't do you any favors. While we updated other classic recipes for modern tastes and dinner parties, we left you jiggling in the dust. But the truth is, you're the total package: easy to make, inexpensive, and amazingly transportable. Plus, nothing brings giggles to a meal or a sense of levity to our cooking like you. So we want to make it up to you. How about a total makeover? We're talking new flavors and fresh looks that will solidify your place at the Southern table for generations to come. Welcome back, old friend. Yours, *Southern Living*

THE NEW INSTANT CLASSIC
SPICED COCONUT-CHERRY MOLD

In order for the cherries to set in a single layer, be sure to stick to the timing instructed in Steps 4-6.

- 1 cup frozen cherries*
- 2 envelopes unflavored gelatin
- 4 cups coconut milk, divided
- 1/2 cup sugar
- 1 tsp. vanilla extract
- 1/4 tsp. ground cinnamon
- 1/4 tsp. ground cardamom (optional)
  Vegetable cooking spray

1. Thaw cherries, reserving juice (about 2 Tbsp.). Sprinkle gelatin over 1 cup coconut milk in a medium bowl. Let stand.
2. Meanwhile, bring sugar, next 2 ingredients, cardamom (if desired), and remaining 3 cups coconut milk to a simmer in a saucepan over medium-low heat, whisking constantly.
3. Pour hot coconut mixture over gelatin mixture. Stir until gelatin dissolves. Stir in reserved cherry juice. Let stand 20 minutes.
4. Lightly grease a 6-cup gelatin mold with cooking spray; place cherries in a single layer in bottom of mold. Pour enough gelatin mixture over cherries to cover halfway. Chill 20 to 30 minutes or until slightly set. (Let remaining gelatin mixture stand at room temperature.)
5. Slowly pour enough remaining gelatin mixture into mold just to cover cherries. Chill 20 to 30 minutes or until slightly set.

6. Slowly pour remaining gelatin mixture into mold, and chill 6 hours or until firm.
7. Gently run a small knife around outer edge of mold to break seal. Dip bottom of mold in warm water for about 10 seconds. Unmold onto a serving plate.

*Fresh pitted cherries may be substituted. Omit cherry juice in Step 3.

Note: We tested with Thai Kitchen Coconut Milk.

Makes 6 servings. Hands-on 35 min.; Total 7 hours, 40 min.

THE LUNCHEON LEGACY
CUCUMBER-TOMATO ASPIC

Mold this tangy aspic in mini muffin pans to make individual condiment-size servings that are delicious with a green salad, chicken, pork chops, or catfish.

- 1 (1-oz.) package unflavored gelatin
- 1 cup cranberry juice
- 3 cups low-sodium tomato juice
- 2 Tbsp. chopped fresh flat-leaf parsley
- 1 Tbsp. olive oil
- 1 tsp. Worcestershire sauce
- 6 to 8 dashes of hot sauce
- 1/2 tsp. celery salt
- 1/2 tsp. garlic salt
- 1 3/4 cups chopped cucumber

1. Sprinkle gelatin over cranberry juice in a bowl. Let stand 3 minutes.
2. Meanwhile, bring tomato juice to a boil in a medium saucepan over

Cucumber-Tomato Aspic

medium-high heat. Pour over gelatin mixture, and stir until gelatin dissolves. Whisk in parsley and next 5 ingredients.

3. Spread cucumbers in a 4-cup mold; pour gelatin mixture over cucumbers. Chill 4 hours or until set. Dip bottom of mold in warm water for about 15 seconds. Unmold onto a serving plate.

Makes 16 to 20 servings. Hands-on 20 min.; Total 4 hours, 20 min.

Mini Tomato Aspics

Prepare recipe as directed in Steps 1 and 2. Spoon about 1 tsp. chopped cucumbers into each cup of a 24-cup miniature muffin pan; top with gelatin mixture, filling completely (about 1 Tbsp. per cup). Chill 1 hour or until set. Unmold as directed in Step 3.

Makes 2 dozen. Hands-on 20 min.; Total 1 hour, 20 min.

THE ENTERTAINING ESSENTIAL

WHITE SANGRIA SALADS

Delicate and sweet, this pairs well with chicken or tuna salad.

- 1 (1-oz.) package unflavored gelatin
- 1 cup cold pineapple juice
- 2 ½ cups white grape juice
- 2 cups chilled sweet sparkling wine (such as Moscato d'Asti)
- 1 cup sliced green grapes
- 1 cup drained mandarin orange segments
- 12 grapefruit sections (about 2 grapefruit)

1. Sprinkle gelatin over pineapple juice in a bowl; let stand 1 minute.

2. Bring 1 ½ cups grape juice to a boil in a saucepan over high heat. Add hot

(continued on page 71)

OUR MOST MEMORABLE MOLDS

NOV. 1983

FIT FOR A KING

Caviar Mousse

Just the mold to make if William and Kate are coming to dinner. Otherwise, we say reserve caviar for blini.

JULY 1984

FRUIT MASTERPIECE

Orange-Pear Salad

Flavored like a Dreamsicle, this salad turned heads with its—dare we say—amazing canned-fruit mosaic.

MARCH 1976

COVER GIRL

Perfection Salad

Our only cover-worthy congealed salad was carrots, peppers, and pimiento suspended in lemon gelatin.

THE FAMILY JEWEL

My hog-farming, quick-witted Grandma Lula Mae was the champion of one particular congealment, a mixture of cream cheese, mayonnaise, marshmallows, and pineapple covered with jewel-toned Lime Jell-O: her Green Top Salad. It was her show pony, and each holiday, with much fanfare, she trotted it out of the refrigerator and onto the buffet table with pride. Although it's never been my favorite thing to eat (one holiday I even made the mistake of telling her so), it will forever be the first thing I scoop from the buffet. It's one of the few recipes that everyone in my family rallies around as a true heirloom, a happy reminder of past gatherings and a dish that embodies the spirit of the cook who championed it. One bite of Green Top Salad brings a smile to my face and feeds my soul with a dose of Grandma's joyous larger-than-life personality.

— *LIBBIE SUMMERS*

21ST-CENTURY GREEN TOP SALAD

"This recipe has the sweet, fruity flavors of Grandma Lula Mae's salad but made for today," Libbie says. "I think Grandma would surely approve."

- 1 **envelope unflavored gelatin**
- 1/2 **cup cold water**
- 1/2 **cup boiling water**
- 1 **(14-oz.) can sweetened condensed milk**
- 1/2 **cup fresh lime juice**
- 1/2 **cup plain Greek yogurt**
- 1 **(8-oz.) can crushed pineapple in juice, undrained**
- 1 **to 4 drops green liquid food coloring (optional)**
- 1 **(7-oz.) jar marshmallow crème**
- 1 **(8-oz.) package cream cheese, softened**
- 1/4 **to 1/2 cup plain Greek yogurt**

1. Sprinkle gelatin over 1/2 cup cold water in a medium bowl. Let stand 2 minutes. Pour 1/2 cup boiling water over gelatin mixture, and stir until gelatin dissolves.

2. Slowly whisk in sweetened condensed milk and next 2 ingredients. Fold in pineapple. Stir in green food coloring, if desired. Pour mixture into a 4-cup mold, and chill 4 hours or until set. Gently run a small knife around outer edge of mold to break seal. Dip bottom of mold in warm water for about 15 seconds. Unmold salad onto a serving plate.

3. Beat marshmallow crème and cream cheese at high speed with an electric mixer until stiff peaks form. Stir in 1/4 to 1/2 cup yogurt. Serve with gelatin salad.

Makes 8 servings. Hands-on 25 min.; Total 4 hours, 30 min.

grape juice to gelatin mixture, and stir until gelatin dissolves. Stir in wine and remaining 1 cup grape juice.

3. Place grapes and citrus fruit in a 12-cup Bundt pan (about ³/₄ cup per mold) or 2 (6-cup) jumbo muffin pans. Top with wine mixture (about ¹/₂ cup per mold). Chill 3 hours or until set.

4. Dip bottom of pan in warm water for about 15 seconds. Unmold onto a serving plate.

Makes 12 servings. Hands-on 35 min.; Total 3 hours, 35 min.

THE SHOW-OFF-AT-A-SHOWER SWEET

LEMON CUPCAKES WITH LAVENDER FROSTING

No time to make the frosting? Simply top the cupcakes with sweetened whipped cream. Find dried lavender buds or tea in spice stores, high-end markets, or at amazon.com. Use food coloring to dye the frosting pale purple, if desired. (Pictured on page 168)

GELATIN CUPCAKES

- ¹/₂ cup sugar
- 2 envelopes unflavored gelatin
- 1 cup coconut water*
- 1 cup lemon-flavored sparkling beverage
- ²/₃ cup fresh lemon juice (about 4 lemons)
  Vegetable cooking spray
- 12 paper baking cups
- 12 (2-inch) round shortbread cookies

FROSTING

- 1 tsp. dried lavender buds
- 1 cup sugar
- 4 large egg whites, at room temperature
- ¹/₄ tsp. cream of tartar
- ¹/₂ tsp. vanilla extract

1. Prepare Cupcakes: Whisk together first 2 ingredients in a medium saucepan; whisk in coconut water and sparkling beverage. Cook over medium-low heat 2 minutes, whisking just until sugar dissolves. Remove from heat, and whisk in lemon juice. Let stand 2 minutes.

2. Lightly grease a 12-cup muffin pan with cooking spray. Spoon ¹/₄ cup

gelatin mixture into each cup of pan. Chill 4 hours or until completely set.

3. Gently run a small knife around the edges of each muffin cup, and invert a baking sheet over muffin pan. Holding baking sheet and pan together, invert and hold under hot running water until gelatin cakes unmold from muffin pan onto baking sheet.

4. Place 12 baking cups on a serving tray; place 1 cookie in each baking cup. Top each with a gelatin cake. Chill 1 to 2 hours.

5. Meanwhile, prepare Frosting: Process lavender and 1 cup sugar in a food processor 1 minute or until lavender is finely crushed.

6. Pour water to depth of 2 inches into bottom of a double boiler over medium-low heat; bring to a simmer. Place egg whites, cream of tartar, and lavender mixture in top of double boiler over simmering water. Cook mixture, whisking constantly, 9 to 10 minutes or until a thermometer registers 165°.

7. Remove from heat, and beat at high speed with an electric mixer, using whisk attachment, 3 to 4 minutes or until stiff, glossy peaks form. Stir in vanilla.

8. Spoon frosting into a zip-top plastic freezer bag. (Do not seal.) Snip 1 corner of bag to make a small hole. Pipe frosting onto each gelatin cupcake. Serve immediately.

*1 additional cup lemon-flavored sparkling beverage may substitute.

Note: Feel free to make these using a jumbo or mini muffin pan.

Makes 1 dozen. Hands-on 45 min.; Total 5 hours, 50 min.

THE REUNION RITUAL

AUNT LAURA'S STAINED GLASS CAKE

Deputy Food Director Whitney Wright's favorite dessert comes courtesy of her aunt, Laura Kazlo, who served it at family events.

- 1 (3-oz.) package orange-flavored gelatin
- 1 (1-oz.) package unflavored gelatin, divided
- 4¹/₂ cups boiling water
- 1 (3-oz.) package lime-flavored gelatin
- 1 (3-oz.) package strawberry-flavored gelatin
- 1 cup graham cracker crumbs
- ¹/₄ cup butter, melted
- ³/₄ cup sugar, divided
- ¹/₄ cup cold water
- 1 cup pineapple juice
- 2 cups heavy cream
- 1 tsp. vanilla extract

1. Stir together orange-flavored gelatin, 1 envelope unflavored gelatin, and 1¹/₂ cups boiling water until gelatin dissolves. Pour into an 8-inch square pan. Repeat with lime- and strawberry-flavored gelatins, placing each mixture in its own pan. Chill pans until firm.

2. Run a small knife around outer edge of each pan. Cut chilled gelatin into ¹/₂-inch squares. Dip bottom of pans in warm water for 10 seconds. Unmold gelatin squares onto a jelly-roll pan. Chill until ready to use (up to 24 hours).

3. Preheat oven to 350°. Stir together graham cracker crumbs, butter, and ¹/₄ cup sugar. Press into bottom of a 10-inch springform pan, and bake 10 minutes. Cool completely (about 20 minutes).

4. Meanwhile, sprinkle remaining 1 envelope unflavored gelatin over ¹/₄ cup cold water. Microwave pineapple juice in a microwave-safe bowl at HIGH 1 minute or until hot. Add hot pineapple juice to gelatin mixture, and stir until gelatin dissolves. Chill until consistency of unbeaten egg whites (20 to 30 minutes).

5. Beat cream, vanilla, and remaining ¹/₂ cup sugar until stiff peaks form.

Fold in pineapple mixture until blended.

6. Gently fold three-fourths of gelatin squares into pineapple mixture; pour over crust in pan. Tap pan sharply on counter to remove air bubbles. Top with remaining gelatin. Tap on counter again. Cover and chill 12 hours.

7. Run a small knife around edge of pan, before unlocking sides, to break seal. Remove sides of pan before serving.

Makes 10 to 12 servings. Hands-on 1 hour; Total 13 hours, 55 min.

THE CELEBRATORY STUNNER

BERRIES AND BUBBLES

The temperature of the Prosecco and club soda are key. Keeping the liquids cold helps the salad congeal faster, before too many of the tiny bubbles disappear. (Also pictured on page 168)

1   (1-oz.) package unflavored gelatin
3   cups chilled Prosecco, divided
1   cup sugar
1/2 pt. fresh raspberries
1/2 pt. fresh blackberries
1   cup cold club soda

1. Sprinkle gelatin over 1 cup cold Prosecco in a large bowl. Let stand 3 minutes.

2. Stir together sugar and remaining 2 cups Prosecco in a medium saucepan. Bring to a boil over high heat, stirring constantly; boil, stirring constantly, until sugar dissolves. Add hot Prosecco to gelatin mixture, and stir until gelatin dissolves. Chill until consistency of unbeaten egg whites (about 40 minutes).

3. Place raspberries and blackberries in a 6-cup gelatin mold. Stir cold club soda into chilled gelatin mixture until blended. Pour over fruit in mold. Chill until set (about 2 hours).

4. If necessary, run a small knife around edge of mold to break seal. Dip bottom of mold in warm tap water for about 15 seconds. Unmold onto a serving plate.

Makes 8 to 12 servings. Hands-on 15 min., Total 3 hours

Berries and Bubbles

GELATIN DO'S AND DON'TS

➔ **DO** BE PATIENT. Wait for gelatin to set fully before unmolding. It makes a big difference in how the mold will transport and hold its shape on a serving platter.

➔ **DON'T** USE SILICONE MOLDS. They make unmolding difficult. Go with metal or plastic, and dip the bottom of the mold into hot water for 10 to 15 seconds before inverting.

➔ **DO** FOLLOW TEMPERATURE GUIDELINES to ensure gelatin dissolves and sets. Cold ingredients should come from the refrigerator and boiled liquids should be brought to a full rolling boil.

➔ **DON'T** ASSUME YOU CAN SUBSTITUTE INGREDIENTS. There's a chemistry to gelatin, and a substitution may affect results. Fresh pineapple, for example, contains an enzyme that prevents gelatin from setting (so stick with canned).

➔ **DO** USE ANTIQUE MOLDS. Old-timey molds come in magical shapes and sizes and transform an old recipe. Find a great selection on *etsy.com*.

Hello, Honey

LIKE A FINE WINE, THE COLOR AND FLAVOR OF EVERY NECTAR REFLECTS
A PARTICULAR TIME AND PLACE. HERE, 13 SWEET AND SAVORY RECIPES.

HONEY FLANS

An elegant make-ahead dessert, these custards sing with faint floral notes and sweet honey. Serving tip from our Test Kitchen: Flans release like a dream if you let the custard cups stand in 1 inch of warm water for 3 to 5 minutes before unmolding. (Pictured on page 169)

- 1/2 cup sugar
- 7 Tbsp. honey (such as orange blossom), divided
- 1 (14-oz.) can sweetened condensed milk
- 1 cup milk
- 3 large eggs
- 1 large egg yolk
- 1/4 tsp. kosher salt

1. Preheat oven to 350°. Sprinkle sugar in a 3-qt. saucepan; place over medium heat, and cook, gently shaking pan, 4 minutes or until sugar melts and turns a light golden brown. Slowly stir in 3 Tbsp. honey. (Mixture will clump a little; gently stir just until melted.) Remove from heat; immediately pour hot caramelized sugar into 6 (6-oz.) ramekins.
2. Process condensed milk, next 4 ingredients, and remaining 4 Tbsp. honey in a blender 10 to 15 seconds or until smooth; pour evenly over sugar in each ramekin. Place ramekins in a 13- x 9-inch pan. Add hot tap water to pan to a depth of 1 inch. Cover loosely with aluminum foil.
3. Bake at 350° for 30 to 35 minutes or until slightly set. (Flan will jiggle when pan is shaken.) Remove ramekins from water bath; place on a wire rack. Cool 30 minutes. Cover and chill 3 hours. Run a knife around edges of flans to loosen; invert flans onto a serving plate.

Makes 6 servings. Hands-on 20 min.;
Total 4 hours, 20 min.

HONEY-ROASTED CARROTS

Substitute apple juice for bourbon, if you prefer. Look for bunches of carrots that are all about the same size so they'll cook evenly. If some are too big—or if you can't find real (sometimes labeled French) baby carrots—just peel the bigger ones and halve them lengthwise before roasting.

- 2 lb. baby carrots with tops
- 2 tsp. olive oil
- 3 Tbsp. butter, divided
- 1/2 tsp. kosher salt
- 1/4 tsp. freshly ground black pepper
- 1 shallot, finely chopped
- 2 Tbsp. bourbon
- 2 Tbsp. honey
- 1 Tbsp. chicken broth or water
- 1/2 tsp. chopped fresh thyme

1. Place a small roasting pan in oven. Preheat oven and pan to 500°.
2. Cut tops from carrots, leaving 1 inch of greenery on each carrot.
3. Stir together olive oil and 1 Tbsp. butter in preheated pan. Add carrots, salt, and pepper; toss to coat. Bake 10 minutes.
4. Meanwhile, melt remaining 2 Tbsp. butter in a small saucepan over medium-high heat. Add shallot; sauté 1 minute. Remove from heat, and stir in bourbon and next 2 ingredients. Return to heat, and bring to a boil, stirring occasionally. Reduce heat to medium, and cook 5 minutes or until mixture is syrupy.
5. Drizzle syrup over carrots; toss to coat. Bake 5 to 7 more minutes or until carrots are crisp-tender. Transfer to a serving dish, and sprinkle with thyme.

Makes 4 to 6 servings. Hands-on 25 min.,
Total 30 min.

SPINACH SALAD WITH HONEY DRESSING AND HONEYED PECANS

Use leftover dressing to marinate meat or perk up plain rice. (Pictured on page 6)

- 1 (6-oz.) package baby spinach
- 1 cup quartered fresh strawberries
- 1/2 cup thinly sliced red onion
- 1/2 cup fresh blueberries
  Honey Dressing
- 3 to 4 cooked bacon slices, crumbled
- 1/4 cup crumbled blue cheese
  Honeyed Pecans (recipe on page 74)

Toss together first 4 ingredients and 1/3 cup dressing. Sprinkle with bacon, cheese, and pecans. Serve with remaining dressing.

Makes 6 to 8 servings. Hands-on 15 min.;
Total 1 hour, 15 min., including vinaigrette and pecans

Honey Dressing

Whisk together 1/3 cup **white balsamic vinegar**, 2 Tbsp. **honey**, 1 Tbsp. **Dijon mustard**, and 1/2 tsp. each **table salt** and **black pepper.** Add 2/3 cup **extra virgin olive oil** in a slow, steady stream, whisking constantly until smooth.

Makes about 1 cup. Hands-on 5 min.,
Total 5 min.

Honey-and-Soy-Lacquered Ribs

Honeyed Pecans

Preheat oven to 325°. Microwave 1/4 cup **honey** in a bowl at HIGH 20 seconds. Stir in 1 cup **pecan halves.** Coat a **parchment paper**-lined jelly-roll pan with **cooking spray;** spread pecans in a single layer on pan. Combine 1 Tbsp. **sugar,** 1/4 tsp. **kosher salt,** and a pinch of **ground red pepper;** sprinkle over pecans. Bake 15 minutes or until toasted, stirring after 8 minutes. Cool completely; break into pieces.

Makes 1 cup. Hands-on 10 min., Total 55 min.

HONEY-AND-SOY-LACQUERED RIBS

Bake these sweet and spicy ribs up to 2 days ahead. Then simply reheat and broil before serving. (Also pictured on page 7)

2 (2- to 2 1/2-lb.) slabs
St. Louis-style pork ribs
1 Tbsp. kosher salt
2 tsp. freshly ground pepper
1/2 cup honey
2 Tbsp. soy sauce
2 Tbsp. Asian chili-garlic sauce
1 Tbsp. fresh lime juice
1 Tbsp. butter
1 tsp. dry mustard
1 tsp. ground ginger

1. Preheat oven to 325°. Rinse slabs, and pat dry. Remove thin membrane from back of slabs by slicing into it and pulling it off. (This will make the ribs more tender.) Sprinkle salt and pepper over slabs; wrap each slab tightly in aluminum foil. Place slabs on a jelly-roll pan, and bake 2 to 2 1/2 hours or until tender and meat pulls away from bone.
2. Bring honey and next 6 ingredients to a boil in a saucepan over high heat, stirring occasionally. Reduce heat to medium-low; simmer 5 minutes or until reduced by half. Transfer to a bowl.

3. Remove slabs from oven. Increase oven temperature to broil on high. Carefully remove slabs from foil; place on a foil-lined baking sheet. Brush each slab with 3 Tbsp. honey mixture.
4. Broil 5 to 7 minutes or until browned and sticky. Brush with remaining honey mixture.

Makes 6 to 8 servings. Hands-on 30 min.; Total 2 hours, 35 min.

HONEY-PINEAPPLE UPSIDE-DOWN CAKE

Fresh pineapple slices work well here too.

2/3	cup honey
1	(15.25-oz.) can pineapple slices in juice, drained
1 1/3	cups sugar
3/4	cup butter, softened
1	tsp. vanilla extract
1 3/4	cups all-purpose flour
1/4	cup plain yellow cornmeal
1	tsp. baking powder
1	tsp. table salt
1/2	tsp. baking soda
3/4	cup buttermilk
3	large eggs
	Honey Glaze

1. Preheat oven to 350°. Pour honey into a buttered 10-inch cast-iron skillet, tilting skillet to spread evenly. Top with pineapple.
2. Beat sugar and butter at medium speed with a heavy-duty electric stand mixer until fluffy. Stir in vanilla. Whisk together flour and next 4 ingredients. Whisk together buttermilk and eggs. Add flour mixture to sugar mixture alternately with buttermilk mixture, beginning and ending with flour mixture. Beat just until blended. Spread batter over pineapple.
3. Bake at 350° for 50 minutes or until a wooden pick inserted in center comes out clean, shielding with aluminum foil after 45 minutes to prevent excessive browning, if necessary. Cool in skillet on a wire rack 10 minutes.
4. Invert cake onto a serving platter. Drizzle with Honey Glaze. Let cool 15 minutes before serving.

Makes 10 to 12 servings. Hands-on 25 min.; Total 1 hour, 50 min., including glaze

Honey Glaze

Bring 1/4 cup **honey,** 1 Tbsp. **light brown sugar,** and 1 Tbsp. **butter** to a simmer in a pan. Cook 1 minute.

Makes about 1/3 cup. Hands-on 10 min., Total 10 min.

GRILLED SALT-AND-PEPPER CHICKEN WINGS

Broiler option: Broil on a foil-lined jelly-roll pan 8 inches from heat 20 minutes or until done, turning halfway through.

2	lb. chicken wings
2	Tbsp. olive oil
1 1/2	tsp. kosher salt
1/2	tsp. black pepper
	Desired Honey Drizzle

Preheat grill to 350° to 400° (medium-high) heat. Toss together wings and oil in a large bowl. Sprinkle with salt and pepper; toss to coat. Grill wings, covered with grill lid, 25 to 30 minutes or until skin is crisp and wings are done, turning occasionally. Toss with desired Honey Drizzle.

Makes 6 to 8 servings. Hands-on 10 min.; Total 35 min., not including drizzle

Cider Vinegar-Brown Butter Honey Drizzle

Cook 1/4 cup **butter** in a saucepan over medium-high heat 5 minutes or until brown and fragrant. Transfer to a small bowl, and cool 5 minutes. Cook 1/2 cup **honey** and 1 Tbsp. **apple cider vinegar** in a saucepan over medium heat, stirring often, 2 minutes or until thoroughly heated. Whisk in browned butter.

Makes about 3/4 cup. Hands-on 10 min.; Total 15 min.

Horseradish-Honey Mustard Drizzle

Cook 1/2 cup **honey,** 3 Tbsp. **prepared horseradish,** and 2 Tbsp. **coarse-grained mustard** in a small saucepan over medium heat, stirring often, 2 minutes or until thoroughly heated.

Makes about 3/4 cup. Hands-on 5 min., Total 5 min.

Cracked Pepper-Rosemary Honey Drizzle

Cook 1/2 cup **honey,** 2 Tbsp. **water,** 1 tsp. cracked **black pepper,** and 1 (3-inch) fresh **rosemary sprig** in a saucepan over medium heat, stirring often, 2 minutes or until thoroughly heated. Discard rosemary.

Makes about 1/2 cup. Hands-on 5 min., Total 5 min.

Chili-Lemon Honey Drizzle

Cook 1/2 cup **honey,** 1/4 cup bottled **chili sauce,** and 2 Tbsp. **fresh lemon juice** over medium heat, stirring often, 2 minutes or until thoroughly heated.

Makes about 1 cup. Hands-on 5 min., Total 5 min.

Lasso Big Texas Flavors

PIONEERING BLOGGER **LISA FAIN** OF *HOMESICKTEXAN.COM* WRANGLES
A LONE STAR MENU FOR CASUAL ENTERTAINING

The Menu

JALAPEÑO-CHEDDAR POPOVERS
. . . .
WEEKEND BRISKET
. . . .
CHIPOTLE SCALLOPED POTATOES
. . . .
GRAPEFRUIT-PECAN SHEET CAKE

Weekend Brisket

JALAPEÑO-CHEDDAR POPOVERS

Make popover batter a day ahead; cover and chill. Bring to room temperature before baking.

3   large eggs, at room temperature
1   cup all-purpose flour
1   cup milk, at room temperature
3   Tbsp. butter, melted
1/2   tsp. kosher salt
1/4   cup (1 oz.) shredded sharp Cheddar cheese
1   Tbsp. minced seeded jalapeño pepper (about 1 pepper)
  Vegetable cooking spray

Preheat oven to 450°. Process first 5 ingredients in a blender 15 seconds or until smooth. Stir in cheese and jalapeño, and let stand 30 minutes. Lightly grease a 12-cup muffin pan with cooking spray; place in a jelly-roll pan, and heat in oven 2 minutes. Spoon batter into prepared muffin pan, filling halfway. Bake 15 minutes. Reduce oven temperature to 375°, and bake 8 to 12 minutes or until puffed and golden brown.

Makes 1 dozen. Hands-on 15 min.;
Total 1 hour, 10 min.

WEEKEND BRISKET

Turn leftovers (if there are any!) into tacos, chili, or egg-and-brisket biscuit sandwiches. (Pictured on page 76)

- 2 garlic cloves, minced
- 1 Tbsp. kosher salt
- 1 Tbsp. freshly ground black pepper
- 2 Tbsp. light molasses, honey, or sorghum syrup
- 2 Tbsp. yellow mustard
- 1/4 tsp. ground red pepper
- 1 (4- to 5-lb.) brisket flat, trimmed
- 1 yellow onion, halved and thinly sliced
- 1 Tbsp. vegetable oil
- 6 garlic cloves, chopped
- 1 cup beef broth
  Horseradish Cream

1. Stir together first 6 ingredients in a small bowl to form a paste. Rub on brisket, and let stand at room temperature 1 hour.
2. Preheat oven to 250°. Cook onion in hot oil in a large Dutch oven over medium-high heat, stirring occasionally, 5 minutes or until tender. Add 6 garlic cloves, and sauté 30 seconds. Remove from heat, and add beef broth, stirring to loosen browned bits from bottom of skillet. Place brisket in Dutch oven, fat side up. Spoon onion mixture over brisket.
3. Bake, covered, at 250° for 4 to 5 hours or until fork-tender. Let stand 30 minutes. Thinly slice brisket across the grain. Serve with Horseradish Cream.

Makes 6 to 8 servings. Hands-on 25 min.; Total 6 hours, 5 min., including cream

Horseradish Cream

Stir together 1 cup **sour cream,** 1 tsp. **prepared horseradish,** 1 minced **garlic clove,** and, if desired, 1 **pickled jalapeño pepper,** stemmed, seeded, and minced, in a small bowl. Add **table salt** to taste. Refrigerate up to 1 week.

Makes about 1 1/4 cups. Hands-on 10 min., Total 10 min.

CHIPOTLE SCALLOPED POTATOES

(Pictured on page 7)

- 1/2 cup half-and-half
- 2 garlic cloves, chopped
- 1 canned chipotle chile in adobo sauce
- 1 1/2 tsp. kosher salt
- 1/2 tsp. freshly ground black pepper
- 1/8 tsp. ground nutmeg
- 2 1/2 cups whipping cream
  Vegetable cooking spray
- 3 lb. russet potatoes, peeled and cut into 1/8-inch slices
- 1 cup (4 oz.) shredded sharp white Cheddar cheese
- 4 cooked bacon slices, crumbled

1. Preheat oven to 400°. Process first 6 ingredients in a blender or food processor until smooth. Transfer mixture to a medium bowl, and stir in whipping cream.
2. Lightly grease a 13- x 9-inch baking dish with cooking spray. Spread one-fourth of potatoes in a single layer in prepared dish; top with one-fourth of cream mixture. Repeat layers three more times with remaining potatoes and cream mixture.
3. Bake, covered, at 400° for 50 minutes. Uncover and sprinkle with cheese and bacon. Bake 20 minutes or until lightly browned and bubbly. Let stand 10 minutes.

Makes 8 to 10 servings. Hands-on 30 min.; Total 1 hour, 50 min.

GRAPEFRUIT-PECAN SHEET CAKE

CAKE

- 1 Ruby Red grapefruit
- 1 cup butter, melted
- 2 cups all-purpose flour, sifted
- 2 cups granulated sugar
- 1 tsp. baking soda
- 1/2 tsp. kosher salt
- 1/2 tsp. ground cinnamon
- 1 cup coarsely chopped toasted pecans
- 1/2 cup buttermilk
- 2 large eggs, lightly beaten
- 1 tsp. vanilla extract
  Shortening

FROSTING

- 1 (8-oz.) package cream cheese, softened
- 1/4 cup butter, softened
- 1 tsp. vanilla extract
- 1 (16-oz.) package powdered sugar

1. Prepare Cake: Grate zest from grapefruit to equal 3 Tbsp. Cut grapefruit in half, and squeeze juice to equal 10 Tbsp.
2. Preheat oven to 375°. Stir together melted butter, 1/2 cup grapefruit juice, and 1/2 cup water in a small bowl.
3. Stir together flour and next 4 ingredients in a large bowl. Stir in pecans, next 3 ingredients, 2 Tbsp. zest, and butter mixture until smooth. Pour batter into a greased (with shortening) and floured 13- x 9-inch pan.
4. Bake at 375° for 20 to 25 minutes or until a wooden pick inserted in center comes out clean. Cool 1 hour.
5. Prepare Frosting: Beat cream cheese and softened butter at medium speed with an electric mixer 1 to 2 minutes or until creamy. Add vanilla and remaining 2 Tbsp. grapefruit juice and 1 Tbsp. zest, and beat until blended. Gradually add powdered sugar, beating at low speed until blended. Spread frosting over top of cooled cake.

Makes 10 to 12 servings. Hands-on 25 min.; Total 1 hour, 45 min.

Spring to the Table

HATCH AN EASY PLAN FOR DINNER WITH CHICKEN RECIPES
THAT CELEBRATE THE SEASON'S FRESHEST GREEN VEGETABLES

SESAME CHICKEN GARDEN SALAD

Dress a double batch of this light but satisfying dinner with the sesame dressing. The flavors get even better overnight in the fridge, and leftovers make a gourmet on-the-go lunch. (Pictured on page 170)

- 1/2 cup reduced-fat sesame dressing
- 2 Tbsp. fresh lime juice
- 1/4 tsp. dried crushed red pepper
- 1 (6-oz.) package regular baby or French baby carrots, thinly sliced lengthwise
- 1 (4-oz.) package fresh sugar snap peas, halved lengthwise
- 1/2 English cucumber, thinly sliced into half moons
- 3 radishes, thinly sliced
- 2 boneless deli-roasted chicken breasts, sliced
- 1/3 cup chopped fresh cilantro
- 2 Tbsp. toasted sesame seeds

1. Whisk together first 3 ingredients; reserve 3 Tbsp.
2. Cook carrots in boiling salted water to cover 2 to 3 minutes or until crisp-tender. Add peas; cook 2 more minutes; drain. Plunge into ice water to stop the cooking process; drain.
3. Toss together dressing, carrot mixture, cucumber, and radishes. Top with chicken and cilantro. Drizzle with reserved 3 Tbsp. dressing. Sprinkle with sesame seeds. Serve immediately, or refrigerate up to 2 days.

Note: We tested with Ken's Steak House Lite Asian Sesame Dressing.

Makes 4 servings. Hands-on 20 min., Total 20 min.

BACON-WRAPPED CHICKEN WITH BASIL LIMA BEANS

- 2 (1-oz.) packages fresh basil
- 2 garlic cloves
- 1/3 cup olive oil
- 1/4 cup fresh lemon juice
- 1 1/2 tsp. kosher salt, divided
- 1 (9-oz.) package frozen steam-in-bag baby lima beans (such as Green Giant)
- 8 thick hickory-smoked bacon slices
- 4 skinned and boned chicken breasts
- 1/4 tsp. freshly ground black pepper
- 2 Tbsp. olive oil
- 1 cup thinly sliced celery (ribs and leaves)
- 1/3 cup loosely packed fresh flat-leaf parsley leaves
- 1/4 cup thinly sliced red onion

1. Preheat oven to 425°. Process first 4 ingredients and 1 tsp. salt in a blender until smooth. Cook limas according to package directions; cool 5 minutes.
2. Microwave bacon in a single layer between paper towels on a plate 2 minutes or until heated through but still limp. (Do not fully cook.)
3. Sprinkle chicken with pepper and remaining 1/2 tsp. salt. Wrap each breast with 2 pieces of bacon. Cook chicken in 2 Tbsp. hot oil in an oven-proof skillet over medium heat 5 minutes or until bacon begins to brown. Turn chicken.
4. Bake chicken, in skillet, at 425° for 20 minutes or until done. Let stand 5 minutes; thinly slice.
5. Stir together celery, next 2 ingredients, limas, and half of dressing. Serve chicken with lima bean mixture and remaining dressing.

Makes 4 servings. Hands-on 25 min., Total 50 min.

CHICKEN BREASTS WITH MUSHROOMS AND ASPARAGUS

- 4 skinned and boned chicken breasts (about 1 1/2 lb.)
- 2 tsp. Sicilian crushed red pepper-and-garlic seasoning (such as McCormick Perfect Pinch)
- 1 tsp. kosher salt
- 8 green onions (optional)
- 1 lb. fresh asparagus
- 1 (8-oz.) package sliced fresh mushrooms
- 3 garlic cloves, sliced
- 4 Tbsp. olive oil
- 2 Tbsp. drained capers
- 2 Tbsp. fresh lemon juice
- 1/4 cup loosely packed fresh dill leaves or chopped fresh flat-leaf parsley
- 2 Tbsp. butter
- 4 French bread loaf slices, toasted

1. Preheat grill to 350° to 400° (medium-high) heat. Place chicken between 2 sheets of heavy-duty plastic wrap; flatten to 1/4-inch thickness, using a rolling pin or meat mallet. Sprinkle with seasoning and salt.
2. Grill chicken, covered with grill lid, 4 to 5 minutes. Add green onions to grill (if desired), and grill chicken and onions 4 to 5 minutes or until chicken is browned and done.

3. Snap off and discard tough ends of asparagus. Cook asparagus and next 2 ingredients in hot oil in a large nonstick skillet over medium-high heat, stirring often, 3 to 4 minutes or until asparagus is crisp-tender. Add capers and lemon juice; cook 1 to 2 minutes, stirring to loosen browned bits from bottom of skillet. Remove from heat; stir in dill and butter, stirring until butter melts.

4. Place chicken and onions on bread, and top with sauce.

Makes 4 servings. Hands-on 30 min., Total 30 min.

CRISPY CHICKEN WITH GREEK GREEN BEAN SALAD

(Pictured on page 171)

- 1 lemon
- 1 (8-oz.) package thin green beans
- 1 medium-size red bell pepper, sliced
- 1 (15-oz.) can chickpeas, drained
- 1/3 cup loosely packed fresh mint leaves
- 1/3 cup bottled Greek dressing
- 1/4 cup crumbled feta cheese
- 4 (4-oz.) skinned and boned chicken breasts
- 1 1/2 tsp. kosher salt, divided
- 1/2 tsp. freshly ground black pepper, divided
- 1/4 cup all-purpose flour
- 2 large eggs, lightly beaten
- 1 cup panko (Japanese breadcrumbs)
- 4 Tbsp. canola oil

1. Grate zest from lemon (about 1 Tbsp.). Halve lemon, and juice it. Cook beans in boiling salted water to cover 3 to 4 minutes or until crisp-tender; drain. Plunge into ice water to stop the cooking process; drain. Stir together bell pepper, next 4 ingredients, lemon juice, and beans.

2. Place each chicken breast between 2 sheets of plastic wrap; flatten to 1/4-inch thickness, using a rolling pin. Sprinkle with 1 tsp. salt and 1/4 tsp. pepper.

Crispy Chicken with Greek Green Bean Salad

3. Place flour and eggs in two separate shallow dishes. Stir together panko, lemon zest, and remaining 1/2 tsp. salt and 1/4 tsp. pepper in a third dish. Dredge chicken in flour, dip in eggs, and dredge in panko, pressing to adhere.

4. Cook half of chicken in 1 Tbsp. hot canola oil in a large nonstick skillet over medium heat 3 minutes or until golden. Turn chicken, add 1 Tbsp. canola oil to skillet, and cook 3 minutes or until done. Keep warm in a 200° oven. Repeat procedure with remaining chicken and canola oil. Serve with bean mixture.

Makes 4 servings. Hands-on 30 min., Total 30 min.

SEVEN REASONS WHY SOUTHERN COOKS WORTH THEIR SALT SHOULD MASTER

Homemade Mayonnaise

Mix Master
A whisk or hand mixer yields softer mayo than the blade of a food processor or blender.

Southern Silk Stir in water 1 tsp. at a time to create a silkier, smoother result.

Good Eggs
Use the freshest organic or pasteurized ones; let them come to room temperature first.

No. 1:

If bourbon is the social lubricant of the South, then mayonnaise is the culinary ball bearings. It makes your deviled eggs, chicken salads, potato salads, pimiento cheese, and tomato sandwiches sing.

No. 2:

Homemade mayonnaise tastes better than store-bought. (Yes, even Duke's.)

No. 3:

It's healthier too.

No. 4:

A certain magic happens when you slowly whip egg yolks with oil. This creamy emulsion is a fundamental lesson in kitchen chemistry.

No. 5:

Got your emulsion down? Now learn the art of enhancing and balancing flavors with vinegar, lemon juice, and salt. (We recommend Diamond Crystal kosher.)

No. 6:

Making mayo will make your grandmother's heart full.

No. 7:

Mayonnaise is *the* Southern mother sauce and the foundation for dozens of other sauces. (See facing page for recipes.) Customize your own by adding everything from herbs to Sriracha.

CLASSIC HOMEMADE MAYONNAISE

Tip: Pasteurized eggs are safest, but eggs from chickens raised healthy and happy taste best.

- 2 large pasteurized egg yolks
- 1 tsp. white wine vinegar
- 1 tsp. fresh lemon juice
- ½ tsp. kosher salt
- ¼ tsp. onion powder
- ¼ tsp. Dijon mustard
- ¼ tsp. hot sauce
- ⅛ tsp. sugar
- 1 cup canola oil

Beat first 8 ingredients at high speed with an electric mixer, using whisk attachment, 15 seconds or until combined. With mixer running, add oil in a very slow, steady stream, beating until smooth and thickened. Add water, 1 tsp. at a time, to thin as desired. Refrigerate 3 days.

Makes 1 cup. Total 5 min.

3 TWISTS TO TRY

COMEBACK SAUCE

The kissing cousin of rémoulade, this versatile spiced sauce originated in Jackson, Mississippi. Try it on chopped lettuce or anything fried.

Stir together 1 cup **mayonnaise**, ¼ cup **chili sauce**, 2 Tbsp. **ketchup**, 1 Tbsp. **lemon juice**, 1 tsp. **smoked paprika**, 2 tsp. **Worcestershire sauce**, 1 tsp. **hot sauce**, ½ tsp. **kosher salt**, ½ tsp. **garlic powder**, ½ tsp. **onion powder**, ½ tsp. **dry mustard**, and ¼ tsp. **freshly ground black pepper.** Cover and chill 30 minutes before serving. Refrigerate 1 week.

Makes 1½ cups. Hands-on 5 min., Total 5 min.

TARTAR SAUCE

This friend of fried fish or shellfish begs to be customized. Add your favorite ingredients.

Stir together 1 cup **mayonnaise**, 1 Tbsp. thinly sliced **fresh chives**; 2 Tbsp. chopped **cornichons** or other small dill pickles; 1 Tbsp. **capers**, drained; 1 large **hard-cooked egg**, peeled and chopped; 1½ tsp. **fresh lemon juice**; ½ tsp. **cornichon juice** from jar; ¼ tsp. **dried tarragon, basil, or parsley**; and ⅛ tsp. **ground red pepper** in a small bowl. Add **salt** and **pepper** to taste. Cover and chill 30 minutes

before serving. Refrigerate up to 3 days.

Makes 1½ cups. Hands-on 10 min., Total 10 min.

WHITE BBQ SAUCE

Use this vinegary, piquant North Alabama specialty as both a basting and finishing sauce on smoked or grilled chicken.

Stir together 1 cup **mayonnaise**, ⅓ cup **apple cider vinegar**, 3 tsp. **water**, 1 tsp. **Worcestershire sauce**, ½ tsp. **kosher salt**, ½ tsp. **garlic powder**, ½ tsp. **onion powder**, ½ tsp. **freshly ground black pepper,** and ¼ tsp. **hot sauce** in a small bowl. Serve immediately or chilled. Refrigerate up to 3 days.

Makes 1½ cups. Hands-on 5 min., Total 5 min.

OUR OWN KING OF THE KITCHEN, NORMAN KING, EXPLAINS

BOUILLON, BASES & BROTH

Save the hours of simmering it takes to make homemade stock. These quick supermarket flavor boosters are a staple of the *SL* Test Kitchen pantry because they add a rich foundation of savory flavor to everything from casseroles and gravies to greens and gumbo. Here are our four favorites and the best uses for each.

OUR TOP PICKS FROM SUPERMARKET SHELVES

BEST BOUILLON CUBE

Made by simmering meat and dehydrating the liquid, these cubes make for easy measuring (1 cube = 1 tsp.). Simply drop a cube into a pot of soup, stew, or greens to deepen the flavor.

BEST BOUILLON POWDER

A little MSG is a good thing. This powdered bouillon makes rich broth on its own, or use it pinch-by-pinch in place of salt to add savory chicken flavor to chicken pot pies, gravies, or slow-cooker braises.

BEST BASE

This concentrated chicken stock is the most versatile option. Reconstitute in hot water to add extra depth and richness to vegetable sautés, sauces, or gumbo. Try brushing on chicken before roasting. It's delicious!

BEST BROTH

Our go-to broth. This healthier version boasts clean chicken flavor and melds with added flavorings and spices for pan sauces or soups. Lower sodium means you can reduce it without making it too salty.

SAVE MONEY!

HOMEMADE REDUCED-SODIUM BROTH

Get more bang for your cluck from a rotisserie chicken (about $3 more!) by using the carcass to make flavorful broth.

Bring 1 **cooked chicken carcass** and 8 cups **water** to a boil in a large Dutch oven over medium-high heat. Reduce heat to medium-low, and simmer 1 hour or until liquid is reduced by half and broth is a rich brown color. Pour through a fine wire-mesh strainer into a large bowl; discard solids. Cool completely (about 30 minutes). Refrigerate up to 1 week or freeze up to 2 months.

Makes about 1 qt. Hands-on 10 min.; Total 1 hour, 50 min.

Roast Three Dinners in One

CYNTHIA GRAUBART SETS THE TABLE

LEG OF LAMB MEANS SPRING TO ME, and not much is easier on the home cook than roasting a large cut of meat to create three easy meals—a perfect candidate for this month's New Sunday Supper. Rubbed simply with fresh herbs, garlic, lemon, and olive oil in the Mediterranean way, the lamb emerges from the oven fragrant with a crisp exterior. Slice and serve with pan juices and potatoes; the texture of the lamb will be nearly fork-tender. Young lamb sold on the market like this has a bright yet earthy flavor, not the gamey flavor associated with older sheep (aka mutton).

I've made this supper easy by calling for a boneless leg of lamb, which is readily available at most supermarkets. The meat that remains after the packagers remove the leg bone isn't uniform in thickness, so they roll the awkward piece and secure it in what is essentially a convenient sack made of string. Cooking the lamb secured in the string means it will cook evenly without any extra work. Coat the lamb with the herb rub directly over the string, and roast the meat surrounded by small potatoes. After cooking, kitchen shears make easy work of removing the string. If you're introducing lamb to potential naysayers, prepare an extra batch of the Yogurt Sauce to serve for dipping. My children always ate anything they could dip.

Chop the remaining lamb for your next two dinners. The stewed tomatoes in the woodsy Rosemary Lamb Stew make it more family-friendly, and the lamb left over will be just enough for a brand-new, fresh-and-lively dish of Lamb Pita Pockets served with Yogurt Sauce. Pass the napkins!

Cynthia's Roasting Tips:

➤ Test the doneness of the lamb with an instant-read thermometer: 125° for rare, or a higher temp as preferred.

➤ Rest the lamb 15 minutes before carving to ensure the juiciest slices of meat.

SUNDAY NIGHT

HERB-ROASTED BONELESS LEG OF LAMB

Look for a roughly 5-lb. boneless leg of lamb rolled in netting; no need to unroll and retie. Roast in the netting, and then remove it with kitchen shears. (Pictured on page 172)

- 1 (5-lb.) boneless leg of lamb, rolled and tied
- 3 1/2 tsp. kosher salt, divided
- 2 tsp. freshly ground black pepper, divided
- 1/4 cup loosely packed fresh rosemary leaves
- 2/3 cup loosely packed fresh flat-leaf parsley leaves
- 1/4 cup loosely packed fresh thyme leaves
- 2 shallots, coarsely chopped
- 6 garlic cloves
- 1 Tbsp. fresh lemon juice
- 10 Tbsp. olive oil, divided
- 2 lb. small new potatoes

1. Rub lamb with 2 tsp. salt and 1 tsp. pepper; let stand 1 hour.
2. Pulse rosemary in a food processor 4 or 5 times or until finely chopped. Add parsley and next 4 ingredients, and pulse 4 or 5 times or until finely chopped. Add 6 Tbsp. olive oil, and pulse 7 or 8 times or until smooth, scraping down sides as needed. Rub mixture over lamb; place in a large roasting pan. Let stand 30 minutes.
3. Preheat oven to 450°. Toss together potatoes and remaining 1 1/2 tsp. salt, 1 tsp. pepper, and 4 Tbsp. oil; place potatoes around lamb in roasting pan.
4. Bake at 450° for 50 minutes to 1 hour or until a meat thermometer inserted into thickest portion registers 125° (rare). Remove lamb from pan; cover loosely with aluminum foil, and let stand 15 minutes before slicing.
5. Dice half of lamb; package in 2 (2 1/2-cup) portions, and reserve for Rosemary Lamb Stew and Lamb Pita Pockets. Serve remaining lamb with potatoes and pan juices.

Note: Peel the centers of the potatoes for a pretty presentation, if desired.

Makes 4 to 6 servings. Hands-on 20 min., Total 3 hours

MONDAY NIGHT

THIS WORKS GREAT WITH BEEF TOO!

ROSEMARY LAMB STEW

Onions, carrots, and garlic give this easy stew its foundation of flavor, and stewed tomatoes make it saucy. Serve it over hot cooked rice.

- 1 cup chopped yellow onion
- 1 Tbsp. olive oil
- 1 (8-oz.) package sliced fresh mushrooms
- 1 cup sliced carrots
- 2 1/2 cups diced cooked lamb
- 2 garlic cloves, minced
- 1 (14 1/2-oz.) can stewed tomatoes
- 1/2 cup chicken broth
- 1 fresh rosemary sprig
- 1 tsp. kosher salt
- 1/2 tsp. freshly ground black pepper
- Hot cooked rice

Sauté onion in hot oil in a 3-qt. saucepan over medium-high heat 3 to 4 minutes or until tender. Add mushrooms and carrots, and cook, stirring occasionally, 5 minutes. Add lamb and garlic, and cook, stirring constantly, 3 minutes. Stir in tomatoes, broth, and rosemary. Bring to a boil; reduce heat to medium-low, and simmer, stirring occasionally, 30 minutes. Stir in salt and pepper. Discard rosemary sprig. Serve stew over hot cooked rice.

Makes 4 servings. Hands-on 30 min., Total 1 hour

TUESDAY NIGHT

READY IN 15 MINUTES!

LAMB PITA POCKETS

Cynthia recommends serving this tangy yogurt sauce when introducing lamb to picky eaters.

Sauté 2 1/2 cups diced **cooked lamb** in 1 Tbsp. hot **olive oil** in a medium skillet over high heat 2 minutes or until hot. Combine 1 1/2 cups chopped **romaine lettuce**, 1/4 cup crumbled **feta cheese**, 2 small sliced **tomatoes**, and 3 Tbsp. bottled **Greek dressing**. Divide lamb among 4 **whole wheat pita rounds**, halved and warmed. Top with lettuce mixture and **Yogurt Sauce**.

Makes 4 servings. Hands-on 10 min., Total 15 min.

YOGURT SAUCE: Stir together 1 cup **Greek yogurt**; 1/3 cup loosely packed **fresh mint leaves**, finely chopped; 1/4 cup **sour cream**; 1 **garlic clove**, pressed; 1 Tbsp. **fresh lemon juice**; 1 medium **cucumber**, peeled, seeded, and chopped; and 1 tsp. **kosher salt.** Serve immediately or chilled. Refrigerate up to 2 days.

Makes 1 1/2 cups. Hands-on 5 min., Total 5 min.

Snack Smarter with Yogurt

SPIN GREEK YOGURT INTO THREE QUICK AND HEALTHY KID-FRIENDLY RECIPES

Freezer Pleasers
CREAMY FROZEN FRUIT POPS

Process 1 1/4 cups **frozen raspberries**, 1 1/4 cups sliced **fresh strawberries**, 1/4 cup **honey**, 1 Tbsp. **fresh lemon juice**, and 1/8 tsp. **table salt** in a food processor until smooth. Stir together 1 (7-oz.) container **low-fat plain Greek yogurt** and 2 Tbsp. **buttermilk.** Fold yogurt mixture into berry mixture. Pour into 10 (2-oz.) pop molds. Top with lids; insert craft sticks, leaving 1 1/2 to 2 inches sticking out of pop. Freeze 4 hours or until sticks are solidly anchored and pops are completely frozen.

Makes 10 pops. Hands-on 15 min.; Total 4 hours, 15 min.

Skinny Dip
CARAMEL-YOGURT DIP

Stir together 1 (7-oz.) container **low-fat plain Greek yogurt**, 1/3 cup **caramel topping**, and 1/8 tsp. **table salt.** Serve with **fruit.**

Makes 1 1/4 cups. Hands-on 5 min., Total 5 min.

Anytime Snack
GREEK YOGURT WITH SAVORY GRANOLA

Top 1/2 cup **low-fat Greek yogurt** with desired amounts of halved **grape tomatoes,** sliced **cucumber,** finely chopped **red onion,** and **Savory Granola.**

Makes 1 serving. Hands-on 5 min., Total 10 min.

Savory Granola

Stir together 1/2 cup crushed **sesame crackers,** 1 Tbsp. assorted chopped **fresh herbs** (such as flat-leaf parsley, basil, mint, and dill weed), 2 tsp. **extra virgin olive oil,** 1/4 tsp. loosely packed **lemon zest,** and 1/8 tsp. **table salt** in a medium bowl.

Makes about 1/2 cup. Hands-on 5 min., Total 5 min.

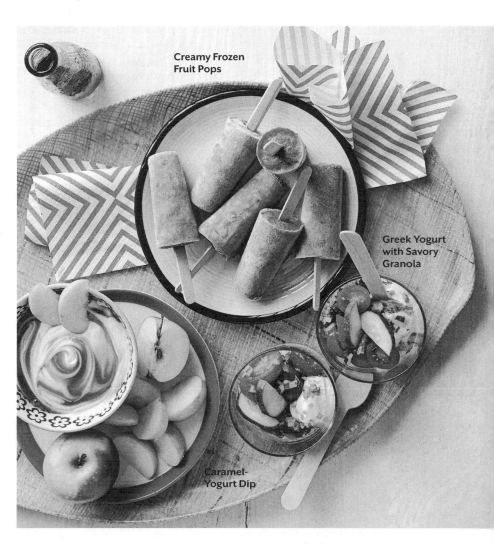

Creamy Frozen Fruit Pops

Greek Yogurt with Savory Granola

Caramel-Yogurt Dip

Community Cookbook

The Junior League of Baton Rouge's definitive collection of Louisiana cooking is now in its 78th printing, with more than 1 million copies sold! Order it at *juniorleaguebr.org*.

CHICKEN SPAGHETTI II

The original recipe for this comforting one-pot dish from River Road Recipes *called for "boiling a hen in seasoned water." We've adapted it for today's cooks.*

- 1 (3-lb.) whole chicken
- 2 large Spanish onions, chopped
- 1 cup chopped celery
- 1 cup chopped green onions
- 1 medium-size green bell pepper, chopped
- 3 garlic cloves, chopped
- 2 Tbsp. bacon drippings
- 1 (15-oz.) can tomato sauce
- 1 (10 3/4-oz.) can tomato soup
- 1/3 cup tomato paste
- 2 Tbsp. Worcestershire sauce
- 1 tsp. hot sauce
- 1 bay leaf
- 3/4 cup chopped fresh flat-leaf parsley
- 1 (16-oz.) package spaghetti, cooked

1. If applicable, remove giblets from chicken, and reserve for another use.
2. Sauté Spanish onions and next 4 ingredients in hot drippings in a large Dutch oven over medium-high heat 8 to 10 minutes or until tender. Stir in tomato sauce, next 5 ingredients, 1 cup water, and chicken. Bring to a boil; reduce heat to medium-low, and simmer 1 hour or until chicken is done. Remove chicken, reserving tomato mixture in Dutch oven. Cool chicken 20 minutes.
3. Meanwhile, simmer reserved tomato mixture, stirring occasionally, 20 minutes.
4. Skin, bone, and shred chicken; stir into tomato mixture. Stir in parsley. Add salt and pepper to taste. Serve over spaghetti.

Makes 8 servings. Hands-on 30 min.; Total 2 hours, 10 min.

SAND TARTS

Serve these savory pecan sandies with tea or on a cheese plate.

Preheat oven to 375°. Beat 1 cup **butter,** softened, and 1/4 cup **powdered sugar** at medium speed with a heavy-duty electric stand mixer 3 to 4 minutes or until fluffy. Stir together 2 cups **all-purpose flour,** 1 1/2 tsp. **baking powder,** and 1/4 tsp. **kosher salt.** Gradually add flour mixture to butter mixture, beating until blended. Stir in 1 cup finely chopped **pecans** and 1 Tbsp. **vanilla extract.** Lightly grease baking sheets with **vegetable cooking spray.** Drop dough by rounded tablespoonfuls onto prepared baking sheets; flatten slightly. Bake 13 to 15 minutes or until golden brown. Cool on baking sheets 5 minutes; transfer to wire racks.

Makes about 3 dozen. Hands-on 20 min., Total 50 min.

Chicken Spaghetti II

April

Set for Spring

GATHER YOUR FAMILY AND FRIENDS AROUND THE TABLE FOR A CANDY-COLORED EASTER CELEBRATION THAT SERVES UP MODERN TAKES ON YOUR FAVORITE HOLIDAY TRADITIONS

THE MENU GLAZED SPIRAL-CUT HOLIDAY HAM –•– EASY PARMESAN-HERB ROLLS
ASPARAGUS WITH RED PEPPER CHOWCHOW –•– CARROT-GINGER PUREE
HOT POTATO SALAD –•– SPRING PEA ORZO –•– EASTER-EGG SHORTBREAD COOKIES

One breezy morning every spring, we don our Easter Sunday best—hat included!—to head to church and laud new beginnings. The crowning moment of the afternoon is always a large family feast that tastes as fresh and new as the day it celebrates. This year, our easy menu and elegant table setting keep things classic, but with an extra helping of flavor and color. Pull up a chair and let us help you plan your own beautiful and festive gathering.

THE SETTING

Event designers Maria Baer and Kelly Seizert of Washington, D.C.'s Ritzy Bee Events (*ritzybee.com*) set an Easter scene that is both classic and modern. The place setting is simple, but details such as gold bands on the china, etching on the stemware, and, of course, grandmother's silver say special occasion.

THE NAPKINS
Forgo the traditional menu card for a printed wrap that stands in as a napkin ring. Tie it with wide satin ribbon in colors that echo your flowers. Be sure to leave the ends extra long for added flair.

THE EGGS
The secret to the best color? Rit dye! You can even mix dyes to get custom colors. Once dry, hand-paint vine and flower designs on your eggs using a fine-tip art brush and water-based gouache paint. Hand-letter initials on some eggs to use as place cards. Note: Use Rit dye for decoration only.

EASY PARMESAN-HERB ROLLS

No time to bake bread from scratch? Here's a recipe to jazz up store-bought canned dough. For the dried herbs, mix together your favorites to make 1 Tbsp.

Parchment paper
Butter
1/2 cup grated Parmesan cheese
1 Tbsp. assorted dried green herbs (such as dill weed, tarragon, and oregano)
1 (11-oz.) can refrigerated French bread dough
1 large egg white, beaten
2 Tbsp. butter, melted
Kosher salt

1. Preheat oven to 325°. Line bottom of an 8-inch round cake pan with parchment paper; grease paper and sides of pan with butter. Stir together cheese and dried herbs in a medium bowl. Cut dough into 8 pieces. Shape each piece into a ball, and brush all sides with egg white. Roll in cheese mixture. Place 1 ball in center of prepared pan. Place remaining 7 balls around center roll. Cut a 1-inch slit in top of each roll.
2. Bake at 325° for 35 to 38 minutes or until golden and done. Remove from oven, and brush with melted butter. Sprinkle with kosher salt to taste. Cool 5 minutes before serving.

Note: We tested with Pillsbury Crusty French Loaf refrigerated dough.

Makes 8 rolls. Hands-on 20 min., Total 1 hour

GLAZED SPIRAL-CUT HOLIDAY HAM

We love a spiral-cut ham, but we don't like the sugary mystery glaze that comes with it. Toss the packet and use one of our three easy and unique glaze recipes instead. (Pictured on page 173)

Preheat oven to 350°. Place 1 (8- to 9-lb.) **fully cooked, bone-in spiral-cut ham half,** cut side down, in a heavy-duty aluminum foil-lined jelly-roll pan; let stand at room temperature 30 minutes. Brush 1/2 cup **desired glaze** over ham. Bake, uncovered, on lowest oven rack 2 1/2 to 3 hours or until a meat thermometer inserted into thickest portion registers 140°, basting every 30 minutes with 1/2 cup glaze. Remove from oven, and spoon pan drippings over ham. Let stand 10 minutes.

Note: We tested with Smithfield All Natural Spiral Sliced Smoked Uncured Ham.

Makes 8 to 10 servings. Hands-on 10 min.; Total 3 hours, 20 min., not including glazes

Pineapple-Prosecco Glaze

- 1 1/4 cups pineapple preserves
- 1/2 cup Prosecco or Cava
- 1/2 tsp. kosher salt

Pulse all ingredients in a food processor 6 or 7 times or until smooth.

Makes 1 1/2 cups

Cola-Dijon-Brown Sugar Glaze

- 1 1/2 cups firmly packed dark brown sugar
- 1/2 cup cola soft drink
- 1/2 cup Dijon mustard
- 1/2 tsp. kosher salt

Stir together all ingredients until smooth.

Makes 1 1/2 cups

Coffee-and-Pepper Jelly Glaze

- 1 1/4 cups red pepper jelly
- 1/2 cup strong brewed coffee
- 1/2 tsp. kosher salt

Stir together all ingredients until well blended.

Makes 1 1/2 cups

HOT POTATO SALAD

Our Test Kitchen Director's grandmother, Jackie Freeman, has been making this genius recipe for decades. It's the perfect marriage of potato salad with a bubbly, cheesy gratin. (Pictured on page 174)

- 1 lb. processed cheese (such as Velveeta)
- 8 baking potatoes (about 4 lb.)
- 1 1/2 cups mayonnaise
- 1 cup half-and-half
- 1/2 cup chopped yellow onion
- 1 cup sliced pimiento-stuffed Spanish olives
  Vegetable cooking spray
- 6 bacon slices, cut into 2-inch pieces

1. Freeze cheese 45 minutes to 1 hour. Meanwhile, cook potatoes in boiling water to cover 25 to 30 minutes or until tender; drain and cool completely.

2. Peel potatoes, and cut into 1-inch cubes. Grate frozen cheese, using large holes of a box grater.

3. Preheat oven to 325°. Whisk together mayonnaise and half-and-half in a large bowl. Stir in onion, olives, potatoes, and cheese until blended. Add salt and pepper to taste. Spoon into a 13- x 9-inch baking dish coated with cooking spray. Top with bacon pieces.

4. Bake at 325° for 55 minutes. Increase oven temperature to broil, and broil 5 minutes or until bacon is crisp. Let stand 5 minutes.

Makes 6 to 8 servings. Hands-on 20 min., Total 2 hours

ASPARAGUS WITH RED PEPPER CHOWCHOW

Use our foolproof blanching method on page 100 and your veggies will look as good as they taste. Serve leftover chowchow with cheese and crackers, ham sandwiches, or burgers. (Pictured on page 174)

- 1 lb. fresh asparagus
- 1 (8-oz.) package fresh sugar snap peas, trimmed
- 1 (6-oz.) package fresh English peas
- 1 Tbsp. butter or olive oil
- 2 Tbsp. Red Pepper Chowchow

1. Snap off and discard tough ends of asparagus. Blanch asparagus, and pat dry with paper towels. (See page 100 for cooking method and tips.) Repeat with sugar snap peas and English peas.
2. Melt butter in a large skillet over medium-high heat. Add asparagus, sugar snap peas, and English peas, and sauté 3 minutes or until thoroughly heated. Stir in Red Pepper Chowchow, and sauté 1 minute. Serve immediately.

Makes 4 to 6 servings. Hands-on 15 min.; Total 15 min., not including chowchow

Red Pepper Chowchow

- 3 red bell peppers, chopped
- 1/2 medium-size sweet onion, chopped
- 3 garlic cloves, finely chopped
- 1/3 cup olive oil
- 1/4 cup white wine vinegar
- 1 1/4 tsp. kosher salt
- 1/2 tsp. dried crushed red pepper
- 1/2 tsp. orange zest

Sauté first 3 ingredients in hot oil in a large skillet 6 to 7 minutes or until tender. Add vinegar and next 3 ingredients to skillet, and sauté 2 minutes. Cool completely (30 minutes). Serve immediately, or refrigerate up to 1 week.

Makes 1 1/2 cups. Hands-on 20 min., Total 50 min.

Spring Pea Orzo

SPRING PEA ORZO

The key to this crowd-pleasing salad is to toss the warm pasta with the dressing so the orzo soaks up flavor. Make it up to two days ahead, and serve any leftovers with ham. (Pictured on page 173)

- 3 to 4 lemons
- 8 oz. uncooked orzo pasta
- 1/4 cup minced shallot or red onion
- 2 Tbsp. extra virgin olive oil
- 1 Tbsp. Dijon mustard
- 1/2 tsp. table salt
- 1/2 tsp. freshly ground black pepper
- 1 1/2 cups cooked fresh or frozen peas
- 1 cup snow peas or sugar snap peas, blanched and chopped
- 1 cup assorted chopped fresh herbs (such as mint, chives, and parsley)
- 1/2 cup sliced almonds, toasted

1. Grate zest from lemons to equal 2 tsp. loosely packed. Cut lemons in half; squeeze juice from lemons into a measuring cup to equal 1/2 cup.
2. Prepare pasta according to package directions. Whisk together shallots, next 4 ingredients, and lemon juice. Toss together pasta and shallot mixture. Cover with plastic wrap, and chill 1 to 48 hours.
3. Toss together pasta, peas, snow peas, next 2 ingredients, and lemon zest just before serving. Add salt, pepper, and additional lemon juice to taste.

Makes 6 servings. Hands-on 20 min.; Total 1 hour, 30 min.

CARROT-GINGER PUREE

You'd never know there's only a table-spoon of butter in this velvety, spiced puree. Make it up to three days ahead. (Pictured on page 174)

- 2 lb. carrots, coarsely chopped (about 4 cups)
- 2 cups milk
- 2 Tbsp. sugar
- 2 tsp. grated fresh ginger or ½ tsp. ground ginger
- 1 tsp. table salt
- ⅛ tsp. ground cinnamon
- 1 Tbsp. butter
- 1 tsp. loosely packed orange zest

1. Bring carrots and milk to a boil in a medium saucepan over medium heat. Reduce heat to low, and stir in sugar and next 3 ingredients. Simmer, stirring often, 25 minutes or until carrots are tender.

2. Transfer mixture to a blender, reserving ½ cup cooking liquid. Add butter and orange zest to carrot mixture, and process until smooth, stopping to scrape down sides as needed. Add reserved cooking liquid, if necessary, 1 Tbsp. at a time, and process to desired consistency. Serve immediately or chilled. Refrigerate in an airtight container up to 3 days.

Note: Organic milk may curdle while simmering. Don't worry; it will smooth out when processed in the blender.

Makes 6 to 8 servings. Hands-on 25 min., Total 55 min.

EASTER-EGG SHORTBREAD COOKIES

Because a large batch of the dough is tricky to work with, we don't recommend doubling this recipe.

- 2 cups butter, softened
- 2 Tbsp. vanilla extract
- 1½ cups powdered sugar
- 4 cups all-purpose flour
- 2 tsp. baking powder
- Parchment paper
- Thin Royal Icing

1. Beat butter and vanilla at medium speed with an electric mixer until creamy. Whisk together powdered sugar, flour, and baking powder. Gradually add sugar mixture to butter mixture, beating at low speed until blended. Flatten dough into a disk, and wrap in plastic wrap. Chill 1 hour to 3 days.

2. Preheat oven to 350°. Place dough on a lightly floured surface; roll to ¼-inch thickness. Cut with desired cookie cutters. Place 8 cookies ½ inch apart on a parchment paper-lined baking sheet.

3. Bake at 350° for 12 to 13 minutes or until edges are lightly browned. Cool on baking sheets 5 minutes. Transfer to wire racks; cool completely (about 20 minutes).

4. Follow the wet-on-wet icing technique to decorate cookies (see box at right). Let dry 1 hour.

Makes 2 dozen. Hands-on 1 hour; Total 4 hours, 10 min., including icing

Thin Royal Icing

This icing is the perfect consistency for decorating as instructed at right.

Beat 1 (32-oz.) package **powdered sugar** (about 7½ cups), 4 tsp. **meringue powder,** and 10 Tbsp. **warm water** at high speed with a heavy-duty electric stand mixer, using whisk attachment, 5 minutes or until glossy. Stir in up to 2 Tbsp. more warm water, 1 tsp. at a time, until mixture reaches desired consistency. Stir in **food coloring,** if desired. Use immediately, or store at room temperature in airtight containers up to 1 week.

Makes about 5 cups

ELEGANTLY ICE WITH EASE

For more instruction on this decorating technique, watch our how-to video at *southernliving.com/icing.*

1 Using royal icing with a wet consistency (recipe at left), pipe a thin border around the edge of the cookie. Fill in the center of the cookie with an even layer of icing.

2 To smooth the surface, swirl a wooden pick in a circular motion around the entire pool of icing, starting at the edges and moving toward the center.

3 Immediately pipe another color of icing, the same consistency as the first, onto the base layer of icing. Manipulate the design gently with a wooden pick.

THE KIDS' TABLE

Give little ones their own pint-size setting with an inexpensive table and chair set and letter decals to personalize each set. Set the table with oversize white plates and glasses dressed up with ribbon accents. And don't forget the jelly beans!

THE CENTERPIECE
Nestle a white chocolate bunny in a glass bowl filled with dried peas for a playful arrangement during dinner and a tasty treat once the table is cleared.

THE GAME
Keep the kids entertained with a round of our Easter Bingo, using jelly beans as the markers. Print your own Easter Bingo cards at *southernliving.com/bingo*.

Bunny Tail Bonbons

BUNNY TAIL BONBONS

Package these white chocolate-cheesecake truffles in clear plastic boxes as a sweet takeaway for guests. Chilled, they'll keep for one week.

1 1/2 (4-oz.) white chocolate baking bars, melted according to package directions
1 (8-oz.) package cream cheese, softened
3/4 cup crushed coconut cookies
1 Tbsp. coconut rum or water
1/8 tsp. kosher salt
Parchment paper
1 1/2 cups shredded coconut

1. Beat chocolate and cream cheese at medium speed with a heavy-duty electric stand mixer until smooth. Add cookies and next 2 ingredients, beating just until blended. Spread in a parchment paper-lined 9-inch pie plate; cover and chill 2 hours.
2. Shape into 1-inch balls (about 2 tsp. per ball), and place in a single layer in a parchment paper-lined jelly-roll pan. Cover and chill 12 to 24 hours. Roll balls in coconut; chill 1 hour before serving. Refrigerate in a single layer in a container up to 1 week.

Note: We tested with Baker's Premium White Chocolate Baking Bar and Pepperidge Farm Sweet & Simple Coconut Cookies.

Makes about 2 1/2 dozen. Hands-on 45 min.; Total 15 hours, 45 min.

Sweeten the Season

JUICY STRAWBERRIES SHINE IN A SEASONAL BOUNTY OF CAKES, PIES, TARTS, DRINKS, AND ONE VERSATILE JAM THAT YIELDS FOUR SURPRISINGLY SAVORY SENSATIONS

MILE-HIGH MINI STRAWBERRY PIES

We used Wilton's nonstick six-cavity Mini Pie Pan. Chill reserved crust rounds while the first batch bakes, and allow the pan to cool completely before beginning the second batch. Or simply bake one big 9-inch pie (see Mega Strawberry Pie at right). (Pictured on page 9)

PASTRY CRUSTS

- 1/4 cup powdered sugar
- 2 (14.1-oz.) packages refrigerated piecrusts

CREAMY LEMON FILLING

- 1 1/2 (8-oz.) packages cream cheese, softened
- 1 Tbsp. sour cream
- 1/2 cup granulated sugar
- 2 tsp. lemon zest
- 1 Tbsp. fresh lemon juice

STRAWBERRY TOPPING

- 1 1/2 cups coarsely chopped fresh strawberries
- 1 cup granulated sugar
- 2 Tbsp. cornstarch
- 1 Tbsp. butter
- 10 cups hulled fresh strawberries

VANILLA CREAM

- 1 cup heavy cream
- 1/4 tsp. vanilla extract
- 3 Tbsp. powdered sugar

1. Prepare Pastry Crusts: Preheat oven to 425°. Sprinkle work surface with 1 Tbsp. powdered sugar. Roll 1 piecrust into a 12 1/2-inch circle on surface, and cut into 3 (6-inch) rounds. Repeat with remaining 3 piecrusts and 3 Tbsp. powdered sugar to make 12 rounds. Fit 6 rounds, sugar sides down, into each mold of a 6-cavity mini pie pan; fold edges under, and crimp. Prick bottom and sides with a fork. Chill remaining 6 rounds.

2. Bake at 425° for 8 minutes or until golden brown. Cool on a wire rack 5 minutes. Remove crusts from pan to wire rack, and cool completely. Cool pan completely. Repeat procedure with remaining 6 piecrust rounds.

3. Prepare Creamy Lemon Filling: Beat cream cheese and sour cream at medium speed with an electric mixer until smooth. Add 1/2 cup granulated sugar and next 2 ingredients; beat until smooth and fluffy. Spread about 2 1/2 Tbsp. filling into each cooled piecrust; cover with plastic wrap, and chill until ready to serve (up to 24 hours).

4. Prepare Strawberry Topping: Process 1 1/2 cups chopped strawberries in a blender or food processor until smooth, and press through a wire-mesh strainer into a 3-qt. saucepan, using back of a spoon to squeeze out juice; discard pulp. Stir 1 cup granulated sugar into juice in pan.

5. Whisk together cornstarch and 1/4 cup water; gradually whisk cornstarch mixture into strawberry mixture. Bring to a boil over medium heat, and cook, whisking constantly, 1 minute. Remove from heat, and whisk in butter. Cool 15 minutes.

6. Toss together strawberry mixture and 10 cups hulled strawberries gently in a large bowl until coated. (Halve some berries; leave others whole.) Cover; chill 3 hours or until cold.

7. Prepare Vanilla Cream: Beat heavy cream and vanilla at medium-high speed until foamy; gradually add powdered sugar, beating until soft peaks form.

8. Spoon about 1/2 cup Strawberry Topping into each pie; top with Vanilla Cream. Serve immediately.

Makes 12 mini pies. Hands-on 1 hour, 35 min.; Total 6 hours, 30 min.

Mega Strawberry Pie

Preheat oven to 425°. Reduce 1/4 cup powdered sugar to 2 Tbsp. and piecrusts to 1/2 (14.1-oz.) package. Sprinkle surface with 2 Tbsp. powdered sugar. Roll 1 piecrust into an 11-inch circle on prepared surface. Fit piecrust, sugar side down, in a 9-inch pie plate; fold edges under, and crimp. Prick bottom and sides with a fork. Bake 10 minutes or until golden. Cool completely on a wire rack. Proceed with recipe as directed in Steps 3 through 8, spooning all of Creamy Lemon Filling into prepared crust, and topping with all of Strawberry Topping and Vanilla Cream.

Makes 8 to 10 servings. Hands-on 40 min.; Total 4 hours, 50 min.

STRAWBERRIES-AND-CREAM SHEET CAKE

- 1 cup butter, softened
- 2 cups sugar
- 2 large eggs
- 2 tsp. fresh lemon juice
- 1 tsp. vanilla extract
- 2 1/2 cups cake flour
- 2 Tbsp. strawberry-flavored gelatin
- 1/2 tsp. baking soda
- 1/4 tsp. table salt
- 1 cup buttermilk
- 2/3 cup chopped fresh strawberries
  Shortening
  Parchment paper
  Vegetable cooking spray
  Strawberry Frosting (recipe, page 96)
  Garnish: fresh strawberries

1. Preheat oven to 350°. Beat butter at medium speed with an electric mixer until creamy; gradually add sugar, beating 4 to 5 minutes or until light and fluffy. Add eggs, 1 at a time, beating until blended after each addition. Beat in lemon juice and vanilla.

2. Stir together flour and next 3 ingredients; add flour mixture to butter mixture alternately with buttermilk, beginning and ending with flour mixture. Beat at low speed just until blended. Stir in strawberries.

3. Grease (with shortening) and flour a 13- x 9-inch pan; line with parchment paper, allowing 2 to 3 inches to extend over long sides. Lightly grease paper with cooking spray. Spread batter in prepared pan.

4. Bake at 350° for 30 to 40 minutes or until a wooden pick inserted in center comes out clean. Cool in pan on a wire rack 30 minutes. Lift cake from pan, using parchment paper sides as handles. Invert cake onto wire rack; gently remove parchment paper. Cool completely (about 1 hour). Spread Strawberry Frosting on top and sides of cake.

Makes 10 to 12 servings. Hands-on 35 min.; Total 2 hours, 50 min., including frosting

STRAWBERRY-RHUBARB TARTLETS

We used a 2 1/2- x 3-inch fluted rectangular cookie cutter to cut the dough for these adorable tarts. You can also cut them by hand or use a round cutter. Serve for breakfast, dessert, or as a sweet snack.

- 2 1/2 cups all-purpose flour
- 1/4 cup granulated sugar
- 1/4 tsp. table salt
- 1/4 tsp. baking powder
- 1 cup cold butter, cut into small pieces
- 2 large egg yolks
- 1/2 cup ice-cold water
- 3 Tbsp. butter
- 1/2 cup sliced fresh or frozen rhubarb
- 1 cup sliced fresh strawberries
- 2/3 cup granulated sugar
- 1 Tbsp. all-purpose flour
- 3 Tbsp. fresh lemon juice, divided
  Parchment paper
- 1 large egg
- 2 1/2 Tbsp. milk, divided
- 1 1/2 cups powdered sugar

1. Pulse first 4 ingredients in a food processor until blended. Add cold butter, and pulse 5 or 6 times or just until mixture resembles coarse meal. Stir together egg yolks and ice-cold water. With processor running, pour yolk mixture through food chute, and process just until mixture forms a ball and pulls away from sides of bowl. Wrap dough in plastic wrap; chill 1 hour.

2. Meanwhile, melt 3 Tbsp. butter in a 1-qt. saucepan over medium heat. Add rhubarb, and sauté 3 minutes. Stir in strawberries and 2/3 cup granulated sugar; cook, stirring constantly and crushing fruit with spoon, 5 minutes.

3. Stir together 1 Tbsp. flour and 2 Tbsp. lemon juice until smooth. Stir juice mixture into rhubarb mixture; bring to a boil. Cook, stirring often, 2 minutes or until thick. Remove from heat, and transfer mixture to a small bowl. Cover and chill 30 minutes.

4. Preheat oven to 350°. Unwrap dough; roll to 1/8-inch thickness on a floured surface. Cut dough into 48 rectangles, using a 2 1/2- x 3-inch cutter and rerolling scraps. Place half of

Strawberry-Rhubarb Tartlets

dough rectangles 2 inches apart on parchment paper-lined baking sheets. Top each rectangle with about 1 Tbsp. strawberry mixture. Dampen edges of dough with water, and top with remaining dough rectangles, pressing edges to seal.

5. Stir together egg and 2 Tbsp. milk, and brush over tops of tarts. Cut a small "X" in top of each tartlet for steam to escape.

6. Bake tartlets at 350° for 30 to 35 minutes or until golden. Transfer tartlets to a wire rack; cool 15 minutes. Whisk together powdered sugar and remaining 1 Tbsp. lemon juice and 1 1/2 tsp. milk; drizzle over tartlets.

Makes 2 dozen. Hands-on 1 hour, 10 min.; Total 2 hours, 25 min.

STRAWBERRY MILK

Process 1 qt. fresh hulled **strawberries** and 3 to 4 Tbsp. **sugar** in a blender or food processor until smooth, stopping to scrape down sides as needed. Press mixture through a wire-mesh strainer into a medium bowl, using back of a spoon to squeeze out juice; discard pulp. Stir in 1 tsp. **vanilla extract** and a pinch of **salt.** Stir strawberry mixture into 3 to 4 cups cold **milk.** Chill 1 hour before serving. Refrigerate up to 3 days.

Makes about 6 cups. Hands-on 10 min.; Total 1 hour, 10 min.

Spiked Strawberry Milk

Stir in 1/4 cup strawberry liqueur (such as De Kuyper Wild Strawberry) just before serving.

Strawberry-Lemonade Layer Cake

STRAWBERRY-LEMONADE LAYER CAKE

You can assemble this glorious cake up to two days ahead; store at room temp. Also, you can freeze cooled layers up to a month in plastic wrap and aluminum foil. (Pictured on page 9)

1	cup butter, softened
2	cups granulated sugar
4	large eggs, separated
3	cups cake flour
1	Tbsp. baking powder
1/8	tsp. table salt
1	cup milk
1	Tbsp. lemon zest
1	Tbsp. fresh lemon juice
	Shortening
	Strawberry-Lemonade Jam (recipe, page 96)
	Strawberry Frosting (recipe, page 96)

1. Preheat oven to 350°. Beat butter at medium speed with an electric mixer until creamy; gradually add sugar, beating until light and fluffy. Add egg yolks, 1 at a time, beating until blended after each addition.

2. Stir together flour and next 2 ingredients; add to butter mixture alternately with milk, beginning and ending with flour mixture. Beat at low speed just until blended. Stir in zest and juice.

3. Beat egg whites in a large bowl at high speed until stiff peaks form. Gently stir one-third of egg whites into batter; fold in remaining egg whites. Spoon batter into 4 greased (with shortening) and floured 9-inch round cake pans.

4. Bake at 350° for 16 to 20 minutes or until a wooden pick inserted in center comes out clean. Cool in pans on wire racks 10 minutes; remove from pans to wire racks, and cool completely.

5. Place 1 cake layer on a serving platter, and spread with about 1/2 cup Strawberry-Lemonade Jam, leaving a 1/2-inch border around edges. Spoon 1 cup Strawberry Frosting into a zip-top plastic freezer bag. Snip 1 corner of bag to make a small hole. Pipe a ring of frosting around cake layer just inside the top edge. Top with second and third cake layers, repeating procedure with filling and frosting between each layer. Top with last cake layer, and spread remaining Strawberry Frosting on top and sides of cake.

Makes 12 servings. Hands-on 45 min.; Total 4 hours, 30 min., including jam and frosting

Strawberry-Lemonade Jam

- 2 1/2 **cups coarsely chopped fresh strawberries**
- 3/4 **cup sugar**
- 1/4 **cup fresh lemon juice**
- 3 **Tbsp. cornstarch**

1. Process strawberries in a blender until smooth; press through a wire-mesh strainer into a 3-qt. saucepan, using back of a spoon to squeeze out juice; discard pulp. Stir in sugar.
2. Whisk together lemon juice and cornstarch; gradually whisk into strawberry mixture. Bring mixture to a boil over medium heat, and cook, whisking constantly, 1 minute. Remove from heat. Place plastic wrap directly on warm jam; chill 2 hours or until cold. Refrigerate in an airtight container up to 1 week.

Makes about 1 2/3 cups. Hands-on 20 min.; Total 2 hours, 20 min.

Strawberry Frosting

- 1 **(8-oz.) package cream cheese, softened**
- 2/3 **cup sugar, divided**
- 2/3 **cup chopped fresh strawberries**
- 1 **drop pink food coloring gel (optional)**
- 1 1/2 **cups heavy cream**
- 3 **Tbsp. fresh lemon juice**

1. Beat cream cheese and 1/3 cup sugar with an electric mixer until smooth; add strawberries and food coloring (if desired); beat until blended.
2. Beat cream and juice at medium speed until foamy; increase speed to medium-high, and slowly add remaining 1/3 cup sugar, beating until stiff peaks form. Fold half of cream mixture into cheese mixture; fold in remaining cream mixture. Use immediately.

Makes about 5 cups. Hands-on 15 min., Total 15 min.

FOUR USES FOR STRAWBERRY-LEMONADE JAM

OUR VERSATILE CAKE FILLING (AT LEFT) DOES DOUBLE DUTY AS A BASE FOR SAVORY SIDES AND ENTRÉES

STRAWBERRY VINAIGRETTE

Toss this pungent dressing with fresh baby spinach or kale, thinly sliced red onion, and toasted pecans.

Whisk 1/4 cup **Strawberry-Lemonade Jam**; 1/4 cup **extra virgin olive oil**; 3 Tbsp. **apple cider vinegar**; 2 Tbsp. **water**; 1 tsp. **sugar**; 1 small **garlic clove**, minced; 1/2 tsp. **kosher salt**; and 1/4 tsp. **freshly ground pepper.**

Makes 3/4 cup. Hands-on 10 min.; Total 10 min., not including jam

JICAMA-AND-BELL PEPPER SLAW

(Pictured on page 173)

Toss together 1 1/2 cups thinly sliced **jicama**, 1/3 cup thinly sliced **red onion**, 1/4 cup **fresh mint leaves**, 1 thinly sliced **red bell pepper**, and 1 thinly sliced **yellow bell pepper**. Sprinkle with 3/4 tsp. **salt**, 1/4 tsp. **ground red pepper**, and 1/4 tsp. **ground black pepper**. Whisk together 1/4 cup **Strawberry-Lemonade Jam**, 3 Tbsp. **olive oil**, and 4 1/2 tsp. **fresh lemon juice**. Drizzle over salad; toss to coat.

Makes 4 to 6 servings. Hands-on 15 min.; Total 15 min., not including jam

CHIPOTLE-STRAWBERRY GLAZE

Use this sauce on roasted or grilled pork or chicken. Set aside half of the sauce for serving, and brush the rest on during the last 10 minutes of cooking. (Pictured on page 173)

Melt 3 Tbsp. **butter** in a small skillet over medium heat. Add 1/2 cup chopped **yellow onion**; 2 **garlic cloves**, minced; and 1 1/2 tsp. minced canned **chipotle pepper in adobo sauce**; sauté 3 minutes. Stir in 1/2 cup reduced-sodium **chicken broth**, 1/3 cup **Strawberry-Lemonade Jam**, 1/4 cup **orange juice**, 3 Tbsp. **apple cider vinegar**, and 1/2 tsp. **kosher salt**. Bring mixture to a boil, and cook, stirring occasionally, 8 minutes or until liquid is thick and syrupy. Process mixture in a blender until smooth. Cool 10 minutes.

Makes about 1/2 cup. Hands-on 25 min.; Total 35 min., not including jam

GRILLED HAM-AND-CHEESE SANDWICHES WITH STRAWBERRY-SHALLOT JAM

Use roasted turkey instead of ham, if you prefer.

Stir together 3 Tbsp. **Strawberry-Lemonade Jam**, 2 Tbsp. minced **shallot**, 1 Tbsp. **olive oil**, and 2 tsp. **Dijon mustard**; spread on 1 side of 4 **sourdough sandwich bread slices**. Top each with 3 thin slices **deli ham**, 1/3 cup (1 1/2 oz.) shredded **Gruyère or other Swiss cheese**, and 1 sourdough sandwich bread slice. Brush 1 Tbsp. melted **butter** on both sides of each sandwich. Cook sandwiches in a large nonstick skillet or griddle over medium-high heat 1 minute on each side or until browned.

Makes 4 servings. Hands-on 15 min.; Total 15 min., not including jam

Raid Your Pantry Tonight

SPRING-CLEAN YOUR CUPBOARD FOR FIVE FAST, FRESH WEEKNIGHT MEALS
MADE WITH CONVENIENT INGREDIENTS

Mix 'n' Match
Spring Pasta
Toss

USE IT UP!
Pasta and
pimiento

MIX 'N' MATCH SPRING PASTA TOSS

Using a mix of different shapes of pasta? Add any larger, thicker shapes to the pot 2 to 3 minutes before smaller pasta. Feel free to veer from the recipe and use up any vegetables that you have on hand. Swap green beans or broccoli for the sugar snaps or ¹/₂ cup chopped red bell pepper for the jarred pimiento. (Pictured on page 8)

- 3 cups uncooked penne, farfalle, or rotini pasta
- 2 cups shredded cooked chicken
- 1 ¹/₂ cups fresh sugar snap peas, cut into ¹/₂-inch pieces
- 1 cup matchstick carrots
- 1 (4-oz.) jar diced pimiento, drained
- 1 cup diced cucumber
- 3 green onions, sliced
- ¹/₂ cup sliced radishes
- ¹/₂ cup bottled Greek dressing
- 1 Tbsp. fresh lemon juice
  Garnishes: fresh dill sprigs, fresh flat-leaf parsley leaves

1. Cook pasta according to package directions for al dente. Add chicken and next 3 ingredients, and cook, stirring often, 1 minute. Drain and place in a large bowl.

2. Stir cucumber and next 4 ingredients into hot pasta mixture until blended. Season with salt and pepper to taste. Serve immediately, or cover and chill up to 48 hours.

Note: We tested with Ken's Steak House Greek dressing.

Makes about 6 servings. Hands-on 25 min., Total 25 min.

SWISS BURGERS IN TOMATO GRAVY

USE IT UP! Diced tomatoes

Simmer ground sirloin patties in a rich tomato gravy to create luscious fork-tender burgers. Serve with steamed green beans.

8	red potatoes, cut into 4 wedges each
2	Tbsp. olive oil
1 1/2	tsp. kosher salt, divided
1 1/2	lb. ground sirloin
1	large egg, lightly beaten
1/2	tsp. ground black pepper
1	medium-size white onion, sliced
2	(15-oz.) cans fire-roasted diced tomatoes
1	chicken bouillon cube
6	(1-oz.) Swiss cheese slices
	Chopped fresh basil (optional)

1. Preheat oven to 425°. Toss together potatoes, oil, and 1/2 tsp. salt in a bowl. Spread potatoes in a single layer in a jelly-roll pan, and bake 35 to 40 minutes or until golden and tender.
2. Meanwhile, stir together sirloin, egg, pepper, and remaining 1 tsp. salt in a large bowl. Shape into 6 (3 1/2-inch) patties.
3. Cook patties in a large skillet over medium-high heat 4 to 5 minutes on each side or until browned. Remove patties, reserving drippings. Sauté onion in hot drippings 2 minutes. Add tomatoes, bouillon, and 1/2 cup water. Cook, stirring occasionally, 3 to 4 minutes or until bubbly.
4. Return patties to skillet; spoon tomato mixture over patties. Cover and cook 15 minutes; uncover and cook 5 minutes. Place 1 cheese slice on each patty. Cover and cook 3 minutes. Sprinkle with basil, if desired. Serve with potatoes.

Makes 6 servings. Hands-on 25 min., Total 45 min.

TUNA CROQUETTES

USE IT UP! Canned tuna

A tangy avocado-buttermilk sauce gives these simple croquettes fresh appeal. Serve them with lettuce or on soft hamburger buns.

1	lime
1/2	cup mayonnaise, divided
1/2	cup chopped fresh cilantro or flat-leaf parsley, divided
1	avocado, mashed
5	Tbsp. buttermilk
1/4	tsp. salt
3	(5-oz.) cans solid white tuna in water, drained
1	large egg, lightly beaten
1/3	cup sliced green onions
1 1/4	cups seasoned panko (Japanese breadcrumbs)
1/4	cup butter
	Butter lettuce leaves
	Lime wedges

1. Grate zest from lime to equal 2 tsp. Cut lime in half; squeeze juice from lime to equal 5 tsp.
2. Process 1/4 cup mayonnaise, 1/4 cup cilantro, next 3 ingredients, 1 Tbsp. water, and 3 tsp. lime juice in a food processor until smooth.
3. Preheat oven to 350°. Stir together tuna, next 2 ingredients, lime zest, and remaining 1/4 cup mayonnaise, 1/4 cup cilantro, and 2 tsp. lime juice. Gently stir in 2/3 cup panko. Shape mixture into 8 (2-inch-wide) patties. Dredge in remaining panko.
4. Melt butter in a large nonstick oven-proof skillet over medium heat; add patties to skillet, and cook 3 to 4 minutes on each side or until browned. Transfer to oven.
5. Bake at 350° for 10 minutes. Serve over lettuce with avocado mixture and lime wedges.

Note: We tested with Bumble Bee Solid White Albacore in Water.

Makes 8 servings. Hands-on 20 min., Total 30 min.

Tuna Croquettes

USE IT UP! Black beans

SHRIMP-AND-BLACK BEAN STIR-FRY

This tropical pairing of sweet and savory will wake up tired taste buds at the dinner table.

- 1/2 medium-size red onion, sliced
- 1 medium-size red bell pepper, sliced
- 3 Tbsp. olive oil, divided
- 1 cup fresh corn kernels (about 2 ears)
- 1 lb. peeled and deveined large, raw shrimp
- 3 garlic cloves, sliced
- 1 cup chopped fresh mango or pineapple
- 1 (15-oz.) can black beans, drained and rinsed
- 1/2 cup teriyaki baste-and-glaze sauce
- 1/4 cup pineapple juice
  Hot cooked rice
  Garnish: cilantro leaves

1. Stir-fry onion and bell pepper in 1 Tbsp. hot oil in a large cast-iron skillet over medium-high heat 2 to 3 minutes or until lightly browned. Remove from skillet.
2. Add corn and 1 Tbsp. oil to skillet; stir-fry 2 to 3 minutes. Remove from skillet.
3. Pat shrimp dry. Add shrimp, garlic, and remaining 1 Tbsp. oil to skillet; stir-fry 2 to 3 minutes or just until shrimp begin to turn pink. Add mango and black beans; stir-fry 2 to 3 minutes or until thoroughly heated. Add teriyaki sauce and pineapple juice, and cook 1 to 2 minutes or until mixture begins to bubble. Stir in corn-and-onion mixture. Serve over hot cooked rice.

Note: We tested with Kikkoman Original Teriyaki Takumi Collection Sauce.

Makes 4 servings. Hands-on 30 min., Total 30 min.

Shrimp-and-Black Bean Stir-Fry

USE IT UP! Cornbread mix

CREAMY TEX-MEX CORNBREAD BAKE

Use ground turkey and low-fat soup and milk to lighten up this hearty casserole.

- 2 lb. ground turkey
- 1 cup sliced green onions
- 1 (10 3/4-oz.) can cream of mushroom soup
- 1 cup milk
- 1 (4-oz.) can chopped green chiles
- 1 cup (4 oz.) shredded pepper Jack cheese, divided
- 1/4 cup chopped fresh cilantro or parsley
  Vegetable cooking spray
- 1 (6-oz.) package buttermilk cornbread mix
- 3 Tbsp. chopped fresh cilantro

1. Preheat oven to 400°. Cook ground turkey in a large skillet over medium heat, stirring often, 5 minutes or until meat crumbles and is no longer pink. Add green onions, and sauté 1 minute.
2. Stir in soup and next 2 ingredients. Bring to a low boil, and remove from heat. Stir in 3/4 cup cheese and 1/4 cup cilantro. Add salt and pepper to taste. Pour turkey mixture into a 2-qt. baking dish coated with cooking spray.
3. Stir together cornbread mix, 3/4 cup water, 3 Tbsp. cilantro, and remaining 1/4 cup cheese. Pour cornbread mixture over turkey mixture in baking dish.
4. Bake at 400° for 20 to 25 minutes or until golden.

Note: We tested with Martha White Buttermilk Cornbread & Muffin Mix.

Makes 6 servings. Hands-on 20 min., Total 40 min.

THE *SL* TEST KITCHEN ACADEMY

COOK PERFECT VEGETABLES

Spring vegetables are in full bloom. Show off their beautiful color and snappy texture by mastering a technique the pros use: big-pot blanching. Your veggies will thank you for making them look—and taste—so good.

THE BLANCHING BLUEPRINT

MASTER THIS BASIC COOKING TECHNIQUE TO ACHIEVE SUPERIOR COLOR AND TEXTURE

① BRING TO A BOIL

Wash and trim vegetables. Bring a large pot of water to a boil. Stir in kosher salt until the water tastes as salty as the sea (about 1 1/2 Tbsp. per every 5 qt. of water). The salt will enhance the flavor of the vegetables. While the water returns to a boil, fill a large bowl halfway with ice cubes. Add just enough cold water to make the ice float.

② COOK AND SHOCK

Working with one variety at a time, boil vegetables until they are bright green and crisp-tender (1 to 2 minutes). Transfer to ice water to set the color and texture, using a slotted spoon or tongs. Chill until ice-cold. Cool tip: Try nestling a colander in the ice bath before adding the vegetables. That allows you to drain without bothering with pesky ice.

③ STORE AND SERVE

Drain vegetables, and pat dry with a kitchen towel. Blanched, shocked vegetables will retain their bright color and crisp-tender texture when chilled up to 4 days or frozen up to 3 months. Store in a zip-top plastic bag. Serve as crudités, use in stir-fries or pasta, or sauté, as in Asparagus with Red Pepper Chowchow (recipe, page 90).

SL TEST KITCHEN SECRET WEAPON: DIAMOND CRYSTAL KOSHER SALT

This salt's small crystals dissolve quickly in boiling water, and their uniform size and texture also make it our go-to salt for seasoning most recipes. When blanching, we recommend salting both the boiling water and the ice bath. Doing so improves flavor, and the salt in the ice water will actually bring the temperature down a few degrees, arresting the cooking and setting the color and texture of the vegetables even faster.

Grow Big Flavors

PLANT TOMATOES IN YOUR BACKYARD FOR A TASTY SLICE OF SUMMER

WE'RE ALL FOR LOCALLY grown foods—and you can't get any more local than right outside your door. Even a tiny, sunny patch of earth can become a planting bed. In the summer, there's nothing simpler or more delicious than a tomato sandwich served on white bread with a little mayo. Step it up and make a BLT, or combine sliced tomatoes with fresh basil and mozzarella for a summer salad. No matter which recipe you choose, growing the key ingredient yourself will definitely make it special. And believe us— it will taste better too.

Select
The smallest slicing tomatoes are about the size of a baseball; the biggest ones can be larger than a softball. Choose from hybrids or heirlooms in a rainbow of hues—red, pink, black, orange, or yellow. For classic reds, try 'Big Boy,' 'Better Boy,' and 'Celebrity.' For pinks, pick 'Arkansas Traveler,' 'Pink Girl,' and 'Watermelon Beefsteak.' Black selections offer some of the most flavorful tomatoes. Try 'Black Krim' or 'Cherokee Purple.' Orange ones such as 'Persimmon' and 'Kellogg's Breakfast' have fruity flavors, while yellows such as 'Taxi' and 'Lemon Boy' are sweet. Buy them online from *totallytomato.com*.

Try
New to many gardeners are grafted tomatoes, created when one plant is cut and joined to a different one with vigorous rootstock. Grafting offers improved yields and disease resistance. It can be a good choice if space is limited and you need maximum production from each plant. Some heirloom tomatoes, for example, are not as productive as new hybrids, but if you love their flavors and want a bigger yield, you can try a grafted heirloom for the best of both worlds. The benefits of grafting come at a price—up to $12 for a grafted tomato plant in a 1-gallon container. Smaller, less expensive grafted plants are available online from *burpee.com*.

Grow
Tomatoes love full sun, whether in your vegetable garden or large containers (*earthbox.com*). They like soil that has been amended with lots of organic matter, such as mushroom compost, chopped leaves, or soil conditioner. Rich soil will nourish your plants. Supplement feeding with organic fertilizers. To keep vines off the ground, use twine to tie them to economical bamboo or wooden stakes. You may need to tie plants every other day as they grow. If you are short on time, invest in convenient, reusable tomato cages; try *tomatocage.com*.

get growing!
TOMATOES

WATER
Regularly

SOIL
Loose, rich, well-drained, and amended with organic matter

MULCH
Use pine straw or straw to conserve moisture, keep roots cool, and discourage weeds.

FERTILIZE
Supplement with a liquid food such as Great Big Tomatoes.

| LIGHT FULL SUN | WATER MEDIUM | CARE MEDIUM |

'Celebrity' tomatoes will ripen red and are a dependable choice for any garden.

EASY TOMATO JAM

Simmer 4 lb. peeled, seeded, and **chopped tomatoes**; 1 cup **sugar**; 2 Tbsp. **orange zest**; 2/3 cup **orange juice**; 2 tsp. **lemon zest**; 1 Tbsp. **lemon juice**; 1/2 tsp. **dried crushed red pepper**; and 1/4 tsp. **kosher salt** over medium-low heat, stirring, 1 hour. Cool, cover, and chill. Serves 6.

TEA SANDWICHES

(FROM MAY 1985)

◄◄ **THE ORIGINAL:** Come tea time, our luncheon spread gave the Brits a run for their money! Sure, these finger sandwiches in '85 were impressive, but who has the time to twirl tomato skins into rosettes? **THE REVIVAL:** Modern dainties crafted for easy entertaining. Make a variety of pretty mosaics by using our all-purpose cream cheese spread and layering method, and choose any seasonal toppings that fit your fancy.

MOSAIC TEA SANDWICHES

(Pictured on page 175)

- 1 (8-oz.) package cream cheese, softened
- 3 Tbsp. fresh lemon juice
- 1 Tbsp. grated white onion
- 1/2 tsp. kosher salt
- 20 thin sandwich bread slices
  Desired toppings (see below)

Stir together first 4 ingredients until well blended. Spread 1 Tbsp. on each bread slice. Top with desired toppings. Cover with plastic wrap, and chill 15 minutes to 12 hours. Trim crusts from chilled slices, and cut each slice into 2 triangles.

Makes 20 appetizer servings. Hands-on 30 min.; Total 45 min., not including toppings

SALMON-CUCUMBER

Cut 1 medium-size English cucumber into thin rounds. Cut rounds into half moons. Divide cucumbers and 4 oz. sliced smoked salmon among prepared bread slices. Gently press to adhere. Sprinkle with fresh dill to taste.

Mosaic Tea Sandwiches

VEGETABLE MEDLEY

Cut 1 medium-size yellow squash, 1 medium cucumber, and 10 radishes into thin rounds. Cut rounds into half moons. Divide vegetables among prepared bread slices. Gently press to adhere. Sprinkle with cracked black pepper to taste.

PROSCIUTTO-ASPARAGUS

Cut 1 lb. blanched fresh asparagus into thin, ribbon-like strips, using a vegetable peeler. (See page 100 for blanching method.) Divide asparagus and 4 oz. thinly sliced prosciutto among prepared bread slices. Gently press to adhere.

SIX REASONS WHY SOUTHERN COOKS WORTH THEIR SALT SHOULD MASTER

Deviled Eggs

The Filling
Grate yolks on a box grater (see page 104) for the creamiest results.

The Whites
Don't overcook the eggs. The whites should still have a little wiggle to them.

The Nest
For a less traditional look than this, halve eggs crosswise so they stand up tall.

No. 1:

They're ours. No, we didn't invent them (thank you, circa-6,000 BC Romans); we just perfected them.

No. 2:

Every self-respecting host needs a go-to recipe for deviled eggs in his or her quiver. Likewise, every guest who brings a platter to the party will guarantee herself a return invitation.

No. 3:

Good stuffed eggs are built on good technique. For the best hard-cooked eggs, simmer them 10 minutes, cool slightly under tap water, and then get cracking.

No. 4:

You can't gossip with authority at the neighborhood potluck about Suzy Jane Smoot's controversial additions of pickle relish, sugar, and bacon fat until you make your own.

No. 5:

Appetizer trends ebb and flow, but deviled eggs are like good manners: They never go out of style.

No. 6:

The possibilities are endless. Learn the rules on page 104 first; then break them with six riffs (also on page 104)—or with your own signature fillings and garnishes.

CLASSIC DEVILED EGGS

12 hard-cooked eggs, peeled
1/2 cup mayonnaise
1 1/2 tsp. white wine vinegar
1 1/2 tsp. Dijon mustard
1/8 tsp. kosher salt
Dash of hot sauce (optional)
Garnish: paprika

1. Slice eggs in half lengthwise, and carefully remove yolks, keeping egg whites intact.

2. Grate egg yolks using small holes of a box grater. Mash together yolks, mayonnaise, and next 3 ingredients. Add more salt or hot sauce, if desired.

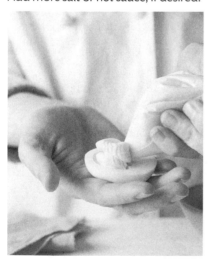

3. Spoon or pipe yolk mixture into egg whites.

Makes 2 dozen. Hands-on 20 min., Total 20 min.

SIX DEVILISH SPINS

TROUT CAVIAR-HORSERADISH

Prepare recipe as directed in Steps 1 and 2 (left). Stir 3 3/4 tsp. **prepared horseradish** into yolk mixture. Spoon or pipe yolk mixture into egg white halves. Top with 3/4 tsp. **trout caviar.**

COUNTRY HAM-BREADCRUMB

Prepare recipe as directed in Steps 1 and 2. Stir 1/2 cup finely chopped cooked **country ham** and 1/4 cup finely grated **Swiss cheese** into yolk mixture. Spoon or pipe yolk mixture into egg white halves. Top with desired amount of toasted breadcrumbs.

AVOCADO-TARRAGON

Prepare recipe as directed in Steps 1 and 2. Mash together 1 1/2 **ripe avocados** and 3 3/4 tsp. **fresh lime juice.** Stir avocado mixture and 1 tsp. **dried tarragon** into yolk mixture. Add **salt** and **pepper** to taste. Spoon or pipe yolk mixture into egg white halves. Top with desired amount of **fresh flat-leaf parsley leaves.**

SPINACH, POPPY SEED, AND BACON

Prepare recipe as directed in Steps 1 and 2. Stir 3/4 cup frozen chopped **spinach,** thawed; 4 1/2 tsp. grated **red onion;** and 4 1/2 tsp. **poppy-seed dressing** into yolk mixture. Spoon or pipe yolk mixture into egg white halves. Top with chopped cooked **bacon.**

SMOKED SALMON, LEMON, AND CAPERS

Prepare recipe as directed in Steps 1 and 2. Stir 1 1/2 Tbsp. finely chopped drained **capers,** 3/4 tsp. loosely packed **lemon zest,** 3 tsp. **lemon juice,** 1/4 tsp. **black pepper,** and 1/8 tsp. **kosher salt** into yolk mixture. Spoon or pipe yolk mixture into egg white halves. Top with desired amount of **smoked salmon.**

CHORIZO-AND-CILANTRO

Prepare recipe as directed in Steps 1 and 2. Stir 3/4 cup cooked and crumbled **chorizo sausage** and 2 1/4 tsp. **sour cream** into yolk mixture. Spoon or pipe yolk mixture into egg white halves. Top with desired amount of **fresh cilantro leaves.**

Roll Out the Roulade

ANY WAY YOU SLICE IT, THIS DIVINE COCONUT CAKE IS AS IMPRESSIVE AS A LAYER CAKE, BUT SO MUCH EASIER TO MAKE

COCONUT-ALMOND ROULADE

If you can't find desiccated coconut, process shredded coconut in a food processor until finely ground. (Pictured on page 8)

CAKE

Vegetable cooking spray
Parchment paper
- 3 large eggs
- 3 large egg yolks
- 3/4 cup granulated sugar
- 1/2 cup coconut milk
- 3 Tbsp. butter, melted
- 1 tsp. almond extract
- 3/4 cup cake flour
- 1/2 cup powdered sugar

FROSTING

- 2 cups heavy cream
- 1/2 cup coconut milk
- 1/2 cup powdered sugar
- 1/4 tsp. table salt

REMAINING INGREDIENTS

- 1/2 cup desiccated coconut
Toasted coconut flakes and toasted sliced almonds

ROLL WAY AHEAD! Wrap the filled, rolled cake with plastic wrap if you want to freeze it longer than 24 hours (up to 5 days).

Coconut-Almond Roulade

1. Prepare Cake: Preheat oven to 400.° Lightly grease an 18- x 13-inch jelly-roll pan with cooking spray, and line with parchment paper. Spray parchment, and dust with cake flour, tapping out excess.
2. Beat eggs, egg yolks, and 3/4 cup granulated sugar at high speed with an electric mixer 5 minutes or until thick and pale.
3. Stir together coconut milk and next 2 ingredients in a small bowl. Gently fold coconut milk mixture into egg mixture. Sift 3/4 cup cake flour into mixture, 1/4 cup at a time, folding until blended after each addition. Spread batter in prepared pan.

4. Bake at 400° for 10 to 12 minutes or until puffed. Cool 10 minutes. Sprinkle 1/2 cup powdered sugar over top of cake. Invert cake onto a parchment paper-lined surface. Peel top layer of parchment from cake. Starting at 1 short side, roll cake and bottom parchment together. Cool completely.
5. Prepare Frosting: Beat cream and coconut milk at medium speed until blended. Gradually add 1/2 cup powdered sugar and salt, whisking until stiff peaks form. Chill 1 1/2 cups frosting.

6. Assemble: Unroll cake onto a flat surface. Spread with remaining frosting, leaving a 1-inch border on all sides. Sprinkle 1/2 cup coconut over frosting. Lift and tilt parchment, and roll up cake in jelly-roll fashion, starting at 1 short side and using parchment paper as a guide. Place cake, wrapped in parchment, on a baking sheet. Freeze 30 minutes to 24 hours. Let stand at room temperature 1 hour before serving. Top with chilled frosting and toasted coconut and almonds. Serve immediately.

Makes 8 to 10 servings. Hands-on 50 min., Total 3 hours

Community Cookbook

Women from all over North Carolina submitted their best recipes and tips to compile this gem of a community cookbook from 1990.

CHEESE-AND-SAUSAGE QUICHE

Adapted from Carolina Cooking, *this is great for breakfast, lunch, or dinner. It also reheats beautifully, so bake an extra and take it to a friend.*

- 1 (1-lb.) package ground pork sausage
- 1/2 cup thinly sliced onion (about 1/4 medium onion)
- 1/3 cup chopped green bell pepper
- 1 1/2 cups (6 oz.) freshly shredded sharp Cheddar cheese
- 1 Tbsp. all-purpose flour
- 1 (9-inch) frozen unbaked deep-dish piecrust shell
- 2 large eggs
- 1 cup evaporated milk
- 1 Tbsp. chopped fresh flat-leaf parsley
- 3/4 tsp. seasoned salt
- 1/4 tsp. garlic salt
- 1/4 tsp. ground black pepper

1. Preheat oven to 350°. Brown sausage in a large skillet over medium-high heat, stirring often, 8 to 10 minutes or until sausage crumbles. Remove from skillet; reserve 1 Tbsp. drippings in skillet.

2. Sauté onion and bell pepper in hot drippings over medium-high heat 3 minutes or until tender. Stir together cheese, flour, sausage, onion, and bell pepper. Place piecrust shell on a baking sheet, and spoon mixture into piecrust.

3. Whisk together eggs and next 5 ingredients in a bowl until smooth; pour over sausage mixture.

4. Bake at 350° for 35 to 40 minutes or until golden brown and set.

Makes 6 servings. Hands-on 25 min., Total 1 hour

BLONDE BROWNIES

Becky Luck, a big fan of Carolina Cooking, *drizzles these blondies with a glaze made from powdered sugar and orange juice.*

Preheat oven to 350°. Beat 1/2 cup softened **butter** at medium speed with an electric mixer until fluffy; gradually add 2 1/4 cups firmly packed **light brown sugar,** beating well. Add 2 large **eggs,** 1 at a time, beating just until blended after each addition. Stir in 2 cups chopped **pecans,** 1 1/2 cups **all-purpose flour,** 1 tsp. **vanilla extract,** and 1/8 tsp. **kosher salt.** (Batter will be thick.) Lightly grease a 13- x 9-inch pan with **vegetable cooking spray.** Spread batter in prepared pan. Bake 25 to 30 minutes or until a wooden pick inserted in center comes out clean. Cool completely on a wire rack (about 1 hour). Cut into 16 squares.

Makes 16. Hands-on 10 min.; Total 1 hour, 35 min.

Cheese-and-Sausage Quiche

May

Country Music's Greatest Eats

FOR OUR NEWEST COOKBOOK, WE TEAMED UP WITH COUNTRY MUSIC TELEVISION TO BRING YOU BACKSTAGE AND INTO THE KITCHEN WITH SOME OF NASHVILLE'S BRIGHTEST STARS. LIKE THEIR GREAT COUNTRY SONGS, EVERY RECIPE TELLS A STORY. HERE'S A SNEAK PEEK.

FLORIDA GEORGIA LINE

Brian Kelley (FL, left) and Tyler Hubbard (GA) earned their grilling marks on the 2012 Country Throwdown tour with Gary Allan. Low men on the totem pole, they were tapped as the "barbecue band," responsible for grilling for the 150-member crew every night after the show. Since then, they've grown into Big Green Egg men. "This summer I'm gonna be cookin' every dang day I'm home. I can't wait to make that sucker rock," Brian says.

SERRANO PEPPER BURGERS

Florida Georgia Line's songwriter friend Craig Wiseman shared his recipe with the band. The secret? Grill-roasted peppers that add spicy heat and a touch of sweetness and smoke to juicy burgers. Use your favorite peppers, including milder Anaheim, Cubanelle, bell, or poblano. (Pictured on page 177)

- 1 lb. serrano peppers
- 2 Tbsp. olive oil
  Kosher salt
- 3 lb. ground chuck
  Freshly ground black pepper
- 1 lb. pepper Jack cheese, thinly sliced
  Butter
- 12 hamburger buns
  Toppings: mayonnaise, ketchup, mustard, lettuce, tomato slices

1. Light 1 side of grill, heating to 350° to 400° (medium-high) heat; leave other side unlit. Toss together peppers and olive oil. Arrange peppers in a grill basket or on an aluminum-foil tray over unlit side, and grill, covered with grill lid, 10 to 15 minutes or until peppers begin to shrivel. Transfer peppers to lit side of grill, and grill, covered with grill lid, 8 to 10 minutes or until lightly charred, turning halfway through. Remove from grill to a wire rack, and cool completely (about 15 minutes).

2. Remove and discard stems; slice peppers in half lengthwise. Remove seeds, and sprinkle peppers with desired amount of salt.

3. Preheat both sides of grill to 350° to 400° (medium-high) heat. Shape

Serrano Pepper Burgers

ground chuck into 12 patties; sprinkle with desired amount of salt and pepper. Grill patties, without grill lid, 4 to 5 minutes on each side or to desired degree of doneness. Place 2 to 3 pepper halves on each patty; top with cheese. Grill, covered with grill lid, 1 to 2 minutes or until cheese melts.
4. Butter buns, and toast on grill. Serve patties on toasted buns with desired toppings.

Makes 12 servings. Hands-on 45 min., Total 1 hour

CRAB-STUFFED CATFISH FILLETS WITH CAJUN RÉMOULADE

Chef Rusty Hamlin feeds the Zac Brown Band members and their fans at big, casual "Eat and Greet" suppers when the band is touring. Here's one of Rusty's favorite dishes, which he serves with Cajun Rémoulade and grits. (Pictured on page 178)

1/2	cup butter
3	celery ribs, diced
1	small onion, diced
1	small green bell pepper, diced
1	Tbsp. minced garlic
1	Tbsp. fresh lemon juice
2	tsp. Cajun seasoning
1/8	tsp. hot sauce
1/2	lb. fresh lump crabmeat, drained
1	cup panko (Japanese breadcrumbs)
6	(7-oz.) fresh catfish fillets
1	Tbsp. olive oil
1	tsp. paprika
	Table salt
	Freshly ground black pepper
	Vegetable cooking spray
	Cajun Rémoulade

1. Melt butter in a large skillet over medium-high heat; add celery and next 3 ingredients, and sauté 6 minutes or until tender. Stir in lemon juice and next 2 ingredients, and cook 1 minute. Gently stir in crabmeat, breadcrumbs, and, if desired, additional Cajun seasoning and hot

sauce. Remove from heat; cool completely (about 15 minutes).
2. Preheat oven to 425°. Butterfly catfish fillets by making a lengthwise cut in 1 side, carefully cutting to but not through the opposite side; unfold fillets.
3. Spoon crab mixture down center of 1 side of each butterflied fillet; fold opposite side over filling. Brush fillets with olive oil; sprinkle with paprika and desired amount of salt and pepper. Place fillets on a wire rack coated with cooking spray in a jelly-roll pan.
4. Bake at 425° for 20 to 25 minutes or until fish flakes with a fork. Serve with Cajun Rémoulade.

Makes 6 servings. Hands-on 40 min.; Total 1 hour, 35 min., including rémoulade

Cajun Rémoulade

Use any leftovers of this piquant condiment as the secret sauce to your favorite fried fish or burger, or as a dressing for hearty salads and slaws.

1/2	cup dill pickle relish, drained
1/2	cup mayonnaise
1/4	cup diced yellow onion
1/4	cup diced celery
1/4	cup diced red bell pepper
1/4	cup chopped fresh flat-leaf parsley
3	Tbsp. ketchup
3	Tbsp. yellow mustard
2	Tbsp. minced garlic
2	Tbsp. Creole mustard
2	Tbsp. prepared horseradish
2	Tbsp. fresh lemon juice
3	dashes of hot sauce
	Table salt
	Freshly ground black pepper

Process first 13 ingredients and salt and pepper to taste in a food processor 30 to 40 seconds or until finely chopped. Serve immediately or chilled. Refrigerate in an airtight container up to 3 days.

Makes 2 cups. Hands-on 20 min., Total 20 min.

ZAC BROWN BAND

When a band takes it upon themselves to feed fans before their concerts, you can assume they're pretty serious about food. Zac and the boys even travel with their own chef and a mobile kitchen nicknamed Cookie. "At our Eat and Greets, we sit down and share a meal with about 150 people, and get to actually visit with them," says Zac. "It's not about autographs, it's about really being one-on-one and connecting with your fans."

LAUREN ALAINA

Growing up as the baby in a large family, Lauren was often kicked out of the kitchen—except by her grandmother. "We'd always sing that song from Winnie the Pooh, 'Up, down, touch the ground, in the mood for food,' over and over and get on everyone's nerves," Lauren says. "Food makes me happy; music makes you feel good. They just go hand in hand."

BLACKBERRY COBBLER

"I remember always wanting my grandmother to make this cobbler for me when I was a little girl," says Lauren.

2 1/2 **cups fresh blackberries***
  1 **cup sugar**
  1 **cup all-purpose flour**
  1 **cup milk**
  2 **tsp. baking powder**
1/2 **tsp. table salt**
1/2 **cup butter, melted**
1/2 **tsp. ground cinnamon**
    Whipped cream or ice cream

1. Preheat oven to 375°. Stir together blackberries and sugar in a medium bowl. Let stand 25 minutes or until some liquid is released and sugar turns pink.
2. Whisk together flour and next 3 ingredients in a medium bowl. Stir in melted butter until blended. Spread batter in an ungreased 8-inch square pan. Spoon blackberry mixture over batter; sprinkle with cinnamon.
3. Bake at 375° for 45 to 50 minutes or until bubbly and golden brown. Serve warm with whipped cream or ice cream.

*Frozen blackberries, thawed and drained, may be substituted.

Makes 4 to 6 servings. Hands-on 15 min.; Total 1 hour, 20 min.

JANA'S CHOCOLATE CHIP COOKIES

Do as Jana does: Tie on an apron, put on a Patsy Cline record, and whip up some of these chewy cookies. Ground oats and chopped pecans give them great texture, and a grated milk chocolate bar gives the chocolate morsels an extraordinary boost. (Pictured on page 176)

2 1/4 **cups uncooked regular oats**
  2 **cups all-purpose flour**
  1 **tsp. baking powder**
  1 **tsp. baking soda**
1/2 **tsp. table salt**
  1 **cup unsalted butter, softened**
  1 **cup granulated sugar**
  1 **cup firmly packed light brown sugar**
  2 **large eggs**
  1 **tsp. vanilla extract**
  1 **(12-oz.) package semisweet chocolate morsels**
  1 **(4.4-oz.) milk chocolate candy bar, grated**
1 1/2 **cups chopped pecans**
    Parchment paper

1. Preheat oven to 375°. Pulse oats in food processor until finely ground. Whisk together flour, next 3 ingredients, and ground oats in a large bowl.
2. Beat butter and next 2 ingredients at medium speed with an electric mixer until fluffy. Add eggs, 1 at a time, beating just until blended after each addition. Stir in vanilla.
3. Gradually add flour mixture to butter mixture, beating at low speed until blended. Stir in chocolate morsels and next 2 ingredients.
4. Drop dough by level spoonfuls 2 inches apart onto 2 parchment paper-lined jelly-roll pans, using a 1 1/2-inch cookie scoop. Flatten each to a 2-inch circle.
5. Bake at 375° for 8 to 10 minutes or until browned. Cool on pans 2 to 3 minutes; transfer to wire racks.

Makes about 4 1/2 dozen. Hands-on 45 min.; Total 1 hour, 10 min.

JANA KRAMER

Jana's first stage might well have been her Grandma Marge's kitchen. "We loved to bake cookies together while we listened to Patsy Cline and Loretta Lynn," Jana recalls. Through baking, she built her musical foundation. She also learned that straying from the recipe can lead to good things—a lesson that's served her well in her career.

BEER-CAN CHICKEN

1 (4-lb.) whole chicken
1 Tbsp. vegetable oil
1 1/2 Tbsp. BBQ Rub
1 1/2 tsp. kosher salt
1 (12-oz.) can beer

1. If applicable, remove neck and giblets from chicken, and reserve for another use. Pat chicken dry with paper towels. Brush cavity and outside of chicken with oil. Stir together BBQ Rub and salt; sprinkle mixture inside cavity and on outside of chicken. Chill chicken 30 minutes to 12 hours.

2. Let chicken stand at room temperature 30 minutes. Light 1 side of grill, heating to 350° to 400° (medium-high) heat; leave other side unlit. Open beer. Place chicken upright onto beer can, fitting can into cavity. Pull legs forward to form a tripod, so chicken stands upright.

3. Place chicken upright on unlit side of grill. Grill, covered with grill lid, 1 to 1 1/2 hours or until golden and a meat thermometer inserted in thickest portion registers 165°. Carefully remove chicken from can. Cover chicken loosely with aluminum foil; let stand 10 minutes before serving.

Makes 4 servings. Hands-on 20 min.; Total 2 hours, 35 min., including rub

BBQ Rub

Stir together 2 Tbsp. **kosher salt,** 1 Tbsp. **smoked paprika,** 1 Tbsp. **onion powder,** 1 1/2 tsp. ground **red pepper,** 1 1/2 tsp. ground **cumin,** 1 tsp. **garlic powder,** 1 tsp. dried **thyme,** 1 tsp. dried **oregano,** and 1 tsp. **freshly ground black pepper.** Store in an airtight container up to 6 months.

Makes 6 Tbsp. Total 5 min.

AVOCADO-AND-FETA DIP

Gloriana's Mike Gossin says this healthy dip is one of his favorite things his mother makes. "I like it so much I may have to write a song about it. Avocado, avocado, avocado dip!" Be sure to fold in the dressing gently so the avocado and feta stay chunky. (Pictured on page 176)

1 lb. tomatoes (about 4 medium), coarsely chopped
3 medium avocados, cubed
1 cup loosely packed fresh basil leaves, chopped
1 (8-oz.) package crumbled feta cheese
2 Tbsp. olive oil
2 Tbsp. red wine vinegar
Tortilla chips

Toss together first 4 ingredients in a large bowl. Whisk together oil and vinegar in a small bowl; pour over tomato mixture, and toss gently to coat tomatoes, avocados, and feta with dressing. Sprinkle with desired amount of salt and pepper. Serve with tortilla chips.

Makes 10 to 12 appetizer servings. Hands-on 25 min., Total 25 min.

GLORIANA

Get Rachel Reinert and brothers Tom and Mike Gossin talking about food, and clear your schedule. This trio loves to eat. "Much like songwriting and performing, when you cook you're creating something," says Mike. Rachel adds, "You could just pop a dish in the microwave, but where's the love in that?" For them, it's all about tasting the love in whatever you're creating, proving nothing's better than home cooking.

Make the Best Biscuit Ever

FLUFFY OR FLAKY? BUTTER OR LARD? EVERYONE HAS AN OPINION ABOUT WHAT MAKES A BISCUIT GREAT. TO SETTLE THE DEBATE, OUR TEST KITCHEN BAKED HUNDREDS OF BISCUITS UNTIL WE LANDED ON OUR ALL-TIME FAVORITE, NO-FAIL RECIPE THAT WILL IMPRESS NEW COOKS AND OLD PROS ALIKE.

OUR FAVORITE BUTTERMILK BISCUIT

- 1/2 **cup butter (1 stick), frozen**
- 2 1/2 **cups self-rising flour**
- 1 **cup chilled buttermilk**
  Parchment paper
- 2 **Tbsp. butter, melted**

1. Preheat oven to 475°. Grate frozen butter using large holes of a box grater. Toss together grated butter and flour in a medium bowl. Chill 10 minutes.

2. Make a well in center of mixture. Add buttermilk, and stir 15 times. Dough will be sticky.

3. Turn dough out onto a lightly floured surface. Lightly sprinkle flour over top of dough. Using a lightly floured rolling pin, roll dough into a 3/4-inch-thick rectangle (about 9 x 5 inches). Fold dough in half so short ends meet. Repeat rolling and folding process 4 more times.

4. Roll dough to 1/2-inch thickness. Cut with a 2 1/2-inch floured round cutter, reshaping scraps and flouring as needed.

5. Place dough rounds on a parchment paper-lined jelly-roll pan. Bake at 475° for 15 minutes or until lightly browned. Brush with melted butter.

Makes 12 to 14 biscuits. Hands-on 25 min., Total 50 min.

STEP 1: Grate frozen butter. It's our favorite fast-and-easy technique to incorporate ice-cold fat into flour.

STEP 2: Stir together all ingredients exactly 15 times to form a ragged, slightly sticky dough.

STEP 3: Fold and roll the dough 5 times before cutting. This creates buttery layers that bake up flaky.

STEP 4: Punch straight down when cutting. Don't twist; it will ruin your layers and reduce the overall rise.

STEP 5: Arrange dough rounds so the sides touch. The biscuits will help each other rise to the occasion.

TRY THIS, TASTE THAT

PUT 1 OF THESE 4 SIMPLE SPINS ON OUR FAVORITE RECIPE (FACING PAGE),
AND YOU'VE GOT A BRAND NEW BISCUIT

1. For Pillowy Dinner Rolls:
Cut in ½ cup cold shortening instead of cold butter. You'll get a soft biscuit that stays tender, even when cool. Plus, shortening has a neutral flavor that will complement anything on your dinner plate.

2. For Sweet Shortcakes:
Add 2 Tbsp. sugar to the flour, and replace buttermilk with heavy cream. The sugar lends the biscuits a subtle sweetness, and the extra fat in heavy cream gives them a crumbly texture like shortbread. They're the perfect base for shortcake desserts.

3. For Pickle Biscuits:
Why didn't we think of these sooner? *Stir 4 Tbsp. drained dill pickle relish into buttermilk before adding to flour mixture.* Split baked biscuits, and top with ham and mustard for the World's Best Ham Sandwich! We promise.

4. For Crunchy-Bottomed Biscuits:
Warm a cast-iron skillet in the oven, and spread a bit of butter in the skillet before adding the biscuits. The bottoms will end up crunchy and golden brown and provide a sturdy base that holds up to a smothering of sausage gravy.

THE 4 ESSENTIAL TOOLS

BOX GRATER
This is our secret weapon for evenly cutting in fat.

ROLLING PIN
It'll keep your warm paws off the dough. (Cold dough is key.)

SHARP CUTTERS
A straight, clean cut will skyrocket a biscuit's rise.

JELLY-ROLL PAN
It's the best surface to achieve a crisp crust and even baking.

THE 3 KEY INGREDIENTS

SELF-RISING FLOUR
Salt? Check. Leavener? Check. And yes, it must be White Lily.

SALTED BUTTER
Freeze it—it'll stay cold longer. And nothing beats the flavor.

BUTTERMILK
The tangy flavor in this Southern staple balances the rich fat.

IT'S ALL GRAVY FROM HERE

SIX BONUS IDEAS TO TAKE YOUR BISCUITS BEYOND THE BASICS

JAM SESSION

What can make a perfect biscuit even better? Homemade jam! Whip up our speedy, any-fruit (use frozen too!), all-seasons recipe.

EASY FRUIT JAM

Keep this jam in the refrigerator up to 1 month.

- 3 cups chopped fresh or frozen fruit (or small whole berries)
- 1 1/2 cups sugar
- 2 lemons
- 2 Tbsp. plus 2 tsp. powdered pectin
- 1 tsp. finely grated fresh ginger (optional)

1. Stir together fruit and sugar in a 4 1/2-qt. saucepan. Let stand 10 minutes. Zest 1 lemon to equal 1 tsp. Cut lemon in half; squeeze juice from lemon into a bowl to equal 2 tsp. Peel and section second lemon, removing seeds and chopping segments.
2. Stir pectin and, if desired, ginger, into fruit mixture, and bring to a rolling boil over medium heat, stirring often. Boil, stirring constantly, 5 minutes. Reduce heat to low; stir in lemon zest, chopped segments, and lemon juice. Cook, stirring occasionally, 3 minutes; remove from heat. Cool 10 minutes.
3. Pour jam into 2 (8-oz.) canning jars, and cool completely (about 30 minutes). Cover with lids, and refrigerate up to 1 month.

Makes 2 (8-oz.) jars. Hands-on 30 min.; Total 1 hour, 20 min.

TRY OUR FAVORITE COMBOS

Peach-Raspberry: 2 cups chopped peaches, 1 cup raspberries

Black and Blue: 2 cups blueberries, 1 cup blackberries

Strawberry-Orange: 2 cups chopped strawberries, 1 cup chopped and seeded orange segments (about 2 large oranges)

THE FORK SPLIT

Now that you've baked a perfect biscuit, don't smush it when you split it. Here's our Test Kitchen's tried-and-true trick: Gently spear the biscuit all the way around the edge with a fork (as you would do with an English muffin). You'll end up with a clean split and an even surface that begs for a pat of butter and/or spoonful of jam.

FROZEN ASSETS

Frozen biscuit dough rises just as well as fresh. Always make a double batch of dough, and freeze half the raw biscuits. To freeze: Arrange the cut biscuit rounds on a flat surface, and freeze. Transfer to a zip-top plastic bag once they're firm. Add 5 to 8 minutes to the bake time.

NEVER THROW AWAY A BISCUIT

Carrie Morey of Callie's Charleston Biscuits in Charleston, South Carolina, knows a thing or two about biscuits; her crew bakes more than 3,000 biscuits a day! Here are her fabulous tips for those cold, sad biscuits you're about to toss.

MAKE BISCUIT CROUTONS
Season cold biscuit crumbles with a little drizzle of olive oil and a sprinkle of salt and pepper, and bake in a 400° oven for about 10 minutes or until crisp.

MAKE BISCUIT BREAD PUDDING
Use biscuits instead of bread in your favorite bread pudding recipe for an outrageously rich sweet or savory casserole.

MAKE BISCUIT CRUMBS
Buzz up cold biscuits in a food processor, and freeze the crumbs until you're ready to use them. Carrie says, "Toasted crumbs add amazing texture to pasta or a trifle."

LAZY DOES IT

It's time to swear off canned biscuit dough for good. How? We're arming you with the easiest recipe ever. No rolling or cutting required!

LAZY BISCUITS

- 2 1/2 cups self-rising flour
- 1/2 tsp. sugar
- 1 1/4 cups chilled buttermilk
- 1/2 cup butter, melted
  Parchment paper
- 2 Tbsp. butter, melted

1. Preheat oven to 475°. Whisk together flour and sugar in a large bowl.
2. Stir together buttermilk and 1/2 cup melted butter in a small bowl. (Butter will clump.) Stir buttermilk mixture into flour mixture until dough pulls away from sides of bowl. Drop dough by level scoops, 1 inch apart, onto a parchment paper-lined jelly-roll pan. (Use a 2-inch cookie scoop.)
3. Bake at 475° for 12 minutes or until golden brown. Brush with 2 Tbsp. melted butter, and serve.

Makes 14. Hands-on 15 min., Total 25 min.

HIT THE ROAD

You really aren't a biscuit guru until you've tasted these famous versions. Visit *southernliving.com/biscuit* to see our other faves.

Loveless Cafe NASHVILLE, TN
The beloved biscuits at this Tennessee institution are so good their own biscuit mix comes with a simple proclamation: "It's the next best thing to the real thing."

Sunrise Biscuit Kitchen CHAPEL HILL, NC
Executive Editor Hunter Lewis recommends Sunrise Biscuit Kitchen for a killer local breakfast and Time-Out for late-night chicken biscuit snacking.

Big Bad Breakfast OXFORD, MS
BBB's biscuits are like religion to devotees who flock to north Mississippi to feast on this all-star creation by the high priest of lard himself, chef John Currence.

Fire Up Salads on the Grill

USE THE GRILL TO SHORTCUT SUPPER AND ADD SMOKY FLAVOR TO FOUR NEW HEARTY ENTRÉES

Grain Salad wtih Grilled Shrimp and Sweet Peppers

WE LOVE GRAINS!
Bulgur is quick-cooking wheat. Substitute brown rice, quinoa, or most any whole grain.

GRAIN SALAD WITH GRILLED SHRIMP AND SWEET PEPPERS

If you use wooden skewers, submerge them in water for 30 minutes before threading on the shrimp.

- 3/4 **cup uncooked bulgur wheat**
- 5 1/2 **Tbsp. olive oil, divided**
- 1 1/4 **tsp. kosher salt, divided**
- 3/4 **tsp. black pepper, divided**
- 1 **lb. peeled, medium-size raw shrimp, deveined**
- 8 **oz. baby sweet peppers**
- 1 **bunch green onions**
- 4 1/2 **tsp. fresh lemon juice**
- 1/3 **cup coarsely chopped fresh flat-leaf parsley**

1. Preheat grill to 350° to 400° (medium-high) heat. Cook bulgur according to package directions. Toss together bulgur, 2 Tbsp. oil, 1/2 tsp. salt, and 1/2 tsp. pepper; spread on a baking sheet. Cool completely (about 15 minutes); transfer to a large bowl.
2. Toss together shrimp, 1 Tbsp. oil, 1/4 tsp. salt, and remaining 1/4 tsp. pepper. Thread shrimp onto skewers. Toss together peppers and 1 Tbsp. oil.
3. Grill shrimp and peppers, covered with grill lid, 2 minutes on each side or just until shrimp turn pink. Brush onions with 1 1/2 tsp. oil, and grill, covered with grill lid, 1 minute on each side. Slice peppers. Cut onions into 1/2-inch-long pieces.
4. Toss together bulgur mixture, peppers, onions, lemon juice, and remaining 1 Tbsp. oil and 1/2 tsp. salt. Top with parsley and shrimp.

Makes 4 servings. Hands-on 30 min., Total 50 min.

GRILLED SAUSAGE SALAD PIZZA

Equal parts salad and pizza, this hearty pie is a fresh, new spin.

- 1 medium-size sweet onion, cut into 1/4-inch-thick slices
- 3 Tbsp. olive oil, divided
- 1/2 lb. smoked link sausage
- 1 (16-oz.) package prebaked Italian pizza crust
- 1 1/2 cups (6 oz.) freshly shredded mozzarella cheese
- 1 1/4 tsp. kosher salt, divided
- 1 cup firmly packed arugula
- 1/2 cup fresh flat-leaf parsley
- 1/2 tsp. ground black pepper
- 1 lemon, halved

1. Preheat grill to 350° to 400° (medium-high) heat. Brush onion with 1 Tbsp. oil. Grill onion, covered with grill lid, 6 minutes on each side. Grill sausage 4 minutes on each side; slice.
2. Brush pizza crust with 1 Tbsp. oil. Grill crust, oil side down, 2 minutes. Turn crust over, and brush with 1 Tbsp. oil; sprinkle with cheese and 1/4 tsp. salt. Grill 2 minutes or until cheese melts.
3. Toss together arugula, parsley, pepper, sausage, onion, and remaining 1 tsp. salt. Top pizza with salad; squeeze lemon juice over salad. Serve immediately.

Makes 6 servings. Hands-on 45 min., Total 45 min.

GRILLED CHICKEN-ASPARAGUS SALAD

- 1 1/2 lb. skinned and boned chicken breasts
- 6 Tbsp. olive oil, divided
- 2 tsp. kosher salt, divided
- 1/2 tsp. black pepper, divided
- 2 lb. asparagus, trimmed
- 4 oz. crumbled goat cheese
- 1/4 cup thinly sliced shallots
- 1/3 cup mayonnaise
- 3 Tbsp. buttermilk
- 2 tsp. fresh lemon juice
- 2 garlic cloves, minced
- 2 Tbsp. chopped fresh mint
- 2 tsp. chopped fresh dill

1. Preheat grill to 350° to 400° (medium-high) heat. Brush chicken with 2 Tbsp. oil; sprinkle with 1 1/4 tsp. salt and 1/4 tsp. pepper. Grill chicken, covered, 5 minutes on each side or until done. Let stand 10 minutes; chop.
2. Toss asparagus with 2 Tbsp. oil, and grill in a grill basket, covered, 1 minute on each side. Cut asparagus into 2-inch pieces. Toss together chicken, asparagus, cheese, shallot, 1/2 tsp. salt, and 1/4 tsp. pepper in a bowl. Whisk together mayonnaise, next 3 ingredients, 2 Tbsp. oil, and 1/4 tsp. salt; drizzle over chicken mixture. Top with herbs.

Makes 6 servings. Hands-on 45 min., Total 45 min.

FLANK STEAK AND CUCUMBER SALAD

Start on the Quick-Pickled Cukes first, so they soak in flavor.

- 1 (1- to 1 1/2-lb.) flank steak
- 1 Tbsp. olive oil
  Kosher salt and pepper
- 2 garlic cloves, minced
- 1 Tbsp. dark sesame oil
- 1/4 cup soy sauce
- 1/4 cup packed brown sugar
- 2 Tbsp. fresh lime juice
- 2 Tbsp. Asian chili paste (such as Huy Fong)
- 1 tsp. cornstarch
  Quick-Pickled Cukes

1. Preheat grill to 350° to 400° (medium-high) heat. Rub steak with olive oil and desired amount of salt and pepper. Let stand 10 minutes. Grill, covered, 5 minutes on each side or to desired doneness. Let stand 10 minutes.
2. Meanwhile, sauté garlic in hot sesame oil in a saucepan over medium heat 1 minute. Stir in soy sauce, next 3 ingredients, and 1/4 cup water; bring to a boil. Whisk together cornstarch and 1 tsp. water, and stir into soy sauce mixture. Bring to a boil; boil, stirring often, 1 minute.
3. Cut steak across the grain into thin strips. Arrange Quick-Pickled Cukes on a platter, and top with sliced steak and sauce.

Makes 4 servings. Hands-on 30 min., Total 40 min., not including cucumbers

Quick-Pickled Cukes

- 4 cups thinly sliced English cucumbers (about 2 large)
- 1/2 cup sliced green onions
- 1/2 cup rice vinegar
- 3 Tbsp. sugar
- 1 garlic clove, minced
- 1 tsp. kosher salt

Place cucumbers and onions in a large bowl. Bring vinegar and next 3 ingredients to a boil in a saucepan, stirring until sugar dissolves. Pour over cucumber mixture. Let stand 30 minutes. Serve with a slotted spoon.

Hands-on 15 min., Total 45 min.

OUR OWN KING OF THE KITCHEN, NORMAN KING, CELEBRATES

SOUTHERN SWEETENERS

Back when refined sugar commanded a premium price, syrups satisfied our collective sweet tooth. When sugar got cheap, these nectars lost their way. It's high time we bring their complex flavors back to the Southern table.

CORN + HONEY

① BLENDED SYRUPS (AKA GOLDEN SYRUP)
A Deep South specialty, especially in Alabama, this pale amber blend is a mixture of corn syrup, cane syrup, and often honey. Not to be confused with British golden syrup, this one's super smooth with a just-sweet-enough caramel corn profile. Use it to sweeten pecan pie or baked beans, brush it on ham, or swirl it into tea. *goldeneaglesyrup.com*

SORGHUM

② SORGHUM SYRUP
The South's most deeply nuanced drizzle, sorghum is made from juice that's been pressed from the stalk of the sorghum plant and boiled down into thick syrup. It boasts an earthy, robust flavor with the subtle tartness of pineapple and notes of roasted coffee. Some say it even has a buttery finish. We use it in zillions of ways: drizzled on biscuits, stirred into coffee or bourbon cocktails, added to barbecue sauce and savory glazes, and more. *muddypondsorghum.com*

SUGAR-CANE

③ CANE SYRUP
Made from fresh-pressed sugarcane juice, cane syrup develops its velvety consistency and sassy, tangy, caramel flavor and floral nose during a long, slow boil in open pots. Move over, maple syrup. This is the divine drizzle for biscuits or pancakes. Look for jars from small producers in the Deep South, or try Abbeville, Louisiana-based Steen's. *steensyrup.com*

④ MOLASSES
Molasses is a by-product of granulated sugar production. Once cane juice is cooked down and begins to crystallize, the sugar crystals are pulled from the brew, leaving thick, dark, nutrient-rich molasses behind. If further refined, almost all the sugar is removed, the flavor intensifies, and you have blackstrap molasses. It lends a rich, deep flavor to quick breads, cookies, cakes, and icing. *store.thesmokehouse.com*

Delight Mom with Brunch

NASHVILLE GENTLEMAN AND COOKBOOK AUTHOR **MATT MOORE** CELEBRATES MOTHER'S DAY WITH AN EASY-DOES-IT MENU

The Menu

FIZZY BERRY PICK-ME-UP

···········

ARUGULA WITH
WARM BACON VINAIGRETTE

···········

CHEESE GRITS AND
ROASTED TOMATOES

···········

SPRING VEGETABLE FRITTATA

···········

CINNAMON-SUGAR
DOUGHNUT BITES

FIZZY BERRY PICK-ME-UP

"Mother's Day is all about a celebration, so I like to start things out with a festive cocktail to keep Mama feeling relaxed and light on her feet," says Matt.

Stir together ⅓ cup fresh **blueberries,** 12 halved fresh **strawberries*,** 4 large fresh **basil** leaves, and 4 tsp. **sugar** in a medium bowl; crush berries and leaves with a wooden spoon. Chill 30 minutes (to release juice from berries). Stir 1 cup chilled **sparkling wine,** such as Prosecco, into fruit mixture, and pour through a fine wire-mesh strainer into a pitcher, discarding solids. Add remaining wine from 750-milliliter bottle to pitcher. Garnish with **lemon slices** and strawberries. Serve immediately, or chill up to 24 hours.

*Frozen, thawed strawberries and frozen blueberries may be substituted.

Makes 4 servings. Hands-on 10 min., Total 40 min.

ARUGULA WITH WARM BACON VINAIGRETTE

"Mama always said, 'Eat your greens,' so start brunch off with a simple salad. The warm vinaigrette melts the goat cheese, creating a magical creamy dressing."

- 4 bacon slices
- 1 shallot, minced
- 4 Tbsp. extra virgin olive oil
- 2 Tbsp. red wine vinegar
- 1/4 tsp. kosher salt
- 1/4 tsp. cracked black pepper
- 1 (5-oz.) package arugula or mixed greens
- 1/3 cup crumbled goat cheese

1. Cook bacon in a 10-inch nonstick skillet over medium heat 6 minutes or until crisp. Remove bacon, reserving drippings in skillet. Crumble bacon. Sauté shallot in drippings 2 minutes or just until tender.

2. Transfer shallot and drippings to a small bowl. Whisk in oil and next 3 ingredients. Toss arugula with vinaigrette on a platter. Top with goat cheese and bacon.

Makes 4 servings. Hands-on 10 min., Total 10 min.

CHEESE GRITS AND ROASTED TOMATOES

Make a double batch of the Roasted Tomatoes, and pair the juicy gems with a cheese tray, salad, or grilled meat.

- 1/2 cup heavy cream
- 2 Tbsp. unsalted butter
- 2 tsp. kosher salt
- 1 cup uncooked stone-ground yellow grits
- 2 oz. cream cheese
- 1/4 cup finely grated extra-sharp Cheddar cheese
  Roasted Tomatoes
  Garnish: fresh chives

1. Bring first 3 ingredients and 3 cups water to a boil in a medium saucepan over medium-high heat. Stir in grits, and reduce heat to medium-low. Cover and simmer, stirring occasionally, 15 to 20 minutes or until tender.

2. Fold in both cheeses, stirring until melted; remove from heat. Cover and let stand 5 minutes. Transfer to a serving platter. Top with Roasted Tomatoes.

Note: Add up to 1/4 cup water after cooking grits, if desired, for a thinner consistency.

Makes 4 servings. Hands-on 25 min.; Total 1 hour, 5 min., including tomatoes

Roasted Tomatoes

Preheat oven to 400°. Toss together 1 lb. halved **cherry tomatoes;** 1 Tbsp. **extra virgin olive oil;** 1 Tbsp. **red wine vinegar;** 1 tsp. **honey;** 1/4 tsp. **kosher salt;** and 1/4 tsp. **freshly ground black pepper** in a baking dish. Let stand 10 minutes. Bake 18 minutes or until tender.

Hands-on 5 min., Total 30 min.

SPRING VEGETABLE FRITTATA

"A frittata is a great brunch dish for entertaining because it makes for an effortless and beautiful family-style presentation."

- 4 oz. fresh asparagus
- 1/2 (8-oz.) package cremini mushrooms, sliced
- 1/2 small yellow onion, sliced
- 1 Tbsp. extra virgin olive oil
- 1/2 tsp. kosher salt, divided
- 1/2 tsp. cracked black pepper, divided
- 2 Tbsp. butter
- 8 large eggs
- 2 oz. crumbled feta cheese

1. Preheat oven to 400°. Cut asparagus into 1-inch pieces, discarding tough ends.

2. Sauté mushrooms and onion in 2 tsp. hot oil in a 10-inch nonstick ovenproof skillet over medium heat 4 to 5 minutes or until onion is tender; remove from skillet. Add remaining 1 tsp. oil to skillet, and sauté asparagus 2 to 3 minutes or until tender; stir in 1/4 tsp. each salt and pepper. Remove from skillet. Wipe skillet clean.

3. Melt butter in skillet over medium heat. Whisk together eggs and remaining 1/4 tsp. each salt and pepper. Add egg mixture to skillet. As eggs start to cook, gently lift edges of egg with a spatula, and tilt pan so uncooked portion flows underneath. Cook 2 to 3 minutes or until almost set. Top with vegetables and feta cheese.

4. Bake frittata at 400° for 16 to 18 minutes or until slightly browned and puffy. Serve immediately.

Makes 4 to 6 servings. Hands-on 20 min., Total 40 min.

CINNAMON-SUGAR DOUGHNUT BITES

"Wash these warm, sugary doughnut bites down with a shooter of ice-cold chocolate milk. I like to stick the milk in the freezer about 10 minutes before serving." (Pictured on page 176)

- Vegetable oil
- 1 1/2 cups all-purpose flour
- 1/3 cup granulated sugar
- 2 1/4 tsp. baking powder
- 1 tsp. ground cinnamon
- 1/4 tsp. kosher salt
- 1 large egg, beaten
- 1/2 cup milk
- 3 Tbsp. unsalted butter, melted
  Garnish: powdered sugar

1. Pour oil to depth of 1 1/2 inches into a 12-inch cast-iron skillet; heat to 350°.

2. Whisk together flour and next 4 ingredients in a large bowl. Make a well in center of mixture; stir in egg and next 2 ingredients until well blended. (Batter will be dry.)

3. Drop batter by level tablespoonfuls, 6 to 8 at a time, into hot oil; fry, in batches, turning occasionally, 2 minutes on each side or until browned. Drain on a paper towel-lined plate. Serve warm.

Makes 2 dozen. Hands-on 30 min., Total 30 min.

Pick Your Squash

GROW FRESH, TENDER SUMMER SQUASH ALL SEASON LONG RIGHT IN YOUR OWN BACKYARD

SUMMER BEGINS with the first picking of yellow squash the color of bright sunshine. This luscious vegetable garden standard is easy to grow—and it's prolific. It's also versatile in the kitchen. You can eat it grilled, roasted, fried, baked, sautéed, stuffed, or pickled. You can also eat it raw, and even eat the flowers.

Select

There are three types of summer squash to grow: yellow, zucchini, and pattypan. Each type has many different selections. For yellow squash, try a straightneck one such as 'Slick Pik,' or plant crooknecks such as 'Gentry' and 'Supersett.' For zucchini, use 'Black Beauty,' 'Tigress,' or 'Raven.' For pattypan, try 'Sunburst' or 'Peter Pan.' Squash needs a good bit of room in the garden. If you don't have much space, plant smaller selections such as 'Sweet Zuke' or 'Saffron,' which will thrive in large containers.

Prep

Summer squash loves warm weather and grows best in full sun. It also prefers rich, well-drained soil amended with a lot of organic matter, such as composted manure, chopped leaves, or mushroom compost. Give your plants a little bit more of a boost with an organic fertilizer such as Happy Frog Fruit & Flower (5-8-4) (planet-natural.com). Add a layer of mulch such as pine straw to help conserve moisture, keep roots cool, and prevent weeds.

Grow

Sow seeds in hills 3 to 4 feet apart in warm soil. Plant two rows of hills side by side for better pollination and fruiting. Sow five to seven seeds per hill 1 inch deep. Firm the soil and gently water. Thin seedlings to the two most vigorous plants. Squash have large orangey yellow, trumpet-shaped flowers. The first blooms are usually male and the females follow. (Female flowers have a tiny squash behind the bloom.) Don't worry if your flowers fall off—male blossoms drop off after shedding their pollen—that's normal, and remember you can eat the flowers. They are best picked right before they open, and are delicious fried.

Protect

Pests include squash vine borers and squash bugs. To deter these culprits, grow your plants under row covers (johnnyseeds.com). Remove covers once flowers appear so bees can pollinate the blooms. Organically control squash bugs by spraying with Neem Oil Extract (lowes.com). Powdery mildew is the most common disease; choose disease-resistant selections, provide good air circulation, and avoid overhead watering. Also, every year rotate where you plant your squash and clean up after the growing season.

---

get growing!
SUMMER SQUASH

WATER
Water weekly, especially while fruiting, to keep soil moist and prevent leaves from wilting.

SOIL
Fertile, well-drained soil amended with organic matter

HARVEST
Cut with sharp scissors or a knife.

| ○ LIGHT FULL SUN | ◆◆◇ WATER MEDIUM | Ⓜ CARE MEDIUM |

Even the blossoms are tasty.

QUICK-PICKLED SUMMER SQUASH

Cut 1 lb. **yellow squash** lengthwise into eighths. Stir together 1 Tbsp. fresh **dill weed**, 1 Tbsp. chopped fresh **mint**, 2 Tbsp. **apple cider vinegar**, 1 Tbsp. **lime juice**, ½ tsp. **kosher salt**, ¼ tsp. **freshly ground black pepper**, and ¼ tsp. dried crushed **red pepper** in a large bowl. Add squash, tossing to coat. Cover and chill 1 hour.

One Slow Cooker, Three Magic Meals

CYNTHIA GRAUBART SETS THE TABLE FOR THREE FAMILY DINNERS: ONE SIMPLE SLOW-COOKED PORK SHOULDER AND TWO FAST AND HEARTY WEEKNIGHT SUPPERS

I CALL IT MAGIC. One pork shoulder roast, a few pantry ingredients, and eight hours on low effortlessly produces the most succulent and tender pork, just as if you waved a magic wand. Although slow cooking is synonymous with fall and winter, as summer beckons, my slow cooker is the workhorse that keeps my kitchen cool. This recipe yields a gracious plenty, making it a wise choice for this New Sunday Supper.

The cooked pork shoulder, also known as pork butt or Boston butt, practically shreds itself when approached with a fork. Serve it with snappy Easy Pickled Sweet Onions and Peppers and a spoonful of the pickle brine, something green, and a side of moist cornbread on Sunday, reserving the extra pork for two additional meals.

Monday's fragrant noodle bowls are light enough for warm weather but substantial enough for dinner. Assemble stoveside, ladling the piping-hot broth into the bowls to coax the flavors of the individual ingredients into perfect harmony. Pass around chopsticks for extra fun.

Serving a popular snack as dinner might be out of character around your family table, but these Tuesday Pulled Pork Nachos are packed with protein and easy to assemble on a weeknight—just the right sign that carefree summer living is close at hand.

SUNDAY NIGHT

5-INGREDIENT SLOW-COOKER PULLED PORK

(Pictured on page 179)

- 2 **large sweet onions, cut into** 1/2-**inch slices**
- 1 **(5- to 6-lb.) boneless pork shoulder roast (Boston butt)**
- 2 **Tbsp. garlic-oregano-red pepper seasoning blend**
- 1 **tsp. kosher salt**
- 1 **(10 1/2-oz.) can condensed chicken broth**

1. Place onions in a lightly greased 6-qt. slow cooker. Rub roast with seasoning blend and salt; place roast on onions. Pour broth over roast. Cover and cook on LOW 8 to 10 hours or until meat shreds easily with a fork.

2. Transfer roast to a cutting board or serving platter; shred with 2 forks, removing any large pieces of fat. Remove onions with a slotted spoon, and serve with pork. (Reserve 4 cups shredded pork for Pork Noodle Bowls and Pulled Pork Nachos, if desired.)

Note: We tested with McCormick Grill Mates Backyard Brick Oven Seasoning.

Makes 8 to 10 servings. Hands-on 10 min.;
Total 8 hours, 10 min.

Easy Pickled Sweet Onions and Peppers

Brine the onions and peppers when you put the pork in the slow cooker so they pickle for at least eight hours. Or make the recipe up to one week ahead—the longer the onions and peppers sit, the better the flavor. The sweet-tart brine is delicious spooned over the succulent pork.

Bring 1 (12-oz.) bottle **rice vinegar,** 1 cup **apple cider vinegar,** 1/2 cup **sugar,** and 1/2 tsp. **dried crushed red pepper** to a boil in a medium saucepan. Toss together 2 sliced **sweet onions,** 6 sliced **sweet mini bell peppers,** 2 **garlic cloves,** hot vinegar mixture, and, if desired, 6 **fresh thyme sprigs** in a large bowl. Let stand 2 hours. Cover and chill 6 hours. Refrigerate in an airtight container up to 1 week.

Makes 1 qt. Hands-on 20 min.;
Total 8 hours, 20 min.

MONDAY NIGHT

PORK NOODLE BOWLS

- 1 **Tbsp. kosher salt**
- 1 **(8.8-oz.) package thin rice noodles**
- 1/2 **(8-oz.) package sliced fresh mushrooms**
- 2 **tsp. olive oil**
- 2 **cups pork from 5-Ingredient Slow-Cooker Pulled Pork**
- 1/2 **(16-oz.) package angel hair coleslaw mix**
- 4 **green onions (white and light green parts only), sliced**
- 1/4 **cup loosely packed fresh cilantro leaves**
- 6 **cups chicken broth**
- 1 **Tbsp. grated fresh ginger (optional)**
  Lime wedges
  Toppings: soy sauce, dried crushed red pepper, chopped dry-roasted peanuts

1. Microwave 8 cups water and salt at HIGH in a large microwave-safe glass bowl 2 minutes. Submerge noodles; let stand 20 minutes or until tender. Drain. Divide noodles among 4 bowls.

2. Sauté mushrooms in hot oil in a medium skillet over medium-high heat 5 minutes or until tender. Spoon over noodles. Add pork to skillet, and cook, stirring occasionally, 5 minutes or until hot; spoon over mushrooms. Divide coleslaw mix and next 2 ingredients among bowls.

3. Bring broth and, if desired, ginger to a boil in a 3-qt. saucepan over medium heat. Remove from heat, and divide among bowls. Serve with lime wedges and desired toppings.

Note: Try Swanson Thai Ginger Flavor Infused Broth as a flavored alternative to chicken broth.

Makes 4 servings. Hands-on 25 min.; Total 45 min., not including pork

PORKED OUT? PULL A ROTISSERIE CHICKEN!

TUESDAY NIGHT

PULLED PORK NACHOS

READY IN 15 MINUTES!

Gussy up these nachos any way you like. Want to use grated cheese instead of queso? Simply spread the chips on baking sheets, sprinkle with cheese, and bake at 350° until the cheese melts. The pulled pork also makes delicious quesadillas, tacos, or sandwiches. (Pictured on page 179(

Layer **tortilla chips** on a platter; top with 1 (15-oz.) can **black beans,** drained and rinsed; 2 cups **pork** from 5-Ingredient Slow-Cooker Pulled Pork, warmed; 1 cup refrigerated fresh **salsa;** 2/3 cup chopped **tomatoes;** 2/3 cup chopped fresh **cilantro;** 1/4 cup sliced **black olives;** 1/4 cup minced **red onion;** and 2 thinly sliced **jalapeño peppers.** Serve with 1 (12-oz.) container refrigerated **queso,** warmed, and 4 **lime wedges.**

Makes 4 servings. Hands-on 15 min.; Total 15 min., not including pork

Bake a Sweet Memory

TRUST US. ONE BITE OF THIS CREAMY BUTTERMILK PIE WILL TAKE YOU BACK IN TIME

CLASSIC SOUTHERN BUTTERMILK PIE

(Pictured on page 176)

1 1/2   **cups sugar**
   3   **Tbsp. all-purpose flour**
   3   **large eggs**
   1   **cup buttermilk**
 1/2   **cup butter, melted**
   1   **Tbsp. loosely packed lemon zest**
   3   **Tbsp. fresh lemon juice**
   1   **tsp. vanilla extract**
      Perfect Pastry Crust
      Garnishes: fresh berries, whipped cream, fresh mint

1. Preheat oven to 350°. Whisk together first 2 ingredients in a large bowl. Whisk eggs and next 5 ingredients into flour mixture; pour into Perfect Pastry Crust.

2. Bake at 350° for 35 to 45 minutes or until almost set, shielding edges with aluminum foil after 15 minutes. Transfer to a wire rack, and cool 1 hour.

Makes 8 servings. Hands-on 15 min.; Total 3 hours, 35 min., including crust

Perfect Pastry Crust

A food processor cuts fat into the flour mixture faster, but you can also do this by hand.

1 1/2   **cups all-purpose flour**
   1   **Tbsp. sugar**
 1/2   **tsp. table salt**
   6   **Tbsp. cold butter, cubed**
   3   **Tbsp. cold shortening, cubed**
   4   **to 5 Tbsp. ice water**
      Parchment paper

1. Pulse first 3 ingredients in a food processor 3 or 4 times or until combined. Add butter and shortening, and pulse 8 to 10 times or until mixture resembles coarse meal. Drizzle 4 Tbsp. ice water over mixture; pulse 4 or 5 times or until dough clumps together, adding up to 1 Tbsp. ice water, 1 tsp. at a time, if necessary. Gently shape dough into a flat disk. Wrap in plastic wrap, and chill 30 minutes.

2. Preheat oven to 400°. Roll dough into a 12-inch circle (about 1/8 inch thick) on a floured surface. Fit into a 9-inch pie plate; crimp edges. Prick bottom and sides with a fork. Line pastry with parchment paper, and fill with pie weights or dried beans.

3. Bake at 400° for 10 minutes. Remove weights and parchment paper, and bake 8 to 10 more minutes or until lightly browned. Transfer to a wire rack, and cool completely (about 30 minutes).

Makes 1 (9-inch) crust. Hands-on 25 min.; Total 1 hour, 45 min.

Classic Southern Buttermilk Pie

Community Cookbook

Nashville homemakers and country crooners alike contributed their favorite recipes to this Nashville Junior League cookbook from 1977. Look for autographs from Loretta Lynn and Tammy Wynette inside. Order it at ebay.com.

FUDGE PIE

Adapted from a recipe in Encore! Nashville, *this simple, decadent chocolate pie filling can easily be used in your favorite purchased or homemade piecrust.*

- ⅔ cup evaporated milk
- ½ (12-oz.) package semisweet chocolate morsels
- 2 Tbsp. butter
- 1 cup sugar
- 2 Tbsp. all-purpose flour
- 2 large eggs
- 2 tsp. vanilla extract
- ¾ tsp. kosher salt
- 1 cup chopped pecans
- 1 (9-inch) frozen unbaked piecrust shell
- Ice cream

1. Preheat oven to 375°. Microwave first 3 ingredients in a large microwave-safe bowl at HIGH 1 to 1 ½ minutes or until melted and smooth, whisking at 30-second intervals.

2. Whisk sugar and flour into chocolate mixture. Add eggs, 1 at a time, whisking just until blended after each addition. Whisk in vanilla and salt. Stir in pecans. Pour mixture into pie shell.

3. Bake at 375° for 35 to 40 minutes or until set. Cool 10 minutes before serving. Serve with ice cream.

Makes 6 to 8 servings. Hands-on 10 min., Total 1 hour

CRISPY CHEESE WAFERS

This rich, crispy snack reminds us that rice cereal isn't just for breakfast. It adds a crunchy texture to this familiar cheese straw treat.

Preheat oven to 350°. Beat 4 cups freshly grated **sharp Cheddar cheese;** 2 cups **all-purpose flour;** 1 cup **butter,** softened; 1 Tbsp. **kosher salt;** and ¼ tsp. **ground red pepper** at medium speed with an electric mixer 30 to 60 seconds or until mixture forms a ball. Gently stir in 2 cups **crisp rice cereal.** Shape into 1-inch balls, and place 1 inch apart on ungreased baking sheets. Flatten each dough ball with a fork dipped in flour. Bake, in batches, 25 to 28 minutes or until golden brown. Transfer wafers to wire racks, and cool completely.

Makes 6 dozen. Hands-on 20 min.; Total 1 hour, 35 min.

Fudge Pie

June

→ Southern Living ←

THE A TO Z GUIDE TO SOUTHERN FOOD

THE RECIPES, TASTEMAKERS, AND TRENDS THAT DEFINE OUR CULTURE RIGHT NOW

A

AGRICULTURAL RENAISSANCE

How the small farm, back-to-the land, edible garden movement is reshaping the way we eat

BY JAMIE COLE

Stephen and Dawn Robertson were computer geeks in another life. Stephen was a software engineer. Dawn was a farm kid from way back, and though her father had gifted her an acre and helped the couple build a house, they had a longing for land.

Today, Stephen's only commute is a tractor ride across East Fork Farm, a pastoral 40-acre valley in the mountains of Madison County, North Carolina, that the couple found after obsessing over real estate ads. After seven years of telecommuting, he quit his job to farm full-time. The goal was to be self-sufficient and sell fresh food—mostly lamb, sometimes poultry and rabbit—locally at farmers' and tailgate markets. His daughters sport muck boots and wash eggs to earn allowance. Dawn has a kitchen garden and barters meat for vegetables. "We go to the grocery store for some things," Stephen begins; then Dawn finishes: "But not a whole lot in the summertime."

The Robertsons made their move during a rural renaissance. At the turn of the 21st century, populations in rural counties—especially across the South and on both coasts—began to grow for the first time since manufacturing drew families out of the agrarian lifestyle of the 1960s. Meanwhile, small farms, such as East Fork, benefited from a fresh food revolution, spearheaded by chefs like William Dissen, who cooks the Robertsons' products along with stock from his own garden at Asheville's Market Place Restaurant. "I watched my grandmother do this for years, with a lot of love for her family and respect for the land," he says.

You don't need a back 40 and commercial kitchen to eat fresh; your backyard and stove will do. Home gardeners crave simpler recipes, while plant breeders have responded to the demand for small-space gardening with more container varieties than ever before. You can grow carrots in a bucket, potatoes in a barrel. Even on a small scale, "it is about control over some aspect of one's life during uncertain times," says Hank Will, a Master Gardener and editor-in-chief of the rural life know-how magazine *GRIT*. "We want to know where the food came from, and that it was produced with our own health and well-being—and not blind profit—in mind," he says.

The "back-to-landers" of the past decade are now settled in that ideal, that life. From downtown to the exurbs, city slickers catch on by maintaining rooftop gardens and urban farms, while chefs continue to ride the crest of the unstoppable farm-to-table movement. It all comes together in programs like Outstanding in the Field—farm tours that set tables for guests right in the pasture. When the Robertsons hosted one such dinner, Dissen cooked up their rabbit in a gumbo and grilled their lamb over coals. It was an ideal expression of a diner's connection to food, but also of a deeper, longed-for connection to the source—the land.

B

BEER

Not so long ago, the predictable pilsner prevailed in Dixie. Red-and-white cans bobbed in our coolers. We lived the High Life at tailgates. But now you'll find us cracking open a different sort of brew. After many grassroots efforts to revise laws governing beer production, the South is now a veritable hop heaven and craft beer destination with the highest annual production rates of any region in the country. If you haven't paid your local brewery a visit, now's the best time to enjoy the beers of summer.
—*Hannah Hayes*

C
CONDIMENTS

Bottle the essence of summer by making your own put ups with the season's peak produce. Bonus: Homemade condiments make great holiday gifts, so get pickling, infusing, and fermenting now.

BOURBON-SOAKED CHERRIES

Kirk Samuels of Chapel Hill, North Carolina, shared this recipe. Stir the cherries and their syrup into anything bourbon-flavored, or use them to gussy up sparkling beverages, such as club soda and ginger ale.

- 1 ½ **cups refrigerated pomegranate juice**
- 1 **cup sugar**
- 1 **lb. fresh cherries**
- 1 ½ **cups bourbon**

1. Bring first 2 ingredients to a simmer in a medium saucepan over medium-high heat, whisking constantly. Cook, whisking constantly, 10 minutes or until mixture is syrupy. Remove from heat, and cool completely (about 30 minutes).
2. Remove pits from cherries, leaving stems intact. Divide cherries among 3 (8-oz.) sterilized jars. Whisk bourbon into juice mixture, and pour into jars, filling to ¼ inch from top; wipe jar rims. Cover with metal lids, and screw on bands. Chill 2 weeks before using. (Will keep in fridge up to 6 months.)

Makes 3 (8-oz.) jars. Hands-on 15 min.; Total 45 min., plus 2 weeks for chilling

CHUNKY HOT SAUCE

Fermentation is the secret to this robust, piquant sauce. Use your favorite chiles here, or blend fiery ones with sweet ones to customize your own. As for the consistency, we love the sauce in all of its chunky glory, but if you want a smooth, looser take, press it through a wire-mesh strainer.

- 1 **lb. fresh hot chiles (such as Fresno), washed and stemmed**
- 2 ½ **Tbsp. kosher salt**
- 2 **cups white vinegar**

1. Process chiles and salt in a food processor about 30 seconds or until minced, stopping to scrape down sides as needed. Transfer chile mixture to a sterilized 1-qt. glass jar. Cover with cheesecloth, and let stand in a cool, dry place 2 days.
2. Remove cheesecloth, and stir in vinegar. Cover mixture with cheesecloth, and let stand in a cool, dry place 5 days. (Skim and discard any film from surface, if necessary.) Cover jar with a tight-fitting lid; refrigerate up to 6 months.

Makes 4 cups. Hands-on 15 min.; Total 15 min., plus 7 days for standing

3 MORE TO TRY

Back 40 Beer Vinegar
The brewers at Gadsden, Alabama's Back 40 Brewery craft this golden elixir by fermenting leftover beer. It's really great with greens. *backfortybeer.com/store*

Kerala Curry Tomato Chutney
Your hot dogs just got 10 times better with this dynamic Pittsboro, North Carolina, sauce. *keralacurry.com*

Pickled Pink Pickles
Our staff goes crazy for former *SL* Test Kitchen Director Lyda Burnette's sweet and sassy pickled goods. *pickledpinkfoods.com*

D
DUKE'S
MAYO

Several friends recently chipped in and surprised me with a painting of a jar of Duke's Mayonnaise. I framed it and hung it above my mantel. "Your mantel?" my mother questioned.

I'm not the only one with a Duke's art collection. As Erin Hatcher, brand manager for Duke's Mayonnaise at the C.F. Sauer Co. in Richmond, Virginia, told me, the company receives countless paintings of Duke's each year, alongside fan letters and pitches for TV commercials. That isn't a new phenomenon. After Eugenia Duke founded her first enterprise, Duke's Sandwiches, in Greenville, South Carolina, in 1917, she was inundated with letters from soldiers who'd been stationed at nearby Camp Sevier. Home after World War I, they requested her mayonnaise recipe: oil, egg yolks, and cider vinegar (for tang) but no sugar (which was rationed during wartime).

It's the same recipe that's praised today—in part, for reasons that first spurred its popularity nearly a century ago. Sold to Greenville drugstore lunch counters, army canteens, textile mills, and the Duke Tea Room in the Ottaray Hotel, Eugenia Duke's mayonnaise has long been an equal-opportunity spread—at home on white bread sandwiches and crudités.

Duke's is a monarch for the people. And a portrait of royalty belongs above the mantel.
—*Emily Wallace*

E
JOHN
EGERTON

Before Brooklyn brunched on buttermilk biscuits and grits guest starred on West Coast menus, there was John Egerton. He died last November, but his legacy—of celebrating and preserving the diversity and complexity of Southern food—is everywhere, starting with the chefs he mentored, the farmers he championed, and the writers he influenced. John's book *Southern Food: At Home, On The Road, In History* will remain a permanent fixture in our libraries. It reveals the beautiful and brutal stories of how we came to know and love cornbread, country ham, and collard greens, while sparking conversations about race and class. He set a table where all could gather over love for Southern food, and to that we raise high our glasses of sweet tea. *—Hannah Hayes*

F
FRIED CHICKEN *AND* CHAMPAGNE

We get that you don't always have time to fry chicken at home. And in this age of convenience, there's no shame in picking up a bucket of bird. But which one's the best? We blind-tasted our way through nine widely available brands—from big-box supermarkets to fast-food chains—in the *SL* Test Kitchen and evaluated the samples (all dark meat, all served at room temperature) for tenderness, crispness, greasiness, and overall flavor. Here, the top five take-out options that have us waving our wings.

1 | POPEYES LOUISIANA KITCHEN
It's tender and juicy with seasoning that goes deep, all the way from crust to bone. (Get this: It *tastes* like chicken.) The Cajun version vaunts a balanced heat that starts up front with white pepper, followed by waves of red pepper for a subtle afterburn. Bonus: The paper packaging is vented, which keeps the crust from steaming to wilted flab inside the box. We wouldn't blame you for trying to pass this off as your own.

2 | PUBLIX
This fowl hits the fried bird trifecta for flavor (we detect celery salt), crunch (deeply satisfying and crust-shattering), and grease factor (extremely low—it's eat-while-you-drive chicken). Leftovers held up well in the fridge, making this a prime candidate for picnics, family reunions, and church suppers.

3 | MRS. WINNER'S CHICKEN & BISCUITS
The golden brown crust, a flour-coated relief map with a glitter-like smattering of black pepper, conceals supremely juicy

meat. While fewer locations of this Georgia-founded chain dot the asphalt landscape than in years past, the chicken still holds court.

4 | LEE'S FAMOUS RECIPE CHICKEN
Modest-size thighs and legs are enveloped in a pale blond, almost buttery crust (our guess: the result of frying in vegetable shortening). At this 48-year-old franchise founded by Lee Cummings, nephew of KFC's Colonel Harland Sanders, they hand-bread, dip in honey, and then pressure-fry every piece of chicken.

5 | KFC
We're betting "finger lickin' good" wasn't an accidental tagline—this chicken was the greasiest of the test. The Original recipe didn't win any fans. But the Extra Crispy got high marks for its beautifully mottled crust and rich flavor. Among those top secret herbs and spices, we nosed out onion and garlic powder and heaps of black pepper. *—Jennifer V. Cole*

BUBBLIN' OVER

There's no better pairing than Champagne and fried chicken—and not just because it's the perfect mix of high and low we Southerners love so much. Its effervescent acidity works as the ultimate grease cutter, keeping your palate crisp and clean as you chow through the salty deliciousness of fried yardbird. You don't have to spend big, but do opt for a dry sparkling wine, such as Spanish cava. Prosecco, with its frothy bubbles and higher sugar, just doesn't cut the fat.

G

GULF

AND

ATLANTIC SEAFOOD

Consider this: "A full 91% of seafood Americans eat comes from abroad," writes author Paul Greenberg in his important new book *American Catch*, even though our local waters often teem with fresh fish and shellfish. This summer, demand local. You may pay a little more, but chances are you'll be buying better quality seafood and supporting local fishermen.

Here's how it works:
At restaurants, ask the chef where the seafood comes from. At the market, develop a relationship with the fishmonger, and use your senses. Do the fish glisten? Is the ice plentiful? Most important, ask to smell everything you buy. Fish should never smell fishy or like ammonia; it should smell briny and clean, just like the sea. —*Hunter Lewis*

WHOLE FISH: *Look for firm flesh that springs back to the touch, bright red gills, and clear eyes, telltale signs of freshness for fish like pompano and red snapper. Bonus: Whole fish costs less per pound than fillets.*

BLUE CRAB: *Buy hard-shell and soft-shell crabs fresh, aka alive, and not foaming at the mouth. Picked crabmeat prices are skyrocketing due to labor costs and historically low catches.*

WHITE, BROWN, AND PINK SHRIMP: *Most "fresh" shrimp have been flash frozen and defrosted, so buy them frozen if you're not cooking them immediately. For defrosted shrimp, buy in the shell and peel yourself; they should feel firm and look plump. Whether you buy large (26-30 per pound) or mediums (41-50 per pound), make sure they're shrimp from North Carolina to Texas.*

FILLETS: *Fillets of white flaky fish such as flounder and denser black grouper should be firm to the touch. Avoid any fillets with an oily sheen or excessive "gapping" in the flesh, or any stored in standing water.*

H
HERBS

Kitchen herbs grown right in my backyard are the fresh secret to my summer cooking. I grill outside every night and use them to add jolts of flavor to marinades, salad dressings, herb butters, and sauces; when I'm grilling or smoking meats, I stuff them into the cavity of chicken or tie hardy ones like rosemary and thyme together to use as basting brushes. What's more, growing herbs is cheaper than buying them. See how I plant them in a strawberry pot. —*Pam Lolley*

HOW TO PLANT

1. Start with a terra-cotta pot with holes (aka strawberry pot). We prefer a 3-gallon one. Fill bottom third with good-quality potting soil.

2. Insert plants into holes; fill soil gently around the roots.

3. Add soil to next level. Repeat all the way to the top. Place in full sun. Water regularly.

TIP: Plant largest herb on the top.

I
INDIE FOOD MEDIA

A whole new wave of writers and photographers are eschewing traditional platforms to share the modern foodscape in their own ways. Welcome to the age of indie food media. The grassroots **Authentic South** (*authenticsouth.com*) podcast serves up a host of genuine characters, from the watermen of Tangier Island to Knoxville's Biscuit Queen. South Louisiana-based **Runaway Dish** (*runawaydish.org*) hosts dinners to bring communities together, and documents all the players (chefs, farmers, and producers) in a culinary journal that, in turn, opens up that community to the outside world. And in **Short Stack** (*short stackeditions.com*), a series of single-topic pamphlets (tomatoes, grits, buttermilk), recipes and their inspiration come together with the soul of a modern community cookbook. —*Jennifer V. Cole*

J
JONES VALLEY TEACHING FARM

The South's most dynamic urban farm is sowing the seeds for Birmingham's next generation

At Jones Valley Teaching Farm in downtown Birmingham, chickens scratch and strut in their coop as rush hour traffic rumbles down U.S. 31 nearby. Young persimmon trees blossom at the edge of the same field where the South's best chefs cook a fund-raising dinner at the end of every summer. It's all too easy to become entranced by the ragged beauty of this urban-pastoral scene, but there's a more meaningful mission under-foot here on this once-vacant lot, one hinted at by local elementary school students digging in the dirt today.

"Students learn best by doing," says Grant Brigham, the farm's executive director. "The goal is to get students to eat more fruits and vegetables. The evidence says it must happen at a young age. Students don't need to be told how or what to do. They need to taste it, feel it, and experience it."

The South's most dynamic urban farm is investing in one of the South's most beleaguered cities by empowering thousands of young students to change their lives. With vegetables. Grant's team takes the farm's curriculum into a handful of Birmingham City Schools through Good School Food, a two-year-old flagship program composed of student-run farmers' markets, grow-your-own tutorials, and cooking classes at *Southern Living* and sister magazine *Cooking Light*. The early results show promise. Four out of every five families who learned how to cook healthy dinners in our test kitchens say they now cook more as a family. The farm's assessments reveal that students who participate in these programs are improving in subjects like math and science and learning skills like critical thinking and creativity. The work forecasts a brighter future for Birmingham. Jones Valley is a lot like those persimmon trees: If you patiently plant, cultivate, and prune, a community will bear fruit for years to come. (To meet student leader Kenneth Taylor, see below.)—*Hunter Lewis*

WHAT I'VE LEARNED
FROM JONES VALLEY TEACHING FARM

EDITOR'S NOTE: We met Kenneth, a sixth-grader at Richard J. Arrington Middle School, through the farm's Good School Food program two years ago. The program is designed to increase access to healthy food and improve school performance.

ON COMMUNITY: "Jones Valley gives kids courage to go out into the community. Sometimes at these city schools, kids don't have things to do at home except play video games or doing the same thing over and over. For me, I can go home, water my plants, taste them. When Mom gets home, I can cook them. I can make something that's successful in life."

ON THE STUDENT FARMERS' MARKET: "I started with the Student Farmers' Market in fourth grade at Glen Iris Elementary School. I've learned about good customer service, how to manage a job, and how to grow plants and food. Show up on time, be helpful, and be open to the customers, employees, and coworkers. Since we did so good [earning $1,600 the first season], we gave half the money to Oliver Elementary to start their farmers' market. That's called paying it forward."

ON ROOTS: "I learned about the life cycle of a plant: the roots, the stem, and the main part. The roots give the plant all the food and water to make it grow and be healthy. I have stronger roots because of Jones Valley."

ON VEGETABLES: "My first favorite is asparagus. My second is okra. My first favorite fruit is strawberries, and my second favorite is blackberries."

ON JVTF'S FAMILY KITCHEN: "We're cooking more as a family now. I'm the chef at home. I make Parmesan Tilapia with Ragu. I entered another recipe, Shrimp and Veggie Sketti, in Michelle Obama's recipe competition. It's really good. We're having it this Saturday night!"

ON THE FUTURE: "When I grow up, I want to become an entrepreneur and make my own business. I thought about making a business like Jones Valley." —*Kenneth Taylor*

K
KITCHEN GADGETS

It was a summertime process my grandmothers knew well. Corn was gathered on the family farms, and within hours they had fresh plump cobs in their kitchens. Both inherited wooden corn creamers that were worn from years in their own mothers' hands. I remember their fingers gracefully sliding the corn down the creamer's blade to force the natural corn milk and crushed kernels into the waiting colored Pyrex bowl. Velvety creamed corn simply can't be replicated with a knife. —*Rebecca Lang*

CREAMED CORN

Keep an eye on the corn as it simmers; it needs to cook only until it's tender. If it starts to dry out and stick to the skillet, add water a little at a time.

- 13 ears fresh corn, husked
- 1/4 to 1/2 cup heavy cream
- 1 Tbsp. unsalted butter
- 1/2 tsp. table salt
- 1/8 tsp. freshly ground black pepper
  Minced chives (optional)

Cut kernels from cobs to yield 6 cups; discard cobs. Cook kernels in a small Dutch oven over low heat, stirring often, about 30 minutes or until tender. (To prevent corn from drying out, add up to 10 Tbsp. water, 1 Tbsp. at a time as needed, during last 15 minutes of cook time.) Stir in cream and butter; cook, stirring occasionally, about 5 minutes or until mixture reaches desired consistency. Stir in salt and pepper. Sprinkle with chives, if desired.

Makes 6 to 8 servings. Hands-on 30 min., Total 1 hour

L
LATTICE PIE

Unexpected but oh-so right, a touch of tangy-sweet balsamic vinegar combined with honey, cinnamon, and a pinch of freshly ground black pepper magnifies the sweetness of blueberries. We love this buttery crust, but if time is short, substitute a store-bought one and simply crimp the edges. —*Marian Cooper Cairns*

HONEY-BALSAMIC-BLUEBERRY PIE

(Pictured on page 11)

CRUST

- 3 cups all-purpose flour
- 3/4 cup cold butter, sliced
- 6 Tbsp. cold vegetable shortening, sliced
- 1 tsp. kosher salt
- 4 to 6 Tbsp. ice-cold water

FILLING

- 7 cups fresh blueberries
- 1/4 cup cornstarch
- 2 Tbsp. balsamic vinegar
- 1/2 cup sugar
- 1/3 cup honey
- 1 tsp. vanilla extract
- 1/4 tsp. kosher salt
- 1/4 tsp. ground cinnamon
- 1/8 tsp. finely ground black pepper
- 2 Tbsp. butter, cut into 1/4-inch cubes
- 1 large egg

1. Prepare Crust: Process first 4 ingredients in a food processor until mixture resembles coarse meal. With processor running, gradually add 4 Tbsp. ice-cold water, 1 Tbsp. at a time, and process until dough forms a ball and pulls away from sides of bowl, adding up to 2 Tbsp. more water, 1 Tbsp. at a time, if necessary. Divide dough in half, and flatten each half into a disk. Wrap each disk in plastic wrap, and chill 2 hours to 2 days.

2. Prepare Filling: Place 1 cup blueberries in a large bowl; crush blueberries with a wooden spoon. Stir cornstarch and vinegar into crushed berries until cornstarch dissolves. Stir sugar, next 5 ingredients, and remaining 6 cups blueberries into crushed berry mixture.

3. Unwrap 1 dough disk, and place on a lightly floured surface. Sprinkle with flour. Roll dough to 1/8-inch thickness. Fit dough into a greased (with butter) 9-inch deep-dish pie plate. Repeat rolling procedure with remaining dough disk; cut dough into 12 to 14 (1/2-inch-wide) strips. (You will have dough left over.)

4. Pour blueberry mixture into piecrust, and dot with butter cubes. Arrange piecrust strips in a lattice design over filling. Trim excess dough.

5. Reroll remaining dough, and cut into 6 (9- x 1/2-inch) strips. Twist together 2 strips at a time. Whisk together egg and 1 Tbsp. water. Brush a small amount of egg mixture around edge of pie. Arrange twisted strips around edge of pie, pressing lightly to adhere. Brush entire pie with remaining egg mixture. Freeze 20 minutes or until dough is firm.

6. Preheat oven to 425°. Bake pie on an aluminum foil-lined baking sheet 20 minutes. Reduce oven temperature to 375°, and bake 20 more minutes. Cover pie with aluminum foil to prevent excessive browning, and bake 25 to 30 more minutes (65 to 70 minutes total) or until crust is golden and filling bubbles in center. Remove from baking sheet to a wire rack; cool 1 hour before serving.

Makes 8 servings. Hands-on 40 min.; Total 5 hours, 5 min.

M

MARINADE

Make your marinades work smarter. This dreamy one for pork doubles as a flavoring agent and a finishing glaze.

JUST PEACHY MARINADE

Whisk together 1/2 cup **peach preserves,** 1/2 cup **olive oil,** 1/4 cup **apple cider vinegar,** 3 Tbsp. fresh **lemon juice,** 2 Tbsp. coarse-grained **Dijon mustard,** 1 1/2 tsp. kosher **salt,** and 1 tsp. black **pepper** in a small bowl. Place 1 cup marinade and 4 pork chops or 2 tenderloins in a large zip-top plastic freezer bag. Seal; turn to coat. Reserve remaining marinade. Chill 2 to 4 hours. Remove pork; discard used marinade. Sprinkle pork with salt and pepper. Grill as desired; baste with reserved marinade during last 5 minutes.

Makes 1 1/2 cups. Hands-on 10 min.; Total 10 min., not including pork

N

NORTH CAROLINA'S

VIVIAN HOWARD

Small-town girl moves to New York City, learns to cook, then moves home to Kinston to open Chef & the Farmer. Fast-forward eight years later. Her PBS show, *A Chef's Life,* wins a Peabody Award, shining a light on her rural region. We asked Vivian to talk about how the show has changed her life. —*Hunter Lewis*

"I FEEL A GREAT responsibility to eastern North Carolina now. We come from an area where we're always apologizing for being from here. Because the series is so popular, people here have a little pep in their step. They say, 'You made me remember the way my grandmother made biscuits or strawberry preserves.' Older folks in our community teach me how to make something very simple. One of the things I like about the show and dislike about modern media in general is that [our culture is] very young-person-new-ideas driven, and I don't think people call on the wisdom of older folks very much. To learn from them and share has been wonderful."

O

OKRA

Okra thrives in the scorching heat of humid summers, soaring skyward in its semitropical glory. Originally from Africa, it is as overtly Southern as sweet tea and kudzu. Luckily for us, we have the inside secret when it comes to the delectable pods—no other people embrace okra as Southerners do. —*Virginia Willis*

SMASHED FRIED OKRA

What a revelation! Use a meat mallet to smash okra and create more surface area for crispy-brown goodness. Try this at home.

- 1 lb. fresh okra
- 1 1/2 cups buttermilk
- 2 cups fine yellow cornmeal
  Kosher salt and freshly ground black pepper
  Canola oil

1. Use a meat mallet to smash okra, starting at tip of pod and working toward stem end. Place buttermilk in a shallow dish, and place cornmeal in another shallow dish. Stir desired amount of salt and pepper into buttermilk and cornmeal. Dip okra in buttermilk; dredge in cornmeal, shaking off excess.

2. Pour oil to a depth of 2 inches into a large Dutch oven; heat to 350°. Fry okra, in batches, 2 to 3 minutes or until brown and crisp, turning once. Remove okra, using a slotted spoon; drain on paper towels. Add salt and pepper to taste; serve.

Makes 4 to 6 servings. Hands-on 40 min., Total 40 min.

SKILLET-ROASTED OKRA AND SHRIMP

Adapted from Virginia Willis' latest book, Okra, *published by The University of North Carolina Press, this fast sauté is great over grits or a bed of arugula.*

- 1/2 **lb. fresh okra, halved lengthwise**
- 3 **Tbsp. olive oil, divided**
- 1 **pt. grape tomatoes**
- 1 **lb. peeled, large raw shrimp, deveined**
- 1/2 **tsp. dried crushed red pepper**
- 3 **garlic cloves, minced**
- 1 **tsp. kosher salt**
- 1/2 **tsp. freshly ground black pepper**
- 2 **Tbsp. chopped fresh flat-leaf parsley**

Sauté okra in 1 Tbsp. hot olive oil in a large cast-iron skillet over medium-high heat 4 to 5 minutes or until lightly browned. Transfer okra to a large bowl. Add tomatoes and 1 Tbsp. oil to skillet; sauté 3 minutes or until skins begin to burst. Transfer tomatoes to bowl with okra. Add shrimp and remaining 1 Tbsp. oil to skillet; sprinkle shrimp with red pepper. Sauté 2 to 3 minutes or just until shrimp turn pink. Add garlic; sauté 30 seconds. Stir in okra mixture, and sauté 1 to 2 minutes or until hot. Stir in salt, pepper, and parsley.

Makes 6 to 8 servings. Hands-on 30 min., Total 30 min.

Macerated Peaches with Ancho-Cinnamon Sugar

P
PEACH TRUCK

I spotted the '64 Jeep Gladiator-turned-farmers'- market-on-wheels in a Nashville parking lot last summer. The truck's owners, Stephen and Jessica Rose, were selling just one thing: peaches. But not just any peaches. These were Georgia peaches from Pearson Farm in—get this—Peach County, and they tasted just as amazing as the story of how Stephen and Jessica have solved Nashville's "peach problem." Stephen grew up in Peach County where his aunt and uncle run an orchard, and he assumed that every peach was as spectacular as the ones he ate there. But when he moved north to Tennessee in 2009, he tasted the local fruit and realized not all peaches were created equal. So, Stephen and Jessica began trucking Georgia's finest into the area, and now they're available to the masses via the couple's Farm to Porch program. Need peaches? Go to thepeachtruck. com. —*Robby Melvin*

MACERATED PEACHES WITH ANCHO-CINNAMON SUGAR

Spoon this incredibly versatile and saucy condiment over vanilla ice cream for an easy summer dessert. Or use it as a topper for pound cake or oatmeal or as the filling for a cobbler or tart. Bonus: It's also a flavorful accompaniment with grilled meats. (Also pictured on page 10)

- 2 **Tbsp. sugar**
- 1 **Tbsp. extra virgin olive oil**
- 1 **Tbsp. thinly sliced fresh mint**
- 2 **tsp. ground cinnamon**
- 1 1/2 **tsp. ancho chile powder**
- 1 **tsp. honey**
  Pinch of kosher salt
- 2 **tsp. lime zest**
- 2 **Tbsp. fresh lime juice**
- 2 **lb. fresh peaches, unpeeled and quartered**

Stir together first 9 ingredients in a large bowl. Add peaches; toss gently to coat. Cover and chill 1 hour.

Makes 6 to 8 servings. Hands-on 15 min.; Total 1 hour, 15 min.

Q

THE CULTURE OF
SMOKE AND FIRE

Nothing fires up a Southern crowd like barbecue. From a modern-day pitmaster to the ultimate whole hog road trip to a succulent smoked chicken recipe, we salute the meat of the matter with an ode to "Q"

KAMADO GRILLS

THE PITMASTER
AARON FRANKLIN

In 2009 Aaron Franklin began serving barbecue out of a trailer in East Austin, Texas. In a region already intimate with exalted smoked meats, Aaron's brisket proved so transcendent that folks practically started speaking in tongues. Two years later, Aaron moved into a funky building near the original site, and the lines grew—all the way down the block. Now, the two-hour-plus wait equates to a pilgrimage. His brisket is the silkiest possible expression of carnivorous rapture, but he also excels in velvety pulled pork. Aaron has appeared as a judge on Destination America's BBQ Pitmasters series, will debut his own instructional PBS show early next year, and is writing his first book. But Aaron is no flash-in-the-pan attention hog. Those trailing lines? So worth it. And behind the service counter, Aaron is ceaselessly friendly to famished customers, making it impossible not to like the guy. His mug may be known across the land, yet he still shows up at 2 a.m. to tend the day's fires—just another reason why Aaron is the new face of BBQ. franklinbarbecue.com

THE UP-&-COMER
GEORGIA BARBECUE

Consider Georgia the great melting pot of 'cue. It eludes a fixed identity and has emerged as an enthralling nexus of styles. Places like **Grand Champion BBQ** (*gcbbq.net*) outside Atlanta and **Southern Soul Barbeque** (*southernsoulbbq.com*) on St. Simons Island specialize in finessed versions of several smoked meats: pork shoulder, ribs, and beef brisket. Georgia joints often offer many regional sauces. **Swallow at the Hollow** (*swallowatthehollow.com*) in Roswell has three: North Carolina vinegar, South Carolina mustard, and a sweet Kansas City tomato. The state's lack of convention allows it to be an incubator for new 'cue frontiers. At Atlanta's **Heirloom Market BBQ** (*heirloommarketbbq.com*), Southerner Cody Taylor and Korean pop star Jiyeon Lee merge backgrounds with dishes like chile-marinated pulled pork with kimchi slaw. Unorthodox? Yes. Delectable? Absolutely. —*Philip Malkus*

Forget the Harley. Forget the F-150. The rig we want for Father's Day is a kamado-style grill. The secret behind smoky ribs, brag-worthy briskets, and pitmaster-perfect pork shoulders, these dynamic ceramic cylinders on steroids have been known to induce OCD, aka Obsessive Ceramic Disorder, in hard-core backyard BBQ enthusiasts. Made for grilling, smoking, roasting, or baking over high or low charcoal heat, their smart design takes inspiration from the ceramic ovens that enterprising GIs brought home from Japan after World War II. Now, Georgia is world HQ for brands like Grill Dome, Big Green Egg, Primo, and Kamado Joe. —*Hunter Lewis*

SMOKED CHICKEN WITH FRESH HERB MARINADE

"Instead of a sauce, [this recipe] features a tasty marinade of fresh herbs and bright lemon juice," writes pitmaster Chris Lilly, in Fire & Smoke. *"By cooking the chicken in a pan instead of directly on the grill grate, the meat gets extra protection from drying out."*

- 6 Tbsp. olive oil
- 1/4 cup peanut oil
- 1/4 cup chopped fresh flat-leaf parsley
- 2 Tbsp. chopped fresh basil
- 2 Tbsp. chopped fresh oregano
- 2 Tbsp. fresh lemon juice
- 2 Tbsp. Dijon mustard
- 4 tsp. dark brown sugar
- 4 tsp. Worcestershire
- 1 garlic clove, minced
- 2 tsp. table salt
- 1/2 tsp. black pepper
- 1 (3- to 3 1/2-lb.) whole chicken, halved
- 1 cup hickory chips

THE BEST 65 MILES OF "Q"

THE TAR HEEL STATE'S flat, fertile coastal plain frames the most sacred sweep of barbecue holy land in the South. Eastern North Carolina is whole hog country. In fragrant clouds of smoke and steam, the region's best pitmasters painstakingly cleave the meat from slow-cooked, wood-scented pigs. The region's time-honored sauce is vinegar-based and administered with a light hand. Discover the singular spin each joint puts on its sublime chopped pork and distinctive sides by making your own scrumptious pilgrimage.

❶ GRADY'S BARBECUE, *Dudley, NC*
Steve Grady buys his hogs from a producer a mile down the road and sleeps only a few hours a night while tending his brick pits solo. His dedication yields smoky pork that melts on the tongue, amped up by the region's spiciest sauce, rife with chile flakes. *919/735-7243*

❷ WILBER'S BARBECUE
Goldsboro, NC
Wilber's basks in its status as a community institution since 1962. Beach-goers make it a habitual stop, as do devotees of the wood-smoked pork (whose sauce thrums with extra zing), oblong hush puppies, and crispy fried chicken thighs. *wilbersbarbecue.com*

❸ JACK COBB AND SON BARBECUE PLACE
Farmville, NC
The only seating at this Wednesday/Friday/Saturday spot is a screened hut with picnic tables. Stop for the pork sandwich, topped with mustardy slaw, and soulful veggies, such as stewed cabbage and vinegar-tinged potatoes. *252/753-5128*

❹ MORRIS BARBEQUE
Hookerton, NC
Arrive at this joint—open only on Saturday—by 1 p.m., lest the locals clean out the place first. Seek this one out for the exquisite harmony among its finely tuned dishes, with frilly, freshly made coleslaw balancing the piquant pork. *morrisbarbeque.com*

❺ BUM'S RESTAURANT, *Ayden, NC*
Less than a mile from Skylight Inn, this charmer with turquoise booths shows how different whole hog 'cue can be, even in the same town. The Dennis family chops pork more coarsely and mixes in less skin for a leaner, more velvety result. *bumsrestaurant.com*

❻ SKYLIGHT INN, *Ayden, NC*
You can't miss the building with a replica of the United States Capitol dome atop its roof. Samuel Jones and his family fold a goodly amount of crispy bronzed skin into the unctuous pork (minced so vigorously they replace the wooden chopping block every year). *skylightinnbbq.com*

R
ROADSIDE STANDS

Take a drive with Georgia poet Betty Gwen Barlow in this excerpt from her poem The Gift:

*Give me the gift of time
to travel the byways
and back roads*

*And fresh eyes to see
fat, contented cows
grazing in green lush pastures
of sweet sweet clover*

*And the privilege to stop
where and when I please
at any roadside stand
for big Vidalia onions
and ripe Elberta peaches*

1. Whisk together first 12 ingredients. Pour mixture into a 1-gal. zip-top plastic freezer bag; add chicken. Seal bag, and turn to coat. Chill chicken 8 to 12 hours.
2. Pile hot coals on 1 side of grill, leaving other side empty. Let grill heat up, covered with grill lid, 10 minutes or until internal temperature reaches 300°. (Go to *southern-living.com/bbqchicken* for gas grill instructions.)
3. Place chicken, skin-side up, in a 13- x 9-inch disposable aluminum foil pan. Pour marinade over chicken. Sprinkle hickory chips over hot coals. Place pan with chicken on unlit side of grill.

4. Grill, covered with grill lid and maintaining internal temperature at 300°, 2 hours or until a meat thermometer inserted in thickest portion registers 175°. Spoon pan drippings over chicken.

Makes 4 servings. Hands-on 30 min.; Total 10 hours, 30 min.

S

SIMPLE SYRUPS

These inventive seasonal tinctures—crafted for you to keep in the refrigerator all summer long—give iced tea or cocktails an extra-fresh zing. Now ain't that sweet?

❶ ORANGE-TARRAGON SYRUP

Bring 2 cups **sugar,** 1 cup **fresh orange juice,** 1 cup water, and ½ cup loosely packed **fresh tarragon** leaves to a boil in a medium saucepan over medium-high heat, stirring just until sugar dissolves. Boil 2 minutes. (Do not stir.) Remove from heat. Press through a wire-mesh strainer into a bowl, using back of a spoon to squeeze out liquid; discard solids. Cool completely (about 30 minutes). Transfer to a jar; cover and refrigerate up to 3 months.

Makes 2½ cups. Hands-on 10 min., Total 40 min.

❷ LAVENDER-MINT SYRUP

Bring 2 cups **sugar,** 2 cups water, 1 cup loosely packed fresh **mint** leaves, and 1 Tbsp. **dried lavender buds** to a boil in a medium saucepan over medium-high heat, stirring just until sugar dissolves. Boil 2 minutes. (Do not stir.) Remove from heat. Press through a wire-mesh strainer into a bowl, using back of a spoon to squeeze out liquid; discard solids. Cool completely (about 30 minutes). Transfer to a jar; cover and refrigerate up to 3 months.

Makes 2½ cups. Hands-on 10 min., Total 40 min.

❸ STRAWBERRY-CHILE SYRUP

Bring 2 cups **sugar,** 2 cups water, 1 cup fresh sliced **strawberries,** and ¼ tsp. dried crushed **red pepper** to a boil in a medium saucepan over medium-high heat, stirring just until sugar dissolves. Boil 2 minutes. (Do not stir.) Remove from heat. Press through a wire-mesh strainer into a bowl, using back of a spoon to squeeze out liquid; discard solids. Cool completely (about 30 minutes). Transfer to a jar; cover and refrigerate up to 3 months.

Makes 2½ cups. Hands-on 15 min., Total 45 min.

❹ PINEAPPLE-BASIL SYRUP

Bring 2 cups **sugar,** 1 cup **pineapple juice,** and 1 cup water to a boil in a medium saucepan, stirring just until sugar dissolves. Boil 2 minutes. (Do not stir.) Remove from heat. Add 1 cup firmly packed **basil** leaves, and steep 10 minutes. Press through a wire-mesh strainer into a bowl, using back of a spoon to squeeze out liquid; discard solids. Cool completely (about 20 minutes). Transfer to a jar; cover and refrigerate up to 3 months.

Makes 2½ cups. Hands-on 10 min., Total 40 min.

T
TOMATO SANDWICH

Whether eaten at a white tablecloth spot or over the kitchen sink, this is the sandwich we wait for all year. Here's how to build an even better one.

1. The Tomatoes: Beefsteaks have an intensely robust flavor, while heirloom yellow tomatoes bring a less acidic, slightly sweet component to the party. Want even juicier tomatoes? Slice and season them with salt 10 minutes before assembling to coax out their juices.

2. The Bread: Whether you go with sourdough or a hearty, seeded, nutty artisanal loaf, slice it thick, smear with butter, and toast or cook on a griddle. The outside will stay crunchy, and the inside will yield just enough to absorb the commingling of tomato and mayo.

3. The Greenery: Totally necessary? No. But peppery arugula and soft, floral herbs like basil and oregano add kicky, fresh flavor, while a touch of fresh lemon juice brings out the acidity in the tomatoes.

4. The Bacon: Don't be a hog and let bacon steal the tomato show, but do cook it perfectly. Done right, thick-cut bacon adds a porcine pop of salt and fat and just enough crunchy chew to contrast the hot mess of everything else.

5. The Salt and Pepper: Season as you build the sandwich to elevate the flavor of every layer. Choose a flaky sea salt for a spark of crunch, and by all means, folks, make sure your pepper is freshly ground.

OVER-THE-TOP TOMATO SANDWICH

(Pictured on page 179)

- 8 artisan sourdough or multigrain bread slices
- 1/2 cup butter, melted
- 1 3/4 lb. ripe beefsteak or heirloom tomatoes (about 5 medium)
- 1/2 cup torn fresh basil leaves
- 2 Tbsp. fresh oregano leaves
- 3 Tbsp. extra virgin olive oil, divided
- 1/2 cup mayonnaise
- 4 1/2 tsp. fresh lemon juice, divided
- 3 cups loosely packed fresh arugula
- 8 thick bacon slices, cooked

1. Brush both sides of bread slices lightly with melted butter. Cook bread slices in a large skillet over medium-high heat 1 to 2 minutes on each side or until toasted.
2. Cut tomatoes into 1/4-inch-thick slices, and place in a single layer on a wire rack in a jelly-roll pan. Sprinkle generously with salt and pepper, and let stand 10 minutes.
3. Process basil, oregano, and 2 Tbsp. oil in a food processor or mini chopper until finely ground. Add mayonnaise and 1 Tbsp. lemon juice to processor; pulse until smooth.
4. Stir together remaining 1 Tbsp. oil and 1 1/2 tsp. lemon juice in a medium bowl; add arugula, and toss to coat. Spread mayonnaise mixture on 1 side of each bread slice. Layer 4 bread slices with tomato slices, arugula mixture, and 2 bacon slices. Top with remaining 4 bread slices, mayonnaise-side down.

Makes 4 servings. Hands-on 20 min., Total 30 min.

U
U-PICK

Want to save money on in-season produce, get outside, and support local business? Head on over to a U-Pick farm! We know picking is hard work, but just like from-scratch pie dough and slow-smoked barbecue, the things that take some effort are also the most satisfying. The South boasts more U-Pick farms than Junior Leagues, so this summer try your hand at everything from blueberries and bell peppers to cantaloupes and cucumbers.

Davey Dempsey, a fourth-generation farmer, has been hosting the public for nearly 40 years at Dempsey U-Pick Farm in St. Helena Island, South Carolina (*dempseyfarms upick.com*). Here are his tips for picking like a pro:

◆ **DON'T WEAR YOUR SUNDAY BEST.** Unless you want to christen your finery with dirt and fruit juice. Do wear a hat and sunscreen.

◆ **CALL AHEAD.** The farmer will tell you the conditions of the field and fruit. Wet produce is prone to bruising and bursting; give the fields a day or two to dry after heavy rain.

◆ **BE THE EARLY BIRD.** Beat the heat and bring home the cream of the day's crop.

◆ **COME HUNGRY.** Nothing beats gobbling up juicy, sun-warmed peaches, one right after the other.
—*Whitney Wright*

V
VEGETABLE PLATES
OF THE SOUTH

Forget steam table cookery. From delicate bites to boldly composed plates, it's a vegetable revolution.

Like pulled pork and fried chicken, the vegetable plate is embedded in the South's culinary DNA. In times when meat was scarce, savvy cooks tended fertile patches behind their homes to nourish their families with seasonal bounty. The practice is budding once again, as the earthen jewels at flourishing green markets entice us to cultivate our own backyards. And the baseline definition of the vegetable plate has started to shift. It once conjured the sprawling steam tables at our meat 'n' threes, where counter staff waited as we studied the daily selection: perhaps turnip greens or collards, fried green tomatoes or crispy okra. And if these regional staples sometimes came out of the kitchen cooked to pap? Well, we were still proud of ourselves for eating our veggies.

But now, inspired by the surging interest in farming, a hotbed of forward-looking chefs is retooling the (ahem) garden-variety vegetable plate. In the same way our kitchen masters embraced snout-to-tail, whole-animal cookery over the last decade, they're forging close relationships with local growers and composing symphonies of produce that show off the region's year-round harvests in center-stage glory. And this isn't a reaction to any kind of health craze: It's really about the ingredients' deliciousness. Welcome to the vegetable renaissance.

At Atlanta's **Miller Union** *(miller-union.com)*, executive chef Steven Satterfield leads the charge with a plate whose humble appearance—four ever-changing dishes mounded into quadrants like an edible pie chart—belies its sophisticated preparation. He considers contrasts in color, flavor, and texture: A succotash of corn and field peas bound with a splash of cream may sidle up to okra fried to order in a sheer cornmeal crust. To cut the richness, he'll also include, say, pickled beets punched up with ginger or sautéed zucchini tossed in a vinaigrette with garlic and just-picked mint. **Bottega** *(bottegarestaurant.com)*, one of Southern food icon Frank Stitt's destination eateries in Birmingham, similarly elevates a seemingly unassuming plate. The Thursday night special in Bottega's café is a montage of vegetables—this time of year expect summer squash, creamed corn, crisp-tender green beans perked with sweet onion, and braised collards—so farm-fresh, the sunshine still practically radiates off of them. The finishing touch: a wedge of jalapeño cornbread baked by the restaurant's beloved pastry chef, Dolester Miles.

Some of our best upscale restaurants reimagine the vegetable plate in bold new visual directions. At

Husk Nashville *(husknashville.com)*, chef-partner Sean Brock and his team present "A Sampling of Summer Vegetables" on a platter carved from a tree trunk. Each dish looks like edible sculpture: charred carrots dappled with their own leafy tops, fried cauliflower sweetened by seared petals of baby onions, butter beans dotted with purple and white garlic flowers. A hearty side bowl of grits in tomato broth with a preserved egg ensures you leave the table full.

It's certainly not easy to finish the cornucopia bursting from a handsome handled pan at Atlanta's **Restaurant Eugene** *(restauranteugene.com)*. A dozen or more individually prepared vegetables—from seared okra to delicate stewed cherry tomatoes to a tempura squash blossom tinted mauve from beet juice—huddle together and flaunt the kitchen's technical prowess.

Obviously, Restaurant Eugene and the other restaurants still serve plenty of meat. Their next-gen vegetable plates, though, enlighten us to the ways that the South's agrarian abundance can star in modern meals. We'll never give up on pork, but we can concede that produce—locally farmed, dazzlingly prepared—might pull focus now and again. —*Philip Malkus*

PARSLIED NEW POTATOES

- 2 Tbsp. butter
- 2 Tbsp. canola oil
- 2 Tbsp. all-purpose flour
- 2 1/2 cups milk
- 2 Tbsp. fresh lemon juice
- 1/2 tsp. garlic powder
- 1/4 tsp. sugar
  Table salt and black pepper
- 2 lb. new potatoes, quartered, boiled until tender and drained
- 1/4 cup loosely packed fresh flat-leaf parsley, chopped

Melt butter with oil in a medium skillet over medium-high heat. Whisk in flour, and cook, whisking constantly, 1 minute. Whisk in milk and next 3 ingredients, and cook, whisking constantly, 5 minutes or until mixture thickens. Add salt and pepper to taste. Pour over potatoes; toss to coat. Sprinkle with parsley; serve hot.

Makes 4 to 6 servings. Hands-on 20 min., Total 45 min.

GREEN BEANS AND CHARRED ONIONS

- 1 lb. fresh green beans, trimmed
- 1 large red onion, cut into 4 wedges
  Table salt and black pepper
- 2 Tbsp. olive oil, divided
- 1 garlic clove, minced
- 6 fresh thyme sprigs
- 2 Tbsp. red wine vinegar
- 1 Tbsp. butter
- 1/4 cup loosely packed fresh flat-leaf parsley, chopped
- 2 Tbsp. thinly sliced fresh chives

1. Cook beans in boiling salted water to cover in a Dutch oven over medium-high heat 4 minutes or until crisp-tender. Plunge beans into ice water to stop cooking process. Drain; pat dry.

2. Sprinkle onion wedges with salt and pepper, and cook in 1 Tbsp. hot olive oil in a large cast-iron skillet over medium-high heat 3 minutes on each side or until charred and tender. Remove onions from skillet; wipe skillet clean.

3. Cook garlic in remaining 1 Tbsp. oil in skillet over medium heat 30 seconds or until fragrant. Add beans and thyme, and cook, stirring occasionally, 3 minutes or until beans are slightly charred. Stir in vinegar, next 3 ingredients, and onion wedges; toss to coat. Remove from heat; sprinkle with salt and pepper. Serve hot.

Makes 4 servings. Hands-on 30 min., Total 30 min.

BUTTERY LADY PEAS

- 2 cups fresh lady peas
- 1/4 yellow onion
- 2 garlic cloves, crushed
- 1 tsp. kosher salt
- 6 fresh thyme sprigs
- 4 fresh flat-leaf parsley sprigs
  Kitchen string
- 2 Tbsp. butter
- 3 green onions, sliced
- 3 Tbsp. coarsely chopped fresh basil leaves
  Black pepper

1. Bring first 4 ingredients and 1 qt. water to a boil in a large saucepan over high heat. Tie together thyme and parsley with kitchen string. Reduce heat to low; add herb bundle, and simmer, stirring occasionally, 25 to 30 minutes or until peas are just tender. Drain peas, reserving 1/4 cup cooking liquid.

2. Melt butter in a medium skillet over medium heat. Stir in peas and reserved cooking liquid; cook 2 minutes. Discard herb bundle and onion wedge. Stir in green onions and basil. Add pepper to taste. Serve immediately.

Makes 4 servings. Hands-on 30 min., Total 55 min.

W

THE

WONDERS

OF

WHITE

Gravy is what we call that happy, inevitable mingling of sauce and drippings at the end of a meal. There is no single recipe for it, and there is no more perfect medium in this world than white bread for sopping up that gravy so indestructibly. Same goes for bacon grease, tomato juice, and mayonnaise. Have you ever tried sopping up those resulting juices with wheat bread? Have you ever tried sopping up anything with wheat bread? If you're a sad sucker like me, still jonesing for the sweet and greasy goodness of what you've just devoured, and stuck without a single slice of white in your health-conscious household, you know the futility of such a substitution. Your favorite barbecue joint probably has this figured out. At Cozy Corner in Memphis, the full rack comes with four untoasted slices. I don't know if it's the sodium stearoyl lactylate or the soy lecithin or the azodicarbonamide that produces such a glutinous miracle. Actually, let's not even go there. To get too deep into ingredients would be to invite the cynicism of nutrition. And this isn't about that. Last I checked, bacon and mayo weren't winning any beauty contests either. Because more than a filler or absorbent, white bread is a fast-fading memory, a time warp to the days when you were knee-high and spoon-fed and your pimiento cheese sandwich was still resolutely stuck to the roof of your mouth well into naptime and you didn't know how happy that would make you feel to remember. —*John M. Martin*

X

The South is no stranger to small-batch spirits. Moonshiners were microdistilling long before such a word existed. But the landscape of legal hooch has changed dramatically. According to the American Distilling Institute, the number of craft distilleries is growing by 30% each year. Southern makers from **Troy & Sons** (heirloom corn whiskey) and **Cathead** (vodka and gin) to **Richland Rum and High Wire Distilling Co.** (sugarcane rum) are just a few of the folks keeping us in good spirits. —*Jennifer V. Cole*

YETI COOLER

Anglers, hunters, and cold drink connoisseurs swear by Austin, Texas-based Yeti Coolers, the marvels of design coveted for their insulating power (they'll hold ice on a boat or at a tailgate during scorching hot days) as well as their legendary durability (the USDA's Interagency Grizzly Bear Committee certified them bear-proof). Hey, if you're gonna buy a cooler, might as well buy a grizzly stopper. —*Hunter Lewis*

FIVE TIPS FOR PACKING A COOLER

1. Freeze meats ahead of time in marinades. They'll help your cooler stay cold longer and will be ready to grill when thawed.

2. Pack all foods in airtight bags or sealed plastic containers to prevent cross-contamination.

3. Prechill your drinks before placing them in the cooler to preserve ice.

4. For long trips, bring one cooler for your food and another for drinks so you can reach for a cold drink anytime.

5. Block ice lasts longer than cubed. Make your own block by freezing water in doubled 1-gallon freezer bags.

AND TWO COOLER-PERFECT TREATS

CHEWY BROWNIES

This thin brownie makes killer ice-cream sandwiches. They also freeze well in a zip-top freezer bag and will slip into a small space in your cooler.

Vegetable cooking spray
3/4 cup butter
1 (4-oz.) bittersweet dark chocolate baking bar (60% cacao), chopped
1 1/4 cups sugar
2 large eggs
1 cup all-purpose flour
1 tsp. vanilla extract
1/4 tsp. baking powder
1/8 tsp. table salt

1. Preheat oven to 350°. Line bottom and sides of a 15- x 10-inch jelly-roll pan with aluminum foil, allowing 2 to 3 inches to extend over sides; lightly grease foil with cooking spray. Microwave butter and chocolate in a large microwave-safe bowl at HIGH 1 1/2 to 2 minutes or just until melted and smooth, stirring every 30 seconds.

Whisk in sugar. Add eggs, 1 at a time, whisking just until blended after each addition. Whisk in flour and next 3 ingredients. Pour mixture into prepared pan.

2. Bake at 350° for 18 to 20 minutes or until a wooden pick inserted in center comes out with a few moist crumbs. Cool completely on a wire rack. Lift brownies from pan, using foil as handles. Remove foil; cut into 24 squares.

Makes 12 servings. Hands-on 20 min.; Total 1 hour, 10 min.

MARINATED TOMATOES

This condiment travels well and is perfect for spooning over grilled fish, chicken, or steak, or tossing with pasta.

8 cups halved assorted grape tomatoes
1/4 cup kosher salt
1 large shallot, sliced
4 garlic cloves, sliced
1 1/2 cups olive oil
14 fresh thyme sprigs
1/3 cup white wine vinegar
1 (1-oz.) package fresh basil, torn
1/2 tsp. black pepper
Pinch of dried red pepper flakes

Toss together first 2 ingredients in a large glass bowl; let stand 30 minutes. Meanwhile, sauté shallot and garlic in hot oil in a medium saucepan over medium heat 6 minutes. Remove from heat, and stir in thyme. Cool completely. Toss together vinegar, next 3 ingredients, tomato mixture, and shallot mixture. Serve, or cover and refrigerate up to 2 weeks.

Makes 9 cups. Hands-on 30 min., Total 50 min.

Z
ZUCCHINI

Zucchini is the Rodney Dangerfield of summer vegetables: "No respect!" Give this underappreciated vegetable its due with two fresh new recipes.

BAKED ZUCCHINI CHIPS

(Also pictured on page 12)

- 1/2 cup panko (Japanese breadcrumbs)
- 1/4 cup loosely packed fresh basil leaves
- 1/4 tsp. kosher salt
- 1/4 cup finely grated Parmesan cheese
- 1/2 lb. zucchini, cut into 1/4-inch-thick rounds
- 1 Tbsp. olive oil
  Vegetable cooking spray

Preheat oven to 450°. Process first 3 ingredients in a food processor 10 to 15 seconds or until finely ground. Stir together breadcrumb mixture and cheese in a medium bowl. Toss zucchini rounds with oil. Dredge zucchini, 1 round at a time, in breadcrumb mixture, pressing gently to adhere. Place rounds in a single layer in a jelly-roll pan coated with cooking spray. Bake 30 minutes or until browned and crisp. Serve hot.

Makes 4 servings. Hands-on 20 min., Total 50 min.

ZUCCHINI-CARROT SALAD WITH CATALINA DRESSING

Dress thinly sliced vegetables with our fresh take on catalina dressing—inspired by two Birmingham chefs, Wil Drake and Roscoe Hall.

- 1 lb. zucchini
- 2 cups matchstick carrots
- 1/2 cup Catalina Dressing
- 1/4 cup firmly packed fresh mint leaves, coarsely chopped
- 2 Tbsp. thinly sliced fresh chives
  Kosher salt and freshly ground black pepper
- 1/2 cup French fried onions

Cut zucchini lengthwise into 1/8- to 1/4-inch-thick slices. Stack 2 or 3 slices on a cutting board, and cut lengthwise into thin strips. Repeat with remaining zucchini. Toss together zucchini, carrots, and desired amount of dressing; let stand 20 minutes, tossing occasionally. Sprinkle mint and chives over zucchini mixture, and add salt and pepper to taste. Top with French fried onions.

Makes 4 servings. Hands-on 15 min.; Total 40 min., including dressing

CATALINA DRESSING

Whisk together 1/2 cup **olive oil,** 1/4 cup **sugar,** 1/4 cup **ketchup,** 1/4 cup **red wine vinegar,** 1/4 cup grated sweet **onion,** 1/2 tsp. **paprika,** 1/2 tsp. **Worcestershire sauce,** 1/2 tsp. **hot sauce,** and salt and pepper to taste.

Makes 1 1/2 cups. Hands-on 5 min., Total 5 min.

Southern Living

THE
SUMMER
5
INGREDIENT
COOKBOOK

MAKE DINNER IN A FLASH WITH OUR
20 SUPER-FAST AND FRESH SEASONAL RECIPES

5 Porch-Perfect Appetizers

QUICK AND SIMPLE BITES MAKE FOR EASY, LAID-BACK SUMMER ENTERTAINING

ORANGE-BASIL YOGURT DIP

(Pictured on page 180)

Grate zest from 1 **orange** to equal 2 tsp. Cut orange in half, and squeeze juice from orange to equal 3 Tbsp. Stir together zest; orange juice; 1 1/2 cups **Greek yogurt;** 1 small **garlic clove,** grated; and 1/3 cup chopped fresh **basil** in a medium bowl. Add salt and pepper to taste. Refrigerate in an airtight container up to 3 days.

Makes 6 servings. Hands-on 20 min., Total 20 min.

PICKLED TINY TOMATOES

(Pictured on page 180)

- 3 pt. assorted grape tomatoes
- 2 cups seasoned rice vinegar
- 3 Tbsp. sugar
- 3 garlic cloves, thinly sliced
- 1 Tbsp. pickling spice
- 1 Tbsp. kosher salt
- 1 (1/2-inch) piece fresh ginger, peeled and sliced (optional)

Pierce each tomato 3 times using a wooden pick or skewer, and place tomatoes in a large glass bowl. Bring vinegar, next 4 ingredients and, if desired, ginger, and 1 1/2 cups water to a boil in a large saucepan over high heat. Remove from heat, and pour over tomatoes. Cool 1 hour. Cover and chill 24 hours before serving. Refrigerate in an airtight container up to 2 weeks.

Makes 12 to 16 servings. Hands-on 20 min.; Total 1 hour, 25 min., plus 1 day for chilling

BUTTERY GARLIC SHRIMP

(Pictured on page 180)

- 1 1/2 lb. peeled, large raw shrimp
- 1/2 cup butter, divided
- 5 garlic cloves, thinly sliced
- 1/2 cup dry white wine
- 1/2 tsp. kosher salt
- 1/2 tsp. freshly ground black pepper
- 1/4 cup chopped fresh flat-leaf parsley
  French bread baguette

1. Devein shrimp, if desired. Melt 2 Tbsp. butter in a large skillet over medium heat; add shrimp, and sauté 3 minutes or just until shrimp turn pink. Remove shrimp from skillet.
2. Add garlic to skillet, and sauté 30 seconds. Add wine, and cook, stirring constantly, 2 minutes. Stir in salt and pepper. Whisk in remaining butter, 1 Tbsp. at a time, and cook, whisking constantly, 2 to 3 minutes or until thickened. Remove from heat, and add parsley and cooked shrimp, tossing to coat. Serve with grilled French bread slices.

Makes 6 to 8 servings. Hands-on 15 min., Total 15 min.

PIMIENTO-STUFFED SUMMER SQUASH

- 1 (4-oz.) goat cheese log, softened
- 3 Tbsp. diced pimiento, drained
- 2 cooked bacon slices, finely chopped
- 1 Tbsp. chopped fresh basil
- 12 to 15 baby squash

1. Stir together goat cheese and next 3 ingredients until smooth; add salt and pepper to taste. If desired, stir in 1 to 2 tsp. water to reach desired consistency. Spoon mixture into a zip-top plastic freezer bag. Snip 1 corner of bag to make a 1/2-inch hole.
2. Cut top from each baby squash, and scoop seeds from bottom, using a small spoon. Pipe cheese mixture into bottom of each squash, and place top of squash over filling. Serve immediately.

Makes 6 servings. Hands-on 20 min., Total 20 min.

BAKED BRIE WITH JEZEBEL PEACHES

(Pictured on page 179)

- 1 Tbsp. hot jalapeño pepper jelly
- 1 tsp. spicy brown mustard
- 1/4 tsp. kosher salt
- 1/8 tsp. freshly ground black pepper
- 1 large ripe peach, peeled and diced
- 1 Brie round (about 13.2 oz.), packed in a wooden box
  Assorted crackers

1. Preheat oven to 350°. Stir together first 4 ingredients; gently stir in peaches until coated.
2. Unwrap Brie; trim and discard rind from top. Return cheese to wooden box bottom, and place box on a baking sheet.
3. Bake at 350° for 10 minutes. Spoon peach mixture over Brie, mounding slightly. Bake 5 minutes or until cheese is melted. Carefully transfer box to a platter, and serve immediately with crackers.

Makes 6 to 8 servings. Hands-on 15 min., Total 30 min.

THE *SL* TEST KITCHEN ACADEMY

Contributing Editor Marian Cooper Cairns, the quick-cooking mastermind behind our Summer Cookbook, shares her tips and tricks to minimizing your grocery list while maximizing flavor.

TAKE A PANTRY PASS
Here's your cheat sheet. The following six ingredients don't count against your total:

1. Olive oil + butter: Good quality fats taste better. Plus, a little bit goes a long way!

2. Flour: This is the key to fuss-free desserts such as fruit cobbler.

3. Sugar: Just a pinch balances flavor in dressings and marinades and helps meat caramelize.

4. Salt and pepper: A sprinkle is all you need to elevate ripe farmers' market finds into the perfect meal. (See seasoning tips at right.)

USE MORE HERBS
Nothing says summer like just-picked herbs. They'll instantly add bright, garden-fresh flavor to any dish. Don't be afraid to mix and match. For tips on growing your own, see page 131.

GRAB FRESH SALSA
Gourmet grocery store pineapple salsa and pico de gallo are colorful, healthy, and convenient. Marian uses them to top grilled meats or to add fresh flavor and bulk up simple side dishes.

GO INTERNATIONAL
Exotic ingredients are flavor bombs—exactly what you need when cooking with only five elements! Miso, a Japanese paste made from fermented soybeans, is a wonder stirred into dressings and sauces. Gochujang, a Korean chili paste, is another one of Marian's favorites. "It's spicy, earthy, and vibrant all at once."

SEASON LIKE A PRO
When used properly, salt and pepper make magic. They enhance flavor without hiding it. Season gently to start; taste and then season again before serving. You can always add, but you can't take away. And remember, cold food needs more seasoning than hot.

5 Easy-Does-It Main Dishes

SPICE UP SUPPER WITH FRESH INGREDIENTS, SMART TECHNIQUES, AND NEW TWISTS ON CROWD-PLEASING ENTRÉES

GRILLED SAUSAGES WITH ASPARAGUS

Mix up the sausages, and use chorizo, spicy Italian, or the turkey and chicken varieties available at the grocery store.

- 3 **lemons, halved and divided**
- 1/2 **cup refrigerated pesto sauce**
- 1/2 **cup toasted walnuts, chopped and divided**
- 2 **lb. fresh asparagus**
- 2 **Tbsp. olive oil**
- 2 **lb. sweet Italian sausage links**

1. Preheat grill to medium-high (350° to 400°) heat. Squeeze juice from 2 lemon halves to equal 2 Tbsp. Stir together pesto, lemon juice, and 1/4 cup walnuts. Snap off and discard tough ends of asparagus; toss asparagus with olive oil.

2. Grill sausage, without grill lid, 10 minutes or until thoroughly cooked, turning occasionally. At the same time, grill asparagus, without grill lid, 4 minutes or until tender. Brush asparagus with pesto mixture, and transfer to a serving platter. Grill remaining 4 lemon halves, cut sides down, 1 minute or until charred. Place on platter with asparagus. Slice sausage, and arrange on serving platter. Sprinkle with remaining 1/4 cup walnuts.

Makes 4 to 6 servings. Hands-on 20 min., Total 35 min.

KOREAN BUTTERMILK CHICKEN KABOBS

Gochujang is a Korean condiment with tons of bright, peppery flavor. It's made with chile peppers but is sweet enough for kids. Try it on grilled meat or stirred into mayonnaise for a sandwich. If you'd like, swap pieces of pork tenderloin or sirloin steak for the chicken.

- 1 1/2 **cups buttermilk**
- 1 **(10-oz.) bottle gochujang (Korean chili paste)**
- 2 **tsp. kosher salt**
- 1 **tsp. freshly ground black pepper**
- 3 **lb. skinned and boned chicken thighs, cut into 2-inch pieces**
- 10 **to 12 (10-inch) wooden or metal skewers**
- 3 **lemons**
  Vegetable cooking spray
- 1/2 **cup torn fresh cilantro leaves**

1. Stir together first 4 ingredients in a large shallow dish or zip-top plastic freezer bag. Add chicken, turning to coat. Cover or seal, and chill 1 to 3 hours.

2. Meanwhile, soak wooden skewers in water 30 minutes. (Omit if using metal skewers.) Cut each lemon into 8 wedges.

3. Coat cold cooking grate of grill with cooking spray, and place on grill. Preheat grill to 350° to 400° (medium-high) heat. Remove chicken from marinade, discarding marinade. Thread chicken and lemon wedges alternately onto skewers, leaving a 1/8-inch space between pieces.

4. Grill kabobs, covered with grill lid, 6 to 8 minutes on each side or until chicken is done. Transfer to a serving platter. Sprinkle with cilantro leaves.

Note: We tested with Annie Chun's Korean Sweet & Spicy Go-Chu-Jang.

Makes 6 to 8 servings. Hands-on 35 min.; Total 1 hour, 35 min.

ROASTED WHOLE TERIYAKI SNAPPER

It's time to embrace whole fish, which makes for easy roasting or grilling. Plus, the bones keep the meat tender and flavorful. Leave gutting and scaling to the fishmonger. (For more buying tips, see page 130.) To serve the cooked fish, peel back the skin, and starting at the backbone, lift the top fillet from the bone with a metal spatula. Then discard the skeleton, freeing the second fillet. (Pictured on page 180)

- 1 (3- to 3 1/2-lb.) red snapper, cleaned, with head and tail intact
  Parchment paper
- 2 tsp. kosher salt
- 1 1/2 tsp. freshly ground black pepper
- 1 large bunch fresh basil, stems and leaves separated
- 2 limes, thinly sliced
- 4 green onions, sliced
- 1/4 cup olive oil
- 1 cup teriyaki sauce

1. Preheat oven to 400°. Cut 3 diagonal slits, 1 1/2 inches apart, on each side of fish. Place fish in a parchment paper-lined jelly-roll pan. Let stand at room temperature 20 minutes. Sprinkle salt and pepper over fish and in cavity. Place basil stems, half of lime slices, and half of green onions in cavity. Drizzle olive oil over fish.
2. Bake at 400° for 35 to 40 minutes or until fish flakes with a fork. Let stand 10 minutes.
3. Transfer fish to a serving platter; drizzle 1/4 cup teriyaki sauce over fish. Top with basil leaves and remaining lime slices and green onions. Serve with remaining teriyaki sauce.

Note: We tested with Soy Vay Veri Veri Teriyaki Marinade and Sauce.

Makes 6 to 8 servings. Hands-on 20 min.; Total 1 hour, 25 min.

TOMATO-ORANGE MARMALADE CHICKEN

If you'd like the tomatoes to have a saucier consistency, once you've added the remaining tomatoes in Step 3, cover and simmer mixture over low heat for up to 10 minutes. (Pictured on page 180)

- 4 (6- to 8-oz.) skinned and boned chicken breasts
- 2 tsp. kosher salt
- 1 tsp. freshly ground black pepper
- 2 Tbsp. butter
- 1 pt. grape tomatoes, halved
- 3 Tbsp. sweet orange marmalade
- 2 tsp. red wine vinegar
- 1/3 cup loosely packed fresh basil leaves, chopped

1. Place each chicken breast between 2 sheets of heavy-duty plastic wrap, and flatten to 1/2-inch thickness, using a small skillet or flat side of a meat mallet. Sprinkle chicken with salt and pepper.
2. Melt 1 Tbsp. butter in a large skillet over medium-high heat. Cook 2 chicken breasts in skillet 4 minutes on each side or until done. Transfer to a serving platter; cover with aluminum foil to keep warm. Repeat procedure with remaining butter and chicken.
3. Reduce heat to medium-low; add 3 Tbsp. water and half of tomatoes. Cook 2 minutes, stirring to loosen browned bits from bottom of skillet. Stir in marmalade and vinegar; cook, stirring occasionally, 4 minutes or until tomatoes burst and sauce begins to thicken. Stir in remaining tomatoes, and cook 2 minutes or until thoroughly heated. Stir in basil; add salt and pepper to taste. Spoon sauce over chicken.

Makes 4 servings. Hands-on 35 min., Total 35 min.

COFFEE-RUBBED SKIRT STEAK

If you don't have chicory coffee, regular ground coffee or espresso works just as well. After grilling, slice the steak against the grain to ensure tender pieces of meat.

- 2 Tbsp. chili powder
- 1 Tbsp. sugar
- 1 Tbsp. kosher salt
- 1 Tbsp. finely ground chicory coffee
- 1 tsp. coarsely ground black pepper
- 2 (1 1/2-lb.) boneless skirt, flank, or tri-tip steaks
  Fresh fruit salsa
  Lime wedges

1. Preheat grill to 400° to 450° (high) heat. Stir together first 5 ingredients; rub over steaks. Let stand 30 minutes.
2. Grill, covered with grill lid, 3 to 5 minutes on each side or to desired degree of doneness. Let stand 5 minutes. Cut across the grain into thin strips; serve with salsa and lime wedges.

Note: We tested with Community Coffee Ground Coffee & Chicory and Whole Foods Pineapple-Mango salsa.

Makes 6 to 8 servings. Hands-on 15 min., Total 50 min.

5 Summery Sides

MIX AND MATCH THESE FRESH AND VIBRANT PAIRINGS WITH ANY MAINS,
OR SERVE THEM TOGETHER FOR A VEGETARIAN FEAST

HOT BACON CAPRESE SALAD

Update the Italian tomato salad with a rich, tart dressing.

- 2 ½ lb. heirloom tomatoes, cut into ½-inch slices
- 1 (16-oz.) package fresh mozzarella cheese, cut into ½-inch slices
- ½ cup fresh basil leaves
- 6 thick bacon slices, coarsely chopped
- 3 to 4 Tbsp. red wine vinegar
- 2 Tbsp. olive oil
- ½ tsp. kosher salt
- ½ tsp. freshly ground black pepper

1. Arrange tomatoes and cheese on a serving platter, placing basil leaves between slices. Sprinkle with desired amount of salt and pepper.
2. Sauté chopped bacon in a large skillet over medium heat 6 to 8 minutes or until crisp. Remove from heat, reserving bacon and 2 Tbsp. drippings in skillet. Let stand 1 minute. Add vinegar and oil, stirring to loosen browned bits from bottom of skillet. Sprinkle with ½ tsp. kosher salt and ½ tsp. black pepper. Drizzle warm bacon mixture over tomatoes and cheese. Serve immediately.

Makes 6 to 8 servings. Hands-on 25 min., Total 25 min.

CHARRED EGGPLANT WITH MISO DRESSING

Miso is a Japanese staple with a slightly salty, pungent flavor. Find it in the international or refrigerated aisle at your grocery store.

- ⅓ cup mayonnaise
- 2 Tbsp. white miso
- 1 Tbsp. fresh lime juice
- ⅛ tsp. freshly ground black pepper
- 2 large eggplants (about 2 lb.)
- ¼ cup olive oil
- ¼ cup torn fresh cilantro leaves

1. Preheat grill to 350° to 400° (medium-high) heat. Stir together first 4 ingredients in a small bowl.
2. Cut eggplants lengthwise into ¾-inch-thick slices. Brush each slice with olive oil, and sprinkle with desired amount of salt and pepper.
3. Grill eggplant slices, without grill lid, 5 minutes on each side or until slightly charred and tender. Arrange on a serving platter, and drizzle with desired amount of miso dressing; top with cilantro. Serve immediately with remaining dressing.

Makes 6 servings. Hands-on 25 min., Total 25 min.

Hot Bacon Caprese Salad

GRILLED MEXICAN CORN SALAD

Here's an off-the-cob play on a popular Mexican street dish.

- 3 limes, divided
- 8 large ears fresh yellow corn, husks removed
- 3 Tbsp. mayonnaise
- ²/₃ cup crumbled feta or Cotija cheese
- ¹/₃ cup sliced fresh chives

1. Cut 2 limes in half, and squeeze juice from lime halves to equal about ¹/₄ cup.

2. Preheat grill to 400° to 450° (high) heat. Brush corn with mayonnaise. Sprinkle with desired amount of salt and pepper. Grill corn, covered with grill lid, 10 to 12 minutes or until done, turning occasionally. (Kernels may char and pop.)

3. Cut kernels from cobs into a large bowl. Stir cheese, chives, and lime juice into kernels. Cut remaining lime into 4 wedges, and serve with corn salad.

Makes 6 to 8 servings. Hands-on 25 min., Total 40 min.

ZUCCHINI-POTATO CASSEROLE

This elegant tian, a French dish of layered vegetables, is delicious warm or at room temp.

- 2 Tbsp. butter
- 2 medium-size sweet onions, chopped
  Vegetable cooking spray
- 1 medium-size Yukon gold potato, sliced
- 1 medium-size zucchini, sliced
- 4 plum tomatoes, sliced
- 1¹/₂ tsp. kosher salt
- ³/₄ tsp. freshly ground black pepper
- 2 Tbsp. butter, melted
- ¹/₃ cup freshly grated Parmesan cheese

Mediterranean Green Beans

1. Preheat oven to 375°. Melt 2 Tbsp. butter in a medium skillet over medium heat; add onions, and sauté 10 to 12 minutes or until tender and onions begin to caramelize.

2. Spoon onions into a 10-inch quiche dish coated with cooking spray. Toss together potatoes and next 4 ingredients. Arrange potatoes, zucchini, and tomatoes in a single layer over onions, alternating and overlapping slightly. Drizzle with 2 Tbsp. melted butter. Cover with aluminum foil.

3. Bake at 375° for 30 minutes. Remove foil, and sprinkle with cheese. Bake 35 to 40 minutes or until golden brown. Let stand 10 minutes before serving.

Makes 6 to 8 servings. Hands-on 35 min.; Total 1 hour, 50 min.

MEDITERRANEAN GREEN BEANS

Use the olive mix to dress other veggies, such as tomato wedges, cooked baby potatoes, or roasted bell peppers.

- ¹/₃ cup chopped pitted kalamata olives
- 1 large shallot, sliced
- 2 Tbsp. red wine vinegar
- 2 tsp. whole grain Dijon mustard
- ¹/₂ tsp. sugar
- 3 Tbsp. olive oil
- 2 (8-oz.) packages haricots verts (thin green beans)

1. Stir together first 5 ingredients in a large bowl. Let stand 10 minutes. Stir in olive oil, and add salt and pepper to taste.

2. Cook green beans in boiling salted water to cover 3 to 4 minutes or until bright and crisp-tender; drain. Plunge beans into ice water to stop the cooking process; drain and pat dry. Toss together beans and olive mixture. Serve at room temperature, or cover and chill up to 2 hours.

Makes 6 to 8 servings. Hands-on 10 min., Total 20 min.

5 Shortcut Desserts

CELEBRATE SUMMER WITH JUICY POACHED FRUIT; ICY FLOATS;
A QUICK CRUMBLE; AND WONDROUS, LEMONY SNOW

RIESLING-POACHED PEACHES AND CHERRIES

When working with a limited palette, good ingredients make all the difference. We call for vanilla beans here because they impart fragrance and thousands of tiny, flavorful specks. They're worth the splurge, but feel free to substitute 2 tsp. vanilla extract for the beans. And if you like, trade the homemade whipped cream for a scoop of ice cream. (Also pictured on page 181)

Riesling-Poached
Peaches and Cherries

2	cups dry Riesling wine
1/3	cup sugar
1	vanilla bean, split
6	medium-size firm, ripe peaches, peeled and halved
2	cups fresh cherries, pitted
1	cup heavy cream
2	tsp. sugar

1. Bring first 3 ingredients and 1 cup water to a boil in a 3- to 4-qt. saucepan over high heat. Reduce heat to medium; add peaches, and simmer 8 to 10 minutes or to desired degree of tenderness. Transfer peaches to a shallow dish, using a slotted spoon. Add cherries to wine mixture, and simmer 3 minutes. Transfer cherries to dish with peaches, using a slotted spoon.
2. Increase heat to high, and cook wine mixture about 10 minutes or until reduced to about 3/4 cup. Pour mixture over peaches and cherries. Cover and chill 4 to 24 hours.
3. Beat cream and 2 tsp. sugar at medium-high speed with an electric mixer until soft peaks form. Divide fruit mixture among bowls, and dollop with whipped cream mixture.

Makes 6 servings. Hands-on 30 min.;
Total 4 hours, 45 min.

STRAWBERRY-GINGER LEMONADE FLOATS

Though the ginger is optional, it gives these refreshing floats their signature zing. If you can't find sparkling lemonade, substitute fizzy lemon-lime soda or ginger ale.

2	cups chopped fresh strawberries
4	Tbsp. fresh lemon juice
1/8	tsp. table salt
2	tsp. grated fresh ginger (optional)
	Premium vanilla bean ice cream
	Sparkling lemonade

Process first 3 ingredients and, if desired, ginger, in a blender until smooth. Divide half of mixture among 4 tall sundae glasses, and top each with desired amount of ice cream. Spoon remaining strawberry mixture over ice cream, and top with desired amount of sparkling lemonade. Serve immediately.

Makes 4 servings. Hands-on 10 min.,
Total 10 min.

LEMONY SNOW

For a grown-up version, drizzle the lemon ice with rum, gin, vodka, or limoncello.

- 2 tsp. lemon zest
- 1/2 cup fresh lemon juice
- 1/3 cup sugar

1. Combine all ingredients and 1 1/2 cups water in a large microwave-safe bowl. Microwave at HIGH 2 minutes; remove from microwave, and stir until sugar dissolves. Cool completely (about 15 minutes). Pour syrup mixture into a 13- x 9-inch pan or baking dish; cover and freeze 2 to 4 hours or until firm.

2. Let frozen syrup stand at room temperature 5 minutes. Break frozen syrup into large chunks, using a large spoon or fork. Pulse chunks in food processor 10 to 15 times or until desired consistency is reached. Spoon into cups, and serve.

Makes 3 to 4 servings. Hands-on 15 min.; Total 2 hours, 35 min.

PEACH-BERRY CRUMBLE

We love this recipe because it's easy enough for busy, weeknight cooking; pop the crumble in the oven when you serve dinner and it'll be ready in about 40 minutes. Blueberries or raspberries may be substituted for the blackberries.

- 3 cups fresh peach slices (about 3 medium)
- 2 cups fresh blackberries
- 1 large egg
- 1 large egg yolk
- 1 cup sugar
- 3/4 cup all-purpose flour
- 1/2 cup uncooked regular oats
- 1/4 tsp. kosher salt
- 1/2 cup butter, melted
  Vanilla ice cream

Preheat oven to 375°. Place first 2 ingredients in an 11- x 7-inch (or 2-qt.) baking dish. Stir together egg, egg yolk, and next 4 ingredients with a fork until mixture resembles coarse meal. Sprinkle over fruit; drizzle melted butter over topping. Bake 40 to 45 minutes or until light brown and bubbly. Let stand 10 minutes; serve warm with ice cream.

Makes 6 to 8 servings. Hands-on 20 min.; Total 1 hour, 20 min.

TROPICAL COCONUT PUDDING

Top this pudding with any ripe fruit. If you're looking for crunchy texture, gild it with crushed banana chips or chopped macadamia nuts.

- 1/2 cup sugar
- 1/4 cup cornstarch
- 1/8 tsp. table salt
- 6 large egg yolks
- 1 1/2 cups milk
- 1 (13.5-oz.) can coconut milk
- 3 cups peeled and diced fresh tropical fruit (such as mango, kiwifruit, or pineapple)

1. Whisk together first 3 ingredients in a medium-size heavy saucepan; whisk in egg yolks and next 2 ingredients until well blended. Cook mixture over medium-low heat, whisking constantly, 10 to 12 minutes or just until mixture thickens and begins to bubble. (Do not boil.) Remove from heat, and pour mixture through a wire-mesh strainer into a bowl.

2. Divide pudding among 6 ramekins or bowls. Place plastic wrap directly on warm custard (to prevent a film from forming); chill 1 hour to 2 days. Top each with fruit just before serving.

Makes 6 servings. Hands-on 30 min.; Total 1 hour, 30 min.

Bring On the Basil

FLAVOR YOUR SUMMER MEALS WITH THE SEASON'S BEST HERB

BASIL IS THE KING OF herbs—it adds fragrance to any garden and is so versatile in the kitchen. Use it for pestos, salads, pastas, or pizzas. In your garden, pair basil with tomatoes, and pick both when needed. It's also a great ornamental. Place it where you can pinch off a few leaves and enjoy the scent whenever you're outside. Cut stems of 'Opal' or 'Thai' basil, and mix with zinnias to add a clean scent and nice color to casual bouquets.

Select

'Genovese' is the classic basil grown for pesto. Plant other selections for a variety of flavors that can be used in different ways in the kitchen. Try 'Mrs. Burns' Lemon' and 'Lime' to enjoy citrus flavors that work well with fish. Use the purple leaves of 'Round Midnight' and 'Purple Ruffles' to flavor vinegars. A single large leaf of 'Mammoth' basil can cover a tomato sandwich. Spicy 'Cuban' basil will pump up your salsas. Order online from *johnnyseeds. com* or *cooksgarden.com*.

Grow

Basil is an easygoing annual herb. It needs warmth and likes four to six hours of sun a day. Plant it in a spot that gets morning light as well as protection from late-afternoon sun. It prefers slightly moist, well-drained soil that has been amended with organic matter. Set out transplants or sow seeds in your garden or in containers. Add mulch such as pine straw or finely shredded pine bark to help keep the roots cool. Don't overwater it. Feed your basil using an organic product, such as Maxicrop Liquid Seaweed & Fish (3-1-1, *planetnatural.com*). Gather it regularly to encourage new leaves and help delay flowering, because once it starts blooming, the leaves will toughen and lose flavor. So bring basil into your kitchen this summer to crown your table with good taste.

Pineapple-Basil Cocktail

Fill a 2-qt. pitcher with ice. Stir in 1 cup **Pineapple-Basil Simple Syrup** (see page 138), ³/₄ cup **gin**, and ¼ cup **fresh lemon juice.** Add 1 (12-oz.) bottle chilled **club soda** just before serving.

Makes about 3 ½ cups. Hands-on 5 min.; Total 5 min., not including syrup

get growing!
BASIL

SOIL
It likes fertile, well-drained soil amended with organic matter.

WATER
Water regularly. Plants in pots may need more attention.

HARVEST
Cut often to stimulate growth.

| LIGHT PART SUN | WATER MEDIUM | CARE MEDIUM |

'Genovese Compact' is a smaller basil that's great for growing in pots.

Community Cookbook

BUILD A BETTER LIBRARY, ONE GREAT BOOK AT A TIME. THIS MONTH: *FUN, FOOD & FLOWERS*

This year, Georgia's Thomasville Garden Club celebrates its 100th anniversary. Join the fun with the organization's spiral-bound cookbook (*thomasvillegardenclub.org*).

ICEBOX CUCUMBER PICKLES

Make these classic pickles from Fun, Food & Flowers *the night before a picnic or barbecue for a sweet-tart side.*

- 2 ½ cups sugar
- 2 cups apple cider vinegar
- ¼ cup canning-and-pickling salt
- ¾ tsp. celery seeds
- ¾ tsp. mustard seeds
- ½ tsp. ground turmeric
- 12 medium cucumbers, cut into ¼-inch slices
- 1 large sweet onion, cut into ⅛-inch slices

1. Cook first 6 ingredients in a large saucepan over high heat, stirring occasionally, about 3 minutes or until mixture is hot and sugar dissolves. (Do not boil.)
2. Place cucumbers and onions in a 4-qt. airtight plastic container. Pour hot vinegar mixture over cucumbers and onions. Cool 30 minutes. Serve immediately, or refrigerate in airtight container up to 2 weeks.

Makes 3 qt. Hands-on 40 min.; Total 1 hour, 10 min.

TIPSY WATERMELON

The easiest and quickest way to cut a watermelon: Cut the top and bottom off so it can sit flat on a cutting board. Run a sharp knife down the sides, taking off the rind. Cut it into rounds, and then cut rounds into chunks.

Place 4 cups chopped seedless **watermelon** in a 9- x 13-inch baking dish. Whisk together ½ cup **tequila,** ¼ cup fresh **lime juice,** and 2 Tbsp. **light agave nectar** in a small bowl. Pour mixture over watermelon, gently stirring to coat. Cover and chill 45 minutes to 8 hours. Sprinkle with ½ tsp. **kosher salt** just before serving.

Makes 6 servings. Hands-on 15 min., Total 1 hour

VANILLA WAFER CAKE

Preheat oven to 300°. Beat 2 cups **sugar,** 1 cup softened **butter,** and 1 tsp. **vanilla extract** at medium speed with an electric mixer 1 minute or until creamy. Add 6 large **eggs,** 1 at a time, beating just until yellow disappears. Add 1 (11-oz.) box **vanilla wafers,** finely crushed, to butter mixture alternately with ½ cup **milk,** beginning and ending with vanilla wafers; beat at low speed just until blended after each addition. Fold in 1 (7-oz.) package **sweetened flaked coconut** and 1 cup **pecans,** chopped. Pour into a greased and floured 13- x 9-inch pan. Bake 55 to 60 minutes or until a wooden pick inserted in center comes out clean.

Makes 12 to 15 servings. Hands-on 20 min.; Total 1 hour, 15 min.

July

Black & Blue

LET SUMMER'S SWEET BERRIES DAZZLE AT EVERY MEAL WITH 14 FRESH AND JUICY NEW RECIPES

BLACKBERRY-BRIE PIZZETTAS

At happy hour, pair these appetizer-size pizzas with a chilly glass of rosé. For an entrée, simply roll dough into larger rounds. (Also pictured on page 14)

- 2 Tbsp. butter
- 1 large sweet onion, thinly sliced
- 1 medium-size fennel bulb, thinly sliced (optional)
- Pizzetta Dough*
- Parchment paper
- 2 Tbsp. extra virgin olive oil, divided
- 12 oz. Brie cheese, trimmed and sliced*
- 1 1/2 cups fresh blackberries, halved
- 3/4 cup chopped toasted pecans
- 2 cups loosely packed fresh arugula
- 1/4 cup torn basil leaves
- 2 tsp. balsamic vinegar

1. Preheat oven to 425°. Melt butter in a large skillet over medium-high heat; add onion and, if desired, fennel, and cook, stirring often, 20 minutes or until golden brown.

2. Flour hands, and shape each Pizzetta Dough ball into a 6- to 8-inch round. Place each round on a small piece of parchment paper. Brush with 1 Tbsp. oil. Top dough rounds with cheese, next 2 ingredients, and onion mixture.

3. Place 4 pizzettas (on parchment paper) directly on oven rack, and bake at 425° for 12 to 14 minutes or until golden. Repeat with remaining dough rounds.

4. Toss together arugula, next 2 ingredients, and remaining 1 Tbsp. oil. Add salt and pepper to taste. Sprinkle baked pizzettas with arugula mixture just before serving.

* 1 lb. store-bought pizza dough and 8 oz. sliced or shredded mozzarella cheese may be substituted.

MAKES 8 servings. **HANDS-ON** 1 hour; **TOTAL** 3 hours, 15 min., including dough

Pizzetta Dough

- 1 (1/4-oz.) envelope active dry yeast
- 1 cup warm water (100° to 110°)
- 1 Tbsp. honey
- 1/4 cup olive oil
- 3 cups plus 2 Tbsp. all-purpose flour
- 2 tsp. table salt

1. Combine first 3 ingredients in bowl of an electric stand mixer; let stand 5 minutes or until foamy. Add oil, 3 cups flour, and 2 tsp. salt. Beat dough at medium-low speed, using dough hook attachment, 5 minutes or until smooth. Gradually add 1 to 2 Tbsp. more flour, if needed, to form a soft dough. Increase speed to medium-high, and beat 4 to 5 more minutes or until smooth and elastic.

2. Place dough in a lightly greased large bowl, turning to grease top. Cover with plastic wrap. Let dough rise in a warm place (80° to 85°), free

Blackberry-Brie Pizzettas

from drafts, 1 hour or until doubled in bulk.

3. Punch dough down; turn out onto a lightly floured surface. Divide dough into 8 portions. Shape each portion into a ball, and place on a lightly greased baking sheet. Cover and let dough stand 15 minutes or chill up to 4 hours.

Note: To make ahead, prepare recipe through Step 2. Cover and chill 24 hours. Proceed with recipe as directed in Step 3.

MAKES Dough for 8 (6- to 8-inch) pizzas or 2 (12- to 14-inch) pizzas. **HANDS-ON** 30 min.; **TOTAL** 1 hour, 50 min.

BLUEBERRY-AND-KALE GRAIN SALAD

Trust us—you're going to want to try this crunchy, sweet, and salty combo. Any variety of kale will do, and feel free to sub cooked farro, wild rice, or quinoa for the wheat berries. (Pictured on page 14)

- 1 cup wheat berries
- 1 tsp. table salt
- 1 (8-oz.) package sugar snap peas
- 4 cups coarsely chopped kale
- 1/2 cup Red Wine Vinaigrette
- 2 cups fresh blueberries
- 1/2 cup chopped toasted pecans
- 3/4 cup crumbled feta cheese

1. Bring wheat berries, salt, and 4 cups water to a boil in a saucepan. Cover, reduce heat to low, and simmer 1 hour.
2. Meanwhile, cook peas in boiling salted water to cover 2 minutes or until crisp-tender; drain. Plunge into ice water; drain and pat dry. Slice in half. Drain wheat berries; rinse under cold water until cool.
3. Toss together kale, wheat berries, and 1/4 cup vinaigrette in a large bowl. Let stand 30 minutes. Stir in blueberries, pecans, and sugar snap peas. Add salt and pepper. Sprinkle with cheese. Serve with remaining vinaigrette.

MAKES 8 servings. **HANDS-ON** 20 min.; **TOTAL** 2 hours, 5 min., including vinaigrette

Red Wine Vinaigrette

- 1/3 cup red wine vinegar
- 1/2 large shallot, minced
- 2/3 cup extra virgin olive oil
- 2 Tbsp. honey
- 2 tsp. coarse-grained Dijon mustard

Stir together red wine vinegar and minced shallot; let stand 10 minutes. Whisk in olive oil and remaining ingredients. Add salt and pepper to taste. Refrigerate in an airtight container up to 1 week.

MAKES about 1 cup. **HANDS-ON** 5 min., **TOTAL** 15 min.

GRILLED PORK CHOPS WITH BLUEBERRY-PEACH SALSA

Go for bone-in center loin chops or loin chops at least 1 1/2 inches thick. Meatier chops ensure a good char while the inside cooks through. (Pictured on page 14)

- 4 (1 1/2-inch-thick) bone-in pork chops (about 3 1/4 lb.)
  All-Purpose Pork Brine
- 1 Tbsp. olive oil
  Blueberry-Peach Salsa

1. Place pork and brine in a large zip-top plastic freezer bag; seal. Place bag in a shallow baking dish, and chill 8 hours.
2. Remove pork chops from brine; discard brine. Let pork stand at room temperature 30 minutes. Light 1 side of grill, heating to 350° to 400° (medium-high) heat; leave other side unlit. Brush pork with 1 Tbsp. oil, and sprinkle with desired amount of salt and pepper.
3. Place pork over lit side, and grill, covered with grill lid, 4 minutes on each side. Transfer pork to unlit side, and grill, covered with grill lid, 8 to 10 minutes on each side or until a meat thermometer inserted into thickest portion registers 150°. Let stand 5 minutes. Arrange pork on a serving platter, and top with Blueberry-Peach Salsa.

MAKES 4 servings. **HANDS-ON** 35 min.; **TOTAL** 10 hours, 40 min., including brine and salsa

All-Purpose Pork Brine

- 1 1/2 qt. hot water
- 3 Tbsp. kosher salt
- 2 Tbsp. chopped fresh thyme
- 2 Tbsp. brown sugar
- 2 tsp. coarsely ground black pepper
- 4 garlic cloves, crushed
- 2 bay leaves
- 1/2 large lemon, sliced

Stir together all ingredients in a large stockpot until salt and sugar dissolve. Let stand 1 hour.

Note: We tested with Diamond Crystal Kosher Salt.

MAKES 1 1/2 qt. **HANDS-ON** 15 min.; **TOTAL** 1 hour, 15 min.

Blueberry-Peach Salsa

This juicy condiment pulls sweet and savory double duty: Liven up a cheese platter with it, or spoon it over goat cheese or a wheel of Brie.

- 1 1/2 cups fresh blueberries
  Zest and juice of 1 lime
- 1 large peach, peeled and finely diced
- 1 small shallot, finely chopped
- 3 Tbsp. chopped fresh basil
- 3 Tbsp. chopped fresh chives
- 2 Tbsp. hot pepper jelly
- 1 Tbsp. olive oil

Coarsely chop half of blueberries. Toss chopped blueberries with whole blueberries and remaining ingredients. Add salt and pepper to taste. Serve immediately, or cover and chill up to 24 hours.

MAKES 3 cups. **HANDS-ON** 15 min., **TOTAL** 15 min.

PETITE BLUEBERRY CHEESECAKES

As pretty as petits fours, these luscious little two-bite gems can be finished with any kind of berry or preserves. Get ahead, and bake the cheesecakes in advance. After baking, they'll freeze up to one month. Thaw and top with preserves and fruit before serving. (Pictured on page 14)

- 12 paper baking cups
- 14 crisp gourmet cookies (such as Lotus Biscoff)
- 2 Tbsp. butter, melted
  Pinch of table salt
- 1 1/2 (8-oz.) packages cream cheese, at room temperature
- 1/3 cup sugar
- 2 Tbsp. fresh lime juice
- 1/2 tsp. vanilla extract
- 2 large eggs
- 1/4 cup blueberry preserves
- 1/2 cup fresh blueberries
  Garnish: lime zest

1. Preheat oven to 325°. Place paper baking cups in 1 (12-cup) standard-size muffin pan. Pulse cookies in a food processor 8 to 10 times or until finely crushed. Stir together cookie crumbs, butter, and pinch of salt. Firmly press about 1 1/2 Tbsp. crumb mixture into bottom of each baking cup.
2. Bake at 325° for 6 minutes. Cool on a wire rack 10 minutes.
3. Meanwhile, beat cream cheese and next 3 ingredients at medium speed with an electric mixer until blended. Add eggs, 1 at a time, beating just until yellow disappears after each addition. Divide mixture among prepared baking cups.
4. Bake at 325° for 15 to 20 minutes or until just set. Cool on wire rack 30 minutes. Cover and chill 4 to 24 hours.
5. Gently remove cheesecakes from pan. Top each with 1 tsp. preserves and a few blueberries.

Note: We tested with Bonne Maman Wild Blueberry Preserves.

MAKES 1 dozen. **HANDS-ON** 30 min.; **TOTAL** 5 hours, 20 min.

DOUBLE BERRY-ALMOND GALETTE

Here's a great baker's secret: Adding a splash of vodka to dough will give you a super-flaky crust, and the alcohol burns off while baking. We prefer to make this dough by hand; you can use a food processor, but the final result will yield a more crumbly, cookie-like texture.

CRUST

- 1/2 cup slivered almonds, toasted
- 2 cups all-purpose flour
- 3 Tbsp. sugar
- 1 1/2 tsp. table salt
- 1/2 cup cold butter, cubed
- 1/4 cup cold vegetable shortening, cubed
- 3 Tbsp. ice-cold water
- 3 Tbsp. vodka, chilled

TOPPING

- 1 cup fresh blueberries
- 1 cup fresh blackberries
- 2 Tbsp. sugar
- 2 tsp. lemon zest
- 1 Tbsp. fresh lemon juice
- 1/4 tsp. almond extract

FILLING

- 1/3 cup sugar
- 3 Tbsp. all-purpose flour
- 1 Tbsp. fresh lemon juice
- 2 cups fresh blueberries
- 2 cups fresh blackberries
- 2 Tbsp. butter, cut into pieces

ADDITIONAL INGREDIENTS

- 1 large egg, beaten
- 1 Tbsp. sugar
  Parchment paper
  Honey Sour Cream (optional)
  Garnish: torn mint leaves

1. Prepare Crust: Pulse almonds in a food processor 15 times or until finely ground. Stir together ground almonds and next 3 ingredients in a bowl. Cut cold butter and cold shortening into flour mixture with a pastry blender until mixture resembles small peas. Gradually stir in ice-cold water and vodka just until dry ingredients are moistened. (Add up to 2 Tbsp. ice-cold water, if necessary.) Shape into a disk. Wrap in plastic wrap; chill 3 to 24 hours.
2. Meanwhile, prepare Topping: Toss together 1 cup blueberries and next 5 ingredients. Let stand, stirring occasionally, 30 minutes. Cover and chill until ready to serve.
3. Unwrap chilled dough, and place on floured parchment paper; sprinkle with flour. Roll to a 14- to 15-inch circle. Carefully transfer dough and parchment paper to a jelly-roll pan.
4. Prepare Filling: Stir together 1/3 cup sugar and next 2 ingredients in a large bowl; stir in 2 cups each blueberries and blackberries. Spoon mixture into center of dough, leaving a 2 1/2-inch border around edges; dot with butter. (Do not make filling ahead or it will become too juicy.) Fold edges of dough around fruit, pleating as you go and sealing cracks. Brush dough with beaten egg, and sprinkle with 1 Tbsp. sugar. Freeze 15 minutes.
5. Preheat oven to 425°. Bake on lower oven rack 30 to 35 minutes or until crust is golden. Transfer to a wire rack; cool 30 minutes. Serve with Topping and Honey Sour Cream, if desired.

MAKES 8 servings. **HANDS-ON** 45 min.; **TOTAL** 5 hours, 30 min.

Honey Sour Cream

Stir together 1 cup **sour cream,** 2 Tbsp. **honey,** and 1 tsp. **vanilla bean paste** or **vanilla extract.** Serve immediately, or chill up to 24 hours.

MAKES about 1 1/4 cups. **HANDS-ON** 5 min., **TOTAL** 5 min.

SEVEN MORE SIMPLE BERRY IDEAS TO TRY ALL SUMMER LONG

❶ BREAKFAST TOPPER

Crush 2 cups of blackberries; add a little brown sugar, a splash of orange liqueur, and vanilla extract. Serve over warm Belgian waffles or pancakes with whipped cream.

❷ SMOOTHIE UPDATE

Riff on an Indian lassi, and blend a heaping handful each of diced mango, any kind of berry, and ice cubes with some yogurt, a splash of milk, spoonful of honey, and a pinch of cardamom.

❸ BLUEBERRY BISCUITS

Stir together a half pint of blueberries, a pinch of sugar, and lemon zest into any biscuit dough; cut and bake biscuits as directed. Serve hot biscuits with berry preserves mashed into softened butter.

❹ BERRY-PECAN RICE PILAF

Fold blueberries, toasted pecans, chopped caramelized onions, and fresh parsley into cooked rice. Serve hot or cold.

❺ BLACK-AND-BLUE STEAK

Toss together a few handfuls of berries, some chopped walnuts, crumbled blue cheese, sliced green onions, and a dash of any vinaigrette. Serve over sliced grilled steak.

❻ GIN MOJITOS

Muddle a few blackberries, mint leaves, and some lime juice in a glass. Fill with ice, and add chilled tonic water. Top with gin, and garnish with mint.

❼ TURKEY-BERRY BURGERS

Fold coarsely chopped blueberries, minced shallots, and freshly chopped parsley and basil into ground turkey. Shape into patties, and grill. Serve on toasted buns with honey mustard and sliced avocado.

BUTTERMILK-BLACKBERRY POPS

Don't have reusable molds? No problem. We found 5-oz. paper cups to be a perfect no-fuss, disposable alternative.

- 1½ **cups fresh blackberries**
- 6 **Tbsp. frozen orange juice concentrate, thawed**
- 1½ **cups whole buttermilk**
- 1 **(8-oz.) container sour cream**
- ⅓ **cup honey**
- 8 **wooden craft sticks**

1. Process first 2 ingredients in a food processor or blender until smooth. Whisk together buttermilk and next 2 ingredients.

2. Pour mixtures alternately into 8 (4-oz.) ice pop molds or paper cups. Swirl mixtures gently, and insert wooden craft sticks. Freeze 8 hours or until completely frozen.

MAKES 8 (4-oz.) ice pops. **HANDS-ON** 15 min.; **TOTAL** 8 hours, 15 min.

BLACKBERRY PISCO SOURS

Pisco is a South American grape brandy popular in Peru and Chile. If you can't find it in your area, feel free to substitute white tequila, grappa, or vodka. Don't be alarmed by the strength of this new classic; it's a cocktail that's meant to be sipped and savored.

- 1 **cup fresh blackberries**
- 1 **cup pisco, chilled**
- ⅓ **cup fresh lime juice**
- 3 **large pasteurized egg whites**
- 5 **Tbsp. simple syrup**
   Angostura bitters (optional)
   Garnishes: fresh basil leaves, fresh blackberries

1. Process blackberries in a blender until smooth. Pour through a wire-mesh strainer into a 1-qt. jar with a tight-fitting lid, discarding solids.

2. Add pisco and next 3 ingredients to jar. Cover with lid, and shake vigorously 30 seconds or until foamy. Pour mixture into 4 (10-oz.) glasses filled with ice. Top each with a dash of bitters, if desired. Serve immediately.

MAKES 4 servings. **HANDS-ON** 15 min., **TOTAL** 15 min.

Blackberry Pisco Sours

Grill Up a Backyard Feast

BROOKE PARKHURST AND **JAMES BRISCIONE** KNOW HOW TO WOW A CROWD.
IT STARTS AT THE GRILL WITH A CASUAL FAMILY-STYLE MENU.

MARGARITA-BRINED CHICKEN

Soak chicken in a citrus-and-tequila-spiked brine to infuse Latin flavors and keep the chicken moist as it cooks. Pat the skin dry before grilling, and start skin-side down to ensure it gets good and crispy. Feel free to sub orange juice for tequila and lemons or oranges for limes, and be sure to grill extra citrus for a pretty and functional garnish. (Also pictured on page 183)

1	cup water
1/4	cup kosher salt
2	Tbsp. light brown sugar
1	cup cold water
1/2	cup tequila
3	Tbsp. orange zest
1/2	cup fresh orange juice
3	Tbsp. lime zest
1	Tbsp. whole black peppercorns
6	bone-in chicken breasts
	Vegetable cooking spray
2	Tbsp. olive oil
1	tsp. kosher salt
1/2	tsp. freshly ground black pepper
6	limes, halved
	Garnish: fresh cilantro

1. Bring first 3 ingredients to a boil in a small saucepan over medium-high heat. Boil, stirring occasionally, 1 to 2 minutes or until salt and sugar dissolve. Remove saucepan from heat; let stand 10 minutes. Pour mixture into a large bowl; stir in 1 cup cold water, 1/2 cup tequila, and next 4 ingredients. Submerge chicken in brine; cover and chill 6 to 12 hours.

2. Coat cold grill grate with cooking spray. Preheat grill to 350° to 400° (medium-high) heat. Remove chicken from bowl; discard brine. Pat chicken dry with paper towels, and brush skin with olive oil. Sprinkle chicken with kosher salt and freshly ground black pepper. Let stand at room temperature 20 minutes.

3. Grill chicken, covered with grill lid, 40 to 45 minutes or until done, turning occasionally. Transfer chicken to a platter. Grill limes, cut sides down, 1 to 2 minutes or until charred. Serve limes with chicken.

MAKES 6 servings. **HANDS-ON** 25 min.; **TOTAL** 7 hours, 40 min.

The Menu

LEMON-MINT SPARKLERS

TOMATO SALAD
WITH GRILLED SHRIMP

MARGARITA-BRINED CHICKEN

GRILL-SMOKED SUMMER PEAS

SMOKY CHOPPED SALAD
WITH AVOCADO

BOURBON-SOAKED PLUMS

KEY LIME CURD CONES

Margarita-Brined Chicken

Lemon-Rosemary-Garlic Chicken
and Potatoes (page 34)

clockwise from top left:

- Curried Shrimp with Peanuts (page 35)
- One-Pot Pasta with Tomato-Basil Sauce (page 35)
- Country Ham-and-Egg Toast (page 33)
- Lemon-Blueberry Quinoa Porridge (page 31)

clockwise from top left:
- Butternut Squash Tortilla Soup (page 40)
- Sweet Potato, Cauliflower, and Greens Casserole (page 25)
- Baked Ziti with Sausage (page 51)

Fried Catfish with Pickled
Peppers (page 52)

Herb-Roasted Pork Loin
(page 50)

Citrus Shortcakes (page 57)

clockwise from top left:
- Lemon Meltaways (page 56)
- Lemon-Lime Pound Cake (page 54)
- Berries and Bubbles (page 72)
- Lemon Cupcakes with Lavender Frosting (page 71)

Honey Flan (page 73)

Sesame Chicken Garden Salad
(page 78)

Crispy Chicken with Greek
Green Bean Salad (page 79)

Herb-Roasted Boneless Leg of Lamb (page 84)

clockwise from top left:
- Chipotle-Strawberry Glaze (page 96)
- Jicama-and-Bell Pepper Slaw (page 96)
- Spring Pea Orzo (page 90)
- Glazed Spiral-Cut Holiday Ham (page 89)

Asparagus with Red Pepper Chowchow (page 90), Hot Potato Salad (page 89), Carrot-Ginger Puree (page 91)

Mosaic Tea Sandwiches
(page 102)

clockwise from top left:
- Cinnamon-Sugar Doughnut Bites (page 119)
- Classic Southern Buttermilk Pie (page 123)
- Avocado-and-Feta Dip (page 111)
- Jana's Chocolate Chip Cookies (page 110)

Serrano Pepper Burgers (page 108)

Crab-Stuffed Catfish Fillets with
Cajun Rémoulade (page 109)

clockwise from top left:
• 5-Ingredient Slow-Cooker Pulled Pork (page 122)
• Pulled Pork Nachos (page 122)
• Baked Brie with Jezebel Peaches (page 145)
• Over-the-Top Tomato Sandwich (page 139)

clockwise from top left:
- Orange-Basil Yogurt Dip, Pickled Tiny Tomatoes, Buttery Garlic Shrimp (page 145)
- Tomato-Orange Marmalade Chicken (page 148)
- Roasted Whole Teriyaki Snapper (page 148)

**Riesling-Poached Peaches
and Cherries (page 151)**

Lemon-Mint Bourbon Sparklers and Tomato Salad with Grilled Shrimp (page 195)

clockwise from top left:

- Margarita-Brined Chicken (page 160)
- Bourbon-Soaked Plums (page 195)
- Asian Slaw with Egg Roll Crackers (page 200)
- Sweet Pea-and-Mint Pasta Toss (page 199)

Key Lime Curd Cones
(page 194)

Red, White, and Blue Ice-Cream Cake (page 201)

clockwise from top left:
- Smoky Field Pea Hummus (page 206)
- Summer Hoppin' John Salad (page 205)
- Bacon, Peach, and Basil Burgers (page 208)
- Tex-Mex Turkey Burgers (page 209)

Sweet Tea-and-Lemonade Cake
(page 213)

**Pork Tenderloin Wraps
with Grilled Corn Salsa
(page 211)**

Parmesan-Herb Cornbread
Pudding (page 225)

**Potato-Crusted Pizza
(page 228)**

Italian-Style Turkey Meatball
Soup (page 228)

Apple Stack Cake
(page 217)

GRILL-SMOKED SUMMER PEAS

Here's a smart new smoky spin on baked beans, substituting field peas for traditional white beans. Use a mix of different kinds, such as crowders, lady peas, and butter beans.

- 1 cup hickory wood chips
  Vegetable cooking spray
- 1 lb. fresh shelled field peas or beans (about 4 cups)
- 4 cups boiling water
- 4 fresh thyme sprigs
- 1 garlic bulb, cut in half crosswise
- 1 bay leaf
- 4 firm medium-size beefsteak tomatoes, cored
- 6 bacon slices, chopped
- 6 garlic cloves, chopped
- 3 Tbsp. molasses
- 2 Tbsp. Dijon mustard
- 2 Tbsp. apple cider vinegar
- 2 tsp. kosher salt
- 1 tsp. ground black pepper

1. Soak wood chips in water 30 minutes; drain. Coat cold grill grate with cooking spray. Light 1 side of grill, heating to 400° to 500° (high); leave other side unlit. Place wood chips in center of a 12-inch square piece of heavy-duty aluminum foil; wrap to form a packet. Pierce several holes in packet; place directly over heat.
2. Combine peas and next 4 ingredients in a 13- x 9-inch disposable aluminum foil pan. Place peas over unlit side of grill, and grill, covered with grill lid, 1 hour or until tender, stirring occasionally. Drain peas, reserving 3/4 cup cooking liquid. Discard garlic bulb, thyme, and bay leaf.
3. Halve tomatoes, and grill, covered with grill lid, 2 minutes on each side. Cool 10 minutes. Discard skins; chop tomatoes.

4. Cook bacon in a large saucepan over medium heat, stirring often, 4 minutes or until crisp. Reserve 2 Tbsp. drippings in saucepan. Add chopped garlic; sauté 30 seconds. Stir in tomatoes, molasses, and next 2 ingredients; bring to a simmer. Reduce heat to low, and simmer, stirring often, 5 minutes. Stir peas, salt, pepper, and 3/4 cup reserved cooking liquid into tomato mixture; cook, stirring often, 10 minutes or until slightly thickened. Adjust seasoning with more vinegar, molasses, salt, and pepper, if desired.

MAKES 6 servings. **HANDS-ON** 45 min.; **TOTAL** 2 hours, 25 min.

Smoky Chopped Salad with Avocado

SMOKY CHOPPED SALAD WITH AVOCADO

- 3/4 cup buttermilk
- 1/4 cup sour cream
- 2 Tbsp. freshly grated Parmesan cheese
- 2 Tbsp. chopped fresh chives
- 1 Tbsp. chopped fresh basil
- 1 Tbsp. fresh lemon juice
- 2 to 3 dashes of Worcestershire sauce
- 1 to 2 dashes of hot sauce
- 1 small garlic clove, pressed
  Vegetable cooking spray
- 2 ripe avocados, peeled and halved
- 3 romaine lettuce hearts, cut in half lengthwise
- 1/2 cup thinly sliced radishes
- 1/2 cup crumbled blue cheese

1. Whisk together first 9 ingredients in a medium bowl, whisking until smooth; add salt and pepper to taste.

2. Coat cold grill grate with cooking spray. Preheat grill to 350° to 400° (medium-high) heat. Lightly coat cut sides of avocados and lettuce with cooking spray; season with salt and pepper. Grill avocado halves and lettuce, cut sides down and covered with grill lid, 1 minute or until grill marks appear.

3. Slice avocados. Chop lettuce, and arrange on a platter. Top with avocado, radishes, and blue cheese. Drizzle with dressing. Add salt and pepper to taste.

MAKES 6 servings. **HANDS-ON** 25 min., **TOTAL** 25 min.

KEY LIME CURD CONES

To prep ahead, make the curd up to two days in advance, and chill. Whip the meringue an hour before your party; assemble just before serving. (Also pictured on page 184)

CURD
- 1/2 cup fresh Key lime juice
- 1 cup sugar
- 6 large egg yolks
- 2 tsp. loosely packed Key lime zest
- Pinch of kosher salt
- 6 Tbsp. butter, cut into 6 slices

MERINGUE
- 2 large egg whites
- 1/2 cup sugar
- 1/8 tsp. cream of tartar

ADDITIONAL INGREDIENT
- 1/2 (16-oz.) box mini ice-cream cones

1. Prepare Curd: Whisk together first 5 ingredients in a medium saucepan. Cook mixture over medium heat, stirring constantly with a wooden spoon, 10 to 12 minutes or until thickened and bubbles form around edges.

2. Remove from heat, and add butter, 1 slice at a time, whisking until blended after each addition. Transfer mixture to a medium-size glass bowl, and place plastic wrap directly on warm curd. Chill 4 to 6 hours.

3. Prepare Meringue: Pour water to a depth of 2 inches into a 2-qt. sauce-

Key Lime Curd Cones

pan. Bring to a boil over medium-high heat. Reduce heat to medium, and let simmer. Beat egg whites and next 2 ingredients in a 2 1/2-qt. bowl at medium speed with an electric mixer until blended. Place bowl over simmering water, and beat at medium speed 9 minutes or until soft peaks form. Remove from heat. Beat at high speed 2 minutes or until stiff peaks form.

4. Divide chilled lime curd among ice-cream cones.

5. Spoon meringue into a large zip-top plastic freezer bag. (Do not seal.) Snip 1 corner of bag to make a small hole. Pipe meringue over curd in each ice-cream cone. If desired, brown meringue using a kitchen torch, holding torch 2 inches from meringue and moving torch back and forth.

Note: We tested with Joy Mini Cups ice-cream cones, and recommend using a pro-style kitchen torch ($20 at *amazon.com* or housewares retailers).

MAKES 22 mini cones. **HANDS-ON** 1 hour, 10 min.; **TOTAL** 5 hours, 10 min.

Key Lime Parfaits

Prepare Key Lime Curd Cones through Step 3. Omit cones. Divide 2 cups **graham cracker crumbs** among 6 bowls or jars; top with lime curd. Proceed with recipe as directed in Step 5.

MAKES 6 servings.

BOURBON-SOAKED PLUMS

Use your favorite kind of plums, or sub nectarines or peaches, if desired. Make sure they're just firm and not too ripe. (Pictured on page 183)

1   lemon
1/4   cup firmly packed light brown sugar
2   Tbsp. butter
1/2   tsp. ground cinnamon
1/4   cup bourbon
1/2   vanilla bean, split*
6   ripe plums, pitted and halved
Vanilla ice cream

1. Using a vegetable peeler, remove thin layer of peel from lemon, leaving white pith intact. Halve lemon cross-wise, and squeeze juice to equal 2 Tbsp. Place lemon juice, lemon peels, brown sugar, next 2 ingredients, and 2 Tbsp. water in a large skillet, and bring to a simmer over medium heat, stirring occasionally. Remove skillet from heat; stir in bourbon and vanilla bean.
2. Return skillet to heat, and add plums, cut sides down. Cook, basting with pan sauce, 3 to 4 minutes or until plums are just tender and lightly caramelized. Remove skillet from heat; discard vanilla bean and lemon peels. Cool 5 minutes. Serve plums and pan sauce with ice cream.

*1 tsp. vanilla extract may be substituted.

MAKES 6 servings. **HANDS-ON** 20 min., **TOTAL** 25 min.

LEMON-MINT SPARKLERS

Make the syrup a week ahead, and keep cold. Chill the club soda, too, but mix the drink just before serving to keep it nice and fizzy. Use leftover syrup to make a boozy version for the grown-ups in your crowd, and set up a self-serve beverage station with fresh lemon and mint leaves.

1 3/4   cups fresh lemon juice (about 10 lemons)
1 1/2   cups Lemon-Mint Syrup
3 1/2   cups chilled club soda
2   cups ice cubes

Stir together all ingredients in a large pitcher. Serve immediately.

MAKES about 1 1/2 qt. **HANDS-ON** 30 min.; **TOTAL** 1 hour, 30 min., including syrup

Lemon-Mint-Bourbon Sparklers

(Pictured on page 182)

Prepare recipe as directed, omitting lemon juice and reducing Lemon-Mint Syrup to 1/3 cup. Stir in 1 1/2 cups bourbon.

MAKES 5 1/3 cups. **HANDS-ON** 10 min.; **TOTAL** 1 hour, 10 min., including syrup

Lemon-Mint Syrup

6   lemons
2   cups sugar
2   tsp. kosher salt
6   to 8 fresh mint sprigs

1. Using a vegetable peeler, remove thin layer of peel from lemons, leaving white pith intact. Reserve peeled lemons for another use.
2. Bring sugar, salt, and 4 cups water to a boil in a medium saucepan over medium-high heat, whisking occa-sionally. Remove syrup from heat, and stir in lemon peels and mint. Cover and let stand 30 minutes. Pour mixture through a wire-mesh strainer into a container; discard solids. Refrigerate up to 2 weeks.

MAKES about 4 cups. **HANDS-ON** 30 min., **TOTAL** 1 hour

TOMATO SALAD WITH GRILLED SHRIMP

Look for beautiful and tasty heirloom tomatoes in a rainbow of colors at your local farmers' market, and keep them at room temperature until you're ready to slice and serve. Refrigerating will give them a mealy texture. (Pictured on page 182)

Vegetable cooking spray
1/3   cup extra virgin olive oil
5   Tbsp. mixed chopped fresh herbs, such as dill, basil, mint, and/or chives
2   Tbsp. white wine vinegar
1   tsp. lemon zest
2   Tbsp. fresh lemon juice
1/4   tsp. dried crushed red pepper
1   garlic clove, minced
1   tsp. kosher salt, divided
2   lb. small tomatoes, sliced or quartered
2   lb. peeled and deveined large raw shrimp
3   Tbsp. olive oil
1/2   tsp. freshly ground black pepper
Garnishes: fresh dill, basil, mint, and chives

1. Coat cold grill grate with cooking spray. Preheat grill to 350° to 400° (medium-high) heat. Whisk together extra virgin olive oil and next 6 ingredients in a small bowl; whisk in 1/2 tsp. kosher salt. Arrange tomatoes on a large serving platter or in a large bowl, and drizzle with 1/4 cup vinai-grette. Sprinkle with desired amount of salt and pepper.
2. Toss shrimp with 3 Tbsp. olive oil, 1/2 tsp. freshly ground black pepper, and remaining 1/2 tsp. kosher salt. Grill shrimp, covered with grill lid, 2 minutes on each side or just until shrimp turn pink.
3. Toss grilled shrimp with remaining vinaigrette, and arrange over toma-toes. Or, if desired, toss together shrimp, remaining vinaigrette, and tomatoes.

MAKES 6 servings. **HANDS-ON** 25 min., **TOTAL** 25 min.

THE *SL* TEST KITCHEN ACADEMY

RESIDENT GRILLMASTER HUNTER LEWIS EXPLAINS HOW TO GRILL THE PERFECT STEAK

THE ART OF THE CHAR

What separates a gorgeous steak house steak and a so-so backyard one? Simple: **a killer crust.** A salty, crispy, expertly charred one gives steak its intensely savory appeal. With the cost of beef at a 30-year high, now's not the time to just slap a steak over fire and call it dinner. Here's how to up your grill game and raise the stakes.

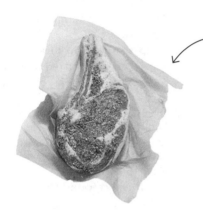

1

FAT OR SKINNY

Go big with bone-in steaks at least 1½ inches thick. They'll develop a crust before the inside overcooks. We love skinny (½-inch-thick) cuts too; just be sure to grill them faster over higher heat. Season any steak liberally with kosher salt and freshly ground black pepper to elevate flavor and add crunch.

2

THE FUEL

Build a two-zone fire with charcoal so you can start the meat over the hot zone and move it to the cooler zone to avoid flare-ups. Grilling with gas? Build a two-zone fire by cranking all the burners up to high. Close the lid to preheat the grates. Then turn the heat down on one side, and get grilling.

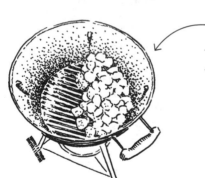

3

ANGLE, ROTATE, AND FLIP FOR A SUPERIOR CRUST

Perfect grill marks are for fast-food burgers. What you're after is a perfect crust. Arrange steaks at a 90° angle across the grill grate to create more surface area, and listen for the sizzle. Don't hear it? Your grill's not hot enough—you want at least 500° at the grate's surface. After two minutes, rotate the steak 90° and cook two more minutes. Flip the steak and repeat, rotating and flipping often to develop the crust. Stop once you reach the desired internal temperature. A digital instant-read thermometer works best for this.

4

THE FINISH

Transfer the steaks to a platter. Season with more kosher salt for extra flavor and texture, and let them rest 5 minutes for maximum juiciness. Slice against the grain with a sharp knife.

NEXT LEVEL

Because of its surface area and even heat, a cast-iron skillet creates the ultimate sear and crust. Preheat a large skillet on the grill for 10 minutes. Swirl in 1 Tbsp. canola oil; then add steak.

5-Ingredient Pasta Salads

MIX AND MATCH THESE FRESH, VIBRANT BEAUTIES WITH ANY
SUMMER CHICKEN, BEEF, PORK, OR SEAFOOD DISH

Penne with
Green Beans
and Tomatoes

LEMON-SHALLOT VINAIGRETTE

Stir together $1/2$ cup fresh **lemon juice** and 1 minced **shallot;** let stand 5 minutes. Whisk in 1 cup **olive oil,** $1/4$ cup minced fresh **flat-leaf parsley,** 1 Tbsp. **honey,** and 1 Tbsp. whole grain **Dijon mustard.** Add **salt** and **pepper** to taste. Refrigerate in an airtight container up to 1 week.

MAKES about 2 cups. **HANDS-ON** 5 min.,
TOTAL 10 min.

PENNE WITH GREEN BEANS AND TOMATOES

Add zing to your salads with fresh dill, or swap it for basil, mint, or parsley.

- 1 (16-oz.) package whole wheat penne pasta
- 1 (8-oz.) package haricots verts (thin green beans), cut into 1 $1/2$-inch pieces
- 1 pt. grape tomatoes, halved
- $3/4$ cup Lemon-Shallot Vinaigrette (recipe above)
- $1/4$ cup chopped fresh dill

Cook pasta according to package directions, adding green beans to boiling water during last 2 minutes of cooking time; drain. Rinse pasta mixture under cold running water until cool; drain. Toss together pasta mixture, tomatoes, and vinaigrette. Cover and chill up to 24 hours, if desired. Just before serving, stir in dill, and add salt and pepper to taste.

MAKES 8 servings. **HANDS-ON** 15 min.;
TOTAL 35 min., including vinaigrette

Tortelloni-and-Grilled
Vegetable Salad

Tomato-and-Gorgonzola
Pasta Salad

TORTELLONI-AND-GRILLED VEGETABLE SALAD

This versatile pasta pairs with any grilled vegetable, so use what you have on hand or what looks best at the farmers' market.

- 3 medium zucchini (about 3/4 lb.), cut in half lengthwise
- 1 (8-oz.) package sweet mini bell peppers, trimmed and seeded
- 1 (20-oz.) package refrigerated cheese-and-spinach tortelloni
- 1/2 cup Lemon-Shallot Vinaigrette (see page 197)
- 1 cup torn fresh basil leaves

1. Preheat grill to 350° to 400° (medium-high) heat. Toss zucchini and peppers with desired amount of salt and pepper.
2. Grill vegetables, covered with grill lid, 4 to 5 minutes on each side or until tender. Remove from grill; let stand 5 minutes. Coarsely chop.
3. Prepare pasta according to package directions. Toss together warm tortelloni, grilled vegetables, and vinaigrette. Add salt and pepper to taste. Serve warm or at room temperature; sprinkle with basil just before serving.

MAKES 6 servings. **HANDS-ON** 15 min.; **TOTAL** 40 min., including vinaigrette

TOMATO-AND-GORGONZOLA PASTA SALAD

We love juicy beefsteaks for their sweet, intense flavor. Colorful small tomatoes and any crumbled cheese work well.

- 1 (16-oz.) package rigatoni pasta
- 1/2 cup Lemon-Shallot Vinaigrette (see page 197)
- 1 1/4 lb. beefsteak tomatoes, seeded and chopped
- 4 oz. Gorgonzola cheese, crumbled
- 1/2 (4-oz.) package arugula

1. Prepare pasta according to package directions. Toss together hot pasta and vinaigrette in a large bowl. Cool completely (about 30 minutes).

2. Stir tomatoes and cheese into pasta mixture. Just before serving, stir in arugula; add salt and pepper to taste.

MAKES 8 servings. **HANDS-ON** 20 min.; **TOTAL** 1 hour, 10 min., including vinaigrette

SWEET PEA-AND-MINT PASTA TOSS

Serve this minty side with grilled shrimp for a quick company-worthy dinner. Can't find torcetti? Use cavatappi or gemelli. (Pictured on page 183)

- 1 (16-oz.) package torcetti pasta
- 1 lb. fresh sugar snap peas
- 1 cup frozen green peas, thawed
- 1 cup loosely packed fresh mint, finely chopped
- 1 cup Lemon-Shallot Vinaigrette (see page 197)

Cook pasta according to package directions, adding sugar snap peas to boiling water during last 2 minutes of cooking time; drain. Rinse pasta mixture under cold running water until cool; drain. Slice sugar snap peas in half lengthwise, if desired. Stir in green peas and remaining ingredients. Add salt and pepper to taste. Serve immediately, or cover and chill up to 1 day.

MAKES 10 to 12 servings. **HANDS-ON** 10 min.; **TOTAL** 30 min., including vinaigrette

WATERMELON-AND-FETA ORZO SALAD

- 1 cup orzo pasta
- 1/2 cup Lemon-Shallot Vinaigrette (see page 197)
- 3 cups seeded and diced watermelon
- 4 cups firmly packed watercress or baby arugula
- 4 oz. crumbled feta cheese

1. Prepare pasta according to package directions. Toss together hot pasta and Lemon-Shallot Vinaigrette in a large bowl. Cover and chill pasta mixture 3 to 24 hours.

2. Gently toss together watermelon, watercress, feta cheese, and pasta mixture just before serving; add salt and pepper to taste.

MAKES 6 servings. **HANDS-ON** 20 min.; **TOTAL** 3 hours, 40 min., including vinaigrette

SNAPPY PEA-AND-HERB SALAD

Serve this fragrant side with just about any grilled meat; it plays well off smoky, charred flavors. Toss in feta cheese and shrimp to turn it into a main.

- 2 cups firmly packed fresh basil, coarsely chopped
- 1 3/4 cups firmly packed fresh mint, coarsely chopped
- 1 1/4 cups firmly packed fresh flat-leaf parsley leaves
- 1 (8-oz.) package sugar snap peas, sliced lengthwise
- 1/2 cup thinly sliced red onion
- 3/4 cup Lemon-Shallot Vinaigrette (see page 197)

Toss together basil and next 4 ingredients in a large serving bowl. Drizzle with 1/3 cup dressing; toss to coat. Serve immediately with remaining dressing.

MAKES 6 servings. **HANDS-ON** 30 min.; **TOTAL** 30 min.

GREEN MACHINE SALAD

There's enough acidity to keep the apples from turning brown if made up to three hours ahead. Use a vegetable peeler to transform asparagus into thin ribbons, a technique that also works well with carrots.

- 1/4 cup red wine vinegar
- 2 Tbsp. honey
- 1 (1-oz.) package fresh basil, chopped
- 1/2 cup olive oil
- 1 tsp. kosher salt
- 1 lb. fresh asparagus
- 1 large Granny Smith apple, cut into thin strips
- 1 (10-oz.) package finely shredded (angel hair) cabbage
- 1 bunch green onions, cut into thin strips

1. Whisk together first 5 ingredients in a small bowl.

2. Snap off and discard tough ends of asparagus. Cut asparagus lengthwise into thin, ribbon-like strips, using a vegetable peeler. Toss together asparagus, apple, next 2 ingredients, and dressing. Cover and chill 10 minutes. Add salt and pepper to taste just before serving.

MAKES 4 servings. **HANDS-ON** 30 min., **TOTAL** 40 min.

STRAWBERRY-TOMATO SALAD

Look for mini multicolored tomatoes at the supermarket. Toss them with strawberries for a surprising combo to serve with grilled salmon, chicken, or pork.

- 1 1/2 cups fresh strawberries, chopped
- 1/2 lb. assorted small heirloom tomatoes, quartered
- 1/3 cup chopped fresh basil
- 1 Tbsp. chopped fresh oregano
- 1 tsp. loosely packed lemon zest
- 1/2 tsp. kosher salt
- 1/4 tsp. ground black pepper

Stir together all ingredients.

MAKES 6 servings. **HANDS-ON** 15 min., **TOTAL** 15 min.

ORIENTAL SALAD BOWL

(FROM JULY 1987)

Cool, Crisp Salads To Beat the Heat

❝ **THE ORIGINAL:** The ingredients for this '80s staple read like a canned goods advertisement. With water chestnuts and baby corn, plus a too-sweet soy dressing, the salad is as authentically Asian as General Tso's Chicken. **THE REVIVAL:** A crisp slaw stars fresh crunchy veggies, including cabbage, bell peppers, and jicama, tossed in a creamy ginger-and-rice vinegar dressing. Bonus: Top it off with chicken, pulled pork, or shrimp. (Also pictured on page 183)

ASIAN SLAW WITH EGG ROLL CRACKERS

DRESSING

- 1/2 cup mayonnaise
- 1 Tbsp. sugar
- 1 Tbsp. loosely packed orange zest
- 1 Tbsp. rice vinegar
- 1 Tbsp. coarse-grained mustard
- 2 tsp. soy sauce
- 2 tsp. Asian hot chili sauce (such as Sriracha)
- 1/2 tsp. sesame oil
- 1/2 tsp. finely grated fresh ginger

CRACKERS

- 6 egg roll wrappers
  Vegetable cooking spray
  Kosher salt
  Freshly ground black pepper

SLAW

- 4 cups shredded green cabbage
- 4 cups shredded red cabbage
- 2 red bell peppers, seeded and sliced
- 1 cup peeled and thinly sliced jicama
- 1/2 cup loosely packed fresh cilantro, chopped
- 1/2 cup fresh corn kernels (from 1 ear)
- 2 green onions, sliced
- 2 tsp. black or white sesame seeds

Asian Slaw with Egg
Roll Crackers

- 4 cups shredded cooked chicken or pulled pork or 1 1/2 lb. peeled cooked shrimp (optional)

1. Prepare Dressing: Whisk together mayonnaise and next 8 ingredients. Cover and chill until ready to use (up to 1 week).

2. Prepare Crackers: Preheat oven to 350°. Arrange egg roll wrappers in a single layer on a baking sheet. Coat generously with cooking spray, and sprinkle with desired amount of salt and pepper. Bake 9 minutes or until golden brown, rotating halfway through.

3. Meanwhile, prepare Slaw: Stir together green cabbage, next 7 ingredients, and, if desired, chicken. Toss with desired amount of dressing. Season with salt and pepper, if desired. Serve immediately on Egg Roll Crackers.

MAKES 6 servings. **HANDS-ON** 30 min., **TOTAL** 30 min.

Celebrate with a Sweet Salute

OUR PATRIOTIC SPIN ON ICE-CREAM CAKE IS THE COOLEST DESSERT OF SUMMER

RED, WHITE, AND BLUE ICE-CREAM CAKE

(Also pictured on page 185)

- 1 (10.75-oz.) **frozen pound cake, thawed**
- 2 **pt. vanilla ice cream, softened**
- 1/2 **cup blueberry preserves**
- 2 **pt. raspberry sorbet, softened**
- 1/2 **cup raspberry preserves**
- 1 (10-oz.) **package frozen raspberries, thawed**
- 1/4 **cup honey**
- 1 **cup whipping cream**
- 1/4 **cup powdered sugar**
  Garnishes: assorted fresh berries, mint leaves

1. Cut 10 (1/2-inch-thick) slices from cake. Arrange slices in a single layer on bottom of a 9-inch springform pan, trimming as needed to snugly cover pan. Save remaining cake for another use.

2. Stir together vanilla ice cream and blueberry preserves in a medium bowl. Spread blueberry ice-cream mixture over cake slices. Cover and freeze 1 hour.

3. Stir together softened raspberry sorbet and raspberry preserves in a medium bowl. Spread raspberry sorbet mixture over blueberry ice-cream mixture. Cover and freeze 3 hours to 2 days.

4. Process frozen raspberries, honey, and 2 Tbsp. water in a blender until smooth. Press raspberry mixture through a wire-mesh strainer using the back of a spoon. Discard pulp and seeds. Chill until ready to serve.

5. Just before serving, beat cream and sugar at medium speed until soft peaks form. Gently run a sharp knife around edge of cake to loosen. Remove springform pan. Spread whipped cream over frozen cake. Drizzle with raspberry-honey sauce.

Note: We tested with Sara Lee All Butter Pound Cake, Bonne Maman Raspberry Preserves, Smucker's Orchard's Finest Northwoods Blueberry Preserves, and Whole Fruit Raspberry Sorbet.

MAKES 8 to 10 servings. **HANDS-ON** 30 min.; **TOTAL** 4 hours, 30 min.

Red, White, and Blue Ice-Cream Cake

Community Cookbook

Just try finding a copy of *Bayou Cuisine*, a compendium of Delta-style recipes from Indianola, Mississippi, without stained and marked pages or a broken spine—all signs of a beloved book.

Sherried Summer Berries

SHERRIED SUMMER BERRIES

In this recipe adapted from Bayou Cuisine, *juicy berries and silken custard called sabayon yield an easy, hot-weather dessert.*

Whisk together 4 large **egg yolks,** 1 cup **sugar,** and ¼ cup **sherry.** Pour water to a depth of 1 inch into bottom of a double boiler over medium-high heat; bring to a boil. Reduce heat to medium-low, and simmer; place sherry mixture in top of double boiler over simmering water. Cook, stirring constantly, 15 minutes. Remove from heat; transfer mixture to a clean medium-size bowl. Cool 5 minutes; cover and chill 30 minutes or until cold. Beat ½ cup **heavy cream** with an electric mixer until soft peaks form. Fold whipped cream into sherry mixture; cover and chill 15 minutes. Divide sherry mixture among 6 to 8 serving bowls; top with fresh **strawberries, halved,** and/or **blueberries, raspberries, or blackberries.**

MAKES 6 to 8 servings. **HANDS-ON** 25 min.; **TOTAL** 1 hour, 15 min.

CREOLE CHICKEN

This one-pot chicken dish comes together in a jiffy at the end of a busy day. Serve over rice.

4	(6- to 8-oz.) skinned and boned chicken breasts
	Kosher salt and ground black pepper
4 ½	tsp. olive oil
¼	cup chopped yellow onion
¼	cup chopped green bell pepper
2	garlic cloves, minced
½	tsp. paprika
½	cup sliced fresh mushrooms
1 ½	cups canned diced tomatoes, drained
1	Tbsp. tomato paste
3	Tbsp. all-purpose flour
2 ½	cups reduced-sodium chicken broth
1	Tbsp. fresh lemon juice
1	tsp. prepared horseradish

1. Sprinkle chicken breasts with salt and pepper. Working in batches, cook 2 breasts in hot olive oil in a Dutch oven over medium-high heat 4 to 5 minutes on each side or until browned. Remove chicken from Dutch oven; cover with aluminum foil to keep warm.
2. Add onion and bell pepper to Dutch oven; sauté 5 minutes or until tender. Stir in garlic and paprika; sauté 1 minute. Add mushrooms; sauté 5 minutes. Stir in tomatoes and tomato paste, and cook, stirring constantly, 2 minutes. Add flour, and cook, stirring constantly, 1 minute. Stir in broth; boil. Reduce heat to medium; simmer, stirring occasionally, 5 minutes. Stir in lemon juice, horseradish, and chicken; simmer 10 minutes or until chicken is cooked through. Add salt and pepper to taste.

MAKES 4 servings. **HANDS-ON** 1 hour, 5 min.; **TOTAL** 1 hour, 5 min.

August

A Field Day
for Peas and Beans

BUY YOUR FAVORITE VARIETIES OF FRESH FIELD PEAS AND BEANS NOW DURING PEAK SEASON, AND KEEP THEM IN YOUR FREEZER TO SAVOR THE TASTE OF SUMMER ALL YEAR LONG

Purple Hull Peas

Lady Peas

Lima Beans

SHELL GAME
Buy limas and field peas at the market in the pod, or pay a little extra for pre-shelled.

SAVE THE BOUNTY

Buy extra peas and beans and put them up for the winter. Here's the best, safest, and easiest way to do it.

Clean Rinse shelled peas and beans with cold water; drain.

Blanch Cook in boiling salted water 1 to 2 minutes; drain. Plunge into ice water to stop the cooking process; drain.

Dry well Pat dry so peas or beans don't clump together when frozen.

Measure and freeze Portion and place each batch in a zip-top plastic freezer bag, and seal, pushing out excess air. Label and freeze up to 6 months.

Take from freezer to table To use, scoop the desired amount of peas or beans directly from the freezer bag, and cook as desired—no need to thaw first. Frozen legumes will cook in about the same time as fresh and retain the same flavor and texture. Most go from freezer to fabulous in less than 45 minutes.

AT THE MARKET

Go early to get first dibs on the best peas and beans before they get picked over or sell out. What's in a name? **Crowder peas** crowd in the pod. **Black-eyed peas** have darker centers than pink-eyes. **Cream peas** (aka creamers) are creamy colored. **Purple hulls** include many types, but they all boast purple hulls. There are hundreds of delicious varieties. Try them!

SMOKY BLACK-EYED PEAS WITH FRIED GREEN TOMATOES

Cooked in an aromatic broth with ham hocks and beer (sub chicken broth, if desired), these Mexican-inspired peas are as delicious on their own as they are with fried tomatoes or grilled steak. (Pictured on page 14)

- 1 cup chopped onion
- 3 Tbsp. canola oil
- 1 garlic clove, minced
- 3 cups fresh black-eyed peas
- 2 Smoked Ham Hocks (recipe, page 207) or purchased smoked ham hocks
- 1 (12-oz.) bottle amber beer
- 2 Tbsp. tomato paste
- 1 bay leaf
- 1 (7-oz.) can chipotle peppers in adobo sauce
- 1 1/2 cups all-purpose flour
- 1 tsp. kosher salt
- 1 tsp. ground black pepper
- 1/2 cup plain white cornmeal
- 1/2 tsp. ground chipotle chile pepper
- 2 large eggs
- 1/2 cup buttermilk
- 3 large firm green tomatoes, each cut into 4 slices
  Canola oil
- 3 large ripe red tomatoes, each cut into 4 slices
- 1/2 cup crumbled feta or Cotija cheese
- 1/4 cup chopped cilantro
  Hot sauce

1. Sauté onion in 3 Tbsp. hot oil in a 3-qt. saucepan over medium-high heat 4 minutes. Add garlic; sauté 1 minute. Stir in peas, next 4 ingredients, 3 1/2 cups water, and 2 Tbsp. adobo sauce from canned chipotle peppers. (Reserve peppers for another use.) Bring to a boil; cover and reduce heat to medium. Simmer, stirring occasionally, 1 1/2 hours. Uncover and cook, stirring occasionally, 20 to 30 minutes or until peas are tender. Discard bay leaf. Remove hocks. Remove ham from bones; discard bones. Chop ham; stir into peas. Add salt to taste; cover and keep warm over low heat.

2. Stir together 3/4 cup flour, 1/2 tsp. salt, and 1/2 tsp. pepper in a shallow dish. Whisk together cornmeal, ground chipotle chile, and remaining 3/4 cup flour, 1/2 tsp. salt, and 1/2 tsp. pepper in a second shallow dish. Whisk together eggs and buttermilk in a third shallow dish.

3. Dredge green tomatoes, 1 slice at a time, in flour mixture, shaking off excess. Dip in egg mixture, and dredge in cornmeal mixture.

4. Pour oil to depth of 1 inch in a cast-iron skillet. Heat over medium-high heat to 375°. Fry green tomato slices, in batches, in hot oil 3 minutes on each side or until crisp. Drain on a wire rack over paper towels. (Let oil temperature return to 375° between batches.)

5. Divide peas among 6 plates. Top each with 1 red tomato slice and 1 fried green tomato slice. Repeat tomato layers once. Sprinkle cheese and cilantro over tomatoes. Serve with hot sauce.

MAKES 6 servings. **HANDS-ON** 1 hour; **TOTAL** 2 hours, 55 min.

Summer Hoppin' John Salad

SUMMER HOPPIN' JOHN SALAD

A New Year's tradition, Hoppin' John is usually served hot, but this cool salad is perfect for a summer picnic or lunch, or as a side salad for grilled meats. Feel free to sub your favorite cooked whole grain instead of rice. (Also pictured on page 186)

- 1 medium-size sweet onion, cut into 1/2-inch slices
- 1 Tbsp. olive oil
- 4 cups drained Classic Fresh Field Peas (recipe, page 206)
  Apple Cider Vinaigrette
- 1 lb. heirloom tomatoes, cut into wedges
- 2 cups loosely packed mixed salad greens
- 3/4 cup chopped assorted fresh herbs (such as flat-leaf parsley, chives, dill, and basil)
- 1 1/2 cups cooked basmati rice, cooled

1. Brush onion slices with olive oil; cook in a hot grill pan over medium-high heat about 5 minutes on each side or until grill marks appear. Coarsely chop onion.

2. Toss together peas, chopped onion, and 3 Tbsp. Apple Cider Vinaigrette in a medium bowl. Gently toss together tomatoes, next 2 ingredients, and 3 Tbsp. Apple Cider Vinaigrette in another bowl.

3. Spoon rice onto a serving platter; top with tomato mixture and pea mixture. Serve with remaining vinaigrette.

MAKES 6 servings. **HANDS-ON** 30 min.; **TOTAL** 3 hours, 45 min., including peas and vinaigrette

Apple Cider Vinaigrette

- 1/4 cup apple cider vinegar
- 1 garlic clove, minced
- 1 tsp. sugar
- 1 tsp. spicy brown mustard
- 1/3 cup olive oil

Whisk together first 4 ingredients; add oil in a slow, steady stream, whisking constantly until smooth. Add salt and pepper to taste.

MAKES about 2/3 cup. **HANDS-ON** 5 min., **TOTAL** 5 min.

SMOKY FIELD PEA HUMMUS

This is our new go-to summer dip. Use any legume you like. (Pictured on page 186)

- 1/3 cup chopped smoked ham from hock
  Vegetable cooking spray
- 4 cups drained Classic Fresh Field Peas (recipe at right)
- 1/4 cup chopped fresh flat-leaf parsley
- 1/4 cup olive oil
- 2 Tbsp. fresh lemon juice
- 1 Tbsp. tahini
- 1 garlic clove, pressed
- 1 tsp. kosher salt
- 1 Tbsp. extra virgin olive oil
- 1/4 tsp. smoked paprika
  Pita chips

1. Sauté ham in a small nonstick skillet coated with cooking spray over medium-high heat 3 to 5 minutes or until crisp.

2. Process peas and next 6 ingredients in a food processor, adding up to 3 Tbsp. water, 1 Tbsp. at a time, as needed to reach desired consistency. Transfer to a bowl, and drizzle with 1 Tbsp. oil. Top with paprika and crisp ham. Serve with chips.

MAKES about 4 cups. **HANDS-ON** 20 min.; **TOTAL** 3 hours, 30 min., including peas

CLASSIC FRESH FIELD PEAS

Smoky ham hocks enrich the broth, yielding a delicious pot of field peas. Try smoking your own hocks—they will yield roughly double what you'll get from store-bought hocks.

- 2 Smoked Ham Hocks (recipe on facing page) or purchased smoked ham hocks
- 1 1/2 cups finely chopped onion
- 3 Tbsp. bacon drippings
- 2 garlic cloves, minced
- 3 cups shelled fresh field peas (about 1 lb.)
- 1 tsp. kosher salt
- 1 tsp. ground black pepper

1. Bring hocks and 2 qt. water to a boil in a large Dutch oven over medium heat; simmer 1 1/2 to 2 hours or until meat is tender.

2. Meanwhile, sauté onion in hot drippings in a medium skillet over medium-high heat 6 minutes. Add garlic; sauté 1 minute. Add peas and onion mixture to Dutch oven with ham hocks; bring to a simmer over medium heat. Cover and simmer, stirring occasionally, 45 minutes or until peas are tender. Remove hocks; drain peas, and sprinkle with salt and pepper.

3. Remove and chop ham from hock bones; discard bones. Stir ham into peas, if desired.

MAKES 4 cups. **HANDS-ON** 45 min.; **TOTAL** 3 hours, 10 min., not including ham hocks

WORTH THE EFFORT
Learn to smoke ham hocks in your backyard. See Test Kitchen Academy on facing page.

OLD-FASHIONED SUCCOTASH

You can make this recipe with limas or butter beans.

- 2 cups fresh lima beans
- 4 fresh thyme sprigs
- 1/2 small onion
- 1 garlic clove
- 1 1/2 cups diced sweet onion
- 2 Tbsp. olive oil
- 4 cups fresh corn kernels (about 6 ears)
- 1 tsp. honey
- 2 Tbsp. unsalted butter
  Kosher salt and freshly ground black pepper
- 3 Tbsp. chopped fresh chives

1. Place lima beans, thyme sprigs, onion half, and garlic in a medium saucepan, and cover with water. Bring mixture to a boil over medium-high heat; reduce heat to medium, and simmer, stirring occasionally, 20 minutes or until beans are tender. Drain beans, reserving 1/2 cup cooking liquid. Discard thyme sprigs, onion, and garlic.

2. Sauté diced onion in hot oil in a large skillet over medium-high heat 5 minutes. Stir in corn and honey; cook, stirring often, 6 minutes or until corn is tender. Stir in beans and 1/2 cup reserved cooking liquid; cook, stirring occasionally, 5 minutes. Stir in butter, and add salt and pepper to taste. Sprinkle with chives.

MAKES 6 servings. **HANDS-ON** 35 min., **TOTAL** 1 hour

RESIDENT PITMASTER PAM LOLLEY EXPLAINS HOW TO

MAKE SMOKED HAM HOCKS

I'll never buy another smoked ham hock from the supermarket again after testing author Cathy Barrow's smart recipe. Smoking your own hocks gives them sweet, rich character without any artificial flavor. Now I make extra batches to keep in my freezer all year 'round to season field peas (recipes, pages 205-206), soups, and stews.

SMOKED HAM HOCKS

Call your butcher days ahead to order fresh hocks. This recipe also works great with fresh turkey wings.

- 3 Tbsp. table salt
- 1 Tbsp. chopped fresh thyme
- 2 Tbsp. honey
- 1 tsp. coarsely ground black pepper
- 4 (10- to 12-oz.) fresh ham hocks
- 4 cups pecan or hickory wood chips
- 2 (9-inch) square disposable aluminum foil pans
- 2 cups beer or apple cider
- ¼ cup maple syrup or molasses

1. Bring first 4 ingredients and 2 qt. water to a boil in a large saucepan. Remove from heat, and cool 1 hour. Divide hocks between 2 (1-gal.) heavy-duty zip-top plastic bags. Pour half of brine mixture into each bag; seal and chill 8 to 24 hours. Remove hocks, and rinse. Discard brine. Chill hocks uncovered on a wire rack over a baking sheet 2 hours, or cover with foil, and chill up to 12 hours.
2. Place 2 cups wood chips in each disposable pan; pour 1 cup beer into each pan. Soak chips 30 minutes.
3. Heat 1 side of grill to 200° (low) heat, leaving other side unlit. Place 1 pan of wood chips on lit side of grill. (Reserve second pan of soaked chips for Step

4.) Cover grill for 20 minutes or until wood chips begin to smoke. Place ham hocks on unlit side of grill; brush with syrup. Grill, covered and maintaining temperature at 200°, 2 hours, brushing with syrup every hour.
4. Remove pan of chips from grill, and discard. Place reserved pan of chips on lit side. Grill, covered and maintaining temperature at 200°, 4 to 6 more hours or until meat is tender. (The longer you cook, the smokier they get.)

MAKES 4 ham hocks. **HANDS-ON** 45 min.; **TOTAL** 18 hours, 45 min.

Revamp Burger Night

ADD ZIP TO YOUR PATTIES. JAZZ UP THE CONDIMENTS. AND GO BEYOND GROUND BEEF.
THESE FIVE EASY SOUTHERN RECIPES WILL INVIGORATE DINNER FROM THE GRILL.

BACON, PEACH, AND BASIL BURGERS

We recommend ground sirloin here because it's lean, which causes fewer flare-ups on the grill. Chopped pickled jalapeños and their juice ramp up the flavor, while bacon, goat cheese, and tangy-sweet chutney balance the heat. (Also pictured on page 186)

1 1/2 lb. ground sirloin
2 Tbsp. chopped pickled jalapeño peppers
2 Tbsp. pickled jalapeño pepper juice
1 tsp. kosher salt
6 thick bacon slices
1 small sweet onion, sliced
1/2 cup peach chutney
4 oz. goat cheese, softened
6 hamburger buns, toasted
1 medium peach, sliced
Fresh basil leaves

1. Preheat grill to 350° to 400° (medium-high) heat. Combine first 4 ingredients. Gently shape mixture into 6 (4-inch) patties.
2. Cook bacon in a large skillet over medium heat 8 minutes or until crisp. Remove bacon, and drain on paper towels, reserving 2 Tbsp. drippings in skillet. Increase heat to medium-high, and sauté onion in reserved hot drippings 6 minutes or until tender. Remove from heat, and stir in chutney.
3. Grill patties, covered with grill lid, 4 to 5 minutes on each side or until beef is no longer pink in center. Top with cheese, and serve on hamburger buns with onion mixture, bacon, peach slices, and basil leaves.

Note: We tested with Alecia's Peach Chutney.

MAKES 6 burgers. **HANDS-ON** 30 min., **TOTAL** 30 min.

Bacon, Peach, and Basil Burgers

SLOPPY JOE CAROLINA-STYLE BURGERS

Eat these over-the-top burgers with a knife and fork, or set out a pile of napkins. Add fresh crisp texture and flavor by mounding slaw atop the burgers. Serve extra slaw on the side, or save it for another day.

1/3 cup mayonnaise
1/3 cup sour cream
1 Tbsp. apple cider vinegar
1 1/2 tsp. kosher salt, divided
3/4 tsp. freshly ground black pepper, divided

1 (16-oz.) package 3-color deli coleslaw mix
1 lb. ground sirloin
2 Tbsp. steak sauce
4 hamburger buns, toasted
1 (16-oz.) can chili, warmed

1. Preheat grill to 350° to 400° (medium-high) heat. Whisk together mayonnaise, sour cream, apple cider vinegar, 1/2 tsp. salt, and 1/4 tsp. pepper in a large bowl. Add coleslaw mix; toss to coat. Cover and chill until ready to serve.
2. Combine ground sirloin, steak sauce, and remaining 1 tsp. salt and

½ tsp. pepper. Gently shape mixture into 4 (4-inch) patties.

3. Grill patties, covered with grill lid, 4 to 5 minutes on each side or until beef is no longer pink in center. Serve on hamburger buns, and top burgers with chili and coleslaw mixture.

Note: We tested with Fresh Express 3-Color Deli Cole Slaw.

MAKES 4 burgers. **HANDS-ON** 15 min., **TOTAL** 25 min.

PIGGY BURGERS

Look for ground pork at the meat counter at the supermarket. We recommend a blend that's not too fatty, such as an 85/15 mix of lean pork to fat.

- 1 lb. ground pork
- 4 thick bacon slices, cooked and crumbled
- 2 tsp. molasses-bacon seasoning blend
- 4 hamburger buns, toasted
  Toppings: Onion-Spiked Pickles, bottled barbecue sauce

1. Preheat grill to 350° to 400° (medium-high) heat. Combine first 3 ingredients. Gently shape mixture into 4 (4-inch) patties.

2. Grill patties, covered with grill lid, 5 minutes on each side or until pork is no longer pink. Serve on buns with desired toppings.

Note: We tested with McCormick Grill Mates Molasses Bacon Seasoning.

MAKES 4 burgers. **HANDS-ON** 10 min.; **TOTAL** 1 hour, 30 min., including pickles

Onion-Spiked Pickles

Remove half the **bread-and-butter pickles** from 1 (16-oz.) jar, leaving juice in jar; reserve removed pickles for another use. Add ½ **onion,** thinly sliced, to jar. Cover tightly with lid, and let stand, upside down, 1 hour. Store at room temperature up to 2 months.

MAKES about 8 servings. **HANDS-ON** 5 min.; **TOTAL** 1 hour, 10 min.

TEX-MEX TURKEY BURGERS

Grab a bag of tortilla chips and a can of black beans to serve alongside the burgers, and whip up a batch of margaritas for a festive cocktail; find your favorite recipe at southernliving.com/margaritas. (Pictured on page 186)

- 1 large lime
- ¼ cup finely chopped red onion
- 2 garlic cloves, minced
- 1 Tbsp. olive oil
- 1 cup fresh corn kernels (about 2 ears)
- 1 avocado, peeled and finely chopped
- ¼ cup finely chopped fresh cilantro leaves
- 1½ tsp. kosher salt, divided
- 1 lb. ground turkey
- 1 (4-oz.) can chopped green chiles
- 1 large egg, lightly beaten
- ½ tsp. ground cumin
- ½ cup fine, dry breadcrumbs
- 6 tostada shells, warmed
  Toppings: salsa verde, crumbled queso fresco
  Garnish: lime wedges

1. Preheat grill to 350° to 400° (medium-high) heat. Grate zest from lime to equal 1 tsp. Cut lime in half, and squeeze juice from lime to equal 1 Tbsp.

2. Sauté onion and garlic in hot oil in a medium skillet 1 minute. Add corn, and cook 2 to 3 minutes or just until corn begins to brown. Transfer mixture to a medium bowl. Stir in lime zest, lime juice, avocado, cilantro, and ½ tsp. salt.

3. Combine turkey, next 4 ingredients, and remaining 1 tsp. salt. Gently shape mixture into 6 (4-inch) patties.

4. Grill patties, covered with grill lid, 4 to 5 minutes on each side or until done. Serve on tostadas with corn mixture and desired toppings.

MAKES 6 burgers. **HANDS-ON** 25 min., **TOTAL** 25 min.

RED BEANS-AND-RICE VEGGIE BURGERS

Stirring the rice as it cooks releases the starch that helps hold the veggie patties together. Want to go beyond vegetarian? Top these burgers with grilled shrimp or sausage.

- ½ cup uncooked long-grain white rice
- 2 (16-oz.) cans red kidney beans, drained and rinsed
- ⅓ cup minced green bell pepper
- ⅓ cup minced sweet onion
- 2 Tbsp. minced celery
- 1 Tbsp. Creole seasoning
- 2 garlic cloves, minced
- 1 large egg, lightly beaten
- 3 Tbsp. olive oil
- 3 Tbsp. mayonnaise
- 3 Tbsp. Creole mustard
- 2 Tbsp. minced green onions
- 2 Tbsp. finely chopped fresh flat-leaf parsley
- 6 butter lettuce leaves
- 6 (½-inch-thick) crusty bread slices, toasted

1. Bring 1½ cups water to a boil in a small saucepan over medium heat; stir in rice. Reduce heat to low. Cook, stirring constantly, 15 minutes or until water is absorbed and rice is tender.

2. Mash red kidney beans in a large bowl with a fork or pastry blender. Stir in bell pepper, next 5 ingredients, and cooked rice until well blended. Shape mixture into 6 (½-inch-thick) patties.

3. Cook 3 patties in 1½ Tbsp. hot oil in a large nonstick skillet over medium heat 5 minutes on each side or until golden. Repeat procedure with remaining oil and patties.

4. Stir together mayonnaise, Creole mustard, green onions, and parsley. Place 1 lettuce leaf on each bread slice; top each with 1 patty and desired amount of mayonnaise mixture.

MAKES 6 burgers. **HANDS-ON** 40 min., **TOTAL** 40 min.

Heat Up the Grill, Not Your Kitchen

CYNTHIA GRAUBART DRAWS YOUR RECIPE ROAD MAP FOR ONE SIMPLE GRILLED PORK TENDERLOIN DINNER THAT YIELDS TWO MORE EASY MEALS

NO NEED TO HEAT YOUR OVEN during these last carefree days of summer. My recipe for spice-rubbed Grilled Pork Tenderloins yields the main dish for a Sunday supper and gives you a head start for Monday and Tuesday nights as well.

There are plenty of reasons why pork tenderloins are so popular: They're lean and cook quickly; you don't have to slather the pork with oil or brush it with a heavy sauce; and grilling them adds an extra layer of charred flavor. I recommend buying tenderloins sold in packs of two that have not been preseasoned or marinated. Season them at home instead with my homemade spice rub to enhance the smoky

flavor from the grill, and double the spice rub to keep on hand for any other grilled meats.

While the grill is still hot and the pork rests, toss on six ears of fresh corn. Then slice the pork, and serve it with the grilled corn and a fresh lemony potato salad. On Monday, combine the reserved pork and grilled corn to make Pork Tenderloin Wraps with Grilled Corn Salsa. Tuesday's dinner is a fresh no-cook salad with pork, mango, lettuce, and tomato drizzled with a tangy-sweet vinaigrette. The lazy days of summer may be coming to an end, but there's still time to fire up the grill to make three smart suppers without breaking a sweat.

Grilled Pork Tenderloins with Corn on the Cob

SUNDAY NIGHT

GRILLED PORK TENDERLOINS WITH CORN ON THE COB

After grilling the pork, divide one tenderloin into three equal portions, and set aside two tenderloins and two-thirds of the divided one to use later in the week. Serve pork and corn with Lemony Potato Salad (southernliving.com/lemony-potato-salad).

1/4 cup firmly packed light brown sugar

2 Tbsp. kosher salt

2 Tbsp. paprika

2 Tbsp. dry mustard

1 tsp. freshly ground black pepper

1 tsp. dried oregano

1 tsp. dried thyme

4 (1-lb.) pork tenderloins

4 tsp. olive oil

6 ears fresh corn, in husks
Kitchen string

1. Process first 7 ingredients in a food processor 30 seconds or until blended.
2. Remove silver skin from pork, leaving a thin layer of fat. Pat tenderloins dry; rub with oil, and coat with spice mixture. Let pork stand at room temperature 30 minutes. Pull back husks from corn; remove and discard silks. Tie husks together with kitchen string to form handles. Rinse and dry exposed cobs.
3. Preheat grill to 350° to 400° (medium-high) heat. Grill pork, covered with grill lid, 10 to 12 minutes on each side or until a meat thermometer inserted in thickest portions registers 145°. Remove pork from grill, and let stand at room temperature 10 to 15 minutes. Thinly slice one and one-third tenderloins; reserve remaining two and two-thirds tenderloins for Pork Tenderloin Wraps and Pork, Mango, and Tomato Salad.
4. Meanwhile, grill corn, covered with grill lid, 15 minutes or until golden brown, turning occasionally. Sprinkle with desired amount of salt and pepper. Reserve 2 ears corn for later use. Serve remaining corn with Grilled Pork Tenderloins.

MAKES 4 servings. **HANDS-ON** 55 min.; **TOTAL** 1 hour, 35 min.

MONDAY NIGHT

READY IN 25 MINUTES!

PORK TENDERLOIN WRAPS WITH GRILLED CORN SALSA

Look for fresh salsa in the refrigerated area of the produce section at most supermarkets, or use your favorite jarred variety. (Pictured on page 188)

2 ears grilled corn (reserved from Sunday supper)

1 1/3 Grilled Pork Tenderloins

1 (16-oz.) container fresh salsa

1/2 cup chopped fresh cilantro

8 (6-inch) fajita-size flour tortillas

1 lime, cut into wedges

Cut kernels from cobs; discard cobs. Chop pork, and cook in a small skillet over medium-high heat, stirring occasionally, 5 minutes or until thoroughly heated. Remove pork from skillet. Add corn kernels to skillet, and cook, stirring often, 2 minutes. Stir together corn, salsa, and 1/4 cup cilantro in a bowl. Warm tortillas according to package directions. Spoon pork and salsa mixture into tortillas; sprinkle with remaining 1/4 cup cilantro, and roll up. Serve with lime wedges.

MAKES 4 servings. **HANDS-ON** 25 min.; **TOTAL** 25 min., not including pork

TUESDAY NIGHT

FRESH NO-COOK SUMMER SALAD

PORK, MANGO, AND TOMATO SALAD

The beauty of this effortless recipe is that you don't even have to heat up your stove; simply slice and serve the pork cold or at room temperature. (Pictured on page 14)

1 1/3 Grilled Pork Tenderloins

1 (10-oz.) package shredded romaine lettuce

1 medium mango, peeled and chopped

1 large tomato, seeded and chopped

1 large cucumber, peeled, seeded, and chopped

1/2 large red onion, thinly sliced

3/4 cup canola oil

1/3 cup balsamic vinegar

3 Tbsp. honey

2 Tbsp. finely grated red onion

1 Tbsp. Dijon mustard

1 tsp. table salt
Freshly ground black pepper

Thinly slice pork. Divide lettuce among 4 plates, and top with pork, mango, and next 3 ingredients. Whisk together oil and next 5 ingredients in a small bowl. Add black pepper to taste. Drizzle over salad.

MAKES 4 servings. **HANDS-ON** 20 min.; **TOTAL** 20 min., not including pork

Grow These Greens

PLANT NOW TO FILL YOUR FALL WITH THE TASTY LEAVES OF THIS ITALIAN HEIRLOOM

TUSCAN KALE has lots of names. It's also called dinosaur kale, black palm, Italian kale, and Tuscan cabbage. With that many titles, it has to be loved—and for good reason. It's easy to grow in the garden and is delicious as well as versatile in the kitchen. Its textured, blue-green leaves are great in salads, stews, pastas, and casseroles. Loaded with vitamins, minerals, and antioxidants, it is one of the most nutritious foods you can eat.

Though it originally hails from Italy, it has been grown in the South for centuries. Thomas Jefferson had it at Monticello, and you can grow it in your own backyard. Buy transplants for a quick start. If you plan to plant a lot of rows, use seeds, which are budget friendly. In smaller spaces, grow it in a container. Or use it as an ornamental—its beautiful foliage pairs nicely with violas. Look for plants at your local nursery, or order seeds online from *territorialseed.com* or *monticelloshop.org*.

Tuscan kale loves the sun. It grows best in rich soil that's been amended with organic matter. Good soil will feed your plants. You can also supplement with an organic fertilizer. Water your kale moderately and consistently. Cut leaves as they're needed. If you want just a little, use a small knife or pop off single leaves by hand, gathering from the bottom of the plant and working your way up. (This way, the plant keeps growing for future use.) If you need a lot, harvest the whole plant. Wash thoroughly before eating. Tuscan kale thrives in cold weather, and the leaves will be even sweeter after the first frost.

KALE POWER SALAD

Whisk together 2/3 cup **olive oil**, 1/4 cup **white balsamic vinegar**, 1 tsp. **orange zest**, 2 Tbsp. **orange juice**, 1 Tbsp. **honey**, 2 tsp. **Dijon mustard**, 3/4 tsp. **salt**, and a pinch each **ground red pepper** and **ground ginger**. Toss 5 oz. chopped **kale**, sections from 3 **oranges**, 1 pt. **raspberries**, and 1/3 cup chopped toasted **almonds** with 1/4 cup **dressing**. **MAKES** 6 servings. **HANDS-ON** 10 min., **TOTAL** 10 min.

---

get growing!
TUSCAN KALE

SOIL
Plant in fertile, well-drained soil amended with organic matter such as composted manure or chopped leaves.

FERTILIZE
Use an organic product such as Dynamite Organic All-Purpose (10-2-8).

| LIGHT FULL SUN | WATER MEDIUM | CARE EASY |

Got kale? These greens offer more calcium per calorie than milk does.

Hit the Sweet Spot

ONE BITE OF THIS ARNOLD PALMER-INSPIRED CAKE AND EVEN GOLFERS WILL AGREE:
THERE'S SUCH A THING AS THE PERFECT SLICE

SWEET TEA-AND-LEMONADE CAKE

Feeling rowdy? Spin this into a tipsy cake by substituting up to 2 Tbsp. vodka or bourbon for the lemon juice in the frosting. (Also pictured on page 187)

	Shortening
1 1/2	cups boiling water
3	family-size tea bags
1	cup butter, softened
2	cups granulated sugar
1/2	cup firmly packed light brown sugar
5	large eggs, at room temperature
3 1/2	cups cake flour
2	tsp. baking powder
3/4	tsp. table salt
1/4	tsp. baking soda
	Lemonade Frosting

1. Preheat oven to 350°. Grease (with shortening) and flour a 13- x 9-inch pan. Pour 1 1/2 cups boiling water over tea bags in a heatproof glass bowl. Cover with plastic wrap, and steep 10 minutes. Lift tea bags from liquid, and press against side of bowl, using back of a spoon; discard tea bags. Cool tea 20 minutes.

2. Beat butter in a separate large bowl at medium speed with an electric mixer until creamy. Gradually add sugars, beating until light and fluffy.

Add eggs, 1 at a time, beating just until blended after each addition. Whisk together cake flour and next 3 ingredients; add to butter mixture alternately with 1 cup tea, beginning and ending with flour mixture. (Discard any remaining tea.) Beat at low speed just until blended after each addition. Pour batter into prepared pan.

3. Bake at 350° for 35 to 40 minutes or until wooden pick inserted in center comes out clean. Cool completely on a wire rack (about 20 minutes). Spread Lemonade Frosting on cake.

Note: We tested with Luzianne Iced Tea tea bags.

MAKES 12 to 15 servings. **HANDS-ON** 35 min.; **TOTAL** 2 hours, 15 min., including frosting

Lemonade Frosting

Beat 1 (8-oz.) package **cream cheese,** softened, and 1/4 cup **butter,** softened, at medium speed with an electric mixer until creamy. Gradually add 6 cups **powdered sugar,** 1 cup at a time, beating at low speed until blended after each addition. Beat in 1 Tbsp. **lemon zest** and 3 Tbsp. fresh **lemon juice** just until blended. Increase speed to high, and beat until light and fluffy.

MAKES about 4 cups. **HANDS-ON** 15 min., **TOTAL** 15 min.

Community Cookbook

BUILD A BETTER LIBRARY, ONE GREAT BOOK AT A TIME. THIS MONTH: *CATCH-OF-THE-DAY*

Catch-of-the-Day is a survey of seafood recipes from the Lowcountry region near Fripp Island, South Carolina. Ginny Lentz and her friends collected the recipes in a slender volume, and they've sold more than 100,000 copies of the timeless book since publishing it in 1978.

Hush Puppies

HUSH PUPPIES

The SL *Test Kitchen raved about the classic flavor of these crispy cornmeal gems. Add chopped fresh herbs or swap chopped green onions for diced onion for variety. (Also pictured on page 14)*

Vegetable oil
- 1 cup self-rising yellow cornmeal mix
- 1/2 cup self-rising flour
- 1 tsp. sugar
- 1/2 tsp. baking soda
- 1 cup diced onion
- 3/4 cup buttermilk

1. Pour oil to a depth of 2 inches into a Dutch oven; heat to 350°. Stir together cornmeal and next 4 ingredients in a large bowl. Add buttermilk, stirring just until moistened. (Mixture will be slightly thicker than cake batter.)
2. Drop batter by teaspoonfuls into hot oil, and fry, in batches, 1 to 2 minutes or until golden brown, turning often. Drain on a wire rack over paper towels; serve immediately.

MAKES about 2 1/2 dozen. **HANDS-ON** 20 min., **TOTAL** 20 min.

BEVIE'S SHRIMP THERMIDOR

This rich and creamy dish makes for an awesome hot appetizer dip. Or spoon it over your favorite cooked pasta for a hearty main course. Catch-of-the-Day co-editor Ginny Lentz also recommends mixing up the seafood and serving it in baked puff pastry shells for an elegant party presentation.

Preheat oven to 400°. Melt 1/4 cup **butter** in a medium skillet over medium heat. Add 1 1/2 cups fresh **mushrooms,** sliced, and sauté 5 minutes. Whisk in 1/4 cup **all-purpose flour,** 1 tsp. **kosher salt,** 1/2 tsp. **dry mustard,** and 1/8 tsp. **ground red pepper.** Whisk in 2 cups **milk,** and cook, whisking constantly, 5 minutes or until sauce is thickened and bubbly. Stir in 1 lb. peeled and deveined raw **shrimp** and 1/4 cup freshly grated **Parmesan cheese.** Transfer mixture to a 9-inch square baking dish. (Or divide among small ramekins.) Sprinkle with desired amount of **paprika.** Bake at 400° for 10 to 15 minutes or until bubbly. Serve with **French bread baguette slices.**

MAKES 6 servings. **HANDS-ON** 30 min., **TOTAL** 40 min.

September

The Lost Apples of the South

HEIRLOOM APPLES ARE BACK. CELEBRATE THEIR NEW GOLDEN AGE WITH A SWEET BITE FROM THE PAST.

SOUTHERN APPLES: A SECOND ACT

by ROWAN JACOBSEN

One blustery day last fall, I sat on the lawn at Monticello with 78-year-old apple guru Tom Burford and sank my teeth into a 'Grimes Golden' apple. It was as sweet and brandied as a praline; it was like nothing I'd ever tasted from a supermarket. It emphatically made the point Tom—whose family has cultivated orchards in Lynchburg, Virginia, since 1713—had been trying to get me to understand, which is that there is a whole universe of Southern apples out there just waiting to be rediscovered. When I think of Southern fruit, apples don't immediately come to mind, yet apples were already a big deal in the South when Jefferson planted 18 different varieties in his Monticello "fruitery" in the early 1800s. They were a huge deal a century later, when the South was the undisputed apple capital of the world, and, after a few decades of eating commercial fruit that anyone who loves apples would rather forget, they are again asserting themselves into Southern life.

Not just any apples. Southern apples. Apples are not native to North America, and there were no apples here until the colonists brought apple seeds with them. Most of these seeds came from varieties that were adapted to English or other Northern climes and did not fare well in the Southern heat and humidity. But a small percentage did, and over time they produced hundreds of new apple varieties no one had ever seen before—apples uniquely adapted to the South. It was one of the greatest explosions of agricultural creativity in history, and it transformed the United States.

Until refrigeration became common in the 20th century, the great challenge for Southern farmers was keeping food fresh year-round. Thank goodness for apples. Some varieties ripened in June; some hung on the tree until November and were so hard they'd keep in the root cellar until almost the following June. There were juicy ones to be fermented into cider and cider vinegar (a major preservative back in the day) and nearly juiceless ones that could be dried and kept forever. There were big, tart ones for pies and fine-grained varieties that cooked into a smooth sauce. It would be an exaggeration to say that apples made rural Southern life livable, but it's fair to say they were what made it sweet.

That way of life ended in the 1920s with the rise of massive orchards out West, which were soon filling the nation's grocery stores with an irresistibly scarlet, cotton-fleshed icon: the 'Red Delicious'. It tasted terrible, but it outsold the cosmetically challenged regional varieties, which orchardists gradually stopped growing. By the 1960s, America had forgotten about the diversity of its apples.

Fortunately, that isn't where our story ends. Apple fanatics like Tom Burford kept the old varieties alive, patiently grafting shoots from old trees onto new rootstocks, tracking down centuries-old trees on abandoned farms, waiting for people to become interested again. And now we are. In a world craving novel flavors and textures, especially those that have regional roots, heirloom apples are suddenly cutting-edge. They can give us a literal taste of the Old South, as that 'Grimes Golden' did for me, or they can simply dazzle us with deliciousness—a reminder that our agrarian elders had some tricks up their sleeves that we've forgotten. For his part, Tom Burford has never been in more demand, helping new cider-makers plan their orchards, leading tastings at places like Monticello, and hitting the road to promote his new book, *Apples of North America*. For a boy who grew up surrounded by 120 varieties of apples, only to watch nearly every one of them fall by the wayside, it's a sweet ending to a long story.

ROWAN JACOBSEN is a James Beard Foundation Award-winning author. His newest book, *Apples of Uncommon Character,* was published by Bloomsbury.

Apple Stack Cake

APPLE STACK CAKE

Use six disposable 8-inch aluminum cake pans to create the layers of this stunning cake. Prepare the filling up to three days before assembling the cake. (Also pictured on page 192)

FILLING

- 3 lb. tart apples (such as Granny Smith), peeled and cut into ½-inch wedges
- 3 lb. crisp apples (such as Braeburn or Honeycrisp), peeled and chopped
- 1 cup firmly packed light brown sugar
- ½ lemon, sliced

CAKE

- Vegetable cooking spray
- 6 (8-inch) round disposable aluminum foil cake pans
- Parchment paper
- 1 cup butter, softened
- 2 cups sugar
- 5 large eggs, separated
- 1½ tsp. apple pie spice
- 3 cups all-purpose flour, divided
- 1 cup buttermilk
- 1 tsp. baking soda
- 1 cup chopped toasted pecans
- 1 cup apple butter
- Apple Cider Glaze (recipe, page 218)

1. Prepare Filling: Bring first 4 ingredients to a light boil in a Dutch oven over medium-high heat. Reduce heat to medium-low, and simmer, stirring often, 25 to 30 minutes or until apples are tender and juices thicken. Discard lemon slices. Cool completely (about 2 hours). Cover and chill until ready to use.

2. Prepare Cake: Lightly grease disposable cake pans with cooking spray; line bottoms of pans with parchment paper, and lightly grease parchment paper.

3. Preheat oven to 350°. Beat butter at medium speed with a heavy-duty electric stand mixer until creamy. Gradually add sugar, beating until light and fluffy. Add egg yolks, 1 at a time, beating just until blended after each addition.

4. Stir together apple pie spice and 2 3/4 cups flour in a medium bowl; stir together buttermilk and baking soda in a small bowl. Add flour mixture to butter mixture alternately with buttermilk mixture, beginning and ending with flour mixture. Beat at low speed just until blended after each addition.

5. Stir together pecans and remaining 1/4 cup flour. Fold pecan mixture and apple butter into batter.

6. Beat egg whites at high speed with an electric mixer until stiff peaks form. Stir about one-third of egg whites into batter; fold in remaining egg whites.

7. Divide cake batter among prepared pans, spreading with an offset spatula.

8. Bake at 350° for 7 minutes; rotate pans from top rack to bottom rack. Bake 7 to 9 more minutes or until a wooden pick inserted in center comes out clean.

9. Remove cake layers from oven, and brush each with 2 to 3 Tbsp. warm Apple Cider Glaze. (Reserve remaining glaze.) Cool cake layers in pans on wire racks 10 minutes. Remove from pans to wire racks; discard parchment paper. Cool completely (about 30 minutes).

10. Assemble Cake: Place 1 layer, glaze-side up, on serving platter. Top with 1 1/2 cups filling. Repeat with remaining layers and filling. Top last layer with any remaining filling, and drizzle cake with desired amount of reserved Apple Cider Glaze.

MAKES 12 to 14 servings. **HANDS-ON** 1 hour, 15 min.; **TOTAL** 4 hours, 15 min., including glaze

APPLE STACK CAKE

Appalachian tradition holds that guests would bring layers of cake to a wedding, and the bride's family would bring the filling. The taller the cake, the more popular the bride, so the saying goes.

Apple Cider Glaze

Bring 1 cup **sugar**, 1/2 cup **apple cider**, 1/2 cup **butter**, and 1 Tbsp. **light corn syrup** to a boil in a small heavy saucepan over medium-high heat, stirring constantly. Reduce heat to medium, and cook, stirring constantly, 4 minutes. Remove from heat, and stir in 1 tsp. **vanilla extract.**

Note: If necessary, microwave glaze in a microwave-safe bowl at HIGH 10 to 20 seconds before drizzling over cake.

MAKES about 3/4 cup. **HANDS-ON** 15 min., **TOTAL** 15 min.

GRILLED PORK CHOPS WITH APPLE-BOURBON GLAZE

The key to success here is to brush the Apple-Bourbon Glaze on the chops during the last few minutes on the grill, turning and brushing often to create a layered, lacquered look. Garnish the chops with grilled halves of small apples brushed with the glaze. (Pictured on page 15)

- 2 Tbsp. dark brown sugar
- 1 1/2 tsp. kosher salt
- 1 tsp. freshly ground black pepper
- 1 tsp. garlic powder
- 1/2 tsp. paprika
- 4 (12-oz.) bone-in pork rib chops
- 2 Tbsp. olive oil
  Apple-Bourbon Glaze

1. Stir together first 5 ingredients. Brush pork with olive oil, and rub both sides with sugar mixture. Place pork in a 13- x 9-inch baking dish; cover and chill 12 to 24 hours. Remove pork from refrigerator, and let stand at room temperature 30 minutes. Meanwhile, prepare glaze.

2. Preheat grill to 350° to 400° (medium-high) heat. Grill chops, covered with grill lid, 6 to 8 minutes on each side or until almost done. Brush chops with glaze; turn and brush other side with glaze. Grill, covered with grill lid, 2 minutes.

3. Repeat process, without grill lid and turning chops every 10 seconds, until glaze thickens and chops are cooked through.

MAKES 4 servings. **HANDS-ON** 25 min.; **TOTAL** 12 hours, 55 min., including glaze

GRILLED PORK CHOPS WITH APPLE-BOURBON GLAZE

Pork. Apples. Bourbon. You can't go wrong with an autumnal trio so ripe for a smoky kiss on the grill.

Apple-Bourbon Glaze

- 1 (12-oz.) can frozen apple juice concentrate, thawed
- 1 cup bourbon
- 3 Tbsp. dark brown sugar
- 1 Tbsp. Dijon mustard
- 1/2 tsp. kosher salt
- 1/2 tsp. dried crushed red pepper

Stir together first 5 ingredients in a medium saucepan. Bring to a boil over medium-high heat. Reduce heat to medium, and simmer, stirring occasionally, 13 to 15 minutes or until mixture has thickened and is reduced to about 1 cup. Stir in red pepper.

MAKES 1 cup. **HANDS-ON** 5 min., **TOTAL** 20 min.

APPLE FLATBREAD

- 1 (11-oz.) can refrigerated thin-crust pizza dough
  Vegetable cooking spray
- 2 crisp, sweet apples (such as Gala, Fuji, or Braeburn)
- 1 1/2 tsp. fresh lemon juice, divided
- 1 cup ricotta cheese
- 1 tsp. firmly packed lemon zest
- 1/2 tsp. kosher salt
- 1/4 tsp. freshly ground black pepper
- 1/2 small red onion, thinly sliced
- 1/2 cup slivered almonds, toasted
- 1 tsp. honey
  Garnish: thinly sliced fresh flat-leaf parsley leaves

1. Preheat oven to 425°. Press pizza dough into a 9- x 14-inch rectangle in a lightly greased (with cooking spray) jelly-roll pan.

2. Bake at 425° on lower oven rack 20 minutes or until lightly browned and crisp. Meanwhile, thinly slice apples; toss with 1/2 tsp. lemon juice.

3. Stir together ricotta cheese, lemon zest, kosher salt, freshly ground black

APPLE FLATBREAD
TWO WAYS

Bake store-bought pizza dough to make a convenient and versatile canvas for apples, cheese, and herbs. Serve as appetizers or the main course.

pepper, and remaining 1 tsp. lemon juice. Spread ricotta mixture over baked crust.

4. Arrange apples over ricotta mixture, and sprinkle with onion slices and almonds. Drizzle with honey. Cut into squares, and serve immediately.

MAKES 6 to 8 appetizer servings. **HANDS-ON** 15 min., **TOTAL** 30 min.

Chicken-Apple Sausage Flatbread

Prepare recipe through Step 2, omitting ricotta, zest, onion, almonds, and honey. Cook 1 (12-oz.) package smoked chicken-and-apple sausage links in a skillet over medium-high heat 6 minutes or until browned; slice. Stir salt and pepper into 1/2 cup whipped cream cheese spread; spread over baked crust. Top with apples and sausage. Sprinkle with chopped fresh chives and basil.

HANDS-ON 20 min., **TOTAL** 40 min.

FENNEL-APPLE SLAW

This vibrant seasonal salad is an ideal way to showcase your favorite apples—just be sure to use ones that are super crisp, tart, and sweet, and keep the peels on to add color and texture.

- 1   **cup thinly sliced celery**
- 1   **cup coarsely chopped fresh flat-leaf parsley**
- 1   **large shallot, thinly sliced**
- 1/4 **cup extra virgin olive oil**
- 1   **tsp. kosher salt**
- 1/2 **tsp. freshly ground black pepper**
- 1   **large fennel bulb**
- 1   **large crisp, sweet apple, thinly sliced**
- 2   **Tbsp. apple cider vinegar**
- 1   **tsp. sugar**

1. Toss together first 6 ingredients in a medium bowl. Slice fennel bulb thinly, reserving fronds. Finely chop fennel

FENNEL-APPLE SLAW

Serve this crunchy, fresh salad as a bracing accompaniment to smoky grilled or roasted meat or fish.

fronds to equal 1 1/2 Tbsp., and sprinkle over salad. Add fennel slices to salad.

2. Toss together apple slices, vinegar, and sugar in a small bowl. Add apple mixture to fennel mixture; toss to combine.

MAKES 4 to 6 servings. **HANDS-ON** 20 min., **TOTAL** 20 min.

CARROT-APPLE SOUP

The smart technique for this simple soup eliminates the need for sautéing the vegetables, which preserves the bright color and flavor of the carrots and results in a brighter, more refreshing soup. To keep it vegetarian, substitute vegetable broth for the chicken broth.

- 1 1/2 **lb. carrots, peeled and chopped (about 8 large)**
- 3   **tart apples (such as Granny Smith) or creamy apples (such as McIntosh), peeled and chopped (about 1 lb.)**
- 1   **large yellow onion, chopped**
- 2   **cups cream**
- 1 1/2 **cups unsalted chicken cooking stock**
- 1 1/4 **cups apple cider**
- 3   **fresh thyme sprigs**
- 1   **tsp. kosher salt**
- 1/2 **tsp. freshly ground black pepper**
  Garnishes: sour cream, diced apples

1. Bring all ingredients to a boil in a Dutch oven over medium-high heat; reduce heat to low, and simmer, stirring occasionally, 50 to 60 minutes or until carrots are tender. Remove from heat, and cool 15 minutes.

2. Remove thyme sprigs. Process soup, in batches, in a blender or food processor until smooth. (For a thinner soup, stir in more broth, 1 Tbsp. at a time.) Spoon into individual bowls, and serve immediately.

MAKES 7 cups. **HANDS-ON** 30 min.; **TOTAL** 1 hour, 45 min.

PICK A BETTER APPLE

THE DIVERSITY OF APPLES AT MANY FARMERS' MARKETS AND SUPERMARKETS HASN'T BEEN THIS RICH IN DECADES. HERE'S HOW TO SHOP SMART.

Apple season in the South runs from summer through fall.

Smart farmers at the market slice samples of each apple, from tart to sweet. Ask for a taste to determine your favorite.

Pick up an apple. It should feel heavy for its size and very firm. Also, redness is not a sign of ripeness.

Mix and match a bag of apples so you can try several different varieties.

At home, store apples in their own refrigerator crisper drawer. Eat or cook any with nicks or bruises immediately so they don't spoil the whole bunch.

You'll find the most diverse apple varieties in the cooler climates of the mountain South. Looking to visit an orchard? See *orangepippin.com* for a state-by-state guide. To order Southern apples online, visit *randaorchards.com* or *mercier-orchards.com*. For apple trees, visit *centuryfarmorchards .com* or *bighorsecreek farm.com*.

ALBEMARLE PIPPIN
QUEENS, NEW YORK, 1720

This NYC native thrived in the Virginia Piedmont and became a favorite of George Washington and Thomas Jefferson. Today, its sprightly lemon-and-pineapple flavor provides the pizazz in a new wave of Champagne-like ciders.

YATES
FAYETTE COUNTY, GEORGIA, 1840s

Little 'Yates' can take heat and humidity, which is why it became a standard on farms throughout the southernmost states. Sweet and tart with a spicy twang, it makes the perfect small snack all winter long.

GRIMES GOLDEN
BROOKS COUNTY, WEST VIRGINIA, 1790

Supersweet with high sugar content and blasts of banana and anise flavors, it became the favorite of moonshiners and children alike. The first 'Golden Delicious' tree sprang from a 'Grimes Golden' seed.

YORK IMPERIAL
YORK, PENNSYLVANIA, 1820

Comically lopsided with a juicy sweetness and a way of melting into fluffy sauce when cooked, it does best in the states near the Mason-Dixon Line. Find it piled high in Maryland and Virginia markets every Thanksgiving.

MAIDEN'S BLUSH
BURLINGTON, NEW JERSEY, 1817

This winsome apple was important to Mid-Atlantic and southern Appalachian farmsteaders. Its cheerful pink cheeks made it an easy sell in the market, and its low-juice flesh made it the top choice for dried apples—a 19th-century staple.

10
APPLES
TO
TRY NOW

ARKANSAS BLACK
BENTONVILLE, ARKANSAS, 1870

A stunning 'Winesap' seedling, it was famed for staying power in the root cellar, where its tart and tannic bite mellowed into delightful flavors reminiscent of a glass of iced tea sweetened with orange-blossom honey.

GOLDEN DELICIOUS
CLAY COUNTY, WEST VIRGINIA, 1890

The second-most-successful apple of all time after 'Red Delicious'. The supermarket version is bland, but the honeyed aromas of a tree-ripened one from a Southern farm capture the very essence of apple.

WINESAP
MOORESTOWN, NEW JERSEY, LATE 1700s

The most important of all Southern apples, it reigned before the advent of controlled atmosphere storage and the rise of 'Red Delicious'. Tart and foxy, it's equally gifted for fresh eating or in pies or cider.

BEN DAVIS
BERRY'S LICK, KENTUCKY, CIRCA 1800

It grew prolifically and was so hard and dry that it survived months at sea. The "Mortgage Lifter" saved countless antebellum farms, which sent barges down the Mississippi to New Orleans and on to Europe.

HEWES CRAB
VIRGINIA, CIRCA 1700

These little pink-and-yellow ornaments are too sour for eating out of hand, but they make the best-tasting hard cider in the country, if not the world. A mainstay at Monticello, 'Hewes Crab' is now being rediscovered around the South.

CARAMEL APPLE CHEESECAKE TART

It may look like a chore, but this cheese-cake tart calls for a relatively straightfor-ward preparation: First, press the crust into the tart pan. Next, mix the cream cheese filling, fill the tart shell, and bake. Finally, gild the pie with sautéed tart ap-ples, and paint them with melted apple jelly for a jewelled effect.

Caramel Apple Cheesecake Tart

CRUST
- 1 cup finely ground gingersnap cookie crumbs (about 24 to 28 cookies)
- 1/2 cup finely chopped toasted pecans
- 1/4 cup butter, melted
- 2 Tbsp. light brown sugar
  Vegetable cooking spray

FILLING
- 2 (8-oz.) packages cream cheese, softened
- 3/4 cup firmly packed light brown sugar
- 1 large egg
- 1/4 tsp. apple pie spice

TOPPING
- 3 lb. tart apples (such as Granny Smith), peeled and cut into 1/2-inch-thick wedges
- 1/3 cup firmly packed light brown sugar
- 1 Tbsp. butter
- 2 Tbsp. apple jelly

1. Prepare Crust: Preheat oven to 375°. Stir together gingersnap cookie crumbs and next 3 ingredients in a medium bowl until moist. Press crumb mixture on bottom and up sides of a lightly greased (with cooking spray) 9-inch tart pan with removable bottom.

2. Prepare Filling: Beat cream cheese and next 3 ingredients at medium-low speed with an electric mixer until smooth. Pour cream cheese mixture into prepared crust, spreading with an offset spatula. Place tart pan on a baking sheet.

3. Bake at 375° for 20 to 25 minutes or until center is almost set. Cool completely on a wire rack (about 40 minutes). Chill 8 to 12 hours.

4. Prepare Topping: Stir together apples and 1/3 cup light brown sugar in a large bowl. Melt 1 Tbsp. butter in a large skillet over medium-high heat. Add apple mixture to skillet, and cook, stirring often, 16 to 18 minutes or until golden brown. Remove skillet from heat, and cool apples completely (about 30 minutes).

5. Arrange apples on top of chilled cheesecake in a decorative fashion. (To achieve the rosette look pictured above, start by arranging apples in an overlapping circular pattern about 1 inch from the edge of the crust. Make a second small circular pattern inside the first. Thinly slice some of the cooked apples, curl them, and place in the center of the tart.)

6. Microwave jelly and 1 tsp. water in a small microwave-safe bowl at HIGH 20 to 30 seconds or until melted and smooth. Brush apples with half of jelly mixture.

7. Preheat broiler with oven rack 5 to 6 inches from heat. Broil tart 2 to 3 minutes or just until apples begin to brown. Remove from oven, and brush apples with remaining jelly mixture. Chill 1 hour before serving.
Note: Tart will hold in refrigerator overnight, but the crust will soften the longer it sits in the refrigerator.

MAKES 8 servings. **HANDS-ON** 1 hour; **TOTAL** 11 hours, 30 min.

CARAMEL APPLE CHEESECAKE TART
This sassy showstopper features a gingersnap cookie-pecan crust, a luscious filling flavored with apple pie spice, and a crown of cooked apples that takes its gilded sheen from melted apple jelly.

KITCHEN DIRECTOR ROBBY MELVIN SHARES THREE SMART WAYS TO USE

APPLE PEELS AND CORES

Shel Silverstein's book *The Giving Tree* features an apple tree for a reason: Every part of the fruit, including the forgotten bits, can be spun into gold. So when you do your fall baking, save the cores and peels to use in these recipes. They'll show you just how generous the apple can be.

① APPLE PEEL-AND-CORE JELLY

Bring **peels** and **cores** of 10 red apples and 6 cups water to a boil in a Dutch oven over high heat. Reduce heat to medium-low; simmer 45 minutes. Pour through a fine wire-mesh strainer into a large saucepan to equal 3 cups liquid. (Add water, if necessary.) Discard solids. Whisk in 3 Tbsp. **powdered pectin** and 1 ½ cups **sugar.** Add 1 **cinnamon stick** and 1 whole **clove.** Bring to a boil. Boil 2 minutes. Remove from heat; discard spices. Pour into 1 (24-oz.) hot sterilized jar, filling to ¼ inch from top; wipe jar rim. Cool completely (about 30 minutes), cover with lid, and chill 12 hours. Refrigerate up to 1 month.

MAKES 3 cups. **HANDS-ON** 35 min., **TOTAL** 14 hours

② APPLE VINEGAR

Use a splash of this to brighten up your dressings and pan sauces, or add tang to your cocktails. Place 10 **apple cores** and 3 fresh **thyme** sprigs in 1 (24-oz.) sterilized jar. Bring 3 cups **white vinegar,** 1 ½ cups **sugar,** and 1 tsp. **kosher salt** to a boil in a small saucepan over high heat. Pour vinegar mixture into jar, filling to ¼ inch from top. Cool completely (about 30 minutes). Cover with lid, and chill 1 week before using. Refrigerate in covered jar up to 3 months.

MAKES 3 cups. **HANDS-ON** 20 min.; **TOTAL** 55 min., plus 1 week for chilling

③ APPLE-BERRY SMOOTHIE

Process 1 cup **orange juice** and peels of 4 large **apples** in a blender 30 seconds or until smooth. Add 1 ½ cups **frozen mixed berries** and 1 Tbsp. **honey.** Process 15 seconds.

MAKES 4 servings.
HANDS-ON 10 min.,
TOTAL 10 min.

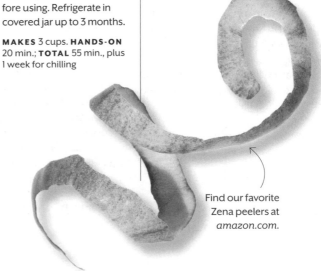

Find our favorite Zena peelers at *amazon.com.*

A Fall Baker's Delight

INSPIRED BY THE COZY FLAVORS OF THE SEASON, THIS BATCH OF SIMPLE BAKING RECIPES WILL RISE TO ANY OCCASION

Mini Apple Cider Pound Cakes

OVER THE TOP

Finish these versatile minis with one of three scrumptious toppings (recipes, page 224).

MINI APPLE CIDER POUND CAKES

Finish the cakes with one of the three toppings that follow. Toss together the Streusel Topping before you start baking. Both glazes can be prepped while the cakes cool.

1 1/2 cups butter, softened
3 cups sugar
6 large eggs
3 cups all-purpose flour
1 tsp. apple pie spice
1/2 tsp. baking powder
1/4 tsp. table salt
1/4 tsp. ground cloves
1 cup apple cider
1 tsp. vanilla extract
6 (5- x 3-inch) disposable aluminum foil loaf pans
Vegetable cooking spray

1. Preheat oven to 325°. Beat butter at medium speed with a heavy-duty electric stand mixer until creamy; gradually add sugar, beating until light and fluffy. Add eggs, 1 at a time, beating just until blended after each addition.
2. Stir together flour and next 4 ingredients. Gradually add flour mixture to butter mixture alternately with apple cider, beginning and ending with flour mixture. Beat at low speed just until blended after each addition. Stir in vanilla.
3. Lightly grease disposable loaf pans with cooking spray. Pour batter into prepared pans, and place on a baking sheet. For streusel-topped cakes, sprinkle about 2 Tbsp. Streusel Topping over batter in each pan.

4. Bake at 325° for 40 to 50 minutes or until a wooden pick inserted in center comes out clean. Cool in pans on wire racks 10 minutes; remove from pans to wire racks, and cool completely (about 1 hour). For glaze-topped cakes, spoon desired glaze over cooled cakes.

MAKES 6 mini loaves. **HANDS-ON** 30 min.; **TOTAL** 2 hours, 20 min., not including topping or glaze

Streusel Topping

Stir together ³/₄ cup **all-purpose flour;** ¹/₂ cup chopped **pecans;** ¹/₄ cup **butter,** melted; 2 Tbsp. **sugar;** 1 tsp. **apple pie spice;** and ¹/₈ tsp. table **salt.** Let stand 30 minutes or until firm. Crumble into small pieces.

MAKES about 1 cup. **HANDS-ON** 10 min., **TOTAL** 40 min.

Bourbon Glaze

Stir together 2 cups **powdered sugar,** 1 Tbsp. **bourbon,** and 3 to 4 Tbsp. **milk.**

MAKES about 1 cup. **HANDS-ON** 5 min., **TOTAL** 5 min.

Lemon-Sugar Glaze

Stir together ²/₃ cup firmly packed **light brown sugar;** 1 ¹/₂ Tbsp. **butter,** melted; 2 tsp. firmly packed **lemon zest;** and 2 Tbsp. fresh **lemon juice** in a small saucepan. Stir in 1 **egg,** lightly beaten, until blended. Cook over low heat, stirring constantly, 10 to 12 minutes or until mixture thickens slightly and begins to bubble around the edges. Use immediately.

MAKES ³/₄ cup. **HANDS-ON** 15 min., **TOTAL** 15 min.

Ben Mims' Perfect Cornbread

BEN MIMS' PERFECT CORNBREAD

Our Test Kitchen granted the "perfect" moniker to Ben's recipe, thanks to the extra flavor and superior texture his browned butter affords. This recipe and Cornbread Pudding with Whiskey Caramel are two of the many treasures in Ben's fresh new cookbook, Sweet & Southern: Classic Desserts with a Twist.

 1   cup plain yellow cornmeal
 1   cup all-purpose flour
 1   Tbsp. baking powder
 1   tsp. kosher salt
¹/₄   tsp. baking soda
 2   cups buttermilk
 2   large eggs
¹/₂   cup butter

1. Preheat oven to 425°. Whisk together first 5 ingredients in a large bowl. Whisk together buttermilk and eggs; stir into cornmeal mixture just until combined. Heat a 10-inch cast-iron skillet over medium-high heat until it just begins to smoke. Add butter, and stir until butter is melted. Stir melted butter into cornbread batter. Pour batter into hot skillet.
2. Bake at 425° for 25 to 30 minutes or until golden and cornbread pulls away from sides of skillet. Invert cornbread onto a wire rack; serve warm.

MAKES 8 to 10 servings. **HANDS-ON** 20 min., **TOTAL** 55 min.

CORNBREAD PUDDING WITH WHISKEY CARAMEL

For a different look, bake in 8 to 10 lightly greased 8-oz. ramekins in a jelly-roll pan. Reduce covered bake time to 25 minutes; reduce uncovered bake time to 10 to 15 minutes.

       Vegetable cooking spray
       Ben Mims' Perfect Cornbread,
       at room temperature
¹/₂   cup butter
 2   cups milk
 1   cup sugar
 1   Tbsp. vanilla extract
1 ¹/₂   tsp. kosher salt
 5   large eggs
       Whiskey Caramel

1. Preheat oven to 350°. Lightly grease a 3-qt. baking dish with cooking spray. Cut cornbread into 2- to 3-inch pieces, and place in prepared dish. (You should have about 10 cups cornbread.) Cook butter in a 2-qt. saucepan over medium heat, stirring constantly, until butter begins to turn golden brown. Remove pan from heat, and whisk in milk and next 3 ingredients until sugar melts. Whisk in eggs; pour mixture over cornbread. Let stand 10 minutes.
2. Bake, covered, at 350° for 30 minutes. Uncover and bake 30 more minutes or until light brown and set. Let stand 10 minutes. Serve with Whiskey Caramel.

MAKES 8 to 10 servings. **HANDS-ON** 15 min.; **TOTAL** 3 hours, including cornbread and sauce

Whiskey Caramel

Stir together 1 cup **sugar** and 1/4 cup water in a saucepan. Cook over medium-high heat, stirring constantly, 3 minutes or until sugar melts. Cook, without stirring, 10 minutes or until medium amber in color. Remove from heat, and stir in 1/2 cup heavy **cream;** 1/2 cup **butter,** cubed; 1/4 cup **whiskey;** 1/4 tsp. **kosher salt;** and 1/4 tsp. ground **nutmeg.** Whisk together 1 large **egg** and 1/2 cup **sugar** in a heatproof medium bowl; slowly whisk caramel sauce into egg mixture. Return mixture to saucepan, and cook over medium heat, stirring constantly, 2 minutes or until thickened.

MAKES 2 cups. **HANDS-ON** 30 min., **TOTAL** 30 min.

Parmesan-Herb Cornbread Pudding

Need a winning side dish? Try our Test Kitchen's savory spin on Ben Mims' sweet recipe. (Pictured on page 189)

Prepare Cornbread Pudding with Whiskey Caramel, omitting vanilla and Whiskey Caramel. Reduce sugar to 2 Tbsp., and cook 1 Tbsp. fresh **thyme** leaves with **butter** in Step 1. Sprinkle 1 cup (4 oz.) shredded **Parmesan cheese** over cornbread just before baking.

MAKES 8 to 10 servings. **HANDS-ON** 15 min.; **TOTAL** 2 hours, 30 min., including cornbread

GRAPE FOCACCIA

Don't be intimidated by homemade bread; even a beginner can master this simple baking sheet focaccia. It's an effortlessly gorgeous dish for entertaining, and the unexpected combination of sweet and savory flavors will impress. As an appetizer, serve the warm slab of bread, sliced, on a large cutting board with a few wedges of your favorite cheese. Try muscadines or figs in place of the grapes. For leftovers, spread the focaccia with peanut butter for a fresh, sophisticated spin on PB&J.

- 1 (1/4-oz.) envelope active dry yeast
- 1 2/3 cups warm water (100° to 110°)
- 4 1/2 cups bread flour
- 1 1/2 Tbsp. kosher salt
- 3/4 cup olive oil, divided
- 2 Tbsp. chopped fresh thyme
- 1 Tbsp. chopped fresh rosemary
- 1 lb. red and green grapes, halved
  Coarse salt
  Freshly ground black pepper
  Garnishes: chopped fresh rosemary, fresh thyme leaves

1. Stir together yeast and warm water (100° to 110°) in bowl of a heavy-duty electric stand mixer; let stand 5 minutes. Add bread flour, salt, and 1/4 cup oil to yeast mixture; beat on low speed, using paddle attachment, 25 seconds or until blended. Add chopped herbs. Switch to dough hook; increase speed to medium-high, and beat 5 minutes. (Dough will be sticky.)
2. Place dough in a large, well-greased bowl, turning to coat top. Cover with plastic wrap, and let rise in a warm place (80° to 85°), free from drafts, 1 hour or until doubled in bulk.
3. Drizzle 1/4 cup olive oil in a half-sheet pan or jelly-roll pan; place dough in pan. Press dough down and into edges of pan, using your fingers. (It's okay if there are holes in the dough.) Cover with plastic wrap, and let rise in a warm place 1 hour.
4. Preheat oven to 425°. Scatter grapes over dough. Drizzle with remaining 1/4 cup olive oil, and sprinkle with coarse salt and freshly ground black pepper. Bake at 425° 30 to 35 minutes or until golden brown. Serve warm or at room temperature.

MAKES 12 to 14 servings. **HANDS-ON** 30 min., **TOTAL** 3 hours

MEXICAN CHOCOLATE PUDDING CAKE

(Pictured on page 14)

- 1 1/2 cups semisweet chocolate morsels
- 1/2 cup butter
- 3/4 cup granulated sugar
- 4 large eggs
- 1 cup all-purpose flour
- 1/2 tsp. ground cinnamon
- 1/4 tsp. baking powder
- 1/4 tsp. ground red pepper
- 1/4 tsp. ground chipotle chile pepper
- 1/2 tsp. kosher salt, divided
- 1/2 cup sliced almonds
- 2 tsp. olive oil
- 1 tsp. light brown sugar

1. Preheat oven to 350°. Microwave chocolate and butter in a large microwave-safe bowl at HIGH 1 to 1 1/2 minutes or until melted, stirring at 30-second intervals. Whisk in granulated sugar. Add eggs, 1 at a time, whisking just until blended after each addition. Whisk in flour, next 4 ingredients, and 1/4 tsp. salt.
2. Pour batter into a greased (with butter) 2-qt. baking dish. Stir together sliced almonds, next 2 ingredients, and remaining 1/4 tsp. salt. Sprinkle almond mixture over cake batter. Bake at 350° for 30 minutes. (Center will be soft.) Cool on a wire rack 5 minutes. Serve warm.

MAKES 6 servings. **HANDS-ON** 30 min.; **TOTAL** 1 hour, 10 min.

Six Fast Weeknight Suppers

USE SMART SUPERMARKET SHORTCUTS TO PUT THESE FRESH RECIPES ON YOUR DINNER TABLE IN A FLASH

Beef Kabobs with Broccoli Slaw and Peanut Sauce

★SHORTCUT★
No. 1
Bagged broccoli slaw

BEEF KABOBS WITH BROCCOLI SLAW AND PEANUT SAUCE

We tested with tri-tip and rib-eye steak, but use your favorite cut.

8	(8-inch) wooden skewers
3/4	tsp. ground cumin
1/8	tsp. ground red pepper
2	tsp. kosher salt, divided
1 1/2	lb. tri-tip or rib-eye steak, cut into 2-inch pieces
3	Tbsp. canola oil, divided
1/4	cup creamy peanut butter
1/4	cup unsweetened coconut milk
3	Tbsp. fresh lime juice, divided
2 1/2	Tbsp. reduced-sodium soy sauce, divided
1	(12-oz.) package fresh broccoli slaw
1/4	cup fresh cilantro leaves
	Garnishes: chopped roasted peanuts, lime wedges

1. Preheat grill to 450° to 500° (high) heat. Soak skewers for 30 minutes.
2. Stir together cumin, red pepper, and 1 1/2 tsp. salt. Thread steak onto skewers. Brush steak with 1 Tbsp. oil; sprinkle with salt mixture. Grill, covered with grill lid, 1 1/2 to 2 minutes on each side or to desired degree of doneness.
3. Whisk together peanut butter, coconut milk, 2 Tbsp. lime juice, and 1 1/2 Tbsp. soy sauce.
4. Whisk together 1/4 cup peanut butter mixture and remaining 2 Tbsp.

canola oil, 1 Tbsp. lime juice, and 1 Tbsp. soy sauce. Toss mixture with slaw, cilantro, and remaining 1/2 tsp. salt. Serve slaw and beef skewers with remaining peanut sauce.

MAKES 4 servings. **HANDS-ON** 20 min., **TOTAL** 50 min.

★SHORTCUT★
No. 2
Peeled garlic cloves

SLOW-COOKER CHICKEN WITH 40 CLOVES OF GARLIC

Look for jars of peeled garlic in the refrigerated cases in the produce section at most major supermarkets. While there, grab a package of poultry herbs, which includes fresh thyme, rosemary, and parsley and can substitute for the individual herbs. Add dried apricots to infuse the rich sauce with a fruity back note, and serve over couscous for a North African-inspired supper.

	Vegetable cooking spray
4	Tbsp. butter, melted
40	peeled garlic cloves
1	cup dried apricots
6	fresh thyme sprigs
1	fresh rosemary sprig
1	(4-lb.) whole chicken
	Kosher salt
	Freshly ground black pepper
1/2	cup unsalted chicken stock
1/4	cup dry white wine
	Cheesecloth (optional)
1	Tbsp. all-purpose flour
1	Tbsp. chopped fresh thyme leaves
	Garnishes: fresh rosemary, thyme sprigs

1. Line bottom and long sides of a 6-qt. oval slow cooker with 1 piece of aluminum foil, allowing 2 inches to extend over sides. Lightly grease foil with cooking spray. Pour 3 Tbsp. melted butter in slow cooker; sprinkle garlic and apricots over butter. Add thyme and rosemary sprigs. Place chicken, breast-side up, on herbs. Brush remaining 1 Tbsp. melted butter over chicken; sprinkle with desired amount of salt and pepper. Add chicken stock and wine to slow cooker. Cover and cook on LOW 8 hours.

2. Transfer chicken from slow cooker to a serving platter, using foil sides as handles. Transfer garlic cloves from slow cooker to platter, using a slotted spoon. Pour cooking liquid through a cheesecloth-lined wire-mesh strainer into a measuring cup; discard solids.

3. Pour 1 cup cooking liquid into a small saucepan (reserve remaining cooking liquid for another use, such as rice or couscous); whisk in flour. Bring to a boil, and cook, whisking constantly, 2 minutes or until thickened. Stir in chopped thyme. Serve with chicken.

Note: We tested with Swanson Unsalted Chicken Cooking Stock.

MAKES 4 servings. **HANDS-ON** 25 min.; **TOTAL** 8 hours, 25 min.

★ EASY SIDE ★

PARSLEY COUSCOUS WITH APRICOTS

Toss some of the cooked garlic cloves from slow-cooker pan juices with couscous, if desired.

Combine 1 cup uncooked plain **couscous,** 1/2 cup chopped **dried apricots,** and 1/3 cup vertically sliced **red onion** in a medium heatproof bowl. Bring 1 3/4 cups **unsalted chicken stock,** 1 Tbsp. **butter,** 1 tsp. **kosher salt,** and 1/4 tsp. freshly ground black **pepper** to a boil in a small saucepan over medium-high heat. Pour broth mixture over couscous; cover and let stand 10 minutes or until liquid is absorbed. Uncover and fluff with a fork. Stir in 1/3 cup chopped fresh flat-leaf **parsley** and, if desired, chopped fresh **rosemary** and **thyme** and additional dried apricots.

MAKES 4 servings. **HANDS-ON** 10 min., **TOTAL** 20 min.

SHORTCUT
★ *No. 3* ★
Chipotle salsa

SOUTHWESTERN MEATLOAF

Use crushed whole grain tortilla chips instead of plain breadcrumbs to flavor this juicy meatloaf and help it hold its shape as it bakes. We love chipotle salsa for its medium heat and smoky notes, but any salsa and heat level will give the meatloaf fantastic south-of-the-border flavor. Make a tasty meatloaf sandwich, or serve a slice alongside Tex-Mex Mashers.

- 1/2 **cup finely crushed whole grain tortilla chips**
- 1 **tsp. ground cumin**
- 1/2 **tsp. garlic powder**
- 1/4 **tsp. freshly ground black pepper**
- 1 **cup plus 1 Tbsp. bottled chipotle salsa, divided**
- 1 **tsp. kosher salt, divided**
- 1 3/4 **lb. ground beef**
- 1 1/2 **cups (6 oz.) shredded sharp Cheddar cheese**
- 2 **large eggs**
  Vegetable cooking spray
- 2 **Tbsp. ketchup**
- 1 **tsp. fresh lime juice**

1. Preheat oven to 350°. Stir together crushed tortilla chips, ground cumin, garlic powder, freshly ground black pepper, 1 cup chipotle salsa, and 3/4 tsp. kosher salt in a large bowl; let stand 10 minutes, stirring occasionally.

2. Gently stir in ground beef and next 2 ingredients just until blended. Line a broiler pan with aluminum foil; coat with cooking spray. Gently shape mixture into a 9- x 5-inch loaf; place meatloaf in prepared broiler pan.

3. Bake at 350° for 50 minutes. Stir together ketchup, lime juice, and remaining 1 Tbsp. salsa and 1/4 tsp. salt in a small bowl. Brush ketchup mixture over top of meatloaf; bake 15 to 20 more minutes or until a meat thermometer inserted into thickest portion registers 160°. Let stand 5 minutes before serving.

Note: We tested with Frontera Gourmet Mexican Chipotle Salsa and Tostitos Multigrain Scoops tortilla chips.

MAKES 6 servings. **HANDS-ON** 20 min.; **TOTAL** 1 hour, 40 min.

★ EASY SIDE ★

TEX-MEX MASHERS

Peel 2 1/2 lb. **russet potatoes,** and cut into 1-inch cubes. Place potatoes in a medium saucepan, and add cold water to 2 inches above potatoes. Bring mixture to a boil over medium-high heat, and boil 15 to 20 minutes or until potatoes are fork-tender; drain. Return hot potatoes to pan, and cook over medium heat, stirring occasionally, 1 to 2 minutes or until moisture evaporates. Remove from heat. Mash potatoes to desired consistency with a potato masher. Stir in 1 to 1 1/2 cups (4 to 6 oz.) shredded sharp **Cheddar cheese,** 1/2 cup **sour cream,** 1/2 cup **buttermilk,** 2 Tbsp. chopped canned **chipotle peppers in adobo sauce,** and 1 tsp. **kosher salt.** Return pan to medium heat, and cook 1 minute or until thoroughly heated. Serve immediately.

MAKES 6 servings. **HANDS-ON** 20 min., **TOTAL** 40 min.

POTATO-CRUSTED PIZZA

We used Ore-Ida Crispy Crowns frozen seasoned shredded potatoes to create a fun and kid-friendly crust. (Pictured on page 190)

- 1 Tbsp. olive oil
- 1 (30-oz.) package frozen seasoned shredded potato rounds
- 1 (28-oz.) can diced tomatoes, drained
- 1 (1-oz.) package fresh basil, torn
- 2 cups (8 oz.) shredded pizza cheese blend

Preheat oven to 450°. Brush a 15 1/2- x 10 1/2-inch jelly-roll pan with oil, and arrange potatoes in a single layer in pan. Bake 10 minutes. Flatten potatoes, using the back of a wooden spoon until rounds touch and cover entire pan. Bake 20 more minutes or until crisp. Top with remaining ingredients. Bake 5 to 10 more minutes or until cheese melts.

MAKES 6 servings. **HANDS-ON** 10 min., **TOTAL** 45 min.

EGGS SIMMERED IN TOMATO SAUCE

This dish is inspired by Middle Eastern shakshuka.

- 1 cup chopped onion
- 3 poblano peppers, chopped
- 2 Tbsp. extra virgin olive oil
- 1 Tbsp. butter
- 1 tsp. ground cumin
- 1 tsp. smoked paprika
- 3 garlic cloves, minced
- 1 (28-oz.) can crushed tomatoes
- 2 tsp. kosher salt
- 1 tsp. red wine vinegar
- 6 large eggs
- 1/2 cup crumbled feta cheese or queso fresco
- 2 Tbsp. chopped fresh cilantro

Sauté onion and peppers in hot oil in a 12-inch skillet over medium-high heat 6 minutes. Add butter and next 3 ingredients; sauté 2 minutes. Stir in tomatoes, salt, vinegar, and 1 cup water; bring to a boil. Reduce heat to medium-low, and simmer, stirring occasionally, 20 minutes. Break eggs, and slip into tomato sauce, 1 at a time. Cover and simmer 3 minutes or until eggs are cooked. Top with cheese and cilantro.

MAKES 4 servings. **HANDS-ON** 25 min., **TOTAL** 45 min.

★ EASY SIDE ★
SPICED PITA WEDGES

Preheat oven to 400°. Brush 3 (6-inch) **pita rounds** with **olive oil.** Slice pitas into wedges, and place on a baking sheet. Bake 6 minutes. Stir together 1/2 tsp. **salt,** 1/4 tsp. **smoked paprika,** and 1/8 tsp. **garlic powder.** Sprinkle pita wedges with salt mixture. Bake at 400° for 2 minutes or until crisp. Sprinkle with 2 tsp. chopped fresh **cilantro.**

MAKES 4 servings. **HANDS-ON** 10 min., **TOTAL** 10 min.

ITALIAN-STYLE TURKEY MEATBALL SOUP

Stir baby spinach into the hot soup; it wilts in just about a minute and adds color. Or sub any herbs or baby greens you have on hand, and add more or less red pepper to vary the level of heat.

- 1 (14-oz.) package frozen turkey meatballs
- 1/4 cup olive oil
- 1 1/2 cups chopped onion
- 1 1/4 cups coarsely chopped carrots (about 2 large)
- 3/4 cup sliced celery
- 6 large garlic cloves, minced
- 1 1/2 tsp. kosher salt
- 3/4 tsp. dried crushed red pepper
- 1 (28-oz.) can whole plum tomatoes, drained and crushed
- 1 (15-oz.) can cannellini beans, drained and rinsed
- 7 cups unsalted chicken stock
- 1 (6-oz.) package baby spinach
  Shaved fresh Parmigiano-Reggiano cheese

Sauté meatballs in 2 Tbsp. hot oil in a large Dutch oven over medium-high heat, stirring often, about 6 minutes or until browned. Remove meatballs, using a slotted spoon. Add remaining 2 Tbsp. oil, and reduce heat to medium. Sauté onion, carrots, and celery 5 minutes or until lightly browned. Stir in garlic, salt, and red pepper; sauté 1 minute. Stir in tomatoes, beans, stock, and meatballs; bring to a simmer over medium heat. Cover and simmer, stirring occasionally, 20 to 25 minutes or until carrots are tender. Remove from heat, and stir in spinach. Spoon into bowls, and top with cheese.

Note: We tested with Armour Turkey Meatballs.

MAKES 6 servings. **HANDS-ON** 20 min., **TOTAL** 55 min.

Relish These Pears

YOU WILL BE SURPRISED BY THE JUICY, SWEET FLAVOR OF THIS CRISP FRUIT

YOU MAY HAVE NEVER heard of Asian pears, but once you've tasted one, you'll want your own tree so you can have all the fruit you can eat. Asian pears are also known as "apple pears" because they're round and firm like apples. The crunchy fruit is wonderful fresh. Chilling it before eating enhances the delicious flavor. You can also enjoy the texture in salads and stir-fries.

Trees can grow up to 25 feet tall, but you can prune in late winter to keep them to a more manageable size. They also can be trained as espaliers against walls or onto wire trellises. Feed your pear trees with a fertilizer such as Ferti-lome Fruit, Citrus and Pecan Tree Food (19-10-5).

For better fruiting, plant two or more different selections. Asian pears are susceptible to fire blight. Choose resistant selections such as 'Hosui' (golden brown, medium-to-large fruit ripens from mid-July to early August and has moderate fire blight resistance), 'Shinko' (brown, medium-to-large fruit ripens from late July to mid-August and has high fire blight resistance), or 'Korean Giant' (brownish olive green fruit is large to very large, can weigh up to a pound, ripens from late August to mid- to late-September, and has high fire blight resistance).

Thin the fruit when it's between the size of a nickel and a quarter, leaving a 4- to 6-inch space between pears. Unlike soft European pears, firm Asian ones should be left on the tree to ripen before picking. Fruit can last three to four months if stored in the crisper of the refrigerator.

Fall is a great time to plant. Look for pear trees at your local nursery, or order online from *justfruitsandexotics.com, johnson nursery.com, petalsfromthepast.com*, and *starkbros.com*.

If you don't have room for Asian pear trees in your yard but want to try the fruit, visit your local farmers' market, or order gift boxes online from Virginia Gold Orchard; *virginiagoldorchard.com*.

ASIAN PEAR SLAW

Cut 2 **Asian pears** into matchstick pieces. Toss pears with 2 Tbsp. chopped **fresh cilantro,** 1 Tbsp. **sugar,** 1 Tbsp. fresh **lemon juice,** 1 Tbsp. **apple cider vinegar,** and 1 tsp. **kosher salt.** Serve immediately. **MAKES** 4 cups. **HANDS-ON** 10 min., **TOTAL** 10 min.

---

get growing!
ASIAN PEARS

NURTURE
Plant in fertile, deep, well-drained soil that's amended with organic matter. Mulch with pine straw or pine bark. Feed with a fruit fertilizer (19-10-5).

PLANT ZONES
Upper, Middle, and Lower South

LIGHT
FULL SUN | WATER
MEDIUM

'Shinko' ripens to a golden brown and has a rich flavor.

Our Easiest Apple Butter

THIS SPREAD IS AUTUMN'S SWEETEST SENSATION, STEALING THE SHOW AS A CONDIMENT AND LENDING FALL FLAVOR TO THREE BONUS RECIPES

Apple Butter-Walnut Thumbprints and Easy Apple Butter

★ ONE MASTER RECIPE ★

EASY APPLE BUTTER

Test Kitchen Tip: Use a wooden spoon to draw a line through the apple butter on the bottom of the pot; if the line holds for 5 seconds before the apple butter merges back together, it's finished cooking.

> 3 lb. crisp and sweet apples, such as Gala, Honeycrisp, and Braeburn, peeled (about 8 apples)
> 1 cup apple cider
> 1 1/2 cups sugar, divided
> 3/4 tsp. ground cinnamon
> 1/4 tsp. ground cloves

1. Cut apples into 1-inch pieces. Bring apples, cider, and 1/2 cup sugar to a rolling boil in a Dutch oven over high heat. Cover, leaving lid slightly ajar, and boil 20 minutes or until apples are tender and most of the liquid has evaporated; stir every 5 minutes.

2. Process cooked apples and cooking liquid in a blender until smooth. Return mixture to Dutch oven. Stir in cinnamon, cloves, and remaining 1 cup sugar. Bring to a boil over high heat. Reduce heat to low, and simmer, uncovered and stirring often, 15 minutes or until thickened. Cool about 45 minutes. Spoon into airtight containers, and refrigerate up to 2 months or freeze up to 6 months.

MAKES about 3 cups. **HANDS-ON** 55 min.; **TOTAL** 1 hour, 50 min.

★ THREE EASY SPINS ★

APPLE BUTTER-WALNUT THUMBPRINTS

For the next three recipes, use our Easy Apple Butter for the best flavor and texture. In a pinch, store-bought apple butter that has been boiled for 5 minutes (to thicken) may be substituted.

2 1/2 cups all-purpose flour
   1 cup toasted walnuts
   1 tsp. kosher salt
 1/2 tsp. baking powder
 1/2 tsp. ground cinnamon
1 1/4 cups powdered sugar
   1 cup unsalted butter, at room temperature
   1 large egg
   2 tsp. vanilla extract
      Parchment paper
 1/2 cup Easy Apple Butter
      Caramel topping

1. Preheat oven to 350°. Pulse first 5 ingredients in a food processor 10 times or until nuts are ground.
2. Beat powdered sugar and butter at high speed with a heavy-duty electric stand mixer 4 minutes or until light and fluffy. Add egg and vanilla, and beat until combined. Add flour mixture, and beat at medium speed 30 seconds.
3. Drop batter by level tablespoonfuls 1 to 2 inches apart on 3 parchment paper-lined baking sheets. Dip finger in cold water, and press into each cookie, forming an indentation. Fill each indentation with 1/2 tsp. apple butter. Dip finger in cold water, and tap down peaks in apple butter.
4. Bake 2 baking sheets at 350° for 14 minutes, placing 1 baking sheet on middle oven rack and 1 sheet on lower oven rack. Rotate pans front to back, and top rack to bottom rack. Bake 4 more minutes or until edges begin to brown. Transfer baking sheets to wire racks, and cool completely (about 10 minutes). Repeat with remaining baking sheet. Drizzle caramel topping over cooled cookies.

MAKES about 40 cookies.
HANDS-ON 40 min.; **TOTAL** 1 hour, 40 min.

APPLE BUTTER-AND-CHEDDAR PUFFS

To get ahead, make these appetizers through Step 2 and freeze up to 1 month. Go straight to the oven from freezer; simply add 5 to 10 minutes to the bake time.

   1 (17.3-oz.) package frozen puff pastry sheets, thawed
   2 large egg whites, lightly beaten
 1/2 cup Easy Apple Butter
1 1/2 Tbsp. fresh thyme leaves
1 1/4 cups (5 oz.) shredded sharp Cheddar cheese, divided
      Parchment paper

1. Preheat oven to 400°. Unfold 1 pastry sheet, and roll to a 12- x 9-inch rectangle on a lightly floured surface. Cut pastry into 9 (4- x 3-inch) rectangles. Brush edges of rectangles with a small amount of egg whites. Stir together apple butter and thyme leaves. Spoon about 1 tsp. apple butter mixture into center of each rectangle. Sprinkle each with about 1 Tbsp. cheese. Fold 2 opposite corners together, and pinch to seal.

2. Gently transfer to a parchment paper-lined baking sheet. Brush pastries with egg whites, reserving remaining egg whites for second batch; sprinkle each pastry with about 1/2 Tbsp. cheese.
3. Bake at 400° for 20 to 25 minutes or until puffed and golden brown. While first batch bakes, repeat procedure with remaining pastry sheet, egg whites, apple butter mixture, and cheese. Serve immediately.

MAKES 1 1/2 dozen. **HANDS-ON** 30 min.; **TOTAL** 1 hour, 10 min.

APPLE BUTTER SPARKLERS

For a kid-friendly version, substitute sparkling apple juice for the Prosecco.

Whisk together 2 Tbsp. **Easy Apple Butter** and 1 1/2 tsp. fresh **lemon juice** until smooth. Whisk in 1 cup chilled **Prosecco.** Strain into a glass, and garnish with a **lemon peel.** Serve immediately.

MAKES 1 serving. **HANDS-ON** 5 min., **TOTAL** 5 min.

Apple Butter-and-Cheddar Puffs

Community Cookbook

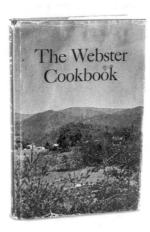

From the hills and hollers of the Blue Ridge Mountains, *The Webster Cookbook* is filled with warm and comforting family recipes from this tiny North Carolina town. Sweet tooths will take note of the extra-long dessert chapter.

CHICKEN BREASTS WITH ALMONDS

Chicken in a creamy white wine sauce makes for simple yet elegant comfort food.

- 6 skinned and boned chicken breasts
- 1 tsp. kosher salt
- 1 tsp. freshly ground black pepper
- 2 Tbsp. butter
- 1 (8-oz.) package sliced fresh mushrooms
- 1/2 cup dry white wine
- 1 (10 3/4-oz.) can cream of mushroom soup
- 1 cup heavy cream
- 1/4 cup toasted sliced almonds
- 1/4 cup loosely packed fresh flat-leaf parsley leaves, chopped
  Hot cooked rice

1. Preheat oven to 350°. Place chicken in a 13- x 9-inch baking dish. Sprinkle chicken with salt and pepper.

2. Melt butter in a medium skillet over medium-high heat. Add mushrooms, and sauté 4 to 6 minutes or until golden brown. Add wine; cook, stirring often, 2 minutes. Stir in soup and cream, and cook, stirring often, 3 minutes. Pour mushroom mixture over chicken.

3. Bake at 350° for 40 to 45 minutes or until bubbly. Remove from oven, and let stand 10 minutes. Sprinkle with almonds and chopped parsley. Serve over hot cooked rice.

MAKES 6 servings. **HANDS-ON** 20 min.; **TOTAL** 1 hour, 10 min.

RICE SOUFFLÉ

Adapted from The Webster Cookbook, *this casserole is a versatile side dish. "This cookbook is one of my prized possessions," says Webster resident Gladys Clark. "It is a historical book of our community with simple, delicious recipes."*

- 1 cup cold cooked long-grain rice
- 3 large eggs, separated
- 1/2 cup milk
- 2 Tbsp. butter, melted
- 1/2 cup freshly grated sharp Cheddar cheese
- 1/2 tsp. kosher salt and 1/4 tsp. freshly ground black pepper
  Vegetable cooking spray

Preheat oven to 300°. Stir together rice and egg yolks in a medium bowl. Stir in milk, melted butter, cheese, salt, and pepper. Beat egg whites at high speed with an electric mixer 2 to 3 minutes or until stiff peaks form; fold into rice mixture. Pour rice-and-egg white mixture into a lightly greased (with cooking spray) 8-inch square baking dish, and bake 30 to 35 minutes or until golden.

MAKES 6 servings. **HANDS-ON** 20 min., **TOTAL** 50 min.

October

Cast Iron Love

RECIPES, TECHNIQUES, AND REVELATIONS FOR THE SWISS ARMY KNIFE OF KITCHEN TOOLS

We tend to store our heirlooms behind glass in a china cabinet or in the shadows of a jewelry box, using them only on special occasions. Not so with cast iron, which belongs next to the tea kettle on the back of the stove. Smart cooks know the more they use cast iron—and the more love they feed it in the form of bacon fat—the better it functions. Cook with your skillet often enough and you'll come to understand that cast iron has an old soul.

If the adage is true that every recipe tells a story, then every old cast-iron skillet is a well-seasoned memoir. Every time we light the stove and swirl fat into a hot iron pan to make cornbread, we turn another page. Listen to its dialogue: the business-like clank against the stove, the hard sizzle-sear of steak, the soothing dull scrape of a wooden spoon dragged through gravy. Pick up a 12-inch skillet; its encyclopedic heft demands two hands and your attention.

As with many durable objects of classic design, like good bicycles or denim, humble cast iron is having a moment. Lodge Manufacturing Company, the family-owned foundry in South Pittsburg, Tennessee, has expanded its factory to keep up with the increasing demand. Welcome to the new iron age. To celebrate, we've created 10 new recipes that speak to the skillet's workhorse versatility. So whether you use yours as an oven-to-table serving piece, as a weight to grill chicken, as a baking pan for the puffiest pancake, or as the best tool for charring vegetables, we ask just one thing: Use it. Put flame to iron, revisit old dog-eared pages, and write new ones.

CHICKEN-AND-WILD RICE SKILLET CASSEROLE

This rustic one-pot meal, a company's-coming riff on the old-school chicken-and-rice number, is held together by a tangy gravy flavored with country ham and mushrooms. Nutty wild rice helps sop up all the good chicken gravy.

- 1 1/4 tsp. kosher salt, divided
- 1 (6-oz.) container uncooked wild rice
- 3 Tbsp. butter
- 1/3 cup all-purpose flour
- 1 cup milk
- 2 1/2 cups chicken broth
- 1 1/2 tsp. dry mustard
- 3/4 tsp. freshly ground black pepper, divided
- 1/2 cup finely chopped country ham or bacon
- 2 Tbsp. olive oil, divided
- 1 cup chopped yellow onion
- 1 large carrot, finely chopped
- 8 oz. assorted fresh mushrooms, chopped
- 3 garlic cloves, finely chopped
- 2 Tbsp. dry sherry or white wine
- 4 skinned and boned chicken breasts (about 1 1/4 lb.)
  Garnishes: fresh flat-leaf parsley, sliced almonds

1. Bring 1/2 tsp. kosher salt and 1 qt. water to a boil in a 3-qt. saucepan over high heat. Stir in rice, and return to a boil. Reduce heat to medium; cover and cook 30 minutes.
2. Meanwhile, melt butter in a heavy saucepan over low heat; whisk in flour until smooth. Cook, whisking constantly, 1 minute. Gradually whisk in milk and next 2 ingredients. Increase heat to medium, and cook, whisking constantly, 3 to 4 minutes or until mixture is thickened and bubbly. Stir in 1/4 tsp. each kosher salt and black pepper.

3. Cook ham in 1 Tbsp. hot oil in a 12-inch cast-iron skillet over medium-high heat, stirring occasionally, 6 minutes or until beginning to brown. Stir in onion and next 2 ingredients. Cook, stirring occasionally, about 6 minutes or until onions are tender. Stir in garlic, and cook 1 minute. Add sherry, and cook, stirring constantly, 1 minute or until sherry is evaporated. Remove mixture from skillet.

4. Preheat oven to 375°. Sprinkle chicken with remaining ½ tsp. each salt and pepper. Add remaining 1 Tbsp. oil to skillet. Cook chicken in hot oil over medium-high heat 4 minutes on each side or until brown. Remove skillet from heat; transfer chicken to a plate.

5. Drain rice. Stir together rice, ham mixture, and sauce in skillet. Place chicken on top of rice mixture.

6. Bake at 375° for 30 minutes or until mixture is bubbly and chicken is done. Let stand 10 minutes before serving.

Note: We tested with Canoe 100% Natural Wild Rice.

MAKES 4 servings. **HANDS-ON** 55 min.; **TOTAL** 1 hour, 40 min.

Top-Shelf Chicken Under A Brick

TOP-SHELF CHICKEN UNDER A BRICK

The "top-shelf" in this recipe speaks to the crispy skin, superior flavor, and juiciness of the bird. It also refers to a novel new technique: cooking potatoes in the heavy cast-iron skillet that's used as a weight on the chicken. The weight presses the chicken flat against the grill grates, cutting the cooking time in half. Plus you'll be cooking your side dish at the same time.

- 1 lb. small red or Yukon gold potatoes, halved
- 3 tsp. kosher salt, divided
- 1 (3- to 4-lb.) whole chicken
- 2 Tbsp. olive oil, divided
- ½ tsp. freshly ground black pepper
- 12 fresh herb sprigs (such as thyme, rosemary, sage, or tarragon)
- 2 lemons, halved

1. Bring potatoes, 1 tsp. salt, and water to cover to a boil in a large saucepan over high heat. Reduce heat to medium, and simmer 5 to 7 minutes or until potatoes are just tender. Drain.

2. Heat 1 side of grill to 300° to 350° (medium) heat; leave other side unlit. Remove and discard giblets and neck from chicken. Place chicken, breast side down, on a cutting board. Cut chicken, using kitchen shears, along both sides of backbone, separating backbone from chicken; discard backbone. Open chicken as you would a book. Turn chicken, breast side up, and press firmly against breastbone with the heel of your hand until bone cracks. Tuck wing tips under. Rub with 1 Tbsp. oil. Sprinkle chicken with black pepper and remaining 2 tsp. salt.

3. Heat a 12-inch cast-iron skillet on lit side of grill 10 minutes. Add remaining 1 Tbsp. oil to hot skillet; place potatoes, cut side down, in skillet. Transfer skillet to unlit side of grill.

4. Place chicken, breast side down, over lit side of grill; top with herbs. Place cast-iron skillet with potatoes on chicken to flatten. Grill, covered with grill lid, 10 to 15 minutes or until chicken is browned. Remove skillet.

CHICKEN HOW-TO

SPATCHCOCK IT
Using kitchen shears, cut along each side of backbone. Remove backbone. Freeze for stock.

FLATTEN IT
Using the heel of your hand, press firmly against the breastbone of the chicken, and crack it.

WEIGHT IT
Grill chicken weighted with a cast-iron skillet full of potatoes, which crisp as the chicken cooks.

Transfer chicken to unlit side of grill. Place cast-iron skillet on chicken. Grill, covered with grill lid, 45 minutes or until a meat thermometer inserted in thickest portion of breast registers 165°. Remove chicken from grill, and let stand 5 minutes. (For crisper skin, place chicken on lit side of grill, and grill, without grill lid, 5 minutes or until crisp.)

5. Meanwhile, place lemons, cut side down, on lit side of grill, and grill, covered with grill lid, about 5 minutes or until charred and softened. Serve chicken with potatoes and charred lemon.

MAKES 4 servings. **HANDS-ON** 45 min.; **TOTAL** 1 hour, 50 min.

APPLE-CINNAMON DUTCH BABY

Straight from the oven, this puffy, airy pancake will elicit major oohs and aahs from your crowd. Be sure to use low-fat or fat-free milk—the pancake will puff higher. Like a soufflé, it will begin to deflate as soon as it leaves the oven, though that won't affect the flavor.

1 large Gala apple, peeled and sliced
1 Tbsp. granulated sugar
3 Tbsp. butter, divided
2 large eggs
1/2 cup fat-free or low-fat milk
1/2 cup all-purpose flour, sifted
1/2 tsp. ground cinnamon
1/4 tsp. table salt
1/4 tsp. ground nutmeg
1 cup sour cream
1/2 cup firmly packed light brown sugar
1 to 4 Tbsp. apple cider or orange juice
Garnish: powdered sugar

1. Preheat oven to 450°. Heat a 10-inch cast-iron skillet over medium-high heat 5 minutes. Toss together apple slices and sugar in a small bowl. Melt 1 Tbsp. butter in skillet. Add apples, and sauté 3 to 5 minutes or until tender. Remove apples from skillet, and wipe skillet clean.

2. Whisk together eggs and milk in a medium bowl. Whisk in flour and next 3 ingredients. Melt remaining 2 Tbsp. butter in skillet over medium-high heat. Immediately pour egg mixture into hot skillet, and top with cooked apples.

3. Bake at 450° for about 20 minutes or until pancake is golden and puffed.

4. Meanwhile, stir together sour cream and brown sugar in a small microwave-safe bowl. Microwave at HIGH 45 seconds. Whisk until sugar dissolves. Stir in apple cider, 1 Tbsp. at a time, until desired consistency is reached. Serve with hot pancake.

MAKES 6 servings. **HANDS-ON** 25 min., **TOTAL** 45 min.

CAST-IRON COWBOY STEAK

This is the best way to cook a thick, juicy bone-in steak restaurant-style without smoking up the house. Use your grill to heat the cast-iron skillet; the skillet surface area promotes a more assertive flavor and better sear than grill grates, yielding a steak with the proper steak house crust. (Pictured on page 16)

Kosher salt and freshly ground black pepper
1 (1 1/2- to 2-lb.) bone-in rib-eye or porterhouse steak (about 2 inches thick)
1 Tbsp. vegetable oil
3 Tbsp. butter
8 fresh herb sprigs (such as thyme, rosemary, and oregano)
3 garlic cloves, peeled and smashed

1. Preheat grill to 400° to 450° (high) heat. Heat a 12-inch cast-iron skillet on grill, covered with grill lid, 15 minutes. Sprinkle salt and pepper generously over steak.

2. Add oil to skillet. (Oil should smoke.) Using tongs, place steak in skillet, and cook on grill, without grill lid, 10 minutes or until dark brown and crusty. Turn steak on fatty edge in skillet, holding upright with tongs, and cook 2 minutes. Place steak, uncooked side down, in skillet. Cook on grill, covered with grill lid, 8 to 10

minutes or to desired degree of doneness. (We recommend an internal temperature of 120° to 125° for medium-rare; temperature will rise as steak rests.)

3. Add butter, herbs, and garlic to side of skillet, and cook 2 to 3 minutes or until butter foams. Tilt skillet slightly, and spoon butter mixture over steak 20 times (being careful not to splatter). Transfer steak, herbs, and garlic to a platter; let stand for 5 to 10 minutes. Slice against the grain.

MAKES 2 to 4 servings. **HANDS-ON** 20 min., **TOTAL** 1 hour

BRAISED WHITE TURNIPS

We based this recipe on one from Atlanta chef Linton Hopkins found in the book Lodge Cast Iron Nation. *Use small Japanese turnips from farmers' markets, or peel and cut larger turnips into 1- to 2-inch cubes.*

Heat a 12-inch cast-iron skillet over medium-high heat 5 minutes. Trim 15 small white **turnips,** and cut in half lengthwise. Melt 2 Tbsp. **butter** in skillet. Place turnips, cut side down, in a single layer in skillet. Cook, without turning, 4 minutes or until golden brown. Pour 3 Tbsp. **apple cider vinegar** over turnips; add water to depth of 1/4 inch. Sprinkle with **kosher salt.** Bring to a boil; cover and reduce heat to medium-low. Simmer 5 minutes or until crisp-tender. Increase heat to medium-high; uncover and return to a boil. Boil 4 minutes or until liquid is almost evaporated. Cook, turning occasionally, 8 more minutes or until liquid has evaporated. Stir in 2 Tbsp. **honey** and 1 Tbsp. **butter.**

MAKES 4 servings. **HANDS-ON** 35 min., **TOTAL** 35 min.

Braised White Turnips; Cast-Iron Blistered Brussels Sprouts; and Charred Peppers with Feta Dipping Sauce

CAST-IRON BLISTERED BRUSSELS SPROUTS

This is the absolute best way to cook Brussels sprouts. High heat searing caramelizes the outside and yields perfect crisp-tender texture inside. Use a 12-inch cast-iron pan, or work in two batches.

Heat a 12-inch cast-iron skillet over medium-high heat 5 minutes. Trim 1 lb. fresh **Brussels sprouts,** and cut in half lengthwise. Add 3 Tbsp. **canola oil** to skillet, and tilt skillet to evenly coat bottom. Place Brussels sprouts, cut side down, in a single layer in skillet. Cook, without stirring, 4 minutes or until browned. Sprinkle with 3/4 tsp. **kosher salt;** stir and cook 2 more minutes. Stir together 1 Tbsp. **honey** and 1 Tbsp. hot water. Stir 1 Tbsp. minced **garlic** (about 2 cloves), 1 Tbsp. **soy sauce,** 1/4 tsp. **dried crushed red pepper,** and honey mixture into Brussels sprouts. Stir in 1/2 cup torn fresh **mint leaves,** and serve immediately.

MAKES 4 servings. **HANDS-ON** 15 min., **TOTAL** 15 min.

CHARRED PEPPERS WITH FETA DIPPING SAUCE

Look for a colorful assortment of baby sweet peppers in the produce section of your local grocer. Hold them by the stems while dipping.

Heat a 12-inch cast-iron skillet over medium-high heat 5 minutes. Whisk together 1/4 cup crumbled **feta cheese,** 1/4 cup **Greek yogurt,** 1 minced **green onion,** 2 tsp. chopped fresh **mint,** 2 Tbsp. **fresh lemon juice,** and 2 Tbsp. **extra virgin olive oil** in a small bowl. Stir in **salt** and **pepper** to taste. Let stand at room temperature until ready to use. Toss 1 (8-oz.) package assorted **mini sweet peppers** with 1 Tbsp. oil; sprinkle with desired amount of salt. Cook peppers in hot skillet over medium-high heat, turning occasionally, 8 minutes or until charred and slightly wilted. Transfer peppers to a plate; drizzle with 2 Tbsp. fresh lemon juice. Serve with feta mixture.

Note: We tested with Pero Family Farms Mini Sweet Peppers.

MAKES 4 servings. **HANDS-ON** 20 min., **TOTAL** 25 min.

SMOKED TROUT- APPLE HASH

Equally at home on your stove or over a campfire, this fragrant skillet breakfast pulls double duty for dinner with a green salad. Try substituting sweet potatoes for russets and your favorite tart apple for Granny Smith. Other smoked fish like bluefish or whitefish also work well here. If using thinly sliced smoked salmon, cut into pieces and drape over hash just before serving.

- 1 cup sour cream
- 2 Tbsp. prepared horseradish
- 4 Tbsp. butter
- 2 medium-size unpeeled russet potatoes, boiled, cooled, and diced
- 1 small yellow onion, finely chopped
- 1 Granny Smith apple, diced Kosher salt and freshly ground black pepper Pinch of ground red pepper
- 1/2 cup heavy cream
- 1 (4-oz.) smoked trout fillet, flaked into 1/2-inch pieces
- 1 1/2 tsp. fresh dill weed
- 1 tsp. thinly sliced fresh chives Lemon wedges

1. Heat a 12-inch cast-iron skillet over medium-high heat 5 minutes. Stir together sour cream and horseradish in a small bowl, and chill until ready to use.
2. Melt butter in skillet over medium-high heat; add potatoes, and cook, turning occasionally, about 10 minutes or until potatoes begin to brown and crisp. Add onions and apples, and cook, stirring occasionally, about 10 minutes or until onions are tender and apples are golden.
3. Add salt and pepper to taste; add ground red pepper. Stir in cream. Cook, without stirring, about 5 minutes or until potatoes are deep golden. Using a metal spatula, gently lift and turn hash. Cook 5 minutes; gently stir in trout and herbs. Remove from heat, and squeeze lemon wedges over hash. Serve immediately with sour cream sauce.

MAKES 4 servings. **HANDS-ON** 55 min., **TOTAL** 55 min.

CRISPY SWEET POTATO-GREEN ONION CAKES

Serve these savory little numbers with a dollop of sour cream and a squeeze of lime as a crunchy appetizer or a dish to accompany roasted or grilled meats or fish.

- 4 medium-size sweet potatoes (about 2 1/4 lb.)
- 2 large eggs, lightly beaten
- 1/2 cup all-purpose flour
- 2 red jalapeño peppers, chopped
- 1 1/2 tsp. kosher salt
- 1/2 cup thinly sliced green onions, divided
- 1/4 cup canola oil
  Lime wedges

1. Pierce 1 sweet potato several times with a fork. Place on a microwave-safe plate; cover with damp paper towels. Microwave at HIGH 8 to 10 minutes or until tender. Let stand 5 minutes. Peel potato, and place in a medium bowl; mash with a fork. Peel remaining sweet potatoes, and grate, using the large holes of a box grater. Stir grated potatoes into mashed potato. Gently stir in eggs, next 3 ingredients, and 1/4 cup green onions just until combined.
2. Pour oil into a 12-inch cast-iron skillet, and heat over medium heat to 350°. Carefully drop mixture by tablespoonfuls, in batches, into hot oil, pressing lightly to flatten. Cook 5 to 6 minutes on each side or until golden brown. Drain on paper towels. Place drained sweet potato cakes on a wire rack over an aluminum foil-lined baking sheet. Keep warm in a 200° oven up to 30 minutes. Sprinkle with remaining 1/4 cup green onions just before serving. Serve with lime wedges.

MAKES 6 to 8 servings. **HANDS-ON** 1 hour; **TOTAL** 1 hour, 5 min.

CAST-IRON SALSA

Turn your skillet into a Mexican comal, aka griddle, by slowly charring onions, garlic, and peppers in a dry skillet. We like to use this traditional dry char technique because it coaxes sweet, earthy flavors from the vegetables and gives them just a hint of smokiness.

- 3 plum tomatoes, halved
- 3 garlic cloves, unpeeled
- 1 red or green jalapeño pepper, halved
- 1 medium-size white onion, cut into 16 wedges
- 1 1/2 Tbsp. fresh lime juice
- 3/4 tsp. kosher salt
- 1/3 cup chopped fresh cilantro leaves

1. Heat a 12-inch cast-iron skillet or griddle over medium heat 5 minutes. Place tomatoes, cut side down, in skillet, spacing evenly; add garlic and jalapeño pepper. Cook, turning occasionally, about 6 minutes or until slightly charred and softened. Transfer tomatoes and jalapeño pepper to a blender or food processor. Peel garlic, and place in blender. Add onion wedges to skillet, and cook 5 to 6 minutes or until slightly charred and softened. Transfer onions to blender.
2. Process vegetables 30 to 40 seconds or to desired consistency. Add lime juice and salt to blender, and process until combined. Cool completely (about 10 minutes). Stir in cilantro. Serve at room temperature, or refrigerate in an airtight container up to 3 days.

Note: For a redder salsa, use red jalapeño peppers.

MAKES 1 1/2 cups. **HANDS-ON** 20 min., **TOTAL** 30 min.

THOU SHALT...

THE 10 COMMANDMENTS OF CAST IRON CARE

(11 written above "10")

Forget all the myths. Follow these tips and your skillet will last forever. Yes, forever.

1
...RESPECT IT.
You are its steward, and it's your duty to pass it on to the next generation.

2
...USE IT OFTEN.
The more you use your cast-iron skillet, the better it will work, and the more you'll care for it.

3
...SAVE THIS PAGE.
Tear it out and tape it to the inside of your pantry door.

4
...CLEAN CAST IRON AFTER EACH USE.
Wash with hot water while pan is still warm.

5
...DON'T USE SOAP. EVER.
And no matter what, don't ever put cast iron in the dishwasher.

7
...DRY IT IMMEDIATELY.
Wipe dry after washing and heat over low flame for 2 minutes to open the pores of the iron. Use a paper towel and tongs to apply an even, light film of vegetable oil or flaxseed oil on the inside of the pan.

9
...UNDERSTAND "SEASONING."
For cast-iron cookware, this is the polymerization of fat bonded to the surface of the pan. In layman's terms, seasoning is the glossy sheen that gives cast-iron cookware its nonstick properties and keeps it from rusting. Protect and maintain the seasoning and your skillet will last forever. See below to learn how.

6
...SCOUR SMARTLY.
Use coarse salt like Morton Kosher Salt for scouring stubborn bits of food without damaging the seasoning. Use a paper towel to rub the salt into the bottom and around the inside edges of the pan. A stiff bristle brush also works well. Still sticking? Loosen residue such as caramel by boiling water in the pan.

10
...BUST THE RUST.
Rub cast iron with steel wool. For the seriously stubborn rust on old, neglected pans, take the cast iron to a machine shop and ask someone to pressure blast it with air or sand. Then start the seasoning process (see below) to build a protective coat.

BEFORE

AFTER

Fry an egg on this surface and it won't stick!

8
...STORE IT IN A COOL, DRY PLACE.
For pans with lids, add a paper towel wad, and keep ajar to let air flow.

11
...RE-SEASON IT.
Here's the best way to rebuild the seasoning and bring your skillet back to life.

WASH VIGOROUSLY
After busting the rust, wash cast iron with warm and—just this once—soapy water. Dry well.

RUB WITH VEGETABLE OIL
Use a paper towel to rub oil inside, outside, and on skillet handle. Wipe away any excess.

BAKE AT 400° FOR AN HOUR
Place upside down on oven rack; line bottom rack with foil. Bake. Repeat oiling and baking until seasoned.

Host a Fall Fun-for-All

CALL YOUR NEIGHBORS, BREAK OUT THE RAKES, AND TACKLE THE FALLEN LEAVES AS A TEAM.
AFTERWARD, CELEBRATE WITH A FAMILY-FRIENDLY OPEN HOUSE.

The Menu

GRAPE-APPLE CIDER

SUGAR-AND-SPICE CARAMEL POPCORN

BUTTERNUT-GOAT CHEESE-
STUFFED MUSHROOMS

SLOW-COOKER TURKEY CHILI WITH QUINOA

PUMPKIN PIE CUTOUT COOKIES

Slow-Cooker Turkey
Chili with Quinoa

SLOW-COOKER TURKEY CHILI WITH QUINOA

Healthy and hearty, this quinoa chili will become a family favorite. The recipe calls for a bottle of beer; use your favorite seasonal brew to amp up the flavor. The alcohol will evaporate as the chili simmers in the slow cooker.

- 2 **lb. lean ground turkey breast**
- 2 **Tbsp. olive oil**
- 2-4 **jalapeño peppers**
- 2 **large poblano peppers**
- 1 **(48-oz.) container reduced-sodium chicken broth**
- 2 **(15.5-oz.) cans great Northern beans, drained and rinsed**
- 2 **(15.5-oz.) cans navy beans, drained and rinsed**
- 1 **(12-oz.) bottle beer**
- 1 **cup uncooked quinoa**
- 2 **medium-size yellow onions, diced**
- 5 **garlic cloves, minced**
- 3 **tsp. kosher salt**
- 3 **tsp. ground cumin**
- 2 **tsp. dried oregano**
  Cilantro Sauce
  Garnishes: shredded Cheddar cheese, sour cream, lime wedges, sliced avocado, diced red bell peppers

1. Cook turkey in hot oil in a large skillet over high heat, stirring often, 10 minutes or until meat crumbles. Transfer turkey to a 6-qt. slow cooker.
2. Using tongs, char each jalapeño and poblano pepper over gas flame, turning occasionally, about 5 minutes or until skins are totally blackened. (If you don't have a gas cooktop, preheat broiler with oven rack 6 inches from heat. Broil peppers 5 minutes or until blackened, turning occasionally.)
3. Place charred peppers in a bowl, and cover tightly with plastic wrap. Let stand 5 minutes to loosen skins. Peel

peppers under running water. Remove and discard seeds and membranes. Dice peppers, and add to slow cooker.
4. Stir in broth and next 9 ingredients. Cover and cook on LOW 6 to 7 hours or until chili thickens. Serve with Cilantro Sauce.

Note: This recipe makes a mild chili. For a spicier chili, add pepper seeds to slow cooker.

MAKES 8 to 10 servings. **HANDS-ON** 55 min.; **TOTAL** 7 hours, 10 min., including sauce

Cilantro Sauce

Swirl our vibrant, tangy topping into the chili before serving. If you don't like cilantro, use parsley instead. The sauce can also be used as a sandwich spread or stirred, like pesto, into hot pasta.

Process 1 bunch fresh **cilantro** (leaves and stems); 3 Tbsp. **olive oil**; 2 Tbsp. fresh **lime juice**; 1 **jalapeño pepper**, seeded and chopped; 1 **garlic clove**; and 1/4 cup **water** in a blender until smooth, adding more water, if needed, to reach desired consistency. Add **kosher salt** to taste. Refrigerate in an airtight container up to 1 week.

MAKES 1 cup. **HANDS-ON** 10 min., **TOTAL** 10 min.

SUGAR-AND-SPICE CARAMEL POPCORN

Old Bay seasoning is our secret ingredient. It's the perfect savory balance for the sweet caramel.

- 3 (3.5-oz.) bags popped microwave popcorn
  Vegetable cooking spray
- 4 tsp. Old Bay seasoning
- 1/2 cup butter
- 1 cup sugar
- 1/3 cup apple cider vinegar
  Wax paper

1. Place popcorn in a large bowl; lightly coat with cooking spray. Sprinkle with Old Bay seasoning, and toss to coat.
2. Melt butter in a 2-qt. heavy saucepan over medium heat. Stir in sugar and vinegar, and bring to a boil. Boil, without stirring, 8 to 10 minutes or until a candy thermometer registers

300°. Immediately pour butter mixture over popcorn mixture, and stir to coat. Spread popcorn on wax paper, and cool completely (about 25 minutes). Break into pieces, and store in an airtight container up to 1 week.

Note: We tested with Newman's Own Natural Tender White Microwave Popcorn.

MAKES 12 cups. **HANDS-ON** 15 min., **TOTAL** 50 min.

PUMPKIN PIE CUTOUT COOKIES

Bake the cookies up to five days ahead, and store in an airtight container.

COOKIES
- 3/4 cup butter, softened
- 3/4 cup granulated sugar
- 1 large egg
- 1 tsp. vanilla extract
- 1 3/4 cups plus 2 Tbsp. all-purpose flour
- 1 3/4 tsp. pumpkin pie spice
- 1/4 tsp. table salt
  Parchment paper

ICING
- 1 (16-oz.) package powdered sugar
- 2 large pasteurized egg whites
  Food coloring (optional)

1. Prepare Cookies: Beat butter and granulated sugar at medium speed with an electric mixer 5 to 7 minutes or until light and fluffy. Add egg and vanilla; beat 1 minute.
2. Sift together flour and next 2 ingredients. Add to butter mixture all at once, and beat at medium speed 1 minute or until combined. Flatten dough into a 1-inch-thick disk, and wrap in plastic wrap. Chill 2 hours.
3. Preheat oven to 375°, with oven racks in 2 middle positions. Place dough on a lightly floured surface; roll to 1/4-inch thickness. (If dough gets too soft to handle, chill 5 to 10 minutes.)
4. Cut dough with desired cutters, and place 1/2 inch apart on parchment paper-lined baking sheets. Reroll scraps as needed. Chill cut cookies 30 minutes.

5. Bake cookies, 2 sheets at a time, at 375° for 9 minutes. Rotate pans front to back, and top rack to bottom rack. Bake 2 to 4 more minutes or until slightly golden around edges. Remove cookies to wire racks, and cool completely (about 15 minutes).
6. Meanwhile, prepare Icing: Beat powdered sugar, egg whites, and 2 tsp. water at low speed 2 minutes. (If necessary, add up to 1 Tbsp. water, 1 tsp. at a time, to reach desired consistency.) Divide icing, and tint with food coloring, if desired. Cover icing with plastic wrap or a damp towel when not in use.
7. Spread a thin layer of icing over each cookie. For a swirled effect, immediately dot cookie with another color of icing, and blend with a wooden pick. Let base layer of icing dry 10 minutes before piping details. Let finished cookies dry 15 minutes before serving.

MAKES about 3 dozen 2-inch cookies. **HANDS-ON** 2 hours; **TOTAL** 4 hours, 45 min.

BUTTERNUT-GOAT CHEESE-STUFFED MUSHROOMS

Stuff the mushrooms a day ahead. Top with breadcrumbs and bake just before company begins to arrive.

- 12 oz. butternut squash, cut into 1/4-inch cubes (about 3 cups)
- 1 Tbsp. olive oil
- 1 1/2 tsp. finely chopped fresh sage leaves
- 3 Tbsp. butter, divided
- 1/4 cup dry white wine (such as Chardonnay)
- 3 (8-oz.) packages fresh mushrooms
- 1 (4-oz.) goat cheese log
- 1/2 tsp. kosher salt
- 1/4 tsp. freshly ground black pepper
- 1/4 cup panko (Japanese breadcrumbs)
  Vegetable cooking spray
  Garnish: chopped fresh chives

1. Preheat oven to 375°. Cook squash in hot oil in a large skillet over high heat, stirring occasionally, 8 to 10 minutes or until browned. Add sage and 1 Tbsp. butter, and cook, stirring constantly, 2 minutes. Add wine, and cook, stirring constantly, 3 minutes or until wine has evaporated. Transfer squash to a medium bowl, and cool about 10 minutes.

2. Meanwhile, rinse mushrooms, and pat dry. Remove and discard stems.

3. Stir goat cheese and next 2 ingredients into squash mixture just until combined.

4. Microwave remaining 2 Tbsp. butter in a medium microwave-safe bowl at HIGH 30 seconds. Stir breadcrumbs into melted butter just until combined. Spoon desired amount of goat cheese mixture into each mushroom cap. Holding each filled mushroom over breadcrumb mixture, press about 1 Tbsp. crumb mixture onto filling. Place mushrooms in a single layer on a lightly greased (with cooking spray) wire rack in a jelly-roll pan. Bake at 375° for 15 to 20 minutes or until breadcrumbs are toasted and golden brown.

MAKES about 12 appetizer servings.
HANDS-ON 45 min., **TOTAL** 1 hour

Gild your mugs with sparkly edges by dipping their rims in apple juice and sanding sugar before ladling in the cider.

GRAPE-APPLE CIDER

Fresh grapes sweeten the cider and turn it a beautiful amber hue. For an adult brew, stir in 1 cup rum just before serving.

- 1/2 gal. apple cider
- 1 lb. Muscadine or red grapes
- 3 (2-inch) cinnamon sticks
- 10 whole cloves
- 1 (1-inch) piece fresh ginger, peeled and sliced
- 1/4 tsp. ground nutmeg
- 1/8 tsp. ground allspice
- 1/4 tsp. anise seeds or 1 star anise pod (optional)
  Garnishes: apple slices, cinnamon sticks, star anise pods

Place first 7 ingredients and, if desired, anise seeds or star anise pod in a covered 4-qt. saucepan, and bring to a boil over high heat. Reduce heat to medium-low; uncover and simmer 5 minutes. Remove from heat. Mash grapes using a potato masher. Cover and let stand 15 minutes. Pour through a fine wire-mesh strainer into a heat-proof pitcher; discard solids. Serve hot or cold.

MAKES 8 cups. **HANDS-ON** 10 min., **TOTAL** 35 min.

Three Simple Slow-Cooker Suppers

THESE COMFORTING, SLOW-SIMMERED DINNERS DELIVER BIG FLAVORS WITH LITTLE EFFORT

TANGY SLOW-COOKER PORK SHOULDER

This will become your new go-to pork shoulder slow-cooker recipe, thanks to the sweet and tangy soy-and-vinegar flavor profile. Pull the pork, and serve it Southern-style over grits or sandwiched between buns, and ladle on plenty of sauce.

Tangy Slow-Cooker Pork Shoulder

- 1 **(4-lb.) bone-in pork shoulder roast (Boston butt)**
- 2 **tsp. kosher salt**
- 1 **tsp. freshly ground black pepper**
- 2 **Tbsp. olive oil**
- 12 **garlic cloves, smashed**
- 2 **bay leaves**
- 1 **onion, cut into 8 wedges**
- 3/4 **cup firmly packed light brown sugar**
- 3/4 **cup reduced-sodium soy sauce**
- 1/2 **cup white wine vinegar or white vinegar**
- 2 **Tbsp. all-purpose flour**
- 2 **Tbsp. fresh lemon juice**

1. Sprinkle all sides of pork roast with salt and pepper. Cook roast in hot oil in a large skillet over medium-high heat 3 minutes on each side or until lightly browned. Transfer pork to a 6-qt. slow cooker, and add garlic, bay leaves, and onion. Whisk together brown sugar, soy sauce, and vinegar until sugar dissolves; pour mixture over pork. Cover and cook on LOW 8 hours.

2. Transfer pork to a serving platter, and cover with foil to keep warm. Pour cooking liquid through a fine wire-mesh strainer into a medium saucepan, discarding solids. Bring to a boil over medium-high heat; boil 8 minutes.

3. Spoon 1/4 cup cooking liquid into a small bowl, and whisk in flour and lemon juice until smooth. Return flour mixture to pan, and boil, whisking constantly, 1 to 2 minutes or until slightly thickened. Serve sauce over pork.

MAKES 4 servings. **HANDS-ON** 40 min.; **TOTAL** 8 hours, 40 min.

Top sandwiches with your favorite crunchy slaw.

Slow-Cooked Cowboy Brisket and Beans

SLOW-COOKED COWBOY BRISKET AND BEANS

Serve this stick-to-your-ribs dish with garlicky slabs of thick Texas toast and a green salad to all of your cowpokes on the range; then take a bow as they tip their hats.

- 1 (20-oz.) package Cajun-flavored dried 15-bean soup mix
- 1 (12-oz.) package frozen diced onion, red and green peppers, and celery
- 1 (4 1/2-lb.) beef brisket, untrimmed
- 2 tsp. kosher salt
- 2 tsp. freshly ground black pepper
- 1/3 cup all-purpose flour
- 2 Tbsp. olive oil
- 2 (1-oz.) containers home-style concentrated chicken stock (from a 4.66-oz. package)
  Garnishes: sliced onion, cilantro leaves

1. Place first 2 ingredients, including soup mix seasoning packet, in a 6-qt. slow cooker. Trim fat from brisket to 1/4-inch thickness; make 1/4-inch-deep cuts, 1 inch apart, in fat. Sprinkle all sides of brisket with salt and pepper, and rub flour over brisket.
2. Cook brisket in hot oil in a large skillet over medium-high heat 10 minutes on each side or until golden brown. Transfer brisket from skillet to a plate.
3. Add chicken stock and 2 1/2 cups water to skillet. Bring to a boil, stirring to loosen browned bits from bottom of skillet; boil, stirring often, 1 to 2 minutes or until sauce is slightly thickened and smooth. Stir stock mixture into bean mixture in slow cooker. Place brisket, fat side up, on bean mixture. Cover and cook on LOW 7 to 8 hours or until brisket is fork-tender.

Note: We tested with Hurst's Ham-Beens Cajun 15-Bean Soup Mix and PictSweet Seasoning Blend frozen diced onion, peppers, and celery.

MAKES 6 to 8 servings. **HANDS-ON** 40 min.; **TOTAL** 7 hours, 40 min.

TORTILLA SOUP

Anaheim peppers are long, slender chile peppers with a sweet, mild heat. Look for Mexican tortilla soup broth on the soup aisle.

- 6 fresh Anaheim or poblano peppers
- 1 (28-oz.) can whole plum tomatoes, crushed
- 12 skinned and boned chicken thighs, trimmed
- 2 (32-oz.) containers Mexican tortilla soup broth
- 1 Tbsp. ground cumin
- 1 Tbsp. smoked paprika
- 1/2 tsp. kosher salt
  Garnishes: crisp tortilla strips, queso fresco, sliced avocado, cilantro, lime wedges

1. Preheat oven to 500°. Place peppers in a single layer on an aluminum foil-lined baking sheet, and bake 10 minutes on each side or until peppers are blistered. Place peppers in a large zip-top plastic freezer bag; seal and let stand 10 minutes to loosen skins. Peel peppers; remove and discard seeds. Coarsely chop peppers, and place in a 6-qt. slow cooker.
2. Add tomatoes and next 5 ingredients. Cover and cook on LOW 6 to 7 hours. Skim fat from top of soup. Remove chicken, using a slotted spoon, and shred. Return chicken to soup, and add salt to taste.

Note: We tested with Swanson 100% Natural Mexican Tortilla Flavor Infused Broth.

MAKES 6 qt. **HANDS-ON** 15 min.; **TOTAL** 6 hours, 45 min.

THE *SL* TEST KITCHEN ACADEMY

ROBBY MELVIN, DIRECTOR OF THE SOUTH'S MOST TRUSTED KITCHEN, SHARES A RECIPE FOR THE

PERFECT POT OF GRITS

Perfect grits begin with good grits. Use stone-ground varieties (see True Grit below) to deliver the best flavor and texture. As for the method, we cover grits as they simmer, a revelatory technique that cuts the cook time in half. Follow this recipe to cook grits like a pro.

① WHISK, WHISK, WHISK
Start by whisking the grits vigorously into a heavy pot of boiling salted water, which encourages even, clump-free cooking.

Bring 2 tsp. **kosher salt** and 1 qt. **water** to a boil in a heavy saucepan over high heat. Whisk in 1 cup **stone-ground grits,** and cook, whisking constantly, 45 seconds. Scrape bottom and sides of the pot.

② PUT A LID ON IT
Covering stone-ground grits while they simmer in a pot reduces the cook time by more than half. Covering also helps the grits retain their texture and corn flavor as they cook to a velvety consistency.

Return to a boil; cover and reduce heat to medium-low. Cook 20 to 25 minutes or until tender. (For a looser consistency, whisk in 2 to 4 Tbsp. water halfway through cooking.)

③ SWIRL IN BUTTER
Adding fat is the final flourish to elevate the toasty flavors and accentuate the natural creaminess afforded by this recipe. Swirl in a pat of butter, grated cheese, or a splash of buttermilk, and season to taste with salt just before serving.

Stir in 2 ½ Tbsp. **butter** until melted, and serve immediately.

MAKES 4 to 6 servings. **HANDS-ON** 5 min., **TOTAL** 30 min.

TRUE GRIT: WHITE VS. YELLOW

White stone-ground grits, the kind milled by crushing dried corn kernels between stone wheels, are the ultimate breakfast grits. Mild in texture and nutty in flavor, they pair dreamily with bacon, sausage, and eggs any way you like them. Yellow stone-ground grits have more hearty and savory tones, making them an ideal companion for grilled pork chops and roasted chicken. They are also ideal for classic shrimp and grits.

One Pot Roast, Three Dinners

SPIN SUNDAY'S ROAST AND ALL THE TRIMMINGS INTO BRAND NEW DISHES FOR BUSY WEEKNIGHT SUPPERS

Zesty Pot Roast, Parmesan Potatoes, and Roasted Carrots

SUNDAY
ZESTY POT ROAST

Serve Parmesan Potatoes and Roasted Carrots Sunday night. Save and chop enough cooked carrots to yield ¹/₂ cup, and refrigerate for Monday's pies.

- 2 (3-lb.) boneless chuck roasts
- 1 Tbsp. kosher salt
- 1 tsp. ground black pepper
- 2 Tbsp. canola oil
- 1 medium onion, chopped
- 1 tsp. minced fresh garlic
- 2 cups beef broth
- 1 Tbsp. lime zest
- 3 Tbsp. fresh lime juice
- 1 (15-oz.) can whole tomatoes, undrained and crushed

1. Preheat oven to 350°. Sprinkle roasts with salt and pepper. Cook 1 roast in 1 ¹/₂ tsp. hot oil in a Dutch oven over medium-high heat 4 minutes on each side. Remove roast; repeat with 1 ¹/₂ tsp. oil and remaining roast. Sauté onion in 1 Tbsp. hot oil in Dutch oven 4 minutes. Add garlic; sauté 1 minute. Return roasts to Dutch oven; add broth, zest, juice, and tomatoes.
2. Bake, covered, at 350° for 3 hours or until beef is tender. Let roasts stand 10 minutes. Slice 1 roast, and serve with 1¹/₂ cups tomato mixture. (Reserve remaining roast and tomato mixture for pot roast pies and soup, if desired.)

MAKES 6 to 8 servings. **HANDS-ON** 35 min.; **TOTAL** 3 hours, 45 min.

PARMESAN POTATOES

Bring 3 lb. peeled **Yukon gold potatoes,** cut into 1-inch cubes; 1 tsp. **salt;** and cold water to a boil in a saucepan over medium-high heat. Reduce heat to medium-low, and cook 16 minutes or until tender; drain. Return potatoes to pan; cook over medium heat until dry. Stir in ¹/₂ cup **half-and-half,** ¹/₂ cup grated **Parmesan cheese,** ¹/₃ cup melted **butter,** 1 tsp. **salt,** and ³/₄ tsp. **black pepper;** cook 30 seconds or until heated. Remove pan from heat. Mash potatoes to desired consistency. (Reserve 2 cups for pot roast pies, if desired.)

MAKES 6 to 8 servings. **HANDS-ON** 20 min., **TOTAL** 45 min.

MONDAY NIGHT

MEAT + POTATOES + FLAKY PASTRY = DIVINE

SHEPHERD'S POT ROAST PIES

Your famiy will love this new spin on calzones, and you'll love the ease and convenience.

- 1 (14.1-oz.) package refrigerated piecrusts Parchment paper
- 2 cups Parmesan Potatoes
- 2 cups chopped Zesty Pot Roast
- ¹/₂ cup sliced Roasted Carrots
- 1 cup frozen English peas, thawed
- ¹/₂ cup tomato mixture reserved from Zesty Pot Roast
- 1 large egg

1. Preheat oven to 400°. Unroll 1 piecrust on a parchment paper-lined baking sheet. Spread 1 cup potatoes over half of crust, leaving a 1-inch border around edge. Toss together chopped roast and next 3 ingredients; spoon half of mixture over potatoes. Whisk together egg and 1 tsp. water; brush a small amount of egg mixture around edge of piecrust. Fold dough over filling, pressing and folding edges to seal. Repeat with remaining crust, potatoes, pot roast mixture, and a small amount of egg mixture. Brush tops of pies with remaining egg mixture; cut small slits in top for steam to escape.
2. Bake at 400° for 25 to 30 minutes or until crusts are golden brown and crisp.

MAKES 6 servings. **HANDS-ON** 20 min.; **TOTAL** 45 min., not including potatoes, roast, or carrots

Roasted Carrots: Preheat oven to 450°. Peel 3 lb. **small carrots** with tops. Trim tops to 1 inch. Toss carrots with 1 Tbsp. olive oil, ³/₄ tsp. **salt,** and ¹/₄ tsp. **pepper.** Place on a 17-x 12-inch jelly-roll pan. Bake at 450° for 20 minutes, stirring once. Reduce heat to 325°, and bake, stirring occasionally, 15 minutes or until carrots are browned and tender.

MAKES 6 to 8 servings. **HANDS-ON** 10 min., **TOTAL** 45 min.

TUESDAY NIGHT

READY IN 35 MINUTES!

BEEF-AND-ORZO SOUP

Pick up a baguette at the market, so you can sop up every drop of this hearty soup. Whip up a fresh spinach salad to serve alongside.

- 1 cup chopped onion
- 1 Tbsp. canola oil
- 1 cup chopped carrots
- 1 (8-oz.) package sliced button mushrooms
- 2 cups chopped Zesty Pot Roast
- 1 cup tomato mixture reserved from Zesty Pot Roast
- ¹/₂ cup uncooked orzo or other small pasta
- 1 (32-oz.) container beef broth

Sauté onion in hot oil in a Dutch oven over medium-high heat 5 to 6 minutes or until lightly browned. Add carrots and mushrooms, and cook, stirring occasionally, 8 to 10 minutes or until mushrooms are tender. Add remaining ingredients, and bring to a boil. Reduce heat to medium, and simmer, stirring occasionally, 5 to 6 minutes or until orzo is al dente and soup is thoroughly heated.

MAKES about 8 cups. **HANDS-ON** 25 min.; **TOTAL** 35 min., not including roast

Trick out Your Treats

MAKE LITTLE GOBLINS GRIN WITH OUR CANDY CORN-COLORED RIFF ON EVERYONE'S FAVORITE COOKIE

CRÈME-FILLED CHOCOLATE SANDWICH COOKIES

Celebrate Halloween by tinting one-third of the filling with orange food coloring and one-third with yellow food coloring; keep one-third white. You can also flavor the colored fillings with 1 tsp. of your favorite extract, such as orange or almond. For adults-only cookies, stir 1 Tbsp. bourbon or rum into filling before dividing to tint.

COOKIES

- 1 2/3 cups all-purpose flour
- 3/4 cup granulated sugar
- 3/4 cup unsweetened cocoa
- 3/4 tsp. kosher salt
- 1/2 tsp. baking powder
- 3/4 cup plus 1 Tbsp. butter, softened
- Parchment paper

FILLING

- 1/2 cup shortening, at room temperature
- 1/2 cup butter, softened
- 3 1/4 cups powdered sugar
- 1/2 tsp. kosher salt
- 1 tsp. vanilla extract (optional)

1. Prepare Cookies: Beat first 5 ingredients at low speed with a heavy-duty electric stand mixer until combined. Add butter, 1 Tbsp. at a time, and beat at medium speed just until blended after each addition.

2. Press dough together with fingers, and divide dough in half. Place each half between 2 sheets of parchment paper, and roll to 1/8-inch thickness. Chill 30 minutes.

3. Meanwhile, prepare Filling: Beat shortening and 1/2 cup butter at high speed 3 to 5 minutes or until smooth. Gradually add powdered sugar, beating until fully incorporated. Beat in salt and, if desired, vanilla. (Do not chill.)

4. Preheat oven to 350°. Remove and discard parchment paper from dough. Working quickly, cut dough with a 2-inch round cutter, and immediately place rounds on parchment paper-lined baking sheets. Reroll scraps, and chill 30 minutes before cutting.

5. Bake cookies on baking sheets at 350° for 6 minutes. Rotate baking sheets front to back, and bake 6 more minutes. Remove from oven to a wire rack, and cool 5 minutes. Transfer cookies to wire rack, and cool completely (about 10 additional minutes). Repeat process with remaining chilled dough.

6. Spoon filling into a zip-top plastic freezer bag. Snip 1 corner of bag to make a small hole. Pipe desired amount of filling onto 1 cookie, and top with another cookie to make a sandwich. Repeat with remaining filling and cookies.

MAKES 12 sandwich cookies.
HANDS-ON 30 min.; **TOTAL** 1 hour, 15 min.

COCKTAIL MEATBALLS

(FROM OCTOBER 1976)

Good Things From Ground Beef

◄◄ **THE ORIGINAL:** A know-it-by-heart recipe (chili sauce + grape jelly + meatballs) Southerners have stabbed with toothpicks from chafing dishes for decades. **THE REVIVAL:** A saucy, Greek-flavored meatball made with briny olives, fresh herbs, and lemon zest. Bonus: We've simplified the cooking.

PARTY-PERFECT MEATBALLS

To make ahead, prepare meatballs through Step 2, and freeze in zip-top plastic freezer bags for up to 1 month. To reheat from frozen, pick up with Step 3 and warm the meatballs in the sauce over low heat. For serving, keep them warm in your slow cooker, in a Dutch oven over low heat, or in a fondue pot.

- 1 **cup pitted kalamata olives**
- 1/2 **small red onion, coarsely chopped**
- 3/4 **cup coarsely chopped fresh mint leaves**
- 1/2 **cup coarsely chopped fresh parsley**
- 2 **tsp. lemon zest**
- 3/4 **cup panko (Japanese bread-crumbs)**
- 1/2 **cup ricotta cheese**
- 2 **large eggs**
- 1 1/2 **tsp. kosher salt**
- 1/2 **tsp. freshly ground black pepper**
- 1 **lb. ground beef**
- 1 **lb. mild Italian sausage, casings removed**
- 1 **(6-oz.) can tomato paste**
- 3 **cups beef broth**
- 1/3 **cup hot pepper jelly**

1. Preheat oven to 450°. Pulse first 5 ingredients in a food processor 8 to 10 times or until chopped. Stir together panko, next 6 ingredients, and olive mixture in a large bowl until well combined. Shape mixture into 1-inch balls, and place 1 inch apart on aluminum foil-lined jelly-roll pans.

2. Bake at 450° for 12 minutes. Cool 5 minutes.

3. Meanwhile, heat a large saucepan over medium heat 2 minutes. Add tomato paste to dry pan, and cook, stirring occasionally, 3 minutes or until paste begins to brown and coat bottom of pan. Increase heat to high, and add beef broth, stirring to loosen bits of tomato paste from bottom of pan. Whisk until smooth. Whisk in hot pepper jelly until combined. Reduce heat to low. Add cooked meatballs, and serve warm.

Note: Sauce may be refrigerated in an airtight container up to 3 days.

MAKES about 20 appetizer servings.
HANDS-ON 35 min., **TOTAL** 50 min.

Community Cookbook

BUILD A BETTER LIBRARY, ONE GREAT BOOK AT A TIME.

We may not be bound by spiral (or by staples anymore, for that matter), but *Southern Living* has been the ultimate community cookbook of the South, publishing the country's best home cooking for nearly 50 years. After poring over 45,000 recipes in our canon, author Sheri Castle collected 200 of the most delicious, including Hummingbird Cake and Classic Deviled Eggs, regional favorites that bind our collective community.

BANANA PUDDING

Perfect custard isn't difficult, but practice makes perfect. Custards are the soul of many great desserts. They are also essential comfort food. In some communities, making proper egg custard was part of the registered nurse licensing exam until the 1970s. Custards do make us feel better.

 1 **cup granulated sugar, divided**
 1/3 **cup all-purpose flour**
    Dash of salt
 2 **cups whole milk**
 4 **large eggs, separated**
 1 **Tbsp. butter**
 2 **tsp. vanilla extract**
 48 **vanilla wafers**
 4 **large bananas (2 ½ lb. unpeeled; about 6 cups when thinly sliced)**

1. Preheat oven to 325°. Whisk together ³/₄ cup sugar, flour, and salt in a large heavy saucepan. Gradually whisk in milk. Whisk in egg yolks. Cook over medium heat, stirring constantly with a heatproof spatula, 8 to 10 minutes or until pudding thickens and just begins to bubble around the edges. Remove from heat, and stir in butter and vanilla.

2. Arrange one-third of the vanilla wafers in the bottom of 6 (6-oz.) custard cups. Cover with one-third of the banana slices. Pour one-third of the warm pudding over the bananas. Repeat the layers twice more.

3. Beat egg whites (at room temperature) in a large bowl at medium speed with an electric mixer until foamy. Increase mixer speed to high, and add remaining ¹/₄ cup sugar, 1 Tbsp. at a time, beating until mixture is glossy and stiff peaks form (2 to 4 minutes). Spread meringue over warm pudding, spreading and sealing to edge of dish.

4. Bake at 325° for 15 to 20 minutes or until meringue is golden. Cool on a wire rack 30 minutes. Serve slightly warm, or cool completely and refrigerate until chilled.

Tips: Use firm, ripe bananas with a few brown speckles. Older bananas quickly darken in the pudding. Bananas keep better when left attached to the crown until needed. If you want them to last, keep them away from fresh apples, which make them ripen quicker. On the other hand, if you need to ripen up green bananas, place them in a brown paper bag with an apple overnight.

MAKES 6 servings. **HANDS-ON** 40 min.; **TOTAL** 1 hour, 25 min.

From the kitchen of
Mrs. Julian Moats
March 1982
BIRMINGHAM, ALABAMA

FROGMORE STEW

Frogmore Stew, otherwise known as Lowcountry boil, is an easy one-pot seafood-and-vegetable dinner, similar to a shrimp or crawfish boil. Although it can be prepared indoors, many people like to tackle a boil outdoors, perhaps in a huge pot, served on a newspaper-covered picnic table, eaten with the fingers, and shared with family and friends.

 ¼ **cup Old Bay seasoning, plus more for sprinkling**
 4 **lb. small red potatoes**
 2 **lb. kielbasa or hot smoked link sausage, cut into 1 ½-inch pieces**
 6 **ears fresh corn, halved crosswise**
 4 **lb. unpeeled, large fresh raw shrimp**
    Cocktail sauce

1. Bring 5 qt. water and ¹/₄ cup Old Bay seasoning to a rolling boil in a large covered stockpot.

2. Add potatoes. Return to a boil, and cook, uncovered, 10 minutes.

3. Add sausage and corn. Return to a boil, and cook 10 minutes or until potatoes are tender.

4. Add shrimp; cook 3 to 4 minutes or until shrimp turn pink. Drain.

5. Sprinkle generously with more Old Bay seasoning, and serve with cocktail sauce.

MAKES 12 servings. **HANDS-ON** 15 min., **TOTAL** 45 min.

From the kitchen of
Richard Gay
August 2003
ST. HELENA ISLAND, SOUTH CAROLINA

November

the
TABLE

**Relax at a table with a natural,
layered look and elevated menu,
both inspired by the season's harvest**

WHAT HAPPENS

when you pair one of the South's most creative stylists with one of its rising culinary stars? Thanksgiving gold. *SL* Style Director Heather Chadduck Hillegas created the season's most inspired table, mixing vintage finds with traditional patterns, alongside Athens, Georgia, cookbook author Gena Knox, who crafted a modern menu full of classic dishes with smart new twists. Follow their leads, and ease up on the formality this year to host your most gracious holiday yet.

GRILL-SMOKED TURKEY

The dry brine used on the turkey is inspired by a wet brine that Gena sells through her brand Fire & Flavor (fireandflavor.com).

1 (10- to 12-lb.) fresh turkey
  Herb-Salt Dry Brine
4 cups applewood chips
3 carrots, halved
1 apple, halved
1 small onion, halved
  Kitchen string
2 (12 $\frac{7}{8}$- x 10-inch) disposable aluminum foil roasting pans
3 Tbsp. canola oil
  Freshly ground black pepper

1. Remove giblets and neck from turkey; pat turkey dry. Rub ¼ cup Herb-Salt Dry Brine into cavity. Rub skin with remaining brine. Cover and chill 14 to 24 hours.
2. Soak wood chips 30 minutes.
3. Meanwhile, rinse turkey; drain cavity well, and pat dry. Place carrots and next 2 ingredients in cavity. Tie ends of legs together with kitchen string; tuck wing tips under.
4. Light 1 side of grill, heating to 300° to 325° (medium-low) heat, leaving other side unlit. Close grill lid, and maintain internal temperature at 300° to 325°.

Roasted Cauliflower-and-Garlic Soup

ROASTED CAULIFLOWER-AND-GARLIC SOUP

Roasting cauliflower brings out a delicious nutty flavor and gives the soup a gorgeous silky texture. Prepare the soup through Step 4 up to two days ahead. Let cool; cover and chill. Reheat just before you're ready to serve. Serve the soup as a seated starter while your turkey rests.

1   large head cauliflower (about 2 1/2 lb.)
4 1/2   tsp. olive oil
1 1/2   tsp. kosher salt, divided
3   garlic cloves, unpeeled
3   cups reduced-sodium chicken broth
1   cup 2% reduced-fat milk
1/2   cup grated Manchego or Parmesan cheese
    Freshly ground black pepper
    Garnishes: olive oil, pomegranate seeds, fresh thyme leaves

1. Preheat oven to 425°. Cut cauliflower into 2-inch florets; toss with olive oil and 1/2 tsp. salt. Arrange florets in a single layer on a jelly-roll pan. Wrap garlic cloves in aluminum foil, and place on jelly-roll pan with cauliflower.
2. Bake at 425° for 30 to 40 minutes or until cauliflower is golden brown, tossing cauliflower every 15 minutes.
3. Transfer cauliflower to a large Dutch oven. Unwrap garlic, and cool 5 minutes. Peel garlic, and add to cauliflower. Add broth, and bring to a simmer over medium heat; simmer, stirring occasionally, 5 minutes. Let mixture cool 10 minutes.
4. Process cauliflower mixture, in batches, in a blender until smooth, stopping to scrape down sides as needed.
5. Return cauliflower mixture to Dutch oven; stir in milk, cheese, and remaining 1 tsp. salt. Cook over low heat, stirring occasionally, 2 to 3 minutes or until thoroughly heated. Add pepper to taste.

MAKES 6 to 8 servings. **HANDS-ON** 30 min.; **TOTAL** 1 hour, 5 min.

5. Drain wood chips, and place in center of a 12- x 20-inch piece of heavy-duty aluminum foil. Wrap to form a packet. Pierce several holes in packet; place directly on lit side of grill.
6. Place 1 disposable roasting pan inside second pan. Place turkey, breast side up, in pan, and brush turkey with oil. Sprinkle with desired amount of pepper.
7. Smoke turkey, covered with grill lid and maintaining internal temperature at 300° to 325°, 2 hours and 45 minutes to 3 hours and 15 minutes or until a meat thermometer inserted in thickest portion registers 165°. Remove carrots, onion, and apple from cavity,

and discard. Let turkey stand 30 minutes at room temperature before slicing.

MAKES 8 servings. **HANDS-ON** 30 min.; **TOTAL** 17 hours, 15 min., including brine

Herb-Salt Dry Brine

1/3   cup kosher salt
1/3   cup sugar
2   Tbsp. chopped fresh rosemary
2   Tbsp. chopped fresh thyme
2   Tbsp. chopped fresh sage

Stir together all ingredients.

MAKES about 1 cup.
HANDS-ON 10 min., **TOTAL** 10 min.

CANE SYRUP-GLAZED ACORN SQUASH

Cane syrup adds old-fashioned Southern sweetness to this stunning side. Feel free to use maple syrup or honey instead.

- 3 acorn squash, halved and seeded
- 4 1/2 tsp. olive oil
- 1 Tbsp. light brown sugar
- 1/2 tsp. kosher salt
  Vegetable cooking spray
- 1/4 cup dried cranberries
- 1/4 cup sherry vinegar
- 1/4 cup cane syrup
- 1 Tbsp. butter, melted
- 1/8 tsp. ground red pepper
- 1/4 cup loosely packed fresh flat-leaf parsley, coarsely chopped

1. Preheat oven to 475°. Slice each squash half into 4 to 5 wedges, and toss with olive oil, brown sugar, and salt. Arrange squash in a single layer on a lightly greased (with cooking spray) jelly-roll pan. Bake 40 minutes or until golden and tender.

2. Meanwhile, microwave cranberries and vinegar in a microwave-safe bowl at HIGH 30 seconds. Let mixture stand 10 minutes; drain. Stir together cane syrup, butter, and red pepper in a bowl.

3. Brush squash with half of syrup mixture. Turn squash over, and brush with remaining syrup mixture. Bake at 475° for 12 more minutes or until golden brown. Transfer squash to a serving platter; top with cranberries and parsley.

MAKES 8 servings. **HANDS-ON** 20 min., **TOTAL** 1 hour

GREEN BEAN SALAD WITH HEARTS OF PALM

If you can't find haricots verts (small, thin French green beans), use regular beans. Make ahead: Blanch the beans up to three days before, wrap them in damp paper towels, and store in a zip-top plastic freezer bag. Compose and dress the salad just before the big feast.

PICKLED ONIONS

- 1 cup thinly sliced red onion (about 1/2 onion)
- 3/4 cup rice wine vinegar
- 1/2 tsp. table salt
- 1/2 tsp. sugar

VINAIGRETTE

- 1 Tbsp. apple cider vinegar
- 2 tsp. whole grain mustard
- 1 tsp. Dijon mustard
- 1/2 tsp. table salt
- 1/4 tsp. sugar
- 2 Tbsp. olive oil

SALAD

- 1 1/2 lb. haricots verts (French green beans), trimmed
- 1 (14-oz.) can hearts of palm, drained and rinsed
  Freshly ground black pepper

1. Prepare Pickled Onions: Toss together first 4 ingredients and 1/4 cup water in a bowl. Cover and chill 1 to 12 hours.

2. Prepare Vinaigrette: Whisk together cider vinegar and next 4 ingredients. Add oil in a slow, steady stream, whisking constantly until smooth.

3. Prepare Salad: Cook beans in 6 qt. boiling salted water in a large Dutch oven over medium-high heat 3 minutes or until crisp-tender; drain. Plunge beans into ice water to stop the cooking process; drain and pat dry.

4. Cut hearts of palm into 1-inch-thick slices, and separate into rings. Toss haricots verts and hearts of palm with vinaigrette; add salt and pepper to taste. Arrange on a platter. Drain onions, and sprinkle over salad. Gently toss, if desired, and serve immediately.

MAKES 6 servings. **HANDS-ON** 25 min.; **TOTAL** 1 hour, 25 min.

HERB-AND-CREAM BISCUITS

The crème fraîche and herbs make these a perfect choice for Thanksgiving dinner. They are so rich you won't even need to butter them before eating.

- 2 cups self-rising soft-wheat flour (such as White Lily)
- 4 Tbsp. cold butter, cut into small pieces
- 1 tsp. fresh thyme leaves, chopped
- 1/2 tsp. chopped fresh rosemary
- 3 Tbsp. crème fraîche or sour cream
- 3/4 to 1 cup buttermilk

1. Preheat oven to 450°. Sift flour into a large bowl. Cut cold butter into flour with a pastry blender or fork until mixture resembles coarse meal. Stir in thyme and rosemary.

2. Stir in crème fraîche, using a fork. Gradually stir in 3/4 cup buttermilk, adding up to 1/4 cup buttermilk, 1 Tbsp. at a time, to make a sticky dough. Gently stir with fork until dough pulls away from sides of bowl.

3. Turn dough out onto a floured (with self-rising soft-wheat flour) surface; sprinkle dough with flour, and pat to a 1-inch thickness.

4. Cut with a floured 2-inch round cutter, and place, with edges touching, in a greased (with butter) 9-inch square pan. Reshape and cut dough until all dough is used.

5. Bake at 450° for 15 minutes or until lightly browned. Serve immediately.

Note: These biscuits can easily be made ahead of time and frozen. Cook biscuits for 10 to 12 minutes or until they're just set but not browned. Remove from oven, cool completely on a wire rack, and place biscuits in a heavy-duty zip-top plastic freezer bag. Seal and freeze. To thaw, remove biscuits from bag, and arrange frozen biscuits on a baking sheet brushed with melted butter. Bake at 450° for 7 to 8 minutes or until thoroughly heated and lightly browned.

MAKES 16 biscuits. **HANDS-ON** 25 min., **TOTAL** 45 min.

WILD RICE-AND-GREENS CASSEROLE

We prefer chopped kale in this casserole, but use your favorite green. For heartier greens like collards, cook them five minutes longer in Step 1. If you want to prepare the dish ahead, cover and chill up to three days before baking. Uncover and bake just before serving.

- 1/2 **lb. fresh kale or other hearty greens, trimmed and coarsely chopped**
- 1 **medium onion, chopped**
- 4 1/2 **tsp. olive oil**
- 3 **garlic cloves, minced**
- 1 **Tbsp. fresh thyme leaves**
- 1/4 **tsp. ground nutmeg**
- 4 **Tbsp. all-purpose flour**
- 1 **cup 2% reduced-fat milk**
- 1 **cup reduced-sodium chicken broth**
- 3 **cups cooked wild rice**
- 1/2 **cup chopped sun-dried tomatoes**
- 1 **cup grated Gruyère cheese, divided***
- **Vegetable cooking spray**
- 1/2 **cup chopped almonds**

1. Preheat oven to 375°. Cook kale in 1 cup boiling salted water in a Dutch oven over high heat, stirring occasionally, 5 minutes; drain.

2. Cook onion in hot oil in a large skillet over medium-low heat, stirring often, 20 minutes or until golden. Add garlic, thyme, and nutmeg, and cook 1 minute. Stir in flour and cooked kale. Gradually stir in milk and broth, and cook, stirring often, 4 minutes or until thickened. Stir in rice, tomatoes, and 1/2 cup cheese. Add salt and pepper to taste.

3. Transfer mixture to a lightly greased (with cooking spray) 2 1/2-qt. baking dish. Sprinkle almonds and remaining 1/2 cup cheese over mixture.

4. Bake at 375° for 18 minutes or until bubbly and lightly browned.

*Swiss cheese may be substituted.

MAKES 8 servings. **HANDS-ON** 50 min.; **TOTAL** 1 hour, 10 min.

BUTTERSCOTCH MERINGUE PIE WITH PECAN CRUST

We won't revoke your pie credentials if you use a purchased piecrust in this recipe, but we love the way the homemade crust's earthy flavor elevates the caramel filling so much that we recommend you give it a try. A few rules of the road: Be sure to finely grind your pecans to ensure the crust will hold together. And if the crust tears just a bit, don't be alarmed. As with all piecrusts, you can easily press it back together with your fingertips or use extra scraps for patchwork.

CRUST

- 1/2 **cup chopped pecans**
- 1 1/4 **cups all-purpose flour**
- 2 **Tbsp. granulated sugar**
- 1/2 **cup cold butter, cut into 1/2-inch pieces**
- 2 **Tbsp. ice-cold water**
- 1 **tsp. vanilla extract**
- **Wax paper**
- **Parchment paper**

FILLING

- 2 **cups firmly packed light brown sugar**
- 2/3 **cup all-purpose flour**
- 1/2 **tsp. table salt**
- 2 1/2 **cups milk**
- 6 **egg yolks, lightly beaten**
- 1/2 **cup butter, cut into 1-inch pieces**
- 2 **tsp. vanilla extract**

MERINGUE

- 6 **large egg whites**
- 1 **tsp. vanilla extract**
- 1/4 **tsp. cream of tartar**
- 6 **Tbsp. granulated sugar**

1. Prepare Crust: Pulse pecans in a food processor 10 to 12 times or until finely chopped. Transfer pecans to a small bowl. Pulse 1 1/4 cups flour and 2 Tbsp. granulated sugar in processor 2 or 3 times to combine. Add 1/2-inch butter pieces, and pulse 10 to 12 times or until mixture resembles coarse meal. Add pecans, and pulse 2 or 3 times to combine. With processor running, pour 2 Tbsp. ice-cold water and 1 tsp. vanilla through food chute, and process just until dough comes together. Transfer dough to a lightly floured surface, and shape into a disk. Wrap disk in plastic wrap, and chill 30 minutes.

2. Preheat oven to 350°. Place dough disk between 2 sheets of lightly floured wax paper, and roll to a 12-inch circle. Fit piecrust into a 9-inch deep-dish pie plate; fold edges under, and crimp. Prick bottom and sides of dough with a fork; line dough with parchment paper, and fill with pie weights or dried beans.

3. Bake at 350° for 20 minutes. Remove weights and parchment paper, and bake 10 to 12 more minutes or until browned. Cool completely on a wire rack (about 1 hour).

4. Prepare Filling: Whisk together brown sugar and next 2 ingredients in a medium saucepan. Gradually whisk in milk. Cook over medium heat, whisking constantly, 8 to 9 minutes or until mixture is smooth and begins to thicken.

5. Gradually whisk about one-fourth of hot sugar mixture into egg yolks; gradually whisk egg yolk mixture into hot sugar mixture, and cook, whisking constantly, 2 to 3 more minutes or until mixture is thick and smooth and just begins to bubble. Remove from heat, and whisk in 1-inch butter pieces and 2 tsp. vanilla. Pour filling into prepared piecrust.

6. Prepare Meringue: Beat egg whites and next 2 ingredients at high speed with an electric mixer until foamy. Gradually add 6 Tbsp. granulated sugar, 1 Tbsp. at a time, beating until stiff peaks form and sugar dissolves. Spread meringue over hot filling, sealing edges.

7. Bake at 350° for 10 to 12 minutes or until golden brown. Remove from oven to a wire rack, and cool completely (about 2 hours). Chill 4 to 6 hours before serving.

MAKES 8 servings. **HANDS-ON** 55 min.; **TOTAL** 8 hours, 5 min.

the TURKEY

**Embrace big flavors and start your
own new turkey tradition
this year with seven bold fresh
takes on the classic roast**

SMOKED SELF-BASTING TURKEY

*Chris Lilly, one of our favorite pitmasters
and four-time Memphis in May grand
champion, taught SL recipe tester and
developer Pam Lolley this cool technique.
The key? Mounding herb butter on top of
the breast, covering the bird with aluminum foil, and cutting a slit in the foil. The
butter will slowly melt and baste the turkey as it cooks, and the smoke will perme-
ate the bird through the hole. Find more
techniques in Chris' book,* Fire & Smoke.

- 1 (12- to 14-lb.) whole fresh or
  frozen turkey, thawed
- 2 Tbsp. kosher salt
- 2 tsp. freshly ground black
  pepper
- 2 fresh thyme sprigs
- 2 fresh sage sprigs
  Kitchen string
- 1 (12 7/8- x 10-inch) disposable
  aluminum foil roasting pan
- 1 cup butter, softened
- 2 tsp. chopped fresh sage
- 1 tsp. chopped fresh thyme
- 1 to 2 cups hickory or oak wood
  chips

1. Light 1 side of grill, heating to 225° to
250°; leave other side unlit. Close grill
lid, and maintain temperature 15 to 20
minutes.

2. Remove giblets and neck from
turkey; pat turkey dry. Sprinkle salt
and pepper over skin and inside
turkey cavity; place thyme sprigs and
sage sprigs inside cavity. Tie ends of
legs together with string, and tuck
wing tips under; place turkey, breast
side up, in pan.
3. Stir together softened butter,
chopped sage, and chopped thyme.
Shape butter mixture into a 2-inch
ball; press ball firmly onto top of turkey
breast. Cover roasting pan with a
double layer of heavy-duty aluminum
foil, sealing edges tightly. Cut a 2- x
1-inch hole in foil directly over butter.
4. Place wood chips directly on hot
coals. Place pan with turkey on unlit
side of grill; cover with grill lid.
5. Smoke turkey, maintaining temperature inside grill between 225° and
250°, for 6 to 7 hours or until a meat
thermometer inserted in thickest
portion of turkey thigh registers 165° to
170°. Peel back foil from turkey during
last 1 to 1 1/2 hours of cooking time.
6. Remove turkey from grill; let stand
15 minutes before carving.

MAKES 8 to 10 servings. **HANDS-ON** 20 min.;
TOTAL 6 hours, 50 min.

DRY BRINED-HERB ROASTED TURKEY

*Skip the cumbersome wet brines that call
for soaking turkey and making the skin
flabby. This classic overnight dry brine—a
simple herb, salt, and sugar mixture—
gives the turkey deep flavor and a crackly
crust. Be adventurous and create your
own signature dry brine using our sugar
and salt ratios as a guide, or try one of our
three variations at right.*

- 3 Tbsp. kosher salt
- 3 Tbsp. dark brown sugar
- 2 tsp. rubbed sage
- 2 tsp. dried thyme
- 1 1/2 tsp. freshly ground black
  pepper
- 1 tsp. garlic powder
- 1 (12- to 14-lb.) whole fresh or
  frozen turkey, thawed
- 1/2 cup butter, softened
  Wooden picks
  Kitchen string
  Vegetable cooking spray

1. Stir together first 6 ingredients.
2. Remove giblets and neck from
turkey; pat turkey dry. Sprinkle
1 Tbsp. brine into cavity; rub into
cavity. Reserve 1 Tbsp. brine, and
sprinkle outside of turkey with
remaining brine; rub into skin. Chill
turkey 10 to 24 hours.

3. Preheat oven to 350°. Stir together butter and reserved 1 Tbsp. brine. Loosen skin from turkey breast without totally detaching skin; spread butter mixture under skin. Replace skin, securing with wooden picks.

4. Tie ends of legs together with string; tuck wing tips under. Place turkey, breast side up, on a lightly greased (with cooking spray) rack in a large roasting pan.

5. Bake at 350° for 2 hours and 30 minutes or until a meat thermometer inserted in thickest portion of turkey thigh registers 165°. Remove from oven; let stand 30 minutes before carving.

MAKES 8 to 10 servings. **HANDS-ON** 25 min.; **TOTAL** 13 hours, 25 min.

Cajun Brine Roasted Turkey:
Prepare recipe as directed, substituting paprika for sage, dried oregano for dried thyme, and 2 tsp. ground red pepper for black pepper.

Jerk Brine Roasted Turkey:
Prepare recipe as directed, substituting allspice for sage and onion powder for garlic powder and adding 2 tsp. ground cumin to brine mixture.

Five Spice Brine Roasted Turkey:
Prepare recipe as directed, substituting Chinese five spice for sage and ground ginger for thyme.

PEPPER BACON FRIED TURKEY

Use black pepper bacon or any bacon to flavor the peanut oil. For you serious spice hounds, try our Nashville Hot Turkey, at right—our ode to the city's incendiary fried chicken.

Peanut oil (about 3 gal.)
1 (12- to 14-lb.) whole fresh or frozen turkey, thawed
2 Tbsp. kosher salt
2 tsp. freshly ground black pepper
1 (1-lb.) package thick pepper bacon

1. Pour oil into a deep propane turkey fryer 10 to 12 inches from top; heat to 350° over a medium-low flame

Nashville Hot Turkey

according to manufacturer's instructions (about 45 minutes).

2. Meanwhile, remove giblets and neck from turkey; pat turkey dry. Stir together salt and pepper. Sprinkle 1 Tbsp. salt mixture inside cavity; rub into cavity. Sprinkle outside of turkey with remaining salt mixture; rub into skin. Let turkey stand at room temperature 30 minutes.

3. Using long-handled tongs, carefully lower bacon, 1 slice at a time, into hot oil. Fry 1 to 2 minutes or until bacon is browned and crisp. Drain bacon on a paper towel-lined baking sheet; reserve bacon for another use.

4. Place turkey on fryer rod. Carefully lower turkey into hot oil with rod attachment. Fry 35 to 45 minutes or until a meat thermometer inserted in thickest portion of turkey thigh registers 165° (about 3 minutes per pound plus an additional 5 minutes).

Keep oil temperature between 325° and 345°. Remove turkey from oil; drain and let stand 30 minutes before carving.

Note: We tested with LouAna Peanut Oil.

MAKES 8 to 10 servings. **HANDS-ON** 25 min.; **TOTAL** 2 hours, 15 min.

Nashville Hot Turkey: Prepare recipe as directed, reserving 1 cup frying oil from fryer. Stir together ¼ cup ground red pepper, 1 Tbsp. dark brown sugar, 1 tsp. paprika, and ½ tsp. garlic powder in a medium saucepan. Carefully whisk in reserved 1 cup frying oil, and cook over low heat, stirring constantly, 5 minutes. Brush mixture over turkey, and serve immediately.

HANDS-ON 25 min.; **TOTAL** 2 hours, 20 min.

TURKEY 101

Turkey is the sun of the Thanksgiving solar system— the timing of every other dish depends on it.
Kitchen Director Robby Melvin explains how to take it from grocer to table.

HOW TO CARVE A TURKEY

Start with a cutting board and a sharp carving knife

1. CUT between thigh and breast down through the joint. Repeat with other leg. Separate each leg from thigh.

2. REMOVE wing tips from breasts. Slice down one side of breast bone, following contour of breast.

3. ROTATE carcass, and repeat with other breast. Slice from breast bone to wish bone, pulling meat away as you go.

4. REMOVE the drumettes to create 10 pieces. Slice breasts crosswise, and slice thigh meat off bone.

BUYING

Freshness and size are key. Plan on 1 to 1½ pounds per person. (This will give you plenty for leftovers.) Look for the word "natural" on the label, which means the turkey has been minimally processed. For the freshest flavor, buy turkey that has been flash-frozen after butchering.

DEFROSTING

Allow two to three days for a 10- to 15-pound bird to thaw properly. Defrost turkey in the original packaging. Set it in a jelly-roll pan at the back (the coldest part) of your refrigerator. Crunched for time? Thaw it in the sink under cold running water, but never on the counter at room temperature.

SEASONING

Let's face it. Turkey without salt is like life without music. Use at least 1 tsp. of kosher salt per pound, and season all over, including the cavity. We like dry-brining (seasoning with a salt-sugar-herb mix) and chilling, uncovered, overnight. The salt will elevate flavors and help keep the skin crisp.

ROASTING

Roast at 325° to 350°. Use a high-sided roasting pan with a V-rack—it holds the turkey upright and allows hot air to flow around it. Kitchen string for tying the legs is optional; an instant-read thermometer is not. Roast until the thickest parts of the leg and breast read 165°. Then let it rest 30 minutes.

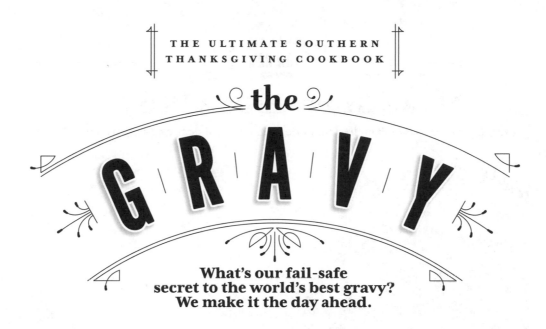

the GRAVY

**What's our fail-safe
secret to the world's best gravy?
We make it the day ahead.**

THE ULTIMATE MAKE-AHEAD GRAVY

- 1/2 **cup butter**
- 1/2 **cup all-purpose flour**
- 4 **cups Easy Chicken Stock**
- 1 **tsp. rubbed sage**
- 3/4 **tsp. kosher salt**
- 1/2 **tsp. garlic powder**
- 1/2 **tsp. dried thyme**
- 1/2 **tsp. freshly ground black pepper**
- 5 **to 6 Tbsp. Easy Chicken Stock (optional)**

1. Melt butter in a Dutch oven over medium heat; whisk in flour, and cook, whisking constantly, 3 to 4 minutes or until mixture is light brown and smooth. Slowly whisk in 4 cups stock. Increase heat to high; bring to a boil, whisking occasionally. Reduce heat to medium; stir in sage and next 4 ingredients. Simmer, stirring occasionally, 10 to 15 minutes or until desired thickness.

2. To make ahead, cool gravy completely. Cover and chill up to 3 days. Cook gravy and, if desired, 5 to 6 Tbsp. stock in a Dutch oven over medium-low heat, stirring occasionally, 15 to 20 minutes or until hot.

MAKES 4 cups. **HANDS-ON** 20 min.; **TOTAL** 30 min., not including Step 2

EASY CHICKEN STOCK

Preheat oven to 400°. Bake 2 lb. **chicken wings** on a baking sheet 20 to 25 minutes or until browned. Bring chicken and 2 (32-oz.) containers **chicken broth** to a boil in a large saucepan over high heat. Reduce heat to medium-low, and simmer 30 minutes. Pour stock through a wire-mesh strainer; discard wings. Cool stock completely. Use immediately, or cover and chill up to 3 days or freeze up to 3 months.

MAKES about 8 cups. **HANDS-ON** 10 min.; **TOTAL** 1 hour, 30 min.

GRAVY STIR-INS

Mushroom Gravy: Heat 1 1/2 Tbsp. **olive oil** in a medium skillet over medium-high heat. Add 1 (8-oz.) package sliced **cremini mushrooms;** sauté 6 minutes or until tender and browned. Stir in 1 Tbsp. **butter** and 1 Tbsp. minced **shallot;** sauté 2 minutes. Add **salt** and ground **black pepper** to taste. Prepare recipe as directed through Step 1 or 2. Add mushrooms. Cook over medium heat, stirring occasionally, 5 minutes.

HANDS-ON 35 min., **TOTAL** 45 min.

Fresh Herb Gravy: Prepare recipe as directed through Step 1 or 2. Stir in 1 Tbsp. chopped fresh **flat-leaf parsley,** 1 tsp. thinly sliced fresh **chives,** 1/2 tsp. chopped fresh **tarragon,** and 1/2 tsp. fresh **lemon juice.** Cook over medium heat, stirring occasionally, 5 minutes.

HANDS-ON 25 min., **TOTAL** 35 min.

Sherry Gravy: Prepare recipe as directed through Step 1 or 2. Remove pan from heat; stir in 1/4 cup **sherry, bourbon,** or **brandy.** Return to medium heat. Cook, stirring occasionally, 5 minutes.

HANDS-ON 25 min., **TOTAL** 35 min.

Make Gravy Like a Pro

Exceptional gravy is built on the foundation of a flavorful stock and simple roux

① DOCTOR STORE-BOUGHT BROTH
Sure, you can simply use chicken broth straight from the box, but try our shortcut for boosting the flavor of store-bought broth by adding roasted chicken wings. Simmering the wings will add more depth of savory poultry flavor to your gravy at minimal cost. The resulting stock will also give your finished gravy a darker, richer brown color.

② MAKE A BLOND ROUX
Roux, the magical marriage of melted fat and flour, kick-starts the thickening process of stews and sauces like gravy and enriches the flavor. Make yours by whisking equal parts melted butter and flour in a pan over medium heat. Whisk and cook, cook and whisk, until the roux smells nutty and takes on a light golden brown color.

③ ADD STOCK, COOK, COOL, THEN REHEAT
Gradually add chicken stock to the roux, which will absorb the stock and begin to thicken into gravy within minutes of cooking. Season accordingly, cook to desired thickness, and serve. Or, remove from heat and let cool. Cover and chill. On Thanksgiving Day, as soon as the turkey comes out of the oven, reheat the gravy slowly with extra tablespoons of stock.

④ IT'S YOUR GRAVY— CUSTOMIZE IT!
We love this gravy as is, but you can also personalize it by using one of the three suggested add-ins on page 259. Pick one flavor; try the mushrooms, herbs, and sherry together; or choose your own favorite traditional Southern riff, from chopped, cooked gizzards to minced hard-cooked eggs. Either way, your turkey and mashed potatoes—and family—will thank you.

the BREAD

Fresh, warm-from-the-oven bread is a must on the Southern table. Fill your basket with new twists on old favorites.

THANKSGIVING
KNOW·HOW

Rise to the Occasion

The Southern bread canon is vast, but four rules reign over all

(1)

ANGEL BISCUITS must be **tender, light as air, and flaky.** Rolling, kneading, and folding produce lovely layers but compromise texture. What to do? Roll away, but leaven with baking powder, baking soda, and yeast for gorgeous height and flaky texture.

(2)

YEAST ROLLS must be **pillowy soft.** For the best texture, add potato flakes to the dough. It reduces the amount of gluten.

(3)

SPOON BREAD promises **creamy** texture. To achieve it, use cornmeal, not flour, and mix by hand.

(4)

BUTTER may be optional, but serving Southern breads **warm** is not; it's a must.

SPOON BREAD CORN MUFFINS

We adapted these custard-like muffins from a recipe in The Gift of Southern Cooking *by Edna Lewis and Scott Peacock and tested with J.T. Pollard Extra-Fine White Corn Meal because our friend Scott Peacock swears by it. To order a bag, call the company at 334/588-3391.*

- 1 1/2 **cups finely ground white cornmeal**
- 1 **tsp. baking soda**
- 1 **tsp. kosher salt**
- 2 **large eggs, lightly beaten**
- 2 1/4 **cups buttermilk**
- 1/4 **cup freshly grated sharp Cheddar cheese**
- 1 **Tbsp. chopped fresh chives**
  Unsalted butter

1. Preheat oven to 425°. Combine first 3 ingredients in a large bowl. Whisk eggs and buttermilk into cornmeal mixture, stirring vigorously until smooth. Stir in cheese and chives. Pour batter into a greased (with unsalted butter) 12-cup muffin tin.
2. Bake at 425° for 13 minutes or until lightly browned. Cool in pan on a wire rack 5 minutes. Remove from pan to rack; cool 5 minutes.

MAKES 1 dozen. **HANDS-ON** 15 min., **TOTAL** 40 min.

GRAHAM CRACKER ROLLS

"This roll recipe was discovered by my wonderful mother, who was an amazing cook and loved to try new recipes. It's still a favorite with my family because of the flavor that the graham cracker crumbs give the rolls."—SL reader Allison Fogle

- 1 **envelope active dry yeast**
- 1/2 **cup warm water (100° to 110°)**
- 1/4 **cup plus 2 1/2 tsp. sugar, divided**
- 1 **large egg**
- 1/4 **cup vegetable shortening**
- 1 **tsp. table salt**
- 1/2 **cup boiling water**
- 2 1/2 **cups all-purpose flour**
- 3/4 **cup graham cracker crumbs, divided**
  Parchment paper
- 3 **Tbsp. butter, melted**

1. Combine first 2 ingredients and 1 tsp. sugar; let stand 5 minutes.
2. Beat egg, shortening, salt, and 1/4 cup sugar at medium speed with a heavy-duty electric stand mixer until creamy. Add boiling water; stir until shortening melts. Stir in yeast mixture. Stir flour and 1/2 cup crumbs into egg mixture.

3. Place dough in a lightly greased (with shortening) bowl; cover, and chill 8 to 24 hours.

4. Punch dough down. Turn dough out onto a lightly floured surface, and knead 4 or 5 times. Roll to 1/2-inch thickness. Cut dough into rounds with a 1 1/2- to 2-inch round cutter, rerolling scraps twice. Place rolls 1 inch apart on a parchment paper-lined baking sheet, and brush with melted butter.

5. Stir together remaining 1/4 cup cracker crumbs and 1 1/2 tsp. sugar. Sprinkle mixture over rolls. Cover and let rise in a warm place (80° to 85°), free from drafts, 45 minutes to 1 hour or until doubled in bulk.

6. Preheat oven to 350°. Bake, uncovered, 15 to 18 minutes or until golden.

MAKES about 2 dozen. **HANDS-ON** 35 min.; **TOTAL** 9 hours, 35 min.

ANGEL BISCUITS

Nestle these yeast biscuits snugly together in the pan and they'll rise even higher when baked. You don't have to use all the dough at once—refrigerate in an airtight container up to five days.

- 1/2 **cup warm water (100° to 110°)**
- 1 **(1/4-oz.) envelope active dry yeast**
- 1 **tsp. sugar**
- 5 **cups all-purpose flour**
- 3 **Tbsp. sugar**
- 5 **tsp. baking powder**
- 1 1/2 **tsp. table salt**
- 1 **tsp. baking soda**
- 1/2 **cup cold butter, cubed**
- 1/2 **cup shortening, cubed**
- 2 **cups buttermilk**
  Parchment paper
- 1/4 **cup butter, melted and divided**

1. Stir together first 3 ingredients in a small bowl. Let stand 5 minutes.

2. Stir together flour and next 4 ingredients in a large bowl; cut butter and shortening into flour mixture with a pastry blender or 2 forks until crumbly. Add yeast mixture and buttermilk to flour mixture,

stirring just until dry ingredients are moistened. Cover bowl with plastic wrap, and chill 2 hours to 5 days.

3. Preheat oven to 400°. Turn dough out onto a lightly floured surface, and knead 3 or 4 times. Gently roll dough into a 3/4-inch-thick circle, and fold dough in half; repeat. Gently roll dough to 3/4-inch thickness; cut with a 2-inch round cutter. Reroll remaining scraps, and cut with cutter. Place rounds, with sides touching, in a 10- or 12-inch cast-iron skillet or on a parchment paper-lined baking sheet. Brush biscuits with 2 Tbsp. melted butter.

4. Bake at 400° for 15 to 20 minutes or until golden brown. Brush with remaining melted butter, and serve.

MAKES about 2 1/2 dozen.
HANDS-ON 30 min.; **TOTAL** 2 hours, 50 min.

HERBED POTATO FLAKE ROLLS

Like magic, packaged potato flakes give these fluffy beauties a lighter-than-air texture that makes them perfect for sopping up gravy. Trust us, they go fast.

- 1 1/2 **cups buttermilk**
- 2/3 **cup sugar**
- 1/3 **cup butter**
- 1/2 **cup instant potato flakes**
- 1 3/4 **tsp. table salt**
- 1 **tsp. baking soda**
- 2 **envelopes active dry yeast**
- 1/2 **cup warm water (100° to 110°)**
- 1 **tsp. sugar**
- 1 **large egg, lightly beaten**
- 4 1/2 **cups bread flour, divided**
  Vegetable cooking spray
- 1/2 **cup butter, melted**
- 2 **tsp. chopped fresh rosemary**
  Parchment paper

1. Stir together first 6 ingredients in a small saucepan, and cook over medium-low heat, stirring constantly, 3 minutes or until butter melts. Cool about 15 minutes or until temperature reaches 110°.

2. Stir together yeast and next 2 ingredients; let stand 5 minutes.

3. Beat buttermilk mixture and yeast

mixture at low speed with a heavy-duty electric stand mixer until blended. Add egg, and beat just until blended. Gradually add 4 cups flour, beating at low speed 4 to 6 minutes or until blended and dough is soft and smooth.

4. Turn dough out onto a lightly floured surface, and knead, adding up to 1/2 cup more flour, 1 Tbsp. at a time, as needed, until dough is smooth and elastic (about 5 minutes). Place dough in a large bowl coated with cooking spray, turning to grease top.

5. Cover and let rise in a warm place (80° to 85°), free from drafts, 1 hour or until doubled in bulk.

6. Stir together melted butter and rosemary. Punch dough down. Turn dough out onto floured surface, and roll into a 22- x 15-inch rectangle. Brush dough with half of butter mixture. (Keep remaining butter mixture at room temperature.)

7. Cut dough into 11 (2- x 15-inch) strips. Cut each strip into 5 (3- x 2-inch) rectangles. Make a crease across each rectangle by pressing lightly with a knife, and fold in half. Place rolls, 2 inches apart, on 2 parchment paper-lined baking sheets. Cover and let rise in a warm place (80° to 85°), free from drafts, 30 to 45 minutes or until doubled in bulk.

8. Preheat oven to 350°. Bake, uncovered, 15 to 18 minutes or until golden. Brush with remaining butter mixture, and serve immediately.

MAKES about 4 1/2 dozen.
HANDS-ON 45 min.; **TOTAL** 2 hours, 50 min.

the SIDES

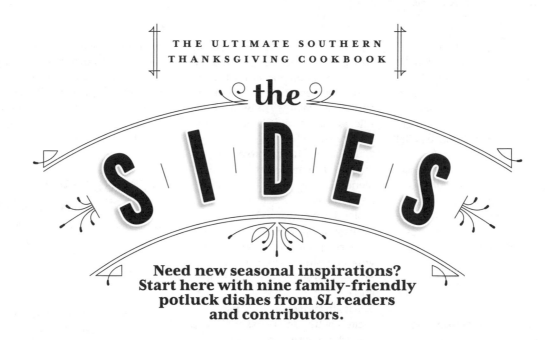

**Need new seasonal inspirations?
Start here with nine family-friendly
potluck dishes from *SL* readers
and contributors.**

Sheri's Creamed Onion Tart

CREAMED ONION TART

"This recipe makes classic creamed onions seem inventive and stylish. A generous wedge is an appealing side dish, but it'll make a nice first course, if paired with a salad. The tart tastes great served warm or at room temperature." —Sheri Castle, author of The *Southern Living* Community Cookbook.

- ½ (14.1-oz.) package refrigerated piecrusts
- 3 thick bacon slices, cut into ½-inch pieces
- 1 Tbsp. butter
- 2 lb. onions, thinly sliced
- ½ cup crème fraîche
- 1 Tbsp. chopped fresh sage
- 1 Tbsp. chopped fresh thyme
- 1 tsp. kosher salt
- ¾ tsp. ground black pepper
- ½ tsp. freshly grated nutmeg
- 3 large eggs, lightly beaten

1. Preheat oven to 400°. Fit piecrust into a 9-inch tart pan lightly coated with cooking spray. Bake crust 8 to 10 minutes or until lightly browned. Cool.
2. Cook bacon in a large skillet over medium-high heat, stirring occasionally until crisp; remove bacon, and drain on paper towels. Reserve drippings in skillet.
3. Reduce heat to medium, and melt

butter with drippings; add onions and a pinch of salt. Cook, stirring often, 5 minutes. Cover and cook about 10 more minutes or until onions are soft and lightly browned. Uncover and cook, stirring often, 2 to 3 minutes or until liquid evaporates. Remove skillet from heat, and cool completely.

4. Whisk together crème fraîche and next 6 ingredients in a medium bowl. Stir in bacon and onions. Spread mixture in prepared crust.

5. Bake at 400° for 25 to 30 minutes or until golden and set. Cool on a wire rack 10 minutes before slicing.

MAKES 8 servings. **HANDS-ON** 45 min.; **TOTAL** 1 hour, 55 min.

Vegetarian Creamed Onion Tart: Omit bacon. Prepare recipe as directed, substituting 1 Tbsp. extra virgin olive oil for bacon drippings.

HANDS-ON 35 min.; **TOTAL** 1 hour, 45 min.

PIMIENTO CHEESE CREAMED SPINACH

"Creamy spinach casserole has always been a favorite in my family, so it's a sure-fire hit for any gathering. The pimiento cheese flavors give it a uniquely Southern twist." —Perre Coleman Magness, author of Pimento Cheese: The Cookbook.

- 3 (10-oz.) packages frozen chopped spinach, thawed
- 2 Tbsp. unsalted butter
- 1/2 medium-size yellow onion, finely chopped
- 3 garlic cloves, minced
- 4 oz. cream cheese, cut into small pieces and softened
- 1 cup milk
- 1 (8-oz.) container sour cream
- 1/4 cup mayonnaise
- 1 Tbsp. Dijon mustard
- 1 large egg, lightly beaten
- 1 (4-oz.) jar diced pimiento, drained and rinsed
- 2 cups (8 oz.) shredded sharp Cheddar cheese, divided
- 1 1/2 tsp. kosher salt
- 1/2 tsp. freshly ground black pepper
- 1/2 cup panko (Japanese bread-crumbs)
- 2 Tbsp. unsalted butter, melted

1. Preheat oven to 350°. Drain spinach well, pressing between paper towels. Melt 2 Tbsp. butter in a large Dutch oven over medium heat. Add onion, and sauté 5 minutes or until tender. Add garlic, and sauté 1 minute; remove from heat.

2. Stir cream cheese into onion mixture until melted and well blended. Stir in spinach, milk, and next 3 ingredients. Stir together egg, drained pimiento, and 1 1/2 cups cheese; stir egg mixture into spinach mixture. Spoon mixture into lightly greased (with cooking spray) ramekins or a 2-qt. baking dish; sprinkle with salt and pepper.

3. Toss together panko, 2 Tbsp. melted butter, and remaining 1/2 cup Cheddar cheese; sprinkle over spinach mixture.

4. Bake at 350° for 50 minutes or until bubbly and golden.

MAKES 8 servings. **HANDS-ON** 30 min.; **TOTAL** 1 hour, 20 min.

OLD-SCHOOL CRANBERRY SALAD

"My cranberry salad has become a staple at our Thanksgiving table because of its beautiful color, taste, and texture. Everyone seems to love this dish. I started adding the maraschino cherries to temper the tartness of the cranberries. The other fruits were added to satisfy family members' tastes. This recipe has a lot of flexibility, and that's why I love it so much." —SL reader Shawn Jackson, Fishers, IN (Pictured on page 2)

- 4 cups fresh cranberries
- 3/4 cup sugar
- 1/2 cup fresh orange juice
- 1 cup drained maraschino cherries
- 1 cup peeled and chopped Bartlett pears (about 2 pears)
- 1/2 cup drained mandarin oranges
- 1/2 cup drained pineapple tidbits

Bring first 3 ingredients and 1/2 cup water to a boil in a large saucepan over medium-high heat, stirring often. Reduce heat to medium, and simmer, stirring occasionally, 20 to 25 minutes

or until cranberries pop and mixture thickens. Remove from heat, and let stand 15 minutes. Stir in cherries and remaining ingredients. Transfer to a bowl; cover and chill 2 to 12 hours.

MAKES 8 to 10 servings. **HANDS-ON** 20 min.; **TOTAL** 2 hours, 55 min.

NEW-SCHOOL CRANBERRY SALAD

We were so inspired by Old-School Cranberry Salad that we created a new version using fresh oranges and pineapple in place of canned and subbing dried cherries for maraschinos. (Pictured on page 2)

- 4 cups fresh cranberries
- 1 cup dried cherries
- 3/4 cup sugar
- 1/2 cup fresh orange juice
- 1 cup orange segments
- 1 cup peeled and chopped Bartlett pears (about 2 pears)
- 1/2 cup chopped fresh pineapple

Bring first 4 ingredients and 1/4 cup water to a boil in a large saucepan over medium-high heat, stirring often. Reduce heat to medium, and simmer, stirring occasionally, 20 to 25 minutes or until cranberries pop and mixture thickens. Remove from heat, and let stand 15 minutes. Stir in orange segments and remaining ingredients. Transfer to a bowl; cover and chill 2 to 12 hours.

MAKES 8 to 10 servings. **HANDS-ON** 25 min., **TOTAL** 3 hours

CHEESY BROCCOLI-AND-RICE CASSEROLE

"The old-school version of this recipe uses canned soup and often calls for frozen broccoli. My new twist is made with fresh, wholesome ingredients. It takes just a smidgen of more time, but the results are absolutely extra-ordinary." —Contributing editor Virginia Willis, author of the forthcoming Lighten Up, Y'all.

- 6 Tbsp. unsalted butter, divided
- 1 cup panko (Japanese breadcrumbs)
- 2 cups (8 oz.) shredded extra-sharp Cheddar cheese, divided
- 3 cups reduced-sodium, fat-free chicken broth
- 2 cups milk
- 1 bay leaf
- 1 fresh thyme sprig
- 2 cups chopped onion
- 1/2 cup diced celery
- 1 (8-oz.) package sliced cremini mushrooms
- 1 tsp. kosher salt, divided
  Pinch of freshly ground black pepper
  Pinch of ground red pepper
- 2 garlic cloves, minced
- 1/4 cup all-purpose flour
- 1 1/2 cups uncooked long-grain rice
- 1/2 cup sour cream
- 1/2 cup mayonnaise
- 1/8 tsp. freshly grated nutmeg
- 3 cups fresh broccoli florets (about 2 heads)

Virginia's Cheesy Broccoli-and-Rice Casserole

1. Preheat oven to 350°. Melt 2 Tbsp. butter. Combine melted butter with panko and 1 cup shredded Cheddar cheese; toss to coat.

2. Bring broth and next 3 ingredients to a simmer in a medium saucepan over medium-low heat. Reduce heat to low; cover and keep mixture warm until ready to use.

3. Melt remaining 4 Tbsp. butter in a large shallow Dutch oven or ovenproof skillet over medium heat. Add onion and celery to Dutch oven, and cook, stirring occasionally, 3 to 5 minutes or until onion is lightly browned. Add mushrooms to Dutch oven, and stir in 1/2 tsp. kosher salt and a pinch each of black pepper and ground red pepper.

Cook, stirring occasionally, 3 to 5 minutes or until mushrooms are tender. Add garlic, and cook, stirring constantly, 45 seconds. Stir in flour until combined. (Mixture will be dry.)

4. Remove and discard bay leaf and thyme from broth mixture. Gradually stir warm broth mixture into mushroom mixture. Add remaining 1 cup cheese, and stir until well blended and smooth. Stir in rice and next 3 ingredients. Cover Dutch oven with a tight-fitting lid.

5. Bake at 350° for 25 to 30 minutes or until rice is tender and liquid is absorbed. Remove Dutch oven from oven; increase oven temperature to broil.

6. Microwave broccoli, 1/4 cup water, and remaining 1/2 tsp. kosher salt in a covered microwave-safe bowl at HIGH about 2 minutes or just until broccoli

is tender and bright green. Drain and pat broccoli dry. Stir broccoli into rice mixture in Dutch oven. If desired, transfer mixture to a broiler-safe serving dish coated lightly with cooking spray.

7. Sprinkle breadcrumb mixture over broccoli mixture. Place on middle oven rack, and broil 2 to 3 minutes or until topping is golden brown. Let casserole stand 5 minutes before serving.

MAKES 8 to 10 servings. **HANDS-ON** 30 min.; **TOTAL** 1 hour, 5 min.

CHEESE CRACKER-TOPPED SQUASH CASSEROLE

"We have a hard time getting our grandson to eat a vegetable. He loves Goldfish crackers, so I came up with this recipe. You can sub any type of crackers," says SL reader Gerri Ellis, of Hazelhurst, MS, whose recipe inspired this dish. To garnish, we crushed a few crackers and tossed the crumbs with paprika to help the whole fish stand out.

- 3 lb. yellow squash, chopped
- 2 lb. zucchini, chopped
- 1 medium onion, chopped
- 2 Tbsp. kosher salt
- 1/2 cup sour cream
- 1/2 cup mayonnaise
- 1 large egg
- 1 (8-oz.) block extra-sharp Cheddar cheese, grated
- 1/2 tsp. ground black pepper
- 2 cups fish-shaped Cheddar cheese crackers
- 2 Tbsp. butter, melted

1. Preheat oven to 350°. Place first 3 ingredients in a Dutch oven; add hot water 2 inches above squash-and-onion mixture. Add salt to Dutch oven, and stir to dissolve. Bring mixture to a boil over medium-high heat. Boil 10 minutes or until squash is very tender when pierced with a fork. Drain vegetable mixture well; let stand at room temperature 15 minutes to cool slightly.
2. Stir together sour cream and mayonnaise in a large bowl. Lightly beat egg, and stir into mayonnaise mixture. Gently stir in cheese, pepper, and cooked squash mixture; spoon mixture into a greased (with butter) 13- x 9-inch baking dish.
3. Bake at 350° for 40 minutes or until bubbly. Combine cheese crackers and melted butter, and toss to coat. Arrange over casserole. Bake 10 more minutes. Remove from oven, and let stand 5 minutes before serving.

MAKES 8 to 10 servings. **HANDS-ON** 20 min.; **TOTAL** 1 hour, 40 min.

ROASTED ROOT VEGETABLES WITH CIDER GLAZE

"A dear friend and great chef, Matthew Wendell, made these rustic vegetables for us while we lived in the White House. They have become a staple at our Thanksgiving because of the simplicity and purity of the dish." —Editor-at-large Jenna Bush Hager

- 1 1/2 lb. parsnips, peeled and chopped
- 1 1/2 lb. medium carrots, peeled and chopped
- 1 1/2 lb. butternut squash, peeled and chopped
- 1 1/2 lb. turnips, peeled and chopped
- 3 Tbsp. extra virgin olive oil
- 1 Tbsp. chopped fresh thyme
- 1 Tbsp. chopped fresh rosemary
- 1 1/2 tsp. kosher salt
- 3/4 tsp. freshly ground black pepper
  Vegetable cooking spray
- 3 cups apple cider
- 1 cup white vinegar
- 1 Tbsp. sugar
- 1 Tbsp. chopped fresh flat-leaf parsley, cilantro, or chives

1. Preheat oven to 425°. Toss together first 5 ingredients in a large bowl. Add thyme and next 3 ingredients; toss. Arrange vegetable mixture in a single layer on 2 lightly greased (with cooking spray) jelly-roll pans.
2. Bake at 425° for 35 to 40 minutes or until vegetables are tender and browned, stirring after 20 minutes.
3. Meanwhile, bring apple cider and next 2 ingredients to a boil in a medium saucepan over high heat. Boil, stirring occasionally, 30 minutes or until reduced to 1/3 cup.
4. Transfer roasted vegetables to a large bowl, and toss with apple cider mixture. Sprinkle with fresh parsley.

MAKES 8 servings. **HANDS-ON** 1 hour, 15 min.; **TOTAL** 1 hour, 15 min.

TWO-POTATO GRATIN

"This luscious gratin strikes a happy middle chord for those hungry for potatoes and those vying for a sweet potato casserole." —Nancy Vienneau, author of Third Thursday Community Potluck Cookbook, *from which this recipe was adapted.*

- 2 shallots, diced
- 1/4 cup butter, divided
- 2 cups heavy cream
- 2 Tbsp. chopped parsley
- 1 Tbsp. chopped chives
- 1 tsp. kosher salt
- 1/2 tsp. ground white pepper
- 1/8 tsp. freshly grated nutmeg
- 1 1/2 lb. Yukon gold potatoes
- 1 1/2 lb. sweet potatoes
- 2 cups milk
- 1 1/2 cups (6 oz.) shredded Gruyère cheese
- 1/4 cup grated Parmesan cheese

1. Preheat oven to 375°. Sauté shallots in 3 Tbsp. melted butter in a saucepan over medium heat 2 minutes. Stir in cream and next 5 ingredients; cook 2 minutes. Remove from heat; cool 15 minutes.
2. Meanwhile, peel and thinly slice all potatoes. Combine sliced potatoes and milk in a large, microwave-safe bowl. Cover with plastic wrap, and microwave at HIGH 5 minutes. Uncover and gently stir mixture. Cover and microwave 5 more minutes. Drain mixture, discarding milk.
3. Layer one-third of Yukon gold potatoes in a well-greased (with butter) 13- x 9-inch baking dish; top with one-third of sweet potatoes. Spoon one-third of cream mixture over potatoes, and sprinkle with 1/2 cup Gruyère cheese. Repeat layers twice, and top with Parmesan cheese. Cut remaining 1 Tbsp. butter into small pieces, and dot over top. Cover with foil.
4. Bake at 375° for 30 minutes. Uncover; bake 20 minutes or until browned. Let stand 10 minutes.

MAKES 10 to 12 servings. **HANDS-ON** 45 min.; **TOTAL** 1 hour, 45 min.

CHORIZO-AND-CORNBREAD DRESSING

"There are two things you'll always find at the Summers' family Thanksgiving table: Julia Child's iconic Cornbread Sausage Stuffing and lively table conversation. A few years ago, I started amping up the spice in Julia's stuffing by adding jalapeño and using chorizo sausage. As the years progressed, I noticed the spicier the stuffing, the livelier the conversation."
—*Libbie Summers, stylist and author of* Sweet & Vicious.

- 4 bacon slices, chopped
- 1 lb. Mexican chorizo sausage, casings removed
- 2 cups chopped celery
- 2 cups chopped sweet onion
- 1 jalapeño pepper, seeded and chopped
- 2 garlic cloves, minced
- 5 cups 1/2-inch cornbread cubes, toasted
- 2 cups cubed French bread
- 2 cups unsalted chicken stock (such as Swanson)
- 1/2 cup chopped fresh flat-leaf parsley
- 1/2 cup butter, melted
- 2 Tbsp. chopped cilantro
- 2 large eggs, lightly beaten

1. Preheat oven to 350°. Cook bacon in a skillet over medium heat, stirring occasionally, 10 minutes or until crisp. Remove bacon; drain. Reserve drippings in skillet.

2. Cook sausage in hot drippings, stirring often, 6 minutes or until no longer pink. Place sausage and bacon in a large bowl. Sauté celery, onion, and jalapeño in hot drippings 10 minutes. Add garlic; sauté 2 minutes. Stir celery mixture into sausage mixture.

3. Gently stir cornbread and next 6 ingredients into sausage mixture. Season with salt and pepper. Spoon into a 13- x 9-inch baking dish coated with cooking spray. Bake at 350° for 35 minutes or until golden.

MAKES 6 to 8 servings. **HANDS-ON** 45 min.; **TOTAL** 1 hour, 20 min.

THANKSGIVING
KNOW·HOW

Start a New Side Dish Playbook

Tired of the same old same old? Here's how to please a crowd while breaking with convention

1. Add a new dish one year at a time. Don't risk a family mutiny by refusing to cook Mamaw's sweet potato casserole, but do bake in new traditions. Start safe by updating an old standby like dressing to Chorizo-and-Cornbread Dressing (at left).

2. Jump-start your sides. Turkey ties up the oven, so get ahead by prepping and baking in advance, if possible. Rewarm as the turkey rests. Or measure and chop at least one day ahead.

3. Piping hot is not mandatory. We love casseroles for their portability and make-ahead qualities, but they take up precious oven space. Balance the buffet with fresh options like Roasted Root Vegetables (recipe on facing page) or salads (recipes, pages 268-269) that can be served at room temperature.

4. Keep a sense of humor. You work hard in the kitchen; laugh a little. Take a page from Cheese Cracker-Topped Squash Casserole (recipe on facing page), and try a whimsical crunchy topper like crackers, nuts, seeds, or chips from your pantry.

Libbie's Chorizo-and-Cornbread Dressing

the SALADS

Balance your menu and add vibrant colors to your buffet with bright and tangy salads

BLOODY MARY GREEN BEAN SALAD

We turned a festive cocktail into a salad by making the drink's crunchy garnishes (green beans and celery) the stars and dressing them with a vinaigrette made with Zing Zang Bloody Mary Mix.

SALAD

- 1 lb. haricots verts (French green beans), trimmed
- 1/2 cup thinly sliced red onion
- 12 pickled okra pods, sliced
- 1 pt. grape tomatoes, halved
- 4 celery ribs, sliced
- 1/4 cup fresh celery leaves

DRESSING

- 1/3 cup Bloody Mary mix
- 2 Tbsp. fresh lemon juice
- 1 1/2 tsp. dry mustard
- 3/4 tsp. kosher salt
- 3/4 tsp. hot sauce (such as Tabasco)
- 1/4 tsp. ground black pepper
- 4 1/2 tsp. prepared horseradish, divided
- 1/2 cup extra virgin olive oil

1. Prepare Salad: Cook beans in boiling salted water to cover 2 minutes or until crisp-tender; drain. Plunge into ice water. Drain and pat dry. Place beans, onion, and okra in a large bowl. Place tomatoes, celery, and celery leaves in a separate bowl.
2. Prepare Dressing: Whisk together Bloody Mary mix, next 5 ingredients, and 4 tsp. horseradish in a medium bowl. Add oil in a slow, steady stream, whisking constantly until blended.
3. Toss bean mixture with 1/4 cup dressing; arrange on a platter. Stir remaining 1/2 tsp. horseradish into 1/4 cup dressing, and toss with tomato mixture. Spoon tomato mixture over bean mixture. Add salt and pepper to taste; serve with remaining dressing.

MAKES 6 to 8 servings. **HANDS-ON** 35 min., **TOTAL** 35 min.

BRUSSELS SPROUTS SALAD WITH HOT BACON DRESSING

Whole Brussels sprout leaves make beautiful little salad greens. If pressed for time, slice the sprouts instead of peeling.

- 2 lb. fresh Brussels sprouts
- 1 large red apple (such as Honeycrisp), thinly sliced
- 5 smoked bacon slices, cut into 1/2-inch pieces
- 1/2 cup apple cider vinegar
- 1 Tbsp. Dijon mustard
- 1 tsp. kosher salt
- 2 tsp. honey
- 1/2 tsp. ground black pepper
- 1 cup thinly sliced red onion
- 1/2 cup olive oil
- 1 1/2 Tbsp. fresh lemon juice
- 1 tsp. sugar

1. Remove and discard stem ends from Brussels sprouts; peel leaves, and place in a large bowl. Add apple slices.
2. Place bacon in a single layer in a large cold skillet. Cook bacon over medium heat 4 to 5 minutes on each side or until crisp. Remove bacon, reserving drippings in skillet. Add cooked bacon to Brussels sprouts mixture.
3. Add vinegar to skillet, and bring to a boil over medium heat, stirring to loosen browned bits from bottom of skillet. Boil 1 minute or until reduced to about 1/3 cup, stirring occasionally.
4. Stir in mustard and next 4 ingredients. Add oil in a slow steady stream, stirring constantly, until blended. Remove from heat, and stir in lemon juice and sugar. Pour hot dressing over Brussels sprouts mixture; toss. Season to taste with salt and pepper; serve immediately.

MAKES 6 servings. **HANDS-ON** 1 hour, **TOTAL** 1 hour

SOUTHERN GIARDINIERA

Set these bread-and-butter-style pickled veggies out on your relish tray so guests can nosh on them before and during dinner. Red pearl onions add vibrant color to the relish, but white onions will work too.

- 1 lb. multicolored baby carrots with tops
- 4 cups apple cider vinegar
- 1 1/2 cups granulated sugar
- 1 cup firmly packed light brown sugar
- 1/2 cup kosher salt
- 1/3 cup molasses
- 1 1/2 Tbsp. yellow mustard seeds
- 1 Tbsp. whole black peppercorns
- 1 (10-oz.) package fresh red pearl onions, peeled and halved
- 2 cups small fresh broccoli florets
- 2 jalapeño peppers, sliced
- 1 (8-oz.) package sweet mini peppers
- 1 medium-size fresh fennel bulb, sliced

1. Trim tops from carrots, leaving 1 inch of greenery on each; peel carrots. Cut carrots in half lengthwise. Bring vinegar, granulated sugar, brown sugar, salt, molasses, mustard seeds, and peppercorns to a boil in a medium-size nonaluminum saucepan over medium-high heat, stirring until sugars and salt dissolve. Reduce heat to medium; add carrots and onions, and simmer 3 minutes, stirring occasionally.

2. Place broccoli and next 3 ingredients in a large heatproof bowl; pour hot vinegar mixture over vegetables. Cool completely (about 1 hour). Stir occasionally while mixture cools.

3. Transfer vegetables to 2 hot sterilized 1-qt. jars, using a slotted spoon and filling to 1 inch from top. Pour cooled vinegar mixture from bowl into a liquid measuring cup with a pour spout. Pour enough vinegar mixture into jars to cover vegetables, and discard remaining vinegar mixture. Cover with metal lids, and screw on bands. Let stand 24 hours before using. Refrigerate in an airtight container up to 2 weeks.

MAKES 12 to 14 servings. **HANDS-ON** 30 min.; **TOTAL** 1 hour, 30 min., plus 24 hours for standing

CITRUS-KALE SALAD

Use your favorite citrus for this refreshing salad. We love the colorful mix and flavor combination of two navel oranges, one blood orange, and Ruby Red grapefruit. No matter what fruit you choose, buy an extra navel orange to juice for the dressing.

- 3 large oranges
- 2 Ruby Red grapefruit
- 3 Tbsp. fresh orange juice
- 2 Tbsp. white wine vinegar
- 2 1/2 tsp. Dijon mustard
- 1 tsp. sugar

Mix It Up a Little (or a Lot)

Salads and relishes pull double duty at the holiday table

As much as we love the holiday onslaught of butter and cream, our taste buds need relief. That's where tart citrus and vinegars, crisp greens and vegetables, and pickles and relishes come in. The acids reset the palate, sharpening the flavors that follow.

- 1 tsp. kosher salt
- 1 tsp. honey
- 1/2 tsp. freshly ground black pepper
- 1/4 cup extra virgin olive oil
- 1 (5-oz.) package baby kale
- 1/2 cup thinly sliced red onion
- 1 (3-oz.) goat cheese log or feta, crumbled

1. Peel oranges and grapefruit; cut away bitter white pith. Cut each orange into 1/4-inch-thick rounds. Holding 1 peeled grapefruit in the palm of your hand, slice between membranes, and gently remove whole segments. Repeat with remaining grapefruit.

2. Whisk together orange juice and next 6 ingredients. Add oil in a slow, steady stream, whisking constantly until smooth. Toss together kale, onion, and 1/2 cup dressing in a large bowl. Add salt and pepper to taste. Top salad with citrus, and sprinkle with cheese. Serve with remaining dressing.

MAKES 8 to 10 servings. **HANDS-ON** 30 min., **TOTAL** 30 min.

Citrus-Kale Salad

the

DESSERTS

**Complete the feast with a
glorious and grand finale of seasonal cakes,
pies, and easy poached pears**

Pumpkin Tart with
Whipped Cream and
Almond Toffee

PUMPKIN TART WITH WHIPPED CREAM AND ALMOND TOFFEE

*Molasses and pumpkin pie spice give
this elegant take on pumpkin pie its deep
autumnal flavor. Buy one 29-oz. can of
pumpkin for the recipe. (Also pictured
on page 1)*

TART

- 1/2 (14.1-oz.) package refrigerated piecrusts
- 3/4 cup granulated sugar
- 1 1/2 Tbsp. all-purpose flour
- 2 tsp. pumpkin pie spice
- 1/4 tsp. ground cloves
- 3 cups canned pumpkin
- 1/2 cup blackstrap molasses
- 6 Tbsp. butter, melted
- 4 large eggs
- 1 (12-oz.) can evaporated milk

ALMOND TOFFEE

- 1/2 cup firmly packed light brown sugar
- 4 Tbsp. butter
- 1 cup slivered almonds
  Vegetable cooking spray
  Parchment paper

WHIPPED CREAM

- 2 1/2 cups heavy cream
- 1/4 tsp. pumpkin pie spice
- 1/2 cup plus 2 Tbsp. powdered sugar

1. Prepare Tart: Preheat oven to 350°. Fit piecrust into a 9-inch deep-dish tart pan with removable bottom; press into fluted edges. Whisk together granulated sugar and next 3 ingredients in a large bowl. Whisk together pumpkin and next 2 ingredients in a separate bowl. Whisk pumpkin mixture into sugar mixture. Add eggs, 1 at a time, whisking until blended after each addition. Whisk in evaporated milk, and pour into crust.

2. Bake at 350° for 1 hour and 30 minutes or until a knife inserted in center comes out clean. Cool completely on a wire rack. Cover and chill 8 to 24 hours.

3. Prepare Almond Toffee: Cook brown sugar and 4 Tbsp. butter in a small skillet over medium heat, stirring constantly, until bubbly. Add almonds, and cook, stirring constantly, 2 minutes or until golden. Pour mixture onto lightly greased (with cooking spray) parchment paper; cool completely. Break into pieces.

4. Prepare Whipped Cream: Beat cream and 1/4 tsp. pumpkin pie spice at medium-high speed with an electric mixer until foamy; gradually add powdered sugar, beating until soft peaks form. Top tart with whipped cream; sprinkle with toffee.

MAKES 8 to 10 servings. **HANDS-ON** 45 min., **TOTAL** 13 hours

CRANBERRY CHEESECAKE WITH CRANBERRY-ORANGE SAUCE

Cut into this fall cheesecake to find a surprising fruit layer on the bottom. Dress it up by pooling sauce on top and garnishing with fresh mint leaves, citrus curls, and sugared cranberries.

CRUST

- 1 1/4 cups all-purpose flour
- 1/2 cup powdered sugar
- 1/4 tsp. kosher salt
- 1/4 tsp. baking powder
- 10 Tbsp. cold butter, cut into small pieces
- 1 large egg yolk
  Vegetable cooking spray

FILLING

- 1 lb. fresh cranberries
- 1 cup firmly packed light brown sugar
- 1/2 cup frozen raspberries
- 2 Tbsp. cornstarch
- 3 Tbsp. orange liqueur
- 2 1/2 Tbsp. coarsely chopped orange zest
- 2 Tbsp. coarsely chopped lemon zest
- 1/4 tsp. kosher salt

CHEESECAKE

- 3 (8-oz.) packages cream cheese, softened at room temperature
- 2 (8-oz.) containers mascarpone cheese or sour cream
- 1 cup firmly packed light brown sugar
- 1/2 tsp. kosher salt
- 5 large eggs
- 2 Tbsp. vanilla extract
  Parchment paper

SAUCE

- 1/4 cup granulated sugar
- 1/4 cup fresh orange juice
- 2 tsp. fresh lemon juice

1. Prepare Crust: Preheat oven to 350°. Pulse first 4 ingredients in a food processor until blended. Gradually add cold butter, and pulse after each addition to combine. With processor running, add egg yolk through food chute, and process until combined. Press mixture onto bottom and up sides of a lightly greased (with cooking spray) 9-inch springform pan. Chill 10 minutes. Bake 10 to 12 minutes or until golden brown; cool in pan on a wire rack 30 minutes.

2. Prepare Filling: Bring cranberries and next 7 ingredients to a boil in a saucepan over medium-high heat; cook, stirring often, 2 minutes or until cranberry skins begin to split and mixture thickens. Let mixture stand 30 minutes. Reserve 1/2 cup cranberry mixture for sauce. Spread remaining cranberry mixture in prepared crust.

3. Prepare Cheesecake: Reduce oven temperature to 325°. Beat cream cheese and next 3 ingredients at medium-low speed with an electric mixer in a large bowl just until blended and smooth. Add eggs, 1 at a time, beating at low speed just until yolk disappears after each addition. Stir in vanilla. Pour cream cheese mixture over cranberry mixture, and smooth top of batter to level. Place cheesecake on a parchment paper-lined baking sheet.

4. Bake at 325° for 1 hour and 10 minutes or until center of cheesecake jiggles. Turn oven off. Let cheesecake stand in oven, with door closed, 30 minutes.

5. Meanwhile, prepare Sauce: Process 1/4 cup granulated sugar, next 2 ingredients, reserved 1/2 cup cranberry mixture, and 1/4 cup water in a blender until smooth. Pour mixture through a fine wire-mesh strainer into a bowl. Discard solids. Cover sauce, and chill until ready to use (up to 1 week).

6. Remove cheesecake from oven, and gently run a knife around outer edge of cheesecake to loosen from sides of pan. (Do not remove sides.) Cool completely on a wire rack (about 2 hours). Cover and chill 8 to 12 hours. Serve with sauce.

Note: We tested with Grand Marnier orange liqueur.

MAKES 12 servings. **HANDS-ON** 1 hour, **TOTAL** 14 hours

Bake a Better Cheesecake

These luscious, silky sweets are back in a big way. Follow SL dessert goddess Pam Lolley's pointers to get perfect results at home every time.

FILLING

Start with room-temperature cream cheese to prevent lumps. Let the cheese stand out at least 2 hours or up to overnight for best results. Be gentle with the batter. Beat at medium-low speed, just long enough to blend the sugar and cheese into a smooth mixture. Incorporate the eggs at low speed, beating just until the yolk disappears.

BAKING

Take your time with baking. An oven temperature of 325° is ideal because the moderate heat bakes cakes evenly and doesn't dry out the filling. Test for doneness by shaking the pan gently. When the cheesecake is cooked, you'll see a 3- to 4-inch circle in the middle that's "jiggly" or slightly loose. It will set fully as the cake cools and chills.

CHILLING

Run a small knife between the edge of cheesecake and pan immediately after removing from the oven to prevent sticking, and let it cool completely in the pan on a wire rack with the sides still attached. Cover and chill at least 8 hours before removing the sides. You can bake and refrigerate the cheesecake up to 2 days ahead.

DECADENT CHOCOLATE-ESPRESSO CHEESECAKE

Dessert and coffee all in one slice, this over-the-top cheesecake is a surefire crowd-pleaser. To garnish with chocolate shards, melt dark bittersweet chocolate, and spread it in a thin layer on a parchment paper-lined baking sheet. Let it stand until set, and break into pieces.

CRUST

Vegetable cooking spray
Parchment paper
- 6 Tbsp. all-purpose flour
- 2 tsp. instant espresso
- 1/4 tsp. table salt
- 1/4 cup butter
- 3 oz. bittersweet chocolate, chopped
- 1/2 cup granulated sugar
- 1/2 cup firmly packed light brown sugar
- 1 large egg
- 1 tsp. vanilla extract

FILLING

- 1 cup bittersweet chocolate morsels
- 1/4 cup heavy cream
- 2 Tbsp. instant espresso
- 2 tsp. vanilla extract
- 4 (8-oz.) packages cream cheese, softened at room temperature
- 1 1/4 cups granulated sugar
- 4 large eggs

TOPPING

- 2 cups heavy cream
- 2 Tbsp. coffee liqueur
- 3/4 cup powdered sugar
Chocolate shavings and shards (optional)

1. Prepare Crust: Preheat oven to 325°. Generously grease bottom and sides of a 9-inch springform pan with cooking spray. Cut parchment paper into a 9-inch circle, and place in bottom of pan; lightly grease parchment paper with cooking spray. Stir together flour and next 2 ingredients in a bowl.

2. Microwave butter and 3 oz. chopped chocolate in a medium microwave-safe bowl at MEDIUM (50% power) 1 minute; stir. Microwave chocolate mixture 1 to 1 1/2 more minutes or until melted and smooth, stirring at 30-second intervals. Whisk in 1/2 cup each granulated sugar and light brown sugar; cool 10 minutes.

3. Whisk 1 egg and 1 tsp. vanilla extract into chocolate mixture. Add flour mixture to chocolate mixture; stir until well blended. Spread mixture in prepared pan.

4. Bake at 325° for 20 minutes. Cool crust in pan on a wire rack 20 minutes.

5. Prepare Filling: Microwave chocolate morsels in a small microwave-safe bowl at MEDIUM (50% power) 1 minute; stir. Microwave morsels 1 to 1 1/2 more minutes or until melted and smooth, stirring at 30-second intervals. Cool 10 minutes. Stir together cream and next 2 ingredients in a 1-cup glass measuring cup until instant espresso dissolves.

6. Beat cream cheese and 1 1/4 cups granulated sugar at medium-low speed with an electric mixer in a large bowl just until smooth. Add melted chocolate and espresso mixture, and beat at low speed just until blended. Add eggs, 1 at a time, beating at low speed just until yolk disappears after each addition; pour into prepared crust.

7. Bake at 325° for 55 minutes to 1 hour or until center of cheesecake jiggles and cheesecake is almost set. Remove cheesecake from oven, and gently run a knife around outer edge of cheesecake to loosen from sides of pan. (Do not remove sides.) Cool cheesecake completely on a wire rack (about 2 hours). Cover and chill at least 8 hours or up to 2 days.

8. Prepare Topping: Beat 2 cups heavy cream and 2 Tbsp. coffee liqueur at medium-high speed until foamy; gradually add powdered sugar, beating until soft peaks form. Dollop on cheesecake.

MAKES 12 servings. **HANDS-ON** 45 min.; **TOTAL** 12 hours, 40 min.

PUMPKIN CHEESECAKE

We use a mix of chocolate and cinnamon graham cracker crumbs here to give the crust a dark color with notes of chocolate and a little spice. You can choose one or the other, so long as you use 1 1/2 cups total. We also like to give the canned pumpkin a whirl in the food processor so it's nice and smooth in the creamy filling.

CRUST

- 3/4 cup cinnamon-flavored graham cracker crumbs
- 3/4 cup chocolate graham cracker crumbs
- 1/2 cup finely chopped toasted pecans
- 5 Tbsp. butter, melted
- 3 Tbsp. granulated sugar
  Vegetable cooking spray

FILLING

- 4 (8-oz.) packages cream cheese, softened at room temperature
- 1 cup firmly packed light brown sugar
- 1 tsp. pumpkin pie spice
- 1 tsp. vanilla extract
- 4 large eggs
- 1 (15-oz.) can pumpkin
- 1 Tbsp. fresh lemon juice

TOPPING

- 1 (16-oz.) container sour cream
- 3 Tbsp. granulated sugar
  Pinch of pumpkin pie spice

1. Prepare Crust: Preheat oven to 325°. Stir together first 5 ingredients in a medium bowl until well blended. Press mixture onto bottom and 1 inch up sides of a lightly greased (with cooking spray) 9-inch springform pan. Bake 10 minutes. Let stand at room temperature until ready to use.

2. Prepare Filling: Beat cream cheese and next 3 ingredients at medium-low speed with an electric mixer in a large bowl just until smooth. Add eggs, 1 at a time, beating at low speed just until yellow disappears after each addition.

3. Process pumpkin in a food processor 1 to 2 minutes or until very smooth. Stir together lemon juice and 1 1/2 cups pumpkin puree; reserve remaining pumpkin puree. Add pumpkin-lemon juice mixture to cream cheese mixture, and beat at low speed just until blended; pour into prepared crust.

4. Bake at 325° for 50 minutes to 1 hour or until center of cheesecake jiggles. (Prepare Topping during last 10 minutes of bake time.)

5. Prepare Topping: Stir together sour cream and 3 Tbsp. granulated sugar; reserve 1/3 cup sour cream-sugar mixture. Stir together remaining sour cream mixture, pinch of pumpkin pie spice, and reserved pumpkin puree.

6. Remove cheesecake from oven. Gently spread sour cream-pumpkin mixture over cheesecake. Dollop with reserved 1/3 cup sour cream-sugar mixture; gently swirl with a knife.

7. Return cheesecake to oven, and bake at 325° for 5 more minutes. Turn oven off. Let cheesecake stand in oven, with door closed, 15 minutes. Remove cheesecake from oven, and gently run a knife around outer edge of cheesecake to loosen from sides of pan. (Do not remove sides of pan.) Cool completely on a wire rack (about 2 hours). Cover and chill 8 to 12 hours.

MAKES 12 servings. **HANDS-ON** 20 min.; **TOTAL** 11 hours, 55 min.

HOW TO MAKE A LEAF GARNISH: Cut refrigerated piecrusts into decorative shapes using seasonal cookie cutters. Arrange cutouts in a single layer on a baking sheet; score dough with the tip of a paring knife to create designs, if desired. Bake dough according to package directions until golden and done. Remove cutouts to a wire rack; cool and decorate as desired.

TENNESSEE WHISKEY-PECAN PIE

We love the combination of pecans and smoky-sweet bourbon in the pie filling. For a booze-free pie, substitute apple juice for the whiskey in the filling, and serve with plain sweetened whipped cream.

CRUST

- 1/2 Tbsp. butter
- 1/4 cup finely chopped pecans
- Pinch of kosher salt
- 1 1/4 cups all-purpose flour
- 2 Tbsp. granulated sugar
- 1/2 tsp. table salt
- 1/4 cup cold butter, cubed
- 1/4 cup cold shortening, cubed
- 3 to 4 Tbsp. buttermilk

FILLING

- 1 cup dark corn syrup
- 1/2 cup granulated sugar
- 1/2 cup firmly packed light brown sugar
- 1/4 cup Tennessee whiskey*
- 4 large eggs
- 1/4 cup butter, melted
- 2 tsp. plain white cornmeal
- 2 tsp. vanilla extract
- 1/2 tsp. table salt
- 2 1/2 cups lightly toasted pecan halves

REMAINING INGREDIENTS

- Vegetable cooking spray
- Whiskey Whipped Cream (optional)

Tennessee Whiskey-Pecan Pie

1. Prepare Crust: Melt 1/2 Tbsp. butter in a small skillet over medium heat, swirling to coat sides of pan. Add 1/4 cup finely chopped pecans, and sauté 2 minutes or until fragrant and lightly toasted. Sprinkle pecan mixture with a pinch of salt. Remove pecans from skillet, and cool completely. Reserve for use in Step 4.

2. Pulse flour and next 2 ingredients in a food processor 3 or 4 times or until well combined. Add cubed cold butter and cold shortening; pulse until mixture resembles coarse meal. Drizzle 3 Tbsp. buttermilk over flour mixture, and pulse just until moist clumps form. (Add up to 1 Tbsp. buttermilk, 1 tsp. at a time, if necessary.) Shape dough into a flat disk, and wrap tightly with plastic wrap. Chill dough at least 1 hour.

3. Meanwhile, prepare Filling: Place corn syrup and next 3 ingredients in a large saucepan, and bring to a boil over medium heat, whisking constantly. Cook, whisking constantly, 2 minutes; remove from heat. Whisk together eggs and next 4 ingredients in a bowl. Gradually whisk about one-fourth of hot corn syrup mixture into egg mixture; gradually add egg mixture to remaining corn syrup mixture, whisking constantly. Stir in 2 1/2 cups lightly toasted pecan halves; cool completely (about 30 minutes).

4. Preheat oven to 325°. Unwrap dough, and roll into a 13-inch circle on a lightly floured surface. Sprinkle dough with sautéed pecans (reserved from Step 1). Place a piece of plastic wrap over dough and pecans, and lightly roll pecans into dough. Fit dough into a lightly greased (with cooking spray) 9-inch pie plate. Fold edges under, and crimp. Pour cooled filling into prepared crust.

5. Bake at 325° for 50 to 55 minutes or until set; cool pie completely on a wire rack (about 2 hours) before slicing. Serve with Whiskey Whipped Cream, if desired.

*Water or apple juice may be substituted.

Note: We tested with Jack Daniel's whiskey.

MAKES 8 servings. **HANDS-ON** 30 min.; **TOTAL** 3 hours, 10 min.

Whiskey Whipped Cream: Beat 1 cup **heavy cream** and 1 tsp. **Tennessee whiskey** at medium-high speed with an electric mixer until foamy. Gradually add 3 Tbsp. **powdered sugar,** beating until soft peaks form.

MAKES about 1 1/2 cups. **HANDS-ON** 5 min., **TOTAL** 5 min.

PECAN SPICE CAKE WITH CARAMEL-RUM GLAZE

Substitute extra cream for rum in the sauce, if you like. For a thicker glaze, add the whole 1 1/3 cups powdered sugar, whisking constantly, as the glaze begins to cool in the pan. For a sheer, saucy glaze, use less powdered sugar.

CAKE

- 2 cups butter, softened
- 3 cups firmly packed light brown sugar
- 6 large eggs
- 3 cups all-purpose flour
- 2 tsp. baking powder
- 2 tsp. ground cinnamon
- 2 tsp. ground ginger
- 1/2 tsp. ground allspice
- 1/4 tsp. baking soda
- 1 cup buttermilk
- 2 cups toasted chopped pecans
- 1 Tbsp. vanilla extract
  Shortening

GLAZE

- 1/4 cup firmly packed light brown sugar
- 1/4 cup granulated sugar
- 1/4 cup butter
- 1/4 cup heavy cream
- 1 Tbsp. rum
- 1/2 to 1 1/3 cups powdered sugar

1. Prepare Cake: Preheat oven to 325°. Beat 2 cups butter at medium speed with a heavy-duty electric stand mixer until creamy. Gradually add 3 cups brown sugar, beating until light and fluffy. Add eggs, 1 at a time; beat until blended after each addition.

2. Stir together flour and next 5 ingredients. Add flour mixture to butter mixture alternately with buttermilk, beginning and ending with flour mixture. Beat at low speed just until blended. Stir in pecans and vanilla. Spoon batter into a greased (with shortening) and floured 15-cup Bundt pan.

3. Bake at 325° for 1 hour and 15 minutes or until a wooden pick inserted in center comes out clean. Cool in pan on a wire rack 15 minutes; remove from pan to wire rack, and cool completely.

4. Prepare Glaze: Bring 1/4 cup brown sugar and next 3 ingredients to a boil in a small saucepan over medium heat, whisking constantly; boil, whisking constantly, 1 minute. Remove from heat, and whisk in rum. Add 1/3 cup powdered sugar; whisk until smooth. Gradually add more powdered sugar, whisking constantly, until desired thickness is reached. Drizzle glaze over cake.

MAKES 12 servings. **HANDS-ON** 30 min., **TOTAL** 3 hours

Apple, Pear, and Cranberry Pie (page 276) and Pecan Spice Cake with Caramel-Rum Glaze

APPLE, PEAR, AND CRANBERRY PIE

Use slightly firm pears and crisp, tart apples here to achieve the best texture in the filling, and let this mountainous pie cool and settle for at least two hours before serving.

CRUST

- 2 1/3 cups all-purpose flour
- 1/4 cup plain yellow cornmeal
- 3/4 tsp. table salt
- 2 Tbsp., plus 2 tsp. sugar, divided
- 3/4 cup cold butter, cut into 1/2-inch pieces
- 1/4 cup cold shortening, cut into 1/2-inch pieces
- 8 to 10 Tbsp. chilled apple cider
- 1 large egg, lightly beaten
- 1/8 tsp. ground cinnamon

FILLING

- 2 1/4 lb. Granny Smith apples, peeled and cut into 1/4-inch-thick wedges
- 2 1/4 lb. pears, peeled and cut into 1/2-inch-thick wedges
- 1 cup sugar
- 1/3 cup all-purpose flour
- 1 tsp. ground cinnamon
- 1/2 tsp. table salt
- 1 cup sweetened dried cranberries
- 1 Tbsp. cold butter, cut into pieces

1. Prepare Crust: Preheat oven to 375°. Stir together flour, next 2 ingredients, and 2 Tbsp. sugar in a medium bowl. Cut butter and shortening into flour mixture with a pastry blender or fork until mixture resembles small peas. Mound flour mixture on 1 side of bowl. Drizzle 1 Tbsp. cider along edge of flour mixture. Gently toss a small amount of flour mixture into cider just until moistened; move moistened mixture to opposite side of bowl. Repeat procedure with remaining 7 Tbsp. cider and flour mixture, adding up to 2 Tbsp. cider, 1 Tbsp. at a time, until a sandy dough forms. Shape dough into 2 disks; wrap in plastic wrap. Chill 1 hour.

2. Roll 1 dough disk into a 13-inch circle on a lightly floured surface. Fit dough into a 9-inch glass pie plate; trim dough 2 inches larger than pie plate. Stir together egg and 1 tsp. water. Stir together 1/8 tsp. cinnamon and remaining 2 tsp. sugar. Set mixtures aside.

3. Prepare Filling: Toss apples with next 5 ingredients; let stand 15 minutes. Stir in cranberries; spoon into piecrust, mounding in center. Dot with 1 Tbsp. butter.

4. Roll remaining dough disk into a 13-inch circle on lightly floured surface. Place dough over filling. Fold edges under; crimp to seal.

5. Brush top with egg mixture, and sprinkle with cinnamon-sugar. Place pie on an aluminum foil-lined baking sheet; cut 4 to 5 slits in top crust.

6. Bake at 375° for 40 minutes. Cover loosely with foil, and bake 50 more minutes. Cool on a wire rack 2 hours before slicing.

MAKES 8 to 10 servings. **HANDS-ON** 1 hour; **TOTAL** 5 hours, 15 min.

POMEGRANATE-POACHED PEARS WITH CREAM

Firm pears will take longer than ripe pears to cook. To test for doneness, slide a skewer or small knife into the centers. The pears are done when the skewer slides effortlessly through the thickest part of the pears. Use extra cooking liquid in cocktails and fizzy drinks, or drizzle over yogurt.

- 4 cups refrigerated pomegranate juice
- 3 cups sugar
- 2 cups no-sugar-added cranberry juice
- 1/2 tsp. kosher salt
- 5 (1- x 1/2-inch) lemon peel strips
- 2 (2-inch) cinnamon sticks
- 1 vanilla bean, split lengthwise
- 8 small firm pears, peeled
- 1/2 (8-oz.) container crème fraîche or sour cream

1. Bring first 7 ingredients and 3 cups water to a boil in a Dutch oven over medium-high heat. Reduce heat to medium, and simmer, stirring constantly, 4 minutes or until sugar dissolves.

2. Add pears. Top pears with a plate; place a small saucepan on plate to keep pears submerged. Reduce heat to medium-low, and simmer 30 minutes. Remove plate and saucepan, and turn pears over. Replace plate and saucepan, and simmer 20 more minutes or until a knife slips easily into pear flesh.

3. Remove Dutch oven from heat. Transfer 2 cups cooking liquid to a small, clean saucepan; bring to a boil over medium-high heat. Boil 8 to 10 minutes or until mixture thickens and becomes syrupy. Remove pan from heat. Transfer syrup to a heat-proof bowl, and cool completely. Cover syrup, and keep at room temperature until ready to use. (You may need to warm syrup 1 to 2 minutes to thin slightly before serving.)

4. Let pears stand in remaining cooking liquid in Dutch oven, uncovered, at room temperature until completely cool. Cover and chill 8 to 12 hours.

5. Uncover Dutch oven, and bring cooking liquid to a boil over medium-high heat. Boil gently 5 minutes or until pears are heated. Carefully remove pears, using a slotted spoon; discard solids in Dutch oven. Reserve cooking liquid for another use, if desired, or discard. Serve warm pears with crème fraîche, and drizzle with reserved syrup.

MAKES 8 servings. **HANDS-ON** 1 hour; **TOTAL** 10 hours, 45 min.

the LEFTOVERS

You plan all month, cook all week, and eat for only an hour. Make the most out of the feast with these 11 smart recipes.

THE BEST LEFTOVER TURKEY SANDWICH EVER

WHAT YOU NEED:

Mayonnaise
Freshly baked sourdough bread slices
Kosher salt and black pepper
Sliced turkey
Apple slices
Thin red onion slices
Spicy Cranberry Salsa (recipe, page 280)
Perfectly cooked bacon
Crisp lettuce

BUILD IT:

Spread mayonnaise on 1 slice of bread, and sprinkle with salt and pepper. (Seasoning sticks to the mayonnaise!) Layer turkey, apple slices, and red onion on bread. Spoon on cranberry salsa. Top with bacon and lettuce, and crown with another slice of bread.

GREEN BEAN QUICHE

What's better than a clever new guise for extra green bean casserole (onion topping and all)? One that takes just 5 minutes to mix.

- 2 cups (8 oz.) shredded Swiss cheese
- 1 cup grated Parmesan
- 3/4 cup all-purpose baking mix
- 1/2 tsp. table salt
- 2 cups 1% low-fat milk
- 1/4 cup butter, melted
- 4 large eggs
- 2 cups leftover green bean casserole
- 1/3 cup sliced almonds

Preheat oven to 350°. Combine first 7 ingredients; fold in casserole. Spoon into a greased (with butter) 10-inch pie plate. Top with almonds. Bake 45 minutes or until set. Cool 10 minutes.

Note: We tested with Bisquick Original Pancake & Baking Mix.

MAKES 8 to 10 servings. **HANDS-ON** 5 min., **TOTAL** 1 hour

NEW TURKEY TETRAZZINI

Loads of spinach and mushrooms freshen up this classic.

- 12 oz. rotini pasta
- 1 (8-oz.) package fresh cremlni mushrooms, sliced
- 5 Tbsp. butter, divided
- 2 cups diced yellow onion
- 3 garlic cloves, minced
- 1/2 cup dry white wine
- 1 (12-oz.) package fresh baby spinach
- 3 cups shredded leftover cooked turkey
- 2 cups stuffing mix, divided
- 1/3 cup all-purpose flour
- 2 1/2 cups milk
- 2 1/2 cups reduced-sodium chicken broth
- 1/2 tsp. table salt
- 1/2 tsp. black pepper
- 2 (5-oz.) packages buttery garlic-and-herb spreadable cheese

1. Preheat oven to 350°. Cook pasta according to package directions. Meanwhile, sauté mushrooms 4 minutes in 2 Tbsp. melted butter in a large skillet over medium-high heat. Add onions and garlic; sauté 3 minutes. Stir in wine, and cook 4 minutes or until liquid almost evaporates. Add half of spinach, and cook, stirring constantly, until wilted; repeat with remaining spinach. Stir together shredded turkey, mushroom mixture, cooked pasta, and 1 cup stuffing mix in a large bowl.

2. Heat remaining 3 Tbsp. butter in a large saucepan over medium heat until foamy. Whisk in flour, and cook, whisking occasionally, 3 minutes. Whisk in milk and chicken broth, stirring until combined and smooth. Increase heat to medium-high, and cook, whisking often, 10 minutes or until mixture begins to bubble. (Do not boil.) Whisk in salt, pepper, and 1 package garlic-and-herb cheese; simmer, whisking often, 4 minutes or until thickened. Add milk mixture to pasta mixture; stir until well blended. Spoon mixture into a well-greased (with butter) 13- x 9-inch baking dish. Dot with remaining package garlic-and-herb cheese; sprinkle with remaining 1 cup stuffing mix.

3. Bake at 350° for 20 to 30 minutes or until browned and bubbly. Cool 5 to 10 minutes before serving.

Note: We tested with Boursin Garlic & Fine Herb Gournay Cheese and Stove Top Stuffing Mix for Turkey.

MAKES 8 to 10 servings. **HANDS-ON** 50 min.; **TOTAL** 1 hour, 15 min.

Sausage-and-Sweet Potato Soup

Lemongrass-Turkey Soup

LEMONGRASS-TURKEY SOUP

The fragrant flavors in this soup are the antidote to a rich Thanksgiving feast. For a heartier spin, serve it over rice or noodles. Can't find fresh lemongrass in the produce section? Try our version that uses Thai ginger-infused chicken broth instead.

- 1 (6-inch) lemongrass stalk
- 6 cups reduced-sodium chicken broth
- 6 garlic cloves
- 1 Tbsp. grated fresh ginger
- 2 cups shredded cooked turkey or chicken
- 1½ cups sliced snow peas
- ½ (8-oz.) package fresh button mushrooms, sliced
- 1 jalapeño pepper, thinly sliced (optional)
  Toppings: hot sauce, sliced green onions, cilantro

1. Trim and discard root end and tough outer leaves of lemongrass stalk; smash with flat side of knife.

2. Bring broth, garlic, ginger, and lemongrass to a boil in a covered Dutch oven over high heat. Reduce heat to medium; simmer 20 minutes. Remove from heat; let stand to infuse 15 minutes. Discard lemongrass and garlic.

3. Bring broth mixture to a boil over medium-high heat; stir in turkey, next 2 ingredients, and, if desired, jalapeño. Boil 3 minutes. Serve with toppings.

MAKES 2 qt. **HANDS-ON** 20 min., **TOTAL** 1 hour

Speedy Lemongrass-Turkey Soup

Omit lemongrass, garlic, and ginger; substitute 1 (32-oz.) container Thai ginger-infused broth for reduced-sodium chicken broth. Omit Steps 1 and 2; prepare recipe as directed in Step 3.

SAUSAGE-AND-SWEET POTATO SOUP

A smart way to repurpose sweet potato casserole, this hearty soup drew rave reviews in our Test Kitchen. If your casserole contains marshmallows, remove them before stirring the casserole into this soup. The flavor will vary depending on your casserole recipe; simply adjust salt and pepper to taste before serving.

- 1 lb. smoked sausage, sliced
- 1 medium-size yellow onion, thinly sliced
- 3 garlic cloves, sliced
- 6 cups reduced-sodium chicken broth
- 2 cups leftover sweet potato casserole (without marshmallow topping)
- 1 medium-size red bell pepper, chopped
- 1 tsp. fresh thyme leaves
- 1 (5-oz.) package baby kale leaves or spinach
  Multigrain crackers

1. Cook sausage in a Dutch oven over medium heat, stirring occasionally, 7 to 8 minutes or until browned. Remove sausage from Dutch oven, using a slotted spoon. Reserve 2 Tbsp. drippings in Dutch oven.

2. Sauté onion in hot drippings in Dutch oven over medium-high heat 5 to 6 minutes or until tender. Add garlic, and sauté 2 minutes. Add broth, next 3 ingredients, and cooked sausage; bring to a boil. Reduce heat to medium, and simmer 20 minutes.

3. Add kale, and simmer 5 minutes. Add salt and pepper to taste. Serve with crackers.

MAKES about 2 qt. **HANDS-ON** 30 min., **TOTAL** 55 min.

CHEESY THANKSGIVING TAMALES

You'll love our way to use leftover stuffing, turkey, or sweet potato casserole by turning it into the starchy outer layer of tamales.

24 dried corn husks
2 cups leftover cooked dressing
1 (4-oz.) block pepper Jack cheese, cut into 12 sticks
    Kitchen string
    Spicy Cranberry Salsa (recipe, page 280)

1. Soak corn husks in warm water to cover 1 hour or until softened. Drain and pat dry.

2. Press 2 Tbsp. dressing into a 3- x 5-inch rectangle along 1 long side of 1 husk, leaving borders along other 3 sides of husks. Place 1 cheese stick in center of dressing. Roll up dressing, starting with long side and using husk as a guide. Press dressing edges together to form a seal, enclosing filling. Fold long side of husk over tamale to enclose.

3. Fold ends toward center to seal. Repeat procedure using remaining husks, dressing, and cheese.

4. Place 6 tamales side by side on work surface, with seam sides inward; tie tamales together with kitchen string, securing bundles at both ends. Repeat procedure to make a total of 4 bundles.

5. Stand tamale bundles on end in a steamer basket; place basket over boiling water in a large Dutch oven. Cover and steam 35 minutes or until dressing is set, adding more boiling water as needed. Serve hot with Spicy Cranberry Salsa.

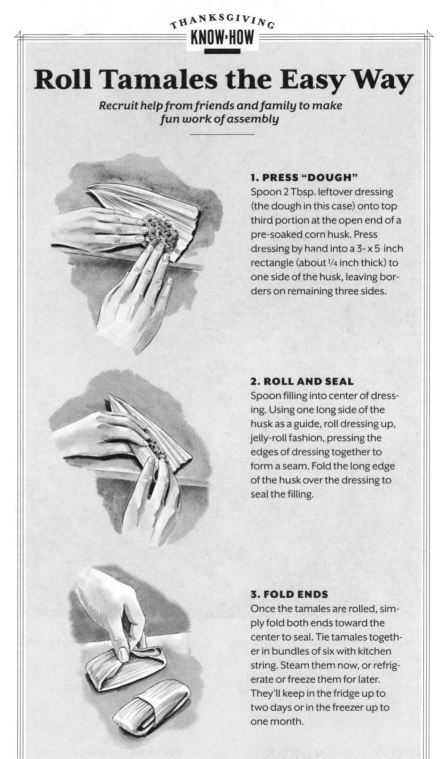

Roll Tamales the Easy Way

Recruit help from friends and family to make fun work of assembly

1. PRESS "DOUGH"
Spoon 2 Tbsp. leftover dressing (the dough in this case) onto top third portion at the open end of a pre-soaked corn husk. Press dressing by hand into a 3- x 5-inch rectangle (about ¼ inch thick) to one side of the husk, leaving borders on remaining three sides.

2. ROLL AND SEAL
Spoon filling into center of dressing. Using one long side of the husk as a guide, roll dressing up, jelly-roll fashion, pressing the edges of dressing together to form a seam. Fold the long edge of the husk over the dressing to seal the filling.

3. FOLD ENDS
Once the tamales are rolled, simply fold both ends toward the center to seal. Tie tamales together in bundles of six with kitchen string. Steam them now, or refrigerate or freeze them for later. They'll keep in the fridge up to two days or in the freezer up to one month.

MAKES 2 dozen. **HANDS-ON** 45 min.; **TOTAL** 2 hours, 20 min.

Turkey Tamales: Omit cheese. Prepare recipe as directed, spooning 1 Tbsp. chopped cooked turkey down center of dressing before rolling in Step 2.

Spicy Cranberry
Salsa

Cheesy Thanksgiving
Tamales

Sweet Potato Tamales: Omit pepper Jack cheese. Prepare recipe as directed, spooning 1 Tbsp. leftover sweet potato casserole down center of dressing before rolling in Step 2.

SPICY CRANBERRY SALSA

Here's our new go-to condiment to use on everything from tamales to turkey sandwiches.

- 2 cups leftover cranberry sauce or 1 (14-oz.) can whole berry cranberry sauce
- 1/3 cup chopped fresh cilantro
- 1 jalapeño pepper, seeded and minced
- 1/2 tsp. lime zest
- 1 1/2 Tbsp. fresh lime juice
- 1/2 tsp. ground cumin
- 1/4 tsp. kosher salt

Stir together all ingredients. Serve immediately, or cover and chill up to 1 week.

MAKES 1 1/2 cups. **HANDS-ON** 15 min., **TOTAL** 15 min.

SWEET POTATO CASSEROLE HOTCAKES

If your sweet potato casserole is very sweet, omit the brown sugar in the pancakes. Does yours come with a marshmallow topping? Even better. Simply stir it into your sweet potatoes, and make the recipe as directed.

- 1/2 cup maple syrup
- 3 Tbsp. leftover cranberry sauce or whole berry cranberry sauce
- 1 1/2 cups milk
- 1 cup leftover sweet potato casserole
- 1/4 cup butter, melted
- 2 large eggs
- 1/2 tsp. vanilla extract
- 1 3/4 cups all-purpose flour
- 2 Tbsp. light brown sugar
- 1 Tbsp. baking powder
- 1/2 tsp. ground cinnamon
- 1/2 tsp. kosher salt
  Toasted pecans

1. Stir together first 2 ingredients.
2. Whisk together milk and next 4 ingredients in a large bowl. Whisk together flour and next 4 ingredients in another bowl. Gradually stir flour mixture into milk mixture just until dry ingredients are moistened.
3. Pour about 1/4 cup batter for each pancake onto a hot (about 350°), lightly greased (with butter) griddle or large nonstick skillet. Cook over medium heat 2 to 3 minutes or until tops are covered with bubbles and edges look dry and cooked; turn and cook 1 to 2 more minutes or until puffed and thoroughly cooked. Serve immediately with syrup mixture and toasted pecans, or place in a single layer on a baking sheet and keep warm in a 200° oven up to 30 minutes.

MAKES about 18 pancakes.
HANDS-ON 30 min., **TOTAL** 30 min.

Grow a Lemon Tree

SWEET, JUICY FRUIT ISN'T THE ONLY THING THAT'S DELICIOUS ABOUT MEYER LEMONS

YOU WILL BE TEMPTED BY more than just the fruit of this citrus tree; the scent of its prolific flowers is amazing!

The Meyer lemon (*Citrus* x *meyeri*) has rounder fruit and fewer seeds than most lemons, with a smooth, thin skin that turns deep canary yellow when ripe. Sweeter and less acidic than other lemons, the Meyer is a hybrid between a lemon and a sweet orange or mandarin, so it's more versatile in the kitchen. You can use it in desserts, drinks, and salads, or roast slices with fish, chicken, or vegetables.

Meyers love sunshine, warmth, and well-drained, slightly acid soil. They are more cold tolerant than true lemons. In the Coastal and Tropical South, use them as specimens or large hedges in ornamental and edible gardens. They grow 6 to 12 feet wide and tall and respond well to pruning. In the Upper, Middle, and Lower South, grow them in containers and bring them inside during cold weather.

For containers, choose a well-drained potting mix and a fertilizer specially made for citrus. Water consistently to keep soil slightly moist but not wet. Never leave your container in a saucer of standing water. Use a soil moisture meter if you're unsure whether your plant needs watering. When your tree is actively growing and fruiting (early spring through late summer), feed it regularly. Meyer lemons prefer temperatures between 50 and 80 degrees. Once temps begin to drop below 50, prepare to bring your tree inside and stop feeding. Place your lemon tree near a south-facing window in a sunny location. Keep it away from heating vents, which can dry out the leaves and make it attractive to spider mites. Deter these pests by regularly misting foliage with water, or treat them using an insecticidal soap or applying organic neem oil (*planetnatural.com*).

The best selection to grow is 'Improved Meyer.' Purchase Meyer lemon trees from your local nursery, or buy online from *logees.com* or *petalsfromthepast.com*.

get growing!
MEYER LEMON

GROW
Plant in well-drained soil that is amended with peat or finely shredded bark.

FEED
Use a citrus fertilizer such as Espoma Citrus-tone (5-2-6).

PLANT ZONES
Coastal and Tropical South

LIGHT
FULL SUN | WATER
MEDIUM

Ideal for use as container plants, Meyer lemon trees can be brought inside when temps cool.

MEYER LEMON VINAIGRETTE

Whisk together 4 Tbsp. fresh **Meyer lemon juice;** 2 Tbsp. minced fresh **oregano;** 1 Tbsp. drained **capers,** chopped; ½ tsp. **honey;** ¼ tsp. dried crushed **red pepper;** ¼ tsp. **anchovy paste;** and 1 minced **garlic clove.** Whisk in ¼ cup olive oil; add **salt** and **pepper. MAKES** about ½ cup.

Community Cookbook

If you die in the South, you can count on one thing: There will be a casserole at your wake. The healing powers of funeral food reflect a distinctly Southern phenomenon, and *Food to Die For,* benefitting the Old City Cemetery in Lynchburg, Virginia, goes way beyond Bundt recipes for the bereaved. The cookbook gives advice on transporting a meatloaf, organizing food delivery, and even writing a condolence note—all with a comforting dose of humor.

CHLOE'S PUMPKIN BREAD

This delicious quick bread disappears as fast as it takes to whisk together.

3 1/2   cups all-purpose flour
3   cups sugar
2   tsp. baking soda
2   tsp. ground cinnamon
1 1/2   tsp. table salt
1/2   tsp. ground nutmeg
1/2   tsp. ground ginger
1   cup chopped toasted pecans
1   (15-oz.) can pumpkin
4   large eggs
1   cup vegetable oil
    Vegetable cooking spray

1. Preheat oven to 350°. Whisk together flour and next 6 ingredients in a large bowl. Stir in pecans. Make a well in center of mixture.

2. Whisk together pumpkin, next 2 ingredients, and 2/3 cup water; add to dry mixture, stirring just until moistened. Pour into 2 lightly greased (with cooking spray) and floured 9- x 5-inch loaf pans.

3. Bake at 350° for 1 hour to 1 hour and 15 minutes or until a long wooden pick inserted in center comes out clean. Cool in pans on a wire rack 10 minutes. Remove loaves from pans to wire rack, and cool 30 minutes. Serve warm or at room temperature.

MAKES 2 loaves. **HANDS-ON** 15 min.; **TOTAL** 1 hour, 55 min.

CHICKEN HASH

Serve this delicious dinner-in-a-flash over biscuits, rice, or pasta.

Melt 2 Tbsp. **butter** in a 2-qt. saucepan over medium heat. Whisk in 2 Tbsp. all-purpose **flour,** and cook, whisking constantly, 1 minute. Gradually whisk in 3 cups reduced-sodium **chicken broth.** Increase heat to high, and bring to a boil, whisking constantly. Reduce heat to medium; simmer, stirring occasionally, 5 minutes or until thickened. Remove from heat, and stir in 4 cups shredded deli-roasted **chicken** (about 1 [2-lb.] chicken), 1/2 cup chopped fresh **herbs** (such as parsley, basil, chives, or thyme), and 1 tsp. fresh **lemon juice.** Add **kosher salt** and **freshly ground black pepper** to taste, and serve immediately.

MAKES 6 servings. **HANDS-ON** 20 min., **TOTAL** 20 min.

CEMETERY GINGER COOKIES

These easy-to-bake cookies have just the right amount of spice.

2   cups all-purpose flour
2   tsp. baking soda
1   tsp. ground cinnamon
1/2   tsp. table salt
1/2   tsp. ground ginger
1/4   tsp. ground cloves
3/4   cup butter, softened
1   cup granulated sugar
4   Tbsp. molasses
1   large egg
1/2   cup Demerara sugar
    Parchment paper

1. Stir together first 6 ingredients.

2. Beat butter and granulated sugar at medium speed with an electric mixer 2 to 3 minutes or until creamy. Add molasses and egg, beating until well blended. Gradually add flour mixture, beating just until blended after each addition. Cover and chill 2 to 4 hours.

3. Preheat oven to 325°. Shape dough into 1-inch balls; roll in Demerara sugar to coat. Place balls 2 inches apart on 2 parchment paper-lined baking sheets. Flatten balls slightly with bottom of a glass.

4. Bake at 325°, in batches, for 12 to 15 minutes. Cool on baking sheets 2 minutes. Transfer cookies to wire racks, and cool 10 minutes.

MAKES 5 dozen. **HANDS-ON** 30 min.; **TOTAL** 3 hours, 20 min.

December

I'll be home...

BREAK OUT THE TINSEL AND MINGLE
TOO AT A COME-AND-GO APPETIZER PARTY
THAT'S EASY ON THE HOST THANKS TO
MAKE-AHEAD NIBBLES

CUBAN SANDWICH SLIDERS

A welcome change from a burger slider,
the key is to crisp the bread by warming
the sandwiches in a hot jelly-roll pan.

- 1/4 **cup olive oil**
- 1 **(12-oz.) package Hawaiian sweet dinner rolls**
- 4 **oz. thinly sliced deli ham**
- 4 **oz. thinly sliced deli-roasted pork**
- 6 **(1-oz.) Swiss cheese slices**
- 1/2 **cup chopped dill pickle chips**
- 3 **Tbsp. yellow mustard**

1. Preheat oven to 400°. Spread olive oil in a jelly-roll pan; place pan in oven to heat.
2. Remove rolls from package. (Do not separate rolls.) Cut rolls in half horizontally, creating 1 top and 1 bottom. Layer ham, pork, and Swiss cheese on bottom half. Spread chopped pickles over cheese. Spread mustard on cut side of top half of rolls, and place, cut side down, on bottom half to make a large sandwich.
3. Remove jelly-roll pan from oven, and carefully transfer rolls to hot pan. Place a cast-iron skillet or griddle on rolls.

4. Bake at 400° for 15 minutes or until cheese melts. Remove from oven, and cool 5 minutes. Cut into 12 sliders, and serve immediately.

Note: We tested with King's Hawaiian Original Hawaiian Sweet Rolls.

MAKES 12 servings. **HANDS-ON** 20 min., **TOTAL** 40 min.

BAKED BRIE

Serve the baked Brie whole on a pretty
cutting board with a cheese knife, and let
guests cut their own portions.

- 1 **(8-oz.) Brie round**
- 1/2 **(16-oz.) package frozen phyllo pastry, thawed**
  Parchment paper
- 1 **cup butter, melted**
- 1/3 **cup sweet orange marmalade**
- 1/3 **cup chopped fresh basil**
- 1/4 **tsp. freshly ground black pepper**
- 1/8 **tsp. kosher salt**
- 1/2 **cup chopped roasted salted almonds, divided**

1. Preheat oven to 375°. Trim and discard rind from sides of Brie. Cut Brie into 1/4- to 1/2-inch slices.

2. Place 2 phyllo pastry sheets side by side, with long sides slightly overlapping, on parchment paper. (You should have an approximately 24- x 17-inch rectangle.) Brush with melted butter (4 to 5 brushes on each sheet). Top with 2 phyllo pastry sheets, and brush with butter. Repeat with butter and remaining 1/2 package of phyllo pastry sheets.
3. Arrange Brie slices across center of phyllo rectangle, overlapping slightly and leaving 3 1/2 inches at each short end. Spread orange marmalade over Brie, and sprinkle with basil, pepper, salt, and 1/4 cup chopped almonds. Fold phyllo into center, covering filling. (Long sides will overlap.) Carefully turn over phyllo packet, and place, seam side down, on parchment paper. Transfer phyllo packet and parchment paper to a baking sheet. Brush with remaining butter, and sprinkle with remaining 1/4 cup almonds.
4. Bake at 375° for 30 to 40 minutes or until golden brown. Cool 15 minutes before slicing. Serve warm or at room temperature.

MAKES 12 to 14 appetizer servings.
HANDS-ON 40 min.; **TOTAL** 1 hour, 25 min.

How to Host an Open House

FOLLOW THESE FIVE KEY TIPS FOR COME-AND-GO PARTY SUCCESS AND MAKE ENTERTAINING LOOK EFFORTLESS

(1) **WELCOME GUESTS WITH REFRESHMENT.** Don't leave guests empty-handed. Set up a drink station at the entry so guests can fill a glass when they arrive. Punch is a great serve-yourself libation.

(2) **TAKE TIME PICKING TUNES.** A great playlist keeps things hopping, even during lulls between crowds. Make it long (at least 2 hours) with a mix of popular songs people can hum along to, holiday tunes, and a few classics sprinkled in the mix.

(3) **PICK A MENU WITH DISHES SERVED** at a variety of temperatures (cold, room temp, and hot). Keep hot foods to a minimum and pick things you can keep warm in the oven. Better yet, pick a dish you can serve in a slow cooker or chafing dish.

(4) **PLACE LITTLE NIBBLES AROUND THE HOUSE.** A bowl of nuts here, an olive boat there. It'll get guests moving from room to room and help control traffic flow around a buffet.

(5) **HIRE SOMEONE TO PARK CARS.** On a blustery night what could be more welcome than pulling up to a party and being greeted by a valet?

CITRUS-MARINATED OLIVES AND ALMONDS

A big batch of this antipasti will last in the refrigerator up to a week. It's the perfect snack to serve unexpected holiday company. For extra flavor, use smoked almonds.

- 1/2 cup extra virgin olive oil
- 3 garlic cloves, crushed
- 2 Tbsp. loosely packed grapefruit zest
- 2 Tbsp. fresh grapefruit juice
- 2 Tbsp. red wine vinegar
- 1 Tbsp. chopped fresh thyme leaves
- 1 Tbsp. loosely packed orange zest
- 2 tsp. sugar
- 1 tsp. kosher salt
- 1/2 tsp. freshly ground black pepper
- 4 cups pitted and drained gourmet olives (such as Castelvetrano and Kalamata)
- 1 1/2 cups roasted salted almonds

1. Stir together first 10 ingredients in a large bowl. Fold olives into marinade. Cover and chill 4 to 24 hours.
2. Remove and discard crushed garlic cloves, and stir in almonds just before serving.

MAKES 10 to 12 appetizer servings.
HANDS-ON 10 min.; **TOTAL** 4 hours, 10 min.

SWEET POTATO CHEESECAKE TARTLETS

- 4 (2.1-oz.) packages frozen mini-phyllo pastry shells, thawed
- 1 (8-oz.) package cream cheese, softened
- 1/2 cup sugar
- 1 cup mashed, cooked sweet potato
- 1/2 cup sour cream
- 1 large egg
- 1 tsp. vanilla extract
  Topping: Pecan Pie-Glazed Pecans
  Garnishes: mint leaves, sweetened whipped cream

1. Preheat oven to 350°. Place mini-phyllo pastry shells on 2 baking sheets.
2. Process cream cheese and sugar in a food processor until smooth. Add sweet potato and next 3 ingredients, and process until smooth. Spoon 1 Tbsp. mixture into each pastry shell.
3. Bake at 350° for 13 to 15 minutes or until center is set. Cool completely on a wire rack (about 40 minutes). Cover; chill 1 hour. Top with Pecan Pie-Glazed Pecans just before serving.

MAKES 5 dozen. **HANDS-ON** 25 min.;
TOTAL 3 hours, 35 min., including pecans

Pecan Pie-Glazed Pecans

- 1/2 cup firmly packed light brown sugar
- 6 Tbsp. dark corn syrup
- 2 cups pecan halves
  Vegetable cooking spray
  Wax paper

Preheat oven to 350°. Stir together sugar and corn syrup in a medium bowl. Add pecans, stirring to coat. Line a jelly-roll pan with aluminum foil; lightly coat with cooking spray. Spread mixture in a single layer in prepared pan. Bake 12 to 15 minutes or until glaze thickens, stirring every 4 minutes. Spread in a single layer on wax paper; cool completely (about 50 minutes), separating pecans as they cool. Store in an airtight container at room temperature up to 1 week.

MAKES 2 cups. **HANDS-ON** 25 min.;
TOTAL 1 hour, 15 min.

BACON-FIG TASSIES

In a pinch, swap the dough for frozen mini-phyllo pastry shells.

- 5 uncooked bacon slices
- 1/3 cup butter, softened
- 2 (8-oz.) packages cream cheese, softened
- 1 cup all-purpose flour
- 1/4 cup fine cornmeal
- 1 1/2 cups diced dried figs
- 1/4 cup sugar
- 3/4 cup red wine
- 1 1/2 tsp. kosher salt, divided
- 8 oz. goat cheese, softened
- 1 tsp. lemon zest
- 2 tsp. fresh lemon juice
- 2 tsp. chopped fresh thyme leaves
- 1/2 tsp. freshly ground black pepper

1. Cook bacon in a skillet over medium heat 8 to 10 minutes or until crisp. Remove bacon, and drain on paper towels, reserving 2 Tbsp. drippings. Finely chop cooked bacon.
2. Beat butter, 1 package cream cheese, and reserved bacon drippings at medium speed with an electric mixer 2 minutes. Gradually add flour and cornmeal, beating at low speed until blended. Shape mixture into about 48 (1-inch) balls. Cover and chill 1 hour.
3. Preheat oven to 350°. Place dough balls in cups of 2 (24-cup) miniature muffin pans, and press dough into and up the sides of the muffin cups, forming shells.
4. Bake at 350° for 22 to 25 minutes or until golden brown. Remove from oven, and cool on a wire rack 10 minutes. (Reshape tart shells, using handle of a wooden spoon, if necessary.) Remove tart shells from pan to a serving platter.
5. Stir together figs, next 2 ingredients, and 1/2 tsp. salt in a medium saucepan. Bring to a simmer over medium heat, and cook, stirring occasionally, 6 to 8 minutes or until thickened and syrupy. Remove from heat, and cool 15 minutes.
6. Meanwhile, beat goat cheese, next 4 ingredients, and remaining 1 package cream cheese and 1 tsp. salt at medium speed until smooth and combined. Spoon goat cheese mixture into a zip-top plastic freezer bag. Snip 1 corner of bag to make a small hole.
7. Spoon 1 tsp. fig mixture into each tartlet shell. Pipe about 2 tsp. goat cheese mixture into each shell, and sprinkle with chopped bacon.

MAKES 4 dozen. **HANDS-ON** 1 hour, 20 min.; **TOTAL** 3 hours, 20 min.

MEXICAN SHRIMP COCKTAIL DIP

Here's a fresh, colorful swap for creamy shrimp dip. Inspired by Porch Club member and reader Carolyn Coleman.

- 1 lb. peeled, medium-size cooked shrimp, deveined and halved
- 3 plum tomatoes, diced
- 3 jalapeño peppers, seeded and diced
- 1 small sweet onion, diced
- 1 garlic clove, minced
- 1/2 cup fresh lime juice
- 1/4 cup extra virgin olive oil
- 1/4 cup chili sauce
- 1/4 cup spicy tomato juice
- 2 Tbsp. hot sauce
- 2 Tbsp. prepared horseradish
- 1/4 cup chopped fresh flat-leaf parsley
- 1/4 cup chopped fresh cilantro
- 1 avocado, diced
  Kosher salt and freshly ground black pepper
  Tortilla chips

1. Stir together first 13 ingredients in a bowl. Cover and chill 1 to 24 hours.
2. Stir in avocado; add salt and pepper to taste. Serve with tortilla chips.

Note: We tested with V-8 Spicy Hot 100% Vegetable Juice.

MAKES 8 to 10 appetizer servings.
HANDS-ON 30 min.; **TOTAL** 1 hour, 30 min.

BENNE-MAPLE ROASTED PECANS

- 4 Tbsp. butter
- 4 cups pecan halves, toasted
- 1/4 cup firmly packed light brown sugar
- 1/4 cup maple syrup
- 3/4 tsp. kosher salt
- 1 Tbsp. soy sauce
- 1/8 tsp. ground red pepper
- 1 Tbsp. sesame oil
  Parchment paper
- 2 Tbsp. sesame seeds, toasted

1. Melt butter in a large saucepan over medium heat. Stir in pecans and next 5 ingredients. Cook over medium-high heat, stirring constantly, 5 minutes or until sugar dissolves and syrupy coating is almost evaporated. Stir in sesame oil; remove from heat.
2. Spread pecans in a single layer in a parchment paper-lined jelly-roll pan; sprinkle with sesame seeds. Cool completely.

MAKES 4 cups. **HANDS-ON** 15 min.; **TOTAL** 1 hour, 5 min.

Bacon-Fig Tassies and Sweet Potato Cheesecake Tartlets

FRIED HOMINY

- 2 (14.5-oz.) cans white hominy, drained
  Canola oil
- 1 cup all-purpose flour
- 1/2 cup plain white cornmeal
- 1/4 cup cornstarch
- 3/4 tsp. table salt
- 1/2 tsp. freshly ground black pepper
  Savory Spice Mix or Cinnamon-Sugar Spice Mix

1. Spread hominy evenly in a paper towel-lined jelly-roll pan; pat dry. Chill 3 to 24 hours. (Do not cover.)
2. Heat 3 inches oil in a Dutch oven over medium-high heat to 350°. Mix flour and next 4 ingredients in a medium bowl. Toss hominy, in 2 batches, in flour mixture, shaking off excess.
3. Fry hominy, in 4 batches, stirring occasionally, 6 to 7 minutes or until kernels float to the top and begin to brown. Remove with a slotted spoon, and drain on paper towels. Immediately sprinkle with desired amount of Savory Spice Mix or Cinnamon-Sugar Spice Mix. Serve immediately, or cool completely, and store in an airtight container up to 24 hours.

MAKES 8 to 10 servings. **HANDS-ON** 40 min.; **TOTAL** 3 hours, 45 min., including spice mix

Savory Spice Mix

Stir together 1 Tbsp. fresh **thyme**, finely chopped; 3/4 tsp. table **salt**; 1/2 tsp. ground **cumin**; 1/2 tsp. ground **coriander**; 1/2 tsp. **paprika**; 1/2 tsp. freshly ground **black pepper**; 1/4 tsp. ground **red pepper**; and 1/4 tsp. dried **oregano**. Store in an airtight container up to 1 month.

MAKES about 4 tsp. **HANDS-ON** 5 min., **TOTAL** 5 min.

Cinnamon-Sugar Spice Mix

Stir together 1/4 cup granulated **sugar**, 1/4 cup firmly packed **light brown sugar**, 3/4 tsp. table **salt**, 1/4 tsp. ground **cinnamon**, and 1/8 tsp. ground **red pepper**. Store in an airtight container up to 1 month.

MAKES about 1/2 cup. **HANDS-ON** 5 min., **TOTAL** 5 min.

Benne-Maple Roasted Pecans, Fried Hominy, and Red Wine-Cranberry Cheese Log

RED WINE-CRANBERRY CHEESE LOG

- 1 (12-oz.) package frozen or fresh cranberries
- 1 cup red wine
- 3/4 cup sugar
- 5 fresh sage leaves
- 3 fresh thyme sprigs
- 1 cinnamon stick
- 1/4 tsp. table salt
- 1/4 tsp. ground allspice
- 1 (8-oz.) package cream cheese
  Assorted crackers

1. Stir together first 8 ingredients in a medium saucepan. Bring to a boil over high heat, stirring occasionally. Reduce heat to medium-low, and simmer, stirring occasionally, 15 to 18 minutes or until about one-fourth of liquid remains. Remove from heat, and cool 20 minutes. Discard sage leaves, thyme sprigs, and cinnamon stick.
2. Place cream cheese on a serving platter. Spoon desired amount of cranberry mixture over cream cheese. Serve with crackers.

MAKES 12 to 14 appetizer servings. **HANDS-ON** 20 min., **TOTAL** 55 min.

GUMBO ARANCINE

Arancine are the ultimate make-ahead party snack. Make the recipe through Step 4 up to two weeks ahead, and freeze. Bread and fry the frozen arancine a few hours before the party starts and hold warm in a 250° oven.

- 1 qt. reduced-sodium chicken broth
- 6 Tbsp. butter, divided
- 1 medium leek, chopped (about 1 cup)
- 1 small yellow onion, chopped
- 2 garlic cloves, minced
- 1½ cups uncooked Arborio rice (short grain)
- ½ cup white wine
- 2 tsp. kosher salt, divided
- ½ tsp. freshly ground black pepper, divided
  Parchment paper
- 1 green bell pepper, finely chopped
- 1 red bell pepper, finely chopped
- 1 lb. peeled cooked shrimp, chopped
- 1½ tsp. filé powder
- ½ tsp. Cajun seasoning
- 3 green onions, thinly sliced
- ½ tsp. hot sauce (such as Tabasco)
- 1 cup all-purpose flour
- 4 large eggs, lightly beaten
- 3 cups panko (Japanese breadcrumbs)
  Vegetable oil
  Spicy Mayo

1. Bring broth to a simmer in a large saucepan over medium-high heat.
2. Meanwhile, melt 2 Tbsp. butter in a Dutch oven over medium heat. Add leeks and onion, and sauté 10 minutes or until tender. Add garlic, and sauté 2 minutes. Add rice, and sauté 1 minute. Stir in wine, and cook, stirring often, 3 minutes. Add 1 cup hot broth, and cook, stirring constantly, until liquid is absorbed. Repeat procedure with remaining broth, 1 cup at a time. (Total cooking time is about 15 minutes.) Stir in 2 Tbsp. butter, 1½ tsp. salt, and ¼ tsp. pepper. Spread rice mixture evenly in a parchment paper-lined jelly-roll pan, and cool 10 minutes.
3. Melt remaining 2 Tbsp. butter in a large skillet over medium-high heat. Add green and red bell peppers, and sauté 6 to 8 minutes or until tender. Stir in shrimp and next 4 ingredients. Stir together rice mixture and bell pepper mixture in a large bowl.
4. Shape mixture into balls, using a 1½-inch cookie scoop. Place in a single layer in a parchment paper-lined jelly-roll pan, and chill 30 minutes to 24 hours.
5. Stir together flour and remaining ½ tsp. salt and ¼ tsp. pepper in a medium bowl. Place beaten eggs in a second medium bowl. Place breadcrumbs in a third medium bowl. Dredge chilled rice balls in flour mixture; dip in eggs, and roll in breadcrumbs to coat. Chill 10 minutes.
6. Pour oil to a depth of 5 inches into a large Dutch oven; heat over medium-high heat to 350°. Fry rice balls, in batches, 3 to 4 minutes or until golden brown; drain on paper towels. Transfer to a wire rack over a baking sheet. Keep warm in a 250° oven until ready to serve. Just before serving, cut in half, and top each half with ½ tsp. Spicy Mayo.

MAKES 35 appetizer servings.
HANDS-ON 1 hour, 45 min.;
TOTAL 2 hours, 40 min., including mayo

Spicy Mayo

Stir together ¼ cup **mayonnaise** and 3 Tbsp. **hot sauce** in a small bowl. Add kosher **salt** and freshly ground **black pepper** to taste.

MAKES about ⅓ cup. **HANDS-ON** 5 min., **TOTAL** 5 min.

Lemon, Herb and Feta Arancine:
Omit green and red bell peppers, shrimp, filé powder, Cajun seasoning, green onions, hot sauce, and Spicy Mayo. Reduce **butter** to ¼ cup. Prepare recipe through Step 1, stirring 3 Tbsp. each chopped fresh **parsley** and chopped fresh **oregano**, 1 Tbsp. chopped fresh **rosemary**, 2 tsp. **lemon zest**, and 1 Tbsp. fresh **lemon juice** into **rice mixture** with **butter**, **salt**, and **pepper**, before spreading to cool. Cut 1 (7-oz.) package **feta cheese** into ½-inch cubes. Omit Step 3, and proceed with recipe as directed in Steps 4 through 6, pressing 1 **feta cheese** cube into each rice ball and reshaping.

HANDS-ON 1 hour, 55 min.;
TOTAL 2 hours, 45 min.

Mushroom-and-Mozzarella Arancine: Omit green and red bell peppers, shrimp, filé powder, Cajun seasoning, green onions, hot sauce, and Spicy Mayo. Prepare recipe through Step 2. Melt remaining 2 Tbsp. **butter** with 1 Tbsp. **olive oil** in a large skillet over medium-high heat. Add 2 (8-oz.) packages sliced **cremini mushrooms**, and sauté 7 to 8 minutes or until tender. Add **salt** and **pepper** to taste. Stir together **rice mixture** and sautéed **mushrooms** in a large bowl. Cut 1 (8-oz.) package fresh **mozzarella cheese** into ½-inch cubes. Omit Step 3, and proceed with recipe as directed in Steps 4 through 6, pressing 1 **mozzarella** cube into each rice ball and reshaping.

HANDS-ON 2 hours; **TOTAL** 2 hours, 55 min.

I'LL BE HOME TO
BAKE COOKIES

*MAKE THE SEASON EXTRA SWEET AND GATHER
IN THE KITCHEN WITH FAMILY AND FRIENDS TO MAKE
OUR FAVORITE SCRATCH-MADE TREATS*

PEPPERMINT MERINGUE COOKIES

Use a paintbrush or buy food coloring gel in a squeeze bottle to make even stripes of color.

- 6 large egg whites
- 1 1/2 tsp. white vinegar
- 1 1/2 cups sugar
- 1 tsp. peppermint extract
  Parchment paper
  Red food coloring gel
- 2 to 3 large disposable decorating bags

1. Preheat oven to 200°. Let egg whites stand at room temperature for 20 minutes. Beat egg whites at high speed with a heavy-duty electric stand mixer, using whisk attachment, 2 minutes or until stiff peaks form. Reduce speed to medium, and add vinegar and sugar, 1/2 cup at a time, beating until blended after each addition. Beat 2 more minutes or until glossy. Beat in peppermint extract.
2. Line 2 baking sheets with parchment paper. Paint 3 or 4 evenly spaced stripes of red food coloring gel on inside of 1 decorating bag, starting at tip and ending three-fourths of the way up bag. Gently spoon meringue into center of bag, filling three-fourths full. Snip end of bag. Pipe about 2 Tbsp. meringue onto 1 prepared baking sheet, leaving 1 inch between each cookie. Repeat with remaining meringue, using a clean piping bag for each batch.
3. Bake at 200° for 2 hours. Turn off oven, and let meringues stand in oven until completely cool (about 3 to 4 hours). Wrap in aluminum foil, and store at room temperature.

MAKES about 7 1/2 dozen.
HANDS-ON 30 min.; **TOTAL** 5 hours, 30 min.

Chocolate-Dipped Peppermint Meringues: Prepare recipe as directed. Melt 2 cups **milk chocolate morsels** in microwave according to package directions. Stir until smooth. Dip bottom of each cooled cookie in melted chocolate, and place on a parchment paper-lined baking sheet. Let stand 15 minutes or until chocolate hardens. Wrap in aluminum foil, and store at room temperature.

HANDS-ON 40 min.; **TOTAL** 5 hours, 55 min.

COFFEE-CHOCOLATE BALLS

Toss the balls in chocolate two at a time for an even coating.

- 1 cup finely chopped almonds, toasted
- 2 cups crushed vanilla wafers (about 56 cookies)
- 1/2 cup powdered sugar
- 2 Tbsp. unsweetened cocoa
- 4 1/2 tsp. light corn syrup
- 6 Tbsp. coffee liqueur
- 3 cups semisweet chocolate morsels

1. Stir together first 6 ingredients until well blended. Shape dough into 32 (1- to 1 1/2-inch) balls.
2. Microwave morsels in a large microwave-safe bowl at HIGH 30 seconds; stir. Microwave 10 to 20 more seconds or until melted and smooth, stirring at 10-second intervals. Using a fork, toss balls in chocolate until thoroughly coated. Remove with fork; place on a parchment paper-lined jelly-roll pan. Chill 30 minutes or until chocolate is set. Refrigerate in an airtight container up to 1 week.

MAKES 32 cookies. **HANDS-ON** 30 min., **TOTAL** 1 hour

How to Assemble a Showstopping Cookie Platter

THINK OF THE PLATTER LIKE A CLOCK AND GROUP COOKIES IN SECTIONS AROUND THE CLOCK

STEP 1

Begin with your neutral colored cookies— everything that's a shade of brown. Alternate shades of brown around the clock, leaving room for more colorful cookies in between.

STEP 2

Incorporating groups of black (dark chocolate) and white (usually powdered sugar-dusted) cookies in between the brown cookies to break up the monotone color.

STEP 3

Fill in the last few open slots with colorful cookies.

STEP 4

Save your prettiest, most colorful cookies for the final touch, and nestle 6 to 8 of these among all the other cookies on a platter. Dot with brightly colored candies or dark chocolate pieces.

Peppermint-White Chocolate Balls: Prepare recipe as directed, substituting **pecans** for almonds, **6 Tbsp. peppermint schnapps** for coffee liqueur, and **white chocolate morsels** for chocolate morsels. Sprinkle with crushed hard **peppermint candies** immediately after coating with white chocolate.

MISSISSIPPI MUD MEDALLIONS

If you can't find chocolate-covered espresso beans, replace them with mini marshmallows.

- 6 whole graham crackers
  Parchment paper
- 2 cups semisweet chocolate morsels
- $2/3$ cup pecan halves, toasted
- $1/4$ cup chocolate-covered espresso beans

1. Place 3 whole graham crackers in a zip-top plastic freezer bag, and roll with a rolling pin until finely crushed. Spoon crushed graham crackers by level $1/2$ teaspoonfuls 1 inch apart onto a parchment paper-lined baking sheet; flatten into 1-inch rounds. Break remaining crackers into $1/2$-inch pieces.
2. Microwave chocolate morsels in a microwave-safe bowl at HIGH 30 seconds; stir. Microwave 10 to 20 more seconds or until melted and smooth, stirring at 10-second intervals.
3. Spoon melted chocolate into a large zip-top plastic freezer bag. Snip 1 corner of bag to make a small hole. Pipe chocolate over each round.
4. Working quickly, press 1 ($1/2$-inch) graham cracker piece, 1 toasted pecan, and 1 espresso bean onto each chocolate round. Chill 15 minutes. Store in an airtight container at room temperature up to 1 week.

Note: To transfer chocolate into zip-top plastic freezer bag, nestle corner of bag in a 1-cup measuring cup and scrape melted chocolate into the opened bag, pooling it in the corner that is nestled in the measuring cup.

MAKES 3 dozen. **HANDS-ON** 25 min., **TOTAL** 40 min.

COOKIE PRESS SANDWICHES

We've punched up this classic with lemon, orange, and peppermint fillings.

- 1 cup butter, softened
- 1/2 cup granulated sugar
- 1/2 tsp. almond extract
- 1/2 tsp. vanilla extract
- 1 large egg
- 2 1/4 cups all-purpose flour
- 1/2 tsp. table salt
- 1/2 cup butter, softened
- 1 (16-oz.) package powdered sugar
- 3 to 4 Tbsp. milk
- 3/4 tsp. flavored extract (such as peppermint, orange, or lemon)
  Food coloring
- 1/2 cup powdered sugar

1. Preheat oven to 400°. Beat first 4 ingredients at medium speed with an electric mixer 1 minute. Add egg, and beat 30 seconds.

2. Sift together flour and salt. Add flour mixture to butter mixture, and beat at low speed 30 seconds. Scrape sides of bowl, and beat 15 more seconds. Divide dough into 3 equal portions.

3. Following manufacturer's instructions, use a cookie press fitted with desired disk to shape dough into cookies, spacing cookies 1 1/2 inches apart on 2 ungreased baking sheets.

4. Bake at 400° for 7 minutes, placing 1 baking sheet on middle oven rack and 1 sheet on lower oven rack. Rotate baking sheets front to back and top rack to bottom rack. Bake 1 to 2 more minutes or until golden brown around edges. Transfer cookies to a wire rack, and cool completely (about 10 minutes). Repeat with remaining dough.

5. Beat 1/2 cup butter and next 2 ingredients at medium speed 2 minutes. Add flavored extract; beat at low speed until blended. Add desired amount of food coloring; beat at low speed until blended.

6. Spoon filling into a zip-top plastic freezer bag. (Do not seal.) Snip 1 corner of bag to make a small hole. Pipe filling onto bottom of 1 cookie.

Top with a second cookie, so bottom sides of both cookies touch filling. Repeat with remaining cookies and filling. Sprinkle with powdered sugar. Serve immediately, or let stand 2 hours. Store in an airtight container up to 2 weeks.

MAKES 3 dozen. **HANDS-ON** 2 hours; **TOTAL** 2 hours, 45 min.

TRIPLE GINGERSNAPPERS

Ship these sturdy spiced cookies to loved ones far away.

- 3/4 cup plus 2 Tbsp. granulated sugar
- 1/2 cup butter, softened
- 2 Tbsp. light brown sugar
- 2 tsp. dark molasses
- 1 large egg white
- 2 Tbsp. grated fresh ginger
- 1 1/3 cups all-purpose flour
- 1 Tbsp. ground ginger
- 1 tsp. ground cinnamon
- 1/2 tsp. baking soda
- 1/4 tsp. table salt
- 1/4 tsp. ground nutmeg
- 1/4 tsp. ground cloves
- 1/3 cup crystallized ginger, minced
  Parchment paper

1. Beat first 4 ingredients at medium-high speed with a heavy-duty electric stand mixer 30 seconds. Add egg white, and beat 30 seconds. Add grated fresh ginger, and beat 30 seconds.

2. Sift together flour and next 6 ingredients in a medium bowl. Add flour mixture to butter mixture, and beat at low speed 30 seconds. Scrape down sides of bowl, and fold in crystallized ginger. Divide dough into 2 (1/2-inch-thick) disks, and wrap tightly in plastic wrap. Chill 4 hours to 3 days.

3. Unwrap 1 dough disk, and generously flour both sides. Place between 2 pieces of parchment paper, and roll to 1/8-inch thickness. Chill 30 minutes. Meanwhile, repeat with remaining dough disk.

4. Cut chilled dough with a 2 1/2-inch round cutter. Place cookies 2 inches apart on 3 parchment paper-lined

baking sheets. Chill 15 minutes.

5. Bake chilled cookies, in batches, at 350° for 12 minutes. Rotate pans front to back, and bake 4 more minutes. (Cookies will puff up, and then collapse.) Cool completely on parchment paper on wire racks (about 15 minutes).

MAKES about 2 dozen.
HANDS-ON 1 hour, 15 min.;
TOTAL 6 hours, 45 min.

PECAN-PEACH LINZER COOKIES

Substitute any flavor of jam for the peach jam, if you like.

- 2 1/4 cups all-purpose flour
- 1 cup pecan halves
- 1 tsp. ground cinnamon
- 1/2 tsp. ground cloves
- 1 cup butter, softened at room temperature
- 1/3 cup granulated sugar
- 1 tsp. firmly packed lemon zest
- 1 large egg
- 1 large egg yolk
  Parchment paper
- 1/4 cup powdered sugar
- 3/4 cup peach jam
  Parchment paper

1. Pulse first 4 ingredients in a food processor 10 times or until pecans are finely ground.

2. Beat butter, sugar, and zest at medium speed with a heavy-duty electric stand mixer 1 minute. Add egg and egg yolk to butter mixture; beat 30 seconds. Scrape sides of bowl, and beat 30 more seconds. Add flour mixture to butter mixture, beating until just combined.

3. Shape dough into 2 (1/2-inch-thick) rectangles. Wrap each rectangle in plastic wrap, and chill 4 hours to 3 days.

4. Preheat oven to 350°. Generously flour both sides of chilled dough rectangles, and place on parchment paper. Roll each into a 14- x 10-inch rectangle about 1/8 inch thick. Cut each dough rectangle into 24 squares, using a 2-inch square cutter. Chill on parchment paper 30 minutes. (Chill, re-roll, and cut scraps, if desired.)

5. Place 24 chilled squares 1 inch apart on 2 parchment paper-lined baking sheets. Cut centers out of half of cookies with a lightly floured 1 1/4-inch square cutter. (If desired, place dough centers on a parchment paper-lined baking sheet; chill 15 minutes, and bake as directed.)

6. Bake at 350° for 12 to 14 minutes or until edges are golden. Cool completely on parchment paper on a wire rack (about 15 minutes). Repeat with remaining cookies.

7. Sprinkle powdered sugar over hollow cookies. Spread about 1/4 tsp. jam onto each solid cookie; top with hollow cookies.

MAKES about 2 dozen. **HANDS-ON** 1 hour; **TOTAL** 6 hours, 10 min.

WREATH MACAROONS

Use your fingers to make a hole in the center of each cookie.

      1 **(14-oz.) package sweetened shredded coconut**
      2 **large egg whites**
   1/2 **cup plus 2 tsp. sugar**
      1 **tsp. vanilla extract**
         Parchment paper
         Holiday nonpareils, finely chopped candied cherries

1. Preheat oven to 350°. Stir together first 4 ingredients until combined. Drop by heaping tablespoonfuls onto 3 parchment paper-lined baking sheets, about 12 per sheet. Make a hole in center of each cookie; pinch each cookie into a wreath shape. Sprinkle with desired amount of nonpareils and cherries.

2. Bake 2 baking sheets at 350° for 14 minutes. Rotate front to back, and bake 1 to 2 more minutes or until coconut around bottom edge begins to brown. Transfer parchment paper with cookies to wire racks, and cool completely (about 15 minutes). Repeat with remaining baking sheet.

MAKES about 3 dozen. **HANDS-ON** 30 min.; **TOTAL** 1 hour, 15 min.

HIDDEN KISSES COOKIES

Use any variety of chocolate kiss you'd like. We love using mint and candy cane kisses for the holidays.

   2 1/4 **cups all-purpose flour**
     2/3 **cup powdered sugar**
        1 **cup sliced almonds**
      1/2 **tsp. table salt**
   1 1/4 **cups butter, softened**
        1 **tsp. vanilla extract**
      1/4 **tsp. almond extract**
           Parchment paper
       42 **chocolate kisses**

1. Preheat oven to 350°. Pulse first 4 ingredients in a food processor 10 to 20 times or until almonds are finely ground.

2. Beat butter and next 2 ingredients at medium-high speed with an electric mixer about 30 seconds or until creamy. Add flour mixture in 2 batches, beating until blended after each addition. Turn dough out onto a lightly floured surface, and knead 4 to 5 times. Divide dough in half.

3. Working with 1 dough portion, drop by heaping teaspoonfuls 1 inch apart on 2 parchment paper-lined baking sheets lined. Press 1 chocolate kiss into center of each cookie. Working with remaining dough portion, cover each kiss with another heaping teaspoonful of dough. Pinch top and bottom edges of dough together to seal.

4. Bake at 350° for 15 minutes, placing 1 baking sheet on middle oven rack and 1 sheet on lower oven rack. Rotate pans front to back, and top rack to bottom rack. Bake 3 to 5 more minutes or until edges just begin to brown. Cool cookies on parchment paper on wire racks 10 minutes. Sprinkle powdered sugar over cookies.

MAKES 3 1/2 dozen. **HANDS-ON** 1 hour; **TOTAL** 1 hour, 30 min.

RED VELVET FUDGE

We like a deep, rich red, but use less food coloring, if you prefer.

           Vegetable cooking spray
           Parchment paper
   1 1/2 **(8-oz.) packages cream cheese, softened**
        1 **Tbsp. milk**
        1 **tsp. vanilla extract**
      1/4 **tsp. table salt**
        1 **(16-oz.) package powdered sugar**
        1 **cup white chocolate morsels**
     2/3 **cup milk chocolate morsels**
        1 **(1-oz.) bottle red liquid food coloring***
        1 **cup toasted chopped walnuts**

1. Lightly grease (with cooking spray) an 8-inch square pan. Line bottom and sides with parchment paper or wax paper, allowing 2 to 3 inches to extend over sides; lightly grease paper.

2. Beat cream cheese and next 3 ingredients at medium-high speed with a heavy-duty electric stand mixer until creamy. Add powdered sugar, 1 cup at a time, beating at low speed until blended after each addition. Increase speed to high, and beat 3 minutes.

3. Melt white chocolate morsels in microwave according to package directions. Add to cream cheese mixture, and beat until well blended. Reserve one-third of white chocolate-cream cheese mixture in a small bowl. Melt milk chocolate morsels in microwave according to package directions. Add melted milk chocolate into remaining two-thirds of white chocolate-cream cheese mixture. Stir in red food coloring until desired color is reached. Fold in walnuts. Pour red velvet fudge mixture into prepared pan. Tap pan sharply on counter to remove air bubbles. Freeze 10 minutes or until surface is firm.

4. Spread reserved white chocolate-cream cheese mixture over red velvet fudge. (If necessary, microwave white chocolate-cream cheese mixture in a microwave-safe bowl at HIGH 10 seconds to soften.) Chill fudge 4 to 24 hours.

5. Lift fudge from pan, using paper sides as handles. Cut into rectangles. Rinse and wipe knife clean between each slice. Chill until ready to serve.

*10 drops food coloring gel may be substituted.

MAKES about 2 dozen (2- x 1 1/4-inch) rectangles. **HANDS-ON** 30 min.; **TOTAL** 4 hours, 40 min.

CREAM CHEESE-CITRUS MINTS

Inspired by a recipe from Southern Living, *December 2003, we added zest for a modern twist.*

- 1/2 (8-oz.) package cream cheese
- 2 Tbsp. butter
- 1 (16-oz.) package powdered sugar
- 1/4 tsp. peppermint extract
- 1/2 tsp. loosely packed lime zest
- 1/2 tsp. loosely packed lemon zest

1. Heat cream cheese and butter in a large saucepan over low heat, stirring constantly, 2 minutes or until butter melts and cream cheese is smooth. Remove from heat. Gradually stir in powdered sugar; add peppermint, lime zest, and lemon zest, stirring until well blended.

2. Divide mixture into 8 (1/4-cup) portions; roll each portion into a 12-inch rope. (If mixture is sticking, sprinkle surface and hands with powdered sugar.) Cut into 1/2-inch pieces. Let stand, uncovered, 4 hours or until firm.

MAKES about 13 dozen. **HANDS-ON** 30 min.; **TOTAL** 4 hours, 30 min.

Red Velvet Fudge, Potato Candy, and Cream Cheese-Citrus Mints

POTATO CANDY

- 1 to 2 large russet potatoes, peeled, cooked, mashed, and cooled (about 1/3 cup)
- 1 Tbsp. milk
- 1 tsp. vanilla extract
- 1/8 tsp. table salt
- 6 to 7 cups powdered sugar Parchment paper
- 1/3 cup creamy peanut butter

1. Beat mashed potatoes and next 3 ingredients at medium speed with a heavy-duty electric stand mixer 2 minutes or until combined. Add 6 cups powdered sugar, 1 cup at a time, beating until well blended after each addition. Add up to 1 cup powdered sugar, 1 Tbsp. at a time, to form dough.

2. Gather dough into a ball, and coat with powdered sugar. Sprinkle powdered sugar over hands and rolling pin. Roll to 1/8 inch thickness on parchment paper, and cut into a 12- x 10-inch rectangle. Generously sprinkle powdered sugar over dough, and place a piece of parchment paper over rectangle. Invert rectangle, and carefully remove and discard parchment paper.

3. Spread peanut butter onto rectangle. Lift and tilt parchment paper, starting at 1 long side, and tightly roll up candy, jelly-roll fashion, using parchment paper as a guide. Wrap in parchment paper, and freeze 1 hour. Cut into 1/4-inch-thick slices, and serve. Refrigerate sliced candy in an airtight container up to 1 week.

MAKES about 3 dozen. **HANDS-ON** 30 min.; **TOTAL** 1 hour, 30 min.

Sugar Cookie Puzzles

*DON'T BE SURPRISED IF YOU HAVE AS MUCH FUN AS YOUR
LITTLE ELVES MAKING THIS KID-FRIENDLY PROJECT. IT'S GUARANTEED
TO BE A NEW CHRISTMAS TRADITION.*

*Choose cutters with simple shapes;
they're easier to handle, and less
likely to break. If you want to make
small puzzles, cut dough into 4-inch
squares, and use a single cookie cutter to cut the center of each square;
cut straight lines from center shape to
edges of square to form puzzle pieces.*

3/4	**cup butter, softened**
3/4	**cup granulated sugar**
1	**large egg**
1 1/2	**tsp. vanilla extract**
2	**cups all-purpose flour**
1/4	**tsp. table salt**
	Parchment paper
1	**(32-oz.) package powdered sugar**
4	**tsp. meringue powder**
10	**to 14 Tbsp. warm water**
	Food coloring

1. Beat first 2 ingredients at medium speed with an electric mixer until creamy. Add egg and vanilla, beating until blended.

2. Sift together flour and salt in a separate bowl. Gradually add to butter mixture, in 2 batches, beating at low speed until just combined after each addition. Flatten dough into 2 rectangles, and wrap in plastic wrap. Chill 2 hours to 3 days.

3. Preheat oven to 350°. Place dough on floured parchment paper, and roll to 1/4-inch thick-ness. Cut into a 7- x 7 1/2-inch rectangle, reserving scraps. Transfer parchment to a baking sheet, and bake 7 minutes. Rotate pan front to back, and bake 7 more minutes or until edges just begin to turn golden brown.

4. Immediately remove from oven; slide parchment onto a flat, hard surface. Working quickly, cut cooked, soft dough with a small cookie cutter, pressing firmly into dough. Cut straight lines from shapes to rectangle edges to form puzzle pieces. Transfer parch-ment paper with cookies to wire rack. Gently separate puzzle pieces. Cool completely (about 10 minutes). Repeat with remaining chilled dough.

5. Beat powdered sugar, meringue powder, and 10 Tbsp. warm water at high speed 5 minutes or until glossy. Stir in up to 4 Tbsp. warm water, 1 tsp. at a time, until mixture reaches desired consistency. Stir in desired food coloring.

6. Pipe a thin border of icing around edge of each cookie piece. Fill center of cookie with an even layer of icing. Swirl a wooden pick in a circular motion around the entire pool of icing, starting at the edges and moving toward the center. Let cookies stand 30 minutes or until icing is dry before decorating with another color on top of base color. Store icing in an airtight container at room temperature up to 1 week.

Note: For crisp cookies, return dough immediately to oven after cutting in Step 4, and bake 3 to 5 more minutes or until golden brown.

MAKES 3 cookie puzzles.
HANDS-ON 1 hour, 30 min.;
TOTAL 5 hours

Ode to a Cookie Tin

The shiny toys, new sweaters, and bow-ladened sedans parked out in snow-covered driveways, they're all well and good. But sometimes all you need is a tin filled with sugar, butter, flour, and a chorus of sprinkles to make a heart sing. In between the gentle folds of wax paper and layers of royal icing is where you will find happiness and cheer, love, and dreams to share as that Charlie Brown Christmas tune goes. But the cookie tin was not born of sentimental circumstances. Bumpy railroad rides that transported fragile, individually packaged foods (a 19th century novelty) in Britain demanded a sturdy vessel, and the British happened to control most of the world's tin ore supply. Efficiency gave way to beauty, and tins became works of art stamped with elaborate patterns and illustrations. Tins have a tendency to take on lives of their own beyond their intended purpose. They become jewelry boxes or crayon catchalls. But no matter who they're from or what they become, they never lose the memories we pack inside them.

PACKING TIPS

BE CHOOSY
Delicate or intricately shaped cookies aren't built for speed. Slice-and-bake or drop cookies are sturdier and more likely to survive the journey to their destination.

SIZE UP
Pick a tin or decorative container that is spacious enough for your cookies along with any cushioning materials that will protect them individually while in transit.

PACK TIGHTLY
Wrap each cookie with tissue paper or bubble wrap if they are particularly fragile. Use wax paper or more bubble wrap as you layer them in the tin to help prevent movement.

DOUBLE DOWN
Once the cookies are snug inside their container, place it in a shipping box. Be sure to cushion the box on all sides to keep the cookies from shifting.

SEND SWIFTLY
To guarantee your cookies arrive fresh and full of cheer, choose a two-day shipping option.

I'LL BE HOME TO

GO CAROLING

FILL YOUR PUNCH BOWL WITH LIQUID COURAGE, SO EVERYONE SINGS LOUDER. WE HAVE SENSATIONAL SIPPERS FOR ALL

CANE SYRUP MILK PUNCH

Bittersweet cane syrup takes the edge off this bourbon-lovers' New Orleans-style frozen punch. Make it ahead, and freeze for up to a week. The boozy punch doesn't freeze rock solid, so set it out as your first guests arrive. Give it a quick stir to create just the right slushy consistency. Keep the punch cold by serving in a chilled metal bowl.

- 2 1/2 qt. milk
- 4 cups bourbon
- 2 1/2 cups heavy cream
- 1 cup cane syrup
- 1/4 cup vanilla extract
- Garnishes: sweetened whipped cream, freshly grated nutmeg

Whisk together first 5 ingredients in a freezer-safe container. Cover and freeze 8 to 12 hours. Remove punch from freezer just before serving; stir until desired consistency is reached. Transfer to a chilled metal punch bowl.

MAKES about 1 gal. **HANDS-ON** 5 min.; **TOTAL** 8 hours, 5 min.

SOUTHERN RUSSIAN PUNCH

Try Cathead Hoodoo Chicory Liqueur from Jackson, Mississippi, to boost the bold chicory flavor. If you can't find chicory coffee, use any strong brewed coffee to make this riff on the White Russian. Rim the cups with turbinado sugar before ladling in the punch.

- 1 cup firmly packed dark brown sugar
- 12 cups hot strong brewed chicory coffee
- 6 cups half-and-half
- 2 cups vodka
- 1 cup chicory liqueur
- 1 Tbsp. vanilla extract

Stir together brown sugar and 1 cup water in a medium saucepan. Bring to a boil over high heat. Remove from heat, and cool 10 minutes. Stir together coffee, next 4 ingredients, and 1/2 cup brown sugar syrup in a punch bowl. (Reserve remaining brown sugar syrup for another use.) Serve punch warm.

MAKES about 5 qt. **HANDS-ON** 10 min., **TOTAL** 20 min.

TEXAS SANTA PUNCH

Use no-sugar-added pomegranate juice and dry sparkling wine so the punch doesn't get too sweet. Freshly squeezed lime juice is best. Float frozen cranberries and an ice ring in the punch bowl for a festive chill.

- 1 cup sugar
- 1 qt. pomegranate juice
- 3 cups blanco tequila
- 1 cup fresh lime juice
- 1 cup cranberry juice
- 1 (750-ml.) bottle dry sparkling wine, chilled

1. Bring sugar and 1 cup water to a boil in a small saucepan over high heat, stirring constantly. Boil, stirring constantly, 5 minutes or until sugar dissolves. Cool syrup completely (about 45 minutes).

2. Stir together pomegranate juice, next 3 ingredients, and simple syrup; chill 4 hours. Pour mixture into a punch bowl, and gently stir in sparkling wine just before serving.

Note: We tested with Ocean Spray 100% Cranberry Juice.

MAKES 3 3/4 qt. **HANDS-ON** 30 min.; **TOTAL** 5 hours, 15 min.

Sorghum-Cider Punch, Texas Santa Punch, and Lemon-Gin Fizzy Punch

CRAN-RASPBERRY-VANILLA PUNCH

Be sure to add the raspberry sorbet right before you serve this nonalcoholic punch.

- 6 cups 100% cranberry-raspberry juice
- 6 cups sparkling cranberry-flavored beverage
- 1 Tbsp. vanilla extract
- 1 pt. raspberry sorbet
  Garnish: frozen whole cranberries

Stir together first 3 ingredients in a large punch bowl; scoop sorbet into punch. Serve immediately.

Note: We tested with Ocean Spray Sparkling Cranberry Flavored Beverage.

MAKES about 3 1/2 qt. **HANDS-ON** 10 min., **TOTAL** 10 min.

LEMON-LIME-ROSEMARY PUNCH

Rosemary and lemon elevate this church basement classic to a higher level.

- 6 cups limeade
- 6 cups lemon-lime soft drink
- 1 pt. lemon sorbet
- 1 pt. lime sherbet
- 2 to 3 fresh rosemary sprigs
  Garnishes: lemon and lime slices

Stir together first 2 ingredients in a large punch bowl. Scoop sorbet and sherbet into punch; add fresh rosemary sprigs. Serve immediately.

MAKES about 3 qt. **HANDS-ON** 10 min., **TOTAL** 10 min.

SORGHUM-CIDER PUNCH

Fizzy hard cider and spicy ginger ale add a subtle effervescence. Add a decorative ice ring to keep it chilled.

- 6 1/2 cups chilled unfiltered apple juice
- 3 (12-oz.) bottles chilled ginger ale
- 2 (12-oz.) bottles chilled dry hard cider
- 2 cups bourbon
- 1/4 cup fresh lemon juice
- 1/4 cup sorghum syrup
- 6 dashes of Angostura bitters
  Garnishes: orange slices, cinnamon sticks

Stir together first 7 ingredients. Garnish with oranges and cinnamon sticks, if desired.

Note: We tested with Blenheim Ginger Ale and Angry Orchard Traditional Dry Hard Cider.

MAKES about 1 gal. **HANDS-ON** 15 min., **TOTAL** 15 min.

LEMON-GIN FIZZY PUNCH

We prefer a more botanical-tasting gin like Bristow in this punch.

- 2 cups sugar
- 4 fresh mint sprigs
- 1 vanilla bean, split
- 1 (750-ml.) bottle gin
- 1 3/4 cups fresh lemon juice
- 1 (750-ml.) bottle dry sparkling wine, chilled
  Garnishes: fresh mint leaves, citrus slices

1. Stir together sugar and 2 cups water in a microwave-safe bowl; microwave at HIGH 5 minutes. Stir to dissolve sugar. Add mint and vanilla bean; cool completely. Discard mint and vanilla bean.
2. Stir together gin, lemon juice, 2 cups water, and 2 1/2 cups mint-vanilla syrup. Cover and chill 4 hours. Combine gin mixture and sparkling wine in a large punch bowl.

MAKES 3 1/2 qt. **HANDS-ON** 20 min.; **TOTAL** 5 hours, 5 min.

I'LL BE HOME TO
ADDRESS CHRISTMAS CARDS

CONNECT IN MORE WAYS THAN ONE WITH A CARDS-AND-CAKE PARTY FEATURING OUR BIG WHITE COVER CAKE, ASSORTED SWEETS, COFFEE, TEA, AND BUBBLY

WHITE CAKE 3 WAYS

White cake is a *Southern Living* Christmas tradition. This year we present three cakes wrapped into one. Bake the Basic White Cake. Then you decide which filling and frosting you like best.

BASIC WHITE CAKE LAYERS

A moist cake perfect for layering.

- 1 cup butter, softened
- 2 cups sugar
- 1 Tbsp. loosely packed orange zest
- 1 tsp. vanilla extract
- 3 1/2 cups all-purpose flour
- 1 Tbsp. baking powder
- 1/4 tsp. table salt
- 1 cup milk
- 8 large egg whites
  Shortening

1. Preheat oven to 325°. Beat butter at medium speed with a heavy-duty electric stand mixer until creamy. Gradually add sugar, beating until light and fluffy. Add orange zest and vanilla, and beat until blended. Stir together flour and next 2 ingredients in a large bowl. Add flour mixture to butter mixture alternately with milk, beginning and ending with flour mixture. Beat at low speed just until blended after each addition.

2. Beat egg whites at high speed until stiff peaks form. Stir about one-third of egg whites into batter; fold in remaining egg whites. Spoon batter into 3 greased (with shortening) and floured 9-inch round cake pans.

3. Bake at 325° for 23 to 26 minutes or until a wooden pick inserted in center comes out clean. Cool in pans on wire racks 10 minutes; remove from pans to wire racks, and cool completely (about 1 hour). Frost as desired.

Note: Cake layers may be baked in 3 (8-inch) square disposable aluminum foil pans. Increase bake time to 26 to 28 minutes.

MAKES 3 (9-inch) cake layers.
HANDS-ON 30 min.; **TOTAL** 2 hours, 15 min.

How to Make the Bow

OUR PEPPERMINT COVER CAKE IS SIMPLE TO PREPARE. TAKE IT OVER THE TOP BY MAKING A FONDANT BOW TOPPER. IT'S EASIER TO MAKE THAN YOU MIGHT THINK. BUT START AT LEAST ONE DAY BEFORE CHRISTMAS, SO IT CAN DRY.

ROLL LONG STRIPS: You need: a rollling pin, pizza wheel, ruler, red and white fondant. Roll a chunk of red and a chunk of white fondant into two long strips (about 1/8-inch thick). Use ruler as a guide to cut white strip into thin strips with pizza wheel.

MAKE STRIPED RIBBON: Moisten finger with water; rub one side of one thin white strip. Turn strip, moist side down, and place on red to form a stripe. Repeat with 2 to 3 white strips. Roll gently with rolling pin. Repeat as needed.

CUT, SHAPE, DRY: Make two bow tails; notch one end of each. Create folds with foil props. Form loops by wrapping ribbon around a cardboard roll, leaving 1/4-inch excess. Pinch ends to seal. Repeat. Cut a small rectangle for knot. Let dry 24 hours.

ASSEMBLE BOW: Drape bow tails on cake. Place loops over straight ends of tails on cake, tipping loops at an angle, if desired, and pressing gently into frosting to secure. (Loop ends should touch.) Cover seam with knot, using frosting as glue, if needed.

WITH PEPPERMINT FROSTING

Kids and grown-ups alike will love this fluffy white cake paired with peppermint frosting and filling. Get your little ones to help you in the kitchen. They can smash mints, stir the frosting, and definitely help put the finishing touches on the cake.

FROSTING
- 1 cup butter, softened
- 1 (8-oz.) package cream cheese, softened
- 1/4 tsp. table salt
- 1 tsp. vanilla extract
- 1/2 tsp. peppermint extract
- 1 (32-oz.) package powdered sugar
- 2 to 3 Tbsp. milk
- 12 round hard peppermint candies

ADDITIONAL INGREDIENT
Basic White Cake Layers

1. Prepare Frosting: Beat first 3 ingredients at medium speed with an electric mixer 1 to 2 minutes or until creamy. Add vanilla and peppermint extracts, and beat until blended. Gradually add powdered sugar alternately with 2 Tbsp. milk. Beat at low speed until blended and smooth after each addition. Add up to 1 Tbsp. milk, 1 tsp. at a time, beating until frosting reaches desired consistency.
2. Reserve 2 cups frosting in a small bowl. Process peppermint candies in a food processor until finely crushed. Stir 1/4 cup crushed candies into reserved 2 cups frosting.
3. Place 1 Basic White Cake Layer on a serving platter. Spread 1 cup peppermint candy frosting mixture over cake layer. Top with second layer, and spread remaining 1 cup peppermint candy frosting over cake layer. Top with third cake layer, and spread top and sides of cake with remaining plain peppermint frosting. Sprinkle top with remaining crushed peppermint candies.

MAKES 10 to 12 servings. **HANDS-ON** 30 min.; **TOTAL** 2 hours, 45 min., including cake layers

WITH CRANBERRY FILLING AND ORANGE BUTTERCREAM

FILLING
- 1 (12-oz.) jar cherry preserves
- 3/4 cup granulated sugar
- 1/4 cup fresh orange juice
- 3 1/2 cups fresh cranberries, divided

BUTTERCREAM
- 1 cup butter, softened
- 1 (8-oz.) package cream cheese, softened
- 1/4 tsp. table salt
- 1 (32-oz.) package powdered sugar
- 2 Tbsp. fresh orange juice
- 1 tsp. vanilla extract
- 1 to 2 Tbsp. milk (optional)

ADDITIONAL INGREDIENT
Basic White Cake Layers

1. Prepare Filling: Bring first 3 ingredients and 3 cups cranberries to a boil in a medium saucepan over medium-high heat. Boil, stirring often, 5 to 6 minutes or until cranberries begin to split and mixture begins to thicken. Transfer 1 cup cranberry mixture to a small bowl, and stir in remaining $1/2$ cup whole cranberries. (This will be the Cranberry Topping.) Transfer remaining hot Cranberry Filling mixture to another small bowl. Cool both mixtures completely. Cover and chill 8 to 12 hours.

2. Prepare Buttercream: Beat butter and next 2 ingredients at medium speed with an electric mixer 1 to 2 minutes or until creamy. Gradually add powdered sugar alternately with orange juice. Beat at low speed until blended and smooth after each addition. Stir in vanilla. If desired, add 1 to 2 Tbsp. milk, 1 tsp. at a time, beating until frosting reaches desired consistency.

3. Place 1 Basic White Cake Layer on a serving platter. Spoon 1 $1/2$ cups orange buttercream into a zip-top plastic freezer bag. Snip 1 corner of bag to make a small hole. Pipe a ring of frosting around cake layer just inside the top edge. Spread cake layer with half of chilled Cranberry Filling (without whole berries), spreading to edge of piped frosting. Top with second cake layer. Repeat procedure with frosting and remaining Cranberry Filling (without whole berries). Top with third layer. Spread remaining orange buttercream over top and sides of cake. Pipe a ring of frosting around top cake layer just inside the top edge. Spread top cake layer with Cranberry Topping (with whole berries), spreading to edge of piped frosting.

*Frozen cranberries, thawed, may be substituted.

MAKES 10 to 12 servings. **HANDS-ON** 45 min.; **TOTAL** 11 hours, including cake layers

WITH BOURBON BUTTERCREAM AND SEVEN-MINUTE FROSTING

BUTTERCREAM
- $1/2$ cup butter, softened
- 1 (16-oz.) package powdered sugar
- 3 $1/2$ Tbsp. milk
- 2 Tbsp. bourbon
- 1 tsp. vanilla extract
- 2 dashes of bitters

ADDITIONAL INGREDIENT
Basic White Cake Layers

FROSTING
- 2 large egg whites
- 1 $1/2$ cups sugar
- $1/8$ tsp. table salt
- 2 tsp. light corn syrup
- 1 tsp. vanilla extract

GARNISHES
Sugar-Coated Orange Slices
Sparkling Cherries

1. Prepare Buttercream: Beat butter in a medium bowl at medium speed with an electric mixer until creamy. Gradually add powdered sugar, beating at low speed until blended after each addition. Gradually add milk and next 3 ingredients, beating at low speed until blended after each addition. Increase speed to medium, and beat until smooth.

2. Place 1 Basic White Cake Layer on a serving platter. Spread half of buttercream over cake layer. Top with second layer, and spread remaining buttercream over cake layer. Top with third cake layer.

3. Prepare Frosting: Pour water to depth of 1 $1/2$ inches into bottom of a double boiler over medium heat; bring to a boil. Stir together egg whites, next 3 ingredients, and $1/2$ cup water in top of double boiler; beat at low speed with a handheld electric mixer until blended. Place top of double boiler over boiling water, and increase mixer speed to high. Beat 7 minutes or until soft glossy peaks form and frosting is spreading consistency. Remove from heat, and stir in vanilla. Spread immediately over top and sides of cake.

MAKES 10 to 12 servings. **HANDS-ON** 45 min.; **TOTAL** 3 hours, including cake layers but not including garnishes

Sugar-Coated Orange Slices

Cut 2 medium **oranges** into thin slices. Stir together 1 cup granulated **sugar,** $1/4$ cup **bourbon,** $1/4$ cup **water,** and 2 tsp. fresh **lemon juice** in a deep, 10-inch skillet. Cook over medium heat, whisking occasionally, 3 to 5 minutes or just until sugar dissolves. Add orange slices in a single layer, and simmer 10 minutes. Turn slices over, and simmer 5 more minutes or until tender. Remove orange slices, 1 at a time, shaking off excess syrup. Transfer to a wire rack, and let dry completely (about 4 hours).

HANDS-ON 15 min.; **TOTAL** 4 hours, 30 min.

Sparkling Cherries

Drain 1 (10-oz.) jar **maraschino cherries** with stems, and return cherries to jar. Pour $1/2$ cup **bourbon** into jar, and add just enough **water** to cover cherries. Cover with lid, and chill 8 hours. Drain cherries, and arrange a single layer on paper towels. Sprinkle 1 envelope **unflavored gelatin** over $1/4$ cup water in a small saucepan; let stand 2 minutes. Cook over low heat, stirring often, 5 minutes or just until gelatin dissolves. Transfer gelatin to a small bowl; whisk until foamy. Dip cherries, 1 at a time, in gelatin, shaking off excess. Sprinkle cherries with $3/4$ cup granulated **sugar;** transfer to **wax paper,** and let dry completely (about 3 hours).

HANDS-ON 20 min.; **TOTAL** 8 hours, 20 min.

GINGERBREAD LAYER CAKE WITH BUTTERMILK BUTTERCREAM

Fiery-sweet ginger and cinnamon combine with bitter coffee and molasses for a fantastic cake that pairs perfectly with the gorgeous tangy buttercream frosting. Look for small jars of crystallized ginger—sometimes called candied ginger—in the spice section at the supermarket. If you don't see it there, check the Asian aisle or specialty markets.

- 3 3/4 **cups all-purpose flour**
- 1/2 **cup chopped crystallized ginger**
- 2 **tsp. baking powder**
- 2 **tsp. baking soda**
- 1 **tsp. ground cinnamon**
- 3/4 **tsp. table salt**
- 1/4 **tsp. ground cloves**
- 1 **cup butter, softened**
- 1 1/2 **cups firmly packed light brown sugar**
- 3 **large eggs, separated**
- 1 1/2 **cups hot strong brewed coffee**
- 3/4 **cup light molasses**
  Shortening
  Buttermilk Buttercream
  Spiced Glazed Pecans

1. Preheat oven to 350°. Process first 7 ingredients in food processor about 1 minute or until ginger is finely ground. Beat butter at medium speed with a heavy-duty electric stand mixer until creamy. Gradually add brown sugar, beating until light and fluffy. Add egg yolks, 1 at a time, beating until blended after each addition.

2. Whisk together coffee and molasses. Add flour mixture to butter mixture alternately with coffee mixture, beginning and ending with flour mixture, beating at low speed just until blended after each addition. Beat egg whites at high speed until stiff peaks form. Stir about one-third of egg whites into batter; fold in remaining egg whites. Spoon batter into 3 greased (with shortening) and floured 8-inch square disposable aluminum foil cake pans.

3. Bake at 350° for 22 to 26 minutes or until a wooden pick inserted in center comes out clean. Cool in pans on wire racks 10 minutes; remove from pans to wire racks, and cool completely (about 1 hour).

4. Place 1 cake layer on a serving platter. Spread 3/4 cup Buttermilk Buttercream over cake layer. Top with second layer, and spread 3/4 cup buttercream over cake layer. Top with third cake layer, and spread top and sides of cake with remaining frosting. Arrange Spiced Glazed Pecans in a ring on top of cake, pressing gently to adhere.

Note: Cake layers may be baked in 3 (8-inch) round cake pans. Decrease bake time to 20 to 24 minutes.

MAKES 10 to 12 servings. **HANDS-ON** 30 min.; **TOTAL** 2 hours, 50 min., including buttercream and pecans

Buttermilk Buttercream

- 1 **cup butter, softened**
- 1 **(32-oz.) package powdered sugar**
- 5 **to 8 Tbsp. buttermilk**
- 2 **Tbsp. fresh lemon juice**
- 1 **tsp. vanilla extract**
  Pinch of table salt

Beat butter at medium speed with an electric mixer 1 to 2 minutes or until creamy. Gradually add powdered sugar alternately with 5 Tbsp. buttermilk. Beat at low speed until blended and smooth after each addition. Stir in lemon juice, vanilla, and salt. If desired, add up to 3 Tbsp. buttermilk, 1 Tbsp. at a time, beating until frosting reaches desired consistency.

MAKES 4 1/2 cups. **HANDS-ON** 10 min., **TOTAL** 10 min.

Spiced Glazed Pecans

- 1/4 **cup sugar**
- 1/4 **tsp. ground cinnamon**
- 1/4 **tsp. ground ginger**
- 1/8 **tsp. ground cloves**
- 1 **cup coarsely chopped pecans**
  Vegetable cooking spray
  Wax paper

Stir together first 4 ingredients in a small heavy saucepan over medium heat. Stir in pecans, and cook, stirring constantly, 7 to 8 minutes or until sugar melts and coats pecans. (Sugar will become grainy before it melts.) Spread mixture in an even layer on lightly greased (with cooking spray) wax paper, and cool 20 minutes.

MAKES 1 cup. **HANDS-ON** 15 min., **TOTAL** 35 min.

MILK PUNCH TRES LECHES CAKE

We love this sheet cake because it's a great traveler. Bake the cake at least a day before you plan to serve it, so it has plenty of time to soak up all the delicious creamy syrup. Top the cake with whipped cream, and take it to your party. Or use a round cutter to cut out small cakes, and top each with billowy sweetened whipped cream and a shaving of fresh nutmeg.

- 1/2 **cup butter, softened**
- 1 **cup granulated sugar**
- 7 **large eggs, separated**
- 2 1/2 **cups all-purpose flour**
- 1 1/2 **tsp. baking powder**
- 1/2 **tsp. table salt**
- 1 **cup milk**
- 1 **tsp. vanilla extract**
  Vegetable cooking spray
- 1 **(14-oz.) can sweetened condensed milk**
- 1 **(12-oz.) can evaporated milk**
- 1/2 **cup coffee liqueur**
- 1 1/2 **cups heavy cream**
- 3/4 **cup powdered sugar**
  Garnish: freshly grated nutmeg

1. Preheat oven to 350°. Beat butter at medium speed with an electric mixer until creamy. Gradually add granulated sugar, beating until light and fluffy. Add egg yolks, 1 at a time, beating until blended after each addition. Stir together flour, baking powder, and salt. Add flour mixture to butter mixture alternately with milk, beginning and ending with flour mixture. Beat at low speed until blended after each addition, stopping to scrape bowl as needed. Stir in vanilla. Wash and dry beaters.

2. Using clean, dry beaters, beat egg whites at high speed until stiff peaks form. Stir about one-third of egg whites into batter; fold in remaining egg whites. Spoon batter into a lightly greased (with cooking spray) 13- x 9- inch pan.

3. Bake at 350° for 23 to 25 minutes or until a wooden pick inserted in center comes out clean. Cool in pan on a wire rack 10 minutes.

4. Pierce top of cake several times with a long wooden pick. Whisk together condensed milk, evaporated milk, and liqueur. Gradually pour mixture over warm cake, about 1/2 cup at a time, allowing mixture to soak into cake before adding more. Let cake stand at room temperature 3 hours. Cover and chill 8 to 12 hours.

5. Beat heavy cream and powdered sugar at medium-high speed with an electric mixer until stiff peaks form; spread over cake.

MAKES 16 servings. **HANDS-ON** 45 min.; **TOTAL** 13 hours, 20 min.

AMBROSIA STREUSEL BARS WITH SHORT-BREAD CRUST

When the baked bars are completely cool, use the foil as a handle to remove the whole recipe from pan, so they're easier to cut.

CRUST

2 1/2 cups all-purpose flour
 1/2 cup powdered sugar
 1/2 tsp. kosher salt
 1/2 tsp. baking powder
1 1/4 cups cold butter, cut into pieces
 2 large egg yolks

FILLING

1 1/2 cups fresh pineapple chunks
 1 cup sweet orange marmalade
 2 Tbsp. granulated sugar
 2 Tbsp. fresh lemon juice
 2 tsp. cornstarch
 1/4 tsp. kosher salt
 1/2 cup drained maraschino cherries, coarsely chopped

STREUSEL

 1/2 cup granulated sugar
 1/2 cup all-purpose flour
 1/8 tsp. kosher salt
 3 Tbsp. cold butter, cut into pieces
 1 cup toasted coconut chips (such as Dang)

1. Prepare Crust: Preheat oven to 400°. Line bottom and sides of a 13- x 9-inch pan with heavy-duty aluminum foil, allowing 2 or 3 inches to extend over sides. Lightly grease foil with butter, and dust with flour.

2. Pulse flour and next 3 ingredients in a food processor 2 to 3 times or until combined. Add 1 1/4 cups cold butter pieces, 2 or 3 pieces at a time, pulsing after each addition. Add egg yolks, 1 at a time, pulsing after each addition. Process until mixture is crumbly. Press mixture into bottom of prepared pan to form a smooth layer.

3. Bake at 400° for 12 minutes; cool in pan on a wire rack 15 minutes.

4. Meanwhile, prepare Filling: Pulse pineapple in food processor until coarsely chopped. Bring pineapple, marmalade, and next 4 ingredients to a boil in a saucepan over medium-high heat. Boil, stirring often, 1 minute. Remove from heat, and let stand 10 minutes. Stir in cherries, and spread mixture in prepared crust.

5. Prepare Streusel: Stir together 1/2 cup granulated sugar and next 2 ingredients in a medium bowl; cut butter into sugar mixture with a pastry blender until mixture resembles coarse meal. Stir in coconut. Sprinkle streusel over pineapple mixture.

6. Bake at 400° for 30 minutes or until golden brown. Cool completely in pan on wire rack (about 45 minutes). Lift bars from pan, using foil sides as handles. Gently remove and discard foil; cut mixture into squares.

MAKES 12 to 16 squares. **HANDS-ON** 30 min.; **TOTAL** 2 hours, 10 min.

COCONUT PUDDING

Look for unsweetened shaved coconut flakes at natural food stores for a pretty not-too-sweet topping on this fantastic custard. Or try the roasted coconut chips that are popping up on snack aisles in many supermarkets. The chips are also available online at retailers such as Amazon.

 1 cup sugar
 5 Tbsp. cornstarch
 1/4 tsp. table salt
1 3/4 cups milk
1 1/2 cups heavy cream
 1 (13.5-oz.) can unsweetened coconut milk
 1/4 cup butter, cut into 1/2-inch pieces
 2 tsp. vanilla bean paste
 Sweetened whipped cream
 Garnish: toasted flaked coconut

1. Whisk together first 3 ingredients in a large heavy saucepan; whisk in milk and next 2 ingredients. Bring mixture to a boil over medium heat, whisking constantly. Boil 1 minute, whisking constantly. Remove from heat.

2. Whisk in butter and vanilla bean paste. Spoon pudding into serving dishes; cover and chill 4 hours. Dollop with sweetened whipped cream.

MAKES about 3 1/2 cups. **HANDS-ON** 20 min.; **TOTAL** 4 hours, 20 min.

Peppermint Pudding: Omit coconut milk and vanila bean paste. Prepare recipe as directed, increasing milk to 3 1/2 cups, and stirring 1/4 tsp. **peppermint extract** into pudding with butter in Step 2. Remove 1 1/2 cups pudding to a 2-cup glass measuring cup, and whisk in 5 to 6 drops **red food coloring gel.** Spoon 2 Tbsp. red pudding into each of 12 (6- to 8-oz.) bowls or glasses; top with remaining uncolored pudding. Cover and chill 4 hours. Top with **sweetened whipped cream** and **crushed peppermint,** if desired.

MAKES 6 servings. **HANDS-ON** 30 min.; **TOTAL** 4 hours, 30 min.

MEXICAN HOT CHOCOLATE TRIFLE

This decadent recipe will wow your guests and feed a crowd. It's actually three amazing recipes rolled into one.

- 6 oz. unsweetened chocolate baking squares, chopped
- 3/4 cup butter, softened
- 1 1/2 cups granulated sugar
- 1 1/2 cups firmly packed light brown sugar
- 3 large eggs, separated
- 1 Tbsp. vanilla extract
- 2 3/4 cups cake flour
- 1/4 cup unsweetened cocoa
- 1 Tbsp. baking powder
- 1 tsp. ground cinnamon
- 3/4 tsp. table salt
- 2 1/4 cups milk
  Parchment paper
  Chocolate Ganache
  Marshmallow Topping

1. Preheat oven to 350°. Microwave chocolate in a small microwave-safe bowl at MEDIUM (50% power) 1 minute; stir. Microwave 2 to 2 1/2 more minutes or until melted, stirring at 30-second intervals. Beat butter at medium speed with a heavy-duty electric stand mixer until creamy; gradually add granulated sugar and brown sugar, beating well. Add egg yolks, 1 at a time, beating until blended after each addition. Add melted chocolate and vanilla, beating at low speed just until blended.

2. Sift together cake flour and next 4 ingredients in a medium bowl. Add flour mixture to butter mixture alternately with milk, beginning and ending with flour mixture. Beat at low speed just until blended after each addition. Wash and dry beaters.

3. Using clean, dry beaters, beat egg whites at high speed until stiff peaks form. Stir about one-third of egg whites into batter; fold in remaining egg whites. Spoon batter into 3 greased (with butter) and floured (9-inch) round cake pans.

4. Bake at 350° for 28 to 34 minutes or until a wooden pick inserted in center comes out clean. Cool in pans on wire racks 10 minutes; remove from pans to parchment paper-lined wire racks,

and cool completely (about 1 hour). Cut cake layers into 1-inch cubes.

5. Layer about one-third of cake cubes in a 4-qt. bowl. Top with one-third each of Chocolate Ganache and Marshmallow Topping. Repeat layers twice.

MAKES 15 to 20 servings. **HANDS-ON** 40 min.; **TOTAL** 3 hours, including ganache and topping

Chocolate Ganache

- 3 (4-oz.) semisweet chocolate baking bars, chopped
- 2 (4-oz.) bittersweet chocolate baking bars, chopped
- 1 1/2 to 1 3/4 cups heavy cream

Microwave first 2 ingredients and 1 1/2 cups cream in a medium-size microwave-safe bowl at MEDIUM (50% power) 1 minute; stir. Microwave 3 to 3 1/2 more minutes or until melted and smooth, stirring at 30-second intervals. Stir in up to 1/4 cup cream,

1 Tbsp. at a time, until desired consistency is reached.

Note: If desired, reserve 3/4 cup ganache to serve with trifle. To reheat, microwave mixture in a microwave-safe bowl at MEDIUM (50% power) for 30 to 60 seconds, stirring at 30-second intervals.

MAKES 3 1/2 cups. **HANDS-ON** 15 min., **TOTAL** 15 min.

Marshmallow Topping

- 3 (7 1/2-oz.) jars marshmallow crème
- 3 cups heavy cream, divided

Beat marshmallow crème and 1 cup heavy cream at low speed with an electric mixer 1 to 1 1/2 minutes or until combined and smooth. Add remaining heavy cream, and beat at medium speed 2 to 3 minutes or until light and fluffy.

MAKES about 7 cups. **HANDS-ON** 5 min., **TOTAL** 5 min.

Mexican Hot Chocolate Trifle

CHRISTMAS EVE

AS THE HECTIC HOLIDAY RUSH SLOWS TO A HUSH, GATHER AROUND THE TABLE WITH LOVED ONES. KEEP A COMFORTING CASSEROLE OR STEW WARM ALL EVENING TO SATISFY EARLY BIRDS AND THE MIDNIGHT MASS CROWD

Chicken Enchiladas

CHICKEN ENCHILADAS

Make the enchilada sauce up to three days ahead; the flavors will meld and only get better.

SAUCE

4 Anaheim chiles or 3 large jalapeño peppers

3 poblano peppers

6 plum tomatoes, halved

1 onion, cut into wedges

7 garlic cloves, unpeeled

1 (28-oz.) can tomato sauce

2 cups chicken broth

1 Tbsp. ground chipotle chile pepper

1 Tbsp. chili powder

1 tsp. ground cumin

1 tsp. dried oregano

1 1/2 tsp. kosher salt, divided

ENCHILADAS

1 (8-oz.) block Monterey Jack cheese

12 (6-inch) corn tortillas

4 cups shredded deli-roasted chicken

1/2 (8-oz.) block sharp Cheddar cheese, shredded

2 avocados, chopped

1/2 cup torn cilantro leaves

2 Tbsp. fresh lime juice

1. Prepare Sauce: Preheat broiler with oven rack 5 inches from heat. Broil first 5 ingredients on a foil-lined baking sheet, 6 minutes or until peppers blister and char. Remove from oven; let stand 10 minutes or until cool enough to handle. Peel and seed peppers; peel garlic. Reduce oven temperature to 375°.

2. Bring tomato sauce, next 5 ingredients, broiled vegetables, and 1 tsp. salt to a boil in a large saucepan over high heat, stirring occasionally. Reduce heat to medium-low; cook, stirring occasionally, 35 minutes. Remove from heat; cool 10 minutes. Process with a handheld blender or in batches in a food processor or blender until smooth.

3. Prepare Enchiladas: Shred 2 oz. Monterey Jack cheese to yield 1/2 cup. Cut remaining Monterey Jack cheese into 12 (4- x 1/2-inch) sticks.

4. Spread 1 cup enchilada sauce in a 13- x 9-inch baking dish coated lightly with cooking spray. Spread a thin layer of sauce on 1 tortilla. Place 1/3 cup chicken and 1 Monterey Jack cheese stick on edge of tortilla, and roll up tortilla. Place in baking dish, seam side down. Repeat with remaining tortillas, chicken, and cheese sticks. Pour 2 1/2 cups sauce over tortillas. Chill remaining sauce for another use. Bake enchiladas at 375° for 30 minutes.

5. Top enchiladas with shredded Cheddar and shredded Monterey Jack cheese; bake 5 more minutes or until cheese is melted. Remove from oven; let stand 10 minutes.

6. Meanwhile, combine avocado, next 2 ingredients, and remaining 1/2 tsp. salt; serve with enchiladas.

MAKES 6 to 8 servings. **HANDS-ON** 45 min.; **TOTAL** 1 hour, 15 min.

SLOW-COOKER SUNDAY SAUCE

Canned whole peeled tomatoes work best in this delicious sauce. Use a pair of kitchen shears to coarsely cut them in the can or squeeze them by hand.

- 3 lb. boneless pork shoulder, cut into 2-inch cubes
- 1 1/2 tsp. kosher salt
- 1 tsp. ground black pepper
- 3 Tbsp. olive oil, divided
- 1 lb. sweet Italian sausage, casings removed, chopped
- 4 oz. pancetta, chopped
- 2 3/4 cups chopped yellow onion
- 1 cup chopped carrots
- 8 garlic cloves, chopped
- 1 cup red wine
- 1 (28-oz.) can whole peeled tomatoes, chopped
- 1 (28-oz.) can tomato puree
- 3 fresh thyme sprigs
- 2 fresh oregano sprigs
- 1 fresh rosemary sprig
- 1/2 cup reduced-sodium chicken broth
  Hot cooked pasta

1. Stir together first 3 ingredients; sauté, in batches, in 2 Tbsp. hot oil in a large skillet over medium-high heat 10 minutes. Transfer to an 8-qt. slow cooker.

2. Sauté sausage in remaining 1 Tbsp. hot oil in skillet 6 minutes or until no longer pink. Transfer to slow cooker; reserving drippings in skillet.

3. Sauté pancetta in hot drippings in skillet over medium heat 7 minutes or until crisp. Add onion, carrots, and garlic; sauté 5 minutes or until tender. Increase heat to high; add wine. Bring to a boil, stirring to loosen browned bits from bottom of skillet. Cook, stirring constantly, 5 minutes or until reduced by half.

4. Add tomatoes and tomato puree; bring to a boil. Transfer to slow cooker; add thyme and next 3 ingredients. Cover; cook on HIGH 1 hour. Reduce to LOW; cook 7 hours. Discard herbs; serve sauce over hot cooked pasta.

MAKES 8 1/2 cups. **HANDS-ON** 1 hour, 10 min.; **TOTAL** 9 hours, 10 min.

FAUX CASSOULET

This Southern version of the French classic comes together in a fraction of the time required to make the original because we use humble chicken thighs and country-style pork ribs. For easy sides, grab a loaf of crusty bread, and toss a tangy vinaigrette with fresh pear slices, toasted pecans, escarole, and frisée or a mix of your favorite winter greens.

- 6 skin-on, bone-in chicken thighs
- 1/4 cup olive oil
- 1 lb. boneless country-style pork ribs, cut into 1 1/2-inch pieces
- 12 oz. thick bacon, chopped
- 1 small onion, chopped
- 2 medium carrots, chopped
- 2 celery ribs, chopped
- 1 (28-oz.) can whole tomatoes, drained and chopped
- 3 garlic cloves, minced
- 1 (16-oz.) package smoked sausage, sliced
- 2 (15.8-oz.) cans great Northern beans, drained and rinsed
- 3/4 cup reduced-sodium chicken broth
- 2 Tbsp. chopped parsley
- 2 tsp. chopped thyme
- 2 tsp. chopped oregano
- 2 tsp. chopped rosemary
- 2 Tbsp. butter, melted
- 1 1/2 cups panko (Japanese breadcrumbs)

1. Sprinkle chicken with kosher salt and freshly ground black pepper; cook half of chicken in 1 Tbsp. hot oil in a large skillet over medium-high heat 5 minutes on each side. Remove from skillet; repeat with 1 Tbsp. oil and remaining chicken. Wipe skillet clean. Sprinkle pork with salt and pepper, and sauté in remaining 2 Tbsp. hot olive oil in skillet, 3 minutes or until browned. Remove pork; wipe skillet clean.

2. Preheat oven to 300°. Cook bacon in skillet over medium heat, stirring occasionally, 8 minutes or until crisp; drain bacon, reserving 2 Tbsp. drippings in skillet. Add onion, carrots, and celery, and cook over medium heat, stirring occasionally, 8 minutes.

Stir in chopped tomatoes, and cook 1 minute. Add garlic, and cook 1 minute.

3. Add bacon, sausage, and reserved pork to tomato mixture; bring to a simmer. Stir in beans and next 5 ingredients. Season with salt and pepper. Arrange chicken in a single layer, skin side up, in a large baking dish. Spoon bean mixture over chicken.

4. Stir together melted butter and breadcrumbs, and sprinkle over cassoulet. Bake at 300° for 2 1/2 to 3 hours or until golden brown and bubbly. Let stand 10 minutes before serving.

MAKES 6 to 8 servings.
HANDS-ON 1 hour, 20 min.; **TOTAL** 4 hours

HARVEST BEEF SOUP

Edamame and kale are colorful and unexpected additions to this comforting soup. Feed a crowd, or freeze some for later.

- 5 thick bacon slices
- 1 onion, halved and sliced
- 8 oz. baby portobello mushrooms, quartered
- 3 garlic cloves, minced
- 1 tsp. kosher salt
- 1 tsp. ground black pepper
- 3 lb. top round steak, trimmed and cubed
- 2 Tbsp. olive oil
- 3 Tbsp. tomato paste
- 1 cup red wine
- 3 (1-oz.) containers concentrated beef stock (from a 4.66-oz. package)
- 1 lb. carrots, peeled and sliced
- 1 lb. parsnips, peeled and sliced
- 1 lb. butternut squash, cubed
- 4 fresh thyme sprigs
- 4 fresh oregano sprigs
- 1 (10-oz.) package refrigerated shelled edamame
- 4 cups baby kale
- 1 to 2 Tbsp. balsamic vinegar Parsley Couscous

1. Cook bacon in a large Dutch oven over medium heat 5 minutes or until crisp. Remove bacon, reserving 1/4 cup drippings in Dutch oven. (Reserve bacon for another use.) Cook onion in hot drippings over medium-high heat, stirring occasionally, 4 minutes. Add mushrooms, and cook, stirring often, 5 minutes. Add garlic, and cook, stirring often, 1 minute. Remove mixture from Dutch oven, using a slotted spoon.

2. Sprinkle salt and pepper over beef. Cook beef in hot olive oil, in 3 batches, over medium-high heat, stirring often, 5 minutes or until browned. Transfer beef to a bowl. Add tomato paste to Dutch oven, and cook, stirring often, 2 minutes. Stir in wine, and cook, stirring often, 4 minutes. Stir in concentrated beef stock, beef, and 8 cups water; bring to a boil. Cover and reduce heat to low. Cook, stirring occasionally, 1 hour.

3. Add carrots, next 4 ingredients, and onion mixture to Dutch oven. Cover and cook over low heat, stirring occasionally, 1 hour.

4. Add edamame and kale to Dutch oven, and cook, stirring often, 3 minutes. Discard herb sprigs. Stir in balsamic vinegar. Serve with Parsley Couscous.

MAKES 4 1/2 qt. **HANDS-ON** 1 hour, 20 min.; **TOTAL** 3 hours, 30 min., including couscous

Parsley Couscous

Cook 1 cup **Israeli couscous** according to package directions. Stir in 1/2 cup chopped fresh flat-leaf **parsley.**

MAKES 1 1/4 cups. **HANDS-ON** 10 min., **TOTAL** 10 min.

CHICKEN-AND-BISCUIT COBBLER

This family-friendly dish is sure to become a new holiday staple. Use fresh herbs in the cobbler.

- 3 Tbsp. butter
- 1 cup sliced carrots
- 1 medium onion, chopped
- 2 (8-oz.) packages fresh mushrooms, quartered
- 2 garlic cloves, minced
- 1/2 cup dry white wine
- 1/3 cup all-purpose flour
- 3 cups reduced-sodium chicken broth
- 3/4 cup whipping cream
- 1 Tbsp. white wine vinegar
- 3 Tbsp. sliced chives
- 3 Tbsp. chopped parsley
- 2 tsp. chopped rosemary
- 2 tsp. chopped thyme leaves
- 8 cups shredded cooked chicken
  Kosher salt
  Freshly ground black pepper
- 2 1/2 cups self-rising flour
- 1/2 tsp. sugar
- 1 1/4 cups chilled buttermilk
- 1/2 cup butter, melted
- 1/2 cup chopped cooked bacon (about 5 thick bacon slices)
  Garnishes: chopped fresh chives, parsley

1. Preheat oven to 400°. Melt 3 Tbsp. butter in a Dutch oven over medium-high heat. Add carrots and onion, and sauté 5 minutes. Add mushrooms, and sauté 5 minutes or until tender. Stir in garlic; sauté 2 minutes. Add wine; cook 2 minutes. Sprinkle with 1/3 cup all-purpose flour, and cook, stirring constantly, 3 minutes. Slowly add broth, stirring constantly; bring mixture to a boil, stirring constantly, 2 minutes or until thickened. Stir in cream and next 5 ingredients. Stir in chicken, and season to taste with salt and pepper. Cover and remove from heat.

2. Whisk together 2 1/2 cups self-rising flour and 1/2 tsp. sugar in a medium bowl. Stir together buttermilk and 1/2 cup melted butter in a small bowl. Stir buttermilk mixture and bacon into flour mixture until dough pulls away from sides of bowl.

3. Return chicken mixture to medium-high heat; cook, stirring constantly, 2 minutes or until bubbly and hot. Spoon mixture into buttered 3-qt. ceramic or glass baking dish. Drop biscuit dough by level 1/4 cupfuls, 1/2 inch apart, onto chicken mixture.
4. Bake at 400° for 30 to 35 minutes or until browned and bubbly.

MAKES 8 servings. **HANDS-ON** 1 hour, 15 min.; **TOTAL** 1 hour, 45 min.

BLACK-EYED PEA, COLLARD, AND SWEET POTATO STEW

Don't be intimidated by the length of the ingredient list for this thrifty Southern stew. The majority of the ingredients are used to make a fantastic stock that starts with the Southern classic: potlikker. Then we use loads of fresh, aromatic vegetables, herbs, and spices to round out the flavor. Serve the stew ladled over hot cooked rice, and sprinkle with the fresh herbs.

- 1 **bunch fresh collard greens (1 lb.)**
- 6 **whole cloves**
- 1 **medium-size yellow onion, halved**
- 2 **Tbsp. vegetable oil**
- 10 **parsley stems**
- 10 **cilantro stems**
- 4 **fresh thyme sprigs**
- 4 **celery ribs, peeled and coarsely chopped**
- 3 **bay leaves**
- 3 **large carrots, peeled and coarsely chopped**
- 1 **garlic bulb, halved**
- 2 **(2-inch) pieces fresh ginger, peeled and crushed**
- 1 **(14.5-oz.) can diced tomatoes, drained**
- 1 **tsp. dried crushed red pepper**
- 4 **Tbsp. sugar**
- 5 **Tbsp. rice vinegar**
- 4 **Tbsp. soy sauce**
- 2 **smoked ham hocks**
- 1 **lb. chicken wings**
- 1 **lb. pork neck bones**
- 1 **(16-oz.) package dried black-eyed peas**
- 2 **medium-size sweet potatoes, peeled and cubed**
- 2 **tsp. kosher salt**
- **Freshly ground black pepper Hot sauce**
- 6 **cups hot cooked rice**
- 1/4 **cup coarsely chopped fresh flat-leaf parsley leaves**
- 1/4 **cup coarsely chopped fresh cilantro leaves**

1. Remove and chop collard stems. Chop collard leaves. Insert 3 whole cloves in each onion half, and place onions, cut sides down, in hot oil in a Dutch oven over medium-high heat. Add parsley stems, next 9 ingredients, and collard stems. Cook, stirring gently, 10 minutes or until vegetables begin to soften. Add 4 qt. water, and whisk in sugar, rice vinegar, and soy sauce; cook 1 minute, stirring to blend. Add ham hocks, chicken wings, and pork necks. Bring to a boil, skimming off foam. Reduce heat to low; simmer 3 hours or until ham hocks are tender and potlikker is rich in flavor, skimming as necessary.
2. Meanwhile, rinse and sort peas. Bring peas and water to cover to a boil in a large saucepan over high heat. Cook 2 minutes, skimming off foam. Drain peas.
3. Pour potlikker through a fine wire-mesh strainer into an 8-cup glass measuring cup, reserving hocks, chicken wings, and pork neck bones. Discard remaining solids. Remove and chop meat from ham hocks, chicken wings, and pork neck bones; discard bones and skin.
4. Wipe Dutch oven clean, and return potlikker to Dutch oven. Add drained peas, chopped ham, chicken, pork, and collard leaves to potlikker. Bring to a boil over high heat, reduce heat to medium-low, and simmer, stirring occasionally, 15 minutes or until peas are just tender. Stir in sweet potatoes, and cook, stirring occasionally, 10 minutes or until peas and sweet potatoes are tender. Stir in 2 tsp. kosher salt. Add freshly ground black pepper and hot sauce to taste. Adjust seasoning, if desired. Serve stew over hot cooked rice, and sprinkle with chopped fresh flat-leaf parsley and chopped fresh cilantro. Serve with hot sauce, if desired.

MAKES 1 1/2 qt. **HANDS-ON** 1 hour, 30 min.; **TOTAL** 4 hours, 20 min.

SPINACH LASAGNA

Always a crowd-pleaser, this lasagna is full of hearty veggies.

- 1 **(24-oz.) jar pasta sauce**
- 1/4 **tsp. dried crushed red pepper**
- 2 1/3 **cups heavy cream, divided**
- 32 **oz. ricotta cheese**
- 1 **oz. fresh basil, chopped**
- 1/2 **tsp. kosher salt**
- 2 **cups freshly shredded Parmesan cheese, divided**
- 4 **large shallots, thinly sliced**
- 1/3 **cup olive oil**
- 8 **garlic cloves, minced**
- 2 **(9-oz.) packages fresh baby spinach**
- 2 **Tbsp. butter**
- 1 **Tbsp. all-purpose flour**
- 12 **no-boil lasagna noodles**
- 1 **(12-oz.) jar roasted red bell pepper strips, drained**

1. Preheat oven to 350°. Combine first 2 ingredients and 1 cup cream. Separately combine ricotta, next 2 ingredients, and 1 cup Parmesan. Sauté shallots in hot oil in a Dutch oven over medium-high heat 3 minutes. Add garlic; sauté 1 minute. Remove shallot mixture.
2. Add one-third of spinach to Dutch oven; cook over medium-high heat 1 minute or until wilted. Place spinach in a colander; drain. Repeat with remaining spinach.
3. Cook butter and flour in Dutch oven over medium heat, stirring constantly, 1 minute. Add 1 1/3 cups cream; bring to a boil. Remove from heat; add spinach and shallots.
4. Pour 1/2 cup sauce mixture in a 13- x 9-inch baking dish coated with cooking spray; top with 3 lasagna noodles. Layer half of spinach mixture, half of roasted peppers, 3 lasagna noodles, and half of ricotta mixture over pasta. Repeat layers; top with 3 lasagna noodles. Pour remaining sauce mixture over top. Place baking dish on a foil-lined baking sheet.
5. Bake at 350° for 1 hour. Top with remaining 1 cup Parmesan, and bake 15 minutes. Let stand 30 minutes.

MAKES 6 to 8 servings. **HANDS-ON** 50 min.; **TOTAL** 2 hours, 35 min.

I'LL BE HOME FOR CHRISTMAS MORNING

WITH MAKE-AHEAD OPTIONS LIKE NUTTY GLUTEN-FREE CAKE, CROISSANT BAKE, AND MINTY AMBROSIA, PRACTICALLY ALL THAT'S LEFT TO DO IS OPEN SOME GIFTS AND JINGLE THE BREAKFAST BELL

CHOCOLATE BREAKFAST WREATH

Be sure to soften butter until it's spreadable. The silky dough is a dream to work with, so even beginning bakers can make this beautiful wreath. Try this chocolate version or Citrus-Cranberry.

½	cup warm milk (100°)
2	(¼-oz.) envelopes active dry yeast
⅓	cup plus ½ cup sugar, divided
4 ½	cups all-purpose flour, divided
2	tsp. kosher salt
1 ½	cups soft butter, divided
3	large eggs, at room temperature
	Parchment paper
1	(4-oz.) bittersweet chocolate baking bar, finely chopped
	Easy Vanilla Glaze

1. Combine milk, yeast, and ⅓ cup sugar in bowl of a heavy-duty stand mixer; let stand 5 minutes or until foamy. Gradually add 1 cup flour, beating at low speed until blended; scrape down sides. Add salt and 1 cup butter; beat at low speed until smooth. Add eggs, 1 at a time, beating until incorporated after each addition and scraping sides of bowl as needed. Gradually add remaining 3 ½ cups flour, beating until blended. Increase speed to medium, and beat until dough forms a ball and begins to pull away from sides. Beat dough 2 more minutes or until smooth and elastic. Turn dough out onto a lightly floured surface, and knead 3 minutes.

2. Place dough in a large greased bowl, turning to grease top. Cover with plastic wrap, and let rise in a warm place (80° to 85°), free from drafts, 1 hour or until doubled in bulk. Punch dough down, and turn out onto lightly floured parchment paper. Roll dough into a 12- x 18-inch rectangle.

3. Brush 6 Tbsp. soft butter over dough; sprinkle with chocolate and ½ cup sugar. Roll up dough, jelly-roll fashion, starting at 1 long side. Press edge to seal, and place dough, seam side down, on parchment paper.

4. Transfer parchment paper with dough onto a baking sheet. Shape rolled dough into a ring, pressing ends together to seal. Cut ring at 2-inch intervals, from outer edge up to (but not through) inside edge. Gently pull and twist cut pieces to show filling. Cover dough.

5. Let rise in a warm place (80° to 85°), free from drafts, 1 hour or until doubled in bulk. Preheat oven to 350°. Uncover dough. Melt remaining 2 Tbsp. butter; brush over dough. Bake 30 to 40 minutes or until golden. Cool on pan 10 minutes. Drizzle Easy Vanilla Glaze over warm bread.

MAKES 10 to 12 servings. **HANDS-ON** 25 min.; **TOTAL** 3 hours, 40 min.

Easy Vanilla Glaze

Whisk together 2 cups **powdered sugar,** 3 Tbsp. **milk,** ½ tsp. **vanilla extract,** and a dash of table **salt.** Whisk in up to 1 Tbsp. milk, 1 tsp. at a

MAKE-AHEAD TIP
FRESHLY BAKED BREAD
Make the dough (through Step 4) a day ahead. Chill overnight. Let the dough come to room temperature and rise in the morning. Then bake and serve.

How to Shape

THIS LUSCIOUS BUTTERY BREAD HAS A GORGEOUS LIGHT-AS-AIR TEXTURE.
AND IT'S AS EASY TO ASSEMBLE AS ONE, TWO, THREE!

STEP 1: ROLL

After sprinkling the sugar and chocolate over the buttered dough, roll it up tightly to form a cylinder, beginning with one of the long sides of dough. Use the parchment paper as a guide to roll, if necessary. Press to seal, and place, seam side down, on the parchment paper.

STEP 2: SHAPE

Transfer parchment paper and dough onto a baking sheet so that it rests horizontally in front of you. Dampen the ends of dough slightly with wet fingers, and bring the dampened ends together, pinching the seam to seal. Stretch and shape dough gently into a nice circle.

STEP 3: CUT

Using a sharp knife, slice the dough at 1 1/2- to 2-inch intervals without cutting all the way up to or through the inner portion of the ring. Turn each section of dough on its side, fanning in the same direction to expose the spiral of filling.

time, until desired consistency is reached.

MAKES 1 1/2 cups. **HANDS-ON** 5 min., **TOTAL** 5 min.

Citrus-Cranberry Wreath: Omit chocolate and Easy Vanilla Glaze. Soak 1 cup sweetened **dried cranberries** in 1 cup boiling water 15 minutes; drain and pat cranberries dry. Prepare Breakfast Wreath recipe as directed through Step 3, sprinkling cranberries over dough and 1 Tbsp. lightly packed **orange zest** over cranberries before rolling. Proceed as directed in Steps 4 and 5. Beat together 3 oz. softened **cream cheese** and 1 Tbsp. softened **butter** in a medium bowl at medium speed with an electric mixer. Gradually add 2 cups **powdered sugar** to cream cheese mixture alternately with 2 Tbsp. fresh **orange juice,** beating at medium speed after each addition. Add up to 2 Tbsp. fresh orange juice, 1 tsp. at a time, until desired consistency is reached. Drizzle over bread.

HANDS-ON 25 min.; **TOTAL** 3 hours, 40 min.

BACON-AND-CHEDDAR GRITS QUICHE

Spread cheese to the edge of the warm, bacony grits "crust" to prevent any custard from seeping out while the quiche bakes.

6	thick bacon slices
2 1/4	cups milk
2	Tbsp. butter
1/2	cup uncooked stone-ground grits
2	tsp. kosher salt, divided
1	tsp. black pepper, divided
2 1/2	cups shredded sharp Cheddar cheese, divided
6	large eggs
2 1/2	cups half-and-half
1	cup heavy cream
1/3	cup sliced green onions

1. Preheat oven to 350°. Cook bacon in a skillet over medium heat until crisp. Remove bacon; drain and crumble. Transfer 2 tsp. bacon drippings to a saucepan.

2. Bring drippings, milk, and butter to a boil over medium heat. Gradually whisk in grits, 1 tsp. salt, and 1/2 tsp. pepper; cook, whisking constantly, 15 minutes or until very thick. Remove from heat; let stand 10 minutes. Stir in 1 cup cheese; let stand 10 minutes. Stir in 1 egg; spread in a 9-inch springform pan coated with cooking spray.

3. Bake at 350° for 25 minutes or until set and browned. Sprinkle remaining 1 1/2 cups cheese over warm grits, spreading to edges. Let stand 15 minutes.

4. Reduce oven temperature to 325°. Combine half-and-half, cream, onions, and remaining 5 eggs, 1 tsp. salt, and 1/2 tsp. pepper. Pour over grits; sprinkle with crumbled bacon. Place pan on a foil-lined baking sheet.

5. Bake at 325° for 1 hour and 15 minutes or until lightly browned and just set. Let stand 20 minutes. Run a sharp knife around edges of quiche; remove sides of pan.

MAKES 10 servings. **HANDS-ON** 1 hour, 5 min.; **TOTAL** 3 hours, 45 min.

AMBROSIA WITH CHANTILLY CREAM

The original ambrosia recipe is simply a layering of orange slices, sugar, and toasted unsweetened coconut. Over the years, folks began to add pineapple, maraschino cherries, and whipped cream to create more of a fruit salad, but the name stuck.

- 1 cup sugar
- 3/4 cup fresh mint, divided
- 3 navel oranges, peeled and sectioned
- 3 blood oranges, peeled and sectioned
- 2 grapefruit, peeled and sectioned
- 6 clementines, peeled and sectioned

1. Bring sugar and 1/2 cup water to a boil; stir until sugar dissolves. Boil 5 minutes. Remove from heat; steep 1/2 cup mint 20 minutes. Strain syrup; discard solids. Cool syrup completely.
2. Toss together citrus sections and 1/4 cup syrup. Cover and chill 8 hours, stirring occasionally. (Reserve remaining syrup for another use.) Chop remaining 1/4 cup mint; toss with fruit. Serve with Chantilly Cream.

MAKES 8 to 10 servings. **HANDS-ON** 50 min.; **TOTAL** 9 hours, 10 min., including cream

MAKE-AHEAD TIP

FRESH MINT SYRUP

Steep fresh mint in hot sugar syrup to make a delightful simple syrup up to a week before Christmas. Section the citrus, and toss it with syrup the day before.

Chantilly Cream

- 1 (8-oz.) container crème fraîche or sour cream
- 3/4 cup whipping cream
- 3/4 tsp. vanilla extract
- 3 Tbsp. powdered sugar

Beat crème fraîche in a large bowl at medium speed with an electric mixer 30 seconds. Add remaining ingredients; beat at high speed 3 minutes or until soft peaks form.

MAKES about 2 1/2 cups. **HANDS-ON** 5 min., **TOTAL** 5 min.

CHEESY SAUSAGE-AND-CROISSANT CASSEROLE

This casserole is rich, delicious, and worthy of Christmas breakfast. Gruyère cheese browns beautifully and adds a nutty flavor to the dish. You can sub Swiss cheese if you prefer.

- 1 lb. hot ground pork sausage (such as Jimmy Dean)
- 1 1/4 cups (5 oz.) shredded Parmesan cheese
- 1 tsp. table salt
- 6 green onions, sliced
- 1 (13.22-oz.) package mini croissants (about 24), torn
  Vegetable cooking spray
- 3 cups milk
- 1 cup heavy cream
- 5 large eggs, lightly beaten
- 2 cups (8 oz.) shredded Gruyère cheese

1. Cook sausage 8 minutes in a skillet over medium-high heat, stirring to crumble. Toss together sausage, Parmesan, and next 3 ingredients; arrange in a 13- x 9-inch baking dish coated with cooking spray.
2. Whisk together milk and next 2 ingredients; pour over sausage mixture. Cover and chill 8 hours.
3. Preheat oven to 350°. Uncover casserole, and sprinkle with Gruyère. Bake 45 minutes or until golden. Let stand 10 minutes.

MAKES 8 to 10 servings. **HANDS-ON** 20 min.; **TOTAL** 1 hour, 15 min.

TANGY GLUTEN-FREE BUTTERMILK-PECAN-WALNUT CAKE

- 6 Tbsp. turbinado sugar, divided
- 4 cups pecan halves, toasted
- 3 cups walnut halves, toasted
- 1 1/2 cups slivered almonds, toasted
- 3/4 cup finely ground plain white cornmeal
- 1 cup butter, softened
- 3/4 cup firmly packed light brown sugar
- 6 large eggs
- 3/4 cup buttermilk
- 1/2 cup half-and-half
- 1 tsp. kosher salt
- 1 tsp. vanilla extract
  Coffee Cream (recipe at right)

1. Preheat oven to 350°. Sprinkle 3 Tbsp. turbinado sugar in a well-greased (with butter) 12-inch cast-iron skillet. Process pecans, walnuts, and almonds in a food processor until coarsely chopped; reserve 2 cups coarsely chopped nuts. Add cornmeal to remaining nuts in processor; pulse until nuts are finely chopped.
2. Beat butter and brown sugar at medium speed with an electric mixer 2 to 3 minutes or until light and fluffy.
3. Whisk together eggs and next 4 ingredients in a medium bowl. Gradually add egg mixture to butter mixture, beating at low speed 2 minutes or until blended, stopping to scrape bowl as needed. Gradually add cornmeal mixture to batter, beating until well blended; fold in reserved 2 cups coarsely chopped nuts. Spoon batter into prepared skillet. Level batter using an offset spatula, and sprinkle remaining 3 Tbsp. turbinado sugar over batter.
4. Bake at 350° for 45 to 55 minutes or until a wooden pick inserted in center comes out clean. Cool completely on a wire rack. Serve with Coffee Cream.

MAKES 10 to 12 servings. **HANDS-ON** 45 min.; **TOTAL** 2 hours, 5 min., including Coffee Cream

Coffee Cream

Stir together 1 cup **heavy cream** and ½ tsp. **instant dark roast coffee** or instant espresso in a medium bowl until well blended. Beat at high speed with an electric mixer 1 minute. Gradually add 6 Tbsp. **powdered sugar**, beating until soft peaks form.

MAKES 2½ cups. **HANDS-ON** 5 min., **TOTAL** 5 min.

CRANBERRY-ORANGE MUFFINS

Sprinkle the tops of the glazed muffins with coarse sugar to add texture and a little sparkle.

- ¾ cup butter, softened
- 2⅓ cups granulated sugar, divided
- 4 large eggs
- 2 Tbsp. orange zest
- 2½ cups plus 1 Tbsp. all-purpose flour
- ½ cup plain yellow cornmeal
- 2 tsp. baking powder
- ½ tsp. table salt
- 1 cup milk
- 2 cups fresh cranberries, coarsely chopped
  Vegetable cooking spray
- 4½ tsp. fresh orange juice
- 4½ tsp. fresh lemon juice
  Turbinado sugar (optional)

1. Preheat oven to 350°. Beat butter with an electric mixer until creamy; gradually add 2 cups granulated sugar, beating until light and fluffy. Add eggs, 1 at a time, beating until blended after each addition. Beat in zest.
2. Stir together 2½ cups flour and next 3 ingredients; add to butter mixture alternately with milk, beginning and ending with flour mixture. Toss cranberries with 1 Tbsp. flour. Fold cranberries into batter. Divide batter evenly between 2 (12-cup) muffin pans coated with cooking spray.
3. Bake at 350° for 25 minutes or until a wooden pick inserted in center comes out clean.
4. Meanwhile, bring orange juice, lemon juice, and remaining ⅓ cup granulated sugar to a boil in a small saucepan over medium heat. Boil until sugar is completely dissolved and syrup has thickened slightly (about 1 minute).
5. Pierce top of each muffin several times with a wooden pick, and brush warm syrup mixture over muffins. Sprinkle tops of muffins with turbinado sugar, if desired. Cool in pans on wire racks 10 minutes.

MAKES 2 dozen. **HANDS-ON** 45 min.; **TOTAL** 2 hours, 15 min.

Blueberry-Lemon Muffins: Omit orange juice. Prepare recipe as directed, substituting **lemon zest** for orange zest and fresh whole **blueberries** or frozen blueberries for cranberries. (Do not chop blueberries.) Increase **lemon juice** to 3 Tbsp.

Brown Sugar-Toasted Pecan Muffins: Omit cranberries and 1 Tbsp. flour. Prepare recipe as directed, substituting **light brown sugar** for granulated sugar and adding 1 tsp. **vanilla** extract with **orange zest** at end of Step 1. Stir 2 cups **chopped, toasted pecans** into batter. Bake at 350° for 18 to 22 minutes.

HANDS-ON 45 min.; **TOTAL** 1 hour, 10 min.

BANANAS FOSTER COFFEE CAKE WITH VANILLA-RUM SAUCE

Substitute extra cream for rum in the sauce, if you prefer.

- 1½ cups mashed ripe bananas
- 7 Tbsp. light rum, divided
- 2 cups brown sugar, divided
- 1½ cups soft butter, divided
- 2 tsp. vanilla extract, divided
- 1 (8-oz. package) cream cheese, softened
- 2 large eggs
- 3¼ cups plus 3 Tbsp. all-purpose flour, divided
- ⅝ tsp. table salt, divided
- ½ tsp. baking powder
- ½ tsp. baking soda
- 1½ cups chopped pecans
- 1 tsp. ground cinnamon
- 1 cup granulated sugar
- 2 cups heavy cream

MAKE-AHEAD TIP

HEAT, SLICE, AND EAT.

Bake the coffee cake and make the sauce on Christmas Eve day. Cool both, and cover. Chill the sauce, and reheat just before serving.

1. Preheat oven to 350°. Cook bananas, 3 Tbsp. rum, ½ cup brown sugar, and ¼ cup butter in a skillet until mixture is bubbly. Cool; stir in 1 tsp. vanilla.
2. Beat cream cheese and ½ cup butter at medium speed with an electric mixer until creamy. Add 1 cup brown sugar; beat until fluffy. Beat in eggs 1 at a time.
3. Stir together 3 cups flour, ½ tsp. salt, and next 2 ingredients; add to cream cheese mixture. Beat at low speed to blend. Stir in banana mixture. Spoon into a greased and floured 13- x 9-inch pan.
4. Combine pecans, cinnamon, remaining ½ cup brown sugar, and ¼ cup flour. Melt ¼ cup butter; stir into pecan mixture. Sprinkle over batter. Bake at 350° for 45 minutes or until a wooden pick inserted in center comes out clean. Cool in pan on a wire rack 10 minutes.
5. Combine granulated sugar, remaining 3 Tbsp. flour, and ⅛ tsp. salt in a saucepan over medium heat. Add cream and remaining ½ cup butter; bring to a boil. Boil, whisking constantly, 2 minutes or until slightly thickened. Remove from heat; stir in ¼ cup rum and 1 tsp. vanilla.

MAKES 8 to 10 servings. **HANDS-ON** 20 min.; **TOTAL** 1 hour, 45 min.

I'LL BE HOME FOR THE FEAST

HERE'S TO EASY-GOING ELEGANCE. LOW-AND-SLOW BRAISES ARE A ONE-POT SLAM DUNK AND WE'VE GOT FIVE SAVORY SIDES FOR PERFECT PAIRINGS

PARMESAN-CRUSTED BRAISED LAMB SHANKS

Authentic Parmigiano-Reggiano is aged, dry, and crumbly and easily grates into a fine powder, making it ideal for creating the beautiful and flavorful crust on these truly luscious shanks.

- 6 lamb shanks
  Kosher salt
  Freshly ground black pepper
- 1/4 cup olive oil
- 2 Tbsp. tomato paste
- 1 cup fruity red wine (such as Merlot)
- 1 (10 1/2-oz.) can beef consommé
- 6 flat-leaf parsley sprigs
- 4 fresh thyme sprigs
- 4 bay leaves
- 3 (1-inch) orange peel strips
- 2 celery ribs, cut into 1-inch-thick pieces
- 1 large carrot, cut into 1-inch-thick pieces
- 1 large yellow onion, cut into wedges
- 1 fresh rosemary sprig
  Parchment paper
- 4 Tbsp. butter, divided
- 1 1/2 cups panko (Japanese bread-crumbs)
- 1 cup finely grated fresh Parmigiano-Reggiano cheese
- 2 1/2 tsp. chopped fresh thyme
- 1 tsp. finely chopped fresh rosemary
  Vegetable cooking spray
  Garnish: chopped fresh thyme

1. Preheat oven to 325°. Sprinkle the lamb with salt and pepper; let stand at room temperature 30 minutes. Cook 3 shanks at a time in 2 Tbsp. hot oil in a large Dutch oven over medium-high heat 2 minutes on each side or until browned. Remove and repeat procedure with remaining shanks and oil; reserve drippings in pan.

2. Cook tomato paste in reserved drippings over medium-high heat, stirring often, about 30 seconds or until tomato paste chars slightly. Add wine, and bring to a boil, stirring to loosen browned bits from bottom. Boil 3 to 5 minutes or until mixture is reduced to 1/3 cup. Stir in consommé, next 8 ingredients, and 1 cup water. Return shanks to Dutch oven. Place parchment paper directly on lamb shanks; cover pot with a tight-fitting lid.

3. Bake at 325° for 3 hours or until meat is very tender and pulls away from bones. Let lamb shanks stand in Dutch oven at room temperature 30 minutes.

4. Melt 2 Tbsp. butter in a skillet over medium-high heat; add panko, and cook, stirring often, 1 minute or until lightly browned. Toss panko mixture with cheese, chopped thyme and rosemary. Place mixture in a shallow bowl.

5. Preheat broiler with oven rack 7 inches from heat. Discard parchment paper. Remove shanks from Dutch oven, reserving cooking liquid. Dredge each shank in panko mixture, pressing to adhere. Spray shanks lightly with cooking spray, and place on a lightly greased rack in a broiler pan. Broil 2 to 3 minutes on each side or until golden. Transfer shanks to a serving platter; cover with aluminum foil.

6. Skim fat from cooking liquid, and pour liquid through a fine wire-mesh strainer into a large saucepan; discard solids. Bring to a simmer over medium-high heat. Simmer, whisking occasionally, 5 minutes or until sauce reduces slightly. Remove from heat. Add remaining 2 Tbsp. butter, and whisk until butter melts and sauce is smooth. Serve sauce with shanks.

MAKES 6 servings. **HANDS-ON** 1 hour, **TOTAL** 5 hours

TANGY-SWEET LEMON CHICKEN

Mediterranean flavors meld deliciously in this chicken dish. Bone-in breasts are meaty and cook perfectly in the moist heat of the braise. Herbed Couscous (page 315) is the perfect side for sopping up the fantastic sauce.

- 1 tsp. freshly ground black pepper
- 2 tsp. kosher salt, divided
- 6 skin-on, bone-in chicken breasts
- 3 Tbsp. olive oil
- 1/4 cup sugar
- 3 lemons, halved
- 1 orange, quartered
- 1 cup pitted prunes or dates
- 3 garlic cloves, crushed
- 1 large onion, chopped
- 1 cinnamon stick
- 3/4 cup white wine
- 3 bay leaves
- 6 fresh thyme sprigs
- 1 cup unsalted chicken cooking stock
  Parchment paper
- 2 Tbsp. cold butter

1. Preheat oven to 325°. Sprinkle pepper and 1 1/2 tsp. salt over chicken. Cook 3 chicken breasts, skin side down, in 1 1/2 Tbsp. hot oil in a large Dutch oven over medium heat 4 minutes or until skin is golden and crisp. Remove chicken; wipe Dutch oven clean. Add remaining 1 1/2 Tbsp. oil, and cook remaining chicken breasts, skin side down, in hot oil 4 minutes or until skin is golden and crisp. Remove chicken; reserve 2 Tbsp. drippings in pan.

2. Sprinkle sugar over cut sides of lemon halves and orange quarters. Cook fruit, cut sides down, in hot drippings in Dutch oven over medium-high heat about 5 minutes or until sugar melts and begins to brown and bubble. Reduce heat to medium-low, and cook 3 more minutes. Add prunes and next 3 ingredients; sauté 3 to 5 minutes or until onion is tender.

3. Increase heat to high, and stir in wine. Bring mixture to a simmer, stirring to loosen browned bits from bottom of Dutch oven. Cook 3 to 5 minutes or until liquid almost evaporates. Stir in bay leaves and next 2 ingredients. Nestle chicken in onion mixture. Place a piece of parchment paper directly on chicken, and cover Dutch oven with a tight-fitting lid.

4. Bake at 325° for 1 hour and 30 minutes to 1 hour and 45 minutes or until chicken is tender. Let chicken stand in Dutch oven at room temperature 30 minutes. Discard parchment paper. Carefully transfer chicken to a serving platter. Cover with aluminum foil.

5. Skim any fat from cooking liquid. Pour cooking liquid through a fine wire-mesh strainer into a saucepan. Reserve lemons and oranges; discard remaining solids. Bring sauce to a simmer over medium-high heat. Add butter, and cook, whisking constantly, until butter melts and sauce is smooth. Garnish chicken with reserved lemons and oranges, and serve with sauce.

Note: We tested with Swanson Unsalted Chicken Cooking Stock.

MAKES 6 servings. **HANDS-ON** 1 hour, **TOTAL** 3 hours

BEER-BRAISED TURKEY LEGS

These Latin-inspired turkey legs are a welcome change of pace from the traditional roast. Serve with Butternut Mash (page 314) or potatoes.

- 1 1/2 Tbsp. kosher salt
- 2 tsp. ground cumin
- 2 tsp. ground chipotle chili powder
- 1 tsp. ground coriander
- 1 tsp. garlic powder
- 1 tsp. onion powder
- 6 fresh turkey legs (about 5 lb.)
- 2 Tbsp. olive oil, divided
- 2 medium carrots, chopped
- 1 medium onion, chopped
- 3 dried chipotle, pasilla, or ancho peppers
- 1 cinnamon stick
- 3 garlic cloves, coarsely chopped
- 3 cups reduced-sodium chicken broth
- 1 (12-oz.) bottle Mexican beer
  Parchment paper
- 2 Tbsp. butter
- 2 limes, halved

1. Stir together first 6 ingredients. Rub salt mixture over turkey legs. Place turkey legs in a single layer on a rack in a jelly-roll pan; chill, uncovered, 12 to 24 hours.

2. Preheat oven to 350°. Let turkey stand at room temperature 30 minutes. Cook 3 turkey legs in 1 Tbsp. hot oil in a large Dutch oven over medium-high heat 10 minutes, browning on all sides. Remove turkey legs from Dutch oven. Add 1 1/2 tsp. oil; cook remaining turkey legs 10 minutes, browning on all sides.

3. Sauté carrots and onion in drippings in Dutch oven over medium-high heat 7 minutes or until tender. Stir in dried peppers and cinnamon, and sauté 2 minutes. Add garlic, and sauté 1 minute. Stir in broth and beer; bring mixture to a boil. Reduce heat to medium, and simmer, stirring occasionally, 5 minutes. Nestle turkey legs in Dutch oven. Place a piece of parchment paper directly on turkey, and cover Dutch oven with a tight-fitting lid.

4. Bake at 350° for 1 1/2 to 2 hours or until meat pulls away from bone. Let turkey stand in Dutch oven at room temperature 30 minutes. Discard parchment paper.

5. Preheat broiler with oven rack 7 inches from heat. Carefully remove turkey from Dutch oven, reserving cooking liquid, vegetables, and cinnamon stick in Dutch oven. Place turkey legs on a lightly greased rack in a broiler pan.

6. Broil turkey 2 to 3 minutes or until skin is crisp and golden brown. Carefully transfer turkey to a serving platter; cover with aluminum foil. Skim fat from cooking liquid in Dutch oven, and pour cooking liquid through a fine wire-mesh strainer into a medium saucepan; discard solids. Bring mixture to a boil over medium-high heat, and boil, stirring occasionally, 5 minutes or until sauce reduces slightly.

Add butter, and cook, whisking constantly, until butter melts and sauce is smooth. Squeeze juice from limes over turkey, and serve turkey with sauce.

Note: We tested with Swanson Natural Goodness 33% Less Sodium Chicken Broth and Dos Equis beer.

MAKES 6 servings. **HANDS-ON** 1 hour, 20 min.; **TOTAL** 15 hours, 50 min.

BRAISED BRISKET WITH MUSHROOM-AND-ONION GRAVY

Flat-cut brisket is available in a range of sizes. If you get a larger, oblong-shaped piece, trim the thin end off, so it will fit in a Dutch oven and cook evenly. Or, braise it in a roasting pan, covered with parchment paper and heavy-duty aluminum foil. Check the water level to keep the brisket partially submerged.

2	Tbsp. kosher salt
1	Tbsp. garlic powder
2 1/2	tsp. freshly ground black pepper
1	tsp. onion powder
1	(5-lb.) beef brisket, trimmed
	Parchment paper
1	(1-oz.) package dried porcini mushrooms
2	cups boiling water
2	Tbsp. olive oil
2	cups reduced-sodium beef broth
12	garlic cloves, smashed
2	large carrots, cut into 1-inch pieces
2	fresh thyme sprigs
1/4	bunch fresh flat-leaf parsley
3	large yellow onions
6	Tbsp. butter, divided
1	lb. whole cremini mushrooms, quartered
2 1/2	Tbsp. cornstarch
	Garnish: coarsely chopped fresh flat-leaf parsley

1. Stir together first 4 ingredients. Rub mixture over both sides of brisket. Place brisket on a parchment paper-lined baking sheet; cover and chill 8 hours.
2. Let brisket stand at room temperature 30 minutes. Preheat oven to 325°. Soak dried porcini mushrooms in 2 cups boiling water 10 minutes. Meanwhile, cook brisket in hot oil in a large Dutch oven 4 minutes on each side or until browned. Add broth, next 4 ingredients, porcini mushrooms, and mushroom soaking liquid to Dutch oven. Cut 1 onion into wedges, and add to Dutch oven. Place a piece of parchment paper directly on brisket, and cover Dutch oven with a tight-fitting lid.
3. Bake at 325° for 4 hours or until tender. Let stand in Dutch oven at room temperature 30 minutes. Discard parchment paper.
4. Meanwhile, thinly slice remaining 2 onions. Melt 2 Tbsp. butter in a large skillet over medium heat; add onion, and sauté 15 minutes or until tender and golden. Transfer mixture to a large bowl.
5. Increase heat to medium-high; melt 2 Tbsp. butter in skillet. Add cremini mushrooms; sauté 8 minutes or until tender and browned. Add sautéed cremini mushrooms to onion mixture.
6. Thinly slice brisket across the grain; transfer to a serving platter. Cover with aluminum foil. Pour cooking liquid through a fine wire-mesh strainer into a medium saucepan; discard solids. Bring liquid to a boil over medium-high heat. Stir in onion-mushroom mixture, and cook, stirring occasionally, 5 minutes.
7. Melt remaining 2 Tbsp. butter in a small saucepan over medium-high heat; whisk in cornstarch. Cook mixture, whisking constantly, 30 seconds. Whisk cornstarch mixture into gravy; bring to a boil, whisking occasionally. Cook, stirring constantly, 1 minute. Remove from heat; add salt and pepper to taste. Serve gravy over brisket.

Note: We tested with Swanson 50% Less Sodium Beef Broth.

MAKES 10 to 12 servings. **HANDS-ON** 1 hour, 15 min.; **TOTAL** 13 hours, 45 min.

BUTTERNUT MASH

Roasted and mashed, winter squash is a comforting side.

3	butternut squash (4 to 5 lb.)
4 1/2	tsp. olive oil
3	Tbsp. butter
	Kosher salt
	Freshly ground black pepper

1. Preheat oven to 400°. Halve squash lengthwise; remove seeds. Brush cut sides with oil, and place, cut sides down, on an aluminum foil-lined baking sheet. Bake 45 minutes or until tender. Remove, and cool on baking sheet on a wire rack 30 minutes. Scoop out pulp; discard shells.
2. Melt butter in a large saucepan over medium-high heat. Stir in squash pulp; cook 6 minutes or until thoroughly heated. Mash with a wooden spoon until desired consistency is reached. Add salt and pepper to taste.

MAKES 6 servings. **HANDS-ON** 15 min.; **TOTAL** 1 hour, 10 min.

BUTTERMILK MASHED POTATOES

Leave the potatoes chunky and rustic, or smash them smooth, depending on what you're serving them with.

2 1/2	lb. russet potatoes, peeled and cubed
	Parchment paper
1 1/2	cups milk
1	cup butter, softened
1 1/2	cups buttermilk
	Kosher salt
	Freshly ground black pepper

1. Preheat oven to 225°. Place potatoes in a large saucepan with cold water to cover by 2 inches. Bring to a boil over medium heat; boil 25 minutes or until potatoes are tender. Drain and spread potatoes in a parchment paper-lined jelly-roll pan. Bake 15 minutes or until potatoes are dry.
2. Bring milk and butter to a simmer in a large saucepan over medium heat, stirring occasionally. (Do not boil.)
3. Transfer potatoes to a large heatproof bowl. Add hot milk mixture, and mash potatoes with a potato

masher. Gradually add buttermilk, and mash until desired consistency is reached. Add salt and pepper to taste. Serve immediately.

MAKES 6 servings. **HANDS-ON** 25 min.; **TOTAL** 1 hour, 5 min.

BROWNED-BUTTER FARRO

Farro is an ancient form of wheat that has seen a resurgence lately. There are countless ways to use this healthy whole grain. We keep it simple, toasting cooked farro in a bit of browned butter for a surprisingly delicious side.

- 1 tsp. kosher salt
- 2 cups uncooked farro
  Vegetable cooking spray
- 3 Tbsp. butter
  Freshly ground black pepper
  Garnishes: finely chopped fresh flat-leaf parsley, chives (or other herbs)

1. Bring 1 tsp. kosher salt and 6 cups water to a boil in a large saucepan over medium-high heat. Add farro; cook, stirring occasionally, 25 minutes or until tender; drain. Spread in a single layer in a lightly greased (with cooking spray) jelly-roll pan; cool completely (about 15 minutes).
2. Melt butter in a large skillet over medium heat. Cook butter, whisking constantly, 7 to 8 minutes or until butter turns golden brown. Add farro to skillet; cook, stirring constantly, 1 to 2 minutes or until thoroughly heated. Remove from heat, and add salt and pepper to taste.

MAKES 6 servings. **HANDS-ON** 15 min., **TOTAL** 1 hour

CREAMY PARMESAN GRITS

Parmesan cheese adds a salty, earthy depth to grits.

- 2 tsp. kosher salt
- 1 cup uncooked stone-ground grits
- 1/4 cup freshly grated Parmesan cheese
- 2 1/2 Tbsp. butter
- 2 Tbsp. heavy cream

Bring salt and 1 qt. water to a boil in a medium saucepan over high heat. Whisk in grits, and cook, whisking constantly, 45 seconds. Return mixture to a boil. Cover, reduce heat to medium-low, and cook 20 to 25 minutes or until grits are tender and have absorbed liquid. Whisk in cheese and butter. Stir in cream, and serve immediately.

Note: We tested with McEwen & Sons Stone Ground Organic White Grits and Yellow Grits.

MAKES 4 to 6 servings. **HANDS-ON** 10 min., **TOTAL** 30 min.

HERBED COUSCOUS

Like a blank canvas, these wonderful fluffy couscous grains pair beautifully with so many flavors. We love the blend of chopped herbs and tangy lemon. Use your favorite herbs to make this versatile side.

- 4 cups reduced-sodium chicken broth
- 2 Tbsp. butter
- 1 Tbsp. extra virgin olive oil
- 1 1/2 tsp. kosher salt
- 2 cups uncooked plain couscous
- 1 Tbsp. chopped fresh flat-leaf parsley
- 1 Tbsp. chopped fresh chives
- 1 tsp. chopped fresh rosemary
- 1 tsp. chopped fresh thyme
- 1 tsp. loosely packed lemon zest
- 1 Tbsp. fresh lemon juice
  Kosher salt
  Freshly ground black pepper

Bring first 4 ingredients to a boil in a medium saucepan over medium-high heat. Stir in couscous; cover and remove pan from heat. Let stand 10 minutes. Uncover and fluff with a fork. Stir in parsley and next 5 ingredients. Add salt and pepper to taste.

MAKES 6 servings. **HANDS-ON** 10 min., **TOTAL** 20 min.

CLASSIC RED WINE-BRAISED BEEF SHORT RIBS

Beef short ribs were made to be braised. As they simmer, the meat becomes tender and pulls away from the bone, adding drama to the plated dish with so little effort. Four pounds of short ribs should give you about 10 good-sized, meaty ribs.

- 4 lb. beef short ribs, trimmed
- 1 Tbsp. kosher salt
- 1 1/2 tsp. freshly ground black pepper
- 4 cups unsalted beef stock
- 1/4 cup olive oil
- 1 3/4 cups red wine
- 1/4 cup brandy or sherry
- 1 cup drained canned whole tomatoes, chopped
- 3 celery ribs, chopped
- 2 medium-size carrots, chopped
- 1 medium-size yellow onion, chopped
- 1 small garlic bulb, cut in half crosswise
- 1 bay leaf
- 3 fresh flat-leaf parsley sprigs
- 3 fresh thyme sprigs
- 2 fresh rosemary sprigs
  Parchment paper
- 2 Tbsp. butter

1. Sprinkle ribs on all sides with salt and pepper; cover and chill 12 to 24 hours.
2. Preheat oven to 300°. Let ribs stand at room temperature 30 minutes. Bring stock to a boil in a medium saucepan over high heat. Reduce heat to medium, and simmer 8 to 10 minutes or until reduced by half.
3. Cook half of ribs in 2 Tbsp. hot oil in a large skillet over medium-high heat 3 minutes on each side or until

browned. Repeat with remaining oil and ribs. Remove from heat, discard drippings, and wipe skillet clean.

4. Pour wine and brandy into skillet and return to medium heat. Bring wine and brandy to a boil; boil 5 minutes or until reduced by half. Stir wine mixture into reduced stock.

5. Place ribs in a large Dutch oven. Add tomatoes and next 5 ingredients, nestling them around the ribs; add parsley, thyme, and rosemary sprigs. Pour stock mixture into Dutch oven; simmer over high heat. Place a piece of parchment paper directly on beef, and cover Dutch oven with a tight-fitting lid.

6. Bake at 300° for 3 1/2 to 4 hours or until meat is tender and pulls away from bone.

7. Let ribs stand in Dutch oven at room temperature 30 minutes. Remove parchment paper. Carefully transfer to a serving platter; cover with parchment paper or aluminum foil. Skim fat from cooking liquid, and pour liquid through a fine wire-mesh strainer into a large saucepan; discard solids. Bring to a simmer over medium-high heat. Simmer, whisking occasionally, 5 minutes or until sauce reduces slightly. Remove from heat; whisk in butter until it melts and sauce is smooth. Serve sauce with ribs.

Note: We tested with Swanson Unsalted Beef Cooking Stock.

MAKES 6 to 8 servings.
HANDS-ON 1 hour, 10 min.;
TOTAL 17 hours, 40 min.

COQ AU VIN

This variation on the classic French wine-braised chicken uses white instead of red wine, giving the finished dish a lovely golden hue.

    Kosher salt
    Freshly ground black pepper
6 **chicken leg quarters (4 to 5 lb.)**
2 **Tbsp. olive oil**
12 **(1-oz.) bacon slices, cut into ½-inch pieces**
2 **(8-oz.) packages fresh cremini mushrooms, chopped**
2 **celery ribs, chopped**
1 **medium-size yellow onion, chopped**
2 **garlic cloves, chopped**
1 **(6-oz.) can tomato paste**
3 **cups dry white wine**
1 **(32-oz.) container reduced-sodium chicken broth**
6 **fresh thyme sprigs**
2 **fresh rosemary sprigs**
1 **(6-oz.) package baby carrots**
    Parchment paper
1 **Tbsp. butter**

1. Preheat oven to 350°. Sprinkle salt and pepper over chicken. Cook 3 chicken leg quarters in 1 Tbsp. hot oil in a large Dutch oven over medium-high heat 5 minutes on each side or until browned. Remove chicken; wipe Dutch oven clean. Repeat with remaining 1 Tbsp. oil and 3 chicken leg quarters.

2. Cook bacon in Dutch oven over medium heat 4 minutes on each side or until crisp. Remove bacon, drain on paper towels, and reserve 2 Tbsp. drippings in Dutch oven. Sauté mushrooms and next 2 ingredients in drippings over medium-high heat 6 minutes or until browned. Stir in garlic; sauté 1 minute. Stir in tomato paste and 1 cup wine; cook over medium-high heat, stirring often, 2 minutes. Add remaining wine, and bring mixture to a boil. Boil, stirring occasionally, about 5 minutes or until reduced by half.

3. Add chicken and bacon to mushroom mixture in Dutch oven. Add broth and next 3 ingredients; bring mixture to a simmer. Place a piece

Coq Au Vin

of parchment paper directly on chicken mixture, and cover Dutch oven with a tight-fitting lid.

4. Bake at 350° for 1 1/2 hours or until meat pulls away from bone. Let chicken stand in Dutch oven at room temperature 30 minutes. Discard parchment paper.

5. Preheat broiler with oven rack 7 inches from heat. Remove chicken from Dutch oven, reserving vegetables and cooking liquid. Place chicken on a lightly greased wire rack in a broiler pan.

6. Broil chicken 2 minutes or until skin is crisp and golden brown. Transfer chicken to a serving platter; cover with aluminum foil. Skim fat from cooking liquid, discard herb sprigs and bring liquid to a simmer over medium-high heat, stirring occasionally. Remove from heat. Add butter, and whisk until butter is melted and sauce is smooth. Serve sauce with chicken.

MAKES 6 servings. **HANDS-ON** 1 hour, 20 min.; **TOTAL** 3 hours, 20 min.

CIDER-BRAISED PORK SHOULDER

Dress up the humble pork shoulder by cooking it in a delicious bath of tangy Dijon mustard, flavorful broth, and sweet apple cider. A slightly cooked apple adds sweet-tart flavor and texture to the dish.

- 2 **Tbsp. kosher salt**
- 2 **tsp. dark brown sugar**
- 1 **tsp. dry mustard**
- 2 **tsp. paprika**
- 1 **tsp. ground red pepper**
- 1 **(4- to 5-lb.) boneless pork shoulder roast (Boston butt)**
- 2 **Tbsp. olive oil**
- 3 **cups reduced-sodium chicken broth**
- 1 **cup apple cider**
- 1 **Tbsp. honey**
- 2 **Tbsp. Dijon mustard**
- 6 **bay leaves**
- 2 **Granny Smith apples**
- 1 **medium-size yellow onion, chopped**
- 1 **garlic bulb, cut in half crosswise**
  Parchment paper

Cider-Braised Pork Shoulder

- 1 **Tbsp. butter**
- 1 **tsp. apple cider vinegar**

1. Stir together first 5 ingredients; rub over pork. Chill pork, uncovered, 8 to 12 hours.

2. Preheat oven to 325°. Let pork stand at room temperature 20 minutes.

3. Cook pork in hot oil in a large Dutch oven over medium-high heat 12 minutes, browning on all sides. Remove from Dutch oven, and wipe pan clean. Boil broth and next 2 ingredients in Dutch oven over medium-high heat. Reduce heat to medium, and whisk in mustard; simmer, stirring occasionally, 5 minutes.

4. Return pork to Dutch oven, and add bay leaves. Cut 1 apple into thick slices. Place onions, garlic, and apple slices around pork. Return to a simmer over medium heat. Place a piece of parchment paper directly on pork mixture, and cover Dutch oven with a tight-fitting lid.

5. Bake at 325° for 3 1/2 to 4 hours or until meat is very tender and pulls away from bone.

6. Let pork stand in Dutch oven at room temperature 30 minutes. Discard parchment paper. Carefully transfer pork to a serving platter; cover with aluminum foil. Skim fat from cooking liquid, and pour cooking liquid through a fine wire-mesh strainer into a large saucepan; discard solids. Bring to a simmer over medium-high heat. Cut remaining apple into thin slices, and add to mixture. Simmer, stirring occasionally, 5 minutes or until sauce reduces slightly. Remove from heat. Add butter and vinegar, and stir until butter melts and sauce is smooth. Serve sauce with pork.

MAKES 6 to 8 servings. **HANDS-ON** 55 min.; **TOTAL** 13 hours, 15 min.

THE HOLIDAY HUNT

*USHER IN THE HOLIDAYS WITH A
FESTIVE TABLE SET WITH A MOUTHWATERING
WOODLAND FEAST INSPIRED BY LOUISIANA FLAVORS*

PROSCIUTTO-WRAPPED DUCK WITH GUMBO GRAVY

Feel free to substitute small skinned and boned chicken thighs when wild duck aren't flying; farmed duck breasts are much too thick and fatty for this preparation.

- 2 **cups buttermilk**
- 2 **Tbsp. hot sauce**
- 1 1/2 **tsp. kosher salt**
- 8 **wild duck breasts or skinned and boned chicken thighs**
- 1/2 **tsp. Cajun seasoning**
- 8 **thin prosciutto slices**
- 2 **Tbsp. vegetable oil**
  Perfect Pot of Rice
  Gumbo Gravy

1. Stir together first 3 ingredients in a large bowl. Soak duck breasts or chicken thighs in buttermilk mixture. Cover; chill 8 to 12 hours.
2. Preheat oven to 400°. Remove meat from buttermilk mixture; discard mixture. Pat breasts or thighs dry; sprinkle with Cajun seasoning. Wrap breast or thighs with 1 prosciutto slice.
3. Cook duck breasts in hot oil in a large skillet over medium-high heat 2 to 3 minutes on each side or until browned. Place duck in a single layer on a wire rack in a jelly-roll pan.
4. Bake at 400° for 6 to 7 minutes (8 to 10 for chicken thighs) or until a meat thermometer inserted in thickest portion registers 145° for duck or 165° for chicken thighs (or desired temperature). Let stand 10 minutes. (Internal temperature will rise during stand time.) Serve with Perfect Pot of Rice and Gumbo Gravy.

MAKES 6 to 8 servings. **HANDS-ON** 20 min.; **TOTAL** 10 hours, 35 min., including rice and gravy

Gumbo Gravy

- 1 **lb. andouille sausage, sliced into 1/4-inch-thick rounds**
- 6 **Tbsp. canola oil, divided**
- 1 **(8-oz.) package button mushrooms, stemmed and quartered**
- 2 **Tbsp. brandy or bourbon**
- 1/4 **cup all-purpose flour**
- 1/2 **tsp. Cajun seasoning**
- 1/4 **tsp. dried thyme**
- 3 **bay leaves**
- 2 **celery ribs, diced**
- 2 **garlic cloves, minced**
- 1 **medium-size green bell pepper, diced**
- 5 **green onions, white and light green parts only, sliced and divided**
- 2 **cups reduced-sodium chicken broth**
  Hot sauce
- 1/8 **tsp. filé powder (optional)**
  Garnish: chopped fresh flat-leaf parsley

1. Cook sausage in 1 Tbsp. hot oil in a Dutch oven over medium-high heat, stirring occasionally, 5 minutes or until browned. Remove sausage, and drain on paper towels, reserving drippings in skillet. Add 1 Tbsp. oil to skillet, and reduce heat to medium. Cook mushrooms in hot oil and drippings, stirring occasionally, 5 minutes or until browned. Transfer mushrooms to a bowl.
2. Remove skillet from heat; add brandy. Return skillet to heat, and cook 1 minute or until liquid has evaporated. Add flour and remaining 4 Tbsp. oil to skillet, and cook over medium-high heat, whisking constantly to loosen browned bits from bottom of skillet, to make a roux. Cook roux, whisking constantly, 8 minutes or until the color of chocolate.
3. Stir in Cajun seasoning, next 5 ingredients, and white parts of green onions; cook over medium heat, stirring constantly, 7 to 8 minutes or until soft. Add broth, and cook,

stirring constantly, 5 minutes or until slightly thickened. Add reserved sausage and mushrooms, and cook, stirring occasionally, about 20 minutes or until thickened. Stir in hot sauce to taste. Remove and discard bay leaves. Sprinkle filé powder over gravy, if desired. Top with green parts of green onions.

MAKES 8 servings. **HANDS-ON** 50 min.; **TOTAL** 1 hour, 10 min.

HARVEST SALAD WITH ROASTED CITRUS VINAIGRETTE

Creole mustard and roasted citrus add depth to this dressing.

- 1 lemon, halved, bottoms trimmed flat
- 1 medium-size orange or 2 satsuma oranges, halved
- 1 Tbsp. sugar
- 1 Tbsp. sherry vinegar
- 2 Tbsp. Creole mustard
- 2 tsp. honey
- 1 garlic clove, minced
  Kosher salt and freshly ground black pepper
- 2/3 cup extra virgin olive oil
- 6 cups packed mixed bitter greens (such as frisée, radicchio, and arugula)
- 1 small red onion, thinly sliced
- 1 pear or apple, thinly sliced
- 2 oz. crumbled blue cheese
  Spiced Glazed Pecans (recipe, page 301)

1. Preheat broiler with oven rack 3 to 5 inches from heat. Pat lemon and orange halves dry with a paper towel, and sprinkle cut sides with sugar. Place, cut side up, on an aluminum foil-lined jelly-roll pan, and broil 5 to 8 minutes or until caramelized and slightly softened. Cool in pan on a wire rack 10 minutes.
2. Squeeze juice from broiled citrus into a small bowl. Stir in vinegar and next 3 ingredients. Add salt and pepper to taste. Let citrus mixture stand 10 minutes. Add oil in a slow, steady stream, whisking constantly until smooth.

3. Gently toss together greens, onion, and pears with desired amount of vinaigrette in a large bowl. Refrigerate any remaining dressing to use later in the week. Season salad with salt and pepper, and toss again. Sprinkle with blue cheese and Spiced Glazed Pecans.

MAKES 6 to 8 servings. **HANDS-ON** 20 min., **TOTAL** 50 min.

ACADIAN GATEAU AU SIROP WITH ROASTED PEARS AND CARAMEL SAUCE

This traditional Louisiana spice cake gains much of its sweet flavor from cane syrup, though you can substitute honey instead. Roast the pears and make the caramel sauce while the cake cools. Then dress it up to serve.

- 3 cups cake flour
- 2 tsp. ground cinnamon
- 1 tsp. ground ginger
- 1 tsp. baking soda
- 1 tsp. baking powder
- 1/2 tsp. table salt
- 1/2 tsp. finely ground black pepper
- 1/4 tsp. ground cloves
- 1 1/2 cups dark cane syrup or honey
- 1/2 cup vegetable oil
- 1 large egg, lightly beaten
- 1 cup buttermilk
  Shortening
  Powdered sugar
  Roasted Pears
  Caramel Sauce
  Spiced Whipped Cream (recipe, page 320)

1. Preheat oven to 350°. Whisk together first 8 ingredients in a large bowl; make a well in center of mixture. Whisk together syrup and next 3 ingredients in a medium bowl; add to dry ingredients. Whisk until blended. Pour batter into a greased (with shortening) and floured 9-inch springform pan.
2. Bake at 350° for 50 to 60 minutes or until a wooden pick inserted in center comes out clean. Cool cake in pan on a wire rack 15 minutes. Remove cake from pan, and cool 1 hour on the wire

rack. Sprinkle powdered sugar over cake, and serve warm immediately or at room temperature with Roasted Pears, Caramel Sauce, and Spiced Whipped Cream.

MAKES 8 to 10 servings. **HANDS-ON** 20 min.; **TOTAL** 3 hours, including pears, whipped cream, and sauce

Roasted Pears

- 8 medium-size firm pears (3 1/2 to 4 lb.), peeled and cut into 1- to 1 1/2-inch wedges
- 2 Tbsp. fresh lemon juice
  Vegetable cooking spray
- 2 Tbsp. butter
- 1/2 cup apple cider
- 1/4 cup cane syrup

1. Preheat oven to 400°. Toss together pears and lemon juice in a large bowl. Line a jelly-roll pan with heavy-duty aluminum foil, and lightly coat with cooking spray. Place pears in a single layer on prepared pan, and dot with butter.
2. Stir together apple cider and cane syrup in a small saucepan, and cook over medium heat, stirring occasionally, 3 to 4 minutes or just until mixture begins to bubble. Drizzle mixture over pears.
3. Bake at 400° for 20 minutes. Stir pears, and bake 30 to 40 more minutes or until golden brown and caramelized, stirring at 10-minute intervals.

MAKES 8 servings. **HANDS-ON** 20 min.; **TOTAL** 1 hour, 10 min.

Caramel Sauce

Bring 1 cup firmly packed **light brown sugar,** 1/2 cup **butter,** 1/4 cup **whipping cream,** 1/4 cup **dark cane syrup,** and a pinch of **salt** to a boil in a small saucepan over medium heat, stirring constantly. Boil, stirring constantly, 2 minutes. Remove from heat, and cool 15 minutes before serving. Refrigerate in an airtight container up to 1 week. To reheat, microwave in a microwave-safe bowl at HIGH 10 to 15 seconds or just until warm; stir until smooth.

MAKES 8 servings. **HANDS-ON** 10 min., **TOTAL** 25 min.

Spiced Whipped Cream

Microwave 1 Tbsp. dark cane syrup in a medium-size microwave-safe bowl at HIGH 10 seconds. Stir in 1 cup heavy cream and a pinch of cinnamon until well blended. Beat at medium-high speed with an electric mixer until soft peaks form.

MAKES 8 servings. **HANDS-ON** 5 min., **TOTAL** 5 min.

SPICED WINE

This soothing drink is a riff on warm German spiced wine.

- 1 (750-ml.) bottle medium-bodied red wine (such as Pinot Noir or Beaujolais)
- 1/2 cup sugar
- 10 whole cloves
- 8 cinnamon sticks
- 4 bay leaves
- 1 medium-size orange or 2 satsuma oranges, cut into 8 wedges
- Garnishes: cinnamon sticks, orange wedges

Bring first 6 ingredients to a boil in a medium saucepan over high heat. Remove from heat, and let stand 10 minutes. Pour through a fine wire-mesh strainer; discard solids. Serve hot or warm.

MAKES 3 1⁄4 cups. **HANDS-ON** 5 min., **TOTAL** 20 min.

HOT BOURBON-ORANGE TEA TODDY

This warming reviver can be served before or after dinner.

- 1 (3-inch) piece fresh ginger, peeled and thinly sliced
- 1 lemon, cut into 8 wedges
- 1/4 cup honey
- 1/8 tsp. dried crushed red pepper
- 3 regular-size orange pekoe tea bags
- 1/2 cup bourbon

Bring first 4 ingredients and 1 qt. water to a boil in a medium saucepan over medium-high heat. Remove pan from heat. Add tea bags; steep 10 minutes.

Remove and discard solids, using a slotted spoon. Whisk in bourbon, and serve hot or warm.

MAKES 4 1⁄2 cups. **HANDS-ON** 10 min., **TOTAL** 25 min.

Perfect Pot of Rice

Rinse 2 cups **long-grain white rice** under running water 3 minutes or until water runs clear. Saute 1 minced **medium onion** in 2 Tbsp. melted **butter** with 2 **bay leaves** and 1/2 tsp. **kosher salt** until soft, 4 to 6 minutes; add rice and cook 2 minutes. Add 2 3⁄4 cups chicken broth or water, and bring to a boil; cook 5 minutes. Cover, reduce heat to low, and simmer 12 minutes. Remove from heat, and let stand, covered, 15 minutes. Fluff rice with fork, and serve hot.

MAKES 6 to 8 servings. **HANDS-ON** 25 min., **TOTAL** 50 min.

ORANGE-GINGER-CHILE-GLAZED CARROTS

Roasting whole carrots in a hot oven, then giving them a final toss in a sweet glaze equals an unforgettable side dish.

- 26 small-to-medium carrots with tops (about 1 3⁄4 lb.)
- 2 Tbsp. olive oil
- 1 tsp. kosher salt
- 1 tsp. ground cumin
- 1/2 cup orange marmalade
- 1/2 cup fresh orange juice
- 1 tsp. ground ginger
- 1/4 tsp. dried crushed red pepper
- 1 tsp. minced fresh rosemary leaves (optional)

1. Preheat oven to 475°. Cut tops from carrots, leaving 1 inch of greenery on each. Peel, if desired. Toss together carrots and oil in a large bowl. Sprinkle with salt and cumin. Spread carrots in a single layer in an aluminum foil-lined jelly-roll pan; bake 25 minutes or just until tender and browned.
2. Meanwhile, bring marmalade and next 3 ingredients to a boil in a small saucepan over medium heat. Boil, stirring often, 4 to 6 minutes or until thickened. Stir in rosemary, if desired.
3. Transfer carrots to large bowl; add

marmalade mixture, and toss to coat. Serve hot or at room temperature.

Note: We tested with Smucker's Sweet Orange Marmalade.

MAKES 6 to 8 servings. **HANDS-ON** 20 min., **TOTAL** 40 min.

BRAISED CABBAGE WITH APPLES AND BACON

Braised, the humble cabbage is an affordable and easy holiday side dish. Serve it with any wild game or roast pork. It's easy to prepare, and just the silky texture we're looking for.

- 4 thick bacon slices, cut into 1/4-inch pieces
- 4 celery hearts, thinly sliced, leaves reserved
- 1 medium onion, thinly sliced
- 2 tsp. fennel seeds (optional)
- 1/2 cup white wine
- 1 head red cabbage (about 2 lb.), thinly sliced
- 1 garlic clove, thinly sliced
- 2 bay leaves
- 1 tart apple (such as Granny Smith), thinly sliced
- 1 cup chicken broth or water
- 1 cup apple cider
- Kosher salt and freshly ground black pepper
- 1 Tbsp. apple cider vinegar

1. Cook bacon in a Dutch oven over medium heat, stirring occasionally, 8 minutes or until crisp; remove bacon, and drain on paper towels, reserving 3 Tbsp. drippings in Dutch oven.
2. Increase heat to medium-high. Add celery, onion, and fennel seeds to Dutch oven, and cook, stirring occasionally, 6 to 8 minutes or until softened. Add wine, and cook 2 to 3 minutes or until reduced by half. Stir in cabbage and next 5 ingredients. Add salt and pepper to taste.
3. Reduce heat to low. Cover and cook, stirring occasionally, about 45 minutes or to desired tenderness. Stir in vinegar just before serving. Sprinkle with celery leaves and cooked bacon.

MAKES 6 to 8 servings. **HANDS-ON** 35 min.; **TOTAL** 1 hour, 20 min.

*RING IN 2015 WITH SOUTHERN FLAIR BY THROWING
A HI-LO DINNER PARTY FEATURING
SOME OF OUR FAVORITE REGIONAL INGREDIENTS*

CHOCOLATE-STICKY TOFFEE-BANANA PUDDINGS

Any remaining sauce makes a great topping for ice cream.

- 1 (18.4-oz.) package fudge brownie mix
- 3 ripe bananas, mashed (about 1 3/4 cups)
- 1 cup sugar
- 1/2 cup light corn syrup
- 1/2 cup butter
- 1/4 tsp. table salt
- 3 1/2 cups heavy cream
  Garnish: chopped chocolate-covered toffee candy bars

1. Prepare brownie mix according to package directions, stirring in mashed bananas just before transferring mixture to a 9-inch square pan. Bake according to package directions.

2. Meanwhile, stir together sugar, next 3 ingredients, and 1 1/4 cups heavy cream in a medium saucepan. Cook over low heat, stirring often, 35 to 45 minutes or until dark amber. Stir in 1 cup heavy cream, and increase heat to medium. Cook, stirring constantly, about 5 minutes or until slightly thickened. Remove from heat, and cool 5 minutes.

3. Cut cooled banana brownies into 3/4-inch cubes. Layer brownie cubes and desired amount of sticky toffee sauce in each of 12 small bowls. Beat remaining 1 1/4 cups heavy cream at high speed with an electric mixer until soft peaks form. Dollop puddings with whipped cream, and drizzle with sticky toffee sauce. Serve immediately.

Note: Refrigerate cooled sauce in an airtight container up to 3 days. To soften, microwave at 30 second intervals, stirring until soft.

MAKES 12 servings. **HANDS-ON** 1 hour, 10 min.; **TOTAL** 1 hour, 15 min.

CHIVE POTATO CHIPS

- 2 large russet potatoes (about 2 1/4 lb.)
- 2 Tbsp. white vinegar
  Peanut oil
- 2 Tbsp. finely chopped fresh chives
  Kosher salt

1. Cut potatoes into thin slices, using a mandoline or sharp knife. (Cut them as thin as you can.) Rinse sliced potatoes under cold water.

2. Bring vinegar and 6 cups water to a boil in a large saucepan over high heat. Add sliced potatoes, and cook 3 minutes. Drain potatoes, and spread on a paper towel-lined baking sheet. Pat dry with paper towels, and chill 15 minutes.

3. Meanwhile, pour oil to depth of 3 inches into a large Dutch oven, and heat to 340°. Fry potatoes, in batches, stirring occasionally, 3 to 4 minutes or until golden brown. Drain on paper towels, and immediately sprinkle with chives and desired amount of salt.

MAKES 6 appetizer servings. **HANDS-ON** 25 min., **TOTAL** 40 min.

HOPPIN' JOHN NOODLE BOWLS

- 1 (16-oz.) package dried black-eyed peas
- 3 qt. reduced-sodium chicken broth
- 1/4 cup minced fresh ginger
- 5 tsp. soy sauce
- 3 tsp. fish sauce

Toppings: Softened rice noodles, Sambal Pickles, Soft-Cooked Eggs, chopped raw collard greens, chopped scallions, deli-roasted chicken, fresh cilantro leaves, pickled okra, Asian hot chili sauce

1. Rinse and sort peas. Boil peas in water to cover in a large saucepan over high heat, 3 minutes; drain peas.
2. Bring chicken broth and ginger to a boil in a large saucepan over high heat. Add peas. Reduce heat to medium, and simmer 10 minutes or until peas are tender. Reduce heat to low, and stir in soy sauce and fish sauce.
3. Place desired toppings in individual bowls, and ladle hot soup over toppings.

MAKES 10 to 12 servings. **HANDS-ON** 15 min., **TOTAL** 35 min.

Sambal Pickles

Stir together 1 cup **bread-and-butter pickles,** coarsely chopped, and 2 Tbsp. **sambal oelek** (chile paste) in a small bowl. Serve immediately, or cover and refrigerate up to 1 week.

MAKES 1 cup. **HANDS-ON** 5 min., **TOTAL** 5 min.

Soft-Cooked Eggs

Bring 6 large **eggs** and **water** to cover to a boil in a small saucepan over high heat; boil 1 minute. Remove from heat, and cover with lid. Let stand 1 minute. Immediately drain eggs, and rinse under cold water until cool. Peel and slice.

MAKES 6 servings. **HANDS-ON** 10 min., **TOTAL** 10 min.

TK Tip: To soften rice noodles, microwave noodles and warm water to cover in a large microwave-safe bowl at HIGH 4 to 8 minutes or until noodles are soft. Drain.

MIDNIGHT SNACK

Southern Cheeses and Fruit

A REGIONAL CHEESE-AND-FRUIT PAIRING IS A TASTY CONVERSATION PIECE

① APPALACHIAN MEADOW CREEK DAIRY, VA
This is the first cheese from this small, sustainable mountain farm. Aged for 60 days, it's bright and buttery with an earthy finish. *meadowcreekdairy.com*

② GREEN HILL SWEET GRASS DAIRY, THOMASVILLE, GA
If you like Camembert, you'll love this silky-sweet cheese. A perfect match for bubbly wines, it's our No. 1 pick for New Year's Eve. *sweetgrassdairy.com*

③ DANCING FERN SEQUATCHIE COVE FARM, TN
An American Cheese Society award winner, this oozy cheese was a Test Kitchen favorite. It's grassy, pungent, and so versatile—it'll go with beer or wine, sweet or savory accompaniments. *sequatchiecovefarm.com*

④ SMOKEY MOUNTAIN ROUND GOAT LADY DAIRY, NC
Smoked over apple wood, this blue ribbon-winner is as tasty smeared on crackers as it is folded into a New Year's Day omelet or crumbled over a salad. *goatladydairy.com*

THE ROADMAP TO BRAISING

Follow these 6 steps to create the perfect holiday entrée

① PICK YOUR CUT Bone-in, economical cuts like pork shoulder, turkey legs, and short ribs that take time to transform from tough to meltingly tender are your best bets for the braising pot.

② SEASON AND SEAR Heat the pan and then add the fat; brown in batches. Overcrowding causes the meat to steam, inhibiting the development of the dark, rich crust that is the first step to building flavor.

③ DEGLAZE Remove the meat and add liquid, like wine or stock, scraping up the crusty browned bits from the pan bottom. Reduce the liquid slightly to concentrate its flavor. Embellish your braise. Add aromatic vegetables and herbs to the liquid when you add the meat back to the pan instead of browning them first to gradually infuse a lengthy braise with flavor as the pot simmers.

④ CREATE THE PERFECT ENVIRONMENT Cover the simmering surface with parchment paper and then the lid to form a tight seal in the oven. In this moist environment the proteins in the meat break down with meltingly tender results.

⑤ TEST FOR DONENESS Pull the meat away from the bone with a fork. It should practically fall off the bone. Give it more time if it resists. Give it a rest. Leave braise at room temperature to let the juices settle back into the meat and to allow the liquid to cool so it is refrigerator-ready.

⑥ CHILL OVERNIGHT and skim the fat from the surface the next day. Reheat the meat in the liquid, remove, and then strain the liquid into a saucepan and reduce slightly. Whisk in butter to create a rich sauce.

Community Cookbook

BUILD A BETTER LIBRARY, ONE GREAT BOOK AT A TIME. THIS MONTH: *SHALOM Y'ALL.*

Savannah's Congregation Mickve Israel never misses a chance to celebrate their faith through food whether it's sharing blintzes at their annual food festival or homemade challah bread at their Sabbath luncheons. Their cookbook *Shalom Y'all* serves up their favorite Jewish recipes with a side of Southern hospitality.

POTATO LATKES

Grate the potato and apple through the large holes of a box grater.

2 1/4   **lb. russet potatoes, grated**
1   **Fuji, apple, peeled, grated**
1   **large egg, beaten**
1/4   **cup matzo meal**
1   **Tbsp. apple juice**
2   **Tbsp. sour cream**
1   **Tbsp. fresh lemon juice**
1   **Tbsp. butter, melted**
1/4   **tsp. ground cinnamon**
1 1/2   **tsp. kosher salt**
1/2   **tsp. ground black pepper**
  Vegetable oil
  Thinly sliced fresh chives
  Sour cream or applesauce

1. Spread grated potatoes and apples onto clean, dry kitchen towels; roll up and wring towels to squeeze out liquid. Combine potatoes, apples, egg, and next 8 ingredients.
2. Pour oil to a depth of 1/4 inch in a large skillet. Heat oil over medium-high heat; drop potato mixture, by tablespoonfuls, in batches; slightly flatten each latke. Cook 2 minutes on each side or until lightly browned. Drain latkes on paper towels. Keep warm on a wire rack in a jelly-roll pan in a 200° oven. Sprinkle with salt to taste and fresh chives. Serve with sour cream or applesauce.

MAKES about 2 dozen. **HANDS-ON** 30 min., **TOTAL** 30 min.

TEMPLE KUGEL

1   **(8-oz.) package cream cheese, softened**
1/2   **cup butter, softened**
1 1/4   **cups sugar, divided**
8   **large eggs, well beaten**
4 1/2   **cups milk**
2 1/2   **tsp. vanilla extract**
1   **tsp. fresh lemon juice**
1/8   **tsp. kosher salt**
1   **(8-oz.) package egg noodles, cooked and drained**
2   **cups cornflakes, crushed**
2   **Tbsp. ground cinnamon**
  Vegetable cooking spray

Preheat oven to 350°. Beat cream cheese and butter in a large bowl at medium speed with an electric mixer for 2 minutes or until creamy. Gradually add 1 cup sugar, beating well. Add eggs, beating until blended. Stir in milk and next 4 ingredients. Transfer mixture to a lightly greased 13- x 9-inch baking dish. Stir cornflakes, cinnamon, and remaining 1/4 cup sugar; sprinkle over noodle mixture. Bake 1 hour and 15 minutes. Cool and cut into squares.

MAKES 6 to 8 servings. **HANDS-ON** 10 min.; **TOTAL** 1 hour, 25 min.

NEW YEAR'S APPLE CAKE

Vegetable oil makes this nondairy cake extra moist and fluffy.

2   **tsp. ground cinnamon**
2   **cups plus 5 Tbsp. sugar**
6   **apples, cut into 1-inch pieces (about 7 cups)**
4   **large eggs**
3   **cups cake flour**
1   **Tbsp. baking powder**
1   **tsp. table salt**
1   **cup vegetable oil**
1/4   **cup fresh orange juice**
2 1/2   **tsp. vanilla extract**

Preheat oven to 350°. Stir together cinnamon, 5 Tbsp. sugar, and apples; toss to coat. Beat eggs at high speed with an electric mixer 2 minutes or until thick and pale yellow. Gradually add remaining 2 cups sugar, beating until blended. Stir together flour, baking powder, and salt. Stir together oil and orange juice. Add flour mixture to egg mixture alternately with oil mixture, beating at low speed until blended. Add vanilla, beating until just blended. Pour half of batter into a greased (with vegetable oil) and floured 15-cup tube pan. Arrange half of apple mixture on top. Top with remaining batter and remaining apple mixture. Bake 1 hour and 30 minutes or until golden and set. Cool in pan 10 minutes. Remove from pan.

MAKES 10 to 12 servings. **HANDS-ON** 30 min.; **TOTAL** 2 hours, 10 min.

Holiday Favorites

Giving Thanks

GATHER AROUND THE TABLE AND CELEBRATE THE YEAR'S BLESSINGS WITH THIS TRADITIONAL HOLIDAY MEAL.

The Menu

GRAPEFRUIT-GINGER BOURBON SOUR*

SPARKLING BLOOD ORANGE COCKTAIL*

PARMESAN-CRUSTED CRAB CAKE BITES
WITH CHIVE AÏOLI

HERB- AND CITRUS-GLAZED TURKEY

CRANBERRY CLEMENTINE RELISH

SWEET AND SAVORY ROASTED GREEN BEANS

PARSNIP PUREE

SAVORY BREAD PUDDING WITH SAGE,
MUSHROOMS, AND APPLE

SPICY SMOKED PECANS WITH BACON SALT

SOUTHERN CHEESE PLATE

DULCE DE LECHE-PUMPKIN CHEESECAKE
WITH CANDIED ALMONDS

double recipe

GAME PLAN

2 days before:
• Prepare Spicy Smoked Pecans with Bacon Salt and Candied Almonds; store in airtight containers.

1 day before:
• Prepare and bake cheesecake; cover and chill overnight.
• Prepare syrup for bourbon sours; cover and chill.
• Prepare blood orange cocktail, omitting sparkling water; cover and chill.
• Prepare crab cake mixture; cover and chill.
• Prepare Chive Aïoli; cover and chill.
• Prepare Citrus Compound Butter for turkey; cover and chill.
• Prepare Cranberry Clementine Relish; cover and chill.
• Assemble bread pudding; cover and chill, unbaked.

4 hours before:
• Prepare and bake turkey.
• Assemble cheese plate; cover and chill.

1 hour before:
• Prepare green beans; keep warm.
• Prepare Parsnip Puree; keep warm.
• Bake bread pudding; keep warm.
• Set out cheese plate.

Just before:
• Stir together blood orange mixture and sparkling water.
• Assemble bourbon sours.
• Slice turkey.
• Garnish cheesecake.

PARMESAN-CRUSTED CRAB CAKE BITES WITH CHIVE AÏOLI

These miniature crab cakes are baked rather than pan-fried and are easy to prepare for a crowd. Use a 1-inch scoop to portion the crab mixture evenly among the mini muffin cups. The crab mixture can be made a day in advance. Cover and store in the refrigerator.

- 6 oz. fresh lump crabmeat, drained
- 2 (3-oz.) packages cream cheese, softened
- 2/3 cup grated Parmesan cheese, divided
- 3 Tbsp. mayonnaise
- 2 tsp. Dijon mustard
- 1 tsp. Worcestershire sauce
- 3/4 tsp. Old Bay seasoning
- 1/2 tsp. lemon zest
- 1 large egg yolk
- 1 1/2 Tbsp. chopped fresh parsley
- 1 1/4 cups panko (Japanese breadcrumbs)
- 1/4 cup butter, melted
- Chive Aïoli

1. Preheat oven to 350°. Generously grease 2 (12-cup) miniature muffin pans. Pick crabmeat, removing any bits of shell.
2. Stir cream cheese in a large bowl until smooth. Add 1/3 cup Parmesan cheese and next 6 ingredients; stir until smooth. Fold in crabmeat and parsley.
3. Combine remaining 1/3 cup Parmesan cheese, breadcrumbs, and melted butter in a medium bowl; toss with a fork until breadcrumbs are moistened. Spoon 1 Tbsp. breadcrumb mixture into each muffin cup; press into bottom and up sides to form crust. Spoon 1 Tbsp. crab mixture into each crust.
4. Bake at 350° for 25 minutes or until golden brown. Cool in pans 5 minutes. Run a knife around edges of crab cakes to loosen; gently lift cakes from pan. Serve warm or at room run temperature topped with Chive Aïoli.

MAKES 12 servings. **HANDS-ON** 18 min.; **TOTAL** 48 min.

Parmesan-Crusted
Crab Cake Bites
with Chive Aïoli

GRAPEFRUIT-GINGER BOURBON SOUR

Put a new twist on this favorite mixed drink by using grapefruit and ginger in a homemade sour mix.

- 1 cup superfine sugar
- 1 (3-inch) piece fresh ginger, peeled and thinly sliced
- 1 3/4 cups fresh grapefruit juice (about 2 grapefruit)
- 1/2 cup fresh lime juice (about 3 large)
- 2 cups bourbon

1. Stir together 1 cup water, sugar, and ginger in a 2-cup glass measuring cup. Microwave at HIGH 3 minutes or until boiling. Stir until sugar dissolves; cool completely (about 1 hour).
2. Remove and discard ginger from syrup. Stir together syrup and juices.
3. Fill 6 double old-fashioned glasses with crushed ice. Add 1/2 cup juice mixture and 1/3 cup bourbon to each glass; stir. Serve immediately.

MAKES 6 servings. **HANDS-ON** 5 min.; **TOTAL** 1 hour, 8 min.

SPARKLING BLOOD ORANGE COCKTAIL

Blood oranges come into season just in time for the winter holidays, their crimson flesh producing a sweet juice with festive color. Paired with good quality tequila and fresh lime for bright acidity, this drink is a great way to spin a new start on the holiday festivities.

- 1 1/2 cups fresh blood orange juice
- 1 cup white tequila
- 1/2 cup red vermouth
- 1/4 cup agave nectar
- 2 Tbsp. fresh lime juice
- 3/4 cup sparkling water
- Garnish: blood orange wedges

1. Stir together first 5 ingredients in a pitcher. Chill until ready to serve.
2. Fill 6 highball glasses with ice. Pour about 1/2 cup blood orange mixture into each glass. Fill each glass with 2 Tbsp. sparkling water; stir. Serve immediately.

MAKES 6 servings. **HANDS-ON** 5 min.; **TOTAL** 5 min.

Chive Aïoli

Prepare this aïoli up to one day in advance; cover and chill.

- ½ cup mayonnaise
- 1 Tbsp. chopped fresh chives
- 1 tsp. Dijon mustard
- 1 garlic clove, pressed

Combine all ingredients in a small bowl. Cover and chill.

MAKES ½ cup. **HANDS-ON** 4 min., **TOTAL** 4 min.

HERB- AND CITRUS-GLAZED TURKEY

Using a compound butter under the skin and stuffing the turkey with citrus and fresh herbs ensures a flavorful, juicy bird.

CITRUS COMPOUND BUTTER
- ½ cup unsalted butter, softened
- 1 Tbsp. table salt
- 2 Tbsp. chopped fresh thyme
- 2 Tbsp. chopped fresh sage
- 1 Tbsp. chopped fresh rosemary
- 1 tsp. freshly ground black pepper
- 1 tsp. tangerine zest
- 1 tsp. lime zest
- 1 tsp. Meyer lemon zest
- 3 garlic cloves, minced

TURKEY
- 1 (12-lb.) whole fresh or frozen turkey, thawed
- 1 Tbsp. table salt
- 1 tangerine, halved
- 1 Meyer lemon, halved
- 1 lime, halved
- ½ cup celery leaves
- ⅓ cup fresh thyme
- ¼ cup fresh sage
- 1½ cups chicken broth

GLAZE
- ½ cup unsalted butter
- ⅓ cup orange marmalade
- 2 Tbsp. honey
- 1 Tbsp. table salt
- 2 tsp. Meyer lemon zest
- 1 tsp. lime zest
- 1 tsp. chopped fresh thyme
- 1 tsp. chopped fresh sage

REMAINING INGREDIENTS
- 2 Tbsp. all-purpose flour
- Table salt and freshly ground black pepper to taste
- Garnishes: clementines, Meyer lemons, pecans, kumquats

1. Prepare Citrus Compound Butter: Stir together all ingredients in a medium bowl until blended.
2. Prepare Turkey: Preheat oven to 325°. Remove giblets and neck, and rinse turkey with cold water. Drain cavity well; pat dry. Loosen and lift skin from turkey with fingers, without totally detaching skin; spread compound butter underneath. Carefully replace skin. Sprinkle cavity with 1 Tbsp. salt. Squeeze citrus halves into cavity; place squeezed fruit, celery leaves, and next 2 ingredients in cavity. Tie ends of legs together with string; tuck wing tips under. Place turkey on a roasting rack in an aluminum foil-lined roasting pan, breast side up. Pour broth in bottom of roasting pan.
3. Prepare Glaze: Place ½ cup unsalted butter, marmalade, and honey in a small saucepan. Cook over medium-low heat until butter melts. Remove from heat; stir in salt and next 4 ingredients. Brush half of glaze over turkey. Loosely cover turkey with foil.
4. Bake at 325° on lowest oven rack for 1 hour and 30 minutes. Uncover and brush with glaze. Bake 1 hour and 25 more minutes or until a meat thermometer inserted into thickest portion of thigh registers 165°, basting with remaining glaze every 30 minutes. Shield with aluminum foil to prevent excessive browning, if necessary. Remove turkey from oven. Let stand, covered with foil, 30 minutes.
5. Place turkey on a serving platter, reserving drippings in pan. Pour about 1 cup pan drippings into 1-cup glass measuring cup. Let stand 10 minutes, and skim fat from drippings, reserving 1 Tbsp. fat. Heat reserved 1 Tbsp. fat in a small saucepan over medium heat; whisk in flour. Cook 1 minute. Gradually add 1 cup reserved drippings, whisking constantly. Cook 5 minutes or until thickened. Add salt and pepper to taste. Serve turkey with gravy.

MAKES 8 to 10 servings. **HANDS-ON** 23 min.; **TOTAL** 4 hours, 19 min.

CRANBERRY CLEMENTINE RELISH

The cranberries in this recipe are left raw and chopped for extra crunch and tartness. Be sure to use clementines, which unlike tangerines, are seedless.

- 4 clementines
- 1 Granny Smith apple, peeled, cored, and cut into eighths
- 1 (12-oz.) package fresh or frozen cranberries, thawed
- ½ cup sugar
- ½ cup honey
- ¼ cup orange liqueur

Grate zest from clementines to equal 4 tsp. Peel clementines, and separate into segments. Process zest, clementine segments, apple, and cranberries in a food processor until chopped. Transfer fruit to a bowl. Stir in sugar and next 2 ingredients. Cover and chill overnight. Serve with a slotted spoon.

MAKES 4 cups. **HANDS-ON** 10 min.; **TOTAL** 8 hours, 10 min.

SWEET AND SAVORY ROASTED GREEN BEANS

In this dish, fresh green beans are roasted to bring out their natural sweetness, then combined with savory bacon for added richness and orange zest for a burst of citrus on the palate.

- 3 lb. fresh green beans, trimmed
- 1 Tbsp. olive oil, divided
- 1 tsp. table salt
- ¼ tsp. freshly ground black pepper
- 6 thick hickory-smoked bacon slices, cut into ½-inch pieces
- 4 large shallots, cut into wedges
- 3 Tbsp. white balsamic vinegar
- 1 Tbsp. honey
- 1 tsp. fresh thyme
- 1 tsp. orange zest
- ⅓ cup chopped toasted hazelnuts

1. Preheat oven to 425°. Place green beans in a large bowl. Drizzle with olive oil; sprinkle with salt and pepper, tossing to coat. Divide green beans between 2 (15- x 10-inch) jelly-roll pans. Bake at 425° for 25 minutes. Stir and bake 10 more minutes or until tender.

2. Meanwhile, cook bacon in a large skillet over medium-high heat 8 to 10 minutes or until crisp; remove bacon, and drain on paper towels, reserving 2 Tbsp. drippings in skillet. Crumble bacon. Sauté shallots in hot drippings until tender. Add vinegar, stirring to loosen particles from bottom of skillet. Stir in honey.

3. Pour shallot mixture over green beans, and sprinkle with thyme, orange zest, hazelnuts, and bacon. Toss well.

MAKES 10 to 12 servings. **HANDS-ON** 43 min., **TOTAL** 43 min.

PARSNIP PUREE

Buttery parsnips are a perfect accompaniment with a holiday meal. Sweeter in flavor than carrots, this side dish is sure to please your guests. Like potatoes, parsnips quickly turn brown when exposed to air, so place in water straight away to avoid oxidation.

    4   lb. parsnips, peeled and cut
        into 1/2-inch slices
    1/2 cup butter
    1/2 cup chicken broth
    1/2 cup half-and-half
    3/4 tsp. sea salt
    1/4 tsp. freshly ground black
        pepper

1. Cook parsnips in boiling, salted water to cover in a large saucepan 30 minutes or until tender. Drain.

2. Process half each of parsnips, butter, broth, and half-and-half in a food processor until smooth, stopping to scrape down sides as needed. Spoon mixture into a large bowl. Repeat procedure with remaining parsnips, butter, broth, and half-and-half; stir in salt and pepper.

MAKES 10 to 12 servings. **HANDS-ON** 15 min.; **TOTAL** 50 min.

SAVORY BREAD PUDDING WITH SAGE, MUSHROOMS, AND APPLE

Bake individual portions of this custard in 8-oz. ramekins 350° for 25 to 30 minutes.

    1   (1-lb.) loaf ciabatta bread,
         cut into 1-inch cubes
    1/2 cup butter, divided
    1 1/2 cups chopped sweet onion
    3/4 cup chopped celery
    2   Tbsp. chopped fresh sage
    3   (4-oz.) packages wild
         mushroom blend
    3   garlic cloves, minced
    2   Golden Delicious apples,
         peeled and chopped
    2   cups heavy cream
    2   cups milk
    5   large eggs
    1 1/4 tsp. table salt
    3/4 tsp. freshly ground black
         pepper

1. Preheat oven to 375°. Place bread cubes on a large rimmed baking sheet. Melt 1/4 cup butter in a large skillet over low heat. Drizzle melted butter over bread cubes; toss to coat. Bake at 375° for 20 minutes or until golden, stirring halfway through. Transfer cubes to a large bowl.

2. Melt 3 Tbsp. butter in skillet over medium-high heat. Add onion and next 4 ingredients to skillet; sauté 12 minutes or until tender. Add mushroom mixture to bread cubes.

3. Melt remaining 1 Tbsp. butter in skillet. Add apple; sauté 4 minutes or until golden. Add apple to bread mixture.

4. Whisk together cream and next 4 ingredients. Pour over bread mixture; toss well. Pour bread mixture into a greased 13- x 9-inch baking dish. Cover and chill at least 8 hours.

5. Preheat oven to 350°. Uncover casserole, and bake at 350° for 1 hour and 10 minutes or until set and lightly browned. Let stand 15 minutes.

MAKES 12 servings. **HANDS-ON** 25 min.; **TOTAL** 10 hours, 10 min.

SPICY SMOKED PECANS WITH BACON SALT

Hickory-flavored bacon salt is the key ingredient in this addictive snack. Guests won't be able to keep their hands out of the nut bowl!

    1/4 cup firmly packed light brown
         sugar
    2   Tbsp. hickory-flavored bacon
         salt
    1 1/2 tsp. crushed chipotle chile
    1 1/2 tsp. smoked serrano chile
         powder
    2   large egg whites
    1   lb. pecan halves
         Parchment paper

1. Preheat oven to 250°. Stir together first 4 ingredients in a small bowl. Whisk egg whites in a large bowl until foamy. Add pecans, tossing to coat. Add spice mixture, tossing to coat.

2. Spread nut mixture in a single layer on a parchment paper-lined baking sheet.

3. Bake at 250° for 1 hour, stirring after 30 minutes. Cool slightly, and break pecans apart. Cool to room temperature. Store in an airtight container up to 2 weeks.

Note: We tested with J & D's hickory-flavored bacon salt and crushed chipotle chile and smoked serrano chile powder from Williams-Sonoma.

MAKES about 5 cups. **HANDS-ON** 5 min.; **TOTAL** 1 hour, 5 min.

QUICK & EASY SOUTHERN CHEESE PLATE

- ½ cup chopped toasted walnuts
- 1 (11-oz.) log Belle Chèvre goat cheese
- 1 cup fig preserves
- 1 lb. Champagne grapes, red grapes, red currants, or pears, sliced
  Assorted crackers
  Wine suggestion: semidry white sparkling wine or Sauvignon Blanc

1. Place chopped walnuts in a shallow dish. Roll goat cheese log in walnuts, pressing gently to coat completely.
2. Arrange log on a serving platter alongside a small bowl of fig preserves, Champagne grapes, and an assortment of crackers.

Variation 1

- 1 lb. Sweet Grass Dairy Asher Blue cow's milk cheese
- 2 cups hickory-smoked almonds
- 1 lb. Medjool dates
  Almond crackers or buttery crackers
  Wine suggestion: Port or full-bodied red wine (such as Cabernet Sauvignon)

Variation 2

- 1 lb. Locust Grove La Mancha Reserve sheep's milk cheese
- 1 (4.2-oz.) container quince fruit paste
- 1½ cups Marcona almonds
  Rosemary crackers
  Wine suggestion: Spanish sherry (such as Amontillado) or White Meritage (such as St. Supery Vertu)

Variation 3

- 1 lb. Sweet Grass Dairy Green Hill (Camembert-style) cow's milk cheese
- 1 cup peach preserves
- 2 cups pecans, toasted (about ½ lb.)
  Assorted butter crackers
  Wine suggestion: Champagne or Vouvray (such as Chenin Blanc)

Note: We tested with Chilton County peach preserves.

Also, for more information about artisanal cheese producers in the South, visit southerncheese.com. These featured cheeses can be purchased online at Fromagerie Belle Chèvre, Elkmont, Alabama, belle-chevre.com Locust Grove Farm, Knoxville, Tennessee, locustgrove-farm.net, Sweet Grass Dairy, Thomasville, Georgia, sweetgrassdairy.com

MAKES 10 to 12 servings. **HANDS-ON** 10 min., **TOTAL** 10 min.

DULCE DE LECHE-PUMPKIN CHEESECAKE WITH CANDIED ALMONDS

Sweet milk caramel, or dulce de leche, takes this decadent cheesecake over the top—be sure to save room for dessert!

CRUST

- 2 (5.3-oz.) packages pure butter shortbread cookies
- ½ cup sliced almonds
- ¼ cup butter, melted
  Vegetable cooking spray

FILLING

- 4 (8-oz.) packages cream cheese, softened
- 1 cup sugar
- ½ cup canned dulce de leche
- 4 large eggs
- 1 (15-oz.) can pumpkin
- 1 tsp. ground ginger
- 1 tsp. ground cinnamon
- ½ tsp. ground cloves

CANDIED ALMONDS

- 1 large egg white
- 3 Tbsp. sugar
- ½ tsp. ground cinnamon
- 1½ cups sliced almonds
  Parchment paper

TOPPING

- ¾ cup whipping cream, divided
- 1 Tbsp. powdered sugar
- ½ cup canned dulce de leche

1. Prepare Crust: Preheat oven to 350°. Process shortbread cookies and almonds in a food processor 30 seconds or until finely ground. Place in a medium bowl; stir in melted butter. Press mixture onto bottom of a 9-inch springform pan coated with cooking spray.
2. Bake at 350° for 12 minutes. Cool in pan on a wire rack. Reduce oven temperature to 325°.
3. Prepare Filling: Beat cream cheese and sugar at medium speed with an electric mixer until blended. Add dulce de leche, beating at low speed until blended. Add eggs, 1 at a time, beating just until yellow disappears after each addition. Add pumpkin and next 3 ingredients, beating at low speed until just blended. Pour batter into prepared crust.
4. Bake at 325° for 1 hour and 15 minutes or until almost set. Turn off oven. Let cheesecake stand in oven, with door partially open, 30 minutes. Remove cheesecake from oven, and gently run a knife around edge of cheesecake to loosen from sides of pan. (Do not remove sides of pan.) Cool on a wire rack 1 hour. Cover and chill at least 8 hours.
5. Meanwhile, prepare Candied Almonds: Preheat oven to 300°. Whisk egg white, sugar, and cinnamon until foamy. Fold in almonds until coated. Spread almonds in a single layer on a parchment paper-lined baking sheet.
6. Bake at 300° for 26 to 28 minutes or until golden brown. Cool completely on pan (about 30 minutes). Remove almonds from parchment paper, and break into small pieces.
7. Prepare Topping: Beat ½ cup whipping cream until foamy; gradually add powdered sugar, beating until soft peaks form. Transfer chilled cheesecake to a serving plate. Spread topping over cheesecake.
8. Combine ½ cup dulce de leche and remaining ¼ cup whipping cream in a small saucepan. Cook over low heat, stirring constantly, 4 minutes or until smooth. Drizzle dulce de leche sauce over topping, and sprinkle with Candied Almonds. Serve immediately.

MAKES 12 servings. **HANDS-ON** 40 min.; · **TOTAL** 11 hours, 37 min.

Festive Pies & Tarts

ENJOY THESE SWEET ENDINGS AT YOUR NEXT HOLIDAY GATHERING.

WHITE CHOCOLATE-PEPPERMINT MOUSSE PIE

This do-ahead frozen dessert makes a perfect ending to a holiday meal.

- 24 cream-filled chocolate sandwich cookies, finely crushed
- 6 Tbsp. butter, melted
- 2 (4-oz.) white chocolate baking bars, chopped
- 3 Tbsp. whipping cream
- 1/2 tsp. peppermint extract or 2 tsp. peppermint liqueur
- 3 large egg whites
- 3/4 cup sugar
- 12 drops of red liquid food coloring
- 1 1/2 cups whipping cream, whipped
  Garnishes: frozen whipped topping, thawed; coarsely crushed hard peppermint candies

1. Stir together chocolate crumbs and melted butter; press firmly into an ungreased 9-inch deep-dish pie plate.
2. Microwave white chocolate in a microwave-safe bowl at HIGH 1 minute, stirring after 30 seconds. Microwave 3 Tbsp. whipping cream in a glass measuring cup at HIGH 30 seconds. Pour hot cream over white chocolate; let stand 1 minute. Stir until smooth. Stir in peppermint extract; cool 10 minutes.
3. Pour water to depth of 1 inch into bottom of a double boiler over medium heat; bring to a boil. Reduce heat, and simmer; place egg whites and sugar in top of double boiler over simmering water. Cook, whisking constantly, 3 minutes or until sugar is dissolved. Beat egg white mixture over simmering water at medium speed with a handheld mixer until soft peaks form. Add food coloring. Increase speed to high, and beat until stiff

White Chocolate-Peppermint Mousse Pie

peaks form. Fold in white chocolate mixture. Fold in whipped cream.
4. Spoon mousse mixture into prepared pie plate; cover and freeze 8 to 12 hours.

MAKES 8 to 10 servings. **HANDS ON** 30 min.; **TOTAL** 8 hours, 41 min.

BUTTERSCOTCH-PECAN TASSIES

Here's an old-fashioned dessert with a butterscotch flavor twist that's sure to be a hit with all ages.

- 1/2 cup butterscotch morsels
- 2 Tbsp. butter
- 1/3 cup light corn syrup
- 2 large eggs
- 1/3 cup firmly packed light brown sugar
- 2 tsp. vanilla extract
- 1/2 cup chopped pecans
  Cream Cheese Pastry

1. Preheat oven to 350°. Microwave butterscotch morsels and butter in a microwave-safe bowl at MEDIUM HIGH (70% power) 1 minute; stir. Continue to microwave at 15-second intervals, stirring until morsels melt and mixture is smooth.
2. Whisk in corn syrup just until blended. Whisk in eggs just until blended. Add brown sugar and vanilla, whisking until blended. Stir

in pecans. Spoon filling evenly into Cream Cheese Pastry shells.

3. Bake at 350° for 26 minutes or until crust is golden. Cool in pans 5 minutes. Run a knife around outer edge of each pastry. Remove from pans, and cool completely on wire racks (about 20 minutes).

MAKES 24 servings. **HANDS-ON** 11 min.; **TOTAL** 2 hours, 16 min., including pastry

Cream Cheese Pastry

- 1/2 **cup butter, softened**
- 1/2 **(8-oz.) package cream cheese, softened**
- 1 1/4 **cups all-purpose flour**

1. Beat butter and cream cheese at medium speed with an electric mixer until creamy. Gradually add flour to butter mixture, beating at low speed just until blended. Cover and chill dough 1 hour.

2. Shape dough into 24 (1 1/4-inch) balls, and place in cups of lightly greased miniature muffin pans; press dough to top of cups, forming shells. Cover loosely, and chill until ready to use.

MAKES 2 dozen. **HANDS-ON** 20 min.; **TOTAL** 1 hour, 20 min.

Make-Ahead: Make this pastry a day ahead, place it in miniature muffin pans, and refrigerate overnight, if desired.

MINI APPLE-CRANBERRY PIES

Classic apple pie takes on a new twist with the addition of cranberries in the filling that's laced with brandy.

- 2 1/2 **cups all-purpose flour**
- 1 **Tbsp. brown sugar**
- 1 **tsp. table salt**
- 1 **cup cold unsalted butter, cut up**
- 6 **to 7 Tbsp. ice water**
- 2/3 **cup firmly packed brown sugar**
- 3 **Tbsp. all-purpose flour**
- 1/4 **tsp. apple pie spice**
- 6 **cups sliced peeled Granny Smith apples (2 1/4 lb.)**

Mini Apple-Cranberry Pies

- 1 1/4 **cups sweetened dried cranberries**
- 1 1/2 **Tbsp. brandy**
- 1 **tsp. vanilla extract**
- 1 **Tbsp. unsalted butter**
- 1 **large egg, lightly beaten**

1. Stir together first 3 ingredients in a large bowl. Cut in 1 cup butter with a pastry blender until mixture resembles small peas.

2. Mound flour mixture on 1 side of bowl. Drizzle 1 Tbsp. ice water along edge of mixture in bowl. Using a fork, gently toss a small amount of flour mixture into water just until dry ingredients are moistened. Move mixture to other side of bowl, and repeat procedure with remaining ice water, 1 Tbsp. at a time, until a dough forms.

3. Gently gather dough into 2 flat disks. Wrap in plastic wrap, and chill 45 minutes.

4. Roll 1 dough disk to 1/8-inch thickness; cut into 4 (7-inch) circles. Fit 1 circle into each of 4 (4 1/2-inch) pie plates. Chill 15 minutes.

5. Meanwhile, preheat oven to 425°. Combine 2/3 cup brown sugar and next 2 ingredients; stir in apples and next 3 ingredients. Spoon about 1 3/4 cups apple mixture into each crust, packing tightly and mounding in center; dot pies with 1 Tbsp. butter cut into pieces.

6. Roll remaining dough disk to 1/8-inch thickness. For double-crust pies, cut dough into 2 (7-inch) circles. Gently place 1 circle over filling in each pie; fold edges under, and crimp, sealing to bottom crust. Cut slits or a hole in top of pies for steam to escape. Brush dough with beaten egg. For lattice-topped pies, cut dough into 1/2-inch-wide strips. Arrange strips in a lattice design over filling; fold excess bottom pie crust under and along edges of top pie crust. Gently press ends of strips, sealing bottom pie crust. Brush lattice with beaten egg. Place pies on a large baking sheet.

7. Bake at 425° for 30 minutes or until crust is golden brown. Transfer to a wire rack, and cool 1 hour before serving.

MAKES 4 servings. **HANDS-ON** 35 min.; **TOTAL** 3 hours, 5 min.

HAZELNUT-CHOCOLATE MOUSSE TARTLETS

Smooth chocolate-hazelnut mousse is mounded in petite chocolate cookie crusts for tiny indulgences that are meant for a holiday tray.

1/3	**cup hazelnuts**
38	**chocolate wafers, finely crushed**
1/2	**cup butter, melted**
	Paper or aluminum foil baking cups
8	**(1-oz.) semisweet chocolate baking squares, coarsely chopped**
2	**cups heavy cream, divided**
1/3	**cup hazelnut spread**
1	**Tbsp. powdered sugar**
	Garnishes: sweetened whipped cream, chopped toasted hazelnuts

1. Preheat oven to 350°. Place nuts in a single layer in a shallow pan. Bake at 350° for 5 to 10 minutes or until skins begin to split. Transfer warm nuts to a colander; using a towel, rub briskly to remove skins. Pulse hazelnuts in a food processor 5 or 6 times or just until finely chopped. Add crushed wafers; pulse 1 or 2 times or until blended. Add melted butter; pulse 2 or 3 times or just until blended. Reduce oven temperature to 325°.

2. Place baking cups in 1 (24-cup) and 1 (12-cup) miniature muffin pans. Spoon about 1 Tbsp. crumb mixture into each cup. Press mixture into bottom and up sides of cups with back of a spoon. Bake at 325° for 7 minutes or just until set. Cool completely (about 20 minutes).

3. Place chocolate and 1 cup whipping cream in a large microwave-safe bowl. Microwave at HIGH 1 minute; stir. Microwave 30 seconds; stir until smooth. Stir in hazelnut spread. Cover and chill 30 minutes or until slightly thickened.

4. Beat remaining 1 cup whipping cream and powdered sugar at medium speed with an electric mixer until stiff peaks form; fold into chocolate mixture.

5. Spoon mousse mixture into a large decorating bag fitted with a metal star tip #1 C. Pipe mixture into prepared crusts. Cover and chill 2 to 8 hours.

Note: We tested with Nutella hazelnut spread.

MAKES 3 dozen. **HANDS-ON** 34 min.; **TOTAL** 3 hours, 24 min.

Make-Ahead: You can bake these chocolaty crusts and freeze them up to 1 week in zip-top plastic freezer bags right in the pan. Then thaw and fill them as needed.

CARAMEL-PUMPKIN PIE WITH CARAMEL SAUCE

To save time, substitute a refrigerated piecrust.

	Buttery Pastry Dough
	All-purpose flour
2	**cups sugar**
2	**Tbsp. light corn syrup**
1 1/2	**cups heavy cream, divided**
2	**Tbsp. butter**
1	**(15-oz.) can pumpkin**
4	**large eggs, lightly beaten**
1/4	**cup butter, melted**
1 1/2	**tsp. pumpkin pie spice**
1/2	**tsp. table salt**
	Sweetened whipped cream

1. Place Buttery Pastry Dough disk on a lightly floured surface; sprinkle dough lightly with flour. Roll dough to 1/8-inch thickness. Starting at 1 edge of dough, wrap dough around a rolling pin. Place rolling pin over a 9-inch pie plate, and unroll dough over pie plate. Trim off excess dough along edges; crimp edges. Cover and chill.

2. Preheat oven to 350°. Combine sugar, corn syrup, and 1/4 cup water in a 3-qt. heavy saucepan, stirring until sugar dissolves. Bring to a boil over medium heat, without stirring. Cook 18 minutes or until mixture is amber colored, swirling pan to incorporate mixture (do not stir).

3. Remove from heat; quickly stir in 1 cup cream and 2 Tbsp. butter. Cook over medium heat, stirring constantly, until caramel is smooth (about 1 minute). Stir in remaining 1/2 cup cream. Cool 10 minutes.

4. Whisk together pumpkin and next 4 ingredients until blended. Gradually whisk in 1 1/2 cups caramel mixture. Pour into prepared crust.

5. Bake at 350° for 40 to 45 minutes or just until center is set. Cool completely on a wire rack (about 1 hour). Serve with sweetened whipped cream and remaining caramel sauce.

MAKES 8 servings. **HANDS-ON** 21 min.; **TOTAL** 3 hours, 10 min., including dough

Buttery Pastry Dough

1 1/4	**cups all-purpose flour**
1/4	**tsp. table salt**
1/4	**cup cold butter, cut up**
1/4	**cup cold shortening, cut up**
2	**Tbsp. ice water**

Pulse flour and salt in a food processor 2 or 3 times or until blended. Add butter and shortening; pulse until mixture is crumbly. Add ice water, 1 Tbsp. at a time, and pulse until mixture holds together when pressed. Shape into a flat disk; wrap in plastic wrap, and chill 30 minutes.

MAKES enough for 1 (9-inch) piecrust. **HANDS-ON** 10 min., **TOTAL** 40 min.

Make Ahead Appetizers

GET THE PARTY STARTED WITH THESE CROWD PLEASERS.

CELERY ROOT LATKES WITH CARAMELIZED APPLE PUREE

Inspired by traditional potato latkes, these petite pancakes are made with a blend of starch-heavy baking potatoes and celery root (also known as celeriac) for an added twist of flavor, then topped with caramelized apple puree and a dollop of crème fraîche. Latkes can be made ahead of time. Cool completely, then layer between sheets of wax paper in an airtight container, and chill or freeze. Reheat in a 375° oven for 10 minutes or until crisp. Caramelized apple puree can be made several days ahead of time and stored in the refrigerator or freezer.

- 2 Tbsp. butter
- 4 Gala apples (about 2 lb.), peeled and coarsely chopped
- 2 Tbsp. sugar
- 2 Tbsp. apple cider
- 2 small baking potatoes (about 1 lb.)
- 1 small yellow onion
- 1 medium celery root (about 3/4 lb.)
- 1/3 cup all-purpose flour
- 3/4 tsp. kosher salt
- 1/4 tsp. freshly ground black pepper
- 1 large egg, lightly beaten
- 1/2 cup vegetable oil
- 6 Tbsp. crème fraîche
  Garnish: watercress leaves

1. Melt butter in a large skillet over medium heat. Add apple to skillet; sprinkle with sugar. Stir in apple cider, and cook 15 minutes or until apples are tender and caramelized, stirring occasionally. Process apple mixture in a food processor until smooth. Transfer to a small bowl. Cool completely; cover and chill until ready to serve.

2. Shred potatoes using the large holes of a box grater. Transfer shredded potatoes to a large bowl of cold water. Drain potatoes. Grate onion. Place potato and onion in a kitchen towel; squeeze out excess liquid. Transfer potato mixture to a large bowl.

3. Coarsely grate celery root; add to potato mixture. Stir in flour and next 3 ingredients.

4. Heat oil in a large nonstick skillet over medium heat. Spoon about 2 Tbsp. batter for each latke into skillet. Cook latkes 3 minutes or until golden brown and edges look cooked. Turn and cook other side. Drain on paper towels. Arrange latkes in a single layer on a serving platter. Top each latke with 1 dollop each of caramelized apple and crème fraîche.

MAKES 3 1/2 dozen.
HANDS-ON 1 hour, 20 min.;
TOTAL 1 hour, 20 min.

Cranberry Salsa

CRANBERRY SALSA

Jalapeño fires up the flavor of this pretty appetizer. Serve it with sweet potato chips or cinnamon sugar pita chips.

- 2 cups fresh or frozen cranberries, thawed
- 1 small Gala, Fuji, or Braeburn apple, cubed
- 1 medium jalapeño pepper, seeded and quartered
- 1 green onion, finely chopped
- 2 Tbsp. chopped fresh cilantro (optional)
- 1/4 cup superfine sugar
- 1 Tbsp. fresh lime juice
- 1 Tbsp. canola oil
- 1/2 tsp. table salt

1. Pulse first 3 ingredients in a food processor 4 times or just until coarsely chopped, stopping to scrape down sides as needed. Transfer to a bowl; stir in green onion and, if desired, cilantro.

2. Add sugar and remaining 3 ingredients, stirring well. Cover and chill 2 to 24 hours. Stir before serving.

MAKES 2 1/2 cups. **HANDS-ON** 8 min.; **TOTAL** 2 hours, 8 min.

BACON-WRAPPED BLUE CHEESE DATES

- 18 bacon slices
- 1/2 cup crumbled blue cheese
- 1/4 cup softened cream cheese
- 1/4 cup chopped toasted pecans
- 36 medium-size pitted dates
  Wooden picks

1. Preheat oven to 400°. Microwave bacon at HIGH 2 to 3 minutes or until almost cooked but still pliable. Drain on paper towels. Cut bacon slices in half.
2. Process blue cheese and cream cheese in a blender or food processor until smooth. Stir in pecans. Spoon mixture into a zip-top plastic freezer bag (do not seal). Snip 1 corner of bag to make a small hole.
3. Cut a lengthwise slit down center of each date, cutting to but not through other side. Pipe cheese mixture into each date (about 1/2 tsp. each), and wrap each with 1 bacon slice. Secure each with a wooden pick. Arrange 1 inch apart on a lightly greased baking sheet.
4. Bake at 400° for 15 minutes or until bacon is crisp. Serve warm.

MAKES 36 appetizer servings. **HANDS-ON** 24 min.; **TOTAL** 40 min.

Make-Ahead: Prepare recipe as directed through Step 3. Cover and chill until ready to bake (up to 24 hours). Proceed as directed.

SMOKED SALMON AND DILL PINWHEELS WITH CITRUS CRÈME

Serve these delicate herbed mini crêpe rollups filled with lemon chive-infused crème fraîche and smoked salmon as an elegant appetizer during the holidays. Crêpes can be made ahead and frozen for up to one month.

- 2/3 cup milk
- 2/3 cup all-purpose flour
- 1 Tbsp. chopped fresh dill
- 2 tsp. butter, melted
- 1/4 tsp. table salt
- 2 large eggs
- 3/4 cup crème fraîche or sour cream
- 1 Tbsp. chopped fresh chives
- 1 tsp. lemon zest
- 1/8 tsp. freshly ground black pepper
  Wax paper
- 8 oz. thinly sliced smoked salmon

1. Process first 6 ingredients in a blender or food processor until smooth, stopping to scrape bowl as needed. Cover and chill 1 hour.
2. Stir together crème fraîche and next 3 ingredients in a small bowl. Cover and chill until ready to serve.
3. Place a lightly greased 10-inch non-stick skillet over medium heat until hot.
4. Pour 1/4 cup batter into skillet; quickly tilt in all directions so that batter covers bottom of skillet with a thin film.
5. Cook about 1 minute. Carefully lift edge of crêpe with a spatula to test for doneness. The crêpe is ready to turn when it can be shaken loose from skillet. Turn crêpe over, and cook about 30 to 40 seconds or until done. Repeat procedure with remaining batter. Stack crêpes between sheets of wax paper until ready to fill.
6. Spread 1 side of each crêpe with 1 1/2 Tbsp. crème fraîche mixture, leaving a 1/4-inch border. Place 2 pieces of smoked salmon on each crêpe; roll up. Cut each rollup into 6 pieces. Secure with wooden picks. Cover and chill 1 to 4 hours.

MAKES 48 appetizer servings. **HANDS-ON** 30 min.; **TOTAL** 2 hours, 30 min.

SWEET AND SAVORY GOAT CHEESECAKES WITH QUINCE GLAZE

These delightful miniature cheesecakes combine almond crackers and black pepper for a savory crust, a blend of goat and cream cheeses for the filling.

CRUST
- 48 miniature paper baking cups
- 1 (8.5-oz.) package almond crackers, crushed (2 1/4 cups)
- 1/2 tsp. freshly ground black pepper
- 6 Tbsp. butter, melted

FILLING
- 1 (11-oz.) package goat cheese, softened
- 6 oz. cream cheese, softened
- 1/4 cup sugar
- 1 tsp. lemon zest
- 2 large eggs

GLAZE
- 1 cup quince preserves

1. Prepare Crust: Preheat oven to 325°. Line 4 (12-cup) miniature muffin pans with miniature paper baking cups. Stir together almond cracker crumbs and black pepper. Stir in butter. Press crumb mixture into bottom of cups.
2. Bake at 325° for 5 minutes or until set. Cool on a wire rack. Reduce oven temperature to 275°.
3. Prepare Filling: Beat first 3 ingredients at medium speed with an electric mixer until blended and smooth. Add lemon zest, beating at low speed until well blended. Add eggs, 1 at a time, beating just until yellow disappears after each addition. Spoon 1 Tbsp. batter into each prepared crust.
4. Bake at 275° for 30 minutes or until center is almost set. Cool completely on wire rack (about 40 minutes). Cover and chill 8 hours.
5. Prepare Glaze: Heat quince preserves in a small saucepan over medium-low heat, stirring constantly, until melted and smooth. Remove from heat; cool 10 minutes. Top each cheesecake with 1 tsp. glaze.

MAKES 24 servings. **HANDS-ON** 35 min.; **TOTAL** 9 hours, 45 min.

Appendices

handy substitutions

ingredient	substitution
baking products	
Baking powder, 1 teaspoon	• ½ teaspoon cream of tartar plus ¼ teaspoon baking soda
Chocolate	
semisweet, 1 ounce	• 1 ounce unsweetened chocolate plus 1 tablespoon sugar
unsweetened, 1 ounce or square	• 3 tablespoons cocoa plus 1 tablespoon fat
chips, semisweet, 6-ounce package, melted	• 2 ounces unsweetened chocolate, 2 tablespoons shortening plus ½ cup sugar
Cocoa, ¼ cup	• 1 ounce unsweetened chocolate (decrease fat in recipe by ½ tablespoon)
Corn syrup, light, 1 cup	• 1 cup sugar plus ¼ cup water • 1 cup honey
Cornstarch, 1 tablespoon	• 2 tablespoons all-purpose flour or granular tapioca
Flour	
all-purpose, 1 tablespoon	• 1½ teaspoons cornstarch, potato starch, or rice starch • 1 tablespoon rice flour or corn flour • 1½ tablespoons whole wheat flour
all-purpose, 1 cup sifted	• 1 cup plus 2 tablespoons sifted cake flour
cake, 1 cup sifted	• 1 cup minus 2 tablespoons all-purpose flour
self-rising, 1 cup	• 1 cup all-purpose flour, 1 teaspoon baking powder plus ½ teaspoon salt
Shortening	
melted, 1 cup	• 1 cup cooking oil (don't use cooking oil unless recipe calls for melted shortening)
solid, 1 cup (used in baking)	• 1⅛ cups butter (decrease salt called for in recipe by ½ teaspoon)
Sugar	
brown, 1 cup firmly packed	• 1 cup granulated white sugar
powdered, 1 cup	• 1 cup sugar plus 1 tablespoon cornstarch (processed in food processor)
granulated white, 1 teaspoon	• ⅛ teaspoon noncaloric sweetener solution or follow manufacturer's directions
granulated white, 1 cup	• 1 cup corn syrup (decrease liquid called for in recipe by ¼ cup) • 1 cup honey (decrease liquid called for in recipe by ¼ cup)
Tapioca, granular, 1 tablespoon	• 1½ teaspoons cornstarch or 1 tablespoon all-purpose flour
dairy products	
Butter, 1 cup	• ⅞ to 1 cup shortening or lard plus ½ teaspoon salt • 1 cup margarine (2 sticks; do not substitute whipped or low-fat margarine)
Cream	
heavy (30% to 40% fat), 1 cup	• ¾ cup milk plus ⅓ cup butter (for cooking and baking; will not whip)
light (15% to 20% fat), 1 cup	• ¾ cup milk plus 3 tablespoons butter or margarine (for cooking and baking) • 1 cup evaporated milk, undiluted
half-and-half, 1 cup	• ⅞ cup milk plus ½ tablespoon butter or margarine (for cooking and baking) • 1 cup evaporated milk, undiluted
whipped, 1 cup	• 1 cup frozen whipped topping, thawed
Egg	
1 large	• ¼ cup egg substitute
2 large	• 3 small eggs or ½ cup egg substitute • 1 large egg plus 2 egg whites
1 egg white (2 tablespoons)	• 2 tablespoons egg substitute
Milk	
buttermilk, 1 cup	• 1 tablespoon vinegar or lemon juice plus whole milk to make 1 cup (let stand 10 minutes) • 1 cup plain yogurt • 1 cup whole milk plus 1¾ teaspoons cream of tartar
fat free, 1 cup	• 4 to 5 tablespoons nonfat dry milk powder plus enough water to make 1 cup • ½ cup evaporated skim milk plus ½ cup water
whole, 1 cup	• 4 to 5 tablespoons nonfat dry milk powder plus enough water to make 1 cup • ½ cup evaporated milk plus ½ cup water

handy substitutions

ingredient	substitution
Milk (continued)	
sweetened condensed, 1 (14-ounce) can (about 1¼ cups)	· Heat the following ingredients until sugar and butter dissolve: ⅓ cup plus 2 tablespoons evaporated milk, 1 cup sugar, 3 tablespoons butter. · Add 1 cup plus 2 tablespoons nonfat dry milk powder to ½ cup warm water. Mix well. Add ¾ cup sugar, and stir until smooth.
Sour cream, 1 cup	· 1 cup plain yogurt plus 3 tablespoons melted butter or 1 tablespoon cornstarch · 1 tablespoon lemon juice plus evaporated milk to equal 1 cup
Yogurt, 1 cup (plain)	· 1 cup buttermilk

miscellaneous

Broth, beef or chicken canned broth, 1 cup	· 1 bouillon cube or 1 teaspoon bouillon granules dissolved in 1 cup boiling water
Garlic	
1 small clove	· ⅛ teaspoon garlic powder or minced dried garlic
garlic salt, 1 teaspoon	· ⅛ teaspoon garlic powder plus ⅞ teaspoon salt
Gelatin, flavored, 3-ounce package	· 1 tablespoon unflavored gelatin plus 2 cups fruit juice
Herbs, fresh, chopped, 1 tablespoon	· 1 teaspoon dried herbs or ¼ teaspoon ground herbs
Honey, 1 cup	· 1¼ cups sugar plus ¼ cup water
Mustard, dried, 1 teaspoon	· 1 tablespoon prepared mustard
Tomatoes, fresh, chopped, 2 cups	· 1 (16-ounce) can (may need to drain)
Tomato sauce, 2 cups	· ¾ cup tomato paste plus 1 cup water

alcohol substitutions

alcohol	substitution
Amaretto, 2 tablespoons	· ¼ to ½ teaspoon almond extract*
Bourbon or Sherry, 2 tablespoons	· 1 to 2 teaspoons vanilla extract*
Brandy, fruit-flavored liqueur, port wine, rum, or sweet sherry: ¼ cup or more	· Equal amount of unsweetened orange or apple juice plus 1 teaspoon vanilla extract or corresponding flavor
Brandy or rum, 2 tablespoons	· ½ to 1 teaspoon brandy or rum extract*
Grand Marnier or other orange liqueur, 2 tablespoons	· 2 tablespoons unsweetened orange juice concentrate or 2 tablespoons orange juice and ½ teaspoon orange extract
Kahlúa or other coffee or chocolate liqueur, 2 tablespoons	· ½ to 1 teaspoon chocolate extract plus ½ to 1 teaspoon instant coffee dissolved in 2 tablespoons water
Marsala, ¼ cup	· ¼ cup white grape juice or ¼ cup dry white wine plus 1 teaspoon brandy
Wine	
red, ¼ cup or more	· Equal measure of red grape juice or cranberry juice
white, ¼ cup or more	· Equal measure of white grape juice or nonalcoholic white wine

Add water, white grape juice, or apple juice to get the specified amount of liquid (when the liquid amount is crucial).

equivalent measures

3 teaspoons	= 1 tablespoon	2 tablespoons (liquid)	= 1 ounce	⅛ cup	= 2 tablespoons
4 tablespoons	= ¼ cup	1 cup	= 8 fluid ounces	⅓ cup	= 5 tablespoons plus 1 teaspoon
5⅓ tablespoons	= ⅓ cup	2 cups	= 1 pint (16 fluid ounces)		
8 tablespoons	= ½ cup			⅔ cup	= 10 tablespoons plus 2 teaspoons
16 tablespoons	= 1 cup	4 cups	= 1 quart		
		4 quarts	= 1 gallon	¾ cup	= 12 tablespoons

ground rules for grilling

meat	cooking time	method	instructions
Beef			
Ground beef patties	8 to 12 minutes	Direct	Cook, without grill lid, until no longer pink.
Steaks (1 to 1½ inches thick)	8 to 12 minutes	Direct	Cook, without grill lid, to at least 145°.
Steaks (2 inches thick)	8 to 10 minutes	Direct	Cook, covered with grill lid, to at least 145°.
Tenderloin	30 to 45 minutes	Indirect	Cook, covered with grill lid, to at least 145°.
Brisket (6 pounds)	3 to 4 hours	Indirect	Cook, covered with grill lid, to at least 145°.
Fish			
Whole fish (per inch of thickness)	10 to 12 minutes	Direct	Cook, covered with grill lid.
Fish fillets (per inch of thickness)	10 minutes	Direct	Cook, without grill lid.
Lamb			
Chops or steaks (1 inch thick)	10 to 12 minutes	Direct	Cook, without grill lid, to at least 145°.
Leg of lamb (boneless or butterflied)	40 to 50 minutes	Indirect	Cook, covered with grill lid, to at least 145°.
Pork			
Pork chops (½ inch thick)	7 to 11 minutes	Direct	Cook, covered with grill lid, to 145°.
Pork chops (¾ inch thick)	10 to 12 minutes	Direct	Cook, covered with grill lid, to 145°.
Pork chops (1½ inches thick)	16 to 22 minutes	Direct	Cook, covered with grill lid, to 145°.
Kabobs (1-inch cubes)	9 to 13 minutes	Direct	Cook, covered with grill lid, to 145°.
Pork tenderloin (½ to 1½ pounds)	16 to 21 minutes	Indirect	Cook, covered with grill lid, to 145°.
Ribs	1½ to 2 hours	Indirect	Cook, covered with grill lid, to 145°.
Poultry			
Chicken (whole, halves, quarters, and thighs)	45 to 55 minutes	Indirect	Cook, covered with grill lid, to 165° or until desired doneness.
Chicken (bone-in breast)	25 to 30 minutes	Indirect	Cook, covered with grill lid, to 165°.
Chicken (boneless breast)	10 to 12 minutes	Direct	Cook, without grill lid.
Turkey (bone-in breast, cut lengthwise in half	40 to 45 minutes	Indirect	Cook, covered with grill lid, to 165°.

baking at high altitudes

Liquids boil at lower temperatures (below 212°), and moisture evaporates more quickly at high altitudes.Both of these factors significantly impact the quality of baked goods. Also, leavening gases (air, carbon dioxide, water vapor) expand faster. If you live at 3,000 feet or below, first try a recipe as is. Sometimes few, if any, changes are needed. But the higher you go, the more you'll have to adjust your ingredients and cooking times.

A Few Overall Tips

· Use shiny new baking pans. This seems to help mixtures rise, especially cake batters.

· Use butter, flour, and parchment paper to prep your baking pans for nonstick cooking. At high altitudes, baked goods tend to stick more to pans.

· Be exact in your measurements (once you've figured out what they should be). This is always important in baking, but especially so when you're up so high. Tiny variations in ingredients make a bigger difference at high altitudes than at sea level.

· Boost flavor. Seasonings and extracts tend to be more muted at higher altitudes, so increase them slightly.

· Have patience. You may have to bake your favorite sea-level recipe a few times, making slight adjustments each time, until it's worked out to suit your particular altitude.

ingredient/temperature adjustments

CHANGE	AT 3,000 FEET	AT 5,000 FEET	AT 7,000 FEET
Baking powder or baking soda	· Reduce each tsp. called for by up to ⅛ tsp.	· Reduce each tsp. called for by ⅛ to ¼ tsp.	· Reduce each tsp. called for by ¼ to ½ tsp.
Sugar	· Reduce each cup called for by up to 1 Tbsp.	· Reduce each cup called for by up to 2 Tbsp.	· Reduce each cup called for by 2 to 3 Tbsp.
Liquid	· Increase each cup called for by up to 2 Tbsp.	· Increase each cup called for by up to 2 to 4 Tbsp.	· Increase each cup called for by up to 3 to 4 Tbsp.
Oven temperature	· Increase 3° to 5°	· Increase 15°	· Increase 21° to 25°

METRIC EQUIVALENTS

The recipes that appear in this cookbook use the standard United States
method for measuring liquid and dry or solid ingredients (teaspoons, tablespoons,
and cups). The information on this chart is provided to help cooks outside
the U.S. successfully use these recipes. All equivalents are approximate.

METRIC EQUIVALENTS FOR DIFFERENT TYPES OF INGREDIENTS

A standard cup measure of a dry or solid ingredient will
vary in weight depending on the type of ingredient.
A standard cup of liquid is the same volume for any type of
liquid. Use the following chart when converting standard cup
measures to grams (weight) or milliliters (volume).

Standard Cup	Fine Powder (ex. flour)	Grain (ex. rice)	Granular (ex. sugar)	Liquid Solids (ex. butter)	Liquid (ex. milk)
1	140 g	150 g	190 g	200 g	240 ml
¾	105 g	113 g	143 g	150 g	180 ml
⅔	93 g	100 g	125 g	133 g	160 ml
½	70 g	75 g	95 g	100 g	120 ml
⅓	47 g	50 g	63 g	67 g	80 ml
¼	35 g	38 g	48 g	50 g	60 ml
⅛	18 g	19 g	24 g	25 g	30 ml

USEFUL EQUIVALENTS FOR DRY INGREDIENTS BY WEIGHT

(To convert ounces to grams, multiply
the number of ounces by 30.)

1 oz	=	1/16 lb	=	30 g
4 oz	=	¼ lb	=	120 g
8 oz	=	½ lb	=	240 g
12 oz	=	¾ lb	=	360 g
16 oz	=	1 lb	=	480 g

USEFUL EQUIVALENTS FOR LENGTH

(To convert inches to centimeters,
multiply the number of inches by 2.5.)

1 in			=	2.5 cm		
6 in	=	½ ft	=	15 cm		
12 in	=	1 ft	=	30 cm		
36 in	=	3 ft	= 1 yd	=	90 cm		
40 in			=	100 cm	=	1 m

USEFUL EQUIVALENTS FOR LIQUID INGREDIENTS BY VOLUME

¼ tsp					=	1 ml
½ tsp					=	2 ml
1 tsp					=	5 ml
3 tsp	=	1 Tbsp		=	½ fl oz	=	15 ml
		2 Tbsp	=	⅛ cup	= 1 fl oz	=	30 ml
		4 Tbsp	=	¼ cup	= 2 fl oz	=	60 ml
		5⅓ Tbsp	=	⅓ cup	= 3 fl oz	=	80 ml
		8 Tbsp	=	½ cup	= 4 fl oz	=	120 ml
		10⅔ Tbsp	=	⅔ cup	= 5 fl oz	=	160 ml
		12 Tbsp	=	¾ cup	= 6 fl oz	=	180 ml
		16 Tbsp	=	1 cup	= 8 fl oz	=	240 ml
		1 pt	=	2 cups	= 16 fl oz	=	480 ml
		1 qt	=	4 cups	= 32 fl oz	=	960 ml
					33 fl oz	= 1000 ml	= 1 l

USEFUL EQUIVALENTS FOR COOKING/OVEN TEMPERATURES

	Fahrenheit	Celsius	Gas Mark
Freeze Water	32° F	0° C	
Room Temperature	68° F	20° C	
Boil Water	212° F	100° C	
Bake	325° F	160° C	3
	350° F	180° C	4
	375° F	190° C	5
	400° F	200° C	6
	425° F	220° C	7
	450° F	230° C	8
Broil			Grill

Menu Index

This index lists every menu by suggested occasion. Recipes in bold type are provided with the menu and accompaniments are in regular type.

Lone Star Supper

SERVES 8
(page 76)

Jalapeño-Cheddar Popovers
Weekend Brisket
Chipotle Scalloped Potatoes
Grapefruit-Pecan Sheet Cake

Mother's Day Brunch

SERVES 4
(page 118)

Fizzy Berry Pick-Me-Up
Arugula with Warm Bacon Vinaigrette
Cheese Grits and Roasted Tomatoes
Spring Vegetable Frittata
Cinnamon-Sugar Doughnut Bites

Backyard Feast

SERVES 6
(page 160)

Lemon-Mint Sparklers
Tomato Salad with Grilled Shrimp
Margarita-Brined Chicken
Grill-Smoked Summer Peas
Smoky Chopped Salad with Avocado
Bourbon-Soaked Plums
Key Lime Curd Cones

Fall Fun-for-All

SERVES 8 TO 10
(page 240)

Grape-Apple Cider
Sugar-and-Spice Caramel Popcorn
Butternut-Goat Cheese-Stuffed Mushrooms
Slow-Cooker Turkey Chili with Quinoa
Pumpkin Pie Cutout Cookies

Giving Thanks

SERVES 6
(page 326)

Grapefruit-Ginger Bourbon Sour
Sparkling Blood Orange Cocktail
Parmesan-Crusted Crab Cake Bites with Chive Aïoli
Herb- and Citrus-Glazed Turkey
Cranberry Clementine Relish
Sweet and Savory Roasted Green Beans
Parsnip Puree
Savory Bread Pudding with Sage, Mushrooms, and Apple
Spicy Smoked Pecans with Bacon Salt
Quick & Easy Southern Cheese Plate
Dulce de Leche-Pumpkin Cheesecake with Candied Almonds

Easter Celebration

SERVES 6 TO 8
(page 88)

Glazed Spiral-Cut Holiday Ham
Easy Parmesan-Herb Rolls
Asparagus with Red Pepper Chowchow
Carrot-Ginger Puree
Hot Potato Salad
Spring Pea Orzo
Easter-Egg Shortbread Cookies

Black & Blue

SERVES 4
(page 156)

Blackberry Pisco Sours
Blackberry-Brie Pizzettas
Blueberry-and-Kale Grain Salad
Grilled Pork Chops with Blueberry-Peach Salsa
Buttermilk-Blackberry Pops
Petite Blueberry Cheesecakes
Double Berry-Almond Galette

Dinner for Your Honey

SERVES 6
(page 73)

Honey-and-Soy-Lacquered Ribs
**Spinach Salad with Honey Dressing
     and Honeyed Pecans**
Honey-Roasted Carrots
Honey Flans

Southern Supper Club

SERVES 8
(page 42)

Southern 75
Ham-and-Greens Crostini
**Butternut Squash-and-Pecan
     Crostini**
Gulf Coast Seafood Stew
Griddle Corn Cakes
Spiced Mayonnaise
Mocha Chocolate Mousse

Fiesty Fiesta

SERVES 6

Cast-Iron Salsa (page 238)
Butternut Squash Tortilla Soup
     (page 40)
Steak Tacos with Charred Salsa
     (page 59)
Grilled Mexican Corn Salad
     (page 150)
Honey Flans (page 73)

Easy Fan Fare

SERVES 8 TO 10

Grape-Apple Cider (page 242)
Classic Deviled Eggs (page 104)
Avocado-and-Feta Dip (page 111)
Serrano Pepper Burgers (page 108)
Deli coleslaw

Tea Party Finger Foods

SERVES 10

Salmon-Cucumber Tea Sandwiches
     (page 102)
**Prosciutto-Asparagus Tea
     Sandwiches** (page 102)
Vegetable Medley Tea Sandwiches
     (page 102)
Pear-and-Blue Cheese Crostini
     (page 43)
**Butternut Squash-and-Pecan
     Crostini** (page 43)
Ham-and-Greens Crostini (page 42)
Strawberry Tomato Salad (page 199)
Mile-High Mini Strawberry Pies
     (page 93)
Lemon Meltaways (page 56)

Sunday Supper

SERVES 6

**One-Pot Pasta with Tomato-Basil
     Sauce** (page 35)
Pillowy Dinner Rolls (page 113)
**Simple Green Salad with Lemon-
     Shallot Vinaigrette** (page 197)

Mediterranean Meal

SERVES 4

Smoky Field Pea Hummus (page 206)
Lamb Pita Pockets (page 84**)**
**Charred Peppers with Feta Dipping
     Sauce** (page 237)
Mediterranean Green Beans
     (page 150)

Weeknight Go-To Meal

SERVES 4

Tomato-Orange Marmalade Chicken
     (page 148)
Cast-Iron Blistered Brussels Sprouts
     (page 237)
Crunchy-Bottomed Biscuits
     (page 113)
Simple green salad

Christmas Cookie Swap

SERVES 12
(page 289)

Peppermint Meringue Cookies
Coffee-Chocolate Balls
Mississippi Mud Medallions
Cookie Press Sandwiches
Triple Gingersnappers
Pecan-Peach Linzer Cookies
Wreath Macaroons
Hidden Kisses Cookies
Red Velvet Fudge
Cream Cheese-Citrus Mints
Potato Candy
Coffee and hot chocolate

Christmas Eve Dinner

SERVES 6

Chicken Enchiladas (page 304)
Mixed salad greens
**Gingerbread Layer Cake with
    Buttermilk Buttercream**
    (page 301)

Christmas Dinner

SERVES 6

**Southern Russian Punch or Texas
Santa Punch** (page 296)
**Parmesan-Crusted Braised Lamb
Shanks** (page 312) or **Braised
Brisket with Mushroom-and-
Onion Gravy**
Buttermilk Mashed Potatoes (page
314) or **Creamy Parmesan Grits**
(page 315)
Mexican Hot Chocolate Trifle
(page 303)

Christmas Breakfast

SERVES 6

Chocolate Breakfast Wreath
    (page 308) or **Tangy Gluten-Free
    Buttermilk-Pecan-Walnut Cake**
    (page 310)
Bacon-and-Cheddar Grits Quiche
    (page 309) or **Cheesy Sausage-and-
    Croissant Casserole** (page 310)
Ambrosia with Chantilly Cream (page
    310) or **Bananas Foster Coffee
    Cake with Vanilla-Rum Sauce**
    (page 311)

The Holiday Hunt

SERVES 6 TO 8
(page 318)

**Prosciutto-Wrapped Duck with
    Gumbo Gravy**
**Harvest Salad with Roasted Citrus
    Vinaigrette**
**Orange-Ginger-Chile-Glazed
    Carrots**
**Braised Cabbage with Apples and
    Bacon**
**Acadian Gateau Au Sirop with
    Roasted Pears and Caramel Sauce**
Spiced Wine
Hot Bourbon-Orange Tea Toddy

New Year's Eve
Gathering

SERVES 12
(page 321)

Chive Potato Chips *(double recipe)*
Hoppin' John Noodle Bowls
Southern Cheeses and Fruit
**Chocolate-Sticky Toffee-Banana
    Puddings**

Recipe Title Index

This index alphabetically lists every recipe by exact title.

Month-by-Month Index

This index alphabetically lists every food article and accompanying recipes by month.

General Recipe Index

This index alphabetically lists every recipe by exact title.

ISBN-13: 978-0-8487-4307-9
ISBN-10: 0-8487-4307-5
ISSN: 0272-2003

Printed in the United States of America
First printing 2014

Oxmoor House

Editorial Director: Leah McLaughlin
Creative Director: Felicity Keane
Art Director: Christopher Rhoads
Executive Photography Director: Iain Bagwell
Executive Food Director: Grace Parisi
Managing Editor: Elizabeth Tyler Austin
Assistant Managing Editor: Jeanne de Lathouder

Southern Living® 2014 Annual Recipes

Editor: Susan Hernandez Ray
Project Editor: Emily Chappell Connolly
Assistant Designer: Allison Sperando Potter
Editorial Assistant: April Smitherman
Senior Production Managers: Greg A. Amason, Sue Chodakiewicz

Contributors

Copy Editor: Donna Baldone
Proofreaders: Polly Linthicum, Barry Wise Smith
Indexer: Mary Ann Laurens
Editorial Interns: Kylie Dazzo, Nicole Fisher
Photographer: Becky Stayner
Photo Stylist: Lydia DeGaris Pursell
Food Stylist: Ana Kelly

Time Home Entertainment Inc.

Vice President and Associate Publisher: Margot Schupf
Vice President, Finance: Vandana Patel
Executive Director, Marketing Services: Carol Pittard
Publishing Director: Megan Pearlman
Assistant General Counsel: Simone Procas

Southern Living®

Editor-in-Chief: Sid Evans
Creative Director: Robert Perino
Managing Editor: Candace Higginbotham
Executive Editors: Hunter Lewis, Jessica S. Thuston
Senior Food Editor: Julie Grimes
Deputy Food Director: Whitney Wright
Test Kitchen Director: Robert Melvin
Recipe Editor: JoAnn Weatherly
Test Kitchen Specialist/Food Styling: Vanessa McNeil Rocchio
Test Kitchen Professional: Pam Lolley
Editorial Assistant: Pat York
Style Director: Heather Chadduck Hillegas
Director of Photography: Jeanne Dozier Clayton
Photographers: Robbie Caponetto, Laurey W. Glenn, Melina Hammer, Hector Sanchez
Assistant Photo Editor: Kate Phillips Robertson
Photo Coordinator: Chris Ellenbogen
Senior Photo Stylist: Buffy Hargett Miller
Assistant Photo Stylist: Caroline Murphy Cunningham
Copy Chief: Susan Emack Alison
Assistant Copy Chief: Katie Bowlby
Production Manager: Mary Elizabeth McGinn Davis
Assistant Production Manager: Rachel Ellis
Office Manager: Nellah Bailey McGough

To order additional publications,
call 1-800-765-6400.

For more books to enrich your life,
visit oxmoorhouse.com

To search, savor, and share thousands of recipes,
visit myrecipes.com

Cover: Basic White Cake with choice of frosting and filling, page 298
Page 1: Pumpkin Tart with Whipped Cream and Almond Toffee, page 270

Favorite Recipes Journal

Jot down your family's and your favorite recipes for quick and handy reference. And don't forget to include the dishes that drew rave reviews when company came for dinner.

Recipe	Source/Page	Remarks

Recipe	Source/Page	Remarks